Television
and
Radio
Writing

STANLEY FIELD

ADJUNCT PROFESSOR
THE AMERICAN UNIVERSITY
AND
CHIEF OF PRODUCTION
RADIO—TV BRANCH — TROOP INFORMATION DIVISION
DEPARTMENT OF THE ARMY

HOUGHTON MIFFLIN COMPANY BOSTON
The Riverside Press Cambridge

The Riverside Press Cambridge, Massachusetts Printed in the U.S.A.

TO JOYCE

Contents

Foreword

To be "all things to all men" is to set oneself an almost impossible task but to be comprehensive rather than fragmentary is still a goal for any serious writer in any area of skill or knowledge.

This book admirably covers the area of writing for broadcast purposes. It distinctly points out the differences in approach to the sound alone and to the sight and sound media together, by making direct comparisons between radio and television writing. But it does not limit itself to these distinctions. It provides a philosophy of approach to the studio which will gladden the heart of many a director and producer and as such, it should do much to eliminate the friction which sometimes develops between writer and director, in achieving a finished product for broadcasting. Elia Kazan, who began as an actor, then became a writer, then a director and, finally, a great producer, has recently looked backward as he has stepped forward and has taken occasion to laud the work of the writer, as a most important part of the production team, hearkening back to the keen estimate of Shakespeare — "the play's the thing."

Not only is "the play the thing" in this valuable guide, written by Stanley Field, an old hand at writing for both the media of radio and television, but the art of teaching is discovered in the sequential materials which the book has assembled together so logically that under the spell of good teaching, we cannot help but learn.

College and university courses in radio and television have so increased in number and in quality over these past few years that we find four hundred and more institutions scheduling such courses with many of them offering credit toward the bachelor's or master's degree. Universities possessing Schools of Communication, such as is to be found in Washington at The American University where the author teaches, present opportunities to major for a doctorate in this particular field. Such achievement on the academic level is the base upon which a fine profession is established. Communication, broadly covering this entire area of a scientific approach to learning, is rapidly assuming this degree of recognition both here and abroad.

Books, such as this one, will go far to set up guide-posts for the ambitious student with creative ideas. It is not "all things to all men" but it approaches, with all deference to human error, being "all things to all writers" of radio and television.

FRANKLIN DUNHAM

Preface

You will find in this book a mixture of the idealistic and the practical: the high-minded criteria that should inspire a potential writer for the broadcast media and the confining exigencies of the market place. If the approach herein is rather personalized, it is because radio and television, despite the most spectacular of "spectaculars," are still beamed to the living room audience. It is an interesting paradox that these mass media must give the impression that they are programmed for the individual. No one was more aware of that paradox than President Franklin D. Roosevelt, who, in his "fireside chats" to tens of millions of listeners, made the man in the easy chair, with his proverbial pipe and slippers, feel that he alone was being addressed. It is a point the beginning writer will do well to remember.

This text, as the title implies, covers both fields of radio and television writing. It attempts to answer many of the questions students of writing continually ask. And because a writer not only learns by writing, but also learns from others' writings, this volume is replete with illustrations.

Today, the emphasis is, naturally enough, on television. But I do not believe that radio should be sold short. There are still some 3,000 radio stations operating in the black. And the four big radio networks are still very much in existence. Predictions, prognostications and speculations on the future of radio are freely expressed in almost every issue of the trade press. My own hat-in-the-ring estimate is that radio is going to be with us for a long time and the budding writer will not go amiss in attempting some writing chore for the local radio station. There are obvious changes. The star-studded variety shows are gone and most of the big-budgeted dramas. However, until TV stations reach their saturation point, the advertiser still needs radio to obtain *complete* coverage. And even then, he will undoubtedly find it necessary to utilize radio as an essential supplement.

Let's take a look at what's happening to radio. This mass medium is rapidly becoming a specialized one. The television set has usurped the living room. So the radio set has moved into the kitchen or the bedroom or the library or the den depending on your economic circumstances. And there is the car radio. Present estimates put the figure at more than 35,000,000 auto radios in use with more to come. The "good music" stations, as exemplified by WQXR in New York, are highly successful and they cater to an audience of discriminating taste in music. NBC's "Monitor" is a new concept: a mechanical Puck girdling the globe, choosing its fare as it will and breaking with the traditional time allotments.

And, of course, for radio, this is the age of the disc jockey, the platter spinner, the ad libber; the delight of the local teen-agers. Newscasts are a mainstay of every radio station. A goodly number of stations, like WGAY, in Silver Spring, Maryland, have identified themselves closely with the community which they serve and garner much of their income from the small retailer who cannot afford the comparatively astronomical rates of television.

This is a time, it seems to me, for the radio broadcaster to take a bold step, to experiment, especially in nighttime radio which has borne the brunt of television competition. Radio must devise programs not readily available on TV. This, to my mind, means a more adult approach. TV is *the* mass medium without peer. Unfortunately, satisfying adult programs are rare. If they became the rule rather than the exception on radio, it is conceivable that a loyal following would be assured, small but concentrated. A perceptive advertiser could slant his copy for this group in the same manner that he does for a magazine like the *New Yorker*. And perhaps this would bring about more freedom, more scope for the truly creative writer. But experimentation takes courage and money, neither of which appear to be expendable.

True, the emoluments would of necessity be small compared to TV, sustaining or commercial, but the writer, known or unknown, would have a market for the unfettered flights of his imagination. The discovery of new writing talent and new formats could prove of immense benefit to both radio and television. And, who knows, the program might even snare a daring sponsor. Witness "Omnibus": adult, experimental, imaginative . . . and it was sponsored! Or as the program producers preferred . . . subscribed. "Omnibus" had its failures, to be sure, but even these were noble, moral victories.

We come now to the inevitable question posed by the student:

how does the beginning writer break in? There is no formula. But this author's survey of the field has resulted in one answer: persistence. Add to that a modicum of luck. This response is based, of course, on the premise that the writer has talent. Generally, when the above question is raised by the student, I find he is thinking, primarily, in terms of free-lancing and that narrows down, almost entirely, to the drama. He overlooks the staff writer, the man or woman who must be a jack-of-all-phrases. The staff writer may be assigned to write an interview, or continuity for a musical program or an introduction to a speaker or a spot announcement. Not as glamorous or as rewarding as writing an hour drama. But, nevertheless, not to be demeaned. For every writing assignment should be regarded as a challenge, no matter how simple or uncreative it appears on the surface.

This book therefore encompasses the requirements of staff writing and of free-lancing. It discusses Commercials, Interviews, Talks, Musical Continuity, Newscasts and the Documentary. These are generally staff assignments, though Documentaries may be farmed out to free-lance writers. Most texts on radio and television writing deal largely in terms of the network. In this book the job of the continuity writer at the local station level is given full consideration. For this is a starting point and a proving ground.

You will find that many chapters are devoted singly to considerations of writing for television. Other chapters include both television and radio techniques. Such chapters as those dealing with "Commercials," "Talks," "Religious Drama," lend themselves readily to a discussion of both media for comparison and contrast. The fact is, also, that in these particular forms of writing much is being done in both radio and television. On the other hand, in respect to free-lance dramatic writing, the emphasis is almost entirely on television in this book as it is on the air.

A full chapter is devoted to "Writing the Government Program." I do not believe any other text covers the field of government information from the standpoint of the radio and television writer. For the scripter who may wish to make a career as an Information Specialist in Radio and Television and for the many thousands of government employees now engaged in allied informational activities and who, at some time or other, may be called upon for a radio or television script, I hope this chapter will prove of value.

If there is any glaring omission in this text, it is a chapter on writing comedy per se, as differentiated from the situation comedy. It is because I believe the gagman, the variety skit writer, is a breed unto himself. If you have a bent for the "yak-provoker" then invest in a typewriter and a file cabinet. The prospecting may be fraught with frustrations for the disciples of Joe Miller but once you strike a vein, it may well turn into a bonanza.

It is amazing to consider the tremendous strides that television has made in the few short years of its existence. Once every area in the United States is fully covered by TV outlets, the influence of this new medium will be unsurpassed. When television first began beaming its programs, there were many expressions of opinion that TV must develop its own art forms; that it must stir in its own cauldron of creativity all the finest ingredients of radio, the stage and the screen, and brew a new concoction for the greater edification and entertainment of mankind. I think we can all agree that TV has brewed a heady concoction but it's something most of us have tasted before. Many radio programs have been taken over lock, stock and barrel with just a camera added to the microphone. Stage plays are presented as great "spectaculars" and old movie films glut the TV screen. Agreed, that it is a sound policy to permit a new generation, or non-playgoers in the hinterlands, to see a fine play, but from the standpoint of the TV writer, this is a limiting process. In the day-to-day business of presenting the tried and true, the proved successful, originality is stifled, and television, instead of creating its own forms, becomes merely another vehicle for the expressions of the past.

This is not to say that no originality exists today in television. "Omnibus," as previously noted, has been creative and imaginative in this new medium. Edward R. Murrow's "Person to Person" has brought a new, fresh approach to the time-worn interview and has taken full advantage of the visual. The creative talents of writers such as Paddy Chayefsky, Reginald Rose and Rod Serling have brought originality and power and adult thinking to the hour- and the 90-minute television play. Educational TV stations have been making giant strides.

After teaching several years at The American University, and at adult education centers, I find the experience enriching and enjoyable. Almost every student of radio and television writing in my classes has labored diligently, shown a keen interest and exchanged lively criticism. I like to believe, also, that if these students have not all turned into professional scripters, they have at least profited from the very discipline of meeting assignment deadlines. I know that during the semester they walked to the typewriter and not around it. The very few who thought they might sit back and listen idly to lectures, soon withdrew. The very many who remained, wrote. I found, as did Albert Perkins of New York University, that "Regular assignments are a spur to creative activity."

I discovered that learning has no age limit, for my classes in the evening division included college freshmen of 19, magazine and newspaper writers in their mid-forties and retired government officials in their sixties.

To all beginning writers, then, no matter their age nor their expectations, I hope this volume will prove a spur in itself.

STANLEY FIELD

Arlington, Virginia
June, 1957

Acknowledgments

I wish to express
my thanks to the copyright holders of the following scripts and other
materials who have granted me permission for reprinting, in whole
or in part:

THE GLORIOUS GIFT OF MOLLY MALLOY by Jameson Brewer,
reprinted by permission of the author. Produced by Revue Productions, Inc., on the "General Electric Theater."

LIFE IS WORTH LIVING, by Bishop Fulton J. Sheen. Excerpt
reprinted by permission of McGraw-Hill Book Company, Inc. Copyright, 1953, by the Mission Foundation, Inc.

MYSTERY WRITER'S HANDBOOK, edited by Herbert Brean.
Excerpt reprinted by permission of Harper & Brothers. Copyright,
1956, by the Mystery Writers of America, Inc.

A CLERK AT OXENFORD, by Gilbert Highet. Excerpt reprinted
by permission of Oxford University Press. Copyright, 1954.

MONGANGA by Lou Hazam. Excerpts reprinted by permission
of Smith, Kline & French Laboratories, and the author.

SINS OF THE FATHERS, by John Meston, written for the series
"Gunsmoke." Reprinted by permission of the author and the Columbia Broadcasting System, Inc. Copyright by Columbia Broadcasting System, Inc., 1956.

CASE OF THE WONDERING WIFE, dramatized by Paul R. Milton, for the series "Treasury Agent." Excerpt reprinted by permission of the producer, Leonard L. Bass, and the author.

BASKETBALLET, TV script for the series, "Mickey Mouse Club."
Reprinted by permission of Walt Disney Productions.

OUR BEAUTIFUL POTOMAC, by Stuart Finley and John Dewitt. Reprinted by permission of WRC-TV.

SKY PILOT OF THE LUMBERJACKS, by Vera Eikel. Excerpts
reprinted by permission of the author and the American Broadcasting Company.

TAMPICO HURRICANES, by Ira Marion, written for the series
"Disaster." Excerpts reprinted by permission of the author and the
American Broadcasting Company.

SIX TELEVISION PLAYS, by Reginald Rose. Excerpts reprinted by permission of Simon and Schuster. Copyright, 1956, by Reginald Rose.

TELEVISION PLAYS, by Paddy Chayefsky. Excerpts reprinted by permission of Simon and Schuster. Copyright, 1955, by Paddy Chayefsky.

THE ART CART. Reprinted by permission of the Houston Independent School District.

DR. JEKYLL AND MR. HYDE, adapted by Robert Esson for "Matinee Theater," National Broadcasting Company. Excerpts reprinted by permission of the author and the author's representatives, Gregory and Fitch.

ANNA SANTONELLO, by Bob Crean. Reprinted by permission of the author.

IS YOUR HAT IN THE RING. Excerpts reprinted by permission of the National Association of Radio and Television Broadcasters.

SPAGHETTI FOR MARGARET and GREAT GUY, by Roswell Rogers, written for the series "Father Knows Best," produced by Rodney-Young Productions and Screen Gems, Inc. Excerpts reprinted by permission of Screen Gems, Inc.

THE BIG GENIUS, by Frank Burt, written for the series "Dragnet." Excerpts reprinted by permission of Mark VII Productions, Ltd.

THE WOOLWORTH HOUR. Musical continuity reprinted by permission of Lynn Baker, Inc.

ERIC SEVAREID NEWS ANALYSIS. Reprinted by permission of Mr. Sevareid and CBS News.

LAWRENCE WELK SHOW. Musical continuity reprinted by permission of Grant Advertising, Inc.

THE BACK OF HIS HEAD, by Steven Gethers. Excerpts reprinted by permission of the author.

GOD AND A RED SCOOTER, by T. J. Mulvey, written for the series "Family Theater," as presented on the Mutual Network. Reprinted by permission of the author and the Reverend Philip A. Higgins, C.S.C.

THE EDGE OF NIGHT, by Vendig and Bixby. Episode #180 reprinted by permission of Procter & Gamble Productions, Inc.

DU PONT commercial "How Are We Doing?", reprinted by permission of the Du Pont Company and Batten, Barton, Durstine & Osborn, Inc. Copyright, 1955, by E. I. du Pont de Nemours & Co., Inc.

CHEVROLET commercials reprinted by permission of the Henry J. Kaufman Agency.

WESTINGHOUSE commercial with Betty Furness. Reprinted by permission of McCann-Erickson, Inc.

SKIPPY commercial, by David Bascom. Reprinted by permission of Guild, Bascom & Bonfigli, Inc.

ESQUIRE SCUFF-KOTE, MANISCHEWITZ WINE, LANOL WHITE commercials reprinted by permission of the Emil Mogul Company, Inc.

PIEL BROS. "Harry and Bert" commercial, by Ed Graham. Reprinted by permission of Goulding-Elliott-Graham.

GROUND OBSERVER CORPS and FUTURE OF AMERICA announcements. Reprinted by permission of The Advertising Council.

RED CROSS TV announcement. Reprinted by permission of the American National Red Cross.

SHAKESPEARE ON TV — Outline Guides by Professor Frank C. Baxter. Excerpts reprinted by permission of the author.

FREEDOM OF EXPRESSION ON THE AIR, an address by Harold E. Fellows, President, of the NARTB. Excerpts reprinted by permission of Mr. Fellows.

I owe a great debt of gratitude to the many members of the television and radio industry, and allied fields, without whose generosity and cooperation this book could not have been written. My deepfelt thanks, particularly, to the following: Gertrude Broderick, David B. Eskind, Alfred Paul Berger, Richard L. MacCartney, Clair R. Tettemer, Mrs. Dorothy Sinclair, Joseph Newman, Layne Beaty, Jacques Renard, Harold E. Fellows, Howard Bell, Professor Willett M. Kempton, Assistant Professor Harvey Pope, Mrs. Pat Hamill, Kenneth Greenberg, Bob Miller, and to General C. V. Clifton, Jr., Colonel H. C. Lyon, Lt. Colonel Samuel S. Kale for reading individual chapters and for their helpful comments; to David E. Durston, Harold L. Blackburn, S. C. Potter, John Gaunt, David Bascomb, Paul Miller, Robert Maurer, Myron Mahler, Lansing B. Lindquist, Selmer L. Chalif, Sig Mickelson, William J. Eiman, Anne Nelson, Rt. Rev. Msgr. Charles M. McBride; to Professors Frank C. Baxter and Gilbert Highet; to Dr. Franklin Dunham; to my good friends at CBS, Don Ball, Lawrence Beckerman and Ted Koop; to Thomas Velotta of ABC; and particularly to Harold M. Wagner of the Mutual Network, and Joseph L. Brechner of WGAY; and an especial thanks for their generosity and assistance to writers Jameson

Brewer, Bob Crean, Ed Graham, John Meston, Roswell Rogers, Steven Gethers, Vera Eikel, Robert Esson, Ira Marion, Timothy Mulvey, Frank Burt, and most particularly to Stuart Finley and Lou Hazam. My deepest gratitude must go to my wife for the many untold hours she labored over this manuscript with me, for her efficiency as a secretary and her devotion as a wife.

General considerations

PART

1

The role
of the writer

1

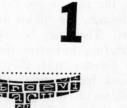

Let us begin with
the observation that the television writer and the radio writer are,
first and foremost, craftsmen. This is not to belittle the media. The
writer for the stage is also a craftsman but he works on a much
larger canvas and he is not bound by the restrictions and taboos of
the broadcast media. Whether a television play will ever be hailed
as great art comparable to the classics of Shakespeare, Ibsen or Shaw,
is debatable.

Although the television drama may not rival the stage play in
aesthetic value, it far outreaches the theater in audience potential.
It would take generations of theatergoers to equal the number of
viewers for a single network performance. And who can predict,
with television ever enlarging its scope in relation to the drama,
that a writer will not appear on the horizon to bring to this new
medium a series of modern classics.

However, our concern in this volume is not solely with the
writer of video or radio drama. There is a vast amount of writing
on the local and the network level which has no relation to the
drama per se. The writers of this essential continuity labor behind

the scenes and their names seldom appear on the visual credits or are heard on the audio credits. And if their output is of a lesser breed than that of the playwrights, it is still true that without them television and radio, in their present form, could not exist. They, too, are craftsmen.

Who are these writers and what are their backgrounds? They are the men and women who write the commercials, the musical continuity, the news copy, the interviews, the talks, the openings and the closings, the fill-ins and a host of other daily or weekly assignments. They may be college graduates on their first job in the broadcasting industry; they may be experienced journalists entering a greener field; they may be enterprising young women with a knack for creating selling slogans. They come from the tenement slums of New York's lower East Side, from a ranch house in Phoenix, Arizona, from an ancient colonial mansion in Savannah, Georgia. In short, the writer's antecedents are everywhere and anywhere. His environment does not matter, nor his heritage. He becomes a writer because of the desire that arises and the ability that develops.

If you have chosen to make writing a career, then you have embarked on a journey which is both fraught with peril and filled with promise. For most writers, the road is rocky, full of detours, and broken by pits of frustration. But the writer who perseveres along the journey may find unparalleled fulfillment.

Let us state, here at the outset, that, exclusive of the genius, writers are made and not born. They are made, as we have noted, of a desire — a compulsion, if you will — to write, a willingness to work long and hard, and to never stop learning and observing. What differentiates writers, in the final analysis, is their degree of talent. But this is true of any profession. There are greater artists and lesser artists, and who is to say that even the lesser artist has not contributed to the growth of civilization and to the communication of ideas. This is not to imply that you ought to compromise on your journey. You should set out to achieve the very heights. But somewhere along the road you may find that the ascent is getting too steep. That is where many writers turn back or give up entirely. Yet it is at this point that the Solonian admonition, "Know thyself," should have its most profound meaning for you. Perhaps you have reached the fullest extent of your powers. If you are able to recognize this factor and maintain your output at your own highest level, there is no need for bitter brooding. Recognition of the extent of your powers is a sign of maturity, and you should have a sense of satisfaction in knowing that you are doing your very best. You should realize that there are other writers of greater or lesser talent than yourself. The paramount question you must ask yourself is: Am I doing the utmost of which I am capable?

Surely you must begin with a set of ideals. The youthful writer always does. He wants to set the world aglow with the beauty of his prose, the wit of his dialogue and the power of his ideas. This is all as it should be. But at some time in his development another question will confront the writer: How far do I compromise?

This may be the supreme question for most writers. Ideally, the writer ought not to compromise; pragmatically, especially in the broadcasting field, he finds he has to, if he wants to make a living at his chosen profession. If he wishes to write a TV play that can be considered dramatic art, he may be balked by many limitations. Should he persist in writing as he pleases, he may discover that he has no market for his wares. He will be told, repeatedly, that television is a mass medium and that he must write for the least common denominator of the audience. Many of his bread-and-butter assignments will be just that: hack work.

Yet, in making your decision to remain a writer in spite of all obstacles, you may learn to compromise outwardly but not inwardly. You will necessarily write within the limitations of your medium, but whatever assignment you are given will be done to the best of your ability. You have an obligation to your audience not to pawn off anything shoddy. That would be a blow to your own integrity. There are many praiseworthy scripts which have been written for radio and television. Whether the broadcasting industry admits it or not, and it has often been reluctant to do so, it depends to a tremendous extent on the writer. His is the inventiveness, the creativeness without which the greater part of the programming would not exist. And despite the many overseers and the restrictive taboos, there can be and there have been some excellent creative productions which may be termed, without equivocation, art.

You may have heard the statement expressed, generally by those of intellectual pretension, that what is popular must be poor. This is a false notion. The writer, who has something to say, wants to reach the largest audience possible. Shakespeare was popular and wanted his plays to be popular. Shaw was not a whit perturbed at *Pygmalion* being a hit play and a very successful film. Dickens was a writer of best sellers. Mark Twain made a fortune out of his books. There is nothing wrong with fame and fortune. Some of our best writers have acquired both!

In your journey you may reach the topmost peak. Let us hope you arrive there with some of your ideals intact.

JOBS AND CAREERS

Writing assignments in broadcasting are many and varied. You may, for example, establish a career as a copywriter or a free-lance dramatist. There is, of course, a world of difference between the two. This difference is an indication of how broad is the field of writing for television and radio. Broadcasting embraces almost every type of writing. No other medium offers such a wide range.

A network may have on its staff creative dramatists, documentary writers, news writers, and general continuity writers. A 50-kilowatt station may employ creative writers, news writers, general continuity writers and commercial copywriters. Smaller stations may hire one or two writers for both general continuity and commercials, and a news reporter who writes his own copy. Both the networks and the larger stations may contract with free-lance writers for special assignments. Advertising agencies have creative departments which may employ both dramatists and copywriters. Many government agencies, particularly the United States Information Agency (USIA), offer careers to radio and television writers. The field, as you can see, is quite extensive.

Presumably all writers, when they begin, set their sights on the highest form of creativeness in their chosen field. In broadcasting, this apex is the drama. But not all of us can be dramatists or, at least, successful dramatists. This type of broadcasting is also the most competitive and the highest paid, for writers, with the exception of gag writers. Yet, as we have observed, the field of broadcast writing is so extensive that, in all probability, the daily output of non-dramatic continuity is far greater than that of the drama. There are some 3,000 radio stations in the United States which utilize a tremendous amount of writing little of which today is in the field of drama. This writing consists of commercials, public service announcements, talks, musical continuity, program introductions, news reports, and the like. Some of this output has been termed "creative" in the sense that an advertising agency's art and copy departments are called "creative." Except for some types of talks, and program notes for symphonic and operatic broadcasts, these forms of writing are hardly cultural and are far removed from the true creativeness of the drama.

Within the broadcast drama itself, there are, as we know all too well, many variations from a standard. Too many television dramas, for example, fall into the potboiler category. This is not a phenomenon peculiar to a new medium. Ever since man learned to tell his fellow men a story, there has been much quantity and comparatively little quality. The true writer is always striving for quality, constantly endeavoring to improve his creative efforts. Nevertheless, economic necessity has made most writers accept hack assignments. In many cases, these assignments prove helpful in that they provide the daily bread and permit the writer to turn out an occasional quality script on which he may have to spend a great deal of time.

Some writers have begun with rather lowly assignments which have, however, qualified them as professionals; they have then found more ready acceptance when submitting a finer type of script to other programs. In other words, the hack assignment may be a stepping stone. The great danger in hack assignments is that the writer may never rise above them. This may be due partly to limited talent and partly to the exigencies of meeting expenses. Yet all through literary history, there are instances of the great having written potboilers. The fact is that the writer, despite his frequent carpings about his profession, would rather write than undertake any other endeavor.

The decision as to the sort of writing career you wish to follow in the broadcasting field is up to you. Not entirely, of course. Circumstances may help shape your destiny. You will find that you are all too infrequently "master of your fate" and "captain of your soul." But you can consider the following aspects of the profession and then make your decision accordingly.

You may begin your career at a small local station as a continuity writer; if you progress upward in the scale you may wind up as chief of continuity for one of the top stations in the country or for a network. You may have a bent towards advertising; again it is possible to learn your craft well at a small station or a small agency. Eventually, you may reach the top rung as chief copywriter for a large advertising agency. Financially, you will be high up in the scale. Or you may, during the course of your career, become a staff writer at a network headquarters. In this capacity, you may be called upon for a wide variety of assignments, from musical continuity to dramas and documentaries. Possibly, after acquiring some experience in the commercial field or after obtaining a college degree with a major, or many courses, in radio and television, you may decide on a government information career.

Suppose, as do so many writers, that you aspire to the most creative goal: free-lance television dramatist. You envision the time when you can work on your own and your plays appear on "Studio One," "Kraft Theatre," "Playhouse 90" or their future equivalents. You earn enough to live well. Some of your video plays sell to the movies. Or perhaps you adapt one of your more successful video dramas for the stage and it becomes a hit. There is no limit to the possibilities. That is one of the great fascinations of writing. Success can be unlimited. Realistically, we must admit, the crown of success is for the very few. Why not for you?

You may begin your free-lance journey in several ways. First, there is the direct approach. You learn how to write a TV play and concentrate entirely on this creative form. Perhaps you are fortunate and sell early. Generally the battle for recognition is a long one. You may be blessed with an income of your own. You may live at home and have indulgent parents who can support you. If not, you may have to follow one of two divergent courses, either of which, you hope, will lead you to the desired end. You get a job as a continuity writer for a radio or television station and pursue your playwriting in your spare hours. Or you may obtain a position completely unrelated to writing and again use your spare hours for dramatic creation.

Even though you may spend only a few hours each week at your typewriter, you will discover, as every writer has, that creativeness cannot be confined by any set rules of time and place. True, you must acquire a discipline of working habits; this you will find stressed further on in this chapter. But a playwright in the throes of creation finds that his play is always with him. He may be on his way to an appointment and snatches of dialogue will flash through his mind. He may be taking part in a conversation in a friend's living room and suddenly lose the thread of it as a new scene abruptly occurs to him. He may lie awake planning the denouement. He may be driving with his wife and his long silences are misconstrued as having nothing to say. Actually, he may be listening to his characters as they harangue each other.

For all this cerebration, this inner working of the creative mind, the writer must be an astute observer of the world about him. The stuff of life is the material from which he weaves his plays. The great dramatists have been keen observers of contemporary life and their comments on the problems, great and small, of daily existence, have wielded immeasurable influence. Many have helped pave the way for social changes. Yet we must remember that the public watches a play primarily to be entertained. Therefore, if you have something to say in your drama, as you should, remember always to say it entertainingly.

QUALIFICATIONS OF THE WRITER

If we were to try to formulate some general qualifications for the potential TV and/or radio writer, we should include the following:

1. Inventiveness
2. A sense of inquiry
3. Discipline
4. Knowledge of the language
5. Knowledge of the media
6. Perseverance

Inventiveness

"It is the divine attribute of imagination that it can create a world for itself."
— *Washington Irving*

If necessity is the mother of invention, then imagination surely is its father. The inventiveness of the writer is his greatest personal asset. He can be taught techniques but no teacher can give a pupil the gift of creativeness. The teacher can only help to develop it.

In studying some of the daily written output for the broadcast media, it becomes apparent that some writers believe inventiveness is exclusively the tool of the fictionizing playwright. That, of course, is a misconception. The writer should bring his imagination into play for every assignment whether it be a twenty-second introduction to a song or an hour drama.

What is inventiveness? Is it dreaming up a plot, an idea, a slogan, even, out of nothingness? No, it is rather the innate ability to build a complete story out of a tiny incident. It is a sort of Aladdin's lamp of the mind which when rubbed with the gauze of imagination turns a hovel into a palace, a pebble into a diamond. It is the wheelwright standing before his shop and conceiving of a coach propelled without a horse, moving more swiftly than ordinary man could ever dream.

The difference between the journalist and the dramatist is that the one records events, the other invents them. Yet the dramatist may lean heavily on the journalist, for the dramatist will take the reporter's random facts and by the power of his imagination transform them into an integrated living entity. This entity will be larger than life. In some instances the dramatist will add deeper tragedy to the fact and in others he will clothe the starkness with a cloak of romanticism.

The writer who toils with words must make an ally of imagination and let it govern his every effort.

A sense of inquiry

"A curious person who searches into things under the earth and in heaven." — Plato

If he is not already endowed with a natural curiosity about people and places, the writer must develop a sense of inquiry. He must be an explorer who is continually making discoveries about his fellow men.

It is not our intention to imply that the writer must become a prying gossip who embarrasses people with intimate questions. Rather he must acquire the reporter's facility in learning the whys and wherefores of any given situation. Besides, people like to talk about themselves and given half a chance, they will. At this point, the writer becomes a rapt listener and makes copious mental notes.

If he has an opportunity to travel, he should do all he can to acquaint himself with the native population, to delve into the customs and traditions of the country, to see for himself what day-to-day existence is really like in this foreign land. This means avoiding the well-trodden tourist paths that afford only a superficial view.

Although travel will broaden the writer's horizon, it is not an essential to his craft. W. Somerset Maugham, a superb craftsman, came upon a wealth of story ideas in his constant travels. But Nobel Prize winner William Faulkner found all the raw material he needed in his home town, Oxford, Mississippi.

A story is generated by an individual; history, by a people.

Discipline

"The art of writing is the art of applying the seat of the pants to the seat of the chair."
— *Mary Heaton Vorse*

The sooner the potential writer learns to discipline himself, the sooner he will transform potential into professional.

Nowhere is the need for discipline more essential than in writing for television or radio. These are deadline media which permit little leeway. The beginning writer ought to set himself a goal, even if it be as little as five hundred words a day. On the face of it, five hundred words a day may appear a trifle. Try it. You will very shortly discover, even within the space of a week, the true meaning of discipline.

Consider this fact: if you are able to write a thousand words a day on a five-day weekly basis, in ten weeks you will have written fifty thousand words. If your output is limited to five hundred words a day, in that same ten-week period you will still have reached twenty-five thousand words. Of course, there will be days when you cannot for the life of you do more than a hundred words or even a sentence. But there will be days when you find you have totaled two thousand. This would probably have been termed piddling by the prodigious Thomas Wolfe, but then genius is in a class by itself.

If you were to begin your writing career at a 250-watt radio station or at one of the mushrooming new television stations, you would be required to turn out a daily stint of copy. You will not be able to wait for a bolt of inspiration to strike you. To paraphrase that ancient French proverb, "The appetite comes with the eating" — for the writer, the inspiration comes with the writing.

The free-lance writer may find it even more difficult to discipline himself. He may not have the work-conducive atmosphere of an office or the daily nine to five routine. If he writes at home and has a family, there are the myriad distractions of which children are so eminently capable. And it is so easy to find things to do to keep the writer from the more arduous task of completing a script. Gardening, if you own a home; a lamp that needs fixing; a new shelf to be put up. Simple and relaxing work, and rewarding, too, but it doesn't pay the bills.

As a result the free-lance writer finds it essential to set a definite time schedule and stick to it. He may not work more than a few concentrated hours a day but the importance of self-discipline, which insures a regular output, cannot be overestimated.

In discussing the free-lancer, we have been speaking in terms of the television or radio playwright who is successful enough to earn his living solely through his writing. There are many free-lance writers who we may term the part-timers. These are writers who do not earn their living exclusively by writing. Their income may be derived from an allied field, such as teaching of English literature, or from some source totally removed from writing, such as clerking. The part-time writer, more than any other, must achieve some form of discipline. He comes home tired after the day's work and the very thought of pushing the typewriter keys is abhorrent. Or he starts to reflect that after all he is already earning a living and the chances are he's only bucking for a rejection slip so why not turn on the television and let someone else do the entertaining. Weekends there's golf and a party or two or the neighbors just invite you in for a couple of drinks. Ah, yes, the many pleasant distractions and who is to say "Satan! Get thee behind me!"

Reginald Rose, one of the better and more successful television playwrights, states in the foreword to his volume, *Six Television Plays*: "I worked as a copywriter for a small advertising agency specializing in men's and women's wear and all of my television writing was done at night and on weekends. I realized that these sixteen-hour days were becoming ridiculous when I found myself referring

to my oldest boy, then four years of age, as "what's-his-name." . . .
I now work a four-hour day and know all four boys' names at all
times." In these three sentences you find the complete success story
of the part-timer who became a full-timer, who has written more
than a dozen hour-long originals for television, two of which,
"Twelve Angry Men" and "Crime in the Streets," were sold for
handsome sums to the movies.

There are very few part-timers who are going to turn into
Reginald Roses but discipline is absolutely essential if the part-timer
is to become a selling writer or achieve that wonderful goal of
earning a living at the work he loves best.

Knowledge of the language

*"The function of
language is twofold: to communicate emotion and to give information."*
— *Aldous Huxley*

The writer is a purveyor of words and should try to maintain
an ever-increasing inventory. He may build up his warehouse of
words from a variety of sources: the speech of the people; reading
books, magazines, newspapers; classroom attendance; listening to
radio; watching television; going to the theater or a movie. A dictionary and a thesaurus are invaluable aids.

This does not mean that the writer has to be a model of erudi-
tion. Many readers, we are sure, after viewing some of the current
television programs will get the impression that they are written in
words of one syllable! While it is true that simplicity is the keynote
of writing for the broadcast media, the apparent simplicity of
many TV dramas, the plays of Paddy Chayefsky, for example, is
very deceptive. Often it is a studied simplicity, consciously and
carefully arrived at by the author.

The writer of drama may conceive of a character whose education, upbringing and economic status are of the highest. Another
character may be at the opposite end of the scale. The writer's
dialogue must be able to portray these widely differing backgrounds.
As Laurence Binyon, the English poet, stated: "A man's language is
an unerring index of his nature."

The commercial copywriter must invent a dozen different ways
to say the same thing and thus his warehouse of words needs con-

stant replenishing. The speech writer must try to avoid the ear-wearying clichés. This is not always possible. As a matter of fact, at times the familiar sentence will help to drive home a point. But new, aptly conceived phrases are always refreshing. The writer of musical continuity should be ever on the search for a new way to describe an old song, and the news writer for the pithy phrase that says so much in so few words.

The beginning writer is an apprentice slowly and diligently learning the use of the master craftsman's tools, in order that he may acquire the master's facility in the use of those tools.

Knowledge of the media

"There is no knowl-edge that is not power." — Emerson: "Society and Solitude"

A craftsman must be familiar with his tools. The television or radio writer should have a working knowledge of the mechanics of the media. He can gain this knowledge in several ways. He may discover a great deal by watching — not casually, to be entertained, but critically, to learn. He may read books which will describe in some detail the complex process by which television and radio programs are broadcast. A list of several such books will be found in the bibliography at the end of this book. He may visit his local television and radio stations and observe the programs in progress. Many universities which give courses in television and radio make it a practice to take a class on a field trip, i.e., either on a guided tour of a broadcasting station or to observe a particular program from sign on to sign off. Workshops enable students to work directly with cameras and microphones and to familiarize themselves first hand with the technical aspects of broadcasting. College and university owned and operated radio and television stations afford practical training opportunities.

Perseverance

"Few things are im-possible to diligence and skill." — Samuel Johnson

The writer must learn early in his career to be persistent. Unless he is one of the very few fortunates who strike a rich vein

article on ten years of television with the provocative title: "What TV is doing to America." The lead sentence of that article is highly significant: "The biggest of the new forces in American life today is television."

How much a part of American life is television? Here are some vital statistics:

The A. C. Nielsen Company in its 1956 report on the Radio and Television Audience stated that 72 per cent of all homes in the United States have TV sets. The average viewing time in these homes is six hours daily. "Daily viewing," the report continues, "starts slowly in the morning hours, picks up steam in the after-noons, then rises to an impressive nighttime high ranging from three hours and 26 minutes (week nights) to 3 hours and 57 minutes on Saturday."

This vast TV audience of 35,100,000 *homes* — and remember that this figure will be larger by the time you read this book — has some rather decided preferences in the matter of programs. The sixty-minute variety show attracts the greatest number of viewers, with the situation comedy, the western drama and the one-hour drama following in that order. Time-wise, the trend for evening network TV is towards the hour and longer program.

Program preference is colored by the composition of the family, depending on whether there are children, and the ages of the children. Unless the parents are very adamant about their children's viewing habits, or have certain programs they insist upon seeing, a great deal of viewing in the family will be decided by the children. If they are younger than teen-age, that influence lasts until 9 P.M., generally, depending on the children's bedtime. The teen-age in-fluence may last perhaps an hour later. A drastic change will arise, of course, when homes have two or more TV sets just as so many homes today have two or more radios.

Television is attempting to make deep inroads into the morn-ing and afternoon audience, most of which is still loyal to radio. Programs such as the Garroway morning show, the "Arlene Francis Show" and "Matinee Theater" have been vying for the multi-million daytime audience.

Many of our readers, we are sure, can remember the days, only a few years back, when most TV stations began their broadcast schedule in the late afternoon or early evening hours. Besides the economic factor — the cost of putting on programs for the entire

day, many of which might have to begin on an experimental, un-sponsored basis — there was the social factor to consider. Would the breadwinner, for instance, have any time, while rushing through breakfast, to view a television program? Would the housewife, busy with her household chores, have any time, during the day, to spend before the TV screen?

Those questions have been answered to some extent. The morning and afternoon programs have found sponsors because they have enticed viewers. The ingenuity of the housewife has enabled her to set up her ironing board and watch the television screen without burning holes in Johnny's shirt or Peggy's dress! We do not know of any survey which has discovered how many housewives watch TV with the vacuum running over the living room rug and it is manifestly impossible for the housewife to keep her eye on the roast and the television set at one and the same time. As a result, the writer of daytime television programs may face a different problem from that of writing evening programs. He may have to concentrate much more on the audio so that the video complements the dialogue rather than having many completely visual scenes. In this way, the housewife, if she has a chore in another room, may still follow the program by hearing what is going on.

We find then, that for many daytime television programs, the writer is combining radio and TV techniques.

THE RADIO AUDIENCE

With the advent of television, there were many gloomy predictions. (1) It would prove the death knell of the movies. Who was going to pay to look at a motion picture screen when you could watch your home screen free? And (2) it would make radio obsolete. Who would want to listen only when now he could both listen and see?

At this writing, and we daresay for the foreseeable future, neither Hollywood nor radio has become extinct nor show any signs of imitating the dodo. No one will question the inroads of television. Run through a current radio log and compare it with a pre-TV log and the change is immediately apparent. The big shows have moved to television. The top comedians, the high rated dramas, the big

variety programs are now firmly entrenched in television with the result that the radio network audience has suffered a tremendous decline in the evening hours.

Note that we say "evening hours." The situation is quite different during the day. The Nielsen report (The Radio and Television Audience 1956) shows that "radio has greater use than TV during 75 per cent of all the hours between 6:00 A.M. and 6:00 P.M. Monday through Friday . . . and until 3:00 P.M., radio reaches an average of more than twice as many homes."

"Since 1950," the Nielsen report states, "radio ownership has increased by 4,000,000 . . . until today over 96 per cent of all U.S. homes have at least one radio. (A big percentage have more than one set in the home plus another in the family car.)" There is a vast number of automobile radios, and they are steadily on the increase. And, as of 1956, there were more than ten million homes in the United States with radio only.

The writer for radio is therefore not sending his scripts into the void. But his opportunities are far more limited than they were before the advent of TV. Some radio "soap operas" still command a large and loyal following. And any night will find a half dozen corpses floating through the radio airwaves as the omnipresent "cops" chase the ubiquitous "robbers" through a mystery script.

The radio audience has become rather nomadic. It listens in automobiles while it travels about the country; it listens at picnics and on the beaches; and even at home it does its listening all over the house: in the kitchen, the den, the bedroom, the workshop. NBC attempted to take advantage of this often sporadic type of listening with its weekend "Monitor" which broke away from the rigid time segments of quarter hour or half hour. "Monitor" spots sometimes run three minutes, one minute, seven minutes, depending on their interest value.

Teen-agers, the pop disc jockeys' mainstays, form a great bulk of the radio audience. Commercial copy for such programs should be geared accordingly. The good music station, which attracts a more adult audience, requires a different copy approach. Many radio stations try to keep to a middle road musically with selections they hope will appeal to a wider audience; this entails still another approach for the writer.

An awareness of audience is, therefore, not only an asset but a decided necessity to the broadcast writer.

AUDIENCE MEASUREMENT

From the beginnings of commercial broadcasting, sponsors, logically enough, wanted to have some precise idea of the size and composition of the audience their programs were reaching. They knew that when they advertised in magazines or newspapers, they had a definite guaranteed circulation. The purveyors of print could quote actual subscription figures and knowledgeable newsstand sales. The task was not so simple for the broadcasting industry. It was comparatively easy to obtain from manufacturers and retailers the number of radio and television sets sold but it was a much more complicated problem to determine who listened to what program and how often.

Several methods were devised by researchers:
1. The Telephone Coincidental Method;
2. The Personal Interview Method;
3. The Diary Method;
4. The Electronic Method.

All four of these methods have their values and their shortcomings. However, we do not believe it is the place of this text to evaluate the different procedures. Rather, it is our purpose to present a short summary of each method to acquaint the reader, *de facto,* of what is current in measurement research. It will also familiarize him with what is meant by a Nielsen, a Trendex, a Pulse, or an ARB rating. There are other audience measurement organizations whose services are available to the broadcasting industry. We have chosen the aforementioned services to illustrate the various techniques because they are each practitioners of a different method.

All surveys, it is to be noted, use the projection method, i.e., a certain sampling of the population is contacted and from this sample there is projected an audience count for the city surveyed or for the entire country. This projection scale is scientifically approved as a research method. Obviously, it would be nearly impossible, physically and economically, to reach every person of listening or viewing age in the United States on a daily, weekly or monthly basis.

Surveys obtain the following information for their subscribers:
(a) Number of sets in use;
(b) Ratings and share of audience;

(c) Sponsor identification;

(d) Audience composition.

Ratings are not intended to be a modern sword of Damocles hanging over every program, although sometimes they appear to have that effect. The audience measurement organizations operate on a purely objective, scientific basis, convinced of their accuracy, despite the criticism that arises, from time to time, by performers and producers, and by competitive measurement firms. Rating figures must be thoroughly analyzed and understood. The important factor of audience composition must be taken into consideration. For example, a shaving cream manufacturer would naturally prefer a large male audience. His program, A, may have a lower rating than program B. However, if program A is shown to have an audience preponderantly male while program B has an audience largely feminine, he is undoubtedly better off with program A.

Nevertheless, it is true that consistently low ratings will sound the death knell of a program and this is certainly of concern to the writer. If the program he is writing for receives high ratings, then his purse will inflate correspondingly. If it rates lowest in the competition, he will probably be searching for another assignment.

THE TELEPHONE COINCIDENTAL METHOD

This method, utilized by Trendex, employs reporters who place calls during the time the program is on the air. There are five specific questions asked by the reporters:

1. Was anyone in your home looking at television just now?
2. What program, please?
3. What station, please?
4. What is advertised? Or, How many men, women, children are looking (listening)?
5. Do you have a television set? (Asked when television is not specifically mentioned.)

Answers to Question 1 will indicate the number of Sets-in-Use, while responses to Questions 2 and 3 give the basis for computing Ratings and Share of Audience. (Trendex offers comparative listener responses in fifteen cities where three or more networks are providing programs at the same time.) The answers to Question 4 serve in computing Sponsor Identification and Audience Composition Indexes. The results of Question 5 are used to obtain a base of television homes from the random sample of all telephone homes.

THE PERSONAL INTERVIEW METHOD

In this method, the viewer or listener is interviewed and asked to recall the program he watched or listened to the previous day, or the hours preceding the interview. For example, in order to ascertain viewing or listening done between the hours of 8 A.M. and 12 noon, the interview would take place between 4 and 5 P.M. For programs scheduled between the hours of 7 P.M. to 12 midnight, interviews would take place the next evening between 6 and 7 P.M.

Interviewers are generally adult, married women who are local residents of the communities they survey.

This personal interview method, as utilized by Pulse, operates, briefly, as follows: "Samples are taken from latest U.S. Census block statistics published for each city. Surrounding areas are studied as blocks. The interviewer has no control over addresses to be called on. She starts in at a designated number in a block, and working clockwise, covers every other home, alternating upstairs and down for two-family dwelling units; one apartment to a floor elsewhere, moving back by apartment size where there are one, two, three and more rooms per apartment."

A printed roster of programs by quarter hours is used by Pulse. However, interviewers determine family activity at home before showing the roster. This is done in order to avoid misleading or inflating statements. If, for instance, it was determined that the set was not in use during the hours to be surveyed, the interviewer would ask routine questions but would not use the roster. On the other hand, if the set were in use, then intensive questioning would be employed. After every survey, Pulse sends out a mail inquiry to check on whether the interview was made as specified. Spot checks are also made by supervisors in the field.

THE DIARY METHOD

This method of audience research consists in obtaining the cooperation of a number of typical families in keeping a diary of all the viewing done by the family during the week. This is the method utilized by the American Research Bureau (ARB). ARB issues two reports each month covering all counties in the United States within a 150-mile radius of any TV signal. Audience studies are also made for individual television markets.

The diary issued to the cross section of families is a compact pamphlet with a page for each day in the week on which can be noted the time of viewing, the station viewed, the name of the program and the number of people watching (men, women, children under 16). There are instructions with each diary to guide the family in accurate reporting.

In addition to actual programs viewed, the diary obtains other pertinent information such as television reception. The family is asked to list all the stations which they can clearly receive. The composition of the household by age and sex is also determined. And there is a query on commercials: "Of all the television commercials you've seen this week, which one did you like the best?" "Which one did you like the least?"

The ARB supervised viewer-diary technique includes three basic interviews: one made during the location of the sample family and two additional ones during the diary week. Samples are completely changed for each separate study.

THE ELECTRONIC METHOD

The A. C. Nielsen Company, which is the world's largest marketing research organization, entered the broadcast measurement field many years ago. It has taken over the former Hooper national network rating service and has concentrated its efforts in utilizing electronics for research. The Nielsen Company developed an "Audimeter," an automatic recorder which records on tape or film, and is attached to the television or radio set; it registers an impulse for every minute of viewing time.

In each of a panel of carefully selected homes, distributed scientifically throughout the United States, an "Audimeter" makes a continuous, minute-by-minute record for each receiver showing the station to which it is tuned. Homes chosen for research purposes include those with and without television, with one, two and three or more radios, with and without telephone, urban and rural, all socio-economic brackets, all ages and family sizes, and each of these groups in its proper proportion. Tapes or films are removed from the Audimeters twice a month and tabulated by special IBM machines.

The Nielsen Company, as do other rating services, believes that it has a large enough sample which can be projected to all United States radio and television homes. These ratings show a program's nationwide appeal or lack of appeal, its standing against competitive hours, and often can forecast a trend.

In order to assure accuracy both in the recording apparatus and the myriad tabulations, the Nielsen Company found it necessary to develop additional apparatus of even greater complexity than the Audimeter:

1. Inspection machines to eliminate defective listening and viewing records.

2. Decoding and keypunching machines to get the data in form for IBM tabulation.

3. Attachments and modifications for IBM tabulating machines. This was necessary since the tabulation of Nielsen Audience Research statistics is one of the most complex operations performed by IBM machines.

4. Automatic typewriting and printing devices.

Some idea of the astronomical tabulations involved may be gained by the following statement from the Nielsen brochure, "Television Audience Research": ". . . 400 full-time (Nielsen) workers . . . produce 5,000,000 new facts each day and perform 50,000,000 statistical computations each day, and each year they print 126,000 copies of report books containing 21,000 different pages and 10,000,000 different figures."

CONCLUSION

It must be obvious that, to coin a phrase, broadcast ratings are not pulled out of thin air. Neither are they drawn from some mathematical wizard's hat. Much effort, study, money and manpower have gone into audience measurement research, and the rating services are continually trying to improve their methods.

Program producers, stars, writers, await each current rating with the same apprehension with which the producer, the cast, the writer of a Broadway play turn to the drama pages the morning after an opening. The cold statistics, like the drama critics' reviews, will always be the subject of warm controversy.

Sources
and resources

3

Material for the writer is as wide as the span of life. His source may be autobiographical: interesting events that have occurred to him or which he has personally witnessed. Hearsay may not be admissible as evidence in a court of law but to the writer of fiction it may provide the basis for a story. The advice to the potential writer, that he dig in his own backyard to unearth a story, has been repeated countless times. It is still true today as it was when first uttered. If you choose a subject about which you know little or write about a strata of society with which you are unfamiliar you may find yourself sailing uncharted seas and unable to navigate safely home.

There are, of course, always exceptions. A recent novel, hailed by critics as an excellent study of the Eskimo, was written by a novelist who gained all his knowledge of Eskimos at the public library. It is difficult to set hard and fast rules for writing, especially writing for television and radio. Once you formulate a rule, you are likely to find that rule broken by the very next television program you watch or radio program you listen to. Yet we must have some general principles which the embryo writer can follow without becoming confused.

We find an analogy in the field of modern art. The true painter does not begin with non-objective or pure abstractionist work. He first learns the elements of composition, the relationship of colors, the demands of perspective. Once he has mastered the fundamentals, he may break away from these basic principles and invent forms of his own. That is the nature of the creative artist.

SOURCES

Many writers find the newspapers and news magazines excellent source material; not the headline stories on page one but the brief items on page four or five. Or you may find an idea for a script in a radio or TV newscast. Some time ago, this author was listening to a CBS year-end roundup and heard a woman relate a few of her experiences when the plane on which she was a passenger was forced down in a heavy snowfall. This incident provided the basis for a prize-winning script, "Together We Live."

A few words of caution regarding the use of factual material will not be amiss here. The laws of libel and slander and the use of actual names are considered in another section of this chapter under the heading "Taboos." However, from the story angle itself, the writer may find that if he hews too closely to the facts, paradoxically enough, the result is a script that may be unbelievable. The maxim that truth is often stranger than fiction is no mere cliché. Transfer the truth verbatim into the guise of a play and you may come up with an incredible tale. Your cries that this is the way it actually happened will move the editors and producers not one whit.

Robert Buckner, screen writer and playwright commented: "The great fault of most true stories is their improbability; it is far simpler to imagine a convincing plot than to borrow one from actual facts." And John Crosby, the syndicated television and radio critic, pointed out in one of his columns the apparent unbelievability of the actual. If the writer were to use as a character a ten-year-old boy who knew more about stocks and investments than most veteran brokers, the reader would insist that this was a figment of fantasy. Yet, as any quiz program fan can tell you, a ten-year-old financial wizard appeared on "The Big Surprise" and won the jackpot of $100,000. If the playwright is looking for any moral, it may very well be the following: build your foundation on facts, if you wish, but brick the house with fiction.

Writers often find other writers a great source of inspiration. This is not to suggest any notion of plagiarizing. But all workers in the arts have gone to the old masters to learn from, to be inspired by and to draw upon. If you were to take a museum tour with an art instructor, he would undoubtedly point out to you how artists have been influenced by their predecessors. A study of Shakespeare reveals that the greatest of all playwrights drew much of his source material from Holinshed's Chronicles.

There is only one criterion: what the artist — and we use the term in its all-encompassing sense — does with the material. If he has only the talent to copy, he will be decried as a mere imitator. But if he is truly creative, he will bring to his work, no matter the source, an air of originality, a breath of invention, a deep draught of imagination. In fact, the source may never be apparent for the writer has now created a thing of his own.

THE WRITER AS RESEARCHER

The writer may be called upon to prepare scripts on so wide a variety of topics that it would be impossible for him to be thoroughly informed on all of them. If he is employed as a staff writer for a network, or under contract to the network, he will be fortunate in having a research department to assist him in obtaining essential background material and to authenticate any statements in his script. If, for instance, he requires correct medical terminology for a hospital sequence, the research department will be able to obtain it for him.

The free-lance writer and the writer on the local level, generally, have no such research department to help them. But they can make use of local library facilities and they will find that in almost all instances, the librarian will be glad to assist them, if not in furnishing the material itself, at least in guiding them to the proper source. They can, of course, avail themselves of any of their friends who are in the professions: a doctor, lawyer, engineer, accountant, and so on.

Only a minority of writers appear to be aware of the research assistance available to them from their federal government. The agencies of government cover almost every facet of our daily lives. If the writer is working on a script which has a military background, he can have it checked for authenticity by the Office of Public Information, Department of Defense. If his script concerns an individual suffering from a malignant disorder, he can secure any available knowledge concerning the disorder from the Information Division of the Public Health Service. The writer will find these government sources and others invaluable when he cannot readily obtain the information from books accessible to him.

How much research should the writer do? The answer depends on the assignment. If he is under contract to write a series of scripts which require scientific or medical knowledge he may have to do a great deal of research in order to fully familiarize himself with the subject; or he may be assigned to write a documentary, which requires extensive travel and preparation. Usually he needs enough knowledge to give an air of authenticity to his script, to use a technical phrase correctly, to place an historic event properly. The writer should have a sense of obligation to his audience and the successful writer will be neither lazy nor slipshod in his search for what is correct.

DEVELOPMENT OF IDEAS

The journey from the opening scene to the closing curtain is a highly personal one. It is a lonely path that no two writers traverse in similar fashion. It is as subjective as the thought process itself.

Many writers will block out a complete script before they start, scene by scene. This is helpful especially in meeting the requirements of the television or radio play. In a half-hour play, you have to plan your sequence of events to build to a crisis at the halfway mark: the first act curtain. Then build to a climax and final resolution in the closing act. In the three-act hour play, you have two crises to lead up to. Your outline will show you where you are going. However, it is altogether probable that somewhere along the route you will encounter many detours of your own making.

Other writers will formulate an idea in their minds, know generally in which direction they are travelling and fill in the route details as they journey.

The development of the idea is generally the most difficult process for the writer. Once the idea has gone through the incubation stage and is fully hatched, the actual writing of the script, for the professional, is comparatively simple. The fear that continually plagues the writer is the possibility of running dry. The enormous amount of material required to meet the needs of the two or three thousand television and radio dramas produced each year make it necessary to depend on numerous adaptations. The creator of original dramas for the broadcast media does not have time for long incubations. Therefore, in order to maintain the essential output, the writer must have these intravenous feedings of adaptations.

Suppose we examine the development of an idea from its inception. The writer is pondering a plot. Through his mind runs a recent incident: He had called on his friend, Joe, one night. Joe had answered the doorbell. He was wearing an apron which he removed hastily and with much embarrassment. No, he couldn't join the poker session. He . . . er . . . had some work to do around the house. Poor, henpecked Joe.

Perhaps there was a story about Joe, a story with a twist. The Cinderella tale. Only, in this case, Cinderella would be a man. Put the man in a modern, easily recognizable setting. He lives in a small suburban home. He has a dominating wife and two grown children. He makes a fairly adequate living but never enough to meet the demands of his wife and his youngsters. His wife is very active in community affairs, president of this and that organization, busy making speeches, etc. So Joe finds himself often cooking dinner and cleaning house since he can't afford a maid. He is weighed down by bills. He has lost the respect of his friends. One night Joe finds himself alone at home. His wife has gone to a meeting. His daughter is out on a date. His son is visiting a friend. Joe is left with the dishes to wash and he is under orders from his wife to vacuum the living room. He is wretched.

Now the idea is beginning to develop. But here the writer pauses and takes a deep cerebral breath. Should he play it straight?

Cinderella was a fairy tale. Perhaps this play ought to be fantasy. Introduce a fairy godmother. But who?

Suppose Joe's wife is continually berating him. He can't even fix an ordinary faucet leak. She blames it on his poor upbringing, a mother who spoiled him. Joe's mother has been dead for a year now and the only time Joe rebels is when a disparaging remark is made about his mother. Maybe that's the answer . . . the fairy godmother? Joe's own mother . . . reappearing out of the blue. Maybe that's your title also: "Out of the Blue."

Perhaps at this moment, the reader should pause and become the writer. How would you develop this story? For a half-hour play or an hour play? What conflicts would you present? How would you show the complete metamorphosis of Joe? What other characters would you bring in? Joe's boss? Joe's neighbors?

Give your mind an exercise in developing an idea. The author could give his version, but the chances are that your version and that of a hundred other readers would be completely at variance. Of most importance to you as a potential writer for the broadcast media is the exercise in training yourself to develop a script from the birth of an idea to a mature and satisfactory conclusion.

Since this book is not confined exclusively to the writing of drama, we must consider the development of ideas in relation to other types of continuity. A great deal of thought and planning, for example, goes into the making of a commercial. Perhaps the reader has at one time or another seen or heard the "Harry and Bert" commercials prepared for the Piel Brothers Brewing Company. These commercials have won unanimous acclaim from the trade press. An American Research Bureau survey (August 1956) found that commercials for Piel's Beer ranked first as those TV announcements most admired by the public. And, of most importance to the sponsor, they have helped to break all sales records.

The creator of "Harry and Bert" is Ed Graham, formerly a copywriter for the Young and Rubicam Advertising Agency and now president of Goulding-Elliott-Graham. Goulding and Elliott are probably better known to radio listeners as "Bob and Ray." They are, incidentally, the voices of "Harry and Bert."

How did Ed Graham develop the idea for these outstanding commercials, "Harry and Bert"? Let him tell you:

The idea for creating "the Piel Brothers" came about when I

looked at the Piel label and noticed, in fine print, a legal line. It read: "A product of Piel Brothers, Brooklyn, N.Y."

Once past this step, however, one thing has distinguished these trade characters from any number of others. And that is the fact that they have individual personalities.

Most of the trademark advertising characters which I can recall seemed only to exist as "shills" for their products. Such quotations as "Folks who know, choose _____," or "Give yourself a _____, the finest," were hardly indicative of a special person speaking to you. Instead, most advertising creations said simply what any advertiser would like to hear and let it go at that.

It was my feeling that in order to make "Harry and Bert" real — they would have to exist as people first, as salesmen second. In order to assure this, I wrote complete biographies on each of the two fictitious gentlemen and thought about them for a week or so before actually writing any commercials.

After this initial step, the commercials seemed almost to write themselves. For given any situation it seemed that the reactions of these two new salesmen would have to follow along certain lines.

The characters were written to exist in every possible selling medium from TV to Dealer Meetings. The radio commercials were the first to go on the air, however. And when their reaction proved favorable to this relatively inexpensive test, the brothers took over on television, in newspapers, on billboards, and at the point of sale.

This is undoubtedly not the way the average copywriter tackles his assignment, which is probably what makes him average. Certainly, the copywriter who has to turn out a raft of commercials at a small agency or a local radio or television station may not have the time to develop ideas to such an extent. It is possible also that he may not have the degree of talent. However, there is a lesson here for every writer: an idea may begin with the flash of inspiration but it takes a great deal of mental application to bring it to fruition.

TABOOS

The broadcast writer, early in his career, must learn to compromise. If he believes that no subject is untouchable, no language, no matter how stark or epithetical, unusable, no scene too revealing, then he had better attempt the stage play or the novel. He will find television and radio too restrictive.

On the other hand, there are enough topics, both adult and compelling, which he can tackle. And, as in any other literary endeavor, the gauge of his writing is only limited by the measure of his talent.

The National Association of Radio and Television Broadcasters issues The Television Code which is a guide to the ethics of the industry. The section on Acceptability of Program Material is pertinent to the writer and we are reproducing below those items which are of particular interest to him. These taboos as outlined in The Television Code (Third Edition, July 1956) apply equally to the radio writer.

Acceptability of program material

Program materials should enlarge the horizons of the viewer, provide him with wholesome entertainment, afford helpful stimulation, and remind him of the responsibilities which the citizen has towards his society. Furthermore:

Profanity, obscenity, smut and vulgarity are forbidden, even when likely to be understood only by part of the audience. From time to time, words which have been acceptable, acquire undesirable meanings, and telecasters should be alert to eliminate such words.

Words (especially slang) derisive of any race, color, creed, nationality or national derivation, except wherein such usage would be for the specific purpose of effective dramatization such as combating prejudice, are forbidden, even when likely to be understood only by part of the audience. From time to time, words which have been acceptable, acquire undesirable meanings, and telecasters should be alert to eliminate such words.

Attacks on religion and religious faiths are not allowed.

Reverence is to mark any mention of the name of God, His attributes and powers.

When religious rites are included in other than religious programs the rites are accurately presented and the ministers, priests and rabbis portrayed in their callings are vested with the dignity of their office and under no circumstances are to be held up to ridicule.

Respect is maintained for the sanctity of marriage and the value of the home. Divorce is not treated casually nor justified as a solution for marital problems.

Illicit sex relations are not treated as commendable.

Sex crimes and abnormalities are generally unacceptable as program material.

Drunkenness and narcotic addiction are never presented as desirable or prevalent.

The use of liquor in program content shall be de-emphasized. The consumption of liquor in American life, when not required by the plot or for proper characterization, shall not be shown.

In reference to physical or mental afflictions and deformities, special precautions must be taken to avoid ridiculing sufferers from similar ailments and offending them or members of their families.

Televised drama shall not simulate news or special events in such a way as to mislead or alarm.

The presentation of cruelty, greed and selfishness as worthy motivations is to be avoided.

Excessive or unfair exploitation of others or of their physical or mental afflictions shall not be presented as praiseworthy.

Criminality shall be presented as undesirable and unsympathetic. The condoning of crime and the treatment of the commission of crime in a frivolous, cynical or callous manner is unacceptable.

The presentation of techniques of crime in such detail as to invite imitation shall be avoided.

The use of horror for its own sake will be eliminated; the use of visual or aural effects which would shock or alarm the viewer, and the detailed presentation of brutality or physical agony by sight or by sound are not permissible.

Law enforcement shall be upheld, and the officers of the law are to be portrayed with respect and dignity.

The presentation of murder or revenge as a motive for murder shall not be presented as justifiable.

Suicide as an acceptable solution for human problems is prohibited.

The exposition of sex crimes will be avoided.

The appearances or dramatization of persons featured in actual crime news will be permitted only in such light as to aid law enforcement or to report the news event.

The copywriter will find the section on Presentation of Advertising of especial value and again we are reproducing several paragraphs which we believe are of particular interest.

Presentation of advertising

Advertising messages should be presented with courtesy and good taste; disturbing or annoying material should be avoided; every effort should be made to keep the advertising message in harmony with the content and general tone of the program in which it appears.

Advertising copy should contain no claims intended to disparage competitors, competing products, or other industries, professions or institutions.

Television broadcasters should exercise the utmost care and discrimination with regard to advertising material, including content, placement and presentation, near or adjacent to programs designed for children. No considerations of expediency should be permitted to impinge upon the vital responsibility towards children and adolescents, which is inherent in television, and which must be recognized and accepted by all advertisers employing television.

Because all products of a personal nature create special problems, such products, when accepted, should be treated with especial emphasis on ethics and the canons of good taste; however, the advertising of intimately personal products which are generally regarded as unsuitable conversational topics in mixed social groups is not acceptable.

A television broadcaster should not accept advertising material which in his opinion offensively describes or dramatizes distress or morbid situations involving ailments, by spoken word, sound or visual effects.

Because of the personal nature of the advertising of medical products, claims that a product will effect a cure and the indiscriminate use of such words as "safe," "without risk," "harmless," or terms of similar meaning should not be accepted in the advertising of medical products on television stations.

LEGAL PITFALLS

There remains a last word of caution to the writer . . . as if he had not been cautioned enough! A legal phrase has arisen in recent years to plague the writer: "invasion of privacy."

Let us explore the meaning of that phrase without getting ourselves entangled in a skein of legal technicalities. The beginning writer is advised to choose his material from the realm of his own experience, to write about people he knows. Yet herein lies the danger. If the writer models one of his characters so closely on an actual living person as to make that fictional character readily recognizable, then the writer is vulnerable to an invasion of privacy suit. It does not matter whether the character is portrayed as a hero or a villain as far as invasion of privacy is concerned. However, the portrayal of an actual person as a villain may have direr consequences since the law of libel or slander may be invoked.

You will note that we have used the qualification, "living person." There is no invasion of privacy if dead persons are portrayed, except under very rare circumstances.

There have been instances where writers have been sued even when they have portrayed a fictional character as good and noble, when that character has been proved to be the counterpart of a living person. Fortunately, in such cases the judge has not awarded any damages since no harm has been done to the person. Such cases do have their nuisance value, however. Punitive damages may be awarded if the character portrayal resulted in loss of prestige or position.

Suppose you wanted to do a play about the woman down the street whose husband came home drunk every night. If the play went on the air and the husband and wife happened to see it and easily recognized themselves, you might very well be sued for invasion of privacy. Truth is a defense where defamation is claimed but it is no defense in cases where actual invasion of privacy is proved.

This then is a legal pitfall the writer must beware of, but it is one he can avoid easily enough. Unless he is writing a fantasy about Martians, he will in the main draw his material from the life about him. Actual incidents will inspire him but then he must put his imagination, his inventiveness and his skill to work. Change the location of the events, perhaps the age of the characters, the jobs they have. Emulate the skillful tailor who can alter Joe's suit so that it fits John perfectly and is no longer recognizable as Joe's. But it still retains the basic cloth.

On the other hand, if someone you knew told you of an experience in his or her life which you believed would make an excellent play, you could ask permission to use the incident. Approval would remove any danger of invasion of privacy.

Anyone who has been involved in a legal suit will know how

complex the law can be. Therefore, the only sage advice we can offer is that if you have any worries about "invasion of privacy," check with a lawyer.

A HAPPY NOTE

Perhaps after reading these restrictions, you may begin to feel that you must approach the typewriter handcuffed. Though it is true that the majority of broadcast dramas are rather innocuous, there are a great many which are stirring in theme, very capably written and thought provoking. When you come right down to it, how many of the novels that are written, plays produced, short stories printed can be classified as great literature or even literature at all.

We suggest that if you wish to write for television that you study the finished product as it comes to you on the home screen. Base your judgements on the better scripts, not the poorer ones. You will never succeed if you approach the medium with a "this is beneath me" attitude. Emulate a script you admire and you will find that if you do have to make a compromise, it will be a happy one.

The video style: a comparative study

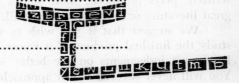

4

When radio made its swift growth in the world of communications, it brought with it a new form of writing. Every other medium in which the writer works is visual or requires the use of visual apparatus, mechanical or human: the camera or the eye. The stage, and even more, the screen, lean heavily on visual action. Radio is different. It exists in an eyeless world and it demands a writing style that is completely aural.

We know now that the lack of the visual was no handicap to radio, that this deficiency was more than compensated for by man's imagination. Television's child may be unaware of the heyday productions of radio but his parents will remember the former splendor of network radio programs, the brilliance, the poetry, the perceptiveness of a script by Norman Corwin or Archibald MacLeish, the fascinating horror of a tale by Arch Oboler.

This "Aural Style of Writing" has been discussed, definitively, by Albert Crews in his book, *Professional Radio Writing*. Our concentration in this chapter will be on the new, visual medium of television, its unique requirements and its similarities to, and differences from, other media.

VIDEO AND RADIO

For radio, the writer has to think in terms of picture words, dialogue which will immediately create an image for the listener. In this, he is aided and abetted by the use of sound and music. Granted that the listener's imagination is of invaluable assistance to the radio writer, the scripter is, nevertheless, obligated to inform his audience of many basic details such as location, time, movement, dress, appearance. These details require comparatively little aural explanation in television. The video writer has the camera, which follows movement; the set, which explains location; the visible actors, whose appearance and dress are obvious.

Now that broadcasting has emerged into the realm of the visual, the writer also has new vistas open to him. He no longer writes for the ear alone. He may make full use of a basic element of drama, the distinguishing element between "blind" radio and visual television: the pantomime. Here, for example, is a scene from a "Father Knows Best" script:

> Eames comes out of the kitchen carrying a tray of wine glasses, which he places on a serving stand near the kitchen door. He glances longingly at the speakers' table, then goes into the kitchen. Jim is the only one in a position to see Eames. At first, he doesn't recognize him, but then he does, and the irony of the whole thing registers in his face. Just before Eames goes back into the kitchen, Kathy starts to turn in that direction, but Jim grabs her so that she won't see him.

This sequence tells its story by movement, facial expression, set and props. It also illustrates the fundamental principle that in visual writing, the dramatist must indicate the movements of his characters and describe their reactions. We will discuss this point further but first let us see what happens if the above scene were to be written for radio presentation. The simplest, and probably the most effective approach, for this particular scene, would be to utilize Jim as the narrator.

JIM: I was seated at the banquet table at Lazarro's restaurant. We were all waiting anxiously for the appearance of our guest of honor. I saw an old man shuffling out of the kitchen carrying a tray of wine glasses. I watched him place the glasses on a serving stand near the kitchen door. At first I didn't recognize the old man. Then I stared in surprise. It was Eames . . . our guest of honor! And there he was working as a dishwasher . . . not knowing this banquet was for him. I looked around quickly. Nobody at the table had seen Eames. Then my daughter, Kathy, turned in Eames' direction. I grabbed her and turned her away.

You will note that the irony of the situation, which is evident in Jim's expression in the video sequence, must be put into words for the radio scene. Each movement, Eames coming into the kitchen, Kathy turning in his direction, must be explained verbally. The location must be specified. Word pictures are called for: "an old man shuffling out of the kitchen."

The differences between the video and the radio style are further illustrated by this excerpt from a radio script:

MUSIC:	FOR TIME PASSAGE FADE FOR
SOUND:	HAMMER ON WOODEN RAIL
MATT:	Hello, Hank.
HANK:	Hi . . .
MATT:	Is my Ma around?
HANK:	She was here a minute ago . . . told me to fix this fence rail 'fore it falls to the ground . . . she went over to the barn.
MATT:	Oh . . . yeah . . . I see her now . . . (CALLING) Ma . . . Ma . . . (FADE OUT)
SOUND:	FOOTSTEPS ON GRAVEL
MATT:	(FADE IN) Ma . . .
MRS. H:	Hello, son.

Here, music has been used for a time transition, later on, a sound effect (FOOTSTEPS ON GRAVEL) has been employed for a place transition; that is, going from one scene to another. To help achieve this latter effect, a FADE OUT of Hank's voice is indicated; that is, he moves back from the microphone to give the illusion of being at a distance.

The radio writer, untroubled by the necessity for physical sets, can utilize many scenes simply by the device of music and/or sound effects for transitions. His script is written in the same manner whether the production is to be live or recorded. But the video writer must ascertain first whether his program is to be live or filmed because his technique will be affected. Transitions may present problems in live productions. Film plays offer more choice and scope of locations. In the foregoing illustrative sequence, a film play could shoot each scene, between Matt and Hank, and between Matt and his mother, at different times. A live teleplay might very well reverse the radio action and have Matt's mother enter the same set which her son and Hank occupy.

In considering the number of scenes, the radio writer has almost as much freedom as the short story writer. The screen writer has the widest latitude in the choice of locations because of the extensive budgets for motion pictures. The stage dramatist is the most limited in the use of physical sets. Television is somewhere in between. These are all factors which influence a writer's technique and with which he must be thoroughly cognizant.

STAGE AND SCREEN

Actually, the video play is more closely allied to the screen play than any other form of writing. Both utilize the same basic mechanical device: the camera. The filming of almost all half-hour dramas and the fact that many of the hour and a proportion of the 90-minute plays are also being filmed are further indications of the close alliance between television and motion pictures.

All three media, stage, screen, television, have common elements: dialogue and pantomime. Yet there is a differentiation in the use of these elements due, in large measure, to the composition of their respective audiences. Both stage and screen plays are presented in a more formal atmosphere than the video play, and to an audience which is at once more homogeneous and gregarious. The stage play reaches mostly an adult audience and generally attracts patrons of higher than average intelligence. This permits the stage dramatist to write in a more literary fashion. He has a much wider range in choice of theme than the video playwright. The ideas he propounds may be more complex, the dialogue, more erudite, and because the stage dramatist has more time, his character and plot development may be fuller and richer.

The video writer, conscious of the fact that his audience is heterogeneous and widely scattered, that his time and subject matter are limited, shapes his style to meet the needs of a very demanding medium, one which requires as much or even greater craftsmanship than the theater.

Television writing must be concise, simple, always coherent. It is directed to all the people, not a select segment. It tends therefore to be idiomatic in style, and avoids the flowery, the formal and the literary phrase. The video writer finds that he cannot indulge in meandering, or pause for philosophic commentary. He must get quickly to the core of his play.

What may often seem a paucity of words on the part of the video writer is more likely an equating of his work with the mass medium, a realistic acceptance of the fact that in day-to-day conversation, the average viewer uses a limited vocabulary. Dialogue is conversation. Even the very learned sprinkle their conversations with idiomatic phrases. The writer to achieve verisimilitude must have an ear for the speech of the people. In normal conversation, for example, most people use a great many elisions: "I'm" instead of "I am"; "I'll" instead of "I will"; "You've" instead of "You have." Note the speech pattern of foreigners who have learned English at their native schools. Their sentence structure is formalized and their speech lacking in idiom and elisions. Even if the foreigner did not have an accent, we would become aware almost immediately of a difference in speech.

The screen play, as we have observed, is allied more closely to the television play than the drama of the theater. Although motion pictures are produced primarily for a captive, paying audience which gathers in an auditorium, in the manner of playgoers, movie theaters are so numerous that, in essence, a screen play caters to a mass audience. In most instances, it is a family audience, such as gathers in the living room to watch TV. Therefore the screen play has many of the restrictions of the video play. The film makers have a Motion Picture Code comparable to the Television Code. An excellent comparison of these Codes is available in Sydney W. Head's comprehensive study: *Broadcasting in America.*

The existence of these Codes is a prime reason why so many motion pictures can be shown on the television screen with little editing except for time. It is only recently that motion pictures, hurt by the competitive sting of television, have turned to more adult themes, and a broader interpretation of subject matter. The Kazan-Schulberg production of "A Face in the Crowd" is a case in point.

Motion pictures have always been haunted by the bugaboo of the "twelve-year-old mind"; that is, any picture which is above the mentality of a twelve-year-old is bound to be a box office failure. The release of a horde of ancient motion pictures for televiewing implies that the television audience is of comparable average mentality. Actually, of course, it is the same audience. But to accept the premise of the "twelve-year-old-mind," unequivocally, would make a hack of every writer, lowering his standards to the level of pulps.

The writer, single-handedly, may not be able to raise the level of programming, but he can maintain the quality of his scripts. We are of the opinion that both the motion picture and the television producers underestimate the intelligence of their audience. Unfortunately, only a comparatively small segment of the audience is vocal in regard to its likes and dislikes. Usually, expressions of opinion come from opposite ends, from highly impressionable "fan club" elements or organized cultural groups. The great body of viewers and listeners, who fall somewhere in between these two groups, are seldom letter writers and their opinions are confined, generally, to their families and friends.

We raise this issue because the demands of an audience will in turn influence the type of programming and, ergo, the style of writing. If an "Omnibus" can continue to interest sponsors and a rather large audience for the more intellectual fare, surely some of its enlightenment may rub off on other programs.

THE NOVELIST'S STYLE

The television writer, unlike the novelist or short story writer, requires a host of collaborators before his work can reach the public. The novelist speaks directly to his audience, and his prose must be all-sufficient. It must convey the sense of action, delineate characters, portray moods, describe locations. There are no cameras, no sound effects, no music, no actors to assist. Reading a novel is a highly personalized experience. It is true that a novel may be read to a group, and there have been readings of novels on the air, but primarily novel reading is an individual experience.

The novelist, unless he is a hack, has no limit to the style of his writing. His prose may be poetic, it may be simple and colloquial, or it may be filled with long, involved Faulknerian sentences. He has no arbitrary length to confine him. The reader also sets his own time in perusing a novel. He may read it in a day, a week or a month. If he were to come across a difficult passage, he may reread it. If he does not understand a word or two, he can stop to ascertain the meaning in a dictionary. Also, since most books are rather widely reviewed, a reader may know its contents beforehand. If he is averse to its subject matter, he may not choose to read it. Conversely, the novelist has an unlimited choice of theme.

On this question of theme, we might mention the existence in the British cinema world of the distinction between "adult only" and general family interest motion pictures. Here in the United States, some motion picture theaters advertise certain features as "adult only." In many instances, this label connotes mere sensationalism. But the point is that television cannot feasibly place an "adult only" label on its productions. The motion picture theater may refuse to sell tickets to minors, but few families can police their own living room, especially when they have little foreknowledge, except for a scant newspaper highlight, of the actual program content. Again, this is a factor which has a direct influence on the writer and of which he must be aware if he is to avoid many fruitless hours of scripting.

For a comparative study of style between the novel and video, here is a paragraph from Oliver Goldsmith's classic, *The Vicar of Wakefield*.

Such vigorous proceedings seemed to redouble Mr. Thornhill's anxiety; but what Olivia felt gave me some uneasiness. In this struggle between prudence and passion, her vivacity quite forsook her, and every opportunity of solitude was sought, and spent in tears. One week passed away; but Mr. Thornhill made no efforts to restrain her nuptials. The succeeding week he was still assiduous; but not more open. On the third he discontinued his visits entirely; and instead of my daughter testifying any impatience, as I expected, she seemed to retain a pensive tranquillity, which I looked upon as resignation. For my own part, I was now sincerely pleased with thinking that my child was going to be secured in a continuance of competence and peace, and frequently applauded her resolution, in preferring happiness to ostentation.

In this one paragraph, Goldsmith has covered a great deal of territory. In one sentence he has given us a vivid picture of Olivia's reactions: her "struggle between prudence and passion, her vivacity quite forsook her" and so on. In this same paragraph there are many intervals of time: "One week passed away," "The succeeding week," "On the third." The video writer, with all his assistance of camera, actors, set, music, would have to enlarge his scope greatly to encompass this one paragraph. Dialogue and pantomime would be necessary to portray Olivia's emotions. It would be possible for her to express her inner feelings in a monologue but dialogue would be preferable. In this instance, it might be a scene between her father, the Vicar, and herself. Or it could be a scene between Mr. Thornhill and Olivia. The television script would also have to make allowances for time passage by means of appropriate transitions. These are details which are discussed fully in the chapters on "The Television Drama" and "Adaptations."

You will note, too, the literary style of the novel and the extensive vocabulary as exemplified by this sentence: "I was now sincerely pleased with thinking that my child was going to be secured in a continuance of competence and peace, and frequently applauded her resolution, in preferring happiness to ostentation." Hardly the type of writing you are likely to encounter in any television script! In video style, this sentence might be translated into dialogue somewhat in this fashion:

VICAR

I'm very happy that your future's going to be taken care of, my child. I've told you many times how wise I think you are in realizing that happiness is more important than living in luxury.

Although most of our contemporary novels are written with a great deal more simplicity of phrase than their eighteenth- and nineteenth-century forerunners, many present-day novels are replete with literary phrasing. And few novelists, past or present, can match the sheer flow of words of a Thomas Wolfe.

In many instances, the television writer must be both a master of condensation and expansion. He might be called upon to adapt the entire *Vicar of Wakefield,* an approximately 300-page novel, to an hour video play. On the other hand, it is possible to choose one episode from this same novel and enlarge upon it for a half-hour or hour drama. This is a skill which comes with experience.

THE VIDEO INTERPRETERS

We have stated that the television writer requires a host of collaborators. This is true for any form of television writing whether it be a commercial, a news story or a professor preparing a lecture for an educational TV station. It is particularly true for the video dramatist. First, he must consider the director. In composing visually, the writer must see each movement of each character and what he sees he must make evident to the director and through him to the audience. Therefore, in writing a script, all action must be indicated. This excerpt from "The Great Guy," another of the "Father Knows Best" series, is a typical example.

INT. CIRCULATION DEPARTMENT — DAY
MEDIUM CLOSE SHOT BUD FREDDY AND A BUNDLE TYER.
Both Bud and Freddy have aprons on, and Freddy is wearing a fingerless glove and finger-cutter on his right hand. He is sweating as he tries to tie a bundle in the accepted manner. Bud is back of the tyers, and he also is sweating as he lifts a tied bundle from in front of the next tyer, and stacks it on the almost-loaded turtle truck. A worker enters the scene (from direction of inserting table) and places another stack of 25 papers in front of the tyer. Bud now moves beside Freddy to pick up Freddy's tied bundle. Both boys look real beat and dirty. They stop working for a moment, breathing heavily.

You will observe how graphic the writer, Roswell Rogers, has been in describing this scene. The actions, known in theater parlance as stage business, are explicit. There are no holes for the director to fill in. How those actions are performed and how they look to the camera are the director's province. But the proficient video writer, detailing the pantomime, the purely visual aspects of his script, demonstrates complete mastery of his subject and leaves no puzzles for the director.

These stage directions, as we will see, are also essential for the other interpreters of the video writer's script, the actors. But first, let us return to the novelist for a moment. His characters are brought to life by his skillful use of word portraits which in turn kindle the reader's imagination. In the video play, however, as in the stage and screen play, the characters are physically alive. The novelist, through prose analysis, gives the reader an insight to the character's thoughts and emotions. He also may use dialogue for this purpose. The video playwright utilizes dialogue and pantomime. Occasionally, he may write a monologue for a character in which that character reveals his inner thoughts, but this is the exception rather than the rule.

The actor, trained to interpret many roles, may possibly grasp each emotional situation without guidance from the writer. Nevertheless, the writer should clarify any line or lines of dialogue which may be open to differing interpretations. For example, note this brief bit of dialogue in which Harry's mother is asking him a simple and natural enough question.

MRS. GREENSPAN
So how's everybody at home . . . Anna and the children?

HARRY
(RATHER BRUSQUELY) Everybody's fine, Mama.

Harry may have replied in several different ways. He may have answered with a sigh of relief, indicating that perhaps there may have been some previous illness. He may have answered without any show of emotion: an everyday response to an everyday query. But the writer has specified an emotional response, "rather brusquely." In this particular scene, Harry was annoyed by a previous action of his mother's and his brusque response was a sign of that annoyance. As we have said, a capable actor, after studying the script, would probably give the correct interpretation. But the writer knows what he wants, or he should know, and, therefore he ought to indicate, wherever he deems it essential, the specific emotional response of the characters. The director and the actors may add more breadth to the play but it must come to them not as a shell but as a complete structure with all the necessary furnishings.

In presenting the video play, there are still other factors of interpretation: sets and music. Both of these elements are discussed fully in other sections of this book, but we will make some comments here. The writer should try to be as familiar with his characters' physical surroundings as he is with their mental makeup. This is especially important where his play takes place in an unusual location. Then he should describe his settings in some detail so that the scenic designer is not left in doubt. However, this is not as essential when dealing with typical locations. In any event, all properties necessary to the development of the plot should be described including their location on the set.

As to music, the video dramatist generally leaves the scoring to the music department as he leaves the specific camera shots and angles to the director. In some local productions, where the writer works closely with the producer-director, he may have a hand in the choice of music. Comparably, the screen writer also has little or nothing to do with the musical scoring; the stage dramatist seldom uses any musical scoring unless he requires it for a special effect; the radio writer, on the other hand, specifies each instance where he feels music is needed, particularly for transitions. In all these media, music serves an important purpose in creating mood and punctuating scenes of high emotion, of suspense and of romance.

So it is that the video writer sets into motion a veritable hive of industry and each workman, to greater or lesser extent, affects the style of the script. No other medium may offer as many cooks stirring the broth, nor breed as many frustrations for the writer, but no other medium equals the potential mass impact of television.

PACING

All forms of writing, particularly fiction, require pacing, emotionally and structurally. There is a necessity for highs and lows much as a musical composition has its fortes and pianissimos. If a play is written in a high pitch throughout, with one breath-taking incident following another, some of the scenes are bound to have their force weakened. Such a production, also, may have a wearing effect on its audience. As an analogy, think of what your reaction would be to a play where the actors spoke continually at the top of their voices!

On the other hand, if a script is written entirely in a low key, it may lead to flagging attention. There are times when a play should be underwritten and, from the actor's standpoint, underplayed. A great tragedy, a scene of horror, will literally speak for itself. A picture of a wounded child, an innocent victim of war, needs no dialogue embellishment. Its pathos is eloquent.

If you were to write a play with tragic overtones, it would be wise to have moments of relief. A classic tragedy such as "Hamlet" has its comic interlude: the gravediggers' scene. Relief scenes give an audience some respite from the grimness and tenseness of the play, a moment to relax the emotional impress upon the senses. This is an important point the video dramatist, especially, should remember. The television viewer, if he feels the play is too "heavy," may easily turn the dial.

Structurally, in order to reach a crisis or climax, there must be a ladder of incident to climb. If you begin on the top rung, you cannot go any higher. The stage play and the screen play, because of their advantage of greater length, can begin on lower rungs than the video drama and ascend more slowly to the climax. The video play may have to start on a middle rung and therefore climb more quickly to the climax. In either event, a curtain scene will be deprived of its power unless it is of greater magnitude than the preceding scene or scenes. Structurally and emotionally, then, a plateau should be avoided.

The principles of pacing apply to other forms of broadcast writing besides the drama. Newscasts, commercials, talks and musical continuity also require pacing. In these types of continuity, pacing may be achieved by building up to important statements, by varying the length of the sentences and by careful choice of words to suit the diverse moods.

What we have discussed in this preliminary chapter, in relation to the video style, is necessarily of a general nature. As you study this book you will find that each type of television writing is analyzed individually and that the specific demands of each are emphasized in the appropriate chapter.

Formats

5

THE TELEVISION SCRIPT

There are, unfortunately for the beginning writer, numerous script formats in television. However, to avoid confusion for both student and instructor, we have made a choice of one of these formats and will use it for both practical and theoretical purposes especially in those chapters dealing with the television drama. It will be noted, nevertheless, that where excerpts from broadcast scripts are utilized in this chapter, they are reproduced generally in their actual format.

It seems to us that there is enough for the newcomer to television to learn without the bewilderment of a maze of varying formats. Some students have difficulty in adjusting themselves to the physical requirements of typing a television script. A note of urgency might well be interpolated here. If you do not own a typewriter, make every effort to obtain one. It is in the realm of possibility that some editor somewhere has purchased a free lance script written entirely in longhand. But, to our knowledge, no professional television or radio writer ever submitted a script in longhand.

We are accustomed in our daily reading of newspapers, magazines, books, to the simple prose format where a sentence begins at the left-hand margin and runs to the end of the right-hand margin.

Some of the published collections of television plays, valuable as they are for study purposes, may also be confusing in regard to format. For the sake of economy, the dialogue in some of these published collections runs the width of the page. But the actual script itself might leave a margin of about a third or a half of the width of the typewriter paper.

Our preference is for the wide margin to appear on the right-hand side. This wide blank space is to allow room for the director to indicate specific camera directions and to note any changes or additions to the stage directions. By keeping this margin on the right-hand side, it appears to us to make it simpler for the writer who does his own typing, either for the original draft or for the final copy. It follows his normal method of beginning from the left-hand side of the page, and by setting the proper marginal stop at approximately one-third to one-half of the width of the page, he will find it easy enough to become accustomed to the new format.

One fact he will discover soon enough is that it takes a great many more pages for a television script than a radio script because the entire width of the page is not utilized. Detailed stage directions in the TV script also require more space.

The page of script reproduced below will illustrate the format for which we have expressed our preference. At times, when inquiring about submissions to advertising agencies or networks, the writer may receive a sample page of script to indicate the format used by the agency or network. Naturally, he will be wise to follow the specifically prescribed format. However, the format designated below will not only serve the purposes of this book but can be used with equanimity by the writer in submitting dramatic scripts.

THE BROTHERS ARE SILENT, SHIFTING
ON THEIR FEET, LOOKING FROM ONE TO
THE OTHER.   THE ELDEST GESTURES
ROUGHLY TO THE MIDDLE WITH HIS THUMB.

          MIDDLE
   Phil?

          POLETTI
   Yes?

                        MIDDLE
            You know -- ah -- the old man
            passed on. You know?

                        PHIL
            Yes. I knew. And I'm sorry --

                        ELDEST
QUICKLY
            It's all right, Phil. What I
            mean is the mourning time is
            ended now.

THE ELDEST TURNS NERVOUSLY TO THE
MIDDLE BROTHER AND GESTURES WEAKLY
TO HIM.

                        MIDDLE
            And that's kind of the reason
            we come to talk to you.

                        YOUNGEST
CONCLUSIVELY
            Yeah.

                        PHIL
            I see ...

Timing

                        It is more difficult
for the writer to time a television script accurately than it is a radio
script. He cannot set an arbitrary number of pages. If he uses a
good many purely visual sequences without dialogue, such as occur
in westerns, his script is apt to take fewer pages than if he uses
dialogue throughout the play.

Generally, the half-hour sponsored television script will run
about twenty-three minutes; the hour script between forty-eight and
fifty minutes. The remainder of time is taken up by the commercials, openings and closings, credits, teasers, or trailers and station
identification.

The writer can time his script with a fair degree of accuracy
by reading it aloud, and he can judge the amount of time consumed

by purely visual action by acting out the sequence. If he possesses a stop watch so much the better. However, the ever-faithful alarm clock or any good watch will serve the purpose.

THE RADIO SCRIPT

Over the years, one type of format has become the standard for radio scripts which simplifies matters for the radio writer at least in that respect.

The sample page reproduced below includes dialogue, sound effects and musical interpolations. You will note that, similar to the television format, the dialogue is in lower case with music, sound effects and emotional reactions in upper case. Both sound and music cues are also underlined, and the script is double spaced. Generally, each line is numbered. This facilitates corrections and changes during rehearsals.

```
 1. SOUND:          (STORM GROWING IN INTENSITY
 2.                  TO HURRICANE PROPORTIONS)
 3. CAPTAIN: (SHOUTING ABOVE STORM)  Belay there!
 4.          Reef those tops'ls!  Move men...move
 5.          ...d'ye want to see us at the bottom!
 6.          Blast ye for a pack o' creepin'
 7.          snails...Hard on that helm....
 8. VOICE:   (OFF)  Rudder's gone!
 9. CAPTAIN: Curse the bloody fool named this ship
10.          the "Great Hope."
11. JOSHUA:  (FADE IN)  Captain...I beg pardon...
12.          Captain....
13. CAPTAIN: Eh?  Who are you and what are you
14.          doin' on my bridge?
15. JOSHUA:  I am Dr. Joshua Maccabee.
16. CAPTAIN: I ordered all passengers below deck.
17. JOSHUA:  So you did, Captain.  But this ter-
18.          rible storm.  I thought you might
19.          need help.
20. CAPTAIN: I don't need help.  It's this blasted
21.          crew o' mine.  Ye'd think they never
22.          heard a wind howl before...wait...
23.          d'ye say ye're a doctor?
```

```
24. JOSHUA:   Yes.
25. CAPTAIN:  Hang on then, might be needin' ye
26.           afore this gale hauls in!
27. SOUND:      (STORM UP IN FURY THEN FADE FOR)
28. (MUSIC:...A QUIET THEME DENOTING THE CALM
29.             AFTER THE STORM)
```

Timing

It is a much simpler task to time a radio script than a television script. A quarter-hour script may run to about twelve pages, a half-hour script to twenty-four or twenty-six pages. Length of commercials, recapitulations and trailers, such as are used for "soap operas," will considerably shorten the script.

The writer may readily time the dialogue by reading it aloud and then adding approximately five to eight seconds for each music bridge and sound effect.

Production
essentials

6

How much technical knowledge should the writer have? What should he know about the operation of cameras, scenic design, wide-angle shots, microphone booms, sound effects?

The amount of essential technical knowledge will vary depending on the writer's situation. If he is employed by a local TV or radio station he may be both a writer and director and it is evident that his store of technical knowledge must be vastly greater than that of the writer, per se.

The staff writer, because of his daily contacts, should rapidly acquire an understanding of many technical aspects of his medium. He will have many opportunities to see the cameramen at work, to note how dissolves, fades, cuts are accomplished. He can see how the participants move about a single set and from one set to another. He can observe how close-ups and long shots are effected.

But the free-lance writer who has no easy access to first-hand observations of these techniques need have no qualms. Although, as we have stated, knowledge of the medium is important, it is not necessary for the writer to immerse himself in a well of technical terminology.

TELEVISION

The television writer's awareness of the scope and limitations of the camera will enable him to turn out a script that takes full advantage of this visual medium. Too often even the professional television writer fails to make the most of this visual asset. As Edward Stasheff and Rudy Bretz have so aptly stated in their text on *Television Scripts* — "When a writer puts action into his scripts, when he has his camera tell the story, when he provides opportunity for movement and discovery, he is contributing to the whole production's originality."

There are some terms with which the television writer should be familiar and which will demonstrate that he is on easy footing with the medium. We will explain them in some detail. A fairly complete list of television terminology will be found in the glossary.

Here then is a list that should prove adequate for the writer. Remember that explicit camera directions are the province of the director.

ESTABLISHING SHOT	PANNING
DISSOLVE	CLOSE-UP
FADE IN	MEDIUM SHOT
FADE OUT	LONG SHOT
SUPERIMPOSURE	INTERCUT

We may as well start at the beginning: the very opening scene of a television drama is known as an ESTABLISHING SHOT. It does in fact establish the location of the beginning sequence. Perhaps your play opens in the kitchen of an average apartment. You might indicate the scene as follows:

ESTABLISHING SHOT: FADE IN THE KITCHEN OF THE McLEAN APARTMENT: IT IS A SMALL KITCHEN WITH THE USUAL APPLIANCES: A GAS STOVE, A REFRIGERATOR, A PORCELAIN SINK WITH LINOLEUM COUNTER TOP. THERE IS ROOM FOR A SMALL TABLE AT WHICH THE McLEANS ARE HAVING BREAKFAST.

The ESTABLISHING SHOT may be an exterior scene, for example, a slum alley.

ESTABLISHING SHOT: FADE IN SILVERS ALLEY. IT IS ONE OF THE MANY NARROW ALLEYS THAT BISECT THE TENEMENTS ON NEW YORK'S LOWER EAST SIDE. A FEW TORN PAGES FROM AN OLD NEWSPAPER ARE SCATTERED ABOUT. AN ASHCAN STANDS GAPING AGAINST THE BRICK WALL. TWO YOUNGSTERS IN THEIR TEENS HAVE FLATTENED THEMSELVES AGAINST THE WALL NEAR THE ASHCAN. EACH HOLDS A BLACKJACK IN HIS HAND. THEY ARE TENSE AS IF EXPECTING SOMEONE TO ENTER THE ALLEY AT ANY MOMENT.

The ESTABLISHING SHOT, or opening shot, may also be one of impact, setting the atmosphere for the play.

Note the use of FADE IN. The FADE IN denotes coming from a blank screen to an actual scene as described above. It is always used for an opening scene.

The FADE OUT indicates the exact reverse, going from a scene to a blank screen. It is also known as going to black. The FADE OUT is always employed as the curtain to mark the end of an act.

If the writer wishes to show a lapse of time, he may do so by having one sequence FADE OUT and the next one FADE IN. The second or two in which the screen is blank also serves the purpose of permitting the audience to adjust to the passage of time whether it is supposed to be a matter of a few hours, days or weeks.

The FADE OUT and FADE IN differ from the DISSOLVE in respect to time. To DISSOLVE is to go immediately from one scene to another. Both scenes will appear on the screen simultaneously for a brief moment until the second scene entirely supersedes the first.

There will be times when the writer, in order to obtain certain effects, will wish to have one scene superimposed on another. The SUPERIMPOSURE technically focuses the pictures from two cameras onto a single scene. Suppose the girl has written a tearful farewell to the boy. We see the girl staring sorrowfully into space, thinking about the boy and his reaction to the letter. At the same time, we see the boy and we hear him reading the letter aloud.

Commercials utilize the device of SUPERIMPOSURE often by having the name of the product appear over a demonstration or other background.

MCU GIRL SPRAYING.   A cool enchanting fragrance
SUPER: Aquamarine Spray Mist
        By REVLON, Inc.

The instant you spray Revlon's
Aquamarine Spray Mist.

The panoramic, or PAN shot, as it is most commonly abbreviated, affords the audience a camera-eye's view of an entire setting. It is generally a long shot because of the amount of space it covers and it is most often a horizontal sweep of the camera. If, for example, one of your scenes is a classroom and you wish to show the attitudes of the students, you will indicate that the camera PANS across the room. It may be a single PAN, from left to right or back again from right to left.

A vertical TILT may also be indicated. The camera may shoot up and down a wall to show an unusual design. It may be used to give an impression of height, or for contrast, as a child looking up at a man.

The CLOSE-UP, the MEDIUM SHOT and the LONG SHOT are all that the terms imply. The CLOSE-UP, or CU, as it is abbreviated, is simply bringing the camera close up. It may be a shot of an individual from the waist or shoulder high or it may be a BIG CLOSE-UP of the face itself or just the eyes. You can readily see the value of the CLOSE-UP for framing a portrayal of tense emotion.

The CLOSE-UP may be employed also for objects. If a knife were a tell-tale clue upon which the writer wished to rivet attention, he would indicate a CLOSE-UP of the weapon.

For the LONG SHOT, the camera is moved back a distance so that the entire setting may be visible. LONG SHOTS are often used for opening scenes so that we may have a full view of a living room or a street or perhaps a courtroom.

The MEDIUM SHOT then would be anywhere between the LONG SHOT and the CLOSE-UP. Your opening scene may show Mary and John sitting on a couch in the living room. You begin with a LONG SHOT so that we can see the entire room. Then you move in for a MEDIUM SHOT so that we get a fuller picture of Mary and John. Part of the room will naturally be cut off as the camera moves in to concentrate on the couch.

To INTERCUT is to move instantaneously from the picture on one camera to the picture on another. This type of camera action may be used to obtain an immediate reaction from one character to another character's statement, or to switch from one person to another in a telephone conversation.

(COME IN ON THE TELEPHONE
AT MATTIE'S HOME.)
SOUND: THE TELEPHONE.
(SARA PICKS IT UP QUICKLY)
INTERCUT
      SARA
Hello . . . hello —

      MIKE
Sara . . . It's me. . . .

      SARA
Oh, Mike — Mike, . . . are
you — all right . . . ?

      MIKE
I couldn't be allrighter,
darling. . . .

Now, in brief, you have acquired a minimum TV vocabulary, that is, sufficient to suit most of the writer's needs. You should become familiar with these terms but do not by any means overload your script with camera directions. Camera directions, as we may have noted, are the province of the director. Make your intent clearly known to him. He will decide what shots to take. He may very well disagree with your close-ups, long shots, etc. But once he has grasped your intent, you may be sure, if the director is worth his salt, that he will do all he can to enhance your play.

RADIO

           In a sense, the radio writer must be more of a craftsman than the television writer, for he does not have the asset of the visual to help move his script. His audience cannot see the change in mood, the wink of an eye, the sweep of a gesture. He must rely on one technical source of output, the microphone. Unlike the television writer, he must indicate the use of music, for transition or for mood, and he should make full use of sound effects. Yet again he need not amass any encyclopedic amount of technical terms. He will find the following necessary and useful:

FADE IN	UNDER
FADE OUT	OFF
SNEAK	STING
SEGUE	COLD
UP AND OUT	IN THE CLEAR
	BACKGROUND

Let us say the radio writer wishes to create the impression of someone entering a room. He may indicate a FADE IN of sound such as footsteps which at first would be heard softly from a distance then increase in volume. He may achieve the same effect by indicating a FADE IN of dialogue so that we hear the character's voice OFF at a distance and gradually growing louder until the speaker is at the microphone.

The FADE OUT is the exact reverse of the above. We hear the footsteps retreating or the voice dying away in the distance.

Music that comes in very faintly and then builds to a more normal level is called a SNEAK. It is a preparation for the establishment of a mood, a sotto voce dramatic foreshadowing:

JOSHUA: The beating of my heart was as loud to me as a jungle drum. I made my way stealthily to the doorway and stole within.
(MUSIC: SNEAK IN OMINOUS MOTIF AND HOLD UNDER)
JOSHUA: There on a rude couch lay a young Negro, breathing heavily. Beside him stood the tall figure of his father, his handsome head bowed in grief.

The term SEGUE (Segway) comes from the Italian signifying to follow. It connotes an immediate transition from one type of music to another or from one musical selection to another without a break. It is often used at the beginning of a program where a transition is made from the theme music to mood music:

ANNCR: Tonight, we bring you a legend of the past; a fantasy which holds in it a strange and haunting key to reality . . . "The Legend of the Great Hope."

(MUSIC: THEME, SEGUE TO MYSTERIOSO MOOD WITH A TOUCH OF
 VOODOO)
 UP AND HOLD UNDER

You will have noted by this time the use of the term UP AND HOLD UNDER which is actually self-explanatory. It indicates the music is to be brought UP. This implies that the music has been held under the dialogue at a low level and now is to be brought UP to a normal listening level, then brought down again and held under narration which follows.

IN THE CLEAR refers equally to dialogue which is not backed by music or sound, or music alone without any admixture of dialogue or sound.

UP AND OUT indicates that the passage of music you have been utilizing is to come to an end. Perhaps we can best clarify this term by an additional example from the script previously referred to. The author had indicated that the music was to be brought up and held under the following monologue by the narrator who was also the lead in the script.

(MUSIC: UP AND HOLD UNDER)
JOSHUA: My name is Joshua Maccabee and I speak to you from out of
    the centuries. If that seems strange, then consider with what un-
    marveling acceptance you sit and listen to this sound box that
    captures voice and melody from the mercurial ether. Think of
    every moment in time eternally writ on waves of light and that you
    have caught one such moment . . . how, unaccountably, you have
    drawn from time, one, Joshua Maccabee, that is myself . . . and the
    legend of the "Great Hope." You who have compelled me, listen. . . .
(MUSIC: UP AND OUT)

Observe that the music has been held under the entire monologue. It served to create a supernatural effect. When the monologue is completed, the music is taken out. The actual story now begins.

Sometimes you will want to underscore a statement, an emotional response, a realization of danger. You can obtain your effect by a STING, a single note held for a few seconds:

NANCY: The child's shivering, Dan. She needs something hot to drink.
    What'd you manage to salvage from the wreck?

DAN: Nothing . . . nothing at all!
(MUSIC: STING)

The term BACKGROUND (BG) is used generally to indicate that the presence of sound is more felt than heard. The audience is to be made aware that an automobile is being driven or an airplane is flying but the sound is kept low so that it does not in any way interfere with the dialogue:

NANCY: What happened, Dan?
DAN: We've hit a freak storm, Nancy. Lightning's put number two motor out of commission. I'm afraid I'll have to try going off course. Maybe get past the storm that way.
NANCY: I'll keep the passengers calm.
DAN: Good girl.
SOUND: MOTORS UP STRONG . . . BLEND WITH STORM . . . THEN DROP STORM AND PLANE TO BACKGROUND
JOHNNY: Dan . . .
DAN: Yes?
JOHNNY: Radio's dead!

The dialogue that follows in this particular scene builds to a crisis of great excitement. The concentration of the audience, therefore, is on the dialogue but there is just enough sound in the background to maintain an awareness of the plane in flight. The writer will indicate this as in the example referred to; the proper mixture of voices and sound is the task of the director. Once he knows the writer's intent, he will instruct the sound effects man accordingly.

Non-dramatic continuity

PART

2

Non-dramatic
continuity

PART

2

The commercial

7

Without the commercial, television and radio, as we know them today in the United States, could not exist. But the commercial is often maligned and seldom praised. It has been called intrusive, distasteful, annoying. Practically every comedy program and every comedian has at one time or another satirized the commercial. A few . . . a very few . . . performers have made it standard practice to "gag up" the commercial. Arthur Godfrey is the prime example. But sponsors who accept this buffoonery at the expense of their product are a tiny minority.

Consider the commercial from the standpoint of the sponsor of a weekly series. He has spent a rather handsome fortune for time and talent in the production of a variety program or a drama. Naturally, he wants the program to be as entertaining as possible, but primarily the broadcast is a vehicle for his sales message. In the sponsor's estimation, the rating his program receives is not as much a measure of the show's popularity as it is an index of the potential buyers of his product. And what shall it avail him if his star is bright and appealing, but his cheese is not!

In the king-size advertising agencies, commercials are conceived with racking labor pains. The copywriter becomes a specialist, often giving all his efforts to one account. He may be taken on a tour of the plant to completely familiarize himself with the product. His agency's research department comes up with pertinent data that will help the copywriter to frame his message. Let us say, hypothetically, 70 per cent of the mothers interviewed buy white bread for their children because it's tastier, but they know brown bread is more healthful. Very well, hit the taste angle. This brown bread is made with honey. Children will love its delicious flavor, etc., etc. . . .

The copywriter at the major advertising agency has another factor in his favor. He generally sits down to write his copy only after a well thought out campaign. And he has opportunities to pretest his copy. J. Walter Thompson, one of the oldest and largest of the advertising agencies, actually installed its own closed circuit television station by means of which television commercials can be judged by the staff as they might be telecast. Changes to make the commercial more effective can then be made before going into expensive rehearsals and filming.

The story is quite different for the commercial copywriter at the small advertising agency or small radio station. He may be called on to write copy for a dozen different accounts. He has no research department to assist him and he doesn't have time to plan a long-range campaign. The radio station time salesman may burst in with a contract from the local used car dealer for a spot announcement campaign to start the next day. It's a grinding task at the local level for the commercial copywriter. And it does not pay very well. But it is excellent training ground and if you want to make a career of it, the top spot of Chief Copywriter at agencies the size of McCann-Erickson may make your income tax payment alone more than the yearly salary you were earning at the local radio or television station, or the small agency.

Radio stations are continually in need of copywriters. This is particularly true of the small or medium-sized station. In a regional meeting of broadcasters, many managers and program directors once discussed the personnel situation. Most of them stated that the degree of talent posed a difficult problem. If they hired a writer with a high degree of talent, he or she was sure to leave after a brief period for a better paying position with one of the larger stations or agencies. The writer with a lesser degree of talent found it more difficult to move up and as a consequence stayed on with the smaller station. It was a question of whether they wanted greater talent for a short term or minor talent for a long term. The general preference was for the long-range view.

Be that as it may, almost every issue of the weekly Broadcasting-Telecasting magazine carries an ad or two for copywriters in its Help Wanted columns. But no matter his talent, the copywriter should be under no illusions regarding his assignment, as this advertisement underscores so pointedly.

> Copywriter, man or woman, capable writing strong sell announcements at retail level. No scripts, no programs, no production or flowery copy but must be able to write hard selling one-minute announcements and lots of them. Volume and speed definite requirements.

Yes, the commercial copywriter's output may be a far cry from literature, but it is a writing assignment and it can be challenging. Possibly every copywriter is a frustrated or a potential dramatist or novelist. The fact that he must keep his nose to the copy grindstone for that weekly pay check does not necessarily inhibit his literary powers. To cite just two examples of several: Charles Jackson, author of one of the most powerful and successful novels of the past decade, "Lost Weekend," served a long stint as copywriter for one of the major advertising agencies; Reginald Rose, one of TV's finest playwrights, kept the pot boiling for many years by writing copy to move merchandise.

There was a story circulated years ago about the brash young man who managed to corner the executive vice-president of one of the larger advertising agencies. "I have the perfect slogan for your cigarette account," he is reputed to have said, and handed the startled executive a slip of paper. The executive stared at the young man and then at the slip of paper containing four words. The brash young man left the advertising agency with another slip of paper: a five-figure check.

In the glamorous and fanciful realm of radio and television, legends abound and some do have a modicum of truth. But the many slogans that are so closely identified with advertisers are usually products of many hours of sweat and concentration. A good slogan . . . a catch phrase . . . is invaluable to the sponsor. Think of some that come readily to your own mind: "You can be Sure if it's

Westinghouse," "Better Things for Better Living Through Chemistry," "They Satisfy," "When You Care Enough to Send the Very Best." On a local level, in New York City, the Emil Mogul Agency made "Calling All Men" synonymous with Barney's clothing establishment.

A slogan is most effective when it includes the name of the product because it leaves no question of sponsor identification. The Westinghouse slogan mentioned above is a case in point. However, the psychological slant, as exemplified by the Hallmark slogan, and the public relations approach of the Du Pont slogan, can be equally effective if repeated often enough in the sponsor's copy.

The ethics of advertising control slogans as much as any other type of copy. It is not ethical to disparage a competitor's product. In preparing copy, the positive approach should always be utilized — not how inferior are the competitor's products, but how good are your own.

A slogan that psychologically had tremendous selling power was one used by the Lucky Strike people some time ago: "Reach for a Lucky instead of a Sweet." It played on the natural vanity of women to keep that fascinating figure, but it brought a storm of protest from the sweets manufacturers who claimed it was unfair and unethical. The slogan was discontinued.

It is a good exercise for the student of writing to devise a number of slogans as a spur to his inventiveness and an aid to his facility in packing maximum sales power into minimum wordage.

The commercial copywriter should have a basic knowledge of psychology and public relations. What makes people buy? What desires can you appeal to in the listening or watching public? How can you arouse and hold interest in your sales message? How do you win good will for your sponsor? The copywriter who can turn out an announcement that will keep your eyes glued to the TV screen or your ears to the radio is literally worth his weight in gold. One columnist some time ago reported a strange phenomenon in his household. Every time the commercial appeared on the screen, the light in his refrigerator went on! The commercial, in many instances, takes on the aspect of the "seventh inning stretch," the time to relax after a gripping first act, to walk into the kitchen for a quick drink or snack. The next time you watch a TV program or listen to a radio broadcast, check your reaction to the commercial. Watch and listen carefully. What is its impact on you? Does it awaken your interest or induce a yawn? Try to analyze its good points or its bad points.

For study purposes, it is useful to classify the various types of commercials. The following categories are not all-inclusive. There is some overlapping of classification and, on the other hand, some commercials employ more than one technique. But we believe this listing will serve the student's requirements.

THE COMMERCIAL AS MONOLOGUE

This type of copy, utilizing one voice in its presentation, is generally referred to as the straight commercial. It is the simplest in format, the most inexpensive from a production standpoint. It uses no gimmicks, no tricks. It can and does sell merchandise effectively. Here is an illustration of the straight commercial prepared for the Chevrolet dealers in the District of Columbia area for radio broadcast.

ONLY CHEVROLET, the biggest selling car in the world, could make you this offer: NOW . . . today . . . you can drive away in a big, new two-door Chevrolet sedan . . . for only seventeen hundred and fifty dollars. You didn't hear me wrong . . . a big, new two-door Chevrolet sedan for only seventeen hundred and fifty dollars! And that's the total price delivered, in the Washington area. Besides big-car comfort with small cost operation, here's what's included at this price: turn signals . . . safety plate glass all around, not just in the windshield . . . a slick Duco paint finish, just like Cadillac's . . . the jet-powerful Blue Flame engine with 115 horsepower . . . and Chevrolet's famous synchromesh transmission. Don't forget this either . . . a Chevrolet not only costs less now . . . it costs less to operate. And, it's worth more when you trade or sell. See your Chevrolet dealer within the next 24 hours. You may well be surprised at his attractive trade-in offer for your present car . . . on a new Chevrolet . . . priced at only seventeen hundred and fifty dollars delivered in the Washington area.

It is written simply and competently. It stresses cost, often the deciding factor to people purchasing cars in the highly competitive field of low priced automobiles. It presents no reading problem to the announcer either from the choice of words or the time allotment of one minute. The good copywriter reads his announcement aloud and times it. But there is a tendency today among many users of local spots to presumably "get their money's worth" by overloading the announcements with verbiage. Generally, a one-minute straight announcement will run from 150 to 175 words, preferably closer to 150. Several announcers have complained, justifiably, that every so often spots are handed to them which exceed 200 words. This means that the announcer has to increase his reading rate considerably with the added hazards of fluffs and lack of clarity. You get that racy, punch technique with the announcer running in high gear, hammering away at you. Fortunately, you are not defenseless against the barrage. You can always turn the dial. Whether it is the advertising agency or the sponsor who insists upon the overload, the copywriter and the announcer are caught in the squeeze. If the retail furniture dealer wants every item he has for sale included in the one-minute spot, or the small variety store requires a mention of almost its entire stock from shoelaces to satchels, the end result is more confusion than sales impact.

This overloading of announcements rarely, if ever, occurs on a network. Timing is exceedingly precise and copywriters adhere to a rigid schedule.

We have considered the straight commercial from the aspect of radio. Now let us see what happens when the visual enters. Here is the Chevrolet commercial prepared for television:

VIDEO	AUDIO
CAM: TIPPY TURNS FROM WEATHER BOARD, MOVES TO STAND BESIDE SMALL SCREEN, CURTAINED TO RESEMBLE MINIATURE STAGE	TIPPY: Now we're going to have a fashion show . . . with the prettiest models you've ever seen!
	— The new Chevrolets!
TIPPY TAKES CORD AND DRAWS ASIDE CURTAINS TO REVEAL RS SLIDE OF 4-DOOR SEDAN	. . . Here's the beautiful 4-door Bel Air sedan — big enough for the whole family! (DROPS CURTAIN)
TIPPY DRAWS CURTAIN AGAIN TO REVEAL CONVERTIBLE	And the exciting Bel Air convertible . . . that looks like all outdoors! (DROPS CURTAIN)
TIPPY DRAWS CURTAIN TO	And then there's the smart-

REVEAL 2-DOOR '150'
SEDAN

DISS. TO SLIDE CHEV. SEAL
. . . SUPER PRICE SLIDE . . .
FLASH PRICE ON & OFF,
KEEPING SLIDES SUPERED

CAM: TIPPY

SLIDE: CHEVROLET SEAL

looking 2-door One-Fifty model — *so* economical to own! (DROPS CURTAIN, TURNS TO FACE CAM DIRECTLY) You can tell right away they're Chevrolets, can't you? You can *own* a wonderful new Chevrolet for as little as $47.88 a month, you know, even less if your present car is worth more than the down payment! You don't make the first payment until 45 days after you get the car! And $47.88 includes *complete* insurance coverage — fire, theft, collision *and* life! So why don't you stop in tomorrow at the Chevrolet dealer nearest you . . . Tell them TIPPY sent you! (TIPPY DOES HAND & EYE ROUTINE) Once you try it . . . I'll bet you buy it!

As effective as radio is as a sales medium, there is little question of the added impact of the visual. Note the number of words used in the TV version as compared with the radio version. You will find that they are almost equal. For most types of commercials, despite the visual, television copy does utilize almost as many words as radio. There are good reasons. The announcer's copy underlines the visual just as the visual emphasizes the audio. And should the viewer turn his attention away from the screen momentarily or leave the room, he can still hear the audio. One picture may be worth a thousand words, but not if it isn't seen.

THE COMMERCIAL AS DIALOGUE

The dialogue commercial may be a simple interview between the announcer and a housewife regarding the qualities of the sponsor's product. It may be a discussion between a simulated husband and wife. Again, it may include the announcer and the star of the show.

Or it may feature two characters especially conceived for the sponsor such as the "Harry and Bert" commercials for Piel Bros. We have described the creation of the "Harry and Bert" characters in our section on Development of Ideas.

PIEL'S
TV FILM COMMERCIAL (1:00)
HARRY AND BERT
"BERT'S OFFENSES"
NO. 87

VIDEO	AUDIO
Open on our two friends making one of their familiar public appearances. Harry is standing in front of a large desk, at which his brother is cheerfully seated.	BERT: This is Bert Piel . . . HARRY: And this is Harry Piel.
Bert's enthusiasm gets a little out of hand. He begins to bang on the desk in order to emphasize certain points.	BERT: Piel's tastes best of all . . . because it's driest of all! Remember that, viewers!
Now he is completely carried away, even climbing up on top of the desk.	Piel's . . .
Well almost, for Harry restrains him at this point.	HARRY: Excuse me, Bert. Friends . . . my brother is so enthusiastic over our wonderful beer . . . that
Harry apologizes to the viewers for his brother's behavior.	. . . well . . . sometimes without meaning to . . . he offends an occasional viewer. . . .
This is the first time Bert has ever actually heard himself referred to as offensive. It hits swiftly and hard.	BERT: Offends?
Harry feels terribly for having hurt his brother's feelings. He tears the letter up.	HARRY: I'm sorry, Bert. We've had some letters, and a lady in New Jersey said that you . . . I'm sorry . . . you go ahead.

But it is too late. Bert is leaving forever.

He goes out the door and closes it behind him.

Harry returns his attention to the viewers. He feels very badly now, but goes on . . . at the sound of the shot, Harry wheels toward the door. He is certain his brother has done away with himself.

Unfortunately, it isn't so. Bert pops back in the door, very much like the old self. He is holding a target with a bullethole in dead center. And in his right hand he carries a smoking pistol.

On word "miss" dissolve to live in which a glass is ostensibly sipped by the viewer, himself.

Fade out to black and bring up legal super.

BERT: No . . . no . . . no. I . . . I've tried to tell people how delicious our beer is . . . how it will bring happiness into their nice homes . . . and somehow . . . I've offended. You tell them Harry. They like you. You're personable. I'm offensive. Goodbye consumers.
SOUND: DOOR SLAMMING SHUT.
HARRY: Well I'm sorry . . . he's so sensitive. I never should have . . .

SOUND: A SHOT FIRED IN THE OTHER ROOM.
Bert, I . . .
SOUND: DOOR BEING OPENED AGAIN.
BERT: Bullseye! Proof Piel's aims for dryness . . . and we don't miss.

HARRY: Well as Bert, thank goodness, says . . . "if you taste it and smack your lips it's a product of Piel Brothers", . . . most likely.
BERT: Unquestionably, Harry.

Some advertisers who prefer the hard hitting technique find that two or more voices carry more impact than one. The copy actually is written much in the same manner as a straight commercial. However, two or three announcers read segments of the copy. Montage effects are often used, that is, having the voices follow each other in rapid succession utilizing succinct phrases or sometimes just one word. For example:

ANNOUNCER 1: For men . . . .
ANNOUNCER 2: For women . . . .
ANNOUNCER 3: For children . . . .

This type of commercial does have the element of variety in voices, but often, because the sponsor or the agency demands punch, the announcers try to outdo each other in forcefulness and the end result is a frontal attack on the eardrums.

This many-voiced commercial is not true dialogue but it has been included under this heading simply because it utilizes more than one voice.

THE COMMERCIAL AS DRAMA

The dramatized commercial is probably the most difficult to present, and yet it can be extremely effective. It calls for a good deal of ingenuity and imagination on the part of the writer to obtain dramatic impact in a minimum of time. If he is able to do so, he can capture his audience's attention and hold it throughout the commercial. If, for example, you want to portray the need for a blow-out proof tire, you can show a family out for a Sunday drive. Then suddenly the tire is punctured. There is a frightening scream. It's all done in a matter of seconds but the drama is an attention-getter. The writer should strive for plausibility of situation and avoid mountain out of molehill scenes. If the young bride goes into hysterics over a soiled napkin and tearfully wails that it will never come clean again, the reaction from the audience may be laughter rather than concern.

The players in the commercial drama should stay in character. We know there will be disagreement about that statement, since many dramatized commercials have one of the actors step right out of the drama to deliver the sales message. However, it may be incongruous for the actress who has just played the part of a harried housewife in the commercial drama to suddenly flash a smile and become a saleswoman. Presumably, the commercial drama attempts to present a tiny vignette of life and to capture some of the essence of reality. That verisimilitude is shattered when the actor steps abruptly out of character. Let the commercial drama remain drama and have the announcer point up the scene with a brief sales message.

This dramatized TV commercial is on the lighter side in keeping with the program "Caesar's Hour."

VIDEO	AUDIO
HUSBAND AND WIFE IN LIVING ROOM. Husband is watching TV	SOUND: (LAUGHTER ON TV) WIFE: You and that TV set. Sometimes I almost wish television had never been invented. HUS: Shhh. I'm watching Caesar's Hour. WIFE: And I'm watching the kids' scuffed shoes pile up. You promised *you'd* do them this time. HUS: After . . . after. (APPLAUSE AND LAUGHTER)
TV SET. TELOP: DOWNS AND LOGO (Or Box of Scuff-Kote)	ANNCR: And now, a word from ESQUIRE SCUFF-KOTE.
DISS TO TV GOBO. MED NELSON & SCUFF-KOTE SIGN.	NELSON: Madam, do you quarrel with your husband about who's going to do the youngster's shoes?
CUT TO HUSBAND & WIFE. (They do a double-take)	Well, quarrel no more.
CUT TO NELSON. (Points to sign)	Just get a bottle of ESQUIRE SCUFF-KOTE . . . the miracle self-shining discovery for children's scuffed shoes.
(He applies)	You just slap ESQUIRE SCUFF-KOTE on any old way and those
DOLLY IN.	scuffs and scrapes disappear. Because it gets deep down into those scuffs and scrapes and practically puts a brand new finish on the leather.
FILM CLIP: "SK-56-2" 35MM. SILENT. (Match Dissolve)	And in a few minutes, those beat-up shoes look like this . . . bright, soft and natural looking without any work for you.
FILM CLIP: "ESQ-56-10" 35MM. SILENT. (Drum Major)	Look for the drum major and the name ESQUIRE on the bright circus package . . .
NELSON IN TV GOBO. (Box in hand.)	and help yourself to the wonderful no-work way of making children's

(Man's hand reaches in
and takes box)

DISS TO HUSBAND & WIFE
IN LIVING ROOM.

CHILD ENTERS. (2 pairs
bright shoes in one hand,
Scuff-Kote box in other)

scuffed shoes look new.
HUS: Thanks!

WIFE: Hm, now that we have
ESQUIRE SCUFF-KOTE you're will-
ing to do them.
CHILD: Nobody has to do my
shoes. I did 'em myself with Es-
QUIRE SCUFF-KOTE. I watch
Caesar, too!

THE COMMERCIAL AS SONG

The theme song

Many programs
have music especially composed for opening and closing their broadcasts, known to us as theme songs. We are concerned here only
with those themes which have lyrics that include the mention of the
sponsor's product. A good example is the "Be Happy, Go Lucky"
tune which opens and closes the Hit Parade programs. This type of
theme heightens sponsor identification and is therefore of decided
advantage.

The jingle

Ever since Pepsi
Cola successfully flooded the airwaves with its singing commercial,
jingles have been on the upsurge. Although jingles have been satirized, burlesqued and gagged without mercy, they go on their merry
way and they do a job for the sponsor. It is essential, of course, that
the jingle have a catchy tune so that anyone, unless he be tone deaf,
can readily whistle or sing it. If the tune stays with him, so will its
association with the sponsor's product. Children, whose memory
process is not as cluttered as adults, will pick up a jingle almost
immediately, and go about singing the praises, in rhyme and rhythm,
of cigarettes, candy or beer!
The writing of jingles is a specialized field. Some agencies

have writers on their staff who can compose singable jingles. Other agencies farm out their requirements to a team of composer and lyricist, banded together for the sole purpose of the creation of jingles. If they can't create an original tune, they will adapt one that's in the public domain, usually a folk tune or the more lively of the Stephen Foster melodies. Again, they are simple, whistleable tunes. If the jingle is not readily hummable, its impact is short-lived. Since many jingles are prepared for use immediately following station breaks, they may not be more than fifteen to twenty seconds in length. The lyric writer may be called on to convey a potent sales message in the briefest span . . . and in rhyme, too!

Here is a combination of jingle and monologue in a commercial which was named as one of the top ten radio commercials by Sponsor Magazine.

RECORDED THEME:
Man, oh Manischewitz!
Man, oh Manischewitz!
Man, oh Manischewitz!
Man!
Manischewitz Fruit Wines!
Manischewitz Fruit Wines!
Delicious Manischewitz Fruit Wines —
There's blackberry, cherry,
And loganberry
Man, oh Manischewitz — what wines!
Man, oh Manischewitz!
Man, oh Manischewitz!
Man, oh Manischewitz!
Man!
One sip and you'll rave a-
'bout the fruit flavor,
Manischewitz Fruit Wines!

Mountain-cool loganberries! That's what makes a MANISCHEWITZ LOGANBERRY COOLER your most refreshing summer drink. For loganberries — like all fruits — refresh you naturally — and MANISCHEWITZ KOSHER LOGANBERRY WINE refreshes you *deliciously,* as well! It captures all the thirst-quenching flavor of ripe, juicy loganberries . . . loganberries picked fresh and frosty from the bush. They're specially sweetened — just right for your MANISCHEWITZ LOGANBERRY COOLER. It's a breeze to make one . . . just fill a glass of ice cubes halfway with MANISCHEWITZ LOGANBERRY WINE. Add ginger ale or sparkling soda. Then sip — and feel refreshed! Enjoy a cooler today. But be sure to use 100% pure . . . kosher . . . delicious MANISCHEWITZ LOGANBERRY WINE. M-m-man, oh Manischewitz, what a wine cooler! Manischewitz Wine Company, New York.

THE COMMERCIAL AS PART OF THE PROGRAM

This type of commercial is generally referred to as the integrated commercial since it is presented as an integral part of the show and usually includes the star or stars of the program. From the writer's standpoint, it is one of the most satisfactory types of commercials because it gives him an opportunity to work with the program. It can be the most creative type of commercial copywriting with the writer exercising his utmost skill to interweave the sponsor's sales message effectively into the body of the program.

One of the most successful and consistent users of the integrated commercial is the Jack Benny program and with all due respect to the Benny writing stable, which has kept him in the top ratings for lo these many years, there have been occasions when the integrated commercial was funnier and more sparkling than the show itself.

In writing the integrated commercial, the copywriter must naturally be familiar with the entire script of the program. The transition from program to commercial must be carefully worked out. It should avoid abruptness. It should not give the impression of putting one over on the listener or viewer. . . . "Didn't think this was going to be a commercial, did you, now?" . . . The smooth transition will have the audience accepting the commercial as it was intended: an integral part of the program. And a well-integrated commercial has the added advantage of keeping the audience's attention throughout since the program will be viewed as a whole without an apparent pause for the sales message.

Not every type of program can utilize the integrated commercial. It is most successful for variety and comedy programs. Most dramatic programs and newscasts must remain apart from the commercial. However, in some cases the dramatic program can utilize the integrated commercial with marked success. An example was the "Martin Kane — Private Eye" series in which there would always be occasion for Kane to appear logically in the cigar store selling the sponsor's tobacco. The commercial can be integrated with telling effect, and yet unobtrusively, as Mollie Goldberg did in placing a can of earth with a plant in a windowbox. The side of the can that faced the audience bore the label of the sponsor's coffee.

From the Emil Mogul Company comes this very cleverly written commercial based on the old vaudeville routine, "Mr. Gallagher and Mr. Shean." Peter Donald, the host of the panel program "Masquerade Party," sponsored by Esquire Polish, steps into a duet with announcer Nelson Case.

VIDEO	AUDIO
SIGN: "DONALD & CASE"	
PETER AND NELSON.	Oh Mr. C.
	Oh Mr. C.
	These white shoes are making life a misery
CU LIMBO DIRTY WHITE SHOES.	Why, they're such an awful sight
	And I have to get them white
	Is there anything that you can do for me?
PETER AND NELSON.	Oh Mr. Donald
	Oh Mr. Donald
	There is no one else who's better qualified
	So I'll quickly set you right
(Nelson holds up box)	With a bottle of Lanol White
	That's ESPECIAL, Mr. Nelson?
	That's ESQUIRE, Mr. D!

THE COMMERCIAL AS AN INSTRUMENT OF PUBLIC RELATIONS

This is the institutional commercial whose aim is to build good will for a sponsor. It is, in essence, an instrument of public relations. Its selling message is implied rather than direct. It may focus attention on the company's policy of incentive rewards to its employees, of promotions from within the ranks. It may stress the company's contribution to the strength of our nation, the integrity, the tradition of fair dealing that the industry has maintained through the many years of its existence. It may be informational in nature describing how the industry's scientists worked for years to discover a new plastic. The format of the institutional commercial may be that of a simple monologue for radio presentation. For TV, the institutional can take advantage of the full range of visual techniques, such as this commercial written for Du Pont and its sponsorship of the "Cavalcade of America" (Copyright E. I. du Pont de Nemours & Company, 1955):

(MUSIC: IN AND UNDER)
FADE IN.
1. MAIN TITLE
DISSOLVE TO:
1-A. MEDIUM SHOT OF ANNOUNCER IN A "GAME" OR HOBBY ROOM SET, WITH FISHING ROD, HUNTING RIFLE, TENNIS RACKET, CAMERA, ALSO A DISPLAY OF GARDENING IMPLEMENTS AND SPRAYS AND PLANT FOODS AND WORLD GLOBE.

ANNOUNCER
You know, in all these things I have here, a Du Pont product plays a part. There's "Tynex" nylon in the fishing leader and the tennis racket strings . . .
(PAN WITH HIM TO RIFLE)
Here's a Remington hunting rifle — film for your camera . . .
(PAN TO GARDEN DISPLAY)
Over here, these sprays and plant foods, for your flower or vegetable garden . . .
(HE TURNS TO FACE CAMERA)
But right now, I'm not going to discuss Du Pont products. The incredible thing is what they represent — the fact that we Americans today have more spare time, more money left over from living expenses to spend on our hobbies and our travel than any people have ever had in the history of the world. Why?
DISSOLVE TO:
2. EXT. DAY. LONG SHOT. MAN AND FAMILY UNLOADING GROCERIES FROM CAR. SUBURBAN SETTING.

ANNOUNCER (O.S.)

Well, here is a typical skilled U.S. factory
worker . . .

CUT TO:

3. CLOSER SHOT.

ANNOUNCER (O.S.)

. . . with his family. They've just arrived home
from their week's grocery shopping.

CUT TO:

4. THE FAMILY IS TAKING GROCERIES OUT OF CAR, CARRYING
THEM INTO HOUSE.

He works a forty-hour week, and that food he is
unloading from his car cost him only six and
three-quarter hours of work.

CUT TO:

5. LONG SHOT OF EUROPEAN MARKET PLACE. (STOCK)

ANNOUNCER (O.S.)

Now let's look at some other average skilled factory workers who live somewhere in Europe.

CUT TO:

6. CLOSER SHOT.

ANNOUNCER (O.S.)

They must work *thirty-eight and a quarter* hours
— almost the entire average American work
week — to buy the *same amount* of food — providing it's available.

DISSOLVE TO:

7. MEDIUM CLOSEUP OF ANNOUNCER.

ANNOUNCER

This comparison — made recently by the United
States Bureau of Labor Statistics is based on
official figures.

(PAN WITH HIM TO WORLD GLOBE)

It illustrates that we Americans do enjoy a better
life with less work.

(HE SPINS WORLD GLOBE TO NORTH AMERICA)

— that we do lead the world in progress. But if
our only desire was for material things alone, we
should soon fail as a nation.

8. PORTRAIT CLOSEUP OF ANNOUNCER.

ANNOUNCER

Standing firmly behind all our advancements are
other, even *more important* interests that are vital
in making us a well-rounded progressive nation.

CUT TO:

9. LONG SHOT OF WORKERS ENTERING GATE OF A DU PONT
PLANT. (STOCK)

ANNOUNCER (O.S.)

For example, a recent survey was conducted
among men and women of the Du Pont Company
in 77 cities throughout the United States. And
these facts were revealed:

CUT TO:

10. STOCK FOOTAGE: PEOPLE ENTERING OR LEAVING A CHURCH.
More than 89 per cent are active church members.

CUT TO:

11. STOCK FOOTAGE: MAN READING NEWSPAPER FROM COMMER-
CIAL #47 SCENE #10.

ANNOUNCER (O.S.)

The first concern most of them have is for the
future of America and the world — *not* for the
state of pocketbooks.

CUT TO:

12. STOCK FOOTAGE OF A COMMUNITY ACTIVITY.
They give freely of their time and effort to every
kind of project from schools to hospital service —

CUT TO:

13. STOCK FOOTAGE: DONOR GIVING TO MARCH OF DIMES OR
OTHER SUCH FUND.
— and take a generous part in the yearly *4 billion dollar* gift Americans give to help their communities and their fellow men.

CUT TO:

14. MEDIUM CLOSEUP OF ANNOUNCER BESIDE WORLD GLOBE.

ANNOUNCER

In short, it is the combination of desires, of
ideals, of interests that have given America the
genius to lead the world in progress. And among

the nation's workers who contribute to this leadership are the men and women of the Du Pont Company . . . producers of . . .

(MUSIC: IN TO FINISH)

15. DU PONT OVAL AND PLEDGE.

"Better Things for Better Living — through Chemistry."

FADE OUT.

The institutional commercial is used primarily by non-competitive public utilities such as the gas, electric or telephone companies, or by large corporations such as United States Steel, Du Pont, and the Aluminum Company of America.

Usually the *kind* of writing for an institutional commercial is on a higher plane than other types of commercials. Since its appeal is on a more intellectual level, its writing tone is elevated accordingly.

THE COMMERCIAL AS THE TESTIMONIAL

This is the familiar type of commercial written for the celebrity: the motion picture star, the sports hero. You see or hear the movie queen telling every woman that she too can have as lovely a complexion as a star simply by using the proper soap. Or the sports personality admits that his physical prowess stems from eating daily portions of an energizing cereal. The testimonial may be written as a monologue or in the form of an interview.

How effective is the testimonial? Check the circulation of fan magazines. Evidently, the aura of the famous casts a wide spell.

However, testimonials are not entirely the province of the star. Mrs. Average Housewife and Mr. Average Breadwinner often take the spotlight to endorse products with whose efficacy they are familiar.

Television Techniques

The foregoing types of commercials can be utilized for both radio and television. However, the advent of the new medium created new techniques. Three broad categories are listed below although it would be possible to make several subdivisions, each of which would merely include minor variations.

THE COMMERCIAL AS DEMONSTRATION

Radio is "blind." The copywriter has to use picture words to bring an image to the listener. But in TV the listener is also the viewer. You not only tell him about the product. You can show it to him. That remarkable refrigerator with its tremendous capacity. The smart lines of the new car. The comfortable looking furniture. The mouth watering cake. The juicy steak so tender it slices at the touch of a knife.

The copywriter must turn out practically full-length copy for most of the demonstration commercials. The announcer-demonstrator underscores the visual as he or she describes the workings of the refrigerator, the stove, the TV set. In other words, you still tell the audience about the product as you show it.

Irving Settel, well known TV consultant and instructor, in enumerating ten "common sense" methods of putting more sell into the TV commercial (Sponsor Magazine, July 26, 1954), listed as his first principle: "Demonstrate wherever possible." Demonstration, as he emphasized, is one of the most effective television techniques. And one of the most effective jobs of demonstrating is that of Betty Furness for Westinghouse. Reproduced below is a typical Westinghouse demonstration commercial, prepared by McCann-Erickson, Inc.

VIDEO	AUDIO
1. TELOP: "WESTINGHOUSE STUDIO ONE"	1. ANNCR: And now . . . let's pause for a moment . . . and turn to Betty Furness with . . . A GUESSING GAME.
2. CU LOAD OF WASH IN WASH BASKET. PULL BACK TO SHOW BETTY IS HOLDING IT UP. IN SYNC, MAT IN, OR SUPER NUMBERS ON SCALE "20 LBS," "40 LBS," "60 LBS," ON "MAN, THAT'S	2. BETTY: Can you guess how many pounds of wet wash a woman lifts and carries out to the clothesline each week? 20 pounds? No. 40 pounds? Wrong again. It's 60 pounds!

WORK" BETTY SETS DOWN BAS-
KET WITH RELIEF.

3. SHE MAKES SWEEPING GES-
TURE INDICATING "FINISHED."
CUT TO DRYER D–100. IN SYNC
SUPER "NO MORE HAULING WET
CLOTHES," "NO MORE HANGING
CLOTHES." IN SYNC, BETTY IN
MCU TAKES CLOTHES FROM LAUN-
DROMAT L–100 NEXT TO DRYER,
SETS THEM ON DRYER'S DOOR.
THEN DROPS THEM ONE BY ONE
INTO DRYER.

4. BETTY FINISHES LOADING
CLOTHES. SHUTS DOOR, INDI-
CATES DRY DIAL. ON "YOU JUST,"
CUT TO TCU DIAL AS SHE SETS IT
TO DRY. OVER TCU SUPER: "SHUTS
OFF AUTOMATICALLY" CUT BACK
TO MCU BETTY.

5. BETTY MOVES TO TWO PILES
OF SIX TOWELS EACH. DRYER
DRIED TOWELS STACK HIGHER
AND FULLER. BETTY HOLDS ONE
OF DRYER-DRIED TOWELS UP TO
HER FACE.

6. CUT TO CU WILD DRYER IN
OPERATION. SHOW STREAMERS
OF RIBBON BLOWING BACK INTO
CLOTHES. SUPER: "DIRECT AIR
FLOW SYSTEM."

7. CUT BACK TO BETTY BESIDE
DRYER. INCLUDE LAUNDROMAT IN
SHOT.

Man, or rather, lady, that's
work!

3. And that's work that could be
completely eliminated . . . finished . . . if you owned this
brand new Westinghouse Electric Clothes Dryer. Imagine!
No more hauling wet clothes.
No more hanging clothes out
on the line. In any weather you
just take the clothes out of your
Laundromat like this, set them
on the Dryer's handy loading
door . . . and slip them in easy
as you please.

4. BETTY: In fact, everything
about this Westinghouse is easy.
For instance, unlike the control
on other dryers, this Westinghouse automatic Dry Dial ends
all guess work. You just set the
Dial to "Dry." The Control
automatically shuts the Dryer
off when your clothes are properly and perfectly dried.

5. And how this Westinghouse
turns out clothes! Just compare these six towels that were
dried out on a line . . . and
these six identical towels dried
in the Westinghouse Clothes
Dryer. They're so much fluf-
fier and they feel so soft.

6. BETTY: The Westinghouse does
such a lovely job because it uses
the exclusive Direct Air Flow
System. It blows the clean
warm air directly into the
clothes . . . dries them faster,
uses less current and saves you
money.

7. See this brand new Westinghouse Electric Clothes Dryer
. . . the Dryer with the hand-

| 8. SUPER IN SYNC: "YOU CAN BE SURE IF IT'S WESTINGHOUSE." | some picture window . . . at your dealer's now. Operates on regular current. Just plug it in. 8. And remember . . . You can be sure if it's Westinghouse. |

THE COMMERCIAL AS CARTOON

Obviously, this form of commercial is entirely visual. It is comparatively costly to produce because of the art and film work involved. But it can be captivating, and may be effective for sponsor identification, as the "SOS" rabbit. The use of the animated cartoon commercial is a natural for a program like Disneyland.

Often there is an interplay of cartoon and live permitting the writer wide latitude for his copy. As in the case of jingles, cartoon commercials are the province of specialists and produced by specialized agencies. Much as the animated cartoon is often the favorite attraction for children at the movies, so the cartoon commercial has a particular appeal to youngsters. And to paraphrase a current slogan: never underestimate the power of a child.

THE COMMERCIAL AS A PRODUCTION NUMBER

Here again, full advantage of the visual can be taken, particularly, the utilization of choreography and costumes. Lucky Strike employed the production number technique dynamically during its sponsorship of the panel program: "This is Show Business." However, the cost factor makes this type of commercial prohibitive for most sponsors.

Although for purposes of study we have classified commercials as distinct types, many commercials do not fall into one particular category. They utilize various techniques, for example, cartoon and jingle, or are semi-integrated — that is, begin with definite program integration and wind up with a straight announcement. Some commercials use humor and trick devices very effectively such as those prepared for Skippy Peanut Butter by David Bascom of Guild, Bascom and Bonfigli. Here is one of the Skippy commercials as presented on the "You Asked For It" program.

VIDEO	AUDIO
OPEN MS Hugh leaning against a prop TV camera or spotlight on stand, in TV studio set.	HUGH: Boy, the more I talk to my friends over at the TV Announcers' Club the more I'm thankful that I do Skippy commercials.
ON WORD "Because" Hugh walks into plain set which holds table, bowl of unidentifiable flaked breakfast food, and box labelled "Abalone Flakes." DOLLY IN TO CU as Hugh holds up a spoonful but doesn't take a bite.	Because, you know, with some products, announcers really have to do a lot of work. For instance, they try a big spoonful of shredded abalone flakes and then they light up, wink, smack their lips,
AFTER WORDS "light up" Hugh pauses and grins broadly. AS HE DOES SO, SUPER QUICKLY the word "YIPPEE!" SUPER OUT.	
AFTER WORD "wink" Hugh winks obviously, pausing in his copy as he does so.	
POP IN SUPER WORD "WOW" with this action. SUPER OUT.	
Hugh pauses and smacks his lips AFTER "smack their lips."	jump up and down,
POP IN SUPER "ZOWIE!" SUPER OUT.	and say,
Hugh bounces up and down after "jump up and down."	
POP IN SUPER "YU 2–6040"	
AS HUGH READS WITH EXAGGERATED ENTHUSIASM "Wow, I could eat."	"Wow! I could eat abalone flakes all the time."
POP IN SUPERS IN QUICK SUCCESSION "TRY 'EM!" and "BUY 'EM!" SUPERS OUT AT END OF THIS LINE.	
DOLLY BACK TO MS as Hugh leaves Abalone Flakes set and moves into directly adjoining set depicting	Well, with Skippy the situation is a little different. We don't shout and jump up and down, because actually Skippy is designed to produce an inner glow.

comfortable, subdued den. Big leather-type chair, side table with jar of Creamy Skippy and plate of crackers. Hugh sits comfortably, opens jar, and proceeds to spread a cracker. TCU this action, keeping jar in picture.

BACK TO MCU as Hugh takes a bite after words "taste it."

ON WORD "furthermore" Hugh picks up jar of Skippy from table in other hand.

ON WORDS "And remember" Hugh picks up cracker he has spread. After he says slogan, he eats cracker. His face is complete deadpan. SUPER SLOGAN.
AFTER RECITING SLOGAN, Hugh finishes off Skippyed cracker.

You spread some Skippy Peanut Butter on a cracker and taste it.

And deep down in your heart of hearts the part of you that likes peanuts says quietly, "Boy, fresh roasted peanut flavor." But all this can go on without one wink or lip smack. Of course, if you'd like to sort of whoop it up after trying Skippy, why, go ahead. It's up to you.

Furthermore, we don't encourage you to do nothing but eat Skippy all the time. You should take time out to go to work, raise a family, play cards —

Why, if you have strong will power, you can probably go for several hours before you take a second helping of the fresh roasted fun that awaits you in Skippy. And Skippy will be there waiting for you. Always fresh, spreadable and digestible, for no other peanut butter's made like Skippy.

And remember — if you like peanuts, you'll like Skippy.

Other species of commercials employ the "repetitive" technique, repeating the same phrase three, four or five times in succession. Many students dislike this approach, terming it "annoyance" technique. But they readily admit its impact for sponsor identification.

Basic Concepts

There are a few additional notes the beginning copywriter ought to remember. As a general rule, sentences should be short. Sentence structure should be confined to one complete thought. However, there may be some variation in length to avoid a completely staccato rendition. One or two longer sentences will provide adequate pacing.

Avoid alliteration. Undoubtedly, alliteration adds beauty to poetry and prose but to the announcer it is merely a reading hazard.

And, finally, these three basic concepts may serve as a guide to the embryonic copywriter:

Simplicity — of words;

Clarity — of ideas;

Repetition — of product.

The public service announcement

Prior to World War II, and during the war, radio stations were flooded with announcements from federal agencies, from state and local governments and from private welfare organizations. These public service announcements — or announcements in the public interest, as they are now termed — all had a vital message to convey to the nation. The problem that beset the station manager or program director was twofold: which messages were to take priority and how many was he expected to schedule? Unlike newspaper or magazine space which can be added to, dependent on the amount of commercial advertising, there is no way of turning an hour into sixty-one minutes.

Therefore, to coordinate the many essential campaigns and to relieve the broadcaster of a daily dilemma, the Advertising Council was established in January, 1942. (For the role of the Office of War Information, see the chapter on "Writing the Government Program.") The Council, which is still in active existence today, established a system of priorities and time allocations. The blood campaign, the bond drive, the need for student nurses, and so on, all receive their due share of time. The Polio drive, the Heart Fund, the Cancer Association, the fight against tuberculosis are given assistance in their fund-raising campaigns.

Copywriters at the cooperating advertising agencies are assigned to write public service announcements. These announcements are donated to the requesting organization or to the government agency as is the time for their presentation on radio and TV.

Formats for announcements in the public interest may parallel those of commercials. For obvious economic reasons, however, public service messages usually employ the simplest format, the straight type of presentation. Kits are prepared by the Advertising Council covering various campaigns in the public interest. These kits include background material on the individual campaign and spot announcements.

Here, for example, is a typical one-minute radio public service message for the Ground Observer Corps campaign, prepared at the request of the United States Air Force and the Federal Civil Defense Administration.

ANNCR: Whenever we think of the American Revolution we think of the citizen-soldier. It was he who *won* our independence. Well, citizen-soldiers of a kind are needed today to *preserve* our independence. Our country urgently needs civilian plane spotters. Much as we hate to think about it we face the possibility of a surprise enemy air attack — at any time. Right now the Soviet Air Force has more than a thousand long-range bombers capable of striking any part of the United States. If we are to survive an attack we must have warning. To be sure our radar network is in operation 24 hours a day — but radar has its limitations. We can't rely on radar alone to detect low-flying aircraft — enemy planes below 5,000 feet. The Air Force calls it the dangerous mile. Only civilian plane spotters can guard this dangerous mile — provide adequate warning. The Air Force needs you as a spotter in the Ground Observer Corps. Join now. Call Civil Defense.

Similar spots of varying lengths (30 seconds and 10 seconds) were included in the Ground Observer Corps kit sent to all radio stations in the United States. It might be well to study the 10-second spot to learn just how much of a message can be successfully conveyed within the limit of approximately thirty-five words.

ANNCR: Much as we hate to think about it, a surprise enemy air attack *is* a possibility. If that attack ever comes, *we must have warning.* Join the Ground Observer Corps. Call Civil Defense.

Both the commercial and the public service announcements are sales messages but their basic appeals differ widely. Whereas the commercial announcement deals with self-interest, how this or that product benefits you or your immediate family, the public service announcement invokes your sympathy for your fellow man and your love of country: your patriotic and your humanitarian instincts. Because of its appeal to your nobler instincts, the public service announcement should be couched in words of an appropriate level. However, the public service message can be hard-hitting. Announcements for the blood campaign, for an organization like Care, or for the National Safety Council, may be written with effective emotional impact, describing a dying soldier, or the child victim of malnutrition, or a serious highway accident. The nature of most public service crusades is so serious that trick devices for radio or TV announcements generally should be avoided. Nevertheless, in some instances a gimmick, such as Smoky the bear in the campaign for prevention of forest fires, can be very effective.

The American National Red Cross, a semi-governmental organization, carries on a year-round informational and public relations campaign with a concentration on fund raising during the month of March. Since its activities include aid to disaster victims, responsibility for the blood banks, service to the armed forces, and other assistance, it has a multifold story to tell. For its public service announcements, it obtains the cooperation of stars of stage, screen, radio and television.

In this illustration of a Red Cross TV announcement, there is literally a complete picture of the agency's services winding up with a plea for funds. Visual effects have been utilized to the utmost demonstrating the wide scope the public service announcement may have even in a brief sixty seconds. The body of the copy becomes in effect a series of captions for the accompanying film clips but integrated through the use of one voice.

VIDEO	AUDIO
OPEN ON MCU OF STAR. RED CROSS BANNER IN BACKGROUND. DOLLY IN SLOWLY.	Hello. This is (Name of Star). Some time this week a Red Cross volunteer will ring your doorbell

	. . . asking you to join your Red Cross. Answer that call, friends, for when you do you'll be answering the call of thousands of people in distress.
CUT TO SHOT OF AREA DESTROYED BY HURRICANE	You'll answer the pleas for help from those families driven from their homes by hurricanes . . .
CUT TO SHOT OF FLOODED STREET, FLOODED HOUSES ETC.	. . . floods . . .
CUT TO SHOT OF FLOODED FARM-LANDS	. . . tornadoes . . .
CUT TO RECONSTRUCTION SCENE	Through your Red Cross you'll help rebuild battered homes . . .
CUT TO RED CROSS CANTEEN FEEDING DISASTER VICTIMS	. . . you'll feed the hungry . . .
CUT TO SHOT OF RED CROSS WORKERS GIVING MEDICAL AID	. . . you'll give help to the sick and injured.
CUT TO SHOT OF RED CROSS WORKERS LOADING BLOOD ONTO TRUCKS	When you answer that call you'll provide the blood that's needed.
CUT TO SHOT OF CHILD IN HOS-PITAL BEING GIVEN TRANSFUSION	. . . to save the life of an ailing child . . .
CUT TO CANTEEN IN FIELD GIV-ING OUT COFFEE TO SOLDIERS	You'll answer the needs of our service men . . . out in the field . . .
CUT TO SHOT OF VET IN HOSPITAL DOING HANDICRAFT WORK	and in V.A. hospitals. You'll brighten their lonely hours . . .
CUT TO SHOT OF BIRTHDAY PARTY IN HOSPITAL	. . . bring them a touch of home . . . help them forget their troubles.
CUT BACK TO CU OF (STAR)	That's what your dollars can do. So when your Red Cross volunteer rings *your* doorbell . . . answer the call . . . give generously.

| PULL BACK AS (STAR) POINTS TO RED CROSS BUTTON ON LAPEL. | And wear your Red Cross button proudly — to remind others to join, too. |

    Both the announcements for the Ground Observer Corps and the Red Cross, illustrated above, have a direct message: the one asking for recruits, the other appealing for funds. But Public Service announcements may utilize an indirect approach, may deal with values in the abstract: announcements to inspire religious faith, to reiterate the principles of democracy, and so forth.

    The Advertising Council's "Future of America" campaign is designed "to reaffirm, with facts and figures, America's dynamic — and continuing — growth." It is geared to tell "the dynamic story of America today . . . of sweeping changes, tremendous needs, vast potentials, all adding up to greater opportunities ahead for practically every person in America!"

    Here is a typical radio announcement for the "Future of America" campaign.

SOUND: BABIES CRYING: UP 3 SECONDS AND UNDER
ANNCR: (STENTORIAN) Maternity Ward, U.S.A. . . .
SOUND: OUT
ANNCR: (STACCATO) More babies are born in America each month than the total population of Syracuse, New York, or Norfolk, Virginia, or Jacksonville, Florida!
SOUND: BABIES CRYING: UP AND OUT
ANNCR: (DRAMATIC) Four *million* new Americans born last year! *America* is growing faster than ever . . . changing more rapidly than ever! (STACCATO) *Americans* are raising more and larger families . . . living longer . . . working more . . . earning more . . . saving more . . . *buying* more! (DRAMATIC) With new and greater need than ever before for more homes and highways . . . schools and hospitals . . . factories and machinery . . . and the electric power to service them. Need for five hundred *billion* dollars worth of goods and services! Five hundred billion dollars worth of *opportunity* — for *you* and *every* American! See how you fit into this greater, growing America. Write *now* to Box 1776, Grand Central Station, New York, for your *free* copy of — "The Future of America." Learn the exciting facts and the exciting promise of tomorrow. Write to Box 1776, Grand Central Station, New York for — "The Future of America." It's free!

It is interesting to note that the public service announcements channeled through the Advertising Council are available for commercial sponsorship. It is assumed that in the event of sponsorship, the announcement would be preceded by a statement such as: "(BLANK) Company brings you the following message in the public interest."

The public service announcements we have considered have been national in scope, that is, either prepared for use on networks or for distribution to stations throughout the United States. The copywriter at the local station will probably be called upon, more frequently than not, to turn out an announcement of purely community interest: the church affair, open house at the public school, the county hospital fund drive, the ladies auxiliary charity affair, and the like. It all comes under the heading of experience and no matter how minor the organization, the writer should not slough off the assignment. Writing habits, as any work habits, pay off in proportion to the sincerity of effort.

The talk

9

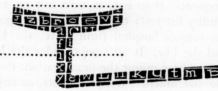

It was 1951 and General Dwight D. Eisenhower, then Chief of our NATO mission, returned home to report to the Congress and to the people of the United States. After his meeting with Congress, he was due to make a television talk to the nation. There was a great flurry of excitement at the Pentagon. The General was to deliver his address from the Pentagon pictorial studio. He did not want to be seated behind a desk reading a script, yet the remarks he was to make were too important to permit of ad libbing.

There was no teleprompter available at the time and after a hurried conference, it was decided to have the entire speech lettered on sheets of bristol board by graphic artists working in relays. The letters had to be large enough so that they could easily be seen at a fair distance since the boards had to be placed beneath the camera. The Defense Department artists worked quickly and accurately, right up to deadline. Last-minute changes in the speech meant swift relettering. During the telecast, two men handled the boards, removing them one by one as the General completed each section.

General Eisenhower chose to stand. He had no script in his hands and he did such a proficient job of reading from the boards that he gave the impression of speaking extemporaneously. He received overwhelming praise for a speech delivered with such ease and such naturalness.

Now this book is not a manual of production or direction, but the above incident was chosen to make a point for the speech writer. What impressed the viewers was the conversational tone and the simplicity of the talk: the ad lib feeling. This is what the writer must strive for whether he is to deliver the address himself or whether he is that anonymous purveyor of words, the ghost-writer.

GHOST-WRITING

Perhaps because the author has engaged in some ghost-writing, he may be forgiven if he has some kind thoughts about the man behind the words. If you enter the greatly expanding field of public relations or if you take a position in the information service of the government, you may be called upon to do your share of ghost-writing. Generally, the high official or the top business executive is invited to speak at many functions. It is part of his job, but since he can seldom find the time to prepare all those speeches himself, he hires a writer or even a staff of writers. A competent ghost-writer, even though he cannot lay any public claim to authorship, does take pride in his output. He learns the speech idiosyncrasies of the man he is working for and he patterns his talks accordingly. Sometimes that pride of authorship suffers a severe blow when the official takes it upon himself to do a complete job of rewriting!

HOLDING ATTENTION

The talk cannot compete with the purely entertainment features of broadcasting. Only during convention days or the final swing of a presidential campaign, nation-wide, or, perhaps a very stirring mayoralty campaign, locally, can the talk begin to hold an audience comparable in numbers to a top entertainment feature. Addresses by the President of the United States on important issues are generally given time by all networks and naturally the audience rating is high. But for lesser officials, representatives of institutions or business organizations, or lecturers, the audience potential is unfortunately not very high.

It is incumbent then upon the talk writer to prepare his statements in such a manner as to win immediate attention. If he has something worth-while to say, he wants to say it to as large an audience as possible. There is no reason why he cannot employ some of the devices that have proven successful for other forms of broadcasting. Let his opening paragraph — indeed, his very opening sentence — be an attention-getter. He has not written a talk merely to fill a time gap in the network or local station schedule. If his opening is flat, or, if he takes too much time getting to the meat of his subject, he will have alienated much of the audience which may be tuned to the station.

The auditorium speaker has a captive audience which may or may not have paid to hear him talk. At least the members of his audience have taken the trouble to leave their homes to hear him. The broadcast speaker, on the other hand, must try to captivate his audience. He has an advantage on television over radio because he may be able to use stills or film clips to illustrate his talk. The radio speaker has only his voice. But they both have one element in common: the words they have written.

Those words should sound conversational. Always bear in mind that your audience is an individual. You are not talking to a crowd gathered in an auditorium. You are talking to Mr. Jones, the man in the easy chair. He may be alone, smoking his pipe. Avoid any sort of bombast. Imagine yourself walking into that living room and haranguing Mr. Jones in a stentorian voice. You would hardly blame Mr. Jones if he jumped to his feet and asked you to pipe down or get out. Yes, pipe down. It is the art of talking *to* you not *at* you.

The National Association of Radio and Television Broadcasters issued a pamphlet, "Is Your Hat in the Ring?" (Revised edition, January 1956). It offers some excellent pointers to political orators, pointers of value to any radio or television speaker. The section on "How to Write the Radio Talk" has a brief, pithy summation: "Pick your purpose. Use short sentences. Use simple words. Use "picture" words. Develop your points interestingly. Write as you feel . . . write conversationally . . . be sincere."

Both radio and television require immediate comprehension. Unless someone owned a tape recorder and took a speech off the air for playback, there is no way a speaker can be halted in mid-sentence and asked to please repeat that phrase. If your sentences are too long and have too many qualifying phrases, they will be difficult to follow. Once your audience loses track of what you are trying to say, they also lose interest and you lose your audience. But let us not make the mistake of thinking that simplicity means catering to the mythical "twelve-year-old mind." We have already noted that it is possible to be highly literate and yet maintain simplicity.

TIMING

Another point the talk writer must consider is the matter of timing. Since time is of the essence in broadcasting, it is absolutely essential to conform to the time allotted. Read your talk aloud and time yourself. If you are ghost-writing, be sure to determine the speaker's rate. If he is a slow speaker you are naturally going to use fewer words. Don't guess. If you overwrite, your speech will be hurried with all the attendant dangers of fluffing on the part of the speaker and lack of understanding on the part of the audience.

THE ART OF THE TALK

Some of our readers, we hope, will be able to recall the late Alexander Woollcott who did make an art of the radio talk. In soft, conversational tones he could tell you about a book he had read and turn it into a best seller overnight. Or he could hold you spellbound as he related a story with a supernatural theme and as you listened your hair would stand on end and the goose pimples would play leap frog down your spine. He needed no sound effects, no music, no mechanical devices, only his voice and the power of the words he had written.

There are others today who make an art of the broadcast talk, men like Bishop Sheen, and Gilbert Highet. Both of them are fully aware of the requirements of the broadcast media: the one for television, the other for radio. Their talks are highly literate and yet maintain that simplicity so essential for broadcasting.

The talks of the Most Reverend Fulton J. Sheen and Gilbert Highet are published in collections which are noted in the bibliography. We recommend them to the reader. However, we are including, in this chapter, a few excerpts from their talks to illustrate style and approach.

A RADIO TALK

Here is the opening paragraph from "The Outsider," a talk included in the volume, *A Clerk at Oxenford,* by Gilbert Highet. Mr. Highet's talks are heard over many radio stations throughout the country and we hope that your local radio station is one of them.

He had no real home. He had not many friends. He did not even like or trust himself very much. His best friend was humanity; he liked the people.

This opening is calculated to hold attention. Our curiosity is piqued. We want to know who the subject is. The sentences in this opening paragraph are simple, short and effective. The second paragraph brings us the answer. It also brings us a change of pace through the lengthening of some of the sentences.

Most of us know his name — at least the name under which he published his books. He called himself "George Orwell." That sounds rather maladjusted, because his real name was much stronger. It was Eric Blair, which somehow suited his long, thin, strong, bony face; while "George Orwell" sounds like one of those dainty young men with wavy hair and brocade waistcoats whom one met in Bloomsbury during the 1930's. Still, let us call him George Orwell, for that is the name he chose.

Then follows a very perceptive study of the famous author of that powerful novel *1984.* In this one brief quarter-hour talk we get to know George Orwell the man and George Orwell, the writer. Gilbert Highet's sensitive, penetrating prose brings us a shuddering but unforgettable picture of young Orwell's anguished days at school.

Long afterward, long, long afterward, Orwell remembered being so hungry that he tiptoed downstairs to steal stale bread from the pantry at two in the morning; and he recalled the filthy metal bowls out of which the boys ate porridge, the rims flaked and scabbed by leavings from yesterday and the day before and the day before that. . . .

In two pithy paragraphs near the close of the talk, Highet gives us his estimation of Orwell's writings.

Returning to Britain, Orwell settled down to become a professional writer. He had many enemies. The Stalin clique and their allies did their best to wreck his work; still he wrote so well that he got into print oftener than they would have liked. His masterpiece is a story already famous: a description of the grim, state-worshipping, police-ridden, torture-dominated socialist future, without permanent truths or permanent values, when the dictatorship of one class has become the dictatorship of one gang, the new Dark Ages, called "1984." It is a splendid book, worthy to be classed with Voltaire's "Candide" and Swift's "Gulliver."

In the remainder of his work, what will last is his extremely sharp social and literary criticisms. His writing is delightfully clear and convincing, without rhetoric or evasiveness. Oh heavens, how hard it is to acquire a good clear style, as honest as decent stitching in a shoe, as clean as a well-laundered shirt, as economical as an efficient surgical operation, as tireless as a fine machine, as graceful as a fast runner! It is particularly hard when one writes about politics, for then one tends to become shrill and excitable, or else to fall into clichés about democratic values and class conflicts and the heritage of history and the mission of the people and so forth, stereotypes which usually conceal an absence of thought. Also when a man is lonely, as Orwell was, it is hard for him not to be savagely bitter, to strike back at personal enemies, to put in poisoned parentheses, to produce a negative effect. But Orwell did manage to maintain his balance, to keep thinking, to continue his kindness to most of his fellow men, to hammer out and to polish into brilliance a sharp, honest style.

If Gilbert Highet will allow, we think you will find in his own radio talks "a sharp, honest style." It is prose you can enjoy listening to, and surely profit from.

A TELEVISION TALK

Now, suppose we consider the television talk as exemplified by the Most Reverend Fulton J. Sheen in his series called "Life is Worth Living." Bishop Sheen uses no notes and his sole working props are a blackboard and some chalk.

As John Crosby has noted in a review of the program, "Bishop Sheen is truly a remarkable man at taking a subject and building it like a three act play from climax to climax."

These talks have been recorded and issued in several volumes. We have chosen a few excerpts from one of them, entitled "For Better or Worse." Bishop Sheen's talks are religious, educational, informative and inspiring. It is evident that he takes no stock in the myth of the "twelve-year-old mind."

This is the opening of "For Better or Worse."

> I wonder why Cupid is always presented as so young? Is it because love never grows up, or because its ideal is always to be young and fresh? Why does he have an arrow? Maybe it is because love is something that wounds and implies sacrifice for others. In any case, in this telecast, we shall discuss, first some tensions that are common to all marriages, and then some problems that are peculiar to certain marriages.
>
> There are three tensions in married love. By tensions, we mean emotions which pull in opposite directions, like a tug of war. There is nothing wrong about them. They are common, in a certain sense not only to the love of a husband and wife, but to human existence and even to the love of souls for God.

The very opening sentence of Bishop Sheen's talk poses a question which most of us probably never considered. And so we sit up and watch, our curiosity is aroused, and our attention is caught. It is held when we learn almost immediately that this talk will concern itself with the tensions of marriage. For this is of interest to us all, married or not.

Bishop Sheen classifies the common tensions and then analyzes them:

> The tension of unity and separateness; the tension of the personal and the social; the tension of longing and satiety.

If you have watched any of Bishop Sheen's talks, you will have found that they are always interspersed with humor, whether purely anecdotal or illustrative. Humor is a priceless ingredient which, if the writer of talks is adept enough to include, will insure a warm response. Here Bishop Sheen injects a note of humor as an illustration of the third tension, "longing and satiety."

This tension may be likened to the boy who asked his mother for a third dish of ice cream; the mother, on discovering he couldn't eat it, said, "See, too much ice cream." He said, "No, not enough boy."

We are not wrong in wanting perfect love. But it so happens that our souls and our hearts are not big enough; thus there is this pull between the two. Jimmy Durante put this thought into a song. I shall be one man who will not attempt to imitate the inimitable. I will merely tell you what Jimmy does. Remember, Jimmy starts to go out the door; he takes off his hat, puts it back on again; takes off his coat, and puts it back on again. Then he says, "Did you ever get the feeling that you wanted to go? And still you got the feeling that you wanted to stay?" That is the way it is with the human heart.

Now this is conversational writing. Actually, of course, it is Bishop Sheen speaking extempore. Fortunately, these talks, as we have stated, have been recorded. A writer studying them will learn the meaning of natural phrasing.

Another aspect of the talk is illustrated in the following excerpt from "For Better or Worse." It is the necessity to make the abstract idea clear by specific illustration.

Now we come to difficulties peculiar to some marriages. For example, there is a marriage in which the husband may be an alcoholic or the wife a spendthrift, or the husband unfaithful or the wife always nagging, or he is a "beast" or she is "impossible."

What is going to be done in a case like that? Stick it out! Remain faithful! Why? Suppose the husband instead of being an alcoholic had pneumonia. Would the wife nurse him and care for him? If he is a sinner, he has moral pneumonia and is spiritually sick; why abandon him? A mother has a child with polio; does she give up the child? St. Paul tells us that "the believing wife sanctifieth the unbelieving husband; the believing husband sanctifieth the unbelieving wife." There can be a transfusion of power from one to the other. Sometimes the condition of making the other better is perseverance and love.

A young German girl, at the close of the last World War, who was very learned and had read Homer at seventeen, was courted by one of our American GIs in Berlin. She married him, and they came to this country, where she discovered that he wanted only to read Western stories, while frequenting saloons and refused to work. While supporting both of them, she wrote to me, saying, "I was thinking of divorce, but I know that if I divorce him, I am contributing to the ruin of civilization. It does not mean very much if I pull my own individual finger out of that dam; just a little water will come through. But if every woman in the world in a similar situation does the same, then the flood tides will sweep the world. So I am going to stick it out; but I cannot do so without faith, and you must help me to get it." We gave her instructions, and God gave her the gift of faith. The husband is now an officer in the Army, a different kind of man, and both are raising a fine family.

Bishop Sheen's talks, since they are in essence, spiritual, always end on a spiritual note, as does this one:

But to love another for God's sake, we must really believe in God.

The interview

10

When radio was in its ascendancy, the rule, generally, was to avoid the ad lib. Security, particularly in the matter of interviews, was favored over spontaneity. The written interview assured accuracy in timing and avoided any embarrassing or inept statements. The goal to be attained, however, was simulated spontaneity, the impression of speaking extempore.

With the advent of television, interviews on the visual medium have become almost entirely extemporaneous. The spectacle of the participants reading from prepared scripts would appear dull and static. In most instances, the interviewer discusses the questions or issues with the interviewee a short time before the actual telecast. A few guiding notes to assist the interview may be noted on a large sheet hung on the base of a camera. This makes it easy for the participants to see the notes while looking directly at the camera; the notes, of course, are invisible to the audience. Another device is to have a few cards hidden from the audience by convenient props.

"PERSON TO PERSON"

Most interviews on television employ a simple set, and utilize only one or two cam-

eras for local presentations and perhaps three for network origina-
tions. But it was Edward R. Murrow who turned the interview into
a full-scale production. Under his guidance and that of his capable
associates, the television interview was no longer simply a radio interview transplanted before a camera. "Person to Person" takes complete advantage of the visual medium. True, it means a great deal
of work and expense to set up the multitude of equipment necessary
to effect the proper pickups. But it also takes imagination. And it
attracts sponsors.

"Person to Person" presents interviews with interesting people
in their homes and immediately there are many visible advantages.
For one, the interviewee is bound to be more at ease in his own home
than in a television studio. He will therefore express himself more
freely, more informally, more conversationally. He is speaking from
the warmth of his home to the welcome of yours. Secondly, the curiosity of the audience is satisfied in getting a first-hand view of where
and how the celebrity lives. Thirdly, because of its wide choice of
people in all walks of life, it aptly illustrates the fundamental principles of telecasting as promulgated in the preamble of the Television
Code, the first paragraph of which reads as follows:

> Television is seen and heard in every type of American home. These
> homes include children and adults of all ages, embrace all races and all
> varieties of religious faith, and reach those of every educational back-
> ground. It is the responsibility of television to bear constantly in mind
> that the audience is primarily a home audience, and consequently that
> television's relationship to the viewers is that between guest and host.

THE WRITER'S FUNCTION

But if interviews
have become almost entirely ad lib, what then is the writer's function?

There are some instances where accuracy of statement is a
prime requisite and the interviewee, particularly for a radio broadcast, prefers to have a script. This is often true when the interview
takes place with a high government official whose statements may be
quoted in the newspapers. It is true also when leaders of the com-

munity are asked to participate in a fund-raising campaign such as the cancer crusade. The community leader may be willing to give his time and lend his name but he may not be familiar with all the details of the campaign. In such instances, a script is prepared for him. The National Institute of Health at one time asked the author to have one of his classes write a series of interviews for nation-wide distribution on the subject of cancer. The Institute furnished the research material. This proved an excellent exercise in many ways: it taught the student how to extract the essential facts from a plethora of data; how to simplify them for mass understanding; how, most important of all, to write an attention-holding interview.

Many stations schedule a daily series of interviews. Each may be an entity in itself or part of the daily women's program, farm program, or news program. Most of them will be ad lib but there will be several occasions, as we mentioned previously, where a written script may be necessary. The writer may be the producer of the program, or a member of the continuity staff. If a government official or a top business executive is to be interviewed, his basic script may be prepared by his public relations aide.

AN INTERVIEW IS A CONVERSATION

The fundamental task of the writer then is to make the script sound as if it were not there! To do this, he must remember one key word: conversational.

This author has had occasion to rewrite or edit dozens of interviews whose main fault was that they were not conversational. The interviews were written in stilted phraseology, in long prosy sentences. On the air, it would be obvious that the interview was being read.

The writer should read the interview aloud and ask himself: is this the way the interviewee speaks? Does this interview sound like a conversation or a lecture?

Remember, also, that it takes two people to make a conversation. Many interviews are merely monologues interspersed by a few obviously leading questions. Granted that the interviewee is the one upon whom attention should be focused, nevertheless there is a loss of interest if the interviewer is written in only as a monosyllabic foil.

We must assume that the interviewee has something to say in which the public is interested, otherwise there would be no point in scheduling him. But if the interviewer is not an integral part of the interview then why not present the program as a talk?

Conversation, the writer should remember, is a continuous flow, yet not an uninterrupted one. An English composition may require that each sentence be complete but a written broadcast interview should simulate spontaneity and the truth of the matter is that we do not always speak in complete sentences. This is not to be construed as an invitation to write ungrammatically. It is rather an entreaty to write realistically.

CLICHÉS

Another common failing of many interviews is the use of clichés. How often have you heard interviews close in this manner: "We are sure our audience has enjoyed this interview today as much as we have." Actually, this is a completely unnecessary assumption on the part of the interviewer. If the audience stayed with the interview to the end, undoubtedly they were interested. The ones who didn't enjoy it wouldn't be there to hear the closing statement!

Prevalent also are the ubiquitous members of the mutual admiration society. They seem to appear on so many interviews on so many different stations. They are readily recognizable:

INTERVIEWER: It's so wonderful to have you on our program.
INTERVIEWEE: It's so wonderful to be here.
INTERVIEWER: Everybody knows what a busy and important person you are and I'm ever so grateful that you could spare a few minutes to be with us today.
INTERVIEWEE: I've heard so much about your program I'm really flattered to be invited.

Are there then to be no amenities? Of course, there should be demonstrated cordiality and politeness which may be the essence of simplicity. A warm "Thank you for being with us" is sufficient for a closing phrase.

CAPTURING ATTENTION

A well-prepared interview should attempt to capture immediate attention. This can be done in the introduction by posing the core of the problem to be discussed: e.g., if the interviewee is a child psychiatrist:

INTERVIEWER: Just what is a problem child? Is your child's unruly conduct natural for his age or is he actually a problem? We know that this is a question which must have occurred to almost every parent. We are pleased to have with us today Dr. _____, the noted child psychiatrist, author of _____, to discuss the so-called problem child.

WHO AND WHY

The above introduction also serves to illustrate two essentials for beginning an interview: the "Who" and the "Why." Tell who the interviewee is and give enough of his background to demonstrate his authority. Explain briefly why he is being interviewed. The order of the Who and the Why will depend on the personality being interviewed. If the interviewee is a celebrated movie star, the magic of his or her name will be enough to hold the audience. The teen-age audience needs only to hear the mention of the reigning popular singing star to stay glued for the interview.

However, for most interviews, some pertinent background about the interviewee is essential. Remember, however, to be brief. Choose only the most important highlights. Your audience wants to hear your guest, not hear about him.

Your closing should recapitulate a briefer version of your introduction:

INTERVIEWER: Thank you, Dr. _____. Today we discussed the problem child with the noted child psychiatrist, Dr. _____, author of _____. Tomorrow, on our (INTERVIEW SERIES) we will bring you _____. We hope you'll join us.

FUNCTIONS OF THE INTERVIEWER

In many instances, preparing a series of interview programs is, to borrow a phrase, a triple-threat job. The interviewer is also writer and producer. He will arrange for the guests to appear on the program. He will meet with the guest to discuss the ground to be covered. Ideally, the guest will ad lib his portion of the interview. In such case, the interviewer may confine himself to preparing a series of questions which should perform the following functions:

(a) Give the audience some insight into the guest's background.

(b) Develop in some rational order the material to be discussed.

(c) Allow for proper transitions.

(d) Permit specific answers.

(e) Take into account the time allotted for the interview.

Whether or not the interview is completely extemporaneous, the interviewer will do well to have in mind a sequence of questions. This will avoid the danger of rambling and the consequent feeling on the part of the audience that the interview "just didn't get anywhere." The interview, like any well-constructed program, should have a beginning, a middle and an end. It is always good technique to recapitulate at the close the points brought out during the body of the interview. No one will expect an interview to compete with an Alfred Hitchcock production, but a series of climaxes can be planned by carefully prepared questions.

THE WARMUP

If you have ever attended a radio or television program as a member of the studio audience, you are probably familiar with what is known in the broadcast idiom as the "warmup." In the few minutes preceding the actual broadcast, the master of ceremonies or the announcer or sometimes the featured performer will regale the audience with a few bits of humor or there will be some good humored banter between the m.c. and one of the performers. This is calculated, literally, to warm up the audience, to make them more receptive to the program.

It is a technique which the interviewer may adapt to good advantage. He can do this by having a few "human interest" questions at the start of the interview. These questions may deal with the personal life of the interviewee. They may show, in the case of a celebrity, that he is the father of two children and that he and his wife have faced the same sort of problems that any other parents have encountered. In the case of interviewees who may be somewhat mike shy, the few simple, personal questions will serve double duty: they will not only help in getting a sympathetic response from the audience; they will also aid in putting the guest at ease. Yes, in this author's experience, even movie stars have had attacks of mike fright.

Musical
continuity

11

On the face of it,
writing musical continuity appears to be a simple task. The writer
merely has to say: "Our next number is . . ." and give the title and
composer. After all, the music's the thing to catch the ear. But if
the writer is content with repetitious, uninteresting copy, he is not
only taking the easiest way, he is in danger of falling into a pattern
of laziness, of doing the least that is expected of him rather than the
best. This is detrimental to the discipline so essential to the writer.
The very simplicity of most musical continuity is a challenge to him.
Can he introduce the same selection in a half dozen different ways
in the space of two or three short sentences? Simplicity, yes, but it
is not simple to do. However, in avoiding the trite, he will sharpen
his facility with words, which, after all, is the essence of his craft.
The repetitious should be left to the commercial which is where it
belongs.

Except for those musical programs, such as operas and symphonies, that may require commentary, brevity must characterize
the usual musical introduction. Otherwise, you cut into the time
allotment for the music. It must be understood that what we are

discussing here is the purely musical program. There is a great deal of music on the air as portions of variety programs, background music, etc. In many instances, particularly in radio, there is a trend toward the uninterrupted musical program. It is not, however, an overpowering trend. One commercial radio station which attempted the ideal of long stretches of music with very brief copy and very limited commercials soon found itself in the red. Even the so-called "good music" stations generally have to effect some sort of compromise as to length of music and frequency of commercials. Only the very few municipally operated non-commercial stations or educational stations can permit themselves the luxury of truly uninterrupted music.

There appears to be a tendency today on the part of more and more network-affiliated radio stations to concentrate on the local scene. This has always been the province, of course, of the independent station. Network stations did more or less local programming, depending on whether they were owned and operated by the network and how much local business they could garner. With the competition of television, the pendulum has swung drastically toward the local scene. Radio, which always had a good percentage of all-musical programs, now has increased that percentage to a point where it is the mainstay of most local stations. That situation has been made possible by the perfection and availability of recordings.

In the early days of broadcasting, recordings were frowned upon and often looked upon as a last resort to be utilized by the poor country cousins. But high fidelity acetates and tapes and the organization of transcription companies to provide complete musical libraries has afforded even the smallest station with the best and latest in music. Where the local station could not possibly have available to it any talent comparable to the lavish live network presentations, it can now compete, musically, via recordings. In the popular vein, Teresa Brewer and Perry Como are as much available to the 250-watter as they are to any network program. For the classics, high fidelity recordings of the great symphony orchestras can be heard through the facilities of any station which wishes to schedule them.

These recordings were not always so readily available because of early protests by the musicians and the recording companies. They feared that if their recordings were played on the air and were listened to, free, by a vast audience, nobody would buy any records. Why pay for something that you can get for nothing? It took the efforts of pioneering disc jockeys to prove to the performers and the recording companies that their reasoning was fallacious. Sales of recordings played on the disc jockey programs doubled and trebled. The situation is now completely reversed. Singers and instrumentalists go out of their way to appear on top-rated disc jockey programs and song pluggers are constantly after the "platter spinners" to feature the newest outpourings of tin pan alley.

Another difficulty had to be ironed out before the music road became a smooth, melodious highway for the broadcasters. This was the all important matter of performance rights. As early as 1914, the American Society of Composers, Authors and Publishers (ASCAP) was formed to protect the rights of their members and to see that the proper royalties accrued to them. In order to avoid a monopolistic situation, a rival organization was formed in 1939, Broadcast Music, Inc. (BMI). All broadcast stations are now licensed by these two major music-licensing organizations. In return for permission to play any selection in the vast music catalogues of ASCAP and BMI, the stations generally pay a percentage of their gross income to the licensing organizations.

Today, the disc jockey holds sway in remote hamlets and in teeming metropolitan centers. He is the phenomenon of the current radio scene. He has a widespread audience and is often the darling of the teen-age set which, with adolescent enthusiasm, forms fan clubs in his honor. In many of our large cities, his earnings are slightly short of fabulous. He has few, if any, counterparts on television. And he is a voluble exponent of the ad lib. This means that at those radio stations which devote the major portion of their time to disc jockeys, there is little opportunity to write musical continuity. The ad lib has the advantage of spontaneity, as we have so often stressed, but the neophyte disc jockey and even his more experienced colleague, often permit this spontaneity to carry them away. The result is an overbalance of verbiage.

There has been some attempt at a return to "live" radio network music programs such as NBC's "Bandstand" and "The Woolworth Hour." The "Voice of Firestone," one of radio's oldest continuous musical programs, is now presented as a simulcast, which means that it is seen on television at the same time as it is heard on radio. Network radio has been in such a constant state of flux since the tentacles of television gripped the nation, that it is impossible, at this writing, to predict what form its programming structure will take from year to year. But music must be a basic ingredient of the radio station or network schedule if the competition of television is to be met. The purely musical program is rare on television. And even when it is scheduled, such as "The Hit Parade," it is full of visual gimmicks, which is, perhaps, as it should be. But it is not music to listen to with your eyes closed, or music to read by, or music to lighten such daily, obnoxious chores as washing the dishes. So here is a mighty stronghold of radio that can still withstand the penetrating onslaughts of TV.

Let us not forget, also, that radio has played and is still playing a large part in advancing the musical culture of the nation. Vast sums have been expended by the networks in bringing the major symphonies and the great operas to the public. Millions of listeners, through radio, were given their only opportunity to listen to the incomparable conducting of Toscanini at the moment he was on the podium, or "Traviata" or "La Boheme" directly from the stage of New York's Metropolitan Opera. The commentaries of a Deems Taylor during the intermission period of a symphony concert, or the stories of the operas as narrated by Milton Cross added much to the musical knowledge of the radio audience.

TYPES OF PROGRAMS

We may classify musical programs, both radio and television, in two broad categories: the Integrated and the Diverse.

In the first category are programs built around a definite theme: e.g., a famous composer; a patriotic occasion; a musical travelogue; a particular period; a sustained mood; a Gilbert and Sullivan program.

Integrated

One of the weekly "Woolworth Hour" programs took its cue from the political conventions and its integrated theme was "the best in music from many other such historic occasions." The script reproduced below is the first half of the hour musical program sans the commercials.

CUE: (THIS IS THE CBS RADIO NETWORK)
(. . . . . .30 seconds. . . . .)
MUSIC: FANFARE.
BRAND: THE WOOLWORTH HOUR . . . presenting "THE BEST IN MUSIC" . . . and coming to you *live* from New York City!
MUSIC: SWEEPS INTO THEME — ORCHESTRA AND CHORUS. UNDER FOR:
BRAND: The more than two thousand Woolworth stores throughout the United States and Canada . . . Cuba and Mexico . . . and the firms that supply F. W. Woolworth Company with high quality merchandise in tremendous variety — present: THE WOOLWORTH HOUR — starring our guest conductor — DAVID ROSE with THE WOOLWORTH ORCHESTRA AND CHORUS . . . today's special guests: TED LEWIS . . . KAY ARMEN and JACK RUSSELL — and, your host — the well-known stage and screen star — DONALD WOODS!
MUSIC: UP AND OUT.
WOODS: Thank you very much, Jack Brand . . . and thanks to all of you for joining us for the sixty-third consecutive broadcast of THE WOOLWORTH HOUR . . . coming to you *live* from New York City. There's history in the making this month in Chicago and San Francisco when our two major political parties meet to nominate their candidates for the coming Presidential elections in November.
MUSIC: IN THE BG — SNARE DRUM BEAT IN TEMPO OF "WINTERGREEN FOR PRESIDENT." GRADUALLY INCREASES IN VOLUME UNDER WOODS.
WOODS: This Sunday, on THE WOOLWORTH HOUR, we salute the Democratic and Republican National Conventions as we turn back the pages of the years to find THE BEST IN MUSIC from many other such historic occasions. DAVID ROSE and THE WOOLWORTH ORCHESTRA AND CHORUS lead the way with the familiar "WINTERGREEN FOR PRESIDENT" march from George and Ira Gershwin's brilliant musical satire . . . "OF THEE I SING."
MUSIC: "WINTERGREEN FOR PRESIDENT" — ORCHESTRA AND CHORUS.
MUSIC: DIRECT SEGUE FROM "WINTERGREEN FOR PRESIDENT" TO "MEMORIES" UNDER NARRATION FOR:
WOODS: Just in the month of August, itself, you'll find a long list of important anniversaries including the first United States census which was held in August of 1790 and showed a population of 3,939,214 in sixteen states and the Ohio Territory . . . or, in August of 1907 — the first taxicab appeared right here in New York City . . . But, suppose we go musically reminiscing with two of our exciting guest stars . . . the dynamic KAY ARMEN . . . and, one of the nation's favorite baritones — JACK RUSSELL . . . as they

join David Rose and The Woolworth Orchestra . . . in person — to sing of many more highlights from the years gone by. . . .
Music: "Dearie": Kay Armen, Jack Russell and Orchestra.
Music: playoff of "Dearie" — under for:
Woods: The Sousa band . . . feathered hats and celluloid collars . . . Yes, we're going back to the 1890's the era of the gay nineties with Jack Russell . . . David Rose and The Woolworth Orchestra . . . and one of the great heart-rending ballads of the day . . . Jack Russell — in person — sings . . . "She's Only a Bird in a Gilded Cage."
Music: She's Only a Bird in a Gilded Cage: Russell and Ork.
Music: in full with "Memories" — under with real corny piano predominating for:
Woods: If you've ever spent a rainy Sunday foraging through the family attic, you've undoubtedly discovered many a memento from the wonderful days of the "Gay Nineties" . . . perhaps it was a theatre program announcing the arrival of the great Sarah Bernhardt . . . an old beaded evening bag or a player piano roll.
Our guest conductor — David Rose — sets such memories to music for us this Sunday, on The Woolworth Hour, with his own special arrangement of one of the most familiar and famous songs of the "Gay Nineties" era . . . with The Woolworth Orchestra — David Rose plays his own colorful variations on "The Bowery."
Music: The Bowery: David Rose and Orchestra
Music: transitional bridge based on "Remember" . . . under for:
Woods: We've passed the turn of the century, now, on our special "Do You Remember?" Woolworth program . . . the year is 1912 . . . the year in which New Mexico and Arizona added two more stars to the national flag and one of the songs being sung from vaudeville stages . . . in tent shows . . . in homes everywhere was the song which the talented singing star and recording artist — Kay Armen — adds next to our list of memory music. With David Rose and The Woolworth Orchestra — Kay Armen — in person — sings . . . "Waiting for the Robert E. Lee."
Music: Waiting for the Robert E. Lee: Armen and Orchestra
Music: segue to introduction for "A Kiss in the Dark" . . . under for:
Woods: Do you remember the opening night of a Victor Herbert operetta on Broadway? In 1922 — with a cast headed by Queenie Smith, Edith Day, Jack Whiting and Hal Skelly . . . Mr. Herbert's big success was "Orange Blossoms" . . . Jack Russell joins

KAY ARMEN — in person — as they sing the beautiful duet from the score called . . . "A KISS IN THE DARK."

MUSIC: A KISS IN THE DARK: ARMEN, RUSSELL AND ORCHESTRA

MUSIC: BRIDGE BASED ON "MEMORIES" — UNDER FOR:

WOODS: Pianist . . . composer . . . orchestra leader — a well-known personality along Tin Pan Alley named TED FIO RITO contributed many happy songs during the twenties and helped to make those musical years the era of the *Roaring* Twenties.

Our special guest conductor — DAVID ROSE — has created a wonderful medley of some of TED FIO RITO's most familiar songs to bring back memories of the days when the cloche hat was in fashion . . . when the Tin-Lizzy jogged noisily along many a hometown street . . . when the Charleston and the Bunny Hug were the popular dances and a raccoon coat the symbol of the smart young collegian. To all those and many other mementos of that carefree, fabulous era — DAVID ROSE with THE WOOLWORTH ORCHESTRA adds the songs of TED FIO RITO . . . "TOOT TOOT TOOTSIE GOODBYE" . . . "I NEVER KNEW" . . . "SOMETIME" . . . "KING FOR A DAY" and "CHARLIE, MY BOY!"

MUSIC: TED FIO RITO MEDLEY: ROSE AND ORCHESTRA.

MUSIC: THEME — UNDER FOR:

BRAND: This is your WOOLWORTH HOUR . . . coming to you live from New York City. After a brief pause for station identification, we'll be back with more of the "BEST IN MUSIC" . . . more information on the best buys on the counters of your local Woolworth store. You'll hear more from your host — DONALD WOODS — and, our exciting guests, who are with us, this Sunday — in person: TED LEWIS . . . KAY ARMEN . . . JACK RUSSELL — together with our special guest conductor — DAVID ROSE, THE WOOLWORTH ORCHESTRA AND CHORUS.

CBS

ANNCR: THIS IS THE CBS RADIO NETWORK

MUSIC: PROGRAM THEME BEHIND FOR:

Diverse

The second category, the Diverse, presents a heterogeneous program: e.g., a group of popular songs, a variety of semi-classical music, a potpourri of old and new songs.

We have remarked that there is a dearth of musical programs per se on television but there is one program which is making up for that lack: the Lawrence Welk Show. This is a program which presents music, not gimmicks — melodic, listenable, popular music which has won an enviable rating. The musical selections are many and diverse and the simplicity of the continuity is in keeping with the program style. As Mr. John Gaunt, vice president of Grant Advertising, Inc., and writer of the program, explained: " — the extreme simplicity of the musical introductory remarks is a reflection of the unpretentious, homey style of our star. . . . It is slanted to suit the specialized talents of a man who has proven himself able to reach the American public in a very special way."

Here are some excerpts from a typical Lawrence Welk Show.

DODGE DIVISION
LAWRENCE WELK SHOW
                    STANDARD OPENING BILLBOARD

FILM — BUBBLES EFFECT	MUSIC: MUSICAL RIFF UP TO SUSPENDED CHORD
LAWRENCE WELK TITLE APPEARS CENTER PICTURE	ANNCR: Direct . . . from Hollywood — the Champagne Music of Lawrence Welk!
BUBBLES SWIRL. ONE BUBBLE SWELLS TO CENTER, WIPES AWAY NAME, WITH CAR IN CENTER OF IT.	MUSIC: SEGUE TO SECOND RIFF INTO HIGHER CHORD SUSPENDED
BUBBLE BREAKS REVEALING CAR	MUSIC: SUDDENLY OUT SOUND: POP! (ON FILM TRACK)
CAR IN CLEAR, BUBBLES AROUND IT	ANNCR: DODGE — the car that says "let's go!" . . . presents — the music that says "let's dance!" (PAUSE) MUSIC: WELK THEME START AND UNDER
	ANNCR: . . . *Champagne* Music with best wishes from the friendly Dodge Dealer in your community . . . the man who sells and services the beautiful new Dodge — Value Leader of the Forward Look — (PAUSE) And here is your host — Lawrence Welk!

MUSICAL CONTINUITY   **119**

DISS TO LS FULL STAGE — LAWRENCE, ORCHESTRA AND ENTERTAINERS	LIVE AUDIENCE APPLAUSE
BOOM IN TO MED. SHOT LAWRENCE AS HE SPEAKS	WELK: BEGIN SHOW Good evening, my good friends from coast to coast. Let's start this Spring evening off with a trip on . . . "Moonlight Bay."
#1 — MOONLIGHT BAY	INSTRUMENTAL TEMPO: MED. Now the lovely little Champagne Lady presents a beautiful new song, descriptive of the . . . "Wayward Wind."
#2 — THE WAYWARD WIND	VOCAL: ALICE LON Very beautiful, Alice. Now Myron Floren is in a Springtime mood and his solo is a reminder that the season can bring . . . "Rain, Rain."
#3 — RAIN RAIN POLKA	INSTRUMENTAL Thank you, Myron. A very beautiful thought is expressed in a new song sung by Jim Roberts . . . "Faith Unlocks the Door."
#4 — FAITH UNLOCKS THE DOOR	VOCAL: JIM ROBERTS TEMPO: MED. Thank you, Jim Roberts. Now let's all dance again, folks, to a real cute tune by LeRoy Anderson featuring our violin section . . . "Plink, Plank, Plunk."
#5 — PLINK, PLANK, PLUNK	INSTRUMENTAL Thank you and now here's Buddy Merrill, ladies and gentlemen, with a tune well designed to show his fine technique . . . "The Third Man Theme."
#6 — THIRD MAN THEME	INSTRUMENTAL TEMPO: MED. Thank you, Buddy. A wonderful thing about young fellows is their enthusiasm. Now here's young Larry Dean, who has something to be enthusiastic about.
#7 — HOT DIGGITY	VOCAL: LARRY DEAN TEMPO: MED. FAST WALTZ Thank you, Larry, you were really carried

away. Ladies and Gentlemen, our distinguished violinist, Dick Kesner, tonight is celebrating his 15th happy wedding anniversary. In honor of the occasion, Dick will play . . . "The Anniversary Waltz."

#8 — ANNIVER-   VIOLIN SOLO
SARY WALTZ   TEMPO: MED. SLOW WALTZ

STYLE

The writer should adapt his style to the type of music. What this actually means is that he is tailoring his script to the level of the audience. A classical music program attracts a smaller but more erudite audience. The writing therefore should have an intellectual appeal. This does not imply any cold formality because as, in any other broadcast program, the audience is in an informal, relaxed attitude. The continuity will vary also depending on whether the program is live or recorded. A broadcast from New York's Lewisohn stadium or the Hollywood Bowl permits additions of "color," that is, descriptions of the surroundings, the crowd in attendance, the arrival of the conductor or the soloist on the stage, even a mention of the weather. Word pictures are essential in radio. When the camera is present, the home audience can see for itself.

Nevertheless, in television, or radio, program notes are helpful. The object is to make those notes as interesting as possible. There are many people who enjoy the classics yet whose knowledge of composers' lives or the background of a particular composition is limited. These notes then can be the "human interest" element in the copy. References to musical theory may also be incorporated as long as the writer does not become too technical. Above all, he must be accurate. Again, the writer-researcher comes to the fore. Any misstatement is bound to bring at least one complaint, if not a great many, from the listening audience.

As an illustration of audience reaction, this author can well remember one occasion on which he wrote and announced the copy for a live symphonic broadcast. An unfortunate slip of the tongue resulted in a slight mispronunciation of a composer's name. It seemed that the error might be lost in the copy that followed. But the next day there were a half dozen post cards calling attention to the fault, one of them a very irate protest from a listener that his favorite composer's name was mispronounced! The point is your copy is listened to and you cannot afford any mistakes, no matter how slight.

If, under circumstances beyond your control, you are called upon to write the continuity for a "rock 'n roll" program, you will be well advised to learn the proper phraseology. Fortunately, most of such programs are in the hands of ad-libbing disc jockeys. But, as we may have mentioned previously, the appellation of jack-of-all-trades is in no way derogatory to the writer. Modern jazz has devised its own idiom and the writer must be aware of it. He may be a scholar versed in semantics, but theory will avail him little against the dictionary-defying terminology of the jazz cults.

THE MOOD PROGRAM

Music, as we know, is most effective in establishing moods, and often musical programs are produced to create a sustained feeling: romance, gaiety, humor, reflection, reverence. As the writer must adapt his style to the level of his audience, so must he attune his words to the mood of the program.

A program of musical humor or sparkling gaiety will call for short sentences, light in flavor. The writing must match the buoyancy of the music.

A program of religious music should have the writer searching for the orotund phrase to equal the dignity of the oratorio or the hymn of piety.

Music of sentiment, of romance will call for flowing phrases, for full-vowelled words that the announcer or narrator may read softly, poetically. The sentences will be longer than for ordinary copy in order to avoid the staccato. Here the writer can use imagery to the fullest. Yet, he must still be brief to permit the maximum of music. Production-wise, he should make his continuity an integral part of the program, by having all of it read with musical background, preferably to the opening strains of each selection. This will insure an uninterrupted flow of words and music, of beauty in the musical and the verbal phrasing.

The news program

12

With hundreds of radio stations inclining towards a news and music format and with television stations presenting news programs several times during the broadcast day, a great many opportunities are open to the writer with a background in journalism. Since many radio stations and an increasing number of television stations employ local newsmen who not only gather news of the area but are also newscasters, it is an asset to have a good voice and an interesting delivery. This does not mean that the newscaster must be gifted with a deep resonant voice with which to emit mellifluous, pear-shaped vowels. Mere resonance has long since been supplanted by intelligence and personality. The tenor is as welcome as the baritone.

However, a very high-pitched voice can be a handicap. It is one of the primary reasons why there are so few women newscasters. For any long stretches of monologue, a low-pitched voice is easier on the ear. Listen with an appraising ear to Edward R. Murrow or John Daly. It will be immediately apparent that a well-modulated voice and an easy command of the language generally will make for more attentive listening than harsh, grating tones. However, as in every other phase of broadcasting, there are always exceptions to every rule, to every formula. The reader is probably aware of some glaring exceptions in this instance.

Some years ago, when news programs were beginning to appear with more and more frequency on the airwaves, this author was asked to engage in a survey whose object was to determine what effect news broadcasts were having on the circulation of newspapers. The survey took place in New York City and editors of all the dailies were interviewed. There were some interesting opinions and caustic comments, freely given. A brief summary of these comments may be of value to the news writer.

There were many points on which the editors agreed: Newscasting had done away with the "extra." It was impossible for newspapers to compete with the broadcasters in the time required to reach the public. You can "stop the press" for a hot story, but it still has to be printed and delivered to newsstands and homes. If the news flash is of great urgency, the broadcaster can break in on any program to relay the news immediately.

Yet the consensus was that news broadcasting increased newspaper circulation. Why? The limited time allotted to news programs, five to fifteen minutes, permits only of capsule reporting. The listener's or viewer's curiosity is whetted to the point where he often turns to the newspaper for a fuller account.

Much of the criticism from editors revolved about the observation that, unlike the newspaper, newscasts had no front page, that each item appeared to have equal weight. One editor remarked that it was possible for a newscaster to color the news by inflection. If the newscaster were to read an item with evident irony, he could conceivably cast doubt on that particular story.

There was a time, and possibly there may still be some instances extant, when several newspapers refused to print radio logs on the ground that radio stations were competitors for the advertising dollar. If the radio station did want its log printed, these newspapers argued, it should pay for the service. However, the old adage which states so emphatically, "If you can't beat 'em, join 'em," has evidently been embraced by a host of newspapers, which now own and operate radio and television stations. It might be added, as a footnote, that one of the editors who was most critical about newscasts, now finds his newspaper owning a radio station which presents news every hour on the hour!

Witness the number of newspapers today which issue weekly television schedules with their Sunday editions. These supplements are presented as weekly magazines or tabloids, replete with news about television programs and people, and with advertisements. They are also a decided asset to the newspaper's circulation.

WIRE SERVICE

The vast press associations, Associated Press, United Press and International News Service, had many conflicts with the broadcasting industry during the early years of radio. The associations looked upon radio's attempt to enter the news field as an intrusion and refused, at first, to lease their news wires to radio stations. This led to the networks establishing their own news services, a step which engendered a great deal of soul searching on the part of the press associations. Finally, the associations decided it was the better part of wisdom to have radio stations as customers rather than competitors. They, therefore, established a radio news service and offered it to the broadcasters on a fee basis. The news copy for broadcasters is written by a special staff of newswriters and tailored for the air, as opposed to the printed page. Most radio and television stations subscribe now to one or more of these services.

For the small radio station, the wire service is a boon. All an announcer has to do is to tear enough items off the news ticker to meet the time requirements and he has a ready made newscast.

The press associations have also taken television in their stride and now provide film scripts, which can be used as inserts for telecasts. These are brief sound on film (SOF) pickups of news of national import, which might not otherwise be available to the station.

However, as the broadcasting industry grew rapidly to maturity, it also became conscious of its power as a news-disseminating medium. The networks organized large news staffs with editors, writers, reporters, commentators, analysts. The larger stations developed comparable local staffs. Today, the trend, even for the smaller stations, is to have a local newsman on the staff who is reporter, writer, newscaster, all in one. In addition, many stations use "stringers" to phone in special stories.

THE PROBLEM OF ACCESS

The broadcast reporter, however, found that in many instances, and unlike his colleagues on the newspaper staff, he was persona non grata. He was not permitted to bring his recorder, remote equipment or his camera to many public hearings. In Washington, he could not gain admission to press conferences granted by cabinet officers. If the broadcast reporter felt personally aggrieved, he soon realized that there was no animosity towards him as an individual, but rather to the tools of his trade. The shorthand notebook was an old and honored acquaintance, although it had proved as much foe as friend. The newcomers, the microphone and the camera, were looked upon with suspicion. The issue is often debated as to whether radio or television equipment may be admitted to the courtroom and, in some instances, to Congressional hearings. There is no question of the tremendous impact on the public when television cameras are permitted at public hearings.

Because they believe the right to know is basic with the American people, the broadcasters have established a Freedom of Information Committee as a standing committee of the National Association of Radio and Television Broadcasters. Its purpose, as outlined in its statement of policy is: "to propose policies and encourage actions which will promote freedom of expression, particularly as such basic freedom relates to the responsibilities of radio and television broadcasters in meeting their public interest responsibilities."

The vigorous stand of the broadcasters has won several victories in recent years. In Washington, both radio and television newscasters now have access, with their equipment, to *news* conferences. The networks have their own "White House reporters." Many Congressional hearings have been televised and, in some locales, court trials have been made accessible to radio and television. The argument has been raised that television cameras in a courtroom are an annoyance, and the glaring lights they presumably require, a hindrance. However, as Harold E. Fellows, President of the NARTB, stated in his address on "Freedom of Expression on the Air": "The truth is that a television camera is noiseless and that it can operate satisfactorily without artificial lights other than ordinary room illumination." As to television or radio "sensationalizing" a trial, the broadcasters' response is that they would be as virtuous or guilty as any newspaper. The fact is that the broadcasters are much more sensitive to public response than the newspaper publishers. The broadcasters have to be. They operate under government license.

Mr. Fellows, in his same address, made a potent appeal for equality of expression:

> These two media (newspapers and broadcasting) perform like functions in unlike manners, one approaching the intelligence through the eye alone and the other approaching through both the ear and the eye. Both entertain. Both inform. Both are instruments of commerce. Both are diversely owned and of varying political and social persuasions. The very addition of the voice of radio and the picture of television gives balance to opinion, since they introduce new expressions of thought and opinion in the market place.
>
> How free should broadcasting be? As free as the press.

EDITORIALIZING

In our survey of newspaper editor opinion, as discussed previously in this chapter, we mentioned one editor stating that newscasts had no "front page." He might well have added that they have no editorial page either. Newspapers are justly proud of their long tradition of fighting for causes, both popular and unpopular. They are outspoken about the influence of their editorials on public opinion. But broadcasters have shied away from taking sides on any issues. This has not been entirely of their own doing. The Communications Act of 1934 and the regulations of the Federal Communications Commission require broadcasters to give equal time to candidates of different political parties. This has led to the present method of paid political broadcasts. Otherwise, it is obvious that in order to bring the candidates before the public and at the same time adhere to FCC regulations, the broadcasters would find their airtime filled with nothing but political speeches during an election campaign.

When a radio station, WAAB of Boston, did take a stand on a controversial public issue, its license renewal was endangered.

The Federal Communications Commission, in effect, ruled that a radio station could not editorialize. This case is referred to, in the industry, as the Mayflower decision. It derives its name from the Mayflower Broadcasting Corporation, which unsuccessfully applied for the WAAB channel. This decision of the FCC, Mr. Fellows states, "had the effect of stifling free comment by broadcasters." The cry of censorship was raised and the Commission subsequently qualified its decision by permitting broadcasters to editorialize, provided equal opportunity for rebuttal was given to the opposition.

It might be well to observe, at this point, that a reader who disagrees with an editorial in a newspaper may write a letter to the editor, which may be printed. There are times when a newspaper may be deluged by a flood of letters and will therefore, because of space limitations, be forced to choose a representative few.

Some of the braver among the broadcasters have already begun to editorialize. This is more particularly true of independent, community stations. One prime example is radio station WGAY, Silver Spring, Maryland, whose general manager, Joseph L. Brechner, believes that the broadcasters are now reaching a point of maturity where they are beginning to think for themselves. WGAY has taken a stand on several controversial issues which affect its listening audience. The station believes it is as much a part of the community as any newspaper. Editorials are labeled as such by the station and bear a tag line somewhat as follows: "You've just heard an editorial. Equal time for rebuttal will be given to a responsible individual or organization."

WGAY has found its editorializing an enlivening experience. The pros have been warmly responsive; the cons have asked for equal time and received it. The gainer has been the public as a whole. The editorials have been successful in bringing the issues to the public and to help clarify its thinking.

As to the future, let us again quote Mr. Fellows:

"In the battle against the insidious evils of silence and censorship, broadcasters have drawn their own battle lines; nor do I believe that they will waver in their obligation to the people to report fairly and comment freely."

WRITING THE NEWS PROGRAM

If we were to choose one word to guide the embryo news writer, it would be: clarity. News programs deal with facts which must be instantly understood by the listener or viewer. There is no opportunity for the audience to say to the newscaster: "Would you mind repeating that statement? I didn't get it."

There are, therefore, several fundamental principles which the news writer should follow, and these principles are applicable to both radio and television:

One thought to each sentence

A multiplicity of ideas strung along in one sentence will tend to confuse your audience. Simplicity of construction, on the other hand, will insure understanding.

Take this example:

> Secretary of State Dulles told his news conference today that differences on fundamental issues in the Suez dispute exist between the United States, on one hand, and Britain and France on the other, and that because of such differences the United States cannot identify itself 100 per cent with the colonial powers if we want friendly relations with anti-colonial countries.

This is, to say the least, an involved sentence. It may have been found on the front pages of some of our newspapers, although truth to tell, newspaper writing, in many instances, is tending more and more to pattern itself on broadcast style. For radio or for video, the above statement would have been broken up into three distinct sentences. Here it is, as actually broadcast over WTOP in Washington:

> Secretary of State Dulles told his news conference today that differences on fundamental issues in the Suez dispute exist between the United States on one hand and Britain and France on the other. Because of such differences, Dulles said the United States cannot identify

itself 100 per cent with the colonial powers. The reason, Dulles explained, is that we want friendly relations with anti-colonial powers.

The almost imperceptible pause by the newscaster after each period definitely marks the end of one thought. It is much easier for the viewer or listener to grasp these three distinct thoughts. On the-other hand, the newspaper reader can reread a sentence two or three times if he does not comprehend its meaning the first time.

Avoid alliteration

Always try to read your copy to yourself; silently, if you must; aloud, if you can. It will help you avoid alliterative or other tongue-twisting phrases. If you find that you stumble over a phrase you have written, then you are setting up a potential fluff. It is not that an announcer cannot read an alliterative phrase. Alliteration is an excellent device for poetry, but it takes a special talent to read poems well. The newscaster who may be handed a late bulletin a few minutes before he goes on the air does not have much rehearsal time. He will appreciate copy that does not present any possible stumbling blocks.

Vary the length

In following the principle of confining sentences to one thought, there may be a tendency to make all sentences brief. This would result in staccato delivery and inevitable monotony. You will find that your newscast will hold attention more effectively if there is variety in the length of your sentences. If your first two statements are brief, make your third statement somewhat longer. This will permit better pacing and a more listenable newscast.

Method of quotation

The "Quote" and "Unquote" technique fortunately has become outmoded. It was an awkward method that stuck out of the news copy like the proverbial sore thumb. Brief quotations may be adequately noted by a change of intonation. Longer quotations may be preceded by the name of the quoted person and the simple verb, said. For example, "Secretary of State Dulles said: 'We are going to meet with the British and French tomorrow.' "

If the quotation consists of several sentences, it is advisable to add at the conclusion of the quotation, an identifying sentence somewhat as follows: "Those were the words of Secretary of State Dulles at his news conference this morning." If there were no such identification, late-tuners might not be aware whether the statements were those of the newscaster or a direct quotation. The problem is lessened, of course, where we have a film insert on television or a tape insert on radio. The picture of the speaker on the screen or the new voice on tape immediately sets up its own visual or aural quotation marks.

Means of identification

You have probably heard the comment that names make news. This is undoubtedly true. Certainly, names like Eisenhower or Stevenson, Marilyn Monroe or Elvis Presley need no introductory statements. Generally, however, most names in the news require some immediate identification, the briefer the better. Your audience should be made instantly aware of the newsmaker's identity. An official title simplifies matters considerably, thus: Secretary of the Treasury Humphrey, or, Senator Johnson.

Here are a couple of typical identifications culled from a local CBS newscast:

"Overseas, Western diplomats report that *Russian Party Boss* Khrushchev has asked *Yugoslav President* Tito to join a new association of European communist countries."

Additionally:

"*Maryland Governor* McKeldin today appointed *Montgomery County Circuit Court Judge* Stedman Prescott to the Maryland Supreme Court."

You will note that it is almost always preferable to have the identification precede the name. This is both a timesaver and an assist to smoother reading. Try the reverse and you will observe these factors on reading the items aloud. Suppose the first news item were written:

"Overseas Western diplomats report that Khrushchev, Russian Party Boss, has asked Tito, Yugoslav President," etc.

The necessary insertion of commas entail a halt and force the reading to become staccato at those points.

In the second news item, it would be awkward to state: "Governor McKeldin, Maryland." We would have to insert the preposition "of."

Clarifying antecedents

In attempting to write your news copy with understandable simplicity, be careful that your word saving does not muddle your antecedents. For example, to write: "John Jones, aide to the Secretary of Defense, died today" might very well be confusing. A late-tuner might just possibly catch the words: "Secretary of Defense, died today." It would be best, in order to avoid any mistaken impression, to write that item as two sentences. "John Jones died today. He was an aide to the Secretary of Defense."

Lead items

The question of which item should be the leadoff for your newscast depends on several factors. A network newscast will generally use an item that is of most significance to the country as a whole. It may be international or national in scope. It may be a story concerning the Middle East crisis or the presidential campaign. Naturally, the news editor has to depend on the news break. He doesn't make the news.

The newscast by a local station, however, will vary from the network lead depending on whether there is any critical occurrence in the local area. If a transit strike has just been declared, which will have a paralyzing effect on the city, it will undoubtedly be the leadoff item for the local newscast because of its direct impact.

Although your lead item should be heavyweight, your closing item, if possible, should be lightweight. Save that bright human interest story or that funny incident for the last. It will leave your listeners or your viewers in a good mood and it makes for a happier transition to a commercial.

Transitions

A newspaper is printed in columns and each column brings you a different story. Your eyes may rove across the headlines, begin one news story, then jump to another. You make your own transitions. But on the air, the newscaster has to make the transitions for you.

Of course, it is possible to prepare an entire newscast without any transitional phrases. The announcer may pause very briefly between news items, the pause acting as a transition. Proper transitional phrases, however, will make for smoother continuity. Again, let us refer to our WTOP newscast.

"The World Series starts at Ebbets Field with Sal Maglie starting for the Dodgers and left hander Whitey Ford hurling for the Yankees. President Eisenhower will be there. His visit is billed as 'Non-political.'

"Definitely political, however, is a farm-storming tour to be made by Agriculture Secretary Benson."

In this instance, "Definitely political" is the transitional phrase that ties in neatly with the preceding news story. It is not always possible to effect a natural transition. If not, it is best to avoid dragging in a transition by the heels.

Taboos

As in every other form of writing for radio and television, news writing also has its taboos. Because they deal with actual occurrences, with news of interest to the public, newscasts generally have more leeway than fictional drama in choice of words and latitude of subject matter. But they are still bound by the "family in the living room" proprieties. When Somerset Maugham's "The Letter" was to be performed on TV, it took a round of conferences before the use of the word "rape" was permitted in the play. Newspaper reporters and rewrite men would hardly hesitate at the use of the word.

Actually, this is not a question of freedom of expression on the air as much as it is a matter of taste and judgment. Obviously, newscasts would avoid vulgarities. And in line with the Radio and the Television Code, there would also be an avoidance of intimate sex details, recitals of sadism, or gory descriptions of crimes. This would tend to place the broadcast news writer on the squeamish side in contrast to some of the sensational copy that appears in several newspapers and magazines. Or even in contrast to some of the routine newspaper reporting. This does not mean that sensational stories have to be omitted on the broadcast media. If the story is being headlined by newspapers throughout the country, then it is evidently of great news value and would undoubtedly be a serious omission from a newscast. In such cases, the news writer becomes a hunter of synonyms which tell the same story but with a softer impact. A spade no longer is a spade but an instrument for digging. Adultery becomes intimacy.

Placement of items is another element which requires good judgment on the part of the news writer or editor. It would be manifestly in poor taste to follow a story of a tragic death by a humorous news item. It would also be poor judgment to conclude a news broadcast with a story of starving refugees when the commercial that follows is one which urges the listener to stock up his refrigerator with Foster's Frozen Foods. On the other hand, many newsmen believe that listeners have become sophisticated enough to recognize the difference between the news story and the commercial and rarely relate one to the other. Nevertheless, you can see that as a radio or television news writer you face many more restrictions and many more problems than your journalistic colleagues. But you do have advantages in speed of reaching the public, and, on the networks, of a vastly greater audience.

General considerations

We have used the term "conversational" as an ideal for broadcast utterance. News copy, because of its very factual nature, tends to formality of approach. Perhaps there ought to be some happy meeting ground. The news writer should strive for naturalness but avoid any "folksiness" or any frequent use of colloquialisms. The radio and television audience wants its news straight without any dramatizing or coloring. Of course, a Will Rogers would have his own droll approach to the news and prove a happy exception.

And always, time is of the essence. If you are writing a five-minute sponsored newscast with commercials fore and aft, you actually have about three and a half minutes. Again, here is a challenge to the news writer to be pithy yet explicit. There is always a good deal happening, internationally, nationally and locally. How many items are to be included in the newscast and how much time devoted to each news item is a matter for careful consideration. The news item, generally, should be judged in relation to the numbers of people it will interest or affect. Availability of tape inserts for radio or film clips for television is an additional determining factor in choice of news events.

NEWSCASTER — COMMENTATOR — ANALYST

The Newscaster, generally, is an announcer, who, among his other duties, handles news broadcasts. At the larger stations and the networks, the copy will be written for him or at least the press association's copy will be edited for him. At the smaller station, he will probably write, edit and even gather his own news. Again, the bulk of his news will be supplied by a wire service.

The Commentator is strictly a newsman who, generally, prepares his own copy or he may have a staff writer or writers, depending on his reputation and his earnings. Like the newscaster, he covers a variety of news items and may inject his views on any or all of the items.

The Analyst is the intellectual of the newsmen. He chooses one major news event, delves into its background, examines it critically and gives the audience the benefit of his own wide experience as he analyzes the situation. One of the nation's outstanding news analysts is Eric Sevareid of the Columbia Broadcasting System. The news analysis reprinted below is typical of his nightly radio broadcasts.

Good evening . . . The Presidential contest, on its national and surface level, continues in a curious air of unreality. On that level it is becoming a speechwriter's contest; it was never realistic to think that any political campaign could become a genuine search for the truth; it was always possible to hope that out of the partisan clash of facts and opinions, the truth would emerge; but the contest is going the other way. The contenders are merely making debating points on most of the specific issues, each hitting at the other's weakest point with his own strongest point, whether pertinent or not; each trying to match a carefully selected virtue of his own against a carefully selected fault of his opponent. It is a kind of Japanese sword dance pantomime, the flashing weapons never quite clashing, always just missing.

But there is a deeper reason for this air of unreality and it is that only now and then, as if by chance, does the substance of the speeches reflect and deal with the true nature of the problem; this is especially the case when the debate concerns the nature of the world beyond our shores. The concept the candidates reflect of the deep and mighty historical forces in motion is the concept of a static problem. Over and over we hear the phrase "a job to be done." It is part of the inbred American notion that if only the right men are appointed, the right sums appropriated, the right legislation passed, then the problem is "solved" and disappears, for good.

By and large this has been the approach to the question of peace. It is valid to speak of the present condition as a condition of peace, since there is no large scale fighting going on, but it is only partially valid; this may be the only kind of peace we shall ever know in our lifetime but "armistice" is the better word for it.

Every day the illusion that armistice is peace is driven deeper. A feeling is taking hold that years of upheaval have given way to years of steadiness, that conflicting forces in the world have somehow settled back, with only an occasional flareup, temporary, restricted, as in the case of Suez. This, surely, is a false reading of our time.

Indeed, it can be logically argued that since World War Two, in these years of armistice in the name of peace, the world has changed more profoundly, more rapidly than in any period since the Industrial Revolution, a century and a half ago. The old alternatives, the old choices by which nations lived have disappeared; it is now peace or annihilation, iron alternatives for which all man's experience has given no one, no philosophers, no diplomats, the slightest shred of preparation.

After three hundred years, the physical safety of the American continent has disappeared.

After a thousand years of weakness or control by others, the majority part of mankind, those who live in the Far East, the Mid-East and Africa, are suddenly casting loose from all previous moorings, off on their own, to a political destination no one can foretell.

Western powers, Occidental civilization can no longer set the terms of human relationships on this globe.

In these recent years of imagined stability, whole empires have collapsed, their military and trading systems torn to pieces.

In these supposedly static years, the political prairie fire of our century, the Bolshevist Revolution, has altered its course, and has revealed to the world another Russian revolution which we never really believed was there — a successful industrial, scientific revolution of such potential that some of our leading technologists believe it is overtaking us, and rapidly.

We do not confront a series of static "problems" to be "solved." We confront a moving ocean of change, moving at a speed and in a worldwide scope beyond all precedent. Our task is not to finish something, our task is to begin; how to live with this in safety; and the start of the beginning is to understand it.

American voters, next month, cannot choose solutions; they can only choose those men who seem to them to most clearly understand.

This is Eric Sevareid in Washington.

WRITING STYLE — BROADCAST VS. NEWSPAPER

We believe it will be of value to the potential newswriter to note some of the precise differences between writing for a newspaper and for broadcast. Many newswriters, perhaps a majority of them, are drawn from the newspaper field. Experience as a newspaper reporter is invaluable, especially at the local level. The leg work the reporter is accustomed to will stand him in good stead when he is called upon not only to be a newscaster but to gather his own news. However, he will have to learn to change his style of writing. To illustrate, we have chosen three similar news items as they were presented in a Kraft

Five Star News script broadcast over the Mutual Network by Frank Singiser, and as they appeared in the New York *Times*.

SINGISER: In less than an hour, Secretary of State Dulles will begin addressing the UN Security Council meeting here in New York. Dulles will be the last of the speakers in public sessions on the Suez Canal situation. This afternoon the Council goes into executive session behind closed doors. The various proposals will then be discussed and presumably voted upon. It is believed that Secretary Dulles will urge that whatever is finally decided should leave the Suez Canal outside the arena of world politics.

It is election day in Alaska. And residents of the big territory are going through the motions of voting for two senators and a congressman, none of whom actually will be able to serve. The decision to vote for members of Congress was taken at the April primary as a way of dramatizing Alaskans' hope that the territory will soon become our 49th state.

The nation's biggest city needs a few bucks for new schools. The New York City Board of Education says just about one billion dollars will do for the present. As a matter of fact, the billion would go for needed new schools over the next ten years. And at the same time some 350 run-down school buildings belonging to Father Knickerbocker would get badly needed repairs and modernization.

Now from the New York *Times*:

The eleven member Security Council is scheduled to start secret negotiations with Egypt tomorrow at 4 P.M. Koca Popovic, Yugoslav Foreign Minister and Secretary of State Dulles, the only representatives who have not made opening statements in the debate, will speak tomorrow morning in that order.

The Singiser newscast is a five-minute strip, actually less than four minutes in duration because there is an approximately fifteen-second introduction plus a minute commercial at the close. Five sentences are devoted to the Security Council meeting. The *Times* story ran some two columns. Granted that the New York *Times* undoubtedly devotes more space to news coverage than other newspapers, it is still very evident that the broadcast newswriter must become a master of condensation.

An additional point to observe in these two items is the immediacy of the radio newscast. Note that this factor of immediacy has been taken advantage of by the phrase: "In less than an hour. . . ." The *Times*, being a morning paper, was running the previous day's dateline on this story in the edition we quoted.

Again from the *Times*:

> A vigorous and possibly historic political campaign ended in Alaska today.
>
> Tomorrow, 27,000 voters in the vast territory will go to the polls to help push the Tennessee Plan for statehood through the United States Congress. Convinced that pleas for admittance must be backed by bold action, Alaskans hope that Congress soon will rule favorably on statehood and invite their Congressmen to take their places in both houses.

The *Times* devoted a column to the Alaskan story; the radio newscast, three sentences. In these two items, you will note that, whereas radio style generally avoids the use of adjectives, newspaper style may make full use of adjectives. Contrast the two lead sentences: "A *vigorous* and *possibly historic political* campaign ended in Alaska today," and "It is election day in Alaska."

Another *Times* item:

> A ten year $1,000,000,000 program for building new schools and a $350,000,000 bond issue for replacing obsolete schools were demanded yesterday by a member of the Board of Education.

We have chosen this particular item to demonstrate the use of figures in both media. The radio newscast has the figure written out: "One billion." This is essential when large figures are used to avoid any possible mistakes by the announcer. Long rows of zeros may well prove a stumbling block to the announcer, especially if he is handed a late bulletin.

On the other hand, the use of numerals in a newspaper story, particularly when there are long rows of zeros, will attract attention to the story. The reader will be drawn by the feeling that this must be a big story since it deals with what are to him, undoubtedly, astronomical figures.

COMMUNITY NEWS

Many stations find it advantageous and a service to the surrounding community to present newscasts of a very localized nature. These newscasts are usually scheduled once weekly, either in cooperation with the weekly community newspaper, or by a local reporter, or by "stringers." The copy is generally very informal and "homey" in nature, as these few items from the Takoma Park *News Report* will illustrate. The reporter is Etta Davis.

Good evening, fellow citizens of Takoma Park.

My intuition was right. Mr. H. M. Pridgen, 6509 Queens Chapel Road, Hyattsville, was appointed Clerk-Treasurer at last Monday's Council meeting.

It took from May 15 to September 24 to do it, but 54 residents, on Philadelphia Avenue, affixed their names to a petition asking that Philadelphia be made one-way from Carroll to Maple Avenue. That street is a State Highway, so there will be little chance of compliance.

The mayor mentioned he has been receiving numerous complaints lately. Here is another case, where we collect for the dog licenses and the money has to be turned over to the county. We should have that money for our own dog catcher. This should be a good test for Home Rule.

The newscast also presented an interview with the Mayor regarding his duties and some of the current problems facing him. Social doings of both the adult and the youthful citizenry were included. Then a few more news items.

The weather Thursday night gave cover to raiders of the coke machine at the C & M and Sunoco filling stations on Carroll Avenue next to the Fire House.

Also on the same night, someone relieved the Flower Delicatessen, Piney Branch Road, of its safe, which contained $1200, by rolling it out the back door. I'd say this Rock 'n Roll is being carried too far.

The final item was a preview of next week's guest.

Chief Carter of our Fire Department will be our guest next Sunday to tell us about Fire Prevention Week and to extend a personal invitation to visit the Fire Department.

And so to sign off.

The drama

PART

3

The television
drama

13

We are concerned, in Part Three, with the truly creative domain of broadcasting: the drama. Here the writer may give full sway to his imagination, may test his ability to create character, his skill in developing a plot, his talent for enthralling an audience. Although, as we have stated often, the writer should approach each assignment as if it were a challenge to his competence, the writing of drama, particularly television drama, is most demanding. It can also be most rewarding.

As you study this section, you will learn that the television drama is a complex organism. To live, it must have characterization, motivation, plot structure, exposition, transitions, dialogue, pantomime. To blend all these elements into a finite whole takes consummate skill and artistry. No doubt you may raise a questioning eyebrow here, for much of the dramatic fare you have seen on TV might hardly qualify as artistic endeavor. But the writer will accomplish little or nothing by either demeaning the medium he works for or by setting his sights too low. Let the finest, not the poorest, of the video dramas be your guide and your inspiration.

You cannot plunge into the writing of TV dramas without adequate preparation and study. It is true, and it has happened on occasion, that a writer has watched two or three dramas on the air and then gone to the typewriter to turn out an immediately salable script. But this is the very rare exception and even in this case, which is an actual one, the writer had had a great deal of experience in allied fields. The able video dramatist is both a dreamer and a practical craftsman. His imagination may roam the heavens but he is fully aware of the down-to-earth requirements of a highly technical medium.

Let us consider, for a moment, our favorite analogy. The professional artist is one who must have a thorough knowledge of perspective, composition, design, of color relationships and space relationships. When he is creating a painting, he must know where to focus the center of attention so that the eye of the viewer, constantly, is drawn to it. He must know how to evaluate his colors to achieve contrast or balance. Observe the professional artist at work. The touch of a brush here and there and, suddenly, magically, the canvas changes. It looks simple, but behind those strokes are years of study and work and experimentation.

When you watch an adroitly written TV play, you sense that it flows smoothly. Your attention is held by the sweep of the drama. You are unaware of the techniques of the play. After it is over, you may say to yourself, as a viewer, it was well done. As a potential video dramatist, you should be asking why. It is the why of the expertly written TV drama that this section attempts to answer.

You may find, when you write your first TV drama, that you are very conscious of technique. You will be thinking, overtly, of exposition, of transitions, of the detailed mechanics of your play. This is all as it should be. With experience, these techniques will become automatic. But in order for them to become automatic, you must learn the fundamentals of your craft thoroughly — so thoroughly that your craft becomes an art.

A NEW ART FORM

The gifted television writer, novelist and dramatist, Gore Vidal, remarked in a magazine article once that the television playwright was going to develop a new art form which would, in time, replace the novel as the novel had replaced poetry. We cannot subscribe to the latter part of Mr. Vidal's prophecy; there is still some excellent poetry being written today. The new poetry may be limited in quantity, but the works of older poets — Carl Sandburg, Archibald MacLeish, Robert Frost, Stephen Vincent Benet, Edna St. Vincent Millay — are not unknown to the rising generation. Despite the sombre predictions that with the advent of television the American public will cease to read, the ranks of the novelists have not noticeably thinned. Best sellers still run into the six figures and the sales of *The Caine Mutiny* have skyrocketed into the millions. Mr. Vidal himself has edited a volume of *Best Television Plays* (Ballantine Books), presumably for reading purposes. Witness also the many other collections of television plays now being published. This in itself is recognition of the television play as an art form.

We do subscribe to the belief that the television playwright is developing a new art form; it will be new in technique but in all else it will be as old as the theater. For the television play can trace its forebears to the ancient Greek drama and many a well-written television play adheres more closely to the classic Greek unities than current stage dramas, a point we will discuss more fully in the section on the dramatic unities.

What we have done today is to add technology to the theater. Our scientists, in developing new means of communication, have also given a new dimension to the art of the theater. This dimension, we must reiterate, is solely technical. The basic principles of good drama are as inherent in the television play as they are in the stage play. It will be wise, therefore, for the budding television playwright, if he has not already done so, to familiarize himself with the great classic plays and with the better products of our contemporary theater. In doing so, he will also come upon some interesting and helpful comparisons, many of which were discussed in Chapter 4 on "The Video Style."

He will note that the stage playwright may think entirely in terms of what he wants to say, whereas the television dramatist is circumscribed as to content and must be wary of earthy dialogue. The theater audience is a captive audience which has had an opportunity to read reviews of the play and has decided to pay a comparatively high price for the performance. Most performances are in the evening hours and attended by adults. This narrowly limits the size of the audience, yet, by so doing, enlarges the scope of the stage dramatist's theme and permits uninhibited dialogue. We can hardly conceive of Tennessee Williams' "Cat on a Hot Tin Roof" ever being presented verbatim on a television screen!

Again, the theater playwright is not only regarded with complete respect and esteem, but he is always present at rehearsals and no script changes are made without his concurrence. The revisions are generally his own unless a "play doctor" is called upon to save a production from an early demise. The broadcast playwright finds his script going through numerous hands: editor, producer, agency, sponsor, network continuity acceptance. All of them offer their expert opinion on what will please the vast American public, or, more often, what will not offend the sensibilities of the viewer.

The stage playwright waits with great anxiety for the critical reviews that may signal success or failure. With great anguish, he reads a devastating critique, or a joyous smile breaks across his face when the review is laudatory. It is true that some plays become resounding hits even after a poor press. But whether they admit it or not, the theater critics are most often the arbiters of public tastes and may very well decide what the public will or will not see to the benefit or detriment of the playwright's royalties.

If the television critics do not wield an influence comparable to their drama colleagues, it is not because of any lack of perception, of analysis, or audience. It is due to the fact that the television play, with some few exceptions, is a "one time thing." John Crosby or Jack Gould may speak very highly of a play which was presented the previous night or the previous week, but if the reader missed the performance there is little likelihood that he will ever be able to see that particular play again. There have been repeats of a few plays that have won unusual acclaim, such as "A Night to Remember" and "Patterns," but these are rare occasions. Not infrequently, suggestions have been made to repeat the better plays.

However, there are some circumstances which prevent repeats. The television play's one performance will have an audience of many millions. In addition, such programs as the "Kraft Theatre," "Studio One," "Theater Guild on the Air," "Playhouse 90," have, it is presumed, a rather constant audience. The sponsor and/or his agency would rather not chance repeating the same play before an audience consisting largely of the same viewers.

We are speaking now of the serious drama, the "one-shot"

play. Many of the episodic dramas, the adventure series, the situation comedies, are often rerun under different titles and at different time periods. This is true of the half-hour filmed series. "Private Secretary" becomes "Susie" for its repeat performances. "Dragnet" becomes "Badge No. 714." It is also the custom for many of these filmed series to repeat the "best" of the year during the summer season.

Nevertheless, the constant demand for new material by both the producers and the audience keeps repeat performances at a minimum. This is both a boon and a hazard to the writer. The insatiable appetite of television requires a multitude of playwrights to keep it fed. At the same time, it is apt to devour the brain that feeds it. The new playwright, on having a drama accepted, is overjoyed. Then he is called on for more and more. Soon he is beset by the fear of running dry. The producer, from his side, is hounded by the weekly deadline. And just as he comes to depend on a coterie of actors to fill his casting needs, so he comes to depend on a stable of writers to meet his script requirements. For the writer it means a greater income but too often it also encourages mediocrity. He would be a rare genius indeed who could turn out a dozen television plays a year, all of high quality.

Paddy Chayefsky, when he was concentrating his efforts in television, stated that it took him six weeks to complete an hour drama. At this rate, simple mathematics will tell you that you can produce some eight or nine hour dramas a year, provided you have eight or nine good ideas. The Chayefsky plays were uniformly good, demonstrating the time and effort he put into each one.

The program producers are not entirely unaware of the writers' problems. They recognize that well-written original plays are few and far between. And so to fill their program demands they turn to other sources: published plays, short stories, novels, articles. This is a tried and true source because the material has already had audience acceptance. It also affords additional income to the professional television writer because he may be called upon to prepare many adaptations. The ideal situation for the writer is to have a number of adaptations on assignment so that he may have more time for developing originals.

We will examine now the various elements of the television drama and then see how they have been carried out in two fine plays: a half-hour filmed drama as produced on the "General Electric

Theater," and an hour live drama as presented on the "Kraft Theatre."

THEME

A play is not a preachment. Yet the serious play does have a message in the sense that the dramatist has something to say to his audience.

You may quite deliberately choose a theme or it may reach you in a burst of inspiration. If, like Reginald Rose, you have a strong social conscience, you will find your theme in the social injustices or the moral ethics of our society. The theme for Rose's "Twelve Angry Men" came to him when he, himself, had served as a juror and had suddenly become aware of a juror's responsibility.

But the playwright cannot be so carried away by his theme, by his own angry conscience, that the theme dominates the story. In other words, don't let your sermon show. First and foremost, you must have a story to tell, and that story must be entertaining and engrossing.

People go to church expecting to hear a sermon. It may be entertaining (in the sense that you enjoy it) but primarily the clergyman has a message for you. You watch a television play, however, chiefly for entertainment; if at the conclusion it has left you with some food for thought, all well and good. Choose your theme wisely, but don't let it overwhelm you.

Your theme, on the other hand, may be a very simple one, with no earth-shaking pretensions. You want to write a love story about Sue and Harry. She is in her early twenties. He is in his late forties. Your theme poses the question: can a marriage be successful when there is a great disparity in age between the bride and groom? A familiar theme, but you are going to give it a new twist.

If you admire the Chayefsky "slice of life" school, your video drama will deal with the "little" man and his "little" problems. The quotations around the word "little" are purposeful. The problems of the "little" man, those of which Chayefsky writes, are basic, not "little."

Much of the time, your theme will come after your story. You want to write a play about your maiden Aunt Sarah. She's really a gay old character, and as you plan your story, you suddenly find yourself with a theme: a spinster's adjustment to life.

Whatever your theme, understatement is generally more effective than overstatement.

PLOT STRUCTURE

In the beginning, there is a situation or there is a character. This is the foundation of your plot structure. You begin to build by putting the proper characters into the situation or inventing a plausible situation for your characters.

You will find a blueprint essential before you proceed. This is your plot outline in which, with more or less detail, you sketch the various scenes. You will have to know, of course, whether your structure is to house a two-act half-hour play, a three-act hour play or a 90-minute drama. The amount of detail with which you can fill out your plot will depend on the time allotment. Your plot outline should also give you a good indication as to whether you have too many or too few scenes. The one will tend to make your play too episodic, the other too static.

There are some books available on plotting a story, generally for the theater, the novel or the short story, which will be of help to you. George Pierce Baker's *Dramatic Technique* has several chapters devoted to plot development. But the actual plotting of your video play becomes a highly personal matter once you have learned the fundamentals of writing the television drama. For example, if you were to hire a half dozen architects, all of them trained in their field, and asked them to design a three-bedroom house, you would find yourself with six different sets of plans, each of which might be very satisfactory. Similarly, given the same basic story elements, a half dozen writers would have six variations of the plot.

Nevertheless, there are certain fundamental principles which are unique to television and of which the playwright must be aware.

The opening

You must establish interest as quickly as possible. The non-captive audience is in the driver's seat. It can, by the flick of a switch, turn off to another road. Therefore, the well-planned play will have an opening incident which quickly sets up the conflict. This may be accomplished by visual action or dialogue or may utilize both action and dialogue. In the "Playhouse 90" filmed production of Bernard Girard's "Four Women in Black," the opening scene was a gunfight between the male protagonist, Webb Carbine, played by Ralph Meeker, and a ranch owner. The sheriff warns Webb that although he fired in self-defense, the wounded rancher and his kin will never rest until they have tracked him down. It is while Webb is escaping his pursuers that he meets the four women in black, nuns en route from Santa Fe to Tucson.

"Four Women in Black" is a western with an unusual plot, the shepherding of four nuns on a hazardous journey by a "bad man." The leader of the nuns is played by Helen Hayes. You will note that even though "Four Women in Black" is a 90-minute drama and therefore has more time for plot development than the shorter video forms, it still begins with a scene of exciting visual action which grips your attention immediately.

Development of conflict

Each scene of your play, whether written in chronological sequence or utilizing the flashback technique, should further the conflict. We may call this "moving the play." Therefore, if you have a scene which does not move your play, it is very likely unnecessary. If you have any doubt about a scene which you have included, test it by eliminating it from your script. See whether the action of your play is clear without it. Is the sequence a beam essential to the support of your plot structure, or is it just decorative? You may have written it with loving care and you would hate to delete it because it adds so much color. But you are always up against the element of time and so your decision must always favor the essentials. It is not that these essentials must be bare but you do not have the scope of a novel in a video play. The novelist may permit himself the luxury of a four-page description of a farmyard. He may write in minute detail so that his completed manuscript numbers eight hundred pages or he may write a tightly compressed novel in less than two hundred pages. The video dramatist has no such leeway. Time, as construction contracts often state, is of the essence.

If we turn once again to "Four Women in Black," we find rapid conflict development. When Webb meets the nuns on the desert, they are stranded. Their covered wagon stands uselessly on the road. The two horses that pulled the wagon are dead. The nuns ask Webb to hitch his horse to the wagon to pull them to the nearest trading post. He faces a powerful conflict now. If he does help the nuns, it will slow his pace considerably and he might be captured by his pursuers and perhaps killed. If he leaves the nuns, they might be set upon by the Apaches who are on the warpath. He decides to help the nuns. This is a decision which wins audience sympathy and at the same time heightens suspense.

Now, we should point out that immediately prior to the above scene, Webb meets a rider coming in the opposite direction. The rider warns Webb to turn back because he is heading directly towards the Apaches who are on the warpath. If you were to eliminate this scene, you would lessen the conflict development in the following scene. It is the fear of the Apaches setting upon the nuns which properly motivates Webb's decision.

Curtain scenes

The technique of the video drama is similar to the theatrical play with respect to curtain scenes. In both media, the playwright develops his plot so that the curtain falls at the end of each act at a point of crisis in the story. This takes precise planning on the part of the video dramatist and he should, therefore, have his plot completely worked out before he starts to write.

In Gore Vidal's thought-provoking fantasy, "Visit to a Small Planet," (*Best Television Plays* — Ballantine Books), Kreton, a visitor from outer space, has landed in a space ship in the garden of the Spelding home. At the first act curtain, he makes the pronouncement that he's come to take charge of the whole world. General Powers and his aide, who have rushed to the Spelding home, try to imprison Kreton but they are stunned by an unknown force. They cannot even come within a foot of the space visitor. Here then is a point of crisis. Act Two ends on an even greater threat: Kreton is planning to plunge the entire world into a war of annihilation.

In the three-act hour video drama, again much as in the standard stage play, the crisis at the end of act two should have more impact than the first act crisis. The play should build to the climax with progressive force, the conflict ever increasing until the final resolution.

In the two-act half-hour play, the big crisis should generally be reached at the first act curtain since your climax must be attained in the second act.

The climax

The climax is the high point of your drama, the apex of your plot. Here the conflicting forces meet in the final round. If the hero wins, it is comedy; if the hero is destroyed, it is tragedy. The well-plotted play will leave us in doubt as to the final outcome until the climax is reached.

In "Visit to a Small Planet" the climax is reached when the visitor from outer space, Kreton, has culminated his plans to plunge the world into war. Apparently, nothing can be done to stop him. In a few minutes the atom bombs will fall. At this point, another visitor arrives in a space ship and forces Kreton to return from whence he came, thus ending the tension and the imminent holocaust. The play has moved forward with progressive force. Movement starts with the sudden awesome and mysterious arrival of Kreton in the first act, his seemingly pleasant manner belying his sinister purpose. The crisis increases with each scene and culminates in the climax.

The plant

Often dramatists will utilize a device either physical, a prop, or visual, a bit of action, or mental, a line of dialogue, which appears innocuous enough at the moment but which later proves to have an important bearing on the play. This is known as a "plant." For example, one character may ask another:

ALAN

Have you seen Don?

BOB

Yes. I guess he's gone hunting.
He had his rifle with him.

Naturally, Don would take his rifle if he were going hunting, but the rifle may later prove to be a murder weapon. The fact that Don had a rifle with him is implanted in the audience's mind.

In "Visit to a Small Planet" Kreton inadvertently drops a lace handkerchief beside the sofa. This action which may appear meaningless at the time eventually is shown to have great significance. The importance of this particular plant is discussed below.

The resolution

Once the climax has been reached, the dramatist proceeds to finish his play. This is the resolution, always a brief scene at the close of the play. Sometimes your resolution may be more implied than specified, as it is in "Visit to a Small Planet." The final scene shows the hands of the clock spinning backwards to the exact time of the first scene, that is, just prior to Kreton's appearance. In the opening scene Roger Spelding, in his broadcast, has discussed the sighting of a flying object which he declares is a meteor. He pooh-poohs the idea of its being a space ship. In the closing scene when John Randolph again mentions the fact that the "meteor" looked like a space ship, Spelding insists it is nonsense. This statement gives the impression that the visit from outer space never occurred. Then suddenly Spelding notices Kreton's handkerchief on the sofa and picks it up. The significance of the "plant" is revealed. The final shot of the play is a stock shot of a starry night with two space ships vanishing into the distance.

Since "Visit to a Small Planet" is a fantasy, its resolution is as highly imaginative as the body of the play.

Whether you write a realistic drama or a fantasy, your audience must be left with the feeling that it has witnessed a satisfactory conclusion to your play. Frank Stockton's "The Lady or the Tiger" is generally offered as the classic example of an unresolved story. The fact that this type of story is so rare is proof that an audience demands a resolution to the stories it reads, or sees, or listens to.

Subplots

The insertion of subplots depends on the length of your video drama. The half-hour drama generally does not permit of any subplot. It requires a concentration on the basic plot structure and if you find yourself veering off into a subplot, it may be that your story is not strong enough to stand by itself. If that is the case, then you must find means of strengthening your main story line or developing a different story.

In the hour drama it is possible to include a subplot, although here again it is best to develop one plot thoroughly. If we examine "Visit to a Small Planet" once more, we find that a subplot exists in the love story of Ellen Spelding, daughter of commentator Roger Spelding, in whose home the visitor from outer space has made his startling entrance. Ellen is in love with John Randolph, but her father frowns upon the romance because he wants his daughter to marry someone important.

The 90-minute drama permits a secondary plot because the playwright has so much more time. "Four Women in Black," which we discussed previously, has for its main plot the hazardous trek of the nuns from Santa Fe to Tucson. The subplot is the escape of Webb Carbine from his pursuers. There is even another subplot in the growing romance between Webb and an orphaned Mexican girl whom the nuns have befriended en route. Webb at first expresses a strong prejudice against Mexicans but is won over by the nuns, one of whom is Mexican herself, and his love for the girl.

Although "Four Women in Black" wove these several plots together successfully, it will be wise for the dramatist not to overload even the longer drama with too many subplots. Subplots are the province of the stage drama which has at least two hours of playing time. This is a full two hours. Remember that your hour video drama is seldom more than 50 minutes and your hour and a half drama seldom more than 70.

THE DRAMATIC UNITIES

Consciously or not, many of our prominent television dramatists have adhered to the dramatic unities as first promulgated by Aristotle. The fact is that the theories put forth by Aristotle might well be more of a guide to the television playwright than the stage dramatist. The dramatic unities are generally translated as the Unity of Action, of Time and of Place. However, many scholars believe that Aristotle considered Unity of Action primary and the other two unities secondary. In other words, if the story has Unity of Action, it does not matter how much time elapses in the story or how many scenes are used. This Unity of Action, Aristotle stated, manifested itself mainly in two ways: "First, the causal connection that binds together the several parts of a play: the thoughts, the emotions, the decisions of will, the external events being inextricably interwoven. Secondly, the whole series of events with all the moral forces that are brought into collision are directed to a single end."

We have previously stated that there should not be any wasted words or actions in a television play. Every line of dialogue, every visual action, should have a meaning. Aristotle commented that the parts of a drama must be "arranged in a fixed order so that none can be removed, none transferred, without disturbing the organism."

The television play, particularly, must adhere to the Aristotelian precept that a drama must have "a certain magnitude." It cannot be "infinitely large" or "infinitesimally small." How large or how small is a matter for debate. There is a tremendous range between "infinitesimally small" and "infinitely large." We might say that Chayefsky's TV plays deal with the smaller problems of mankind. He himself called it, "the marvelous world of the ordinary." He is the "slice of life" exponent. His people are the everyday variety whose lower-middle-class problems are common to many, are familiar to all of us. Vidal's "Visit to a Small Planet," on the other hand, approaches the far end of the scale. The concepts are very broad: the issues of war and peace; the possibilities of man's self-destruction. Both types of plays possess the Aristotelian prerequisite, "a certain magnitude."

Aristotle's description of the ancient Greek tragedy would aptly fit the current television drama, as a play "which begins almost at the climax, the action proper is highly compressed and concentrated."

If we were to choose any one television play to exemplify the dramatic unities, it would probably be Reginald Rose's "Twelve Angry Men." For here is a drama that truly has unity of action, a jury whose decision can mean life or death to the accused; unity of place, the scene is entirely in the courthouse; actually, except for the brief scene with the judge, all the action takes place in the jury room; unity of time, the playing time is the actual time.

Certainly, it is not necessary to follow the dramatic unities as precisely as "Twelve Angry Men." As we stated previously, unity of action is the prime requisite. This means, baldly, there should be one major plot. Aristotle was opposed to plurality, but not to variety within the unified action. You cannot have two major plots within your television play, but you certainly can have a variety of incidents to further your basic plot.

Even from this brief commentary, we believe you can see that Aristotle's theories of the drama are of particular significance to the television playwright. It will be of interest and value to you to read or, perhaps, reread a translation of Aristotle's theories of poetry and fine art.

CONFLICT

The essential ingredient of any drama is conflict. The stronger the conflict, the more powerful the play. The writer must be skillful in building up opposing forces until at the climax, one of the forces is the victor. There are certain basic conflicts which we may identify as follows:

1. Man against man;
2. Man against his conscience;
3. Man against the forces of nature.

Under these very broad headings, we have an unlimited number of variations: (1) Rivalry for the love of a woman; struggle for control of wealth; competition for power, for political ascendancy, for social position, and so on. The conflict may be between mother and daughter, father and son. It may be that of the nonconformist against the dictates of convention; the dreamer against the practicalities of life. The struggle may be between two individuals, (man, singly) or between an individual and society, (man in the aggregate).

"Twelve Angry Men" is one of Reginald Rose's most potent television plays (*Six Television Plays* by Reginald Rose, published by Simon and Schuster). It deals with a trial for murder and almost all the action takes place in the jury room. A nineteen-year-old boy has been accused of killing his own father. On the first ballot, there are eleven votes for Guilty. Only Juror No. 8 has voted Not Guilty. The remainder of the play details, in powerful dramatic fashion, the battle of Juror No. 8 against his fellow jurors to convince them they are wrong in their judgment. At the conclusion, he wins his battle.

(2) "Conscience is God's presence in man," wrote the Swedish religious philosopher, Emanuel Swedenborg. The conflict of man against himself is one which involves a question of ethics and of spiritual values. A man lives by certain principles dictated by his environment. The influence of his parents, his wife and children, his religion, his education, will affect the strength or weakness of those principles.

If you have read Jessamyn West's book or seen the movie version of "Friendly Persuasion," you were made aware of the conflict between the young son and his Quaker conscience. As a Quaker, he was brought up not to fight under any circumstances, yet he feels he should defend his home against the Southern rebels. After a long, inward struggle with his conscience, and despite the entreaties of his mother, he joins the Union forces.

In Rod Serling's TV play, "The Strike" (*Best Television Plays* — Ballantine Books), we have another powerful instance of the conflict between man and his conscience. Major Gaylord has sent twenty men on a patrol mission to the Korean front. The Major has under his command five hundred men, all that are left of a decimated division. They are pinned down by heavy Chinese artillery fire which threatens to destroy them. Finally contact is made with the Air Force which is planning an airstrike to wipe out the enemy artillery and permit the escape of Gaylord's entrapped men. However, at the same time, word is received from the patrol. Their position is the same as that of the Chinese artillery. As a matter of fact, it was a message from the patrol that gave the Air Force the Chinese position. However, although the Major's Command Post is able to receive the patrol's signal, its own signal cannot be picked up by the patrol. The Air Force is awaiting the go ahead from the Major for the airstrike. Major Gaylord wrestles with his conscience. He sent the patrol out. He is responsible for the lives of those twenty men. If he gives the Air Force the signal, those twenty men will be destroyed. If he doesn't, the 500 men will undoubtedly be annihilated. He feels, at first, that he cannot order the destruction of the patrol. But he is finally forced to weigh 20 against 500 and makes his decision to save the 500. As his men start to move out to safety, the tears stream down the face of Major Gaylord.

(3) No conflict is more elemental than the eternal battle of man against the forces of nature. For man, from his earliest beginning, has come into conflict with the contrasting ravages of flood and drought, cold and heat, storm and calm. Yes, even calm, for in the days of sailing ships, a vessel becalmed for several days or weeks faced great danger. However, as a theme for a television play, this third category of conflict is seldom used in comparison to the first two categories. At times, this type of conflict is combined with one of the other two.

Two mountain climbers are caught in an avalanche and struggle towards safety. The question of whether they will ever be able to extricate themselves involves a battle against the elements. But your play will present an even stronger conflict if, in the struggle to safety, one of the men is seriously injured. The conflict arises as to whether the uninjured man should try to carry his companion which might result in the death of both of them or go on alone. This, then, becomes a conflict of man against his conscience.

CHARACTERIZATION

From the earliest days of playwriting, the perceptive delineation of character has been the mark of a good play. As George Pierce Baker has observed: "The permanent value of a play rests on its characterization." Think of Euripides' Medea, of Shakespeare's Macbeth, Shaw's Liza Doolittle, O'Neill's Anna Christie, Ibsen's Nora. These are masterpieces of characterization. They are worthy of study and restudy by the television playwright who has any ideals about his profession.

True, the television playwright does not have the scope of the legitimate theater but he can learn from it and, as many television writers have already done, contribute to it. Because of time limitations, he cannot create the full-length portraits of the stage play. The closest he can come now is in the 90-minute drama. Rod Serling's "Emmy" Award-winning "Requiem for a Heavyweight," written for the Columbia Broadcasting System's "Playhouse 90," presented an unforgettable portrait: the decline of a contender for the heavyweight crown, sensitively portrayed by Jack Palance.

It is difficult, and a tremendous challenge for the writer, to create a full-blown character portrait within the space of the half-hour drama. The result is that most half-hour TV dramas rely heavily on plot rather than characterization. Many mystery plays eschew characterization entirely. Their reliance is on action and suspense.

The hour and the hour and a half dramas permit much more leeway for character delineation. Although Paddy Chayefsky has turned almost entirely to the theater and the movies, his collection of *Six Television Plays* (Simon and Schuster) still remains a model for study by the embryo playwright. Chayefsky's forte is characterization. Read "Marty," "The Mother," "The Big Deal," "The Bachelor Party." The characters stay with you. If you have not known a "Marty" or a "Joe Manx" in your own experience, you have come to know them now and understand them. The TV writer's canvas, although not so large as the stage dramatist's, can still hold a full-length portrait.

You, the writer, have to paint this portrait so that its likeness is readily recognizable. To do so you should have a model. That model may be an actual person or a synthesis of several individuals.

All dramatists have their own particular approach to their writing problems. But it is safe to say that if you do see an especially well-drawn characterization on the air, the playwright has spent a good deal of time getting to know his character.

You will find it an excellent habit to prepare brief biographies of your leading characters. You probably have a fairly clear mental picture of your protagonist. However, the business of actually spelling out his background will help you immeasurably in defining your character. Where was he born? What was his home environment? What schools did he attend? Did he have to struggle for a livelihood? Is he successful now? How does he get along with people? Is he an introvert or an extrovert? Does he have any special physical characteristics? These are just a few of the questions the TV playwright can ask himself about the character into whom he is going to breathe life. As you answer each question, you begin to learn a little more about your dramatis personae.

Sometimes you will hear a writer remark that his play "practically wrote itself." The fact is that once a character is created he appears to take over from the writer. He will have a specific reaction to specific situations. His emotions, his responses are individual and they follow a pattern based on his particular characteristics. He is as much a product of his environment and heredity as any living being. It is true that the author has given the character his environment and heredity but once the character has been so endowed he must act henceforth in accordance with his background.

Shading

The reaction you must seek from your audience is the belief that your characters are true to life. They will not give this impression if they are one-dimensional. Think for a moment of the people you do know: relatives, friends, acquaintances, colleagues. Is there anyone among them who is wholly good or wholly bad? Very unlikely. Some sentimental poet once observed that there is "so much good in the worst of us and so much bad in the best of us." If you will forgive the cliché, this observation is more truth than poetry.

In the bygone melodrama, the villain was thoroughly black, the heroine virtuously white. There was no shading. A vestige of that era remains in some of the westerns seen on our TV screens today. The "bad guy" is one-dimensionally bad; the "good guy" one-dimensionally good. This even applies to costuming. The villain wears a black hat and rides a black horse. The hero wears a white hat and rides a white horse. Presumably this makes it very simple for the child viewer to distinguish between good and evil. But to the mature viewer, this type of western soon loses its credibility and its interest. This may explain why there has been a trend toward the so-called "adult western" which places more reliance on characterization.

Proper shading, then, is an essential ingredient of characterization. People tend to be gray. They are composed of faults and virtues. The most honest man has, on occasion, told a lie. The faithful wife has indulged in a flirtation or two. The thief has helped the beggar.

Empathy

The perceptive playwright strives to achieve empathy, that subconscious identification of the viewer with the player. The viewer knows that his own character is at least two-dimensional, generally multi-dimensional. He, therefore, expects to see these various dimensions reflected in the characterizations. He can identify himself with an individual, not with a stereotype.

Sympathy

It is axiomatic that your protagonist must be sympathetic. If we do not care what happens to the leading character, we will soon lose interest in the play. This means that even if your principal character is a villain, he must have some redeeming features.

MOTIVATION

An assumption common to all sciences is that every event must have a cause. In like manner, every human action must have a reason, a motivating force. The motivation may be elemental. A man drinks because he is thirsty. He eats because he is hungry. He builds a home because he needs shelter. Sometimes we may feel that a person acts unreasonably or abnormally. Psychologists will tell us that such unorthodox behavior does have its reasons, rooted deep in the subconscious of the individual.

What impels people to act as they do? This is a question to which the playwright must have a proper answer, and to obtain that answer he must be a student of human nature. The great writers were also great psychologists. Long before the term "schizophrenia" had become an everyday word, Robert Louis Stevenson had plumbed its meaning in "Dr. Jekyll and Mr. Hyde."

Painters often do many self-portraits. Of course, in some instances it may simply be a matter of economics; the artist cannot afford a model at the moment. But most of the time, this self-portraiture is a learning process for the painter. The playwright will do well to emulate the painter and set down a verbal portrait of himself. Understanding yourself will help you to understand others.

Drives

There are certain basic drives which affect all of us. Physical drives, such as hunger, thirst, sex, and physical needs such as shelter and clothing. There are the social drives of love, hate, fear, anxiety, ambition, pride. The list might be extended endlessly if we were to divide and subdivide each human drive. The drives we have enumerated are representative and, like primary colors, we can mix them to achieve various hues. We must remember that human drives or motivations depend on circumstances and may vary in degree from one person to another, indeed from one country to another. A hermit will have little need of material things, in terms of money, and will therefore not be driven to obtain wealth. Social concepts among the Arabs are far different from our own and this affects the relationship between the sexes.

Some specific instances

Reginald Rose's hour TV play "Tragedy in a Temporary Town" is an excellent study in *fear*. The engineer, in a settlement of migratory workers, has rebelled against a vigilante group formed to ferret out an alleged attacker of a young girl. He stands forthright against vigilantism but when he discovers that his own teen-age son was the one who awkwardly tried to kiss the girl (that was the extent of the "attack"), the father becomes fearful of the vigilantes. He hides his son's "guilt" until a wrongly accused Puerto Rican boy is dreadfully beaten by the mob. His sense of justice now overcomes his fear and in a climactic scene, whose power has seldom been matched on television, he scathingly denounces the bloodthirsty mob.

In Paddy Chayefsky's "The Big Deal" it is Joe Manx's *pride* which keeps him from accepting a low-paying building inspector's job. Manx was once a successful builder who has since failed and is now on the verge of poverty. He keeps trying to make a "big deal" which will return him to his former status but one deal after another falls through. He continually talks about the days when he was a great success. The resolution is achieved when Manx realizes how much he has come to depend on his daughter who has a well-paying job, and that he has almost borrowed her wedding money for another "big deal." He is finally resigned to his situation and accepts the building inspector's job.

In "Sincerely, Willis Wayde," John Marquand's novel dramatized for "Playhouse 90," it is Wayde's *ambition* which brings him financial success but marital unhappiness.

Character change

Many plays have as their theme the regeneration of the protagonist. A major change takes place in the character of the protagonist by the time we reach the final curtain. You are undoubtedly familiar with this type of drama: the timid soul who acquires courage, the avaricious merchant who becomes generous, the misogynist who falls in love, the proud celebrity who turns humble, the disbeliever who finds faith. These major changes in character must be carefully motivated. The failure of many such plays is traceable, generally, to the fact that the character transformation is not fully motivated and therefore not believable. The essence of good drama is plausibility and the greatest aid to plausibility is proper motivation.

DIALOGUE

Dialogue is the prime mover of the drama. It is possible to present a drama purely in pantomime but this is not the norm, for speech is normal to people and it is primarily through speech that our thoughts are conveyed in our daily living. Professor Baker has stated that "the chief purpose of good dialogue is to convey necessary information clearly." In the television drama, dialogue is aided and abetted by visual action. In the radio drama, the dialogue portrays the action.

But dialogue in drama must not only convey information, it must depict emotion. If it lacks emotion, it has no power to hold our attention. The skill of the dramatist reveals itself in his ability to combine these two elements of dialogue: information and emotion.

However, the playwright may often have to qualify the emotional content of a line of dialogue since the same line may have many different meanings.

For example, in the following brief scene, the father has just returned from work and meets his boy in front of their home. He asks about the boxing tournament in which his son participated at the Boys Club.

WILMINGTON

How'd you come out in the boxing tournament, son?

DAN

I won.

WILMINGTON

Good for you. That makes you champion of the club, doesn't it?

DAN

(DEPRESSED) I guess so.

WILMINGTON

(STUDIES HIS SON ANXIOUSLY) You're not hurt?

DAN

Not from any punching, Dad.

WILMINGTON

I see. (GENTLY) Tell me what happened, son.

The son's response, "I guess so," could have been made with some modesty, but happily, which would indicate that he was glad to have won the decision. However, the emotional quality indicated is that of depression which informs us that something must be troubling the boy. No youngster would normally sound depressed about winning a boxing match.

You will note that in response to his father's question, "You're not hurt?", the boy replies, "Not from any punching, Dad." No emotional qualification is needed for this line. The line implies that he

is hurt but not physically. Had Dan merely answered "No," a qualification would have been needed. An unemotional "No" would
merely indicate that the boy was not hurt physically, without other
implications. However, even the "No," properly expressed by the
actor, could convey the desired emotion.

Characterization by dialogue

You have probably
read a critique or heard someone say that this or that dramatist has
a "good ear for dialogue." When Paddy Chayefsky was writing his
television plays, the comment was made that he might have followed
his characters with a tape recorder. As the jacket blurb for Chayefsky's *Television Plays* states: "The author brings these people startlingly close to the reader by means of dialogue that captures the precise nuance of speech and, at the same time, reveals the most secret
levels of character." These are objectives of dialogue. But they are
objectives not easily attained.

The beginner often has difficulty keeping his characters in
character. When this happens, the fault lies primarily in the fact
that the characters are not complete entities in the writer's mind.
You can try a simple test with any script on which you are working.
Transpose the lines from one character to another. If it appears that
each character could just as easily have been given the lines of the
other, then the dialogue has failed in one of its most important functions: to create and reveal character.

Again, go back to your models, your prototypes, your friends of
long standing, your relatives, acquaintances, fellow employees,
teachers, the milkman, the postman, the boy who delivers your
papers. Listen to them speak. Attune your ear to their natural
dialogue. Each individual has his own idiosyncrasies of speech.
Some vary slightly. Some greatly. But remember, each is an individual and you want to create individuals.

Often, it will be necessary for you to exaggerate to some extent
a speech peculiarity of a character. This will have the effect of in-
delibly stamping the character in the minds of the viewers. However, you must be careful not to turn your character into a caricature
by over-exaggeration.

In delineating character, you may use both a direct and an
indirect approach.

Direct: (a) the character describing himself:

MRS. DIXON

Henry, you're wonderfully persistent and I adore
you for it. But I really would be hard to live
with. I've had to fight all my life. When I was
left a widow, and Martha just a baby then, I had
to struggle for a living. I remember how I fought
with the Board of Trustees to have them pay me
the same wages as the men teachers. Everywhere
I went, they were prejudiced against me, because
I had to work, and they penalized me because I
was a woman.

WOODSON

I understand. Only recently, a young woman
applied for admission to the medical college. I
was the only one voted for her admittance.

MRS. DIXON

It's bitterly unfair, Henry. We're supposed to be
living in an enlightened age . . . the very end of
the 19th century . . . but women are still shack-
led, still treated as inferior beings. I've dedicated
myself to fight for equality.

(b) Delineation of the character by another with whom he is
in conversation:

WOODSON

You're tired, Clara. I mustn't keep you any longer.

MRS. DIXON

No, Henry, please sit down. Just a few minutes
longer. Sometimes I think I ought to be like any
other woman of my generation . . . like Donna,
perhaps. I imagine it would make life so much
simpler. But I can't, Henry, I can't.

WOODSON

Of course not. You're Clara Dixon . . . a woman
of great ambition . . . of high ideals . . . and prob-

ably very hard to live with. But I'm willing to
chance all that.

Indirect: Two characters describing a third:

MRS. ANDERSEN

Clara's such a remarkable woman. I believe she's
the most brilliant woman I've ever known. And
so daring. Don't you think so, Dr. Woodson?

WOODSON

I do, indeed.

Thus, we have actually three different approaches in the use
of dialogue to delineate character. The portrait of Clara Dixon is
not the work of one painter for there are many who have sketched
her and, indeed, she has added a self-portrait.

Selectivity

Because of the ar-
bitrary time limits of television drama, dialogue must be highly selec-
tive. Each line should have some bearing on the progression of the
play. Again, you can make another test for yourself by eliminating
any dialogue of which you are not sure. If the story line remains
clear, if no necessary information is deleted, then, in all probability,
the lines are superfluous. The experienced television playwright has
learned the value of words and has acquired the ability to choose
those which tell the most in the least time.

Remember that the information your dialogue conveys is for
the benefit of the audience yet it must not appear obvious. All the
information must come through natural dialogue. This principle is
more explicitly enunciated in the section on Exposition.

Author and protagonist

We have spoken of
the necessity for maintaining the individuality of your characters.
This is not a simple task, especially when it involves the expression

of ideas. Often, and this is true of some of our leading playwrights, the protagonist is obviously the author speaking rather than the character. We sense the protagonist stepping out of character to deliver a message. The dialogue performs its function of giving information but its overtness will lessen its impact. Keep your ideas within the framework of your drama and let them be expressed through the personality with which the character is invested.

Dialect

Dialect will add flavor to your play, but it has both advantages and pitfalls. First, the writer must be sure of his ground. If he knows the dialect of a region from personal experience, then he can probably set it down with a great deal of verisimilitude. There is no need, however, for the writer to portray the speech pattern completely phonetically. What he wants to get across is the "feel" of the dialect. In some cases, if his transcription is too verbatim, the audience will have a difficult time understanding the character. Clarity must not be sacrificed for the sake of dialect. Overdoing the dialect often leads to burlesque. Proper use of dialect can be a prime factor in characterization. As Professor Baker commented: "Nothing more quickly characterizes than dialect."

For an example of dialect in a television play, the reader is referred to Jameson Brewer's "The Glorious Gift of Molly Malloy," reprinted on pages 205–228.

PANTOMIME

The next time you take a walk through your neighborhood, observe the reactions of people meeting each other. Do they smile? Do they shake hands vigorously? Do they pass each other by with a curt nod? Do they embrace? Do they seem embarrassed?

Jot down a few notes describing your reactions. You think these two people like each other; you think the other two are rather unfriendly. In other words, the physical reactions of people to each other are informative. Even the lack of emotion is enlightening. It tells you the individual is a cold fish, or inhibited or very placid.

Thus, the emotional reactions of your characters, their facial expressions, their gestures, in effect, become another tool for characterization and for exposition. Suppose you are writing a crime drama. You have a scene where the heroine is in her room alone. There is a knock at the door. She goes to open it. A man enters. She steps back, her face contorted in fright. The pantomime is revelatory. It informs you that she is afraid of the man. The dialogue will tell you why.

There is a story which went the rounds about the super-salesman who tried to convince a skeptical manufacturer that daytime TV dramas reached a tremendous women's audience. Even if the women become too busy with their housework to keep their eyes on the screen, they can still enjoy the programs, the salesman insisted enthusiastically. "There's never a pause in the dialogue. As a matter of fact, it's just like radio!"

Of course television isn't just like radio, and if there is one single factor which differentiates the two media, it is visual action: the pantomime. Television brought sight and movement to its "blind" predecessor, and the capable television craftsman takes full advantage of the great opportunity which this new medium affords him. He learns to think visually, to decide where action can stand alone and where it can supplement dialogue.

In the following scene from "The Great Guy," an episode of the "Father Knows Best" series, there are some excellent illustrations of pantomime. Bud, the teen-age son of the Andersons, has decided to take a job after school at the newspaper plant. His parents warn him that the strain will be too much but he is determined. After an evening of pushing loads of newspapers, tying them into bundles, etc., Bud returns home, to say the least, weary.

INT. HALLWAY — NIGHT
MEDIUM CLOSE SHOT MARGARET
She is coming down the stairs. We hear the front door o.s. She halts on the stairs and reacts slightly to what she sees.

MEDIUM CLOSE SHOT BUD FROM MARGARET'S POV
He is shuffling, completely worn out, toward the bench in the hallway. He is carrying his jacket, or rather dragging it. He also has a few copies of the newspaper. He flops down on the bench, gives a big, weary sigh, and his head droops. His jacket slips from his hand and falls to the floor in a heap. The papers slide to the floor also.

BUD
(moans softly)
Ohhhhh . . .

Kathy, Bud's younger sister, enters, spies Bud and reminds him that he has promised to teach her how to "bop." She is going to a party soon and she wants to learn to dance. Bud wearily waves her away. Kathy is insistent and Margaret (Mrs. Anderson), who has been watching the scene, tells Kathy to let her brother alone, he's exhausted. This brings Bud to his feet and, in a show of bravado, he insists he feels great at which point Kathy demands he teach her to dance.

KATHY
All right then, if you feel so good, why don't you teach me to bop?

Bud shoots her a quick, dirty look, then smiles gayly for Margaret's benefit.

BUD
Well, I'm going to. I'm dying to. Have to use up all this energy someway.

KATHY
Well, good! Come on, let's rock!

Kathy starts humming a rock and roll tune, as she grabs Bud's hands and starts executing some vigorous bop steps. Bud, covertly glancing at Margaret, tries to respond, but it's mostly his shoulders that do the responding. His feet will hardly move. Margaret watches this a moment, completely unsold on Bud's attempts at gay activity, and then she walks out of scene toward the dining room. The minute she is out of sight, Bud pulls away from Kathy.

In both the foregoing scenes, Bud's actions reveal his weariness more effectively than any amount of dialogue could.

Pantomime can also be an effective tool for characterization. Gestures, physical idiosyncrasies are often very revealing. If you saw the stage or video version of "The Caine Mutiny Court-Martial," you were undoubtedly aware of Captain Queeg's constant rolling of the two steel balls in his hand, a gesture revealing inner uneasiness.

There are some gestures, which although stereotyped are very revelatory: the backslapping extrovert, the shy retreat of the sheltered maiden, the finger pointing of the self-righteous.

The pantomime the dramatist indicates for his play must be as much in keeping with the characters as the dialogue. The physical reactions of an elderly person will differ from those of a youth. The environment which has helped to mould your characters will also influence their reactions. A young woman reared in luxury may manifest her distaste if suddenly brought into an ancient tenement. Her facial expression of disgust or displeasure may be her first outward reaction.

The interplay of pantomime and dialogue makes for greater emphasis, as in this scene, also taken from "The Great Guy." Bud and Freddy, after accepting jobs in the circulation department of a newspaper, find that the circulation manager is a difficult taskmaster, a Simon Legree of the press to their young minds. Their feeling towards him, at the moment, is unmistakable.

Unable to think of anything sufficiently devastating, Freddy finishes his sentence by spreading his fingers and forming two large cups and bringing them together with a diabolical slow crushing effect. . . . As his fingers nearly meet he twists the cups viciously.

BUD

(in the mood — diabolically)

Have you ever seen that machine they got out at
the quarry for crushing rocks?

FREDDY

Look — how much more we going to take off
that little guy? Let's quit.

BUD

(wavering)

I don't know . . . I gotta think this over. I gotta
think this over.

DISSOLVE TO:

INT. KITCHEN — NIGHT

CLOSE SHOT BUD

He is supposed to be drying dishes but he's pretty oblivious of the fact.
He slowly moves the towel around on a small bowl he's drying. The
CAMERA PULLS BACK to INCLUDE Betty, washing the dishes. She stops

and watches Bud curiously. Now his face becomes grim, and with the towel and bowl he makes some of the same crushing and twisting gestures that Freddy made in the last scene.

The question as to how visual your video drama ought to be depends entirely on the type of play. A western or adventure drama may be mostly visual. A drawing room comedy will depend, more than likely, on the dialogue. A drama of suspense may place a good deal of emphasis on the pantomime. A "Jimmy Valentine" story, which reaches its climax in the necessity for a reformed burglar to open a safe in which a child is imprisoned, makes very effective use of pantomime. This scene concentrates entirely on Valentine's deft fingers as he manipulates the dial of the safe.

Let us say then that pantomime should be used whenever action alone can tell the story without the necessity of explanatory dialogue.

EXPOSITION

One of the important hurdles confronting the dramatist is the problem of exposition. Since time is of the essence and since the writer has been told repeatedly that every line of dialogue and every action must move the play, he may sometimes feel at an impasse when faced by the necessity of exposition. How does he explain the relationship of his characters to one another? If he is writing a half-hour play, which requires an almost immediate unfolding of plot, how does he reveal the details which must have preceded the opening sequence? How is a new character introduced? What is the time period of the play?

All these elements are necessary in order to present a coherent story. A viewer is not apt to be absorbed in a play which confuses him. Yet the exposition must not be self-evident. As a lovely gown conceals its stitching, so must a well-made play veil its mechanics. It is the "art which conceals art."

There are at least three tools which the writer can manipulate for effective exposition:

1. Monologue;
2. Dialogue;
3. Sets and Costumes.

Monologue

In utilizing monologue, the writer may employ a narrator to set the scene, to explain the passage of time and to comment on the action. This is the simplest and most direct way of handling exposition. Although the device of the narrator may present less of a challenge to the writer, there are instances where the narrative technique may serve very effectively. The "Dragnet" series utilizes this technique, as the following excerpt from the episode entitled "The Big Genius" illustrates:

FADE IN:

INT. JUVENILE SQUADROOM — DAY — 7:57 A.M. — TUESDAY, APRIL 10TH (SILENT)

We see CLOSEUP of locker. OFFICER FRANK SMITH walks into the scene, opens the locker, and hangs up his topcoat.

> JOE'S VOICE
>
> It was Tuesday, April 10th. We were working the Morning Watch out of Juvenile Division. My partner's Frank Smith. The boss is Captain Powers.

Frank starts to close the locker, and a jar of vitamin pills falls off the shelf. JOE'S HAND enters the scene. He catches the pills. As he does so, CAMERA PANS UP for CLOSE SHOT of SERGEANT JOE FRIDAY's face, for:

> JOE'S VOICE
> (continuing)
> My name's Friday.

Joe hands Frank the pills. Frank replaces them on the shelf in the locker and closes the door. The door to the squadroom opens and DAVE NEFF enters. Dave is in his forties, well-dressed, usually self-controlled, but at the moment extremely agitated. In pantomime, Joe and Frank introduce themselves. Dave ignores the introductions and speaks what are obviously angry words.

> JOE'S VOICE
> (continuing)
> The parent of a teenage boy came in to see us. He was understandably upset. Five hours earlier we had arrested his son.

CAMERA MOVES into a CLOSE SHOT of Dave. His face is tense and he is trying to suppress his anger.
FADE OUT:

You will observe that in this brief sequence, the narrator has imparted to us a great deal of information: who the protagonists are, what their jobs are, and the time period of the play. We will have a further analysis of this particular scene and the entire episode of "The Big Genius" in the Chapter on the Series Plays.

Dialogue

The most effective method of incorporating the necessary exposition in your play is through dialogue. The natural flow of conversation should perform the double duty of carrying along the play and, at the same time, including the necessary explanatory details.

Suppose we examine some illustrations of exposition through dialogue. Here, to begin with, is an example that is the essence of simplicity and yet thoroughly demonstrates our premise.

This is a scene which takes place in a small, neighborhood grocery store. An elderly man is behind the counter. The door opens and a young man enters. He walks up to the counter.

YOUNG MAN

Hello, Pa.

As you see, there are no more than two words of dialogue but immediately they inform the audience of the relationship of the two characters: father and son. Had the writer merely written, "Hello," it would have taken at least another line of dialogue or perhaps a few more to establish the relationship. Perhaps you may think that this illustration is cutting it pretty fine. But the fact is that since the television writer always has to be conscious of time, every line should have its value. Exposition, especially, requires a maximum of information with a minimum of wordage.

The dramatist is in the unusual position of a host who not only must introduce his guests to each other but also to an audience which is aware of his every action and yet invisible to him. It is an audience that wishes to remain unseen but still expects all the courtesies.

Therefore, the writer-host must proceed to enlighten his invisible
guests while seemingly unaware of them.

From one of the episodes of the "Father Knows Best" series,
entitled "Spaghetti for Margaret," we have an interesting example of
exposition.

FADE IN:

INT. KITCHEN — DAY

CLOSE SHOT MARGARET (PATIO DOOR IN BG)
She has on rubber gloves and is cleaning the stove, as the patio door flies
open, and Bud barges in, causing Margaret to cringe in fear of her life.
He is waving a small card.

> BUD
>
> Hey, mom! Guess what, mom! You — *you are
> a winner!* An E-flat, gold-plated, souped-up
> winner!

> MARGARET
>
> I am? Winner of what?

> BUD
>
> Winner of what, she says. Mom, don't you re-
> member the chance I sold you for a buck? You
> know, when we were raising money for the Hi-Y,
> and the merchants put up prizes and all that?

> MARGARET
>
> Oh, yes . . . that.

> BUD
>
> Yes, that. And today we had the drawing, and
> you — oh little gray haired mother of mine —
> you are a big, fat winner!

> MARGARET
>
> You mean I actually won that television set?

> BUD
>
> Oh no, that was *first* prize.

MARGARET

Oh. Well what was the second prize?

BUD

Second prize was a hickory-smoked, sugar-baked
Virginia ham!

MARGARET

Oh, really?!

BUD

But you didn't win that either. You got the thirteenth prize.

MARGARET

Thirteenth?

BUD

And here's the little beauty right here.
(shows her the card)
A spaghetti feed for one at Lazarro's Pizza House.
Pretty cool, huh?

MARGARET
(taking card)
Downright freezing.

This opening sequence is written in a style particularly suited
to the situation comedy. For our purposes of study, it is an instruc-
tive instance of exposition informing the audience of actions preceding the opening scene which are pertinent to the plot. Even if this
were the first episode a viewer had witnessed of the "Father Knows
Best" series, he would be informed immediately of the relationship
of the two people who first meet his eyes. Bud's first words are
"Hey, mom!"

From Bud's excited conversation with his mother, we learn
about the fund-raising raffle that led to Margaret's winning the free
spaghetti dinners. This incident eventually leads to the climax of
the play. The dialogue is natural. It holds our interest and it en-
lightens us.

It is entirely plausible to us that in the press of household
duties, Margaret would hardly keep in mind the dollar she had once

donated to the Hi-Y fund. It is therefore perfectly normal for Bud to refresh her memory. In using this device, the writer, Roswell Rogers, is managing his exposition expertly. Bud, apparently refreshing the memory of his mother, is actually informing the audience. We will also have a detailed analysis of this episode from "Father Knows Best" in the section on Situation Comedy.

Sets and costumes

The physical scenes themselves may be valuable aids to exposition. A set which depicts a living room with the wallpaper peeling in spots, the sofa old and soiled and a few rickety chairs, speaks eloquently of its occupants. Obviously, they are poverty-stricken.

A set which shows a den with a large-screen television set and an Eames chair tells us that this is a contemporary home whose occupants have very modern tastes. If yours is a period play, let us say of the colonial or Victorian era, the set, with its appropriate furnishings, will inform us of the time period. In like manner, the costumes of the actors are visual aids to our recognition and understanding.

The writer may go into fairly elaborate detail in describing the various sets of his play and the costumes of the cast. On the other hand, he may use just a few explanatory lines, and leave the details to the scenic designer. But whether he elaborates or is brief, he will be contributing to the exposition.

His scene description may simply indicate:

FADE IN:

THE DINING ROOM OF THE FOSTER HOME, A TYPICAL DINING ROOM OF A TYPICAL MIDDLE INCOME SUBURBAN HOME.

Or he may elaborate:

FADE IN:

THE KITCHEN-DINING ROOM OF THE BLEAKER FLAT. ITS POVERTY IS ALL TOO EVIDENT, FROM THE ANCIENT, WHEEZY REFRIGERATOR, THE EQUALLY ANCIENT GAS STOVE, TO THE WALLS SADLY IN NEED OF PAINT. A LARGE ROUND TABLE, ONE OF WHOSE LEGS IS WOBBLY, STANDS IN THE CENTER OF THE LARGE ROOM. THERE ARE A HALF

DOZEN HARD BACKED CHAIRS AROUND THE TABLE. A WORN OILCLOTH
SERVES AS A TABLECLOTH. IT IS EVENING, NEAR THE DINNER HOUR.
THE ROOM IS POORLY LIT AS IF THE LIGHT BULBS WERE OF A SMALLER
SIZE THAN NECESSARY, WHICH THEY ARE. THE TIME OF YEAR IS LATE
NOVEMBER. MRS. MARY BLEAKER IS AT THE STOVE ON WHICH A SOUP
POT IS BEING HEATED. SHE IS OF MEDIUM HEIGHT, THIN AND PEAKED.
SHE IS IN HER EARLY FORTIES BUT LOOKS MUCH OLDER. SHE WEARS
A WORN APRON AND AT THE MOMENT IS STIRRING THE SOUP WITH A
WOODEN LADLE.

The advantage of using more detail should be apparent from
the preceding examples. The latter description is full and shows
that the writer has a very definite picture in mind. Evidently, poverty is the theme of the play. In either case, brief or detailed scene
description, the writer should be sure to indicate any properties
essential to the plot.

TRANSITIONS

When you watch
an engrossing, well-constructed play, you are unaware of all the hidden devices the playwright has used to make his drama run smoothly.
You see the clock ticking away but you do not see the clockwork.
You may be certain that in the well written play, the transitions have
been carefully thought out. If they weren't, the mechanism of the
play would be visible and the end result would be to destroy the
illusion.

The functions of transitions are to show the passing of time
and to provide a smooth passage from scene to scene. There are
several transitional devices which the television playwright can
employ:

1. Dissolve   3. Film Inserts
2. Fade   4. Defocus.

These are camera devices as distinct from the verbal devices,
dialogue and narration, which may also be utilized to effect transitions.

Dissolves

The Dissolve, as
we have previously explained, generally is used to indicate the im-

mediate passage from one scene to another. In this sequence from "The Great Guy," a "Father Knows Best" episode, Bud and Freddy are beginning to question the wisdom of their having accepted jobs in the newspaper circulation office.

> SINK
> C'mon, we'll go punch in your cards, and then
> cover you with a little blood, sweat and ink.

Sink walks out of the scene. Bud and Freddy stand there a moment, and exchange glances that indicate they're not sure they like what they're getting into. They obviously have little love for this man Sink.

> FREDDY
> (sotto)
> Let's quit.

> BUD
> Quit? We haven't started workin' yet. You
> can't quit till *after* you start.

> FREDDY
> Let's start then.

> SINK'S VOICE (O.S.)
> C'mon, c'mon, c'mon!

The boys jump as though they've been shot with a poison arrow.

CLOSE SHOT   SINK

He is standing near the inserting table looking at the boys o.s.

> SINK
> They tell me the art of conversation is a lost art.
> Let's don't try to revive it right now, eh? C'mon!

He turns and strides off as the boys run into the scene following him, and we:

> DISSOLVE TO:

INT. CIRCULATION DEPARTMENT — DAY

MEDIUM CLOSE SHOT   BUD   FREDDY AND A BUNDLE TYER

Both Bud and Freddy have aprons on, and Freddy is wearing a fingerless glove and finger-cutter on his right hand. He is sweating as he tries to tie a bundle in the accepted manner. Bud is back of the tyers, and he also is sweating as he lifts a tied bundle from in front of the next tyer, and stacks it on the almost-loaded turtle truck. A worker enters the scene (from direction of inserting table) and places another stack of 25 papers in front of the tyer. Bud now moves beside Freddy to pick up Freddy's tied bundle. Both boys look real beat, and dirty. They stop working for a moment, breathing heavily.

The Dissolve may also be used to show simultaneous action in two different scenes as in this sequence from "The Edge of Night." Sara has received a telephone call from her fiancé, Mike, a Lieutenant in the police force. During the conversation she hears a couple of shots.

> SARA
>
> (THIS IS WHAT FRIGHTENS HER) Grace — right after Mike said wait a minute — he said something else and — and then I — I'm sure I heard two shots. . . . (GRACE'S FACE SHOWS HER FEAR)

> GRACE
>
> Now — how could you tell it was a shot — over the telephone —

> SARA
>
> (IN THE PHONE) Mike — Mike . . . ! Hello, hello . . . !

> GRACE
>
> It could have been a — a truck back-firing, or a bad connection. . . . Sometimes you hear all sorts of popping noises on a phone —

> SARA
>
> (IN THE PHONE) Oh, please, please. . . . Hello, hello —

> GRACE
>
> Rap on it with something . . . (SHE PICKS UP A PENCIL FROM THE PHONE TABLE) Here use this —
> (SARA RAPS SHARPLY ON THE TRANSMITTER WITH THE PENCIL)

SOUND: PENCIL TAPPING HARD ON TRANS-
MITTER.

SARA

Hello — hello — Mike — Charlie — somebody —

DISSOLVE TO —

SCENE IB

(THE FRONT HALLWAY "OUTSIDE OF ROSE'S
DRESSING ROOM," IN THE PHONE AREA. COME
IN ON THE DANGLING PHONE FROM WHICH WE
CAN HEAR THE RASPING INDISTINCT FILTERED
VOICE)

SARA

Hello, hello — Mike — Mike . . . !

SOUND: THE TAPPING OF THE PENCIL ON THE
TRANSMITTER.

(PULL BACK TO SHOW MIKE LYING ON THE
FLOOR, MOTIONLESS. CHARLIE ENTERS THE
HALLWAY WITH DRAWN GUN. HE SEES MIKE
AND RUNS TO HIM.)

Here we actually have the use of sound combined with the
Dissolve. The pencil tapping in both scenes is indicative of simultaneous action. Music can also be utilized with the Dissolve to
maintain the transitional mood. However, where the writer always
indicates musical transitions (bridges) in the radio play, he seldom
indicates music in his television script. This is generally left to the
director and musical arranger.

Matching dissolves

This is a device
which affords a flowing transition. It involves the use of a similar
prop or action at the end of one scene and the beginning of the next.

LOUIS

LOOKS UP AT HIS MOTHER, SMILING.
Mama . . . you're wonderful.

SHE EXITS. LOUIS TURNS BACK TO STUDY HER PAINTING ON THE
EASEL. THE CAMERA RESTS ON THE ABSTRACT FOR A MOMENT, THEN
DISSOLVE TO A CEZANNE PRINT WHICH HANGS ON THE WALL OF THE
KITCHEN.

The above is an instance of using stationary props for the
matching dissolve. Here is an example of action.

LOUIS TURNS TO THE WALL AND CHECKS ONE OF THE PICTURE
HANGERS. IT APPEARS LOOSE TO HIM SO HE PICKS UP THE HAMMER
WHICH IS LYING ON A CHAIR AND BEGINS TO TIGHTEN THE PICTURE
HANGER. THE CAMERA FOCUSES ON THE ACTION OF THE HAMMER.
DISSOLVE TO COURTROOM WHERE CAMERA PICKS UP GAVEL HAMMER-
ING ON JUDGE'S BENCH.

There are innumerable matching dissolve devices which the
writer may employ for denoting time passage. He may, for example,
show a flower pot with the seed just beginning to sprout. In the
following scene, the plant is full grown. Or he may use this device
in reverse. We see a vase with roses in bloom. In the next scene,
the roses have withered. Actually, such devices are only limited by
the playwright's inventiveness.

Although the matching dissolve provides an interesting device,
there is a danger of the writer becoming so enamored of his own
inventiveness that he overdoes. Matching dissolves should be used
sparingly in the course of a play, otherwise their effectiveness is
lessened.

Fades

Suppose the writer
wishes to show the passage of a few hours. To do this, he may employ the familiar clock device.

JOHN IS PACING THE FLOOR. WE SEE THE HARRIED LOOK ON HIS FACE.
HE STARES UP AT THE CLOCK ON THE WALL. IT IS THREE P.M. THE
CAMERA FOCUSES ON THE CLOCK FOR A FEW SECONDS. FADE OUT.
THEN FADE IN AGAIN ON THE CLOCK. IT IS FIVE P.M. PULL BACK TO
SHOW JOHN STILL PACING THE FLOOR.

If the passage of time calls for days, weeks, months or even
years, another tried and true device is the use of the calendar. Here

the camera may be brought in for a Closeup of a calendar showing the date and then by using the FADE OUT, FADE IN technique we would bring the camera in again showing the advanced date or, if this were a flashback, the past date. Films often employ the trick device of showing calendar pages turning or falling.

The FADE OUT is always used for a curtain scene at the end of an act or preceding the commercial. In this scene from "The Great Guy" a climax is reached as Bud Anderson believes he is being fired.

SINK

(without looking toward the boys)

Anderson, the Personnel Manager wants you to report to his office.

Bud and Freddy react. As Sink tosses his match away he glances at Bud, and then exits. It takes a moment for the boys to recover.

FREDDY

You got the sack, boy.

BUD

(grimly)

Yeah! . . . Didn't have enough nerve to tell it to my face! Well, boy, I'm going to report to the Personnel Manager all right. And the report's going to be about — *one Mister Sink! !*

FADE OUT.

COMMERCIAL

FADE IN:

INT. KITCHEN — NIGHT

MEDIUM CLOSE SHOT   BETTY   JIM AND MARGARET

Margaret, halting her operation of slicing a cucumber into a salad, is looking apprehensively at Betty. Jim, evening newspaper in hand, is also looking at Betty, who has on jacket and is carrying school books.

JIM

Well, now wait, you say Freddy told you this?

BETTY

Yes, he was just coming from the newspaper office when I saw him. He said Bud and this Sink fellow had this awful fight, and then —

The FADE IN, of course, always follows a FADE OUT since you have gone to a blank screen and have to bring the picture completely back whereas in a DISSOLVE, both pictures may be visible simultaneously, for a very brief time. Where you wish to denote the passage of several hours or days, during an act, you may employ the device of FADING OUT TO BLACK, a transitional method which has the screen dark for an instant.

Film inserts

The use of film inserts or film clips as transitional devices applies specifically to live video dramas. This technique is employed quite often and very skillfully. However, if you find it necessary to call for film inserts in your play, they should be of the type that are readily available from film libraries, otherwise special film inserts are quite expensive to produce. An auto chase, mob scenes, horses galloping into the distance, planes flying, ships at sea, these types of sequences fall into the stock category. If you were writing a video play about the Korean conflict, or about World War Two, for live production, there would be no problem in obtaining film footage of an artillery barrage, a patrol in action, and the like.

In this scene, Matt and Bill are out on night patrol but have lost contact with the main body of the patrol in the darkness.

MATT
Don't like this quiet, Bill . . . it's too quiet. . . .

BILL
Yeah . . . and so blasted dark, can't see a thing
. . . we sure lost our patrol. . . .

SUDDEN BURSTS OF RIFLE FIRE
Hey . . . that's them . . . over to the right . . .
let's go, Matt. . . .

DISSOLVE TO:
FILM INSERT . . . RIFLE FIRE . . . ARTILLERY BURSTS . . . MEN SCURRYING FOR COVER IN THE DARK . . . A SHELL BURST LIGHTS UP THE SKY.
DISSOLVE TO:
BILL LYING WOUNDED ON THE GROUND, MATT BENDING OVER HIM.

MATT

Bill . . . Medic . . . Medic. . . .

Dissolving from live to film to live is readily accomplished but film inserts, like matching dissolves, should be used sparingly. The too frequent use of film clips would imply that perhaps the play should have been filmed entirely.

Defocus

This is a device which is used generally for flashbacks and since we are devoting a section of this chapter to the flashback, the defocus will be discussed in that section.

Verbal transitions: dialogue

In utilizing dialogue for transitions, it is essential, as we have continually stressed, that the transition speeches be an integral part of the play. The time transition can be accomplished by a very direct reference, as in the following scene.

Senator Archer has just read in the morning newspaper that Clara Dixon is going to run for president of the United States, a decision which greatly annoys him. He tells his wife, with whom he is having breakfast:

SENATOR ARCHER

I'm still hopeful this story is a complete exaggeration. I shall investigate it as soon as I reach my office. If it's the truth, I am going to take it upon myself to warn Mrs. Dixon that she is being both reckless and foolish.

HE RISES AND WALKS TO THE DOOR. MRS. ARCHER RISES ALSO. SHE SPEAKS WITH A GREAT EFFORT JUST AS HE REACHES THE DOOR.

MRS. ARCHER

Hiram, I forbid you!

HE STOPS DEAD. THEN HE TURNS SLOWLY AND FACES HER, LOOKING AT HER AS IF HE COULD NOT HAVE HEARD CORRECTLY.

SENATOR ARCHER

(WITH COLD FURY) You . . . forbid me! . . .
forbid me! . . . Am I facing rebellion in my own
home! You spend a few minutes speaking to that
Dixon woman and this is the result. Emily,
you've had a bad morning. You'd better come to
your senses. And, most of all, remember your
place!

HE STALKS OUT. MRS. ARCHER SINKS BACK SLOWLY INTO HER CHAIR,
VISIBLY SHAKING. THE CAMERA MOVES IN TO CATCH THE STRUGGLE
IN EMILY ARCHER'S FACE AS SHE STRIVES TO CONTROL HER TEARS.
FADE TO BLACK.

FADE IN CLARA DIXON'S OFFICE. CAMERA MOVES IN FOR CLOSEUP
OF MRS. DIXON, AMUSED AND EXPECTANT, THEN DOLLIES BACK TO
CATCH SENATOR ARCHER STORMING INTO HER OFFICE.

MRS. DIXON

Good afternoon, Senator, how nice to see you
again. Won't you sit down.

Verbal transitions: narrative

In the hour drama
series, "Robert Montgomery Presents," Mr. Montgomery introduced
each act of the play with a few words about the time and place of
the scene and the events about to occur. Many other series employ
a "host," such as "Lux Video Theater," "G. E. Theater," "Alfred
Hitchcock Presents."

The narrative technique is employed by some adventure and
crime drama series, such as "Dangerous Assignment." In this series
the narrator, Brian Donlevy, is also the hero. The narrator in such
series handles transitions by direct statements: "I had a tough time
getting out of Budapest, but I made it and headed for the Austrian
border with a dozen refugees." Or, "It was ten o'clock when the
plane landed in Lisbon. An hour later I was at the Café."

Transitions may be made very readily from first to third person,
as in the following scene.

SHOT OF INSIDE OF TRAIN COACH. MOVE IN FOR CLOSEUP OF JOE
JENSEN. HE IS STARING THOUGHTFULLY OUT OF THE WINDOW.

JENSEN

It all began when I decided to go home. I hadn't
been home in ten years. I didn't know what kind
of a welcome I'd get. I knew Ma would be at the
station. I guess I hadn't realized how much a
person can change in ten years.

DISSOLVE TO FILM INSERT OF TRAIN SPEEDING ALONG. THEN DIS-
SOLVE TO STATION PLATFORM. WE SEE THE SIGN "PLATTSVILLE."
THE CAMERA PICKS UP MRS. JENSEN, TIRED LOOKING, AND OLD. JOE
COMES ON SCREEN WALKING SWIFTLY TOWARDS HIS MOTHER.

JENSEN

Ma . . . Ma . . .

Cover scenes

In the filmed play,
there is no need for the writer to be concerned with the time it takes
for costume changes or for actors to get from one set to another.
However, the writer of the "live" play must be aware of these requirements. He cannot have the same character appear at the conclusion of one scene and at the very beginning of another if a change
of costume is necessary. The writer must also realize that, physically, sets may be many feet apart and even the fastest sprinter
among the thespians will need a few seconds between sets. Therefore, the video dramatist has to plan transitions to take care of these
physical factors. Your cover scene must appear to the audience as
an essential part of the play and not as a discernible device.

In the following script example, Mrs. Dixon, a lawyer, is seen
dressed formally for a party at her home. The next scene, which
requires a complete change of costume, takes place in her office, a
few mornings later.

WOODSON

And now I mustn't keep you any longer. It's
been a wonderful party, Clara.

MRS. DIXON

(REGARDS HIM FONDLY)
Thank you, Henry. Good night.

He rises, then bends over to kiss her cheek.
Fade out.
Fade in reception room of Mrs. Dixon's office. It is a few mornings later. Hannah, her secretary, is at her desk. She is busily typing.
Alice Colton enters. She is in her late thirties, thin faced, a small woman physically, but very high spirited.

COLTON
(SPRIGHTLY)
Good morning, Hannah, good morning.

HANNAH
(STOPS TYPING ABRUPTLY AND LOOKS UP STARTLED OUT OF HER CONCENTRATION.)
Oh . . . Miss Colton . . . good morning.

COLTON
Is Mrs. Dixon in?

HANNAH
She hasn't returned from court yet, but I believe she'll be here soon. Was she expecting you?

COLTON
I'm afraid not, but I'll wait.
SEATS HERSELF.

HANNAH
Mrs. Dixon told me this would probably be a brief session.

COLTON
What case is she trying now?

HANNAH
It's the Rogers case, Miss Colton.

COLTON
Rogers? . . . Oh, yes, the young lad accused of murder. I've read about it in the papers . . . sordid business. How on earth did Mrs. Dixon get mixed up in that one?

Hannah

The boy's mother came in here, crying. She told
Mrs. Dixon she didn't have the money the lawyers
wanted to defend her boy and she didn't want to
throw herself on the mercy of the court, or take
any lawyer the court appointed. She pleaded
with Mrs. Dixon to take the case and you know
how Mrs. Dixon is . . .

Colton

I know . . . I know . . . a perfectly splendid,
generous person. . . .

CLARA DIXON ENTERS BRISKLY, CARRYING A BRIEF CASE. SHE STOPS
AS SHE SEES ALICE COLTON.

This cover scene gives Clara Dixon ample time to change her
costume. It has also added information regarding the character of
Mrs. Dixon and helped the progression of the play. It has, therefore, served a threefold purpose and is an essential part of the play.

THE FLASHBACK

The flashback is a
device for portraying an episode of the past which bears a relation to
the current action of a play. It is a step backward into time. The
flashback can be very effective if used skillfully and sparingly. However, it is important for the writer who wishes to utilize this device
to be aware of the technicalities involved.

The viewer is accustomed to seeing progressive action. It is
also easier for him to follow a play that moves forward in a straight
line. If you have ever watched or listened to a daily serial, you may
have observed that the flashback is rarely, if ever, employed. It is
also true that most television dramas, whether one-shot or series, use
the flashback only occasionally. Nevertheless, there are times when
the writer finds that the flashback is extremely helpful to his play.

Since the flashback is a retrogression in time as opposed to the
normal progression of the play, it requires, as it were, special handling. The viewer must be prepared for this backward flight. He

is watching a play move forward. Suddenly, the writer, in essence, says to him: "Now, let's stop here for a moment and go back a day or a year or a decade." Since all of us are blessed with some imagination, we generally do not find it too difficult to accept this premise. But we cannot be hurtled into this past time sequence abruptly.

In order that the flashback sequence may take place smoothly, the camera must be put to most effective use. One common method is to have the camera go out of focus so that the screen is blurred and we achieve a sort of mystic effect preparing us for a non-normal sequence. Then the camera comes back into focus and we are now in the past. This effect is called defocusing. The process is repeated in returning from the past to the present action. Music is generally blended with the defocus to heighten the effect. In radio, music plays a major role in effecting flashbacks. If two or more flashbacks are used in the play, it is good practice to utilize the same musical theme whenever the flashback occurs. The familiar strain serves to alert the viewer or listener to the oncoming flashback.

Another device the writer can employ is that of matching dissolves, which we have discussed previously in the section on transitions. If his story, let us say, were about an old charwoman who had known better days, he might have a scene of the old woman down on her knees scrubbing the floor of a deserted office. The camera focuses on her weary, gnarled hands; then there is a slow dissolve and we see another pair of hands, young, immaculate, lovely. They are, of course, the hands of the charwoman when she was young.

In like manner, the same device can be used with settings. We see a garden, or what used to be a garden, before ugly weeds took full control. The rustic fence that surrounds the garden is falling apart. An elderly man comes on. He stands there looking sadly at the towering weeds. Again there is a slow dissolve and we see the same garden but now the weeds are gone, the fence looks new and there is a host of flowers blossoming in the sunlight.

It should be noted at this time that it will make a good deal of difference to the writer, as far as the flashback is concerned, whether the play is to be filmed or live. If the play is live, a cover scene may be necessary. For example, if the flashback were used to portray an incident which occurred to the heroine a year or two ago, a change of dress would be necessary and the actress would have to have time to make that change. The writer would have to provide time for the costume change much as he would in a forward transition where the same character appears in one scene immediately following the preceding scene. A cover scene would not be necessary for a filmed play. On the other hand, even in a live play, no cover sequence would be necessary if the flashback were to take place many years ago. For example, if a young man were to recall an incident in his childhood, naturally, a child actor would play the role in the flashback scene.

For purposes of study, we may classify flashbacks into three categories:

1. Thought Sequence;
2. Narrative Device;
3. Memory Image.

Thought sequence

To illustrate the use of this type of flashback, here are several scenes from a live half-hour television play. The flashback technique is utilized throughout the play and demonstrates the Thought Sequence to the full.

THE SCENE IS A FOXHOLE ON A KOREAN HILL. IT IS NIGHT AND CORPORAL MATT HERKIMER IS ON SENTRY DUTY . . . A LONELY VIGIL. SOMETIMES STABS OF LIGHT TEAR ACROSS THE DARKNESS AND THE RUMBLE OF ARTILLERY IS HEARD IN THE DISTANCE. THEN IT IS QUIET. WE CAN MAKE OUT CORP. HERKIMER'S FACE DIMLY. HE IS ABOUT 23, BUT HIS FACE HAS THAT MATURE SERIOUSNESS ABOUT IT WHICH YOUNG MEN ACQUIRE WHO HAVE GONE THROUGH THE HELL OF COMBAT. HIS CARBINE IS GRIPPED IN HIS HANDS AS HE SITS IN THE FOXHOLE. HE STARES OUT INTO THE NIGHT AND WE CAN HEAR HIS THOUGHTS.

MATT

(RECORDED)
I don't like it. It's too quiet. The gooks ain't usually this quiet. Usually they'd be lobbin' mortars, or their artillery'd be breakin' loose. Not that they hit anythin'. Just nuisance value. Tryin' to break up our sleep. Maybe they're asleep too. Maybe they're dreamin' of home. What kind of homes do the gooks dream about?

(A LIGHT FLARES IN THE DISTANCE. IT MOVES BACK AND FORTH,
LINE A SIGNAL. THEN IT IS GONE.)

MATT
(RECORDED)
What's that? Must be some sort of signal. Came
from down in the valley. Don't know what it
could be. Don't look like anythin' to report.

(THERE IS THE EERIE WHISTLE OF THE SOUND FIELD PHONE. MATT
PICKS UP THE RECEIVER FROM THE FOXHOLE)

(LIVE)
Corporal Herkimer . . . no . . . Captain Blake
hasn't been by this hole yet . . . okay . . . I'll
tell him.

(HE PLACES THE RECEIVER BACK ON THE GROUND)

(RECORDED)
Wish I could smoke. Better not. In this darkness, it'd be like a beacon. A match'd flare up
like that light. Well, it won't be long now. I'll
be goin' home . . . leavin' these black ridges of
Korea . . . the back breakin' hills of Korea . . .
the smell of the valleys. Home to the Blue Ridges
of Virginia . . . the clean, sweet air of the
Shenandoah valley.

(THE CAMERA DOLLIES BACK SO THAT MATT IS NO LONGER VISIBLE.
WE SEE ONLY THE BG. AND THE STABS OF LIGHT IN THE DISTANCE
BUT WE STILL HEAR MATT'S VOICE)

And the nights, blue and bright with a million
stars. Remember, Elly? . . . It was Saturday
night and we were just comin' out of the movies.
Jim and Claire were ahead of us.

FADE OUT

(FADE IN FRONT OF MOVIE. THE MARQUEE ABOVE IS BARELY VISIBLE.
JIM AND CLAIRE COME ON FRAME AS IF EXITING FROM MOVIE. THEY
STAND BEFORE ENTRANCE AND WAIT.)

JIM
(LOOKS BACK)
What happened to Matt and Elly?

CLAIRE

If you can remember, Jim, before we were married, we used to walk very slowly, too, arm in arm.

JIM

Even comin' out of a movie?

CLAIRE

Even comin' out of a movie.

MATT

(COMING ON, HOLDING TIGHTLY TO ELLY'S ARM. IT IS JUNE AND HE WEARS AN OPEN SHIRT. ELLY WEARS A SUMMER DRESS WITH A STAR PATTERN. SHE LEANS AGAINST MATT AS THEY STOP BESIDE JIM AND CLAIRE.) That was a pretty good show, don't you think so, Jim?

Since this play was written for live production, you will note the cover scenes which permit Matt to make a quick change of costume. Just before the flashback, we hear Matt's voice but he is no longer on camera. His voice has been prerecorded for this scene. Then as the flashback sequence opens, we see Matt's friends, Jim and Claire, first and they have a brief conversation, which also serves as exposition. In this instance, we learn from Jim and Claire's conversation that Matt and Elly are very romantically attached.

As the scene progresses, Matt and Elly are alone and Matt proposes to her. We discover also an element of conflict. The following dialogue occurs just before we leave the flashback to return to the present.

MATT

I'm the one who cares for you, Elly. It don't matter what Ma thinks. I want you to marry me, Elly.

ELLY

I will, Matt. I will.

MATT

(HE EMBRACES HER) My darlin' . . . my darlin'
. . . my Elly.
(THEN HE RELEASES HER. SHE LEANS BACK)
Let me look at you, Elly. I just want to look at
you.

(CU OF ELLY. THERE IS A LOOK OF RAPTURE ON HER FACE. WE
HEAR MATT'S VOICE OVER FRAME.)

MATT

I remember you sittin' there, Elly, leanin' against
the haystack . . . and all the stars were in your
eyes. I remember that, Elly.

FADE OUT.

(FADE IN KOREAN HILL. MATT IS IN FOXHOLE. HE IS LEANING FOR-
WARD, ALERT, HIS CARBINE HELD IN FIRING POSITION. A FIGURE
CRAWLS TOWARDS THE FOXHOLE.)

MATT

Halt! (HE GIVES THE PASSWORD — FIRST
HALF OF IT) Forest!

BLAKE

Green!
(CAPTAIN BLAKE SITS UP AT THE EDGE OF THE
FOXHOLE)
How are you doing, Matt?

MATT

(RELAXED NOW)
Fine, Captain Blake.

BLAKE

Seen anything out there?

MATT

No, sir. Everythin's quiet and still. There's
been some artillery thrown over there, usual nuisance stuff, sir. Command Post wants you to
call, sir.

For the cover scene this time, we have a close-up of Elly with

Matt now off camera. Again his voice is prerecorded. There is a long shot of the Korean hill which not only gives Matt a few additional seconds for his costume change but serves to reorient the viewer. Now the cycle is complete. We have met Corporal Matt Herkimer in the present. We have followed his thought sequence to the past and returned to the present.

The device is sound and appears to be properly motivated. A soldier alone on sentry duty would very naturally have thoughts of home. Therefore the device is acceptable to the viewer and he will have no difficulty in moving with the play from the present back to the past.

Narrative device

This method of utilizing the flashback is a good one, particularly for children's stories. Youngsters, if they have loving parents, are accustomed to having stories read to them and if the parents are both loving and imaginative, then the child may be treated to tales never found in any anthology! In any event, the role of the storyteller is a familiar one to the child.

Programs such as "Mr. I-Magination" (which, unfortunately, did not have the long run it deserved) and the former "Gabby Hayes Show" made good use of the narrative device. Generally, this genre of program features a narrator and a child. The narrator, or storyteller, is often depicted as an ancient garrulous soul who has had an infinite number of adventurous experiences. After some brief prodding by the youngster, the oldster begins his tale with a few expository remarks regarding time and locale. Then comes the flashback to an actual dramatization of the story. They may be personal stories in which case the narrator always plays the hero. Or they may be tales of legendary figures such as Paul Bunyan.

In the utilization of the narrative device, the story may be told entirely by flashback. If the play is of a half hour duration with a first act curtain, it is acceptable technique to return to the narrator at the end of the first act. He may then add impetus to the situation which has ended the first part of his story and additionally whet our curiosity as to the outcome of the events. When we return to Act Two, after the commercial, the storyteller is on stage again with the omnipresent youngster and a few pertinent remarks that lead us into the second half of the story. At the conclusion of the play, the story-teller returns again and this time he may give a brief preview of his story for the coming week.

The following illustration will serve to demonstrate this form of the Narrative Device:

FADE IN: A SHACK WITH A SMALL PORCH. AS THE CAMERA MOVES IN FOR A M.C.U., WE SEE AN OLD MAN SITTING ON THE STEPS AND WHIT-TLING AWAY AT A PIECE OF WOOD WITH A HUNTING KNIFE. HE IS WEARING A COSTUME OF THE OLD WEST. HE IS BAREHEADED AND WHAT IS LEFT OF HIS HAIR IS GRAY AND FRIZZLED. A YOUNGSTER OF ABOUT EIGHT ENTERS. HE APPROACHES THE OLD MAN FAMILIARLY.

> BOY
>
> Hi, Pete.

> PIONEER
>
> LOOKS UP
> Hi, there, Andy. Come on an' sit down.

> BOY
>
> Sure.

HE SEATS HIMSELF NEXT TO THE OLD MAN. FOR A FEW SECONDS THERE IS SILENCE WHILE THE OLD MAN KEEPS WHITTLING. THE BOY LOOKS AT HIM EXPECTANTLY. THE OLD MAN STOPS WHITTLING AND GRINS AT THE BOY.

> PIONEER
>
> Waitin', huh?

> BOY
>
> I sure am.

> PIONEER
>
> Wal, I ain't one to keep a youngun waitin'. Now,
> you let me light up my pipe.
> HE TAKES A CORN COB FROM HIS SHIRT POCKET,
> LIGHTS UP AND PUFFS CONTENTEDLY.
> Lemme see. Did I tell you about the time I rode
> smack into a whole herd of Comanches on the
> warpath. . . .

> THE BOY NODS.

Uh . . . huh . . . reckon I did. But not about the
time the Apaches made me a blood brother?

THE BOY SHAKES HIS HEAD.

I reckon it all started when I was on my way
to the old fort. . . .

LAP DISSOLVE TO SHOT OF MAN RIDING HORSEBACK. . . .

The Narrative Device may have several variations. Instead of
a single narrator, many characters may relate their version of a story.
"The Remarkable Incident at Carson Corners," by Reginald Rose
(*Six Television Plays,* Simon and Schuster), is an outstanding
example of this technique. A youngster, Billy McGinnis, has been
killed in a fall at school because of a faulty railing. His classmates
gather in the evening at the schoolhouse to which they have invited
their surprised parents. The children conduct a trial accusing the
janitor of the death of the boy. During this startling trial, some of
the children and the adults give their version of the events leading
up to the death of Billy McGinnis. Each witness begins with a
narrative lead-in to a flashback.

Memory image

As its title implies,
this type of flashback utilizes the device of an object, a setting or an
individual to fan the spark of memory in the protagonist. The
Memory Image differs from the Thought Sequence in that the
former conjures up memories of deceased individuals while the latter
generally is concerned with living persons. For example: the son
comes upon an old watch which belonged to his departed father
and the timepiece brings back memories of his parent; the widow
visits the grave of her husband and recalls the struggles and joys
they shared; a man sees a child playing in the street and is reminded
of the daughter he lost in an accident; a soldier orders a beer in a
London pub and as he looks into the sparkling foam, he sees the
dead buddy with whom he had many a drink. The Memory Image
definitely calls for the use of the defocus to serve the purposes of
illusion.

OPEN WITH LONG SHOT OF EXTERIOR OF PROSPEROUS LOOKING HOME.

A GARDENER IS TENDING A FLOWER BED. AN ELDERLY MAN COMES ON SCENE. HE WALKS SLOWLY, LEANING HEAVILY ON A CANE. HE IS DRESSED RATHER SHABBILY. HE STOPS BEFORE THE HOUSE AND STARES AT IT. MOVE IN FOR CLOSEUP OF THE MAN. WE SEE AN INTELLIGENT FACE BUT ONE THAT IS LINED WITH CARE. PULL BACK TO BRING IN GARDENER WHO NOW SPEAKS TO THE MAN.

GARDENER

Something I can do for you?

MAN

No . . . no . . . I . . . er . . . this is the Desmond residence, isn't it?

GARDENER

It was.

MAN

Was? . . . Mrs. Desmond . . . she doesn't live here any longer?

GARDENER

She died a year ago.

MAN

Oh . . .

GARDENER

You knew her?

MAN

Yes . . . yes . . . I did . . . she was my wife. . . .

THE GARDENER STARES AT HIM IN ASTONISHMENT. THE CAMERA GOES OUT OF FOCUS FOR THE FLASHBACK. IN FOCUS WE SEE THE WELL FURNISHED LIVING ROOM OF THE DESMOND HOME.

LIVE VS. FILM

While watching television dramas you may have noted the following tag lines: "This program has come to you *live* from New York," or "This program has come to you *filmed* from Hollywood."

It is most natural that filmed dramas originate from the West coast. Hollywood is the home of the film industry, still the giant of the entertainment world. The screen writers, the movie actors, the technicians, the vast studios are all there in abundance. Hollywood has the film know-how. The big motion picture companies have organized their television subsidiaries, e.g., Columbia Pictures has Screen Gems which produces such filmed series as "Father Knows Best," "77th Bengal Lancers," "Circus Boy," "Ford Theater," etc. There are also many independent producers: Desilu Productions, Hal Roach, Ziv Productions, etc. They are all used to working with film and to them it is the ideal method of presenting drama.

There are several advantages to film presentation:

More variety in locales;
The use of extensive outdoor sequences;
No fluffs;
Immediate transitions.

The basic assets of "live" programs are:

Lower production costs;
Spontaneity of performance;
Flexibility for last-minute changes.

There appears to be a trend to more and more film programs. The half hour dramas are almost entirely filmed now and the "live" half-hour drama is the exception. As for the hour drama, the reverse situation is still true. CBS "Playhouse 90," pioneering in a regular weekly series of hour and a half dramas, presents a filmed play once each month. The other plays in the series are "live."

How does this question of "live" vs. film affect the writer? In many ways. The "live" drama presents more of a challenge to him because his scope is narrowed. He cannot write in a sequence where the villain dives off a ship and is seen swimming to shore with a police boat in hot pursuit. The writer must introduce "cover" scenes for transitions to give his heroine time to change a dress or to get from one set to another. Film clips may be inserted, but these, generally, must be stock shots, readily available, to avoid added expense.

The film writer has no comparable transition problems. He can have his characters appear immediately in one scene after another because each scene is shot individually. He can write in scenes of actual pursuit and of exotic locale. Many film series are shot on location. The film writer thinks more in terms of a screen play rather than a television play, and if you have access to any scripts of filmed dramas, more than likely you will find that the title page bears the statement: "Screenplay by. . . ."

Credits for a film play follow the standard lineup of motion pictures, while live plays more often utilize the television technique of rolling credits on a drum.

The argument has been advanced that the actor on the stage usually can give a more rounded performance than the screen actor. This is because a film, generally, is produced in a bits and pieces technique; in other words, the climax may be filmed before the opening scene. Also, if two scenes occur in the same setting, even though they are apart in sequence in the script, they will probably be shot successively, in order to save the expense of putting the set up again. The "live" performer, on the other hand, works up naturally and chronologically to each crisis and to the climax therefore adding the spark of spontaneity.

VIDEOTAPE

What effect such mechanical developments as the Ampex Company's Videotape will have on television film is not fully answerable at this writing. But since the videotape provides so remarkable an apparatus for instantaneous filming, it is bound to have a decided influence.

The Videotape records sound and picture simultaneously and, like its radio counterpart, this film tape can be played back immediately. No developing procedure is necessary. The advantage of this process is patently obvious. Scenes can be observed immediately. There is no need to wait for film rushes. This method affords a saving in both time and money.

The Videotape also affords a much better image than kinescopes, which are films made of the original production directly from a picture tube. These kinescopes, although definitely of broadcast quality, are inferior in clarity to the live production. The Videotape offers the possibility of equalling the quality of the live program.

SETS

Before the writer begins to plan his play, he must know whether he is writing for a filmed or live production. It may make a difference as to the number and type of sets. A live production is necessarily more limited in physical area than a filmed play. Even with the huge studios available for live network productions, they cannot begin to compare with the "on location" possibilities of film. Nevertheless, with the technical facilities now available for live productions, the writer does have great leeway.

Sets for a TV play are not as much a factor in budget considerations as those for a stage play, but they can be costly. The television dramatist, then, must keep his set requirements in reasonable bounds without sacrificing the needs of his story. He has to strike a happy medium. A one- or two-set play would narrow the action and may cause his play to appear static. This again is in contrast to a stage play where the beginning playwright has more of an opportunity for consideration of his drama if it requires only one set. The stage producer is taking a gamble. He does not know whether the play will be a success, and if it is the work of an unknown writer, it is imperative to keep the initial cost low.

Where the one-set video drama may prove static, the play with too many sets may be too episodic, or choppy. Nevertheless, as is the way with creative art, the creator, more often than not, confounds the rules. One of the most dynamic of TV plays was Reginald Rose's "Twelve Angry Men," since made into a film. The entire action of the play, except for a very brief scene of the jury box, takes place in the jury room.

Although it is possible, as we have stated, for the writer to indicate the use of film clips for certain scenes, it is advisable to keep the film inserts to a minimum. If the film clip can be obtained from stock footage, it presents no problem, physically or financially. Stock footage refers to film sequences which may be obtained from film libraries, either maintained by the networks or by newsgathering organizations. For example, if the writer required a scene of a presidential inauguration, a crowd at a basball game, shots of the Cherry Blossom Festival, or scenes of soldiers marching, such film clips are readily available. But if the film insert requirement were for a unique occurrence or if it were an auto pursuit sequence which called for the participants in the cars to be identifiably visible, added expense would be incurred for the individual shooting of this film insert.

Therefore, in outlining your play for live production, you must be aware of set limitations. A play about skin divers would best be written for film where advantage could be taken of many underwater shots. However, the advances of video camera techniques permit the writer of live dramas more scope. Many of you may have seen the Kraft Theatre production of Walter Lord's "A Night to Remember," the story of the sinking of the Titanic. At first glance, this story would have appeared to present an impossible task for a live production. But the many sets, both in the interior of the ship and on deck, and the cast of hundreds, were handled with great skill and precision. Still, it must be admitted that "A Night to Remember" was an exceptional production for live television.

Local production

The local television station has neither the budget nor the staff of the network and its programming is limited accordingly. Therefore, a drama for local presentation must confine itself to a minimum of sets, generally interiors. However, many sets may be represented by fragments. The skillful use of the "cameo" technique will also permit more flexibility in the number of scenes. The writer should consult with the local producer before he begins to write his play so that he may be aware of set possibilities.

A NOTE TO REMEMBER

Unlike the novelist, short story writer, poet who speak directly to their audience, the television playwright must reach his audience through a host of interpreters: directors, actors, cameramen, scenic designers, musicians, lighting experts, stage hands. If the video dramatist has an opportunity to see all these craftsmen in action, he will understand the magnitude of network television presentations and he will never cease to marvel at the precisioned coordination.

A play in performance may be likened to a symphony orchestra with all its instruments blending harmoniously. The orchestra may possibly perform without a conductor, but the genius of a Toscanini inspires it to great heights of performance, evokes all the nuances the composer envisioned and many that go beyond the original composition. So a talented director may fashion script, cast, camera technique, settings into the living, breathing creation the playwright imagined. Paddy Chayefsky paid deserved tribute to director Delbert Mann: "an extremely gifted director who has a precise affinity for my kind of writing and a sharp understanding of his own needs in conveying the values of the script to the actors and cameramen."

The play, like music, requires performance. Although it is true that a play may be read with a good deal of enjoyment and benefit to the reader, even so, the play has been written to be acted and full satisfaction can only come about with a competent performance. The playwright, however, must never lean on the performer. Characterizations must be full blown with no blank spaces to be filled in by the actor. A great actress like Helen Hayes may possibly transcend inadequate writing, but with all due respect to our talented stars, the drama is basic. Therefore, the dramatist must give the actor proper food to feed his talent or the play will suffer from malnutrition. A well-written drama plus an able cast equals a gratifying performance.

The half-hour
filmed drama

14

The half-hour television play, with few exceptions, is now produced on film. This change from the early preponderance of live half-hour television dramas to the current situation where such productions are a rarity, is directly traceable to the Hollywood influence. When Hollywood producers, large and small, entered the television field, they, naturally enough, turned to film. To them, television was a form of movie making: little pictures in big doses. They had the advantage of a concentration of film technicians. They had the Hollywood know-how. They thought in terms of technical perfection rather than artistic spontaneity. It is an interesting commentary that very few of even the top movie directors have been successful when assigned to live television programs. On the other hand, many of television's leading directors, such as Delbert Mann, have made the transition to film easily.

There are a great number of half-hour anthology series on the television airwaves. As any other type of TV program, they come and go but it is safe to say that the half-hour drama, in greater or lesser numbers, will always be with us. It was a well-established form in radio and has been a stronghold of video from the very beginning of television networks. You can probably name a dozen shows with which you are familiar, among them "The General Electric Theater," "The Loretta Young Show," "Du Pont Cavalcade Theater," "Schlitz Playhouse," "Fireside Theater," "Studio 57," and "Ford Theater."

There are very few dramatic anthology series produced by local TV stations. Most of the TV stations either take their dramas from the network with which they are affiliated or utilize film dramas from packagers, such as ZIV TV programs, for local sponsorship. There have been instances of locally sponsored half-hour original drama programs which afford an excellent opportunity for local talent. These programs, of course, are presented live. University dramatic groups, in cooperation with either the local commercial or educational TV station, can and do present half-hour dramas. These local productions must be comparatively simple to produce. Sets must be few and inexpensive and camera tricks generally avoided.

The half-hour play is almost always divided into two acts and requires a crisis of some magnitude to occur at the first act curtain. Length of the half-hour sponsored play runs about twenty-three minutes, with both acts rather evenly divided.

The script and analysis which follow will illustrate in specific terms the elements of a successful half-hour filmed drama. The play is "The Glorious Gift of Molly Malloy," written by the very talented Jameson Brewer. It was originally produced by Revue Productions for the "General Electric Theater" and starred Greer Garson.

"THE GLORIOUS GIFT OF MOLLY MALLOY" *

FADE IN:

EXT. METROPOLITAN ELEMENTARY SCHOOL — DAY — FULL SHOT — (STOCK). A MODERN CITY GRADE SCHOOL SHOWING, IF POSSIBLE, SMALL CHILDREN AT PLAY IN THE YARD. THE SOUND OF A CLASS BELL IS HEARD.

DISSOLVE

INT. SCHOOL ROOM — DAY — FULL SHOT
THIS ROOM HOUSES THE FIRST GRADE AND IS FUNCTIONALLY

* For actual film script format, see the "Mickey Mouse Club" script in Chapter 22.

MODERN. THERE ARE NO SAND TABLES, TOY BOXES OR INTRI-
GUING GADGETS TO OCCUPY THE CHILDREN. IT HAS THE CLIN-
ICAL ATMOSPHERE AND APPEARANCE OF AN OPERATING THEATRE
IN A MEDICAL COLLEGE. ONLY THE SMALL DESKS AND LOW
BLACKBOARDS INDICATE THAT TINY HUMANS GATHER HERE FOR
LEARNING. AN ASSORTMENT OF SIX-YEAR-OLDS IS FILING INTO
THE ROOM AS THE TEACHER, MOLLY MALLOY, STANDS AT THE
FRONT OF THE ROOM SMILING FONDLY AT EACH AND EVERY ONE.
SMALL CHAIRS HAVE BEEN ARRANGED IN A SEMI-CIRCLE NEAR
MOLLY AND THE KIDS EAGERLY TAKE PLACES THERE. IT IS EVI-
DENT THAT THERE IS GREAT AFFECTION BETWEEN CHILDREN
AND TEACHER. FOR THAT MATTER, MOLLY MALLOY CAPTIVATES
EVERYONE WITH HER LITTLE TOUCH OF BROGUE AND HER MORE
THAN A LITTLE BLARNEY. WHEN THE KIDS ARE ALL SEATED
THEY FALL SILENT AT ONCE, LARGE EYES TURNED EXPECTANTLY
UPON MOLLY.

MOLLY: You managed that quietly and I'm proud of you.
(BRIGHTLY) Now, then, who'd be knowing where we left our
wonderful tale of the wee people yesterday?

BOY (EAGERLY): Danny McDuff was walking home at night
through the meadow!

MOLLY: Ah, yes, so he was. (DRAMATICALLY) It was a misty night,
and Danny ran swoosh up against a strong rail fence.

THE CHILDREN LEAN FORWARD TO FOLLOW THE STORY WITH
BATED BREATH AS MOLLY CONTINUES WITH THE TRUE GIFT
FOR FANTASY.

MOLLY: Danny was that startled, you may be sure, and even
more astonished by the nine cats all sitting atop the gate-
post!

BOY (SCOFFINGLY): Aw, there's nothin' so wonderful about nine
cats.

MOLLY (WINKING): Isn't there, now? When they're all singing
Rose of Shannon in perfect harmony?

THE CHILDREN GIGGLE DELIGHTEDLY AND THE SKEPTICAL BOY
IS ABASHED. MR. DIETZ, THE STERN-FACED PRINCIPAL,
APPEARS IN THE DOORWAY. HE EASES INTO THE ROOM
QUITE UNNOTICED DURING THE FOLLOWING.

MOLLY (CONTD) (TO CHILDREN): Poor Danny was horrified
when one cat suddenly spoke to him saying, "Danny McDuff,
tell Patrick Riley that Peg Powson is dead!"

Mr. Dietz, who has remained unobtrusively in the bg., is startled by this line from Molly and moves closer, as if doubting his ears.

MOLLY (CONTD) (TO CHILDREN): Danny ran home fast as his legs would take him and told his wife this marvelous story. They were both puzzled and wondering who Patrick Riley might be when their old brindle cat by the fireplace leaped up and cried, "I'm Patrick Riley and if Peg Powson is dead then I'm the king of the cats!" And with that he sprang up the chimney and was never seen again!

The children applaud delightedly as Dietz stands in shock for a moment. Suddenly Molly notices him and nods respectfully.

MOLLY: Children, we're honored! Our Principal, Mr. Dietz, has favored us with a visit this fine morning!

The faces of the children fall at once and the room freezes noticeably.

DIETZ (FINDING HIS TONGUE): Miss Malloy, what was that fantastic nonsense you were telling the children?

MOLLY: Faith, it's not nonsense, Mr. Dietz. It's the true story of Danny McDuff, a leprechaun living in County Donegal.

DIETZ: A leprechaun!

MOLLY (TWINKLING): Seen by my very own father, he was.

DIETZ: Your fath. . . . ! (TROUBLED) Miss Malloy, may I speak to you privately a moment?

MOLLY: It's a privilege, sir.

Mr. Dietz hurriedly leads the way to the back of the room away from the children. He turns to face Molly.

Two shot — Molly and Dietz

Molly looks at the man curiously.

DIETZ: Miss Malloy, the moulding of young minds is a tremendous responsibility.

MOLLY: I love young minds.

DIETZ: Then why don't you conform to the prescribed curriculum? You can do great harm by using improper methods.

MOLLY: I only add a little something of my own . . . a personal touch.

DIETZ: Such personal touches will completely wreck progressive education! We try to curb fantasy . . . instill reality!

MOLLY (SOFTLY): Childhood is a time for dreaming, Mr. Dietz. Realities will come soon enough.

DIETZ: You're paid to teach, not to theorize.

MOLLY (EARNESTLY): Children live in a special world of their own, a land of magic and miracles . . . of mermaids and pirates . . . pixies . . . wee people and talking rabbits. The more fantastic to us, the more real it is to the dear babes.

DIETZ: Witches and hobgoblins! What possible good can tales like those serve?

MOLLY: They stimulate the imagination and that's very important, Mr. Dietz. Otherwise, where will we find our poets and artists and inventors and composers and designers and all for tomorrow?

DIETZ (SUSPICIOUSLY): Haven't you been following the curriculum as outlined by Professor Meyerdal of State University and approved by our Board of Education?

MOLLY: Oh, I follow it, sir.

DIETZ: Good.

MOLLY (TWINKLING): When I'm able to sort of work it in and around my own curriculum.

DIETZ (SHOCKED): Don't you understand! Professor Meyerdal is a brilliant man, an internationally known authority on education.

MOLLY: Does he teach the first grade?

DIETZ (EXASPERATEDLY): Of course not! He's at the University!

MOLLY: Ah, that's it then. Children are only statistics to him. He sees them as one huge mass of pegs, all to be rounded and squared and fitted into so many sockets of uniform size.

DIETZ (SIGHING): I'm sorry, Miss Malloy. I've tried to be lenient but I must *insist* that you observe our methods now or I'll be forced to ask the Board for your dismissal. (WITH COLD FINALITY) You have just twenty-four hours to fall in line with our methods or I'll ask the Board for your immediate dismissal!

HAVING DELIVERED HIMSELF OF THIS ULTIMATUM, DIETZ WHEELS AND STRIDES OUT OF THE ROOM. MOLLY LOOKS AFTER HIM, PERHAPS A BIT CONCERNED FOR HIM BUT NOT AT ALL TROUBLED IN HER OWN CONSCIENCE.

DISSOLVE

EXT. RESIDENTIAL STREET — DAY — FULL SHOT
MOLLY COMES DOWN THE SIDEWALK, DRESSED IN THE BRIGHT

ATTIRE ONE MIGHT EXPECT OF A WOMAN WITH SUCH A
VIVID IMAGINATION AND TWINKLING EYE. SHE CARRIES AN
ARMLOAD OF BOOKS AND HOMEWORK. SHE TURNS IN AT
THE GATE OF A MODEST HOME, STARTS UP THE WALK TO
THE PORCH THEN IS STOPPED IN HER TRACKS BY THE EX-
CITED APPROACH OF A DECREPIT OLD CAR WEAVING
WILDLY TOWARD HER HOUSE, HORN HONKING URGENTLY.
IT PULLS TO A SKIDDING STOP AT THE GATE AND A ROTUND,
ELDERLY LITTLE MAN LEAPS OUT FROM BEHIND THE
WHEEL. HE LOOKS ABOUT QUICKLY, WIDE-EYED AND AP-
PREHENSIVE, THEN HURRIES UP THE WALK TO MOLLY.
THIS IS DENNIS MALLOY, HER FATHER, AND THE ONE FROM
WHOM SHE INHERITED HER VIGOROUS IMAGINATION AND
FORTHRIGHT MANNER.

TWO SHOT — MOLLY AND DENNIS

SHE BEAMS HAPPILY AT THE OLD MAN AS HE HURRIES UP TO
HER.

MOLLY: Sure, it's himself, Dennis Malloy!

DENNIS (URGENTLY): Molly, into the house, lass!

HE LOOKS ABOUT WORRIEDLY AND MOLLY SMILES SOFTLY AND
    WITH UNDERSTANDING.

MOLLY: Is it the leprechaun again?

DENNIS: The same! Been on me track all day, laughin' and tor-
    mentin' the very life out of me! Hurry along, now!

HE GRASPS HER ARM AND HUSTLES HER UP THE STEPS TO THE
    FRONT DOOR, OPENING THE DOOR AND SHOVING HER INSIDE
    QUICKLY. HE LOOKS ABOUT OUTSIDE ONCE AGAIN, THEN
    DARTS INSIDE AFTER HER.

INT. LIVING ROOM OF MALLOY HOME — FULL SHOT

THIS IS A WARM AND COZY PARLOR REFLECTING THE WARMTH
    AND FRIENDLINESS OF ITS OWNERS. MOLLY WATCHES
    WITH AMUSEMENT AS HER FATHER SLAMS AND BOLTS THE
    DOOR THEN HURRIES TO THE FRONT WINDOW AND PEERS
    CAUTIOUSLY OUT AT THE STREET THROUGH A SLIT IN THE
    CURTAINS.

MOLLY (TWINKLING): About the leprechaun, father . . . I suppose
    now he tormented you when you went to see about that job at
    the factory?

DENNIS (HELPLESSLY): That he did! Gave me such a turn I never
    did get inside to ask the good man about employment.

MOLLY (KNOWINGLY): And he was waiting for you down at the union hiring hall?

DENNIS (STARTLED): Why, that's the size of it exactly, lass!

MOLLY: And you didn't get over to see about the janitor's job at the school, I've no doubt. (GENTLY) The vacancy won't be open long, I'm thinking, father.

DENNIS (AGHAST): Molly, colleen! Ye wouldn't ask me to be leadin' that spalpeen of an imp over to the school where he might be doin' great and lastin' damage to the dear gossoons and girleens?

WITH A WRY SMILE, MOLLY PUTS HER BOOKS ON THE TABLE AND DROPS INTO AN EASY CHAIR.

MOLLY: I'm afraid he's already done a bit of damage at the school, that leprechaun.

DENNIS LOOKS AT HER SHARPLY, NOTES HER WORRIED AIR AND CROSSES TO HER, PUTTING A GENTLE AND COMFORTING HAND ON HER SHOULDER.

DENNIS (SOFTLY): It wasn't Danny McDuff, lass . . . he's me own private leprechaun, more or less.

MOLLY: It was Danny, all right.

DENNIS (OBJECTINGLY): Now, Molly, it can't be! Ye see . . . well, now . . . (SUSPICIOUSLY) Did he pop out of a bottle of any sort?

MOLLY GLANCES UP AT HIM WITH AN UNDERSTANDING SMILE.

MOLLY: He popped out of my mouth.

DENNIS (UNDERSTANDINGLY): Aye, I'd be knowin' what ye mean. You spoke about Danny to folks with no talent for seein' beyond their noses and they didn't believe your tales, that's it.

MOLLY (SOFTLY): That's it, father. I was telling the children about Danny and . . .

DENNIS (SORROWFULLY): Ah, it's a sad state of affairs when children start doubtin'.

MOLLY: It was Mr. Dietz, the principal, who doubted.

DENNIS (DISGUSTEDLY): Och, he's a miserable, shrunken up specimen of a creature from all I've heard tell!

MOLLY (SERIOUSLY): Father?

DENNIS (TENDERLY): Aye, lass?

MOLLY: When I was a little girl you told me wonderful tales of goblins and elves and pixies and fairies.

DENNIS (FONDLY REMINISCENT): And demons and dragons and

monsters and giants! Aye, that's a glorious, entrancin' time for tots . . . a moment to be captured. If passed, it may never be caught again.

MOLLY (RISING): And when you cheat a tot of this time of magic, he makes up his own adventures.

DENNIS: Aye, Molly Malloy.

MOLLY (THOUGHTFULLY): If all he knows of adventure is the cold, hard facts of real life, he may very well choose the brutal, primitive adventures of the juvenile delinquent.

DENNIS: Now you're leadin' me into deep waters, lass. All I know is there's more strange and mysterious things in this world than most men dream of . . . and leprechauns is one of them!

MOLLY LAUGHS DELIGHTEDLY AND WRAPS HER ARMS ABOUT HIM.

MOLLY (WARMLY): And I love you dearly for helping me to know them.

DENNIS GIVES HER A LOVING KISS ON THE CHEEK THEN BACKS OFF AND LOOKS CONTRITE.

DENNIS (WITH FAINT DETERMINATION): I'll be goin' to inquire about that janitor's job first thing in the mornin'.

MOLLY (SMILING): But what about the leprechaun?

DENNIS (WINKING): With clever maneuverin', I may well be able to escape him till quite late in the day . . . tomorrow's election day. The pubs don't open!

MOLLY CHUCKLES AND HUGS HIM AFFECTIONATELY AS HE BEAMS.

DISSOLVE

INT. PRINCIPAL'S OFFICE — FULL SHOT

A VISITOR IS SEATED IN THE ROOM AWAITING THE PRINCIPAL. HE IS PROFESSOR MEYERDAL, A TALL, GAUNT, ANGULAR MAN WITH A FURIOUS SCOWL AND AN AIR OF RAWBONED GENIUS. MR. DIETZ BURSTS INTO THE ROOM ANGRILY, SLAMS THE DOOR BEHIND HIM THEN STOPS SHORT IN SURPRISE AT SIGHT OF THE VISITOR.

DIETZ (OVERWHELMED): Professor Meyerdal! This is a great honor! A personal visit from the greatest educator in the country!

THE PROFESSOR WAVES OFF DIETZ' EFFUSIONS WITH A LANGUID HAND.

PROFESSOR: I called to commend you for the wonderful results you've obtained with my elementary school curriculum which was inaugurated throughout the nation last semester.

DIETZ (DELIGHTEDLY): Thank you, sir.

PROFESSOR: Results of recent tests show that this institution has the highest rating of any school in the nation which has adopted the curriculum.

DIETZ (AWED): We've been very diligent in its application.

PROFESSOR: The accomplishments of one of your teachers is especially amazing . . . Miss Malloy, I believe.

DIETZ (BLANCHING): No! Not Malloy!

PROFESSOR: The first grade teacher?

DIETZ (GROANING): That's Malloy.

PROFESSOR: I'd like to see her at once.

DIETZ (WILDLY): Well, I don't know about interrupting the class. You know your own theory in that respect, Professor!

PROFESSOR: No need to interrupt. We'll just drop into the classroom and watch. (EAGERLY) I've got to see how this woman applies my techniques to get such startling results!

DIETZ (BESEECHINGLY): Really, I think it would be much better another time . . . another day . . . another semester . . . !

PROFESSOR (IMPATIENTLY): Nonsense, Dietz. I can't be running over here every other day! Come along now.

THE PROFESSOR HEADS FOR THE DOOR AND THE MISERABLE MR. DIETZ FOLLOWS, RESIGNED TO THE INEVITABLE CATASTROPHE TO FOLLOW.

DISSOLVE

INT. SCHOOL ROOM — FULL SHOT

SEATED IN A CHAIR FACING A SEMI-CIRCLE OF YOUNGSTERS, MOLLY IS CAREFULLY SCISSORING A DOLL FROM THE FOLDED PIECE OF COLORED PAPER AS SHE SPINS A TALE FOR THE CLASS. AS SHE TALKS, DIETZ AND PROFESSOR MEYERDAL SILENTLY ENTER THE ROOM AND STAND TO ONE SIDE. MEYERDAL PUTS A FINGER TO HIS LIPS, CAUTIONING DIETZ, AND STUDIES MOLLY WITH GREAT INTEREST.

MOLLY (TO CHILDREN): Now, you see, this cave was guarded by a dreadful dragon who devoured man and beast . . . until Sir John of the Thumbs came along!

THE PROFESSOR GLANCES QUIZZICALLY AT DIETZ WHO SHRUGS MISERABLY.

MOLLY (CONTD): The good man acquired this strange name because he had four thumbs on each hand. Now, he heard about this fiery monster which might often be seen at midnight flying about the countryside breathing flame and smoke and snatching up young children who roamed about too late.

A LOOK OF DISBELIEF HAS SLOWLY CREPT OVER THE FACE OF THE PROFESSOR AND DIETZ WINCES IN AGONY.

DIETZ (ROARING): Miss Malloy!

MOLLY STOPS SHORT, STARTLED. THE CHILDREN ALL TURN TO LOOK AT THE MEN. THE PROFESSOR AND DIETZ START TOWARD MOLLY AS SHE UNCONSCIOUSLY UNFOLDS THE STRING OF DOLLS BEFORE HER, THE FIGURE IN THE CENTER OF THE SERIES BEING CONSIDERABLY LARGER THAN THE REST BUT OF THE EXACT DESIGN.

DIETZ: Clear the classroom immediately! (SHARPLY TO KIDS) Take a short recess, boys and girls!

MOLLY (OBJECTINGLY): But they just had one.

DIETZ: Let them have another! (TO CHILDREN) Go!

THE KIDS HOP UP AND STREAM QUICKLY OUT OF THE ROOM, CHATTERING EXCITEDLY OVER THE UNEXPECTED RECESS. MEYERDAL HAS NOTICED THE DOLLS IN MOLLY'S HAND AND HAS FIXED THEM WITH A GLITTERING STARE OF FASCINATION.

PROFESSOR (AWED): Amazing! Very, very clever!

MOLLY FOLLOWS HIS GLANCE TO THE DOLLS, STUDIES THEM A MOMENT, THEN LOOKS BACK AT HIM CURIOUSLY.

MOLLY: Oh, they're not really amazing . . . just something I do while telling stories.

DIETZ (STIFFLY): Miss Malloy, this is Professor Meyerdal.

MOLLY: Ah, is it now? I've read your books, sir.

PROFESSOR (IMPATIENTLY): Thank you. May I see those paper things, please? And perhaps you'd explain them to me.

MOLLY: Certainly, sir. And perhaps you'd explain your books to me?

GREATLY PUZZLED, MOLLY GIVES THE DOLLS TO MEYERDAL WHO EXAMINES THEM INTENTLY. DIETZ IS JUST AS PUZZLED BY HIS BEHAVIOR AS MOLLY, BUT FLASHES HER A WARNING SCOWL.

PROFESSOR (VASTLY INTRIGUED): Amazing magic! Even more baffling than the famous Hindu rope trick.

MOLLY (BACKING OFF FROM HIM WORRIEDLY): Sure, there's

no magic to it. Anybody with a pair of sharp scissors can do it.

PROFESSOR (WINKING AT HER): Oh, come, come. Everyone knows a string of paper figures are all of equal size . . . they never have a large one in the center like this!

MOLLY AND DIETZ ARE MOMENTARILY STUNNED AS THEY STARE AT THE DOLLS AND NOTICE THE ODD FACT FOR THE FIRST TIME.

MOLLY (FLABBERGASTED): Whist, now, it never struck me before this very minute! It's not a trick . . . it must be a special knack I have.

PROFESSOR (STAGGERED): Not a trick? (SUSPICIOUSLY) Do it again.

MOLLY: Cut more paper dolls?

PROFESSOR: Yes, yes . . . quick, woman!

DIETZ (NERVOUSLY): Perhaps you could see Miss Malloy later, Professor.

PROFESSOR (BRUSHING HIM ASIDE): Please! (TO MOLLY) Cut!

MOLLY (HESITANTLY): Well, now, what would I cut?

PROFESSOR: Anything! Dogs, cats, rhinoceros, Mongolian sheep . . . anything! Just cut!

MOLLY SELECTS A SHEET OF PAPER FROM THE DESK AT HER SIDE AND FOLDS IT OVER SEVERAL TIMES AS THE PROFESSOR AND DIETZ WATCH CLOSELY.

MOLLY: I do a rather fancy rabbit.

PROFESSOR: Cut! (WITH BATED BREATH) This could be a discovery fraught with significance!

DIETZ: You think so?

PROFESSOR: This woman may inadvertently have made a startling addition to the science of physics. It all depends on how she folds the paper.

MOLLY: There, that's the way I fold it.

PROFESSOR (PUZZLED): But that's the way anyone would fold it!

MOLLY: Yes, I suppose it is, now.

PROFESSOR (AWED): Then cut, please.

MOLLY CUTS NEATLY FROM THE FOLDED PAPER, FASHIONING A SMALL, SIMPLE RABBIT IN OUTLINE.

PROFESSOR (DRAMATICALLY): It must have been just such a moment when Benjamin Franklin caught the first spark of electricity on his kite string!

DIETZ (HELPFULLY): Perhaps like the moment when Joseph Priestley discovered oxygen with a sprig of mint and a wax candle!

PROFESSOR: No, no, it would have to be compared more to John Dunning's first demonstration of nuclear fission!

HE SCARCELY WAITS FOR THE LAST SNIP OF MOLLY'S SCISSORS TO GRASP THE DOLLS AND UNFOLD THEM. THERE IS A VERY LARGE RABBIT IN THE STRING OF SMALLER RABBITS. MEYERDAL STARES IN STUNNED SILENCE FOR A MOMENT THEN TURNS A GLITTERING EYE ON MOLLY.

PROFESSOR: I'd like you to come to the University tomorrow morning at nine o'clock sharp.

MOLLY (STARTLED): Me? Whatever for?

PROFESSOR (MOMENTOUSLY): I don't believe you quite realize, Miss Malloy . . . what you've just done can't possibly be done!

MOLLY RECOILS FROM HIM A BIT AS HE FIXES HER WITH A WILD GLEAM OF SCIENTIFIC DISCOVERY.

FADE OUT

FADE IN:

INT. UNIVERSITY LABORATORY — DAY — CLOSE SHOT OF STRINGS OF PAPER DOLLS HANGING FROM LINES LIKE WASHING. CAMERA PANS ALONG THE LINES, DISCLOSING SERIES OF DOLLS OF ALL SHAPES, SIZES AND SUBJECTS. THERE ARE DARK COLORED ONES, LIGHT COLORED ONES, OPAQUE ONES, TRANSPARENT ONES, SOME CUT FROM CLOTH, SOME FROM LEATHER, SOME FROM PLASTIC. THERE ARE EVEN SOME THAT LOOK SUSPICIOUSLY LIKE BATHROOM TISSUE. SUBJECTS RANGE FROM SIMPLE TREES TO COMPLICATED SUNBURSTS AND FILIGREED DESIGNS. AND IN EACH AND EVERY CASE THERE IS A LARGE FIGURE IN THE CENTER OF THE STRING OF EXACT SHAPE AND DESIGN.

FULL SHOT — THE ROOM

THIS IS AN AUTHENTIC RESEARCH AND EXPERIMENTAL LAB, NOT A FRANKENSTEIN NIGHTMARE. THERE ARE TABLES HOLDING LAB EQUIPMENT AND MANY ELECTRONIC AND PRECISION INSTRUMENTS. SEVERAL TECHNICIANS IN WHITE GOWNS ARE STUDYING THE STRINGS OF PAPER DOLLS. ONE

MEASURES A DOLL WITH CALIPERS, FURIOUSLY MAKING NOTES ALL THE WHILE. ANOTHER TRAINS THE EYE OF AN X-RAY MACHINE ON A SERIES OF DOLLS. STILL ANOTHER IS DUNKING DOLLS IN AN ACID BATH. THE MEN PAUSE NOW AND THEN TO GLANCE CURIOUSLY OVER AT A TABLE IN THE CORNER WHERE MOLLY MALLOY SITS, FORLORNLY AND MECHANICALLY SNIPPING MORE DOLLS. ALL ABOUT HER ARE HEAPS OF SCRAPS FROM PREVIOUS CUTTINGS AND THE PILE OF MATERIAL SHE HAS YET TO CUT THROUGH IS FORMIDABLE. THE DOOR BURSTS OPEN AND PROFESSOR MEYERDAL ENTERS, ACCOMPANIED BY A SHORT, STUBBY MAN WHO HAS A WILD SHOCK OF STEEL-GREY HAIR AND GLASSES WITH LENSES MORE POWERFUL THAN THE ONE AT PALOMAR. THIS IS DR. HARNISH, INTERNATIONALLY FAMOUS PHYSICIST. THE TWO HURRY TO MOLLY.

PROFESSOR (BRIGHTLY TO MOLLY): Well, how are we doing today, Miss Malloy?

MOLLY (PLAINTIVELY): I've been cutting things for three days, Professor. I've never missed a day of school before and I'm so worried about the children.

PROFESSOR (REASSURINGLY): Now, now, everything is all arranged at school. Your work here is much more important.

MOLLY (WRYLY): What sort of work is this now, I ask you?

PROFESSOR (MAKING INTRODUCTIONS): Miss Malloy, this is Dr. Harnish.

HARNISH (PEERING AT HER CLINICALLY): A great pleasure, Miss Malloy. I'm indeed very happy to meet you.

MOLLY (GRATEFULLY): A doctor, is it? Well, I'm very happy to meet you. (PRESSING HER BACK) I've a spot right here that's torturing me. It's all this sitting and cutting and then . . .

PROFESSOR: No, Miss Malloy, Dr. Harnish —

MOLLY (HEEDLESSLY): And then there's this blister on my thumb from so much snipping with the scissors and my poor numb . . .

PROFESSOR (HASTILY): Dr. Harnish is an internationally known physicist!

MOLLY (DISAPPOINTEDLY): Ah, that's a shame.

THE TWO MEN EXCHANGE SHOCKED GLANCES BUT THEIR CURIOSITY OVERCOMES THEIR VANITY.

HARNISH (TO MOLLY): Professor Meyerdal has described your trick to me.

PROFESSOR: He came all the way from Paris to see it.

MOLLY (WEARILY): I've said over and over, it's no trick . . . and I don't know how I do it. (INDICATING LAB MEN) And by the looks of those poor souls, neither does anyone else!

HARNISH: Well, no doubt there's a very simple explanation.

PROFESSOR: Dr. Harnish is a little skeptical. Would you cut out some dolls for him, please?

MOLLY (POINTING O.S.): There's dolls from here to next Tuesday! Take your pick.

HARNISH: I'd like to see you cut them, if I may.

MOLLY SIGHS, PICKS UP A PAPER AND STARTS TO FOLD IT. QUICK AS A FLASH, HARNISH WHIPS OUT AND AFFIXES TO HIS GLASSES A SMALL JEWELER'S LENS. HE LEANS CLOSE TO THE PAPER MOLLY IS FOLDING AND SHE FINDS HERSELF STARING INTO THE WILD, TANGLED BRUSH OF HIS HAIR. WORKING AROUND THIS HANDICAP, SHE COMPLETES THE FOLDING. HARNISH LOOKS AT MEYERDAL.

HARNISH (CONTD): That's all?

PROFESSOR: That's all.

HARNISH (TO MOLLY): Cut, please.

HE LEANS CLOSE TO THE PAPER AGAIN AS MOLLY TAKES HER SCISSORS IN HAND. SHE EXPERIENCES A MOMENTARY URGE TO SHEAR HIS MOP OF HAIR, BUT RESTRAINS HERSELF AND QUICKLY CUTS OUT A SIMPLE DOLL. HARNISH FOLLOWS HER EVERY MOVE, MEASURING THE STROKE AND THE BITE OF THE BLADES. SHE FINISHES AND HE GRABS THE DOLLS FROM HER, UNFOLDS THEM AND IS FACED BY THE PHENOM-ENON OF A LARGE DOLL IN THE MIDDLE. HIS FACE FALLS. HE SHAKES HIS HEAD AS IF TO CLEAR HIS BRAIN. HE STARTS TO CHUCKLE WITH A KIND OF HYSTERICAL UNDER-TONE.

HARNISH: No . . . oh, no . . . no, no, no . . . it's utterly impossible! Quite inconceivable!

PROFESSOR: I promised you'd be intrigued. What do you make of it, doctor?

HARNISH (THOUGHTFULLY): She's broken something.

MOLLY (HOTLY): If anything's broken, it's my poor back!

HARNISH: No, no, you've broken some law . . . I'm not just sure which. (MUSINGLY) Things equal to the same thing are equal to each other. Well, of course that one's shot to pieces.

MOLLY (SNIFFING): I never considered it too important, any-how.

MOLLY SUDDENLY GETS AN IMPISH GLEAM IN HER EYE. UNTIL THIS MOMENT, THE IMPLICATIONS OF HER STRANGE TAL-ENT HAVE NEVER STRUCK HER.

PROFESSOR: If I'm not mistaken, doctor, this pretty much finishes the Pythagorean Theory, too, don't you think?

HARNISH (BLANCHING): You're right! It may eventually wipe out many other laws of mathematics and physics! Just when I was beginning to understand the quantum theory, there it goes!

MOLLY (MUSINGLY): I had a thought. If I can do this with paper, why can't I do it with other things? It may be quite a money-making gift I have.

PROFESSOR (STARTLED): What do you mean?

MOLLY: Now, take the automobile industry. Oh, wouldn't they be happy if, for every ten wee sports cars coming out on the as-sembly line, there'd be a huge limousine in the middle and at no extra cost or trouble!

HARNISH: That's impossible!

MOLLY (SERENELY): They said the same about the dolls. (WARM-ING UP) And the clothing business . . . for every ten tiny suits, a big one in the middle! (REALLY INSPIRED) And the United States mint!

PROFESSOR (APPREHENSIVELY): What about the mint?

MOLLY: For every ten nickels coming out of the minting machine, one silver dollar in the middle!

THE TWO MEN LOOK AT EACH OTHER IN COMPLETE DISMAY AND MOLLY GLANCES AT THEM WITH A SLY TWINKLE.

HARNISH (WORRIEDLY): Miss Malloy, you're talking wildly. This business has upset you, of course.

MOLLY (BLANDLY): Upset? I'm feeling glorious! Since you gen-tlemen seem to be getting no place with my little gift, I'll just be seeing what I can do on my own. No doubt when the news-papers hear. . . .

PROFESSOR (HORRIFIED): You mustn't tell the press!

MOLLY: And why not, I'd like to ask?

THE MEN EXCHANGE WORRIED, DESPERATE LOOKS.

HARNISH (PERSUASIVELY): You're an intelligent woman, Miss Malloy. You can see what a devastating effect such a premature announcement might have on the world. It could seriously affect education, for example.

PROFESSOR: Certainly. You're a teacher. I know your first and foremost consideration is the advance of education!

MOLLY (CUNNINGLY): Indeed, that it is. Well, if I'm to keep quiet, I may be asking a few favors on your part, also.

HARNISH: Anything you wish later! (PLEADINGLY) But you must give us more time to find the answer to your strange ability.

MOLLY (KNOWINGLY): Yes, it wouldn't look well at all for me to be walking around doing something you wise gentlemen couldn't explain, now would it?

PROFESSOR (BESEECHINGLY): Promise you won't say a word to the papers until we reach a solution!

MOLLY: I'll give my promise, right enough, but it's almost impossible to stop an Irishman from talking.

HARNISH: We'll keep you under observation every minute!

MOLLY (SMILING SOFTLY): That's well and good, gentlemen, but my father is running about loose and he's every bit as Irish as myself!

THE MEN LOOK AT EACH OTHER IN CONSTERNATION AND SHE SMILES UP AT THEM WITH DISARMING INNOCENCE.

DISSOLVE

EXT. MALLOY HOME — DAY — FULL SHOT AT PORCH

ACROSS THE FRONT OF THE PORCH IS A HUGE SIGN PROCLAIMING: "HOME OF MOLLY MALLOY!" A SMALL SANDWICH BOARD NEXT TO THE FRONT DOOR ANNOUNCES "ADMISSION 50¢ — ORIGINAL FURNITURE — NOTHING CHANGED — SEE HER BED, HER DISHES, HER CLOTHES!" DENNIS MALLOY, IN HIS BEST BLUE SERGE, STANDS BY THE FRONT DOOR COLLECTING ADMISSIONS AS SEVERAL PEOPLE FILE INTO THE HOUSE. WHEN THEY HAVE ENTERED, HE PICKS UP A MEGAPHONE AND GOES TO THE STEPS TO DRUM UP MORE BUSINESS.

DENNIS (SHOUTING THROUGH MEGAPHONE): All right, now, step up and see the home of Molly Malloy! The very place where the greatest scientific wonder of the age was born!

LONGER SHOT — TOWARD HOUSE FROM STREET

SEVERAL PEOPLE CLUSTER NEAR THE GATE AND LISTEN. A CAR OR TWO PULLS TO A STOP AND CURIOUS PEOPLE ALIGHT TO LINE THE FENCE AND STARE AT THE HOUSE.

DENNIS (BARKING): It's Dennis Malloy I am . . . the one and only
father of Molly Malloy! Sure, you've been readin' in the papers
the story of me Molly's great mystifyin' and magical gift! And
it's here you may get the straight and honest truth of the matter!
INTRIGUED, THE PEOPLE DRIFT INTO THE YARD AND UP TO
DENNIS.
GROUP SHOT — DENNIS AND PEOPLE
DENNIS LOWERS THE MEGAPHONE AND ADDRESSES THE PEOPLE
IN DRAMATIC, HUSHED TONES.
DENNIS: Ye'll be wantin' a look at the marvelous creation that has
all the world agog and here it is!
FROM HIS POCKET, HE WHIPS A STRING OF PAPER DOLLS AND
HOLDS THEM UP. THERE IS A BIG DOLL IN THE MIDDLE
DENNIS (CONTD): Have ye ever seen the likes of it, now? It defies
all the men of science because . . . (DRAMATICALLY) . . . it's
magical! An art learned from the wee people!
THE CROWD BUZZES.
DENNIS (CONTD): In this very house the well known leprechaun,
Danny McDuff, pops up at all hours. It was him, without a
doubt, who so gifted me dear lass. Now I can't be makin' ye
a promise the leprechaun will put in his appearance just at
the moment, but there's always the possibility. So for the small
fee of fifty cents, step up and enter the house of the most
startlin' woman of the day . . . Molly Malloy!
THE PEOPLE HURRY UP THE STEPS AND DENNIS TAKES ADMIS-
SIONS.
DENNIS (CONTD): On your way out ye may be wantin' photographs
of the dear colleen. They'll be sellin' at twenty-five cents
apiece. (MODESTLY) And there's a very few of meself now
goin' at the bargain price of two for a quarter!

DISSOLVE

INT. TELEVISION STUDIO — NIGHT — MED. SHOT
THE SET IS SIMPLE: A DESK CONTAINING BOOKS AND A WORLD
GLOBE. THERE IS A WELL STOCKED BOOKCASE BEHIND THE
DESK. MILTON HOLMES, THE NEWS ANALYST, SEATED AT THE
DESK, REFERRING TO NOTES IN FRONT OF HIM, IS DIGNIFIED
AND SCHOLARLY. HE LOOKS UP AND ADDRESSES CAMERA,
HIS MANNER UNTHEATRICAL, BUT HIS VOICE BETRAYING
THE DRAMATIC IMPORT OF HIS NEWS.
HOLMES: Good evening. Well, tonight we are confronted with a

phenomenon which has leading scientists of the world baffled. While some men struggle to prove that such basic truths as peace, freedom, tolerance and liberty can exist, other men are literally stampeding to belief in hysterical fiction of all kinds . . . flying saucers . . . reincarnation . . . regression through hypnosis . . . and now the mystery of Molly Malloy!

HOLMES PICKS UP FROM HIS DESK A STRING OF PAPER DOLLS AND EXHIBITS THEM. THERE IS A BIG ONE IN THE MIDDLE.

HOLMES: This, believe it or not, ladies and gentlemen, is what has confounded the distinguished thinkers of the world! (BITINGLY) Yes, science is bleeding profusely from a deep wound inflicted by a simple Irish school teacher with a pair of sharp scissors! And scientists are hanging their heads in shame. Gathered in emergency session at State University, they will give out no word. Could it be they don't know the word? (GLANCING TO ONE SIDE) There is only one man who presumes to be an authority on the subject and we are happy to have him with us in the studio tonight. Mr. Dennis Malloy, father of Molly Malloy!

HOLMES SMILES OFF AND CAMERA PANS OVER SLIGHTLY TO REVEAL DENNIS SEATED IN AN EASY CHAIR SMOKING A CIGAR, NOW OBVIOUSLY A MAN OF AFFLUENCE. HE SMILES AT THE CAMERA WITH THE EASY ASSURANCE OF A PERSON ACCUSTOMED TO BEING IN THE PUBLIC EYE.

DENNIS (TO AUDIENCE): It all started with a small green leprechaun named Danny McDuff!

DISSOLVE

INT. UNIVERSITY LABORATORY — NIGHT — FULL SHOT

AN EMERGENCY CONCLAVE IS IN SESSION. SCIENTISTS FROM ALL OVER THE WORLD ARE SEATED IN A CIRCLE ABOUT THE DESK WHERE MOLLY IS STILL CUTTING DOLLS. AT THE MOMENT, A THIN, SWARTHY SCIENTIST, POSSIBLY A TURK, IS STANDING BESIDE MOLLY CUTTING DOLLS FROM FOLDED PAPER. WITH AN AIR OF IMPENDING TRIUMPH, HE COMPLETES THE CUTTING AND SPREADS OUT THE DOLLS. THEY ARE ALL OF EQUAL SIZE, EVEN THE ONE IN THE MIDDLE. HIS FACE FALLS TO HIS FEET AND, WITH A SHRUG OF HELPLESSNESS, HE SITS DOWN. THE DOOR BURSTS OPEN AND THERE IS A CLAMOR FROM OUT IN THE HALLWAY.

PROFESSOR MEYERDAL, LOOKING HAGGARD AND DISTRAUGHT, DASHES INTO THE ROOM, CLOSELY FOLLOWED BY MEMBERS OF THE PRESS WITH CAMERAS AND NOTEPADS. THE PROFESSOR TURNS TO RESTRAIN THEM.

PROFESSOR (AGITATEDLY): Please, gentlemen! We have no statement to make at this time! Shortly, I promise you!

HE FORCES THEM BACK OUT OF THE DOOR AND SLAMS THE DOOR, TURNING THE KEY IN THE LOCK. THE OTHERS IN THE ROOM HAVE WITNESSED THE FOREGOING IN STRAINED SILENCE. THE PROFESSOR COMES OVER TO FACE THE GROUP. HE STOPS NEXT TO MOLLY, WHO SMILES UP AT HIM BRIGHTLY.

MOLLY: You missed some fine speeches, Professor. There was an Irish scientist here . . . spoke pure Gaelic, he did. We had a splendid talk.

PROFESSOR (WORRIEDLY): Professor Kennedy from Dublin. Where is he now?

MOLLY: He left with Danny McDuff.

PROFESSOR (PUZZLED): Danny McDuff?

MOLLY: The leprechaun I've spoken of!

PROFESSOR (GROANING): No!

MOLLY (WINKING): I didn't see Danny myself, but the Professor said he saw him plain as anything. He went out laughing and talking away to the wee creature.

MEYERDAL WIPES BEADS OF PERSPIRATION FROM HIS FOREHEAD AND TURNS TO THE OTHERS IN THE ROOM.

PROFESSOR: I take it no one has come up with a theory yet?

THE MEN SIT IN STONY SILENCE.

PROFESSOR (PRESSING): Have we exhausted every avenue? Tried every known kind of material that can be cut, for instance?

MOLLY: You've used five hundred kinds of material and twenty-eight kinds of scissors!

PROFESSOR (GRIMLY): Well, gentlemen, the pressure on us is enormous. The public is clamoring for an answer . . . also the newspapers . . . the universities . . . even the government! Do you have any suggestions?

MOLLY (EARNESTLY): Wouldn't it be better all around if you just swallowed your pride and admitted there's things no wee human brain can cope with?

PROFESSOR: We're scientists, Miss Malloy. The world won't accept evasive philosophy from us . . . it expects logical, realistic explanations.

MOLLY: And have you ever been able to explain why two and two makes four?

PROFESSOR (UNEASILY): That's a mathematical proposition a priori. Two and two just make four, that's all.

MOLLY: Now I ask you, what kind of a logical answer is that, Professor?

THE PROFESSOR LOOKS AT HER AS THOUGH HE WISHES HE HAD NEVER SEEN HER.

PROFESSOR (DULLY): Miss Malloy, I suspect there's something insidiously evil about you.

HARNISH (RISING): You know, this inexplicable trick of hers is dangerously disruptive when you analyze it.

MOLLY (STUNNED): Evil? Dangerous? Me?

PROFESSOR (GRASPING AT STRAWS): It is! Look what she's done to education. Struck at the very foundation of learning.

HARNISH: A teacher of six year olds!

PROFESSOR (EAGERLY): An ideal time to fashion young minds as they turn from the impulsiveness of five to the creative thrusts of six!

HARNISH: She can destroy the inwardness of seven, the expansiveness of eight, and completely curb the self-motivation of nine!

MOLLY (BEWILDERED): I don't even know what all that gibberish is, now! How can I destroy it?

PROFESSOR (TO HARNISH): You believe we can prove she's dangerous and a menace?

HARNISH (SHRUGGING): Anything would be easier to prove than her trick.

PROFESSOR: But even if we can prove it, that won't explain how she cuts those dolls.

HARNISH: It will divert public attention from them . . . in time, it will all fade . . . we can simply explain it as a magic trick which she refused to divulge.

PROFESSOR: Excellent. We can wash our hands of her and let the authorities handle this hot potato a while! They've been screaming for a solution . . . well, let them supply it!

MOLLY LOOKS APPREHENSIVELY AT THE GRIM FACES AROUND HER.

DISSOLVE

EXT. CIVIC CENTER — DAY — FULL SHOT — STOCK
OVER THIS SCENE THE VOICE OF MILTON HOLMES IS HEARD.

HOLMES' VOICE (DRAMATICALLY): Today, the entire nation awaits news of the fate of Miss Molly Malloy. Not since the days of Salem has this country seen such a witch hunt! Is she a sorceress or is she a genius? Is she another Lucrezia Borgia or another Joan of Arc? In a room in the Civic Center of this city, Miss Malloy is undergoing gruelling questioning at a closed hearing by a special investigating committee!

DISSOLVE

INT. COMMITTEE ROOM — DAY — MED. PANNING SHOT DOWN A LONG TABLE AT WHICH ARE SEATED A NUMBER OF IMPOSING INVESTIGATORS, ALL STARING WITH DRAMATIC INTENSITY O.S. TOWARD THE END OF THE TABLE. AT THE VERY END SITS MOLLY, A PERKY LITTLE HAT PERCHED DEFIANTLY ATOP HER HEAD. SHE FACES A BATTERY OF MICROPHONES AND LOOKS TINY AND LOST. ON HER LEFT SIT PROFESSOR MEYERDAL AND MR. DIETZ, PLAINLY MORE AT EASE NOW THAT THE AUTHORITIES ARE CARRYING THE BALL. DENNIS MALLOY SITS AT HER ELBOW, SUBDUED AND IMPRESSED BY THE SCENE. MEYERDAL IS SPEAKING TO THE COMMITTEE.

PROFESSOR: Eminent scientists from around the world have watched this woman cut her paper dolls and all agree the result is a scientific impossibility!

FULL SHOT — THE TABLE
ONE KINDLY LOOKING INVESTIGATOR ADDRESSES MEYERDAL.

INVESTIGATOR: Then what conclusion have you reached, Professor Meyerdal?

PROFESSOR: We have unanimously concluded that it is a trick . . . a sleight of hand feat.

INVESTIGATOR: And how does she do it?

PROFESSOR (SQUIRMING): She refuses to tell.

THE QUESTIONER TURNS A KINDLY EYE ON MOLLY.

INVESTIGATOR: Young lady, you've thrown this tired old world into quite an uproar, do you realize that?

MOLLY (SORROWFULLY): I'm that sorry about it, sir, I wish I'd never had a pair of scissors in my hand!

INVESTIGATOR (GENTLY): Would you be kind enough to tell me and these other gentlemen at the table just how you perform your magic trick?

MOLLY (SIGHS): I'm thinking of offering a reward to the one who can tell *me* how I do it!

INVESTIGATOR: I beg your pardon?

MOLLY (UNHAPPILY): It's not a trick, your honor, just a knack I have . . . a sort of gift, I suppose it is.

DENNIS (LOUDLY): Given to her by Danny McDuff, the leprechaun!

THE INVESTIGATOR IS TAKEN ABACK AND GLANCES AT HIS COLLEAGUES WHO ARE EQUALLY UNCERTAIN AS TO HOW TO PROCEED.

INVESTIGATOR (TO MEYERDAL): Do you have a suggestion as to how to resolve this dilemma, Professor?

PROFESSOR: We feel Miss Malloy is highly destructive to the cause of learning. Her views on education are strange to say the least, almost frightening. We suggest she be committed indefinitely for further observation.

MOLLY IS SHOCKED AND DENNIS LEAPS TO HIS FEET IN ANGER.

DENNIS (FURIOUSLY): Committed, is it! The man's gone daft just because there's somethin' in the world he hasn't an answer for! And never will have, I might add!

AN OFFICER HURRIES UP TO FORCIBLY SIT DENNIS DOWN IN HIS CHAIR. THE COMMITTEE LOOKS EXTREMELY ILL AT EASE.

INVESTIGATOR (TO MEYERDAL): I hardly see how we can commit the woman just because she cuts paper dolls. Besides, that won't explain the mystery of *how* she cuts them.

PROFESSOR: It will distract public attention and allow the whole thing to die quietly.

DENNIS (LEAPING UP ANGRILY): You're fools, the lot of you! Don't ye know the truth never dies quietly?

MOLLY PLACES A HAND GENTLY ON HIS ARM AND PULLS HIM BACK TO HIS CHAIR. DENNIS LOOKS AT HER SHEEPISHLY AND SHE SMILES.

MOLLY (SOFTLY): The time has come to make a complete confession, father.

INVESTIGATOR: About the dolls, Miss Malloy?

MOLLY FACES THE ARRAY OF MEN, BITES HER LIP THEN MAKES HER DECISION.

MOLLY: It might very well be that my trick *is* just sleight of hand.

PROFESSOR: I knew it! We'll inform the press immediately!

MOLLY (WARNINGLY): One moment, now. I only said it *might* be sleight of hand.

INVESTIGATOR (WARILY): What are you driving at, Miss?

MOLLY (TO PROFESSOR): I'll not say how I do it but I'll be willing to tell the world it's a trick. In return you must do me a favor of admitting here and now there's certain mysterious, wonderful things in the world that no man can explain.

PROFESSOR (EAGERLY): Yes, yes, certainly . . . I'll agree with that.

MOLLY (TO DIETZ): And I'll get my first grade back? And be allowed to instruct in my own manner?

PROFESSOR (IMPATIENTLY): He'll do it. Just make your statement to the press.

MOLLY (TO EVERYONE): You see, when you study him closely, the most brilliant man is only a child grown up. You wise men of learning comprehend things you can't see, like the tiny atom, and believe in things you can't comprehend, like infinity. Isn't that so?

PROFESSOR (UNEASILY): Yes, it's an amusing paradox.

MOLLY: Well, I believe in teaching children the same . . . teaching them how to believe in things they can't comprehend. (TWINKLING) Perhaps one of my students will become as wise as you, Professor.

PROFESSOR (MOVED): Let's hope they become as wise as their teacher.

MOLLY: Let's hope they're different than either of us. When everyone is more or less the same . . . all conforming, all agreeing . . . there's an end to progress. There must always be a new crop of dreamers and planners. They lift our sights and keep us from ever falling into the dreary and humdrum rut that dulls men's minds and crushes their souls.

INVESTIGATOR (MOVED): There's a good deal of magic about you, indeed, Miss Malloy.

MOLLY: About everyone, sir. Man has invented his own moons and satellites, but he can't invent a simple blade of grass. That takes a special magic . . . aye, a magic . . . the mystery of the secret forces in nature. (RISING — QUIETLY) Now I'll be giving my story to the papers.

THE MEN AT THE TABLE RISE OF ONE ACCORD, BEAMING HAPPILY AT THIS OUTCOME AND ALL DEEPLY MOVED.

DISSOLVE

INT. SCHOOL ROOM — DAY — FULL SHOT
ONCE MORE MOLLY IS BACK WITH HER CLASS, STANDING AT THE
FRONT OF THE ROOM FACING THE SEMI-CIRCLE OF PUPILS.
SHE IS SPINNING A STORY AS SHE CUTS PAPER DOLLS.

MOLLY (TO CHILDREN): Now, at one time wild ducks had made
such a shambles of Finn McCall's corn fields that the good
man shot one of the birds and ate it. The other ducks took
to the air and circled about, grieving and raising a terrible
noise.

THE DOOR QUIETLY OPENS AND MR. DIETZ AND THE PROFESSOR
STEAL INTO THE ROOM.

MOLLY (TO CHILDREN): Goll McNorma, a local magician, heard
the cries and straightaway put the dead and eaten duck back
together again, sending it into the air to rejoin its flock.

THE TWO MEN HAVE SMILED IN FRIENDLY FASHION AT MOLLY
BUT NOW FREEZE IN HORROR.

PROFESSOR: Miss Malloy!

STARTLED, MOLLY LOOKS UP. THE MEN HURRY TO HER AGI-
TATEDLY.

MOLLY (BRIGHTLY): The top of the morning to you, gentlemen!

DIETZ (POINTING IN HORROR TO DOLLS IN HER HAND): You
promised, Miss Malloy!

PROFESSOR: You even told the investigating committee you'd never
cut those dolls again!

MOLLY (REASSURINGLY): Tut, now, I gave my promise and that's
that. I said I'd not cut dolls with a big one in the middle again
and I'll not do it, you may be sure.

DIETZ (APPREHENSIVELY): You're positive?

MOLLY: You have my solemn oath, Mr. Dietz.

PROFESSOR (RELIEVED): Good. We'll be running along, then.
Keep up the good work, Miss Malloy.

MOLLY: Thank you, gentlemen. Good day to you.

THE MEN HEAD FOR THE DOOR AS MOLLY CONTINUES HER STORY
TO THE CHILDREN AND FINISHES CUTTING THE DOLLS.

MOLLY (TO CHILDREN): But alas, the magician had left out some
of the bones in the duck's legs, giving it a most strange manner
of walking.

TWO SHOT — PROFESSOR AND DIETZ AS THEY HEAD FOR THE
DOOR.

MOLLY'S VOICE: All the other ducks being very sympathetic imitated his walk to save him embarrassment . . . which is why to this very day all ducks waddle!

AT THE DOOR THEY HAVE STOPPED TO LOOK BACK AT MOLLY. THEIR EYES BUG IN HORROR AT WHAT THEY SEE.

CLOSE SHOT — MOLLY

SHE HAS COMPLETED THE DOLLS AND UNFOLDED THEM, HOLDING THEM UP FOR THE CHILDREN. SHE HAS KEPT HER PROMISE. THERE IS NOT A LARGE DOLL IN THE CENTER. NOW THERE IS A VERY TINY ONE IN THE MIDDLE! MOLLY SMILES TENDERLY AT THE CHILDREN AS WE:

FADE OUT.

SCRIPT ANALYSIS

"The Glorious Gift of Molly Malloy" is a charming fantasy and yet it has more than charm for beneath its delightful Irish humor lies a meaningful philosophy: conformity stifles imagination and the stifling of imagination in turn halts progress. Jameson Brewer wrote a very entertaining play but he also had something to say. This is an ideal combination and places the play far above the average half-hour TV drama.

In examining what we may term the physical structure of the play, we find that there is a good deal of fluid movement which filming permits. Nine sets are used including several exteriors. Two of the exteriors, the Elementary School and the Civic Center, are noted as Stock shots which means they are readily available from a film library.

Act I

We meet the protagonist of the play, Molly Malloy, immediately. The setting of the schoolroom also serves as exposition, both of locale and of Molly's occupation. And it only takes a few lines of dialogue for us to discover that she is a proud daughter of Erin with the Irish gift for storytelling. The children's rapt attention tells us that she enjoys their confidence.

When Mr. Dietz enters, he is identified for us simply and naturally with Molly announcing to the children: "Our principal, Mr. Dietz, has favored us with a visit this fine morning!" We also receive an immediate insight into the principal's character from the reaction of the children. Their faces fall "and the room freezes noticeably." Evidently, Mr. Dietz is not a warm, likeable soul!

Conflict arises quickly. Molly and the principal are in complete disagreement on teaching methods and this conflict leads to a swift crisis. Dietz gives Molly twenty-four hours to conform. Since we have been as enchanted with Molly's story as her pupils, there is no question where our sympathies lie.

The next scene is a residential street, and we see Molly walking along dressed in "bright attire," etc. Since this is a filmed play, no cover scene is necessary and we may call for a dissolve from one scene to another with the same character immediately in view, even if a change of costume is necessary. This is because the scenes are shot separately. The action, that of a "decrepit old car weaving wildly toward the house" is also indicative of the advantage of film in respect to movement.

The moment we meet Dennis Malloy and hear his first lines of dialogue, we are aware of Molly's heritage. Dennis is not a man to take his leprechauns lightly. The dialogue between Molly and her father is replete with exposition and characterization. We learn that Dennis is jobless, that he is not eager to work, that he is a nonconformist, that he possesses a fine sense of humor. His daughter's affection for him empathically induces our own affection. Their philosophies are identical: childhood is a time for dreaming.

We note, too, the savor of the Irish in the dialogue yet it is not smothered in dialect. There are phrases that flavor: "Molly, colleen! . . . ," "the dear gossoons and girleens. . . ."

With the entrance of Professor Meyerdal, there is a buildup of both humor and suspense. (Remember that there has been a foreshadowing of the Professor's appearance when Dietz questioned Molly as to whether she were following Meyerdal's curriculum. In other words, the Professor's name was not thrown idly into the dialogue. All dialogue must have a purpose in your play.) And so we look forward now with great anticipation to the meeting between Meyerdal and Molly Malloy. But the turn of events is totally unexpected, as we view the symbolic incident of the paper dolls. This is the element of surprise, an instance of the writer's imagination at its peak. The humor is heightened by the comparison of this incident by Meyerdal and Dietz, with the great scientific discoveries such as the demonstration of nuclear fission.

We are now approaching the first act curtain and the attendant crisis is underscored by the Professor's momentous observation: "Miss Malloy, what you've just done can't possibly be done!"

Technically, the curtain is indicated by a FADE OUT. Filmed half-hour plays seldom use fade outs to black except for the end of an act. Movies, as you are probably aware, do not utilize the dark screen effect for passage of time or any other transitions. Since filmed TV dramas are a form of screenplay, the technique in writing for TV film is closely allied to that of the cinema.

Act II

Correlatively, FADE IN is indicated for the opening of the second act. Here, in this opening scene, props are used to good advantage adding greatly to the imaginative humor of the situation. The writer keeps his play in the comedy vein, avoiding outright farce by stressing that the lab be authentic in every respect and not "a Frankenstein nightmare." The situations are comical enough and any burlesque would prove detrimental to the structure of the play. It would destroy the illusion and break the thread upon which the "suspension of disbelief" hangs.

Molly Malloy, as we have come to know her, is honest, forthright and gifted with a wonderful imagination. She believes there are things in this world beyond man's earthly reasoning and so she accepts the phenomenon of the dolls. Her attitude presents a strong contrast to Professors Meyerdal and Harnish whose scientific training does not permit them to accept any phenomenon which does not adhere to the laws of science.

As Molly realizes the impact of her "strange talent," she becomes aware of her own power and "impishly" paints its potentialities to the worried professors. This is all in keeping with her own whimsical imagination and innate humor. When she says "I may be asking a few favors on your part" for keeping quiet about her "impossible" accomplishments, it is not to take advantage, in the derogatory connotation of the word; as we learn later, the favors she desires are all for a good cause.

Molly's closing lines of dialogue in this scene, referring to her father ("... it's almost impossible to stop an Irishman from talking") prepare us for the events of the next scene in which we find Dennis Malloy in his element. The confidant of leprechauns is naturally enough a master of the blarney and again we can understand why the routine workaday world is not for such as Dennis Malloy.

Both the Dennis Malloy "barker" sequence and the commentary of the news analyst, Milton Holmes, serve to move the play by showing the widespread interest Molly Malloy has aroused. It is this public interest and the clamor of the press which leads the distraught scientists to attempt to divert attention from their own inability to explain the phenomenon. They accuse Molly of being the possessor of dangerous gifts. This aspect of the play is allegorical in nature. The analyst's comments may be satiric . . . "Is she a sorceress or is she a genius?" . . . but the thoughtful viewer will recognize the incident as having had many a serious counterpart in history.

We find that the investigating committee acts in a sane and kindly manner toward Molly. This adds balance and pacing to the drama. If the investigating committee were pictured as distraught as the scientists, the play would run on one high-pitched level and would lack contrast, much in the manner of a musical composition played entirely fortissimo.

The stature of Molly is increased in our eyes by the decision which she makes. Although the decision is contrary to her own principles, she feels it will be for the greater good. She lies . . . "It might very well be that my trick is just sleight of hand." She has eased the untenable position of the scientists and the committee. Furthermore, she will be permitted to teach as she believes. To that end, she has made a sacrifice. This is an illustration of one of the basic elements of conflict: man against his conscience.

It is also in the above scene that the philosophy of the play is so succinctly stated by Molly Malloy: "When everyone is more or less the same . . . all conforming, all agreeing . . . there's an end to progress."

Now the play has come full round. It opened on the classroom scene where the conflict began. We have seen the resolution of the conflict as Molly Malloy has won her battle . . . fully . . . for the magic is still within her. And as comedy should, "The Glorious Gift of Molly Malloy" leaves us with the warmth of an appreciative smile.

The hour and
the 90-minute
drama

15

Much of the credit for some of the peaks the hour television drama has reached belongs to Fred Coe, who for several years produced the Sunday night "Television Playhouse." Under his guidance and inspiration many of our top-flight video dramatists were developed and had an opportunity for truly creative work. To Coe, the writer was of prime importance, the creator of dramas of literary merit, not merely vehicles for stars. Although, at this writing, the "Television Playhouse" appears to have seen its last season, the hour video drama has become a mainstay of the networks. The Kraft TV Theatre is a veteran of more than a decade, presenting hour dramas fifty-two weeks a year and its recent offering of a $50,000 award for the best play produced on the series during the span of a year is a golden boon for the TV dramatist. The purpose of the award is, of course, to attract the finest writers to the program. "Studio One" has been in the forefront in the presentation of some very excellent hour plays. And some very fine dramatic and suspenseful writing has been done for such programs as "Climax!",

"Kaiser Aluminum Hour," "United States Steel Hour," "Wire Service," etc. Hour-long dramatic series have come and gone, for the television program structure is in a constant state of flux.

There have been two bold ventures in the realm of drama: NBC's "Matinee Theater," a daily series of hour-long dramas, and CBS's "Playhouse 90," a weekly series of hour and a half productions. The number of scripts consumed by "Matinee Theater" is phenomenal. Its producer, Albert McCleery, runs what critic John Crosby has termed "the greatest show business factory in the world." McCleery won his fame back in 1952 when he directed the "Cameo Theater" and introduced experimental techniques to television. His use of "cameo" technique — that is, the production of plays without the use of full sets or expensive backdrops — cut the costs of TV drama considerably. This technique permits little or no use of the long shot and most camera actions are close-ups or medium close-ups. Full advantage is also taken of TV's fluid movement from scene to scene. McCleery utilized this technique when he was producing the "Hallmark Hall of Fame" series and now employs it for his "Matinee Theater" productions. Since "Matinee Theater" runs on a limited budget, sometimes producing five shows each week at the cost of one night-time hour drama, the "cameo" technique appears to be perfectly devised for the series.

Before the advent of "Playhouse 90," most hour and a half productions on TV were in the nature of so-called "spectaculars," presented on a once a month basis, such as "Producer's Showcase," or an even less frequent basis. The "spectaculars" are still with us and they include musical comedies, variety shows and dramas. However, "Playhouse 90" was the first program to present hour and a half dramas on a regular weekly basis. The success of the CBS series will undoubtedly inspire other hour and a half weekly dramatic shows.

Both the hour and the 90-minute programs offer the TV dramatist wider scope for, freed from the time limitations of the half-hour drama, the playwright actually has a "first act" to work with. He also has more time for plot and character development, more opportunities for heightening conflict. He may even permit himself the luxury of a subplot.

In most instances, the hour drama is presented in three acts, although one of the hour series, for a time, used a two-act format. In the hour play, therefore, the video dramatist plans in terms akin to the theater playwright, at least insofar as having first, second and third act curtains. However, there is still a wide divergence in time. The theater play may run two to two and a half hours; the hour TV drama from 48 to 50 minutes; the hour and a half drama from 68 to 70 minutes.

The craftsmanship of the TV dramatist becomes apparent in his ability to cope with the requirements of the medium. Each of his three acts for the hour play vary in length from 15 to 17 minutes, approximately. A crisis must occur at the end of Act One and Act Two, and there must be a climax and final resolution in Act Three.

The weekly hour and a half drama, as exemplified by "Playhouse 90," has about five curtains, that is, there are five interruptions for the commercials. The expense of these weekly productions has forced the network to sell portions of the time to several different sponsors. We have mentioned previously that the astronomical costs of full-scale TV productions necessitated dual sponsorship of programs so that the Kraft Theatre with its single sponsor is more the exception than the rule. Therefore the 90-minute drama has to be written with these commercial breaks in mind. Bill Barton, columnist of Radio-Television Daily, averred that the "success of 'Playhouse 90' was due in part to the care in selecting good breaks in the strong story lines for the 'money' interruptions."

There was some conjecture when "Playhouse 90" began its series as to whether or not the many interruptions would prove fatal. The danger of too many "curtains" is that the audience may become restless and that the mood of the play is constantly disrupted. However, the fact is that "Playhouse 90" has proved highly successful in holding a large audience, despite protests against the frequent commercials. Exceptionally well written plays such as Rod Serling's "Requiem for a Heavyweight" and Tad Mosel's "If You Knew Elizabeth" are the reason for the success of the hour and a half series.

These two innovations, "Matinee Theater" and "Playhouse 90," point up the fact that the writer who wishes to make a career of writing television drama must be aware of TV's changing needs. The writer finds that he must be not only a doer but a watcher. He must be aware of the special requirements of many television programs. "Matinee Theater," for example, prefers that casts be limited, preferably to about eight. The "cameo" technique permits rare use of crowd scenes. As the writer studies the current crop of hour dramas appearing on his TV screen, he will discover the types of plays each series prefers.

Right now, we believe it will serve a very practical purpose for the writer to study the hour TV play we have included in this text. *The script of "Anna Santonello" is reproduced as below for study purposes. (For actual typing format see Chapter 5.)*

"ANNA SANTONELLO"

"Anna Santonello" was written by Bob Crean and presented on the Kraft TV Theatre. It is the story of an Italian-American family and the title role was played by one of television's finest actresses, Eileen Heckart. If you were fortunate enough to have seen this play, you will not have forgotten her performance.

Jack Gould of the New York *Times,* in reviewing the play, called it a "poignant and sensitive study," a story written "with grace, understanding and an economy of words that aided its gentle emotional strength." *Variety's* reviewer was of the opinion that author Crean's "capacity to conquer a mood with his simple dialogue and vibrant characterizations of a people and their way of life certainly holds forth promise of an exciting addition to the ranks of topflight video dramatists."

Here is the play.

CAST

ANNA SANTONELLO (About 28)
HER BROTHERS:
    THE ELDEST (35)
    THE MIDDLE (32)
    THE YOUNGEST (26)
THE PRIEST (About 60)
JOHN KELLY (A plumber — about 30)
TERESA (An upstairs neighbor — about 26)
PHILIP POLETTI (A grocer — about 38)
MAMA POLETTI (About 60)
JERRY (A plumber's assistant) (Bit)
MOOSE (A bartender) (Bit)

SETTINGS — 4

INTERIORS:

Unit — The Santonello kitchen, bedroom and laundry room.
The bar at the Crescent Moon, a neighborhood cafe.

EXTERIORS:

The vegetable stands before Poletti's grocery.
An outdoor shrine.

(See text for descriptions and special requirements of settings.)

KRAFT TELEVISION THEATRE

FULL SCREEN HEXAGONAL "K"

ANNOUNCER: The Kraft Television Theatre comes to you LIVE
from New York. The play is performed at the moment you see
it . . . living theatre for your best television entertainment.

PAUSE — MUSIC — THEME — THE KRAFT TELEVISION THEATRE
SYMBOL DOLLIES INTO CENTER OF SCREEN AND TURNS. MODEL
CAMERA NEVER STOPS FACING FORWARD BUT ALWAYS TURNS SO
WE CAN SEE THE LETTER "K" ON THE SIDE.

ANNOUNCER: Good evening. This is Charles Stark speaking for the
Kraft Foods Company makers of the world's favorite cheese
— who bring you each week all year long, a fine play with a
fine cast on . . .

DISSOLVE TO FILM:

KRAFT
TELEVISION
THEATRE

ANNOUNCER: The Kraft Television Theatre.

DISSOLVE TO FILM

SUPER TITLE

"ANNA SANTONELLO" by Bob Crean.

"ANNA SANTONELLO"

ACT ONE

OPENING SHOT:

ANNA SANTONELLO AT WORK IN HER KITCHEN ON A HOT JUNE AFT-
ERNOON. THE SANTONELLO HOUSE, IN AN ITALIAN COMMU-
NITY OF A SMALL CITY, IS OLD. YET, ANNA'S KITCHEN
BOASTS GLEAMING APPLIANCES — A FINE SINK, STOVE,

REFRIGERATOR. THE KITCHEN HAS BEEN "MODERNIZED."
FORMICA SURFACES SHINE ATOP OLD WOODEN COUNTERS:
NEW CABINETS HANG ALONG THE WALLS.
BUT THE KITCHEN IS LARGE, AND ANNA'S MODERN UNITS FILL
ONLY ONE END. IN CONTRAST, THERE IS A LARGE OLD
TABLE WITH FOUR MATCHING CHAIRS, PLUS AN EASY CHAIR
IN THE CONSPICUOUS "HEAD-OF-THE-TABLE" POSITION. THE
EASY CHAIR IS OLD AND WORN, ALMOST MOLDED TO THE
SHAPE OF A STOOPED OLD MAN.
THREE DOORS OPEN OFF THE KITCHEN. A SWINGING DOOR
LEADS TO A DINING ROOM (WHICH THE CAMERA DOES NOT
ENTER). ANOTHER DOOR LEADS DIRECTLY OFF THE
KITCHEN INTO THE BEDROOM OF ANNA'S BROTHERS. A
THIRD DOOR LEADS TO AN ENTRYWAY WHICH HAS BEEN
CONVERTED TO A LAUNDRY ROOM. FROM THE ENTRYWAY
WE LOOK THROUGH A SCREEN DOOR DOWN A SMALL PATH
ROOFED WITH GRAPE VINES TO A CEMENT ALLEY.
THOUGH THE HOUSE IS NOW IN MOURNING, THIS ATMOSPHERE
HAS NOT INVADED THE KITCHEN. THE AFTERNOON SUN
SHINES BRIGHTLY THROUGH THE WINDOWS. BUT ANNA
MUST GRADUALLY REVEAL TO US THAT SHE IS TAUT WITH
MOURNING: THAT BENEATH HER FULL APRON IS A BLACK
DRESS. ANNA, HER FACE DRAWN, IS WORKING INDECI-
SIVELY BETWEEN STOVE AND SINK. THE BACK DOORBELL
RINGS — TWO LOUD BLASTS ON AN EXCEPTIONALLY JAR-
RING BELL. ANNA STARTS, HER WHOLE BODY TREMBLING,
HER HANDS FLYING TO HER FACE.
SHE HURRIES THROUGH THE LAUNDRY ROOM WITH ITS AUTO-
MATIC WASHER AND DRYER.
STANDING OUTSIDE THE SCREEN DOOR IS A BIG MAN IN WHITE
OVERALLS. HE WEARS NO UNDERSHIRT AND THE WHITE
STRAPS CROSS HIS BROWN SHOULDERS. HIS FACE IS BIG
WITH LARGE HONEST FEATURES. ON HIS MASS OF DARK
HAIR IS A WHITE CAP BEARING THE WORDS "MCAVOY
PLUMBING." HIS NAME IS JOHN KELLY.
KELLY: You got a clothes dryer needs connecting?
ANNA: Yes. My new dryer.
KELLY (ENTERING): Where's it at?
ANNA: You going to hook it up now?
KELLY SETS DOWN HIS TOOLS, CONSULTS PAD.

KELLY: I got it on my schedule sheet, lady. Thursday. Four P.M. It's four P.M.

ANNA: Will you mind not to hook it up today?

KELLY (STUDYING DRYER): Make your mind up. It's your machine.

ANNA: I dunno.

KELLY: Make your mind up yes or no. I got no time for any debating society.

ANNA STARES, NUMBED BY THIS PRESSURE. KELLY TURNS AND LOOKS AT HER. WE MUST SEE THE IMPACT OF THEIR MEETING — ANNA OVERWHELMED BY THE POWER OF THIS MAN; KELLY RECOGNIZING ANNA'S FEMININE RECEPTIVITY TO THIS POWER.

KELLY: Lady! Yes or no? No? Yes? *Yes?*

ANNA (SHATTERED): Yes, I guess. I dunno! SHE CLAMPS HER HANDS OVER HER FACE AND RUNS FROM THE ROOM.

CU:
KELLY'S FACE — INTERESTED, CONFUSED

CUT TO:
KITCHEN. ANNA RUSHES ACROSS KITCHEN INTO THE BEDROOM OF HER THREE BROTHERS. AS SHE SHUTS THE BEDROOM DOOR, HER "MIDDLE" BROTHER ENTERS THE KITCHEN ANGRILY FROM THE DINING ROOM.

MIDDLE: Hey what's with the doorbell ringing? You shoulda stuffed that up with cotton.

NOT FINDING ANNA, HE STOPS IN THE CENTER OF THE KITCHEN. THE MIDDLE BROTHER IS ABOUT 32 AND IS LEAN AND WIRY. HE IS THE MOST ALERT OF THE THREE BROTHERS AND, LIKE THE OTHERS, HE IS GRUFF, HANDSOME, AND WELL BUILT. HE WEARS A BLACK SUIT AWKWARDLY, HIS WRISTS JUTTING FROM THE CUFFS, HIS NECK IRRITATED BY THE STIFF COLLAR.

FROM THE LAUNDRY ROOM COMES THE RATTLE OF KELLY UNPACKING HIS TOOLS.

MIDDLE (TO KELLY): Hey . . Wha' you think you're doing!

KELLY: Connecting the dryer.

MIDDLE (ENTERING LAUNDRY): We don't want nothing fixed up today. Take your stuff out of here.

KELLY (STILL WORKING): If I don't get it today, buddy, I don't get back around for two weeks.

MIDDLE: I told you get out of here!

KELLY: Look! The lady told me to go head. This is the time she re-quisitioned on the schedule.

MIDDLE: I don't care what she said.

KELLY CONSULTS A BIG TURNIP WATCH FROM A "VEST" POCKET.

KELLY: It's four P.M. I'm always on the schedule. Two minutes after.

MIDDLE: I told you! Out!

WITH A VICIOUS SWEEP OF HIS FOOT, HE SENDS KELLY'S TOOL BOX ACROSS THE FLOOR. IT HITS THE SCREEN DOOR, TOOLS TUMBLING OUTSIDE.

KELLY'S BIG FISTS RISE INTO FIGHT POSITION.

KELLY: Hey!

THE BROTHER GRABS KELLY BY THE VEST OF HIS OVERALLS, PUSHING HIM BACK TOWARDS THE DOOR.

MIDDLE: I told you get out of here!!

KELLY: Keep ya hands off!

MIDDLE (WITH TWO SHOVES): Get out! Get out!

KELLY BANGS AGAINST THE DOORJAMB. HE JERKS HIS HEAD AND WITH ONE QUICK SWIPE HE BRUSHES OFF THE BROTHER'S HANDS FROM THEIR GRIP. THEN, WITH A DEEP ANIMAL GRUNT, HE SWINGS POWERFULLY, SLAMMING THE BROTHER'S SHOULDER WITH HIS BROAD PALM.

THE BROTHER IS HURLED ACROSS THE ROOM, THUDDING AGAINST THE CLOTHES DRYER. HE IS THROWN BACK OVER IT, HIS BACK PROSTRATE AGAINST IT.

KELLY APPROACHES SLOWLY, HIS FISTS WEAVING. THE BROTHER MASSAGES HIS SHOULDER, PANTING, GLARING UP AT KELLY IN ANGRY FEAR. HE MAKES NO MOVE AND KELLY STOPS BEFORE HIM, HIS FISTS STILL READY.

MIDDLE (HUSKILY): Listen . . . We got a *death* in this house.

KELLY (IMPRESSED): A death . . . ? You coulda told somebody.

KELLY SAGS, ANGRY YET SHEEPISH WITH GUILT.

KELLY (CONT'D): The — the girl didn't say anything.

KELLY TURNS TO HIS TOOLS, RETRIEVING THEM, READY TO LEAVE. THIS IS AS GOOD AS A VICTORY TO THE BROTHER. HE STANDS ERECT, STILL MASSAGING HIS SHOULDER, AND FROWNING DOWN UPON KELLY HE COMMANDS.

MIDDLE: Fix the machine! Fix it! Then get out!

THE BROTHER LEAVES THE ROOM QUICKLY. HE CROSSES

KITCHEN, BREATHING HEAVILY, MASSAGING HIS SHOULDER, ON THE VERGE OF SOBBING. HE PUSHES OPEN THE BEDROOM DOOR AND ENTERS.

CUT TO:

THE BROTHER'S BEDROOM CONTAINING TWO DOUBLE BEDS AND A SINGLE. THE WINDOWS ARE SHADOWED BY THE WALL OF THE HOUSE NEXT DOOR AND THE ROOM IS DIM. ANNA STANDS AT THE WINDOWS, CLUTCHING THE LACE CURTAINS, AND LOOKING OUT AT A TREE WHICH GROWS IN THE FEW FEET BETWEEN THE TWO BUILDINGS.

THE MIDDLE BROTHER, ENTERING, IS SURPRISED BY HER PRESENCE.

MIDDLE: Anna.

ANNA: You scared me.

MIDDLE: You shouldn't of let that guy fix the dryer.

ANNA SAYS NOTHING. SHE REMAINS AT THE WINDOW, STARING OUT. THE BROTHER SITS ON A BED, RUBBING HIS SHOULDER.

MIDDLE: That's a wise guy out there. (NO ANSWER) HE RUBS SOME MORE, LOOKS UP. What's the matter with you? Why are ya in here?

ANNA SEEMS HUDDLED AT THE WINDOW AND THE BROTHER WAXES SYMPATHETIC.

You crying?

ANNA: No. I don't feel like crying.

MIDDLE: Not for the old man?

ANNA: Who's got to cry for Papa. Papa's got perpetual light shining on him.

MIDDLE: Got what?

ANNA: You know the prayer — May he rest in peace; and let perpetual light shine upon him.

THE BROTHER BREAKS DOWN WITH HOARSE SOBS. ANNA REMAINS STARING OUT THE WINDOW. THE BROTHER STRUGGLES FOR CONTROL, WIPING HIS EYES ON THE BEDCLOTHES.

MIDDLE: I'm sorry. I'm sorry. You shouldn't of said the prayer, that's all. Agh — if the old man seen me!

ANNA (FLATLY): His big strong son.

MIDDLE: Papa should have some tears!

ANNA: Don't you worry about the tears. Tonight the old women will come. Oh, they'll cry all right. They will be crying and crying and crying for Papa. Like they're all his *wives* or something. Even the ones that hardly know him. Papa will have tears all right.

MIDDLE: But not from his own daughter?

ANNA (HER THROAT TIGHT): I don't have no tears. Didn't you know that? I never got so fat and full of tears like them other women. I only dried up like. (HER VOICE RAW WITH SORROW) And I miss Papa — but I couldn't cry for the life of me.

MIDDLE: What's all this talking with you all of a sudden! (ANNA LOOKS AT HIM, BEGGING FOR UNDERSTANDING) Anna, what's the matter at you?

ANNA: I don't know. I'm mixed up.

MIDDLE: You better stop talking so crazy.

ANNA GOES TO DOOR.

MIDDLE: You understand! You better start acting right!

ANNA (QUIETLY): Who you telling. Who you telling to act right, hah? The big man. Bawling like a baby. The big strong son!

MIDDLE: Shut up!

ANNA EXITS.

CUT TO:

KITCHEN WHERE KELLY THE PLUMBER STANDS, HAT IN HAND, AT THE DOOR TO THE LAUNDRY ROOM.

ANNA SEES HIM AS SHE LEAVES THE BEDROOM. SHE CATCHES HER BREATH, THEN SHUTS THE BEDROOM DOOR QUIETLY BEHIND HER.

KELLY: I'm — I'm sorry for your troubles.

ANNA (QUIETLY): Thank you.

KELLY: The guy told me. You got a death in the house.

ANNA: My father.

KELLY: I'm sorry.

ANNA: He was eighty-two.

KELLY: It's okay to use the machine. The installation is completed.

ANNA: Thank you.

KELLY: I'll come back next week if you want and show you the operation.

ANNA: Now's as good a time.

THEY ENTER LAUNDRY ROOM

KELLY: You see, it's very simple. You set it here. For wool and cotton. For knits. For delicate fabrics. Like your underwear, you know?

HE THROWS A GLANCE WITH ANNA. ANNA BATS HER EYES AND FOLDS HER ARMS ACROSS HER BREAST IN AN UNCONSCIOUS GESTURE OF MODESTY.

KELLY: Yeh. You put your load in. It's better if you shake the clothes out first. The timing you set here. The timing is different for how much weight you put in. Here's a book tells you all about it.

ANNA: It sounds hard.

KELLY: It's easy once you get used to it.

ANNA: I didn't want the dryer. My brothers wanted I should have it.

KELLY: One of your brothers must be smart. It's a good machine.

ANNA: I suppose.

KELLY: How many brothers you got?

ANNA: Three.

KELLY: I guess that one was mad with me, huh?

ANNA: He didn't say he was.

KELLY: Would you sign this here?

ANNA SIGNS ORDER FORM. THEN KELLY STUDIES THE SIGNATURE.

ANNA: Anna. Anna Santonello.

KELLY: Santa — ?

ANNA (IN ROLLING ITALIAN): Santonello. (SHE SPELLS IT OUT) S-a-n-t-o-n-e-l-l-o.

KELLY: Thanks, Miss Santanelli. (AT DOOR) And, like I said, I'm sorry for your troubles. If I'd of known —

ANNA: It's all right.

KELLY (THROUGH SCREEN DOOR): You shouldn't have no trouble with it. If you do — my name's on the tag.

HE TURNS TO GO AND COLLIDES WITH TERESA WHO IS DESCENDING FROM A STAIRWAY THAT OPENS INTO THE ENTRYWAY. SHE IS CARRYING A CAKE. THEY DO NOT SPEAK. KELLY MOVES TO DOOR. TERESA GIVES KELLY THE ONCE OVER.

KELLY (TO ANNA): So long.

HE EXITS. WE SEE HIM GO DOWN PATH AND ANNA WATCHES HIM BLANKLY AS TERESA SPEAKS.

TERESA: Hi. I brought you down a cake.

ANNA: You didn't need to. Oh Teresa — you didn't need to do that.

THEY ENTER KITCHEN

TERESA: How good it is — there's no guarantee.

ANNA: Everybody is been sending stuff over. Cakes, pies, meat loaf. Chicken.

TERESA (GLANCING TO STOVE): So you're still cooking!

ANNA: What else I should do beside cooking? Anyway — my brothers don't like the sweets.

TERESA: A meat loaf is sweet?

ANNA: Well, you know, they like their dishes special ways prepared and —

TERESA: Anna, you sit down for a cup of coffee!

ANNA (SITTING): I should finish up and be going in there.

TERESA (HEATING COFFEE): There's none of the women arrived yet. I been looking out the upstairs window. — Where's your cups? — You should go in there and sit with all the old men?

ANNA: I should stand up next to my brothers.

TERESA: You sit down at the table. We'll have a cup. I got a couple of minutes while the baby's asleep.

ANNA (JUMPING UP): Do I owe you a jar of baby food?

TERESA: Forget it. Sit.

ANNA: At least I won't be borrowing your baby food no more when I run out. Nobody in the house except Papa eats baby food.

TERESA (BRINGING COFFEE): Here. Sit.

ANNA SITS AT ONE END OF THE TABLE. SHE STIRS HER COFFEE IDLY, STARING AT THE ARM CHAIR AT THE TABLE'S OTHER END.

ANNA (MUSING): Just like a baby . . .

TERESA: Humn?

ANNA: I was remembering . . . how Papa couldn't eat so well. He wasn't so — *neat!* You know? I had to spoon feed him. Just like a baby. And one time, it was before you moved in upstairs — I'll never forget him — I sewed him up a kind of bib, you know? To save on ironing the shirts. Oh, you should have seen him! He couldn't talk, you know, but his eyes — them black eyes — just looked at me. If looks could kill! So he hammers on the table with his spoon and one of the boys come in and took the bib off him. Oh he was mad with me! For two days he wouldn't eat. Umhumn . . .

SHE IS EMOTIONALLY SHATTERED BUT SHE DOES NOT WEEP
You know, I sit here, and I almost can see him sitting in that chair. You know . . . I'm going to miss Papa.

TERESA: You know who's going to miss him? The baby. Did she like your father! And he liked her!

ANNA: They was two of a kind.

ANNA RISES

TERESA: Sit down, finish your coffee.

ANNA SITS
You got to stop working at a time like this. Everybody is going to help out.

ANNA'S ELDEST BROTHER ENTERS FROM THE DINING ROOM THROUGH THE SWINGING DOOR. HE IS ABOUT 35, A GRIM WORK-HARDENED MAN BUT LIKE THIS OTHER BROTHER HE HAS HANDSOME ITALIAN FEATURES AND A RUGGED PHYSIQUE. UNCOMFORTABLE IN HIS BLACK SUIT, HE CARRIES A DELICATE ORNAMENTED DISH IN HIS FIST.

ELDEST (GRUFFLY): Give some more biscotti.

ANNA HURRIES, FILLING THE DISH FROM A LARGE TIN OF PASTRIES. THE ELDEST GETS TWO BOTTLES OF WINE FROM A CABINET. WITH SURE STRENGTH, HE PULLS THE CORKS. THE WOMEN ARE SILENT. THEN:

TERESA (RISING): Mister Santonello. I want to tell you: I'm sorry for your trouble.

WITH A GRAVE SWEEP OF HIS HAND HE BRUSHES ASIDE ANY ANSWER.
Well, I guess I better be getting back upstairs, huh? (AT DOOR) Yell up if you want anything.

ANNA: Thank you, Teresa.

TERESA EXITS.

ANNA GIVES HER BROTHER THE REFILLED DISH.

ELDEST (STUDYING HER): You better get dressed up.

ANNA: Under my apron I'm dressed up.

SHE SHOWS HER BLACK DRESS. THE BROTHER GRUNTS AND EXITS. THE DOOR SWINGS TO.

ANNA (RUSHING TO DOOR): What you want for supper?

THERE IS NO ANSWER.

ANNA IS RELIEVED TO BE ALONE. SHE MAKES WORK FOR HERSELF IN THE KITCHEN, PUTTERING AT THE STOVE. UNCONSCIOUSLY SHE STARTS TO HUM. CROSSING TO THE

CUPBOARD SHE TAKES DOWN A JAR OF BABY FOOD. STILL HUMMING, SHE STARTS TO PRY THE TOP OFF.

THE MIDDLE BROTHER ENTERS THE KITCHEN FROM THE BEDROOM. HE IS SOUR AND DOES NOT LOOK IN HER DIRECTION UNTIL HE HEARS THE HUMMING. THEN HE GLARES AT HER.

MIDDLE: Anna!

SHE STOPS HUMMING. HIS LOOK SEARS HER. HE EXITS INTO DINING ROOM. ANNA LOOKS AT THE BABY FOOD JAR IN HER HAND. THEN SHE LOOKS AT THE ARMCHAIR. IT IS EMPTY. SHE STANDS AND WONDERS.

THE PRIEST ENTERS FROM THE DINING ROOM. HE IS OLD AND HIS ROUND FACE HAS A CLARITY OF SPIRIT. BUT HE IS A MAN OF ROUGH MANNERISMS, HIS VOICE LOW AND GRAVELLY.

PRIEST: Anna . . .

ANNA: Father. I didn't know you was here.

PRIEST: How are you, Anna?

ANNA: Fine, Father. You'll have some wine, Father?

PRIEST RAISES HIS HAND, SHOWS A SMALL WINE GLASS.

PRIEST (SOLEMNLY): Anna, what's this I'm hearing about you.

ANNA (BEWILDERED): Me, Father?

PRIEST: Anna. You are always close to the Church, eh? Daily Masses, evening devotions, the Altar Society. You are a good girl, Anna.

ANNA: Not so good, Father.

PRIEST: But you have the — the spiritual understanding about your Papa. Do you?

ANNA: Yes, Father. I know Papa is in heaven.

PRIEST: Anna — your brothers are very upset.

ANNA (UNDERSTANDING NOW): Oh . . .

ANNA GIVES NO DEFENSE AGAINST HER BROTHERS' COMPLAINTS.

PRIEST: This is a bad time. For everyone, eh?

ANNA: Yes, Father.

PRIEST: But you, Anna, you have the spiritual strength to help your brothers now. They don't come to the church so often. They limp a little, eh?

ANNA: I'll try, Father.

PRIEST: Anna — is there anything you want to talk out?

ANNA: Nothing, Father.

PRIEST: You got my help if you need it.

ANNA: I'm nervous, you know? And tired out from the heat. That's all.

PRIEST: You have some wine yourself.

ANNA: No thank you, Father.

PRIEST: Drink up. For helping the nerves.

HE HANDS HER HIS OWN GLASS. ANNA OBEDIENTLY TAKES A SMALL SIP.

PRIEST: I'm going to lead the Rosary now. You will be in?

ANNA: Yes, Father.

THE PRIEST EXITS INTO DINING ROOM.

ANNA PUTS DOWN THE WINE UNFINISHED. SHE SCURRIES AROUND THE KITCHEN MAKING WORK FOR HERSELF. FROM THE FRONT ROOMS COMES THE DEEP MALE CHANT OF THE ROSARY. ANNA REACHES INTO HER APRON POCKET. SHE TAKES OUT HER BEADS AND AS SHE WORKS SHE JOINS IN THE PRAYERS. WE HEAR ONLY HER SIBILANT WHISPER AGAINST THE CHANT OF THE MEN. (THE PRAYER IS THE APOSTLES' CREED, "I believe in God, the Father Almighty," etc.)

THE DINING ROOM DOOR OPENS. ANNA'S YOUNGEST BROTHER STICKS HIS HEAD IN THE DOOR. HE IS ABOUT 28 WITH THE INNOCENT FACE OF A PLUCKY YOUNG PRIZE FIGHTER. HE FROWNS AT ANNA, PULLS HIS HEAD TOWARD THE FRONT ROOMS. ANNA QUICKLY PUTS HER WORK DOWN. THE BROTHER PULLS HIS HEAD BACK AGAIN. ANNA TAKES OFF HER APRON. THE BROTHER EXITS. ANNA SMOOTHS HER HAIR AND HER DRESS. SHE GRIPS THE ROSARY IN HER HAND AND EXITS.

FADE OUT.

BLACK SCREEN SIGNIFYING PASSAGE OF TIME. THEN ON FADE-IN WE HEAR WHISTLING. THE TUNE: "O Caterina."

FADE IN:

THE LAUNDRY ROOM WHERE A SECOND REPAIRMAN IS POKING ABOUT THE DRYER. HE WHISTLES AS HE WORKS. THE PLUMBER WEARS A SWEATY T-SHIRT, BLUE JEANS, AND A POCKET HANDKERCHIEF KNOTTED AROUND HIS NECK. HIS NAME IS JERRY. HE STOPS WORKING AND SHOUTS TO KITCHEN.

JERRY: You say it makes a funny noise?

ANNA (OFF CAMERA): A kind of grinding noise.

Jerry resumes whistling, looks inside dryer with a flashlight.

Anna enters from the kitchen. She wears a wraparound printed housedress.

ANNA: You're not the one was here before.

JERRY: Big fella? Black hair?

ANNA: Yes.

JERRY: Kelly. He's waitin' on me out in the truck. You want to see him? (HE BELLOWS OUT THE DOOR.) O, Kel! Hey, Kel!

ANNA: I was only asking only . . . I didn't . . .

JERRY: It's only in the alley.

KELLY ENTERS. DESPITE THE INTENSE HEAT, HIS OVERALLS ARE STILL NEAT AND WHITE. HE BARGES IN, TAKES OVER THE JOB. HE SEEMS NOT TO SEE ANNA.

ANNA: I didn't say I wanted to see you.

KELLY (TO JERRY): What's the trouble?

JERRY: I dunno. She says it's a kind of grinding noise. Parts defect maybe?

KELLY TAKES THE FLASHLIGHT AND POKES HIS HEAD INSIDE THE DRUM.

KELLY: Parts defect, baloney. (HE COMES OUT) You're not using this machine right, lady. (TO JERRY): Get me the tools.

JERRY EXITS

ANNA: I followed the book.

KELLY: Well, you ain't using it right. (HE AIMS FLASH INSIDE) Look.

ANNA: What? (SHE STOOPS, PEERS IN)

KELLY: A screw — stuck in the cylinder.

ANNA: It must have fell out of someplace.

KELLY: It fell out of somebody's pocket! You supposed to go through the pockets for foreign objects.

ANNA: Oh.

KELLY (REACHING INSIDE): You got to treat this machine right, you know? This ain't some kid's toy.

ANNA: I'm sorry.

KELLY IS WORKING BLIND, HIS ARM STRETCHED INTO THE MACHINE AS HE TRIES TO PRY OUT THE SCREW WITH HIS FINGERS. SUDDENLY HE BURSTS INTO A ROAR, LIKE A GREAT WOUNDED LION.

KELLY: Aargh!

HE YANKS HIS HAND OUT OF THE DRYER. THE INDEX FINGER IS
BLEEDING. HE PUTS THE FINGER IN HIS MOUTH AND
CLEANS IT OF BLOOD.

ANNA (BACKING AWAY): Excuse me, huh?

KELLY HOLDS HIS INJURED FINGER IN THE AIR. WITH HIS OTHER
HAND HE REACHES INTO HIS CHEST POCKET AND TAKES OUT
A BANDAID. WITH HIS TEETH HE TEARS THE TISSUE FROM
THE BANDAID, SPITTING THE PAPER FROM HIS LIPS. ANNA
WATCHES NERVOUSLY, THE FRIGHTENED MOUSE WATCH-
ING THE INJURED LION.

ANNA (EDGING TO DOOR): I'm baking for the Bingo.

KELLY WRAPS THE BANDAID AROUND HIS FINGER. THIS ENTIRE
OPERATION HAS BEEN DONE WITH PROUD EFFICIENCY.

KELLY: Okay. I got no need for you.

HE REACHES INTO THE MACHINE AGAIN WITHOUT LOOKING AT
ANNA.

ANNA MOVES INTO KITCHEN. SHE STOPS, CATCHING HER
BREATH WITH DIFFICULTY. SHE IS FRIGHTENED BY THIS
MAN. SHE CROSSES TO TABLE, STILL CATCHING SHORT
BREATHS. SHE TAKES AN EMBROIDERED HANDKERCHIEF
FROM HER POCKET AND DABS THE PERSPIRATION FROM
HER FACE. THEN, UNTHINKINGLY, SHE SINKS INTO THE
BIG ARM CHAIR. WHEN HER ARMS TOUCH THE CHAIR, SHE
JUMPS TO HER FEET. SHE STARES. IT IS HER FATHER'S
CHAIR.

KELLY (IN DOORWAY): Hey.

ANNA STARTS — AS IF RUDELY AWAKENED.

KELLY (BLANKLY): I scare you or something?

ANNA: No. No. I was just sitting. In the chair there.

KELLY: If I scared you, I'm sorry. (HE STUDIES HER) You had a
death in the family, right?

ANNA: My father.

KELLY: It slipped my memory. You know?

ANNA (POLITELY): It wasn't your father.

KELLY: No. (HE CROSSES TO HER) All I wanted to show you was
I got the screw out.

HE LIFTS HER HAND, DROPS THE SCREW INTO HER PALM. SHE
LOOKS AT HIM, CLOSES HER PALM ON THE SCREW. THEY
STARE AT ONE ANOTHER. THEN THERE IS A NOISE FROM

THE LAUNDRY ROOM. SOUND OF JERRY ENTERING WITH THE TOOLBOX.

KELLY (WITHOUT TURNING): Jerry? I don't need them tools.

JERRY (OFF CAMERA): Yeah?

KELLY: Take them to the truck. I'll be right with you.

KELLY CROSSES TO LAUNDRY ROOM DOOR. THEN TURNS.

KELLY (TO ANNA): You're baking for the Bingo you said?

ANNA: Cookies.

KELLY: The Saint Anthony's Bingo?

ANNA: Yes.

KELLY: Maybe tonight I'll see you Saint Anthony's. (HE ENTERS LAUNDRY ROOM.) Treat this machine right, huh?

HE EXITS, SLAMMING THE SCREEN DOOR. ANNA OPENS HER PALM, LOOKS AT THE SCREW. SHE CROSSES TO SINK AND LOOKS OUT THE WINDOW INTO THE ALLEY AS WE HEAR THE TRUCK START AND MOVE AWAY. AS THE SOUND FADES, ANNA BECOMES AWARE OF THE SCREW — AS IF IT BURNS HER PALM. SHE DROPS IT INTO THE WASTE BASKET QUICKLY AND RUBS HER PALM WITH HER FINGERTIPS. TERESA STICKS HEAD IN THE DOOR.

TERESA: Hi.

ANNA JUMPS.

TERESA ENTERS. SHE IS WEARING SHORTS, ELABORATE STRAW SANDALS, AND A MATERNITY BLOUSE.

TERESA: Boy, you're jumpy like a churchmouse.

ANNA: Hello Teresa. (SHE LAUGHS.) I'm sorry. You know, that's the second time today I jumped like that. You want some coffee?

TERESA (COMIC A LA DANNY THOMAS): Uhhh-ummm . . .

ANNA: How's the baby in the heat?

TERESA (SITTING AT TABLE): You know something. Someday I'm going to murder that kid.

ANNA: Teresa. God forgive you.

TERESA: I am. All day I'm trying to get her to go "nappy-time." Now it's almost suppertime — she falls asleep.

ANNA (COOING): Ahh . . .

ANNA BRINGS COFFEE TO THE TABLE, THE CUPS AND SAUCERS RATTLING IN HER HANDS.

TERESA: You know something? Every day you're getting more nervous. You got the heebie-jeebies!

ANNA: Since Papa died, every day, you know, I don't have enough to do anymore.

TERESA: You're working all the time!

ANNA: Well, it's lonesome, for one thing. I dunno. I need a what-you-call-it — adjustment.

TERESA: Adjustment yet! (THEY LAUGH. AFTER A SILENCE) You know, Anna, I heard a priest say once in high school: There's only two states of life for a woman — the marriage state or the religious state.

ANNA SIPS COFFEE; PUSHES MILK TO TERESA.

TERESA: Thanks. So it means you should be either married or a nun.

ANNA: There's lots of women aren't married and aren't nuns.

TERESA: The priest said it.

ANNA STIRS COFFEE IN SILENCE; THEN:

ANNA: I would of made a good nun.

TERESA: Anna!

ANNA: I mean it. When I was a little girl I'd tell the Sisters I wanted to be a nun.

TERESA: Agh! Every girl in the parochial school wants to be a nun once. I did! Oops! Imagine — me!

ANNA: I even told the Sisters. But they were scared to tell Papa.

TERESA: Scared?

ANNA: Oh you didn't know Papa before he got sick. Everyone was scared of him. Anyway he would of never let me go in the convent. Leave this house? He wanted to watch after me.

TERESA: To watch after you?

ANNA: You know. To take care of me. Papa always wanted him and my brothers to watch after me.

TERESA: Yeah . . .

ANNA: And they did. I mean my brothers do. Look at my kitchen. My stove. My own telephone. My dryer.

TERESA: And your sport clothes . . . and your jewels.

ANNA: Ah. I never cared for such things.

TERESA: Anna, whyn't you wear just a touch more of makeup?

ANNA: You going to start that again! A touch more!

TERESA (ELABORATELY): I beg your pardon!

ANNA: You know cosmetics ruin your complexion? Did you know that? You keep wiping that stuff on you and your skin's going to get all splotched.

TERESA (LAUGHING): Splotched! Oh Anna!

ANNA (GIGGLING): That's not a word?

THEY ARE BOTH GIGGLING WHEN THE SCREEN DOOR SLAMS. THE
TWO OLDER BROTHERS ENTER. THEY ARE WEARING SERV-
ICE STATION COVERALLS WITH THE WORDS: "SANTONELLO'S
SERVICE STATION." AS THEY ENTER, ANNA JUMPS UP.
BUT THEY CROSS THE KITCHEN WITHOUT A WORD AND
ENTER THE BEDROOM. THEY CLOSE THE DOOR.

ANNA: My supper! I never been so late with my supper. I been
making cookies for the Bingo, you know. And then the man
to fix the dryer came.

SHE BEGINS WORKING FEVERISHLY AT THE STOVE.

TERESA: Anna, you're a slave to them guys.

ANNA: You're a slave. You're a slave to your husband.

TERESA: He's my husband.

ANNA: There's a difference?

TERESA: That's just it. There *is* a difference. There's —

THE YOUNG BROTHER ENTERS, HAVING GARAGED THE TRUCK.

YOUNGEST: Where's supper?

ANNA (WORKING): Ten minutes.

YOUNGEST: Ten minutes!

ANNA: I said ten minutes!

THE YOUNGEST GLARES AT TERESA. HE OPENS THE BEDROOM
DOOR. WE HEAR A RADIO BASEBALL GAME AND SEE THE
OTHER BROTHERS STRETCHED OUT ON THEIR BEDS IN THEIR
STOCKING FEET.

YOUNGEST (TO ANNA): Wise guy?

HE ENTERS BEDROOM AND SLAMS THE DOOR.

TERESA: Good girl.

ANNA: What do you mean — good girl?

TERESA: For talking up.

TERESA WINKS AND EXITS.

ANNA: Hmmm?

BUT SHE'S TOO BUSY WITH DINNER TO WONDER.

FADE OUT.

FADE IN AS SOON AS POSSIBLE.

THE THREE BROTHERS ARE SEATED AT THE TABLE WOLFING
DOWN THEIR SUPPER. THE FATHER'S CHAIR REMAINS
EMPTY. THE BROTHERS ARE IN THEIR UNDERSHIRTS.

ANNA COMES TO THE TABLE WITH A SECOND SERVING IN A DISH.
    SHE SITS (NOT, OF COURSE, IN THE FATHER'S CHAIR) AND
    BEGINS HER MEAL.
MIDDLE: You seeing somebody or something?
ANNA: What?
MIDDLE: Some boyfriend or something — on the sly?
ELDEST: What's that for talk?
MIDDLE: Supper was ten minutes late.
ELDEST: So she's seeing somebody?
YOUNGEST: She's seeing Teresa upstairs. That's who she's seeing.
MIDDLE: Yeah. She live down here now or something?
ANNA: She comes for coffee.
YOUNGEST: Sitting big as life. Smoking a cigarette and giving out
    free advice.
ANNA: I don't take no advice from Teresa.
MIDDLE: You're smarter and I thought.
ELDEST: Will you stop with the talking! We're eating!
THE MEN CONCENTRATE ON THEIR FOOD IN GLUM SILENCE.
    ANNA WATCHES. WE MUST UNDERSTAND THAT HER EYES
    ARE OPENING; BUT THAT SHE CANNOT YET GRASP THE REAL-
    IZATIONS THAT ARE COMING UPON HER.
ANNA (QUIETLY): You know, I look at you and I get surprised.
ELDEST: Hurh?
ANNA: I said I sit here and I look around and I'm surprised, that's all.
THE MEN CONTINUE EATING. ANNA LOOKS DOWN THE TABLE
    TO HER FATHER'S EMPTY CHAIR.
FADE OUT.

ACT TWO

OPENING SHOT:
ANNA IS SITTING ON A BENCH WHICH IS PROTECTED BY SOME
    SHRUBBERY. BEHIND HER, AND TO THE RIGHT, IS A SHRINE
    CONSTRUCTED IN REPLICA OF THE GROTTO OF LOURDES.
    A STATUE OF THE VIRGIN STANDS HIGH IN A NICHE. A
    CANDLE STAND IS CHAINED TO THE SHRINE AND TWO CAN-
    DLES BURN IN THE STILL HOT SUMMER NIGHT. BEHIND
    THE SHRINE AND THROUGH THE SHRUBS WE SEE STRINGS
    OF BARE LIGHT BULBS WHICH HAVE BEEN FESTOONED IN
    PROFUSION OVER THE CHURCH GROUNDS.

A RECORDING IS BLARING OVER A LOUD SPEAKER IN THE DIS-
TANCE. IT IS A NEOPOLITAN TUNE AND ITS MESSAGE OF
LILTING SENTIMENTALITY COMES THRU THE SCRATCHING
OF ELECTRONIC EQUIPMENT. UNDER THE RECORD WE HEAR
THE SOUND OF A BINGO GAME IN PROGRESS:
ANNA IS IN A CHEAP SHEER BLACK DRESS. SHE WEARS WHITE
"SUMMER SHOES" AND WHITE GLOVES. AS SHE SITS, SHE
CLUTCHES A WHITE PURSE IN HER HANDS.
SHE IS WAITING WITH THE EXPECTANCY OF A SMALL CHILD.
THERE IS A SOUND OF SOMEONE APPROACHING AND SHE
JUMPS TO HER FEET.
IT IS THE PRIEST — BUT SHE WAS NOT EXPECTING HIM.
ANNA: Buona sera, Father.
PRIEST: Anna. How are you?
ANNA: Fine, Father.
PRIEST: I took my personal taste of those cookies of yours, Anna.
(HE THROWS A KISS FROM HIS FINGERTIPS) Muuh!
ANNA: Thank you, Father.
PRIEST: You waiting for somebody, Anna?
ANNA: Just sitting here, Father. Listening to the music.
PRIEST: You like the music, eh?
ANNA: It's beautiful.
PRIEST (ALMOST IN REVERY, HIS LIPS SAVORING THE RICH SYL-
LABLES): Bella. Bella musica . . . (THEN) I'll tell you, Anna,
about that music. The younger ones are mad with me. (HE
STOPS, HUMS.) You hear? Napoli! (HE CHUCKLES SOFTLY.)
I have had those records long before I came to the parish.
Scratchy? Maybe. But what should I play instead over the
loud speaker? The rock and the roll? Eh?
ANNA: Beautiful . . .
PRIEST: Uhmmm . . . (THEY LISTEN; THEN, SOFTLY) You know
why I come by the shrine, Anna? When the Bingo tables are
filled and the Bake Sale is going along, I come back here and I
stop to tell the Blessed Mother. "Oh, I know it!" I tell her. "I
know they are here for the Bingo prize and for Anna Santonello's cookies — "
ANNA (MODESTLY): Father.
PRIEST (WAGGING A FINGER): Oh yes! "But," I tell her, "still they
are next to your Son's house. And the money coming in will
keep the roof over your Son's head. (POINTING TO STATUE)

And your head. (POINTING TO HIS CHEST WITH A GRIN)
And my head." There! I have said it. Now I can go. (HE
GRINS AT HER) Buona notte, Anna.

ANNA: Good night, Father.

ANNA SITS AGAIN AND FOLDS HER HANDS OVER HER POCKET-
BOOK. BUT SHE CANNOT FEIGN PATIENCE. SHE FROWNS.
THEN SHE GLANCES UP AT THE VIRGIN AND SMILES. EM-
BARRASSED AT HER JOYFUL IMPATIENCE, SHE COVERS HER
FACE WITH HER HANDS.

KELLY ENTERS. HE IS CARRYING TWO HOT DOGS AND TWO BOT-
TLES OF COKE. HE WEARS SMARTLY PRESSED SUMMER
SLACKS AND A DIAPHANOUS SPORT SHIRT OF A SYNTHETIC
MATERIAL. NOT ONLY IS THIS FASHIONABLE, BUT HE IS
PROUD THAT HE IS GENTLEMAN ENOUGH TO WEAR A CLEAN
UNDERSHIRT BENEATH IT.

KELLY: Hey . . .

ANNA (LIFTING HER HEAD): Oh! Thank you.

KELLY: What was you doing? Crying?

ANNA: I never cry. (SHE SMILES) I was thinking only.

KELLY (SITS BESIDE HER): What about? (MUNCHES HIS HOT
DOG)

ANNA: Oh, we been talking so much tonight. I got a lot to think
about.

KELLY: Like what?

ANNA: You know, it's funny, me meeting you here tonight.

KELLY: I told you back in the kitchen I might see you here.

ANNA: I never saw you before around Saint Anthony's.

KELLY: I go Saint Michael's.

ANNA SMILES SECRETLY AT THIS AND THROWS A GLANCE TO THE
VIRGIN.

KELLY HAS FINISHED OFF HIS HOT DOG AND ANNA, WHO HAS
BEEN CONTENT TO SIP HER COKE, OFFERS HERS.

ANNA: You eat mine. (HE ACCEPTS WITHOUT CEREMONY AND
SHE WATCHES HIM FOR A MOMENT AS HE EATS.) Sometimes
I run over Saint Michael's for Mass. I never seen you there
either.

KELLY (CHEWING): I don't go much.

ANNA: You're like my brothers. You should go. I want to tell you
something. My Papa never went to church. And when he was
dying he got scared and he was crying for the priest. I mean,

crying like a baby. Then he couldn't even talk to say his confession. You want to be like my Papa?

KELLY: Why you always talking about your Papa?

ANNA: I don't know.

KELLY: Why?

ANNA: After all, he was my Papa. For years I took care of him.

KELLY: You talk like he was your baby or something, for crying out loud.

SHE TURNS AWAY, LOOKING AT THE BINGO LIGHTS THROUGH THE BUSHES.

KELLY TAKES OUT A CLEAN FOLDED HANDKERCHIEF AND WIPES HIS MOUTH CAREFULLY. HE RETURNS IT TO HIS POCKET, STILL UNFOLDED.

ANNA: What do you *want* to talk about?

KELLY: I want to talk about you. And I want to talk about Kelly. (POINTING A THUMB TO HIS CHEST) But I don't know how to do that.

ANNA (COYLY): I thought you was Irish.

KELLY: What?

ANNA: I said I thought you was Irish. Irish are supposed to have silver tongues.

KELLY: Silver tongues? What you talking about?

ANNA: Whatever you call it — blarney.

KELLY: You're always talking about Irish and Italian. What difference does that make, Irish and Italian?

ANNA: It makes a difference to me. I'm an Italian girl and inside me I still got whatever it is to be Italian. I mean, Italy is a certain place and Italians are a certain way because they live in Italy. And Irish is another place.

KELLY: If I was Italian I'd be different?

ANNA: You would. Believe me, you would!

KELLY (WITH SARCASM): Sure —

ANNA: More passionate. (QUICKLY) I don't mean it that way. I mean more — hot blooded. Skip it!

KELLY (ANGRILY): What kind of crazy talk! (HE STANDS)

ANNA (LAUGHING): You know, you get mad like an Italian. Honest, sometimes you're just like my Papa.

KELLY: Will you forget your Papa.

HE GRABS HER ANGRILY AND KISSES HER. SHE PULLS AWAY, CLAMPS HER HANDS OVER HER MOUTH AND CHOKES UP.

ANNA: I love my Papa!

SHE BURSTS INTO TEARS AND SITS ON THE BENCH WEEPING. KELLY STANDS, LOOKING THROUGH THE BUSHES, AT THE BINGO GAME. AFTER A TIME, ANNA RECOVERS. KELLY HANDS HER HIS FOLDED HANDKERCHIEF.

ANNA: Ah . . . I haven't cried since he died, you know? Since I was a little girl. I don't know what —

KELLY: Let's try the Bingo, huh?

ANNA: I couldn't do that. Not in the parish. Not so soon after Papa's dead.

KELLY: You wait here, I'll win you something.

ANNA: I'm sorry —

ANNA WATCHES KELLY GO, LIFTS HER FINGERS TO HER LIPS. THEN SHE OPENS HER PURSE — WHEN HE IS OUT OF SIGHT — AND CAREFULLY PUTS HIS FOLDED HANDKERCHIEF IN-SIDE. SHE'S ABOUT TO SNAP IT SHUT WHEN SHE GLANCES AT THE VIRGIN. SHE SCRAMBLES IN HER PURSE FOR A DIME, LOOKS FOR A COIN SLOT IN THE CANDLE STAND; BUT THERE IS NONE SO SHE PLACES THE DIME ON THE STAND. SHE LIGHTS A CANDLE. THERE IS A RUMBLE OF THUNDER AS SHE KNEELS AT THE SHRINE. THE FIRST GUST OF WIND FROM A SUMMER STORM BLOWS ALL THE CANDLES OUT. ANNA RISES AND, STRUGGLING AGAINST THE WIND, SHE CAREFULLY RELIGHTS THE THREE CANDLES. THUNDER.

FADE OUT.

FADE IN:

THE SANTONELLO KITCHEN. THE ELDEST IS IN THE KITCHEN OPENING A BOTTLE OF WINE. HE IS IN STOCKING FEET AND WEARS TROUSERS WITHOUT A SHIRT. IN THE BEDROOM THE OTHER TWO BROTHERS ARE STRETCHED OUT IN THEIR UNDERWEAR LISTENING TO A NIGHT BALL GAME. THE WINDOWS ARE WET BUT IT IS NO LONGER RAINING.

ANNA ENTERS, HUGGING A GLASS PITCHER. INSIDE THE PITCHER ARE TWO GLASSES. SHE HOLDS TWO MORE GLASSES. UN-DER HER ARM IS A SMALL ROUND TRAY. THERE ARE NO GREETINGS.

ANNA: I got caught in the storm. Everybody had to wait inside the church for the rain.

YOUNGEST (FROM BEDROOM): Some rain! It's more hot than before.

ANNA STRUGGLES WITH HER PURSE AND HER PRIZE, SETTING
  THE PITCHER ON THE TABLE AND TAKING THE GLASSES
  FROM INSIDE. THERE ARE SOME FEW DROPS OF WATER
  ON THE PITCHER AND SHE TAKES THE FOLDED HANDKER-
  CHIEF FROM HER PURSE AND DABS AT THEM CAREFULLY.

ELDEST: What you got there?

ANNA: A service. Pitcher and four glasses. Them stripes are real
  gold.

YOUNGEST RISES AND COMES INTO KITCHEN.

YOUNGEST: Yeah? Where'd you get that?

ANNA: At the Bingo.

MIDDLE (STILL ON BED): You was playing Bingo? With the old
  man not dead a month!

YOUNGEST: What's wrong with playing Bingo?

MIDDLE: The dead should be mourned.

ANNA (QUICKLY): I wasn't playing Bingo.

ELDEST: You said you won this in the Bingo.

ANNA: I didn't win it. Somebody won it for me.

ELDEST: Who?

ANNA: What?

YOUNGEST: He said: who won it for you?

ANNA: Just a fella.

MIDDLE (SITTING UP IN BED): A fella . . .

ELDEST: What fella?

ANNA: Only the fella that installed my dryer, that's all. I saw him
  at the Bingo and he said he'd win something for me.

ELDEST: Who's this fella?

ANNA: The dryer man, I told you.

YOUNGEST: What's his name, this guy?

ANNA: I dunno. Kelly or something. John Kelly.

YOUNGEST: Kelly . . . Kelly . . .

MIDDLE (COMING IN KITCHEN): Sure, Kelly. You know him.

YOUNGEST: I don't know him.

MIDDLE: I mean you seen him. The big mick hangs around the
  Crescent Moon. You know? He works on the truck for
  McAvoy Plumbing.

YOUNGEST: Yeah . . . The big mick.

ELDEST: You seeing this — this big mick again?

ANNA: I don't know. How do I know if I'll see him. Maybe if my
  dryer breaks down or something . . .

THE ELDEST SEEMS SATISFIED. HE POURS WINE INTO THREE OF THE NEW BINGO GLASSES. BUT:

MIDDLE: You meeting him again?

ANNA: I didn't *meet* him. Gee, what is this? A quiz program or something?

THIS SPURT OF BRAVADO RENEWS THE ELDEST'S SUSPICIONS. HE TAKES A DRINK FROM THE BINGO GLASS, WIPES HIS MOUTH WITH THE FOLDED HANDKERCHIEF BELONGING TO KELLY, AND PUTS IT IN HIS BACK POCKET.

ELDEST: You going to see this fella again?

ANNA: Why?

YOUNGEST: Because you don't know nothing about him. That's why!

ANNA (ONE LAST PANICKY TRY): I brung some cookies over to the Bingo. I ran against this fella, he won the prize in —

ELDEST (WITH FINALITY): You going to see him again?

ANNA (DEFINITELY DEFEATED): No . . .

THE BROTHERS GRAB THE GLASSES OF WINE AND RETURN TO THE BEDROOM.

THE REMAINING GLASS AND THE PITCHER ON THEIR ROUND TRAY STAND LIKE A BIZARRE PLACE SETTING BEFORE PAPA'S EMPTY CHAIR. ANNA STARES AT IT.

ANNA (UNDER HER BREATH): Papa . . . Papa . . .

MIDDLE (OFF CAMERA): How 'bout a dish biscotti?

IN QUICK OBEDIENCE, ANNA LEAVES THE TABLE. THE CAMERA MOVES IN ON THE TRAY AND THE GLASSWARE.

FADE OUT.

FADE IN.

THE EMPTY KITCHEN, FILLED WITH THE SUNLIGHT OF LATE AFTERNOON. THE "PLACE SETTING" REMAINS ON THE TABLE. THERE IS A KNOCKING AT THE SCREEN DOOR.

PRIEST (OFF CAMERA): Anna.

AGAIN, THE KNOCKING.

CUT TO:

PRIEST SEEN THROUGH SCREEN DOOR.

PRIEST: Anna. Anna Santonello.

TENTATIVELY, HE OPENS THE SCREEN DOOR. HE IS CARRYING THE SAME ORNAMENTED DISH WE SAW IN ACT I.

ANNA (OFF CAMERA): Father?

PRIEST: Yes, Anna.

ANNA COMES TO DOOR, WRAPPING A FLOWERED ROBE AROUND HER. UNDER IT SHE WEARS A SLIP. HER HAIR IS MUSSED, HER FEET SCUFF IN SLIPPERS.

ANNA: Father . . . I was laying down.

PRIEST (RETREATING): Ahh . . . I woke you up.

ANNA: No, Father. Come in, Father. It's time anyway to be starting supper.

THEY ENTER KITCHEN.

ANNA (LAUGHING FEEBLY AT HERSELF): Lazy bones . . .

PRIEST: Anna, you look tired out.

ANNA: These hot nights, I haven't been sleeping so good.

PRIEST: And that's why I haven't seen you at daily Mass?

ANNA: I'm there on Sunday, Father.

PRIEST: Yes. (PAUSE) I came only to bring back your dish from the Bake Sale.

ANNA: Will you sit down, Father?

THE PRIEST IS ABOUT TO SETTLE IN THE ARMCHAIR.

PRIEST: When this heat will end —

ANNA: Would you mind, Father! Here?

SHE GUIDES HIM TO ANOTHER CHAIR AT THE TABLE. THE PRIEST SITS, EYES THE CHAIR — AND THE PITCHER AND GLASS — WITH CURIOSITY. THEN HE ATTEMPTS TO BREAK THE SOMBER MOOD WITH JOCULARITY.

PRIEST: Heh! So it's you is running off with all my Bingo prizes!

ANNA: Yes.

PRIEST: That's real gold around those rings.

ANNA: Father — Remember you asked me if I wanted to talk.

THE PRIEST CONCEALS HIS EAGERNESS TO HELP HER WITH THE WISE IMPERSONAL WITHDRAWAL OF HIS CALLING. HE FOLDS HIS HANDS OVER HIS STOMACH AND LOWERS HIS HEAD, NODDING SLOWLY.

ANNA: First thing — First I want to ask you, Father, is it true there's only two states of life for a woman? Married or religious?

PRIEST: Who told you that?

ANNA: A friend.

PRIEST: And you are worried about it?

ANNA: You didn't answer my question, Father.

PRIEST: You answer my question. You are worried about it. And you think maybe you should join the convent.

ANNA: Yes . . .

PRIEST: Anna. Anna. You're getting too old to think so young and foolish. But maybe you are fooling *me,* eh? Maybe what you want is marriage?

ANNA: No . . . I didn't say that.

PRIEST: Maybe you want a husband and a home?

ANNA: I got a home.

PRIEST: But a husband — and babies of your own?

(ANNA HANGS HER HEAD.) Is it so shameful?

(HE TURNS TO HER.) Anna — your brothers also want the normal life for you. They came to see me at the rectory.

ANNA LOOKS UP IN AMAZEMENT.

PRIEST: They want you should meet some nice man. Some nice man from the parish.

ANNA: They *asked* you?

PRIEST: Oh . . . they hinted around the bush. Your brothers love you, Anna. They worry.

ANNA: They must be worried pretty hard for them to come to the church!

PRIEST: Anna, that is not charitable.

ANNA: I'm sorry, Father. So — did you find anyone? Anyone for me, I mean.

PRIEST: Anna, Anna. So bitter? Is this the woman who used to come every day to the church?

ANNA: That's what I wanted to talk about with you before, Father. My religion.

PRIEST: Your religion?

ANNA: I love the church. I love the devotions. But do I know my religion, Father?

PRIEST (PATIENTLY): Such as?

ANNA: Such as — Papa. I know he's in heaven. I know that. But — I don't know where he is. So you understand that, Father?

PRIEST: Yes.

ANNA: Then where is he?

PRIEST: With you. If you want to think of it that way.

ANNA IS SILENT. THEN:

ANNA: I still love my Papa.

PRIEST: Of course . . . Of course.

ANNA: Is that wrong?

PRIEST: Anna . . . Is that wrong! You are a grownup woman. Is there suddenly so much trouble figuring what is right and wrong?

ANNA: No . . .

PRIEST: Then you know what is your right and what is your wrong. And you do what is right.

ANNA: But — when other people . . .

PRIEST: Other people! Since when has other people made a right or wrong? (STERNLY) Anna! You are a woman with a free will. God *made* you free — to do whatever is right for you.

THEY SIT SILENTLY. THE DISCOVERY OF HER SPIRITUAL FREEDOM BEGINS TO SHINE IN ANNA'S EYES.

PRIEST: Better now?

ANNA SMILES AND THE PRIEST RISES, READY TO LEAVE.

ANNA: Thank you, Father.

HE SMILES, TAKES HIS HAT AND WALKS OUT INTO LAUNDRY ROOM.

ANNA (SUDDENLY): Father! Father! Will you do me one favor? Per favore. I am thinking of having somebody tonight to the house. Would you be here, Father? I'd like for you to be here, too.

PRIEST (SMILING): That's not a favor, Anna. That's an invitation.

ANNA: Would you come?

PRIEST: Tonight is Saturday. I am hearing confession.

ANNA: After confessions?

PRIEST: At nine o'clock. I'll be here.

ANNA: Oh Father. (THEN QUICKLY) You'll stay one more minute? While I make a telephone call.

THE PRIEST SMILES AT HER GLOWING EXCITEMENT. HE PUTS HIS HAT ON THE TABLE AND SITS.

ANNA RUSHES INTO THE LAUNDRY ROOM. SHE RIPS A TAG OFF THE DRYER AND GOES TO THE TELEPHONE ON THE KITCHEN WALL. SHE CONSULTS THE TAG AND DIALS.

PRIEST: Ah this heat . . .

ANNA (WAITING FOR CONNECTION): Terrible, Father. (BUT SHE IS SMILING) (INTO PHONE): Hello. Hello? Is this McAvoy Plumbing? Could I speak, please, to Mister Kelly. I see. I see. I'll call back. In a little while I'll call back.

FADE OUT.

FADE IN:

THE BAR AT THE CRESCENT MOON. THE CRESCENT MOON IS A NEIGHBORHOOD HOSTEL, SMALL, DIM AND SLEEPY. ITS FURNISHINGS ARE OLD. THE SNAPSHOTS TUCKED IN THE MIRROR BEHIND THE BAR ARE CHANGELESS: SOMEBODY'S BABY, A COUPLE OF GUYS IN SERVICE, A LOCAL PRIZE FIGHTER. THERE'S A PAIR OF PRINTED PLAQUES WITH WEAK JOKES ABOUT CREDIT AND DRUNKENNESS. ON THIS HOT SUMMER AFTERNOON, A BALL GAME IS IN PROGRESS ON THE TELEVISION SET WHICH IS ELEVATED HIGH IN THE AIR AT ONE END OF THE BAR.

MOOSE, A FAT AND LETHARGIC BARMAN, IS PORING OVER A TABLOID NEWSPAPER AT ONE END OF THE BAR. HE WEARS A T-SHIRT AND THE STRINGS OF A BAR APRON ARE WRAPPED AROUND HIS MIDDLE.

BENEATH THE TELEVISION SET, THE BROTHERS SANTONELLO LEAN OVER THE BAR AND THEIR BEERS. THE TELEVISION SCREEN WAVERS AND FLICKERS AND THE SOUND BUZZES.

YOUNGEST: Hey, Moose! Why-n't you fix this set!

MOOSE LEAVES HIS PAPER RELUCTANTLY, WALKS DOWN, AND STRETCHING HIS ARMS UPWARD HE TRIES TO ADJUST THE SET. THE MEN KEEP THEIR EYES RIVETED ON THE GAME.

YOUNGEST: You oughta buy a new TV. Nobody can see nothing on that.

MOOSE (WALKING AWAY): Why-n't you buy one yourself. Stay home once in a while.

YOUNGEST (GRINNING): What's the matter? You don't want no business?

THE HUMOR FAILS TO MOVE MOOSE. HE RETURNS TO HIS NEWS-PAPER. THE DOOR OPENS FROM THE OUTSIDE, LETTING IN A BLAST OF SUNLIGHT.

KELLY ENTERS. HE WEARS HIS WORK CLOTHES. HE PAYS NO ATTENTION TO THE BACKS OF THE SANTONELLO BROTHERS, GOES DOWN THE BAR TO MOOSE.

KELLY: Moose . . .

MOOSE: Hi . . .

KELLY: Gimme a beer.

KELLY SETTLES AT THE BAR, LOOKS UP AT THE TELEVISION. MOOSE BRINGS HIM THE BEER.

What's the score?

MOOSE COMMITS THE CARDINAL SIN OF THE BARTENDER.

MOOSE (CARELESSLY): Who knows?

HE RETURNS TO HIS PAPER.

CUT TO:

SANTONELLO BROTHERS.

THE MIDDLE BROTHER WHO HAS GLANCED DOWN THE BAR WHILE DOUSING A CIGARETTE, SEES KELLY, REACTS, THEN MUTTERS TO HIS BROTHERS.

MIDDLE: That's the guy. Kelly.

THE OTHER BROTHERS LOOK.

MIDDLE (NEEDLING): Drives for McAvoy Plumbing?

THE ELDEST FROWNS. THEN HE TURNS BACK TO THE TELEVISION SET AND WATCHES THE GAME GRIMLY. THE MIDDLE BROTHER WANTS SOME ACTION. WITH A COUPLE OF NUDGES, SOME ROLLS OF HIS EYES, AND THE WORKINGS OF HIS JAW, HE EGGS ON THE YOUNGEST BROTHER.

THE YOUNGEST BROTHER TAKES THE BAIT. HE STROLLS DOWN THE BAR TO KELLY'S SIDE. BEHIND HIM, THE MIDDLE BROTHER EYES THE ELDEST WHO IS STILL PINNED TO THE BALL GAME.

YOUNGEST: Your name Kelly?

KELLY (DISINTERESTED): Yeh.

THE YOUNGEST RESTS HIS ELBOWS ON THE BAR. IN DOING SO HE BLATANTLY KNOCKS OVER KELLY'S BEER.

MOOSE: Hey, watch it!

AS MOOSE WIPES UP THE BEER, THE YOUNGEST WATCHES KELLY WITH A BRAVE GRIN. BUT KELLY IGNORES THE CHALLENGE OF THIS YOUNG KID.

KELLY (TO MOOSE): Draw me another beer.

YOUNGEST (TO KELLY): My name is Santonello.

KELLY: I *know* what your name is.

YOUNGEST: You think it's a good name — Santonello?

KELLY: I don't think about it. One way or the other.

KELLY TURNS HIS BACK ON THE YOUNGEST SANTONELLO.

YOUNGEST: Hey! I'm talking to you!

HE SLAMS KELLY ON THE ARM. KELLY TURNS AND FINDS THE YOUNGEST WAITING FOR HIM WITH HIS FISTS UP. KELLY GRABS HIM BY THE SHIRT WITH ONE BIG FIST.

KELLY: Listen, Kid . . .

BUT, LOOKING PAST THE YOUNGEST'S HEAD, KELLY SEES THE

TWO OTHER SANTONELLO BROTHERS MOVING DOWN THE
BAR TOWARDS HIM, INTENT ON "DEFENDING THE HONOR"
OF THEIR KID BROTHER. MOOSE SEES THEM, TOO. STILL
BENT OVER HIS PAPER, HE KEEPS HIS CONTRIBUTION
VOCAL.

MOOSE: Hey you guys . . .

KELLY FLINGS THE YOUNGEST AWAY. HE'S READY TO TAKE ON
ALL THREE. AND HE DOES. BUT THE MELEE IS QUICK TO
TAKE A FIXED SHAPE. THE SANTONELLOS WORK AS A TEAM.

MIDDLE (AS FISTS FLY): Grab him! — Grab him!

SUDDENLY KELLY IS PINNED BACK AGAINST THE BAR. THE
YOUNGEST HAS HIM PINNED ON ONE SIDE: THE ELDEST ON
THE OTHER. THE MIDDLE, WHO HAS PLANNED IT THIS
WAY, MOVES IN SLOWLY ON KELLY. HE SLAPS HIM HARD
ACROSS THE JAW.

MIDDLE: You keep your hands off my sister.

HE SLAPS HIM ACROSS THE JAW AGAIN. BEHIND THE BAR, MOOSE
LEANS OVER HIS PAPER.

MOOSE: Hey you guys!

IT'S OBVIOUS THAT KELLY IS GETTING BEATEN UP — BAD.

MOOSE: Hey you guys . . .

FADE OUT.

FADE IN:

THE SANTONELLO KITCHEN. THE PRIEST STILL SITS AT THE
TABLE. ANNA IS MOVING NERVOUSLY AROUND THE
KITCHEN. THE DELAY HAS HEIGHTENED HER EXCITEMENT.

ANNA: You'll wait another minute, Father? This man. This fella
should be back by now.

PRIEST (NODDING): A fella.

ANNA (BEAMING): You knew that. You knew that all the time.
(ANNA CROSSES TO PHONE) I'm try again.

SHE DIALS. THERE IS A LOUD ANGRY BANGING AT THE SCREEN
DOOR. ANNA CRINGES, BUT STAUNCHLY CONTINUES.

ANNA (GLANCING TOWARD DOOR): Could I please speak to Mister
Kelly.

THERE IS A STOMPING IN THE LAUNDRY ROOM, A SLAM OF THE
SCREEN DOOR. ANNA TURNS FROM THE PHONE. HER FACE
BLANCHES AT WHAT SHE SEES. SHE REPLACES THE PHONE
ON THE HOOK. KELLY STANDS IN THE DOORWAY. HE IS

LIKE A MADDENED ANIMAL. HIS FACE IS BATTERED, HIS
WHITE OVERALLS STAINED WITH BLOOD.

KELLY: What did you tell your brothers?

ANNA STANDS FROZEN.

KELLY: What did you tell your brothers about me! You tell them
I did something?

PRIEST: Stop yelling at this woman!

ANNA: No, Father — he's bleeding!

PRIEST (TO KELLY): What is this matter!

KELLY: I had to fight three of her brothers, that's what's the matter!

ANNA: Fight?

KELLY: What you tell your brothers!

ANNA IS SOBBING. SHE TURNS TO SINK.

ANNA: Sit. Sit. You got to have your face fixed up. Sit.

SHE WETS A CLOTH IN THE SINK. KELLY IS SWAYING ON HIS
FEET. THE PRIEST LEADS HIM TO PAPA'S CHAIR, SEATS
HIM.

ANNA TURNS. SHE STARTS AT SEEING KELLY IN HER FATHER'S
CHAIR. BUT SHE GOES TO HIM AND BEGINS TO CLEAN HIS
FACE. HE IS AN ANGRY AND PAINED THING, HEAVING WITH
ANIMAL BREATHING. SHE IS FRIGHTENED AS SHE WORKS
— AS IF MINISTERING TO A BLOODY BEAST.

ANNA (SOBBING): What did they do? What did they do?

THE PRIEST GETS A BOTTLE OF WINE.

KELLY: At the Crescent Moon they ganged up on me. I took on all
three your brothers. Three!

ANNA: I don't know why. I don't know why.

THE PRIEST IS POURING WINE IN ONE OF THE BINGO GLASSES.

PRIEST: Why you come here to upset her? If you fight in barrooms,
don't bother this woman about it.

KELLY: This woman is telling stories about me. No reason for her
brothers to beat me up. No reason.

PRIEST (GIVING WINE GLASS): Drink! Drink and go!

THE PRIEST LOOKS FIERCELY AT KELLY. KELLY LOOKS AT HIM,
THEN HANGS HIS HEAD AND SHOVES THE GLASS ASIDE.

KELLY: Okay, Father. I'm going.

AS HE STRUGGLES TO RISE FROM THE CHAIR, THERE IS THE
ROAR OF A TRUCK IN THE ALLEY.

ANNA: That's the truck. My brothers —

PRIEST (TO KELLY): Go in the other room.

KELLY: They don't scare me off.

PRIEST: I said go in the other room!

KELLY: Father, I'm a man. (WITH A CRUEL GLANCE AT ANNA)
I ain't one of your church biddies.

PRIEST: Listen to me — man! Maybe you got no respect for the
priest. But I want you should have some respect for this girl.
She don't want no more fighting.

KELLY GOES THROUGH THE SWINGING DOOR INTO THE DINING
ROOM. THE PRIEST GESTURES TO ANNA TO SIT DOWN. HE
TAKES THE WINE GLASS IN HAND. ANNA SITS AT THE
TABLE, CLUTCHING THE BLOODY CLOTH IN HER LAP. SHE
STARES GLASSILY AT HER FATHER'S CHAIR.

THE TWO OLDER BROTHERS ENTER.

PRIEST: Good afternoon, *men.*

ELDEST: Father.

MIDDLE: Hello, Father.

PRIEST (EYES FLARING): You say hello to your sister?

MIDDLE: Hello, Anna.

ELDEST (GRUFFLY): You excuse us, Father. We got to change.

THE BROTHERS WALK INTO THE BEDROOM. THE PRIEST RISES
AND FOLLOWS THEM.

PRIEST: I excuse you — (HE BLOCKS THE CLOSING OF THE DOOR
WITH HIS HAND) — from some things!

THE PRIEST ENTERS THE BEDROOM. THE BROTHERS ARE
STARTLED.

CUT TO:

CU OF ANNA WHO SITS FROZEN AT THE TABLE AS WE HEAR THE
PRIEST OFF CAMERA.

PRIEST (OFF CAMERA): You don't come to my church. That's
your business. You are big men. But there is something that
is my business. Your sister Anna is my business.

BROTHER (ANGRILY; OFF CAMERA): Father —

PRIEST (OFF CAMERA): Anna is a good woman. But she is also a
free person!

THE YOUNGEST BROTHER ENTERS THE KITCHEN. HE HEARS
THE NOISE, STOPS, LOOKS AT ANNA. ANNA LOWERS HER
HEAD. THE YOUNGEST BROTHER GOES TOWARD BEDROOM.

PRIEST (OFF CAMERA): You want a servant, you go hire a servant.
You want a sister, you love her and give her what is best for her

happiness and her salvation. (TO YOUNGEST BROTHER) You come in too. Come in!

WE HEAR BROTHER WALK IN. THERE IS A NEW AUTHORITY IN THE PRIEST'S VOICE. THIS AFTERNOON, AFTER YEARS OF PRIESTLY POLITENESS, HE HAS COME INTO HIS OWN. THE PRIEST'S NEW-FOUND STRENGTH EXPLODES IN ONE DECLARATION OF SCATHING CONTEMPT.

PRIEST (OFF CAMERA): Agh! I am just an old priest, right? But I am *so sick* of these big . . . strong . . . men!

THE PRIEST SLAMS THE DOOR. HIS VOICE IS MUFFLED AWAY AS HE LIGHTS INTO THE BROTHERS BEHIND THE CLOSED DOOR.

ANNA RAISES HER HEAD. SHE STANDS, WALKS TO DINING ROOM DOOR, PUSHES IT OPEN AND STANDS HOLDING IT, WAITING.

KELLY COMES INTO THE KITCHEN. THEY DO NOT LOOK AT ONE ANOTHER. HE CROSSES KITCHEN, GOES INTO LAUNDRY ROOM AND STOPS, HIS HAND SMOOTHING THE TOP OF THE DRYER. ANNA COMES INTO LAUNDRY ROOM AND SPEAKS QUIETLY TO HIS BACK.

ANNA: I want you to know something. I didn't tell my brothers nothing bad about you.

KELLY: Then they're nuts or something.

ANNA: They're my brothers!

KELLY: One by one I could lick them. One at a time!

KELLY POUNDS HIS FIST ON THE DRYER. HE WALKS TO SCREEN DOOR, THEN TURNS TO HER — REGRET BURNING IN HIS EYES.

ANNA: You get out. And don't you come back again! I got enough animals here! Don't you come back here never!

ANNA TURNS, RUSHES BACK INTO KITCHEN.

ANNA STOPS AT FATHER'S CHAIR AND CLUTCHES IT WITH HER HANDS. SHE HEARS THE SCREEN DOOR SLAM. HER FACE IS GRIM. SHE DOES NOT CRY. SHE RUNS HER FINGERS OVER THE ARMS OF THE CHAIR. THEN SHE LIFTS ONE HAND. THERE IS BLOOD ON HER FINGER. SHE TAKES THE CLOTH AND KNEELS, SCRUBBING THE CHAIR WITH FURY. AS SHE SCRUBS SHE LOOKS UP TO HEAVEN WITH COLD ANGER.

ANNA: I don't want no man. I don't need no man.

FADE OUT.

ACT THREE

THE EXTERIOR OF PHILIP POLETTI'S GROCERY. IT IS A SMALL STORE — A VERY SMALL STORE. IN FACT, MOST OF IT IS ON THE OUTSIDE. BUT WE KNOW THAT POLETTI HAS NO FEAR OF THE LAVISH CHAIN GROCERY WHEN WE SEE THE RICH AND RARE FRUITS AND VEGETABLES PILED IN BOXES AND BASKETS, STACKED ON BIG TRAYS, AND HUNG IN ABUNDANCE FROM THE AWNINGS AND WINDOW FRAMES. SO PROFUSE IS THE EXTERIOR DISPLAY THAT WE SCARCELY SEE THE INTERIOR. WHEN WE DO, WE ONLY GLANCE IN, DOWN ONE SHORT CENTER AISLE. ON EITHER SIDE OF THE AISLE, CANNED GOODS ARE PILED AND SHELVED.

ALONG THE SIDEWALK, THE THREE SANTONELLO BROTHERS APPROACH LIKE REFUGEES FROM THE SILENT MOVIES. THEIR THREE-MAN UNIT MAKES A BUMBLING, NERVOUS PROGRESS. THEY HALT AT THE FRUIT STANDS, ALMOST BOUNCING OFF ONE ANOTHER. THEY WEAR THEIR WORK COVERALLS. NERVOUSLY, THEY TAKE A SELF-INVENTORY. THE ELDEST TRIES TO COAX THE COLLAR POINTS OF HIS SERVICE-STATION COVERALLS TO STAY DOWN. THE YOUNGEST USES SPIT AND A THUMB TO REMOVE A SPOT ON HIS SHIRT-FRONT. THE MIDDLE SHIFTS NERVOUSLY, HIS HANDS DIGGING INTO HIS POCKETS.

THE THREE MEN THEN UNITE WITH A GLANCE. THEY MOVE FORWARD. THEN THEY BEND OVER, PEERING INTO THE STORE AND DOWN THE LITTLE AISLE. THE THREE HEADS SEE A VERY FAT OLD LADY WITH A BIG MOON FACE WHO IS SITTING ON A BOX, SMACK AT THE END OF THE AISLE. THE MOON FACE NODS. THE THREE MEN WITHDRAW, STANDING ERECT. THEY LOOK AT EACH OTHER IN CONFUSION. THEN THEY BEND FORWARD AGAIN, PEEKING INTO THE STORE. THE MOON FACE BURSTS INTO A BEAMING SMILE AND MAMA POLETTI — FOR THIS IS SHE — NODS AGAIN. SHE THEN LOOKS TO HER LEFT, CATCHES SOMEONE'S EYE AND SIGNALS TOWARD THE DOOR WITH HER THUMB.

PHIL POLETTI'S HEAD NOW COMES INTO VIEW AS HE BENDS FORWARD OVER THE MEAT COUNTER INTO THE AISLE,

LOOKING OUT AT THE BROTHERS SANTONELLO. HE SQUINTS,
MAKES THEM OUT.

POLETTI: One moment!!

HIS HEAD DISAPPEARS. MAMA POLETTI NODS AGAIN TO THE
BROTHERS SANTONELLO. THE BROTHERS SMILE WEAKLY,
THEN STAND ERECT.

POLETTI COMES OUT OF THE STORE. HE IS AN INGRATIATING
ITALIAN IN HIS LATE 30'S. HIS HEAD IS BALD AND HIS FACE
IS SHINY AND INNOCENT.

POLETTI: Boys . . .

MIDDLE (ONE BY ONE): Hi Phil.

ELDEST: Phil.

YOUNGEST: Hiya . . .

POLETTI: I can help you?

ELDEST: Well — (RUBBING HIS CHIN) maybe you will.

THE BROTHERS ARE SILENT, SHIFTING ON THEIR FEET, LOOKING
FROM ONE TO THE OTHER. THE ELDEST GESTURES
ROUGHLY TO THE MIDDLE WITH HIS THUMB.

MIDDLE: Phil?

POLETTI: Yes?

MIDDLE: You know — ah — the old man passed on. You know?

PHIL: Yes. I knew. And I'm sorry —

ELDEST (QUICKLY): It's all right, Phil. What I mean is the mourning time is ended now.

THE ELDEST TURNS NERVOUSLY TO THE MIDDLE BROTHER AND
GESTURES WEAKLY TO HIM.

MIDDLE: And that's kind of the reason we come to talk to you.

YOUNGEST (CONCLUSIVELY): Yeah.

PHIL: I see . . .

ELDEST: You see — our sister Anna. She's a woman. And the
women take these things hard. You know?

POLETTI: Yeah. Oh, I know.

MIDDLE: Yeah.

YOUNGEST: Oh, hard. Yeah.

THERE IS SILENCE AGAIN.

POLETTI (STUDYING THEM): Very hard.

MIDDLE (QUICKLY): We thought it would do her good maybe to
have some company in the house. Gives her a chance to do
something — ah — special.

ELDEST: Fix up things special like.

YOUNGEST: Yeah. She's good that way!

AFTER TUMBLING OVER ONE ANOTHER THEY AGAIN COME TO A STOP.

CUT TO:

MAMA POLETTI WHO IS MOVING HER BULK DOWN AISLE, STRAIN-ING, AND CATCHING EVERY WORD OF THE CONVERSATION.

ELDEST (GETTING UP STEAM): For company, you know, she'd want to cook up special dishes.

MIDDLE: She's a good cook, my sister.

YOUNGEST: Great cook.

POLETTI (SMILING POLITELY): Yes . . .

HE NODS RHYTHMICALLY. THIS SIGN OF AGREEMENT LENDS COURAGE TO THE BROTHERS.

ELDEST: Anyway, we thought maybe you'd like to come over the house. Play some pinocle.

THE THREE BROTHERS AWAIT THE ANSWER. BUT POLETTI DOESN'T SEEM TO HAVE GOTTEN THE MESSAGE.

POLETTI (IN INNOCENCE): I'm not such a good pinocle player.

MIDDLE: Aw, that don't matter, Phil.

YOUNGEST (GRINNING BRILLIANTLY): You come on over.

ELDEST (GRUFFLY): Maybe tonight, huh?

POLETTI (CAREFULLY): Well, I'm busy till late in the store. Saturdays I got a lot of business.

THE MIDDLE BROTHER LOOKS OVER THE STORE.

MIDDLE: You got a good business, Phil.

THE OTHER BROTHERS LOOK OVER THE STORE, TOO. THEY ARE ALL IN AGREEMENT.

YOUNGEST: Yeah.

ELDEST: A *fine* business.

THIS INSPIRES THEM TO FORGE AHEAD WITH RENEWED DE-TERMINATION, AFTER PHIL HAS NODDED IN MODEST CON-TENTMENT:

POLETTI: Thank God . . .

MIDDLE: You want to come over, Phil? My sister would be — ah — glad to meet you.

YOUNGEST: She'd like that.

POLETTI (BEAMING): Anna — I *know*. She's nice girl.

THIS IS MUSIC TO SANTONELLO EARS.

SANTONELLOS (ALMOST IN UNISON): She's nice girl!

At this moment, Mama Poletti forces her bulk through the fruit stands and into the group. The men back aside. Mama Poletti nods deeply to each Santonello.

Mama Poletti (to Eldest): Mister Santonello . . . (to Middle) Mister Santonello . . .

Youngest (as Mama nods to him): Missus Poletti . . .

Mama Poletti: I am hearing dis. (she nods again, solemnly) Yes . . .

Middle: We'd like Phil over the house.

Mama Poletti: I know dat.

Youngest (with brilliant grin): And sometime maybe we'd like you over the house, Missus Poletti.

Mama Poletti: Dat's nice . . . Your sister — she's Anna Santonello.

Eldest: Yuh.

Middle: We was telling Phil here —

Mama Poletti: Dat's all right. I unnerstand. You know?

Youngest: We was trying —

Mama Poletti stops him short with a lift of her hand. Silence.

Mama Poletti (nodding): Philippe will be dere at your house. (looking up lovingly at Phil) I will talk to my son.

Eldest (glancing at his brothers): Yeah . . .

Middle: Yeah. Well, thank you, Missus Poletti.

Youngest: Thanks.

Middle (backing away): See ya tonight, Phil.

Eldest: Phil . . .

Youngest: See ya . . .

The three brothers leave in a polite and disorganized bunch.

Mama Poletti is beaming up at her son, still holding his hand. He smiles weakly in response. Gently she pats his hand in soothing rhythm. A woman approaches the vegetable counters. Mama Poletti jerks her head.

Mama Poletti: Customer.

Phil turns obediently to serve the customer.

CU: Mama Poletti, beaming and bowing her head.

Fade out.

FADE IN:

THE SANTONELLO KITCHEN, EARLY EVENING. ANNA IS DRESSED
UP AND IN THE MIDDLE OF BIG PREPARATIONS. FOR THE
FIRST TIME, SHE IS NOT IN BLACK. SHE WEARS AN INEX-
PENSIVE SLEEVELESS DIMITY. TERESA, VERY PREGNANT,
IS SEATED AT THE TABLE IN A KNEE-LENGTH PEIGNOIR. SHE
IS BARE-LEGGED AND WEARS SLIPPERS.

TERESA: It's a lot of fuss if you ask me.

ANNA: It's a party, that's all.

TERESA: The Santonello brothers are entertaining now?

ANNA: It's only a friend.

TERESA: A friend for who.

ANNA: For my brothers. They got a lot of friends.

TERESA: Oh Anna! I know what the friend is for!

ANNA: Huh?

TERESA: Everybody knows what the friend is for. I know who it is
even. Philip Poletti.

ANNA: The grocer man?

TERESA: You didn't even know! Oho! I thought you knew.

ANNA: My brothers only told me — a friend.

TERESA: Hey! Everybody knows. The whole neighborhood. The
Santonellos are getting a boyfriend for Anna.

ANNA: I'm glad everybody knows because I don't.

TERESA: Since when are your brothers having men into this house?
Throwing parties?

ANNA: Well, the mourning time is ended for Papa. (SHE PONDERS)
Poletti the grocer man, you said?

TERESA: One, he's got money. Two, his old lady wants he should
get married.

ANNA: He's a nice enough man.

TERESA: So what about the Irish?

ANNA: Teresa, you're fresh tonight, you know?

TERESA: So I'm fresh and what about Irish?

ANNA: The whole neighborhood told you about that also?

TERESA: Everybody knows, sure. You don't have a free-for-all in
the Crescent Moon and have it a secret from the world.

ANNA GIGGLES NERVOUSLY

TERESA: What's the matter?

ANNA: I'm not used to being such a topic of conversation.

TERESA: You don't kid me. You like this Irish Kelly.

ANNA: I never said that.

TERESA: You don't kid me.

ANNA: Teresa, I'm sorry. I got a lot of work to do.

TERESA: Okay. And I'll mind my own business. You know what the baby called me yesterday? She called me Fat Mama! Fat Mama! You hear what I said?

ANNA: Yuh. That's nice.

TERESA: That's nice! Anna, you're crazy if you don't call up that Kelly or something.

ANNA: I couldn't do that.

TERESA: Why not for Heaven's sake. The phone's on the wall.

ANNA: There's reasons I couldn't call him up.

TERESA: Your brothers?

ANNA: I got no business talking against my brothers. They're watching after me.

TERESA: Yeah. I give up with you.

ANNA: Teresa, I want you to get this story right. And I want everybody that's wagging their heads to get it right. It was me sent the dryer man away from here. And he wanted to go. And it was nothing to begin with. We met at the Bingo. And my brothers didn't have nothing to do with it. Because the man — he wanted to go.

TERESA: Okay.

ANNA: I'm sorry if I yelled at you.

TERESA: He was a real big guy, that Kelly. What shoulders, huh?

ANNA: If you want to know, he scared me. He's a very *grup* man.

TERESA (LAUGHING): Grup . . . ? The word's *gruff*!

ANNA GIGGLES, THEN BURIES HER FACE IN HER HAND. HER SHOULDERS SHAKE — BUT SHE IS NOT LAUGHING NOW.

TERESA: Anna . . . I'm sorry. I didn't mean — you're always asking me: correct your language.

ANNA (SNIFFING): It's all right, Teresa. That ain't the reason —

TERESA: You never going to see this guy?

ANNA (TRYING TO LAUGH AT HERSELF): I don't know. Someday my machine might break down or something.

TERESA: Hit it with a hammer!

ANNA: Oh no! You got to treat that machine right! But, I pray, you know. Every night I pray — for grace and God's will be done. But I also pray to the Blessed Mother special. Let my machine break down, I say. Please. Let it break down.

TERESA (FIGHTING OFF TEARS): What to do, huh? We each got
   our sorrows. And what to do?
ANNA (LOOKING AT TERESA'S STOMACH): Teresa. You meditate
   on your joys, all right?
TERESA (SNIFFING BACK TEARS; GRINNING): Some joy!
SHE RUBS HER SIDES.
FADE OUT.

FADE IN:
THE SANTONELLO KITCHEN LATER THAT EVENING. THE THREE
   BROTHERS ARE AT THE KITCHEN TABLE PLAYING CARDS
   AND DRINKING WINE. THE FATHER'S CHAIR IS STILL THERE
   AND EMPTY. IN A FIFTH CHAIR SITS PHILIP POLETTI. THEY
   PLAY IN SILENCE, ALL IN SHIRTSLEEVES. BUT POLETTI HAS
   HIS TIE NEATLY TIED AND HIS SUITCOAT NEATLY HUNG
   OVER THE BACK OF THE CHAIR. ANNA SITS QUIETLY TO ONE
   SIDE ON A HIGH KITCHEN STOOL, WATCHING THE MEN.
   PHILIP POLETTI LOOKS UP AT HER. HE SMILES. ANNA
   SMILES IN RETURN. SHE JUMPS TO HER FEET AND BRINGS A
   FRESH BOTTLE OF WINE TO THE TABLE.
ANNA: Some more wine for anyone?
THE ELDEST GIVES HER THE GUEST'S GLASS — A BINGO GLASS.
ELDEST: Fill it up, eh?
ANNA POURS. ONE BY ONE THE BROTHERS RISE SELF-CON-
   SCIOUSLY. THEY STRETCH, LEAN ON THE BACK OF THEIR
   CHAIRS.
ELDEST: You excuse us a minute, Phil?
MIDDLE: Yeah. Excuse us?
POLETTI: Sure. Certainly.
THE BROTHERS MOVE ACROSS THE ROOM. THE TWO ELDEST GO
   INTO THE BEDROOM.
YOUNGEST: Excuse me.
HE BACKS NERVOUSLY INTO THE DINING ROOM. POLETTI SMILES
   AT ANNA. THE YOUNGEST, HAVING DISCOVERED HIS ERROR,
   COMES OUT OF THE DINING ROOM, GRINS NERVOUSLY, AND
   RETREATS TO HIS BROTHERS IN THE BEDROOM. POLETTI,
   WHO ROSE WHEN THE BROTHERS EXCUSED THEMSELVES,
   STAYS ON HIS FEET.
POLETTI: Your brothers are good pinocle players.
ANNA: They play a lot.

Anna moves to sit down.

Poletti (moving back a chair): Let me help you.

Anna: No. You sit down.

He sits in the father's chair. Anna moves to stop him, then allows it. She studies him in her father's chair and moves his glass of wine over to him.

Poletti: You'll have some wine?

Anna: Only a little. (she smiles) In your honor.

Poletti pours the wine. He raises his glass in a toast.

Poletti: To — the happy times.

Anna: Yes.

Poletti: You're bashful girl, huh?

Anna: Yes.

Poletti: I like bashful people. Because I'm kind of bashful myself. You know?

Anna: Yes.

Poletti: I think the bashful ones should stick together.

He laughs. Anna watches him. his kindness, his unaffected good nature would please a saint.

Poletti: I was watching you tonight. And you was watching me. What are you thinking?

Anna: What are you thinking?

Poletti: I asked you first.

They both laugh.

Anna: You're a nice man. I always thought so in your grocery.

Poletti: Anna — would you be interested in the movies, Sunday night? I know there's the television. But sometimes the movies are nice.

Anna: I don't go to the movies so much. (fumbling) My eyes.

Poletti: Maybe the dancing then. At the casino?

Anna: I don't really dance so well.

Poletti: Oh, that don't matter.

Anna: I don't dance, Mister Poletti.

Poletti: Maybe the Bingo on Tuesday. I seen you before at the Bingo.

Anna: I'm sorry. No thank you.

Poletti: I guess I don't understand.

Anna: Mister Poletti — I don't want to hurt nobody. But the truth is I just don't go out much — with nobody.

Poletti: Is there some boyfriend you got?

ANNA: Yes! Yeh, there is a man comes calling. God forgive me!

POLETTI: What?

ANNA: There isn't no man. I don't want no man.

POLETTI: But your brothers —

ANNA: My brothers don't know my mind.

POLETTI: It was a mistake?

ANNA: Yes. I'm sorry.

POLETTI: You think maybe I better say goodnight?

ANNA: Goodnight.

HE PICKS UP HIS SUITCOAT. ANNA LEADS HIM THROUGH THE
LAUNDRY ROOM. AS HE PASSES HER TO EXIT, HE SMILES.
ANNA SMILES.

POLETTI: Buona notte, Anna.

HE EXITS. ANNA LEANS ON THE DRYER, SOOTHING HER PALMS
ON ITS COOL SURFACE.

THE BROTHERS ENTER KITCHEN, LOOK IN AT ANNA.

ELDEST: We hear the door slam?

MIDDLE: Where's Phil Poletti?

ANNA: He went.

MIDDLE: Where?

ANNA: Because he didn't see no use in hanging around here.

MIDDLE: What'd you tell him?

ANNA: I told him I got a boyfriend.

YOUNGEST: You ain't got no boyfriend!

ANNA: I know it.

SHE WALKS PAST THEM INTO KITCHEN.

ELDEST: Anna! What's this for crazy talk!

MIDDLE: I'll tell you what's the crazy talk! She's thinking of that
mick!

ELDEST: Anna. Is that how you're thinking?

ANNA: No. I wouldn't commit no crime like that.

YOUNGEST (FISTS UP): Have him over here. Go ahead.

ANNA TURNS HER HEAD AWAY WITH A GROAN. THE ELDEST
PUSHES THE YOUNGEST'S FISTS DOWN AND WALKS TO ANNA.

ELDEST: Anna — Phil Poletti is a nice fella. We'll have him over
the house again. For pinocle.

ANNA: It won't matter.

MIDDLE: What you mean it won't matter?

ANNA: Because I'm not going to marry anybody. It's too late now
for marrying.

YOUNGEST: Too late? What's she mean — too late?

ANNA (SMILING): I'm staying with my brothers. After all, who would cook for you? Who could keep the coveralls neat?

ANNA WALKS BEHIND HER FATHER'S CHAIR AND LOOKS AT THE BROTHERS. SHE IS PLEASED AT GIVING THEM WHAT THEY WANT. THE BROTHERS BUNCH TOGETHER LIKE A GROUP OF NERVOUS ELDERS. THEN, AS IF EMBARRASSED AT HIS OWN WORDS, THE ELDEST SPEAKS:

ELDEST: Anna — uh. The priest — the Father told us some things . . .

ANNA: He told me also — to follow my own way. I decided my own way.

ELDEST: He told us: your sister should be married. The priest said we got the responsibility for that.

ANNA: I can't do what I want?

THE BROTHERS EXCHANGE GLANCES. THEN LIKE AN UNEASY CULPRIT, THE ELDEST GOES TO ANNA'S SIDE. HE HAS DIFFICULTY STARTING HIS SPEECH.

ELDEST: Anna. We want you should understand something. You're not a servant. You understand?

THERE IS NO AFFECTION IN THE STATEMENT. IT IS THE STUMBLING ATTEMPT BY A CONFUSED MAN TO RIGHT SOME WRONG WHICH HE IS NOT SURE EXISTS.

ANNA: I know that.

ELDEST: You're a sister. And — and you got your brothers' love.

YOUNGEST (CHILDISHLY EMPHATIC): You're a sister.

ANNA: But not a mama.

ELDEST: A mama?

ANNA: I said — yes, not a mama. I am not your mama.

ELDEST (CONFUSED): No. No . . .

ANNA: You are not my sons. And Papa is not my little baby.

SHE HAS MOVED AROUND TO THE FRONT OF THE CHAIR, LOOKING AT IT INTENTLY.

MIDDLE: What kind of crazy talk!

ANNA: I said — Papa's not my baby.

SHE SITS IN THE FATHER'S CHAIR.

ELDEST: Get out the old man's chair.

ANNA: This isn't Papa's chair. Papa's dead. He don't need no chair.

ELDEST: Get out the old man's chair!

ANNA: Papa's in heaven. Maybe if you went to the church more and think about God more, you'd know it! Papa's in heaven. Is the chair a shrine?

ELDEST: Get out! Get out!

HE SLAPS HER SWIFTLY ACROSS THE CHEEK. ANNA RUNS TO THE LAUNDRY ROOM AND CLINGS TO THE DRYER. THE THREE BROTHERS STAND TOGETHER LOOKING AT THE CHAIR. THEY ARE EMOTIONALLY SHATTERED, BREATHING SPASMODICALLY, LIPS TREMBLING. TEARS POUR DOWN THE CHEEKS OF THE MIDDLE BROTHER AND HE SOBS GUTTURALLY. ANNA TURNS AND WATCHES THEM.

ANNA: You want to know someone else sat in your shrine chair? Your mick! He sat there when I washed off the blood that you put on him!

THE ELDEST LUNGES AT THE TABLE. WITH A SWEEP OF HIS HANDS HE SENDS THE BINGO GLASSES AND PITCHER CRASHING TO THE FLOOR. HE LOOKS FIERCELY AT ANNA.

ANNA: Does that scare me? Because I'm not scared anymore of what you do.

ELDEST: Shut up!

ANNA: Because that mick you call him can beat up all of you! One by one! He told me! One by one!

ELDEST: I curse the time he come to this house! I curse the time we give you that machine! (HE THUNDERS TO LAUNDRY ROOM) I curse it!

HE SLAMS HIS FOOT ON THE OPEN DOOR OF THE DRYER WITH ALL HIS WEIGHT AND FURY. IT CLATTERS TO THE FLOOR. THE ELDEST BROTHER CONTINUES HIS FURIOUS PATH. AT THE SCREEN DOOR, HE SLUMPS, LOOKING OUTSIDE. THE TWO OTHER BROTHERS, WHO HAD DASHED AFTER HIM, FEARING ANOTHER ATTACK UPON ANNA, STOP AT THE KITCHEN ENTRANCE TO THE LAUNDRY ROOM. ANNA HAS CRINGED BACK TO THE WALL IN FEAR. NOW SHE SEES THE DRYER DOOR ON THE FLOOR. ALL ARE SILENT. SPENT.

ANNA (QUIETLY): It's broken.

THE ELDEST, DRAINED OF ANGER, TURNS TO HER.

ELDEST (ALMOST TENDERLY): Anna. Anna . . .

ANNA (HER JOY RISING): It's broken. It's broken.

THE OTHER BROTHERS ARE RELIEVED TO TAKE THEIR CUE FROM THE ELDEST.

MIDDLE (EAGERLY): Anna, we'll fix it for you.

YOUNGEST: We'll buy you another.

ANNA GRABS UP THE DOOR AND CLUTCHES IT TO HER BREAST.

ANNA: You don't know how to fix it.

SHE STANDS, CLUTCHING THE DOOR TO HER BREAST, SWAYING
ECSTATICALLY, HER EYES TURNING HEAVENWARD.

ANNA: It's broken . . . Oh, it's broken. It's broken . . . It's broken.

FADE OUT

END ACT THREE

EPILOGUE

AS CREDITS ROLL, WE SEE THE LAUNDRY ROOM IN THE MORNING
SUNLIGHT. KELLY IS WAITING OUTSIDE THE DOOR. ANNA
LETS HIM IN, HANDS HIM THE BROKEN DOOR.

AS HE WORKS THEY SPEAK TENTATIVELY TO ONE ANOTHER. WE
WATCH THEM — BOTH UNSURE AS THEY VERY CAREFULLY
START THEIR ASSOCIATION OVER AGAIN. THERE IS NO LOVE
SCENE — NO KISSES. SLOWLY, THEY ARE FINDING THEIR
WAY.

THE END

ANALYSIS

Act I

You will note, first
of all, that author Bob Crean's description of the Santonello home is
quite thorough. It gives evidence of the writer's familiarity with
such a home; and the details of the setting are of great assistance to
the scene designer and to the director. Since environment does play
so large a part in influencing our daily lives, the writer should be
familiar with the environment of his characters.

The drama brings its two leads, Anna Santonello and John
Kelly, on screen immediately and in a brief scene of visual dramatic
foreshadowing sets the stage for the impending romance: ". . . the
impact of their meeting. Anna overwhelmed by the power of this
man; Kelly recognizing Anna's feminine receptivity to this power."
The very opening scene, then, holds our attention and arouses our
interest in the possible romance.

The fight scene, which follows, illustrates the belligerency of the Middle brother, an important indication of his character, of which we will have further evidence in Acts Two and Three. It is this belligerency which adds fuel to the rising conflict between Anna and her brothers. The fight is, obviously, excellent visual action.

The dialogue gives us an insight to Anna's background. "I never got so fat and full of tears like them other women. I only dried up like." Evidently, she has not had much formal education, but she is a person of quiet strength and she wins our sympathy immediately. When the Middle brother, "the big man," admonishes her for "talking so crazy," she does not shout back at him but in quiet, forceful tones puts him in his place. "Who you telling. Who you telling to act right, hah? The big man. Bawling like a baby. The big strong son!"

Anna has led a sheltered life and she is shy. It is indicated by her reaction when Kelly describing the operation of the dryer tells her: "For delicate fabrics. Like your underwear, you know?" Anna folds her arms across her breast in an unconscious gesture of modesty.

Sympathy is invoked for John Kelly in the scene between Anna and the plumber. Kelly offers his condolences for her father's death and apologizes for his insistence in setting up the dryer at such a time. We take a liking to Kelly and thus we look forward to a successful romance. Once sympathy for the protagonists has been established, any future tensions between the two will be shared by the audience. In the conversation between Anna and her upstairs neighbor, Teresa, we have a good example of exposition through natural dialogue. Friends normally do exchange confidences. In this instance, we learn of Anna's attachment to her aged father. Similarly, when the priest speaks to Anna, we discover that she is a faithful churchgoer.

For a time passage transition, there is a Fade Out to Black after the Rosary sequence. The Fade Out to Black is, figuratively, a curtain. Fade In implies the curtain rising again, much as it does on the theater stage with the set coming slowly into view.

The scene where Jerry, the repairman, is working is actually a cover scene. All "Kraft Theatre" plays are produced live and the playwright must therefore allow time for changes in costume, and for actors to move from one set to another. The device in this particular scene is an acceptable one to the audience: a repairman called in to fix the recently purchased dryer. It is an incident of probability.

While the camera is focused on the visual action of Jerry "poking about the dryer," it gives Anna time to change to a "wraparound printed housedress."

The device of the inoperable dryer serves also to bring Kelly back to the Santonello household and therefore moves the play. The romance is furthered when Anna remarks that she is baking cookies for the Saint Anthony's Bingo and Kelly tells her, "Maybe tonight I'll see you Saint Anthony's."

Anna is evidently receptive to Kelly's friendship, but her whole life has been devoted to taking care of her father and her brothers. Her own individuality has been submerged. This is a point the dramatist wants to stress and so once again he employs the device of conversation between Teresa and Anna to clarify the issue and inspire the conflict.

Teresa, for all her bubbling chatter, is well aware of Anna's deeply hidden frustrations and she knows that Anna's brothers have taken advantage of her sense of obligation. As Teresa bluntly phrases it: "Anna, you're a slave to them guys." Much as Anna rationalizes her position, Teresa's shrewd observations have a telling effect which manifests itself almost immediately by Anna's sharp reply in answer to the Youngest brother's inquiry as to when supper will be ready. "I said ten minutes!" Teresa praises her for talking up.

At the first act curtain, Anna is beginning to realize the servitude of her position. We are waiting now to see what she will do about regaining her own individuality.

Act II

In Act Two, the play gathers momentum. There is a good deal of action and a strong crisis is developed. If you had seen this second act of "Anna Santonello," the chances are you would have enjoyed it to the fullest. There are no chinks, no faults, no creakings here.

The extensive description of the opening scene again demonstrates the writer's familiarity with the play's locale. We are treated . . . and we mean that in its happiest sense . . . to a delightful portrayal of the priest whom we had met briefly in the first act. This is excellent character drawing. A sense of warmth pervades us as we listen to the priest explain to Anna why he has come by the shrine tonight. He knows the people have come to Saint Anthony's for the Bingo prize and, he gallantly observes, for Anna Santonello's cookies.

"And the money coming in will keep the roof over your Son's head," he says, with wry humor, to the statue of the Blessed Mother, "And your head . . . and my head."

The scene between Anna and Kelly at the church grounds is a very poignant one but it has its humor too, the finest type of humor, arising naturally out of a situation: Anna discussing the difference between the Irish and the Italians. Before that, there is a revealing note of exposition when Anna tells Kelly that for years she has taken care of her Papa. It is another indication of her servitude, of how circumscribed her life has been, and of her devotion to her father. It leads us to understand her reaction to Kelly's kiss. She is shocked, but inwardly she knows this is the sort of affection she needs. Her exclamation, "I love my Papa," is a troubled cry to justify her long years of dedication. The gesture of Kelly offering Anna his handkerchief and his promise to win a prize for her at the Bingo game are both utilized to maintain a sympathetic portrayal.

The opening of Scene Two in the Santonello kitchen is a cover scene. The camera is on the Eldest brother opening a bottle of wine. This is only a brief bit of visual action but it gives Anna time to pick up the props: the glass pitcher, the tray and the glasses, and to move from the church set to the kitchen set.

An illustration of denoting time passage through natural dialogue is seen in the Middle brother's statement: "You was playing Bingo? With the old man not dead a month!"

There is no wasted dialogue. When the Middle brother remarks: "The big mick hangs around the Crescent Moon," it may, at first, appear to have little or no significance but as the act progresses, we find that the Crescent Moon plays an important part in the plot structure of the drama.

The scene between Anna and her brothers builds to a crisis. We are aware from their questioning that they have no love for Kelly. They warn Anna to stay away from him. Her acquiescence and her almost panicky replies reveal that she is not yet ready to assert her individuality.

Once again there is a cover scene with the arrival of the priest. He is off camera at first so that all we see is the empty kitchen; then the camera picks up the priest coming in the door and Anna calls to him off camera. This is a natural bit of visual action and dialogue which gives Anna time to change her costume. In other words, your cover scenes must never be obvious.

There is another visual indication of the father complex as Anna guides the priest away from her father's old armchair. The "shrine" is sacred even from the priest.

The dialogue now between Anna and the priest reaches the crux of the play and it is the priest's stern but sympathetic summation that marks the turning point of the drama. "Anna! You are a woman with a free will. God made you free — to do whatever is right for you." This, as the writer indicates, is the discovery of Anna's spiritual freedom. It leads her to immediate action, telephoning John Kelly.

Now the element of suspense is introduced. Anna is unable to reach Kelly on the phone. At the time of her call, he is at the Crescent Moon Bar, so we have a simultaneous action sequence. The brothers Santonello have been waiting for Kelly and the scene builds to a crescendo of violence, with the plumber beaten up badly. This fight is a physical manifestation of the brothers' bigotry, much as they have verbalized their contempt for Kelly by referring to him as "the mick."

Kelly's subsequent entrance into the Santonello home, his face battered, his overalls stained with blood, is a scene of tremendous impact. You will note that for this transition, we have another cover scene. We fade from the Crescent Moon to the Santonello kitchen. Anna has a bit of dialogue with the priest and then anxiously she tries calling Kelly again, all of which moves the play and at the same time allows for adjustments to Kelly's makeup and costume.

There is good symbolism in the priest leading Kelly to "Papa's chair." Anna starts at seeing Kelly seated there, but she accepts it and tends to his wounds. It is another step in freeing herself.

The scene between the priest and the brothers, with the priest finding new strength within himself, is a very heartwarming one. It also fills a need for the audience. The average viewer's social environment is such that he yearns to see justice done: in this instance, the viewer has been angered by the unfairness of the three brothers in setting upon Kelly. When the priest rebukes the brothers with scathing contempt, he is, in a dramatic sense, speaking for the viewer and granting him the satisfaction he anticipates.

The staging of the above scene, with the priest admonishing the brothers off camera, and the play of the camera on Anna, is very effective. It permits the actress to display her powers of pantomime.

In addition, it helps to move the play physically: the priest closes the door behind him, which is a cue for Anna to release Kelly.

Kelly, naturally enough, is still very bitter. His anger, belatedly, turns to contrition, but now Anna is furious and sends him on his way. She grips her father's chair, seeking comfort from it and then scrubs the contaminating blood from it. The curtain descends on a grave crisis in the drama. We are anxious to know what will happen next.

Act III

There are sharp contrasts in the opening scene of Act Three. It is a very humorous yet very poignant sequence, and full advantage is taken of the visual. Note how much pantomime there is in the brothers' embarrassed approach to the grocer, Philip Poletti.

A minor point, but one of essential interest to the potential video drama writer, is that of name identification. The Middle brother greets Poletti, "Hi Phil." He could have said merely, "Hi," which would have been natural enough but would not have given any information to the viewer.

Bob Crean has drawn another vivid portrait in Phil Poletti. The grocer's inability to grasp the underlying significance of the Santonello invitation, his obeisance to his mother, his awkward responses, delineate him finely as a shy, socially unresponsive individual. Withal, he is likeable, and sympathetically drawn. The scene at the Santonello home, when Poletti inevitably becomes the rejected suitor, is written with great sensitivity and understanding. We are sorry for the shy grocer but we know that Anna could not have responded in any other way.

The preceding scene between Anna and Teresa served to prepare us for Anna's rejection of Poletti. Teresa, shrewdly again, realizes that Anna, much as she may protest, is in love with Kelly. And there is dramatic foreshadowing in Anna's remark that, "Someday my machine might break down or something." There is a deft contrast portrayed between the characters of Anna and Teresa. The forthright Teresa would hit the dryer with a hammer. The shy, gentle Anna turns to prayer.

The symbolism of the father's chair is utilized again when

Poletti seats himself in the armchair. Anna studies him as if meditating whether he could replace her father in her life.

The scene between Anna and her brothers is sensitively written. Awkwardly, they try to tell her that they want to do the right things for her, that she is not a servant in the house. But it is Anna who finally finds herself, who realizes the truth now, as she tells her brothers, "I am not your mama . . . you are not my sons. And papa is not my little baby." Her ultimate freedom is achieved with her declaration, "This isn't Papa's chair. Papa's dead. He don't need no chair."

The truth of her statement leads to a violent reaction on the part of the Eldest. He slaps his sister who runs out to the laundry room and clings to the dryer which is now her symbol of strength. The violence of the Eldest results in his breaking the door of the dryer and Anna's outspoken bid for freedom has had the happy consequence of having her prayer answered. This is the climax of the play and the third and final act can well end on this note. However, the brief epilogue, actually the resolution, with Kelly coming to fix the dryer may have given the viewer more satisfaction.

There is a somewhat analogous situation in the movie version of Chayefsky's TV play, "Marty," when Marty, despite his mother's remark that she doesn't like the girl he has met and his friend's disparagement of the girl as a "dog," still decides to call her. In the movie version, we saw the girl waiting anxiously at home for her phone to ring, trying hard to keep the tears from streaming as the time passes without a call. In the final sequence, we see Marty in the telephone booth dialing her number. The screen play ends there. Many moviegoers we spoke to expressed the wish that the play had had an additional scene: the girl answering the phone and the happiness that must, perforce, have lighted up her face. This would have been akin to the epilogue for "Anna Santonello."

The question may be raised, would the additional "Marty" scene have been anticlimactic? And what of the "Anna Santonello" epilogue? The epilogue is very brief. As a matter of fact, it was played while the credits rolled. The "Marty" scene would have taken a few brief seconds. In the last analysis, the final curtain is the writer's choice. He may debate it with himself or with the director but each writer will reach his own individual conclusion.

Adaptations

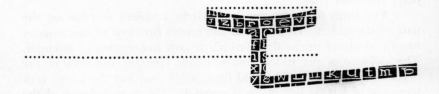

16

A large percentage of the current television dramas are adaptations. There is a twofold reason for this: television's insatiable need for scripts, and the fact that the primary source is proven material. A short story published in a national magazine has already met the test of popular approval. A successful play or novel has won the plaudits of a large audience. The word "large" is used here only in a relative sense. A hit play, running for a year on Broadway, might be seen by an estimated quarter of a million people. This is the proverbial drop of water compared to the oceanic size of the audience viewing a highly rated television program. It is obvious, therefore, that even the most successful stories, plays or novels will have been read or seen by only a comparative minority of the television audience. Therefore, most adaptations are, for all intents and purposes, new material to the vast majority of viewers.

Literary rights

For the professional, adaptations are an added source of income; for the beginning writer, they are excellent exercises. This statement is not meant to be facetious. Most TV adaptations are written on assignment. The producing agency or network obtains the rights to a copyright work and then assigns a known writer to adapt the vehicle. The unknown dramatist will find it difficult, if not almost impossible, to obtain the rights to any successfully published story. Prominent writers are invariably represented by leading literary agents and they, in turn, are constantly attempting to sell their clients' output to other suitable media.

In the case of public domain works, the beginner will find again that even with such literary properties, the producers prefer to work on assignment. However, since so many adaptations are utilized on television, it is of vital importance that the neophyte be trained in this phase of writing.

Liberties of the adaptor

The question we are most frequently asked by students is: how much liberty can be taken in adapting a short story, a novel or a stage play to television?

It is not a question which can be answered in one brief statement. At times, the adaptor may hew very closely to the original. At other times, it may seem as if only the title remains of the original. On the surface, there would appear to be little point in a producer purchasing a story and then having an adaptor turn in a play which had little or no resemblance to the original. Presumably, the story property was purchased in the first place because it had appealed to many readers. Since radio and television are mass media, rights for short stories are generally purchased from the mass circulation magazines; novels are chosen from the ranks of best sellers, and plays from former Broadway hits.

Nevertheless, the requirements of the broadcast media are such that it takes an expert craftsman to make a skillful adaptation. What sufficed for the novel or the short story may not be valid for the drama. The novelist, for example, may permit himself the luxury of detailed descriptions, of many subplots, of dozens of minor characters, of many changes of scene. He can write: "Kenneth left his office, walked swiftly down the hall and into the waiting elevator. In the lobby, he stopped at the newsstand for his evening paper, glanced briefly at the headlines and then went out to the street. There he hailed a cab which made its way tortuously through the rush hour traffic to Grand Central Station. It was getting late so he ran through the station and along the platform, catching his train just as it was about to depart." In these four sentences there are seven changes of scene, and these scenes would also call for a flock of extras. It is true that a filmed TV play could encompass all these details by the use of stock clips and perhaps a couple of sets, but then the element of time enters, a problem which does not beset the novelist. The adaptor is always conscious of the fact that he has an arbitrary time limit.

The art of compression

The adaptor must make a decision as to which characters and which scenes of the original story he will retain. Christopher Isherwood, commenting in *Variety* on his adaptation of the Romain Rolland novel, *Jean Christophe,* for the films, stated that where two or more characters exerted the same kind of influence on Christophe, they could be fused into one character. Also, he went on, with some levity, "Romain Rolland in his novel creates enough romantic female characters to stock a harem. We have limited ourselves to four."

You will find, therefore, that in adapting many short stories and novels, you will have to fuse two or more characters into one. The novelist may bring in a minor character, for a chapter or two, who has some bearing on the main plot. In another chapter, a different character assists in the progression of the story. It is possible for the adaptor to assign both actions to the same person.

In the matter of scenes, an adaptation for a live TV play will face more difficulties than preparing an adaptation for filming. There is a limit in the number and the expanse of sets for the live production. Again, it will be necessary to combine several scenes into one, much in the manner of fusing characters. Two vital actions occurring in different scenes may be transposed to one scene.

In the novel or the full-length stage play, there are usually one or more subplots. If the adaptation is to be a half-hour video or radio play, the subplots, almost always, will have to be eliminated. For the hour or 90-minute adaptation, a subplot may be included.

The half-hour adaptation will begin practically at the climax of the story to be adapted. The novel can open with a lengthy description of the protagonist, can delve deeply into his ancestry, can probe into his every thought. There is no time for these excursions in the half-hour or even the hour video drama. But the video dramatist does have the advantage of the visual. Where the novelist may take many paragraphs to describe the physical appearance and the dress of a character, the dramatist has the actor and his costume.

It is generally simpler to adapt the stage play to television than the novel or short story. The stage play is written in dialogue so that it may be possible to use much of the original, and since the stage play is visual, much of the action and business may also be incorporated in the adaptation. Radio presents more of a problem because the adaptor may have to rewrite a good deal of the dialogue to compensate for the visual action. In either case, the arbitrary time limits of the broadcast media make compression essential.

The novel or the short story may have a minimum of dialogue with much of the prose devoted to the thought processes of the characters. The adaptor must translate thought into action. This can be done through dialogue, by having the character express his thoughts, in a conversational give and take, to another character, assuming that the thought passages you have chosen are essential to the play's progression. It may be possible also to translate the thought process into visual action.

Outlines

The suggestion has been offered by many instructors, and it is a valuable one, that the adaptor make a scene-by-scene outline of the story. This skeleton of the novel, play or short story will enable the adaptor to view with more clarity the underlying structure of the work. He can then more readily make a decision as to which scenes or characters may be combined or eliminated, and, most important, whether he is to follow the original story line faithfully or incorporate any major changes.

So much then for the generalities. Let us now examine a specific instance, an adaptation for television.

"Dr. Jekyll and Mr. Hyde"

The classic tale of "Dr. Jekyll and Mr. Hyde," by Robert Louis Stevenson, lends itself admirably to dramatization. The fact is, it has been dramatized for both stage and screen and recently a very fine adaptation was made of the story by Robert Esson for NBC's "Matinee Theater." By comparing the original Stevenson story with the Esson adaptation, we will achieve a very practical lesson.

It must be noted, first of all, that the adaptor was faced not only with the task of turning a prose story into a drama but also that he had to meet the unique requirements of "Matinee Theater." Some of these requirements we have mentioned previously, but they will bear repeating: the cast to number a maximum of eight, the play to open with a teaser of about a minute and a half in length, the scenes planned so that they fit into the cameo technique, the drama to be divided into three acts and to run some 47 minutes.

There was no problem here of literary rights since the story is in the public domain. We might suggest that if you have never read "Dr. Jekyll and Mr. Hyde," you ought to do so. It is a very compelling story and it is one you are not likely to forget. You might term it a long short story. In some editions, it runs to 65 pages. Perhaps it might be classified as a novelette.

Robert Esson's adaptation of the Stevenson classic answers very thoroughly the question of how much liberty the adaptor may take with the original story. The basic Jekyll-Hyde transformation has remained, of course, in the adaptation, but beyond that it is largely Esson's story.

Many of the major and minor characters are omitted including Dr. Lanyon, Jekyll's colleague, and Richard Enfield, close friend of Utterson, who is Dr. Jekyll's lawyer. The characters appearing in the adaptation are as follows: Dr. Henry Jekyll, Polly Bannon, Utterson, Peter, Mr. Hyde, a double for Polly, and Poole, the butler. There is no Polly Bannon or Peter in the original story. These characters are the invention of the adaptor.

Presumably the introduction of Polly Bannon, a dancer, as a major character, was to lend romantic interest which the original story lacked. The "Matinee Theater" audience, being composed almost entirely of women, would be more favorably inclined, it is assumed, to a drama which had a feminine lead as well as a male lead.

The adaptation opens with a teaser sequence which shows Peter, a stage doorman, warning Polly that it is not safe for her to go home alone. A fearsome, ugly man has been waiting for her at the stage door, but Peter has sent him away. However, Polly insists on going home alone. She is not afraid. At the close of the teaser, we see the wheel of a carriage and from behind a curtain Mr. Hyde peers out ominously. This teaser sequence, with its presentiment of danger, is bound to hold our interest. The commercial follows this scene and then the first act begins. In this act, Polly is discovered lying in the street. Her ankle is broken. Mr. Hyde's carriage has deliberately run over her. Dr. Jekyll appears, seemingly out of nowhere, and takes her to his office to treat the broken ankle. This begins a strange, romantic interlude.

Now, it is possible that the introduction of Polly Bannon and the accident was a complete invention of the adaptor. However, there is a scene in the original story in which Mr. Hyde on one of his nocturnal adventures jostles a young girl and then steps on her cruelly as she falls to the ground. This scene may have inspired the Polly Bannon episode.

We have spoken of the necessity for the adaptor to combine characters and scenes. This Robert Esson has achieved very effectively. In the original story, Edward Hyde murders Sir Danvers Carew, a member of Parliament. But in the adaptation, it is Utterson, the lawyer, who is murdered. Utterson is absolutely essential to the story. Therefore, the same end is achieved, that of having Hyde commit the ultimate crime, but an extra character and an extra scene is eliminated. Utterson actually serves a threefold purpose in the adaptation. In the Stevenson story, it is Dr. Lanyon who first witnesses the Jekyll-Hyde transformation. We learn of this episode only from a letter left by Dr. Lanyon in which he describes his emotions on seeing the metamorphosis. But in the adaptation, it is Utterson who is the spectator at this most horrifying transformation. This is translating thought into action. The scene where Utterson discovers the good Dr. Jekyll changing to the evil Mr. Hyde is the curtain scene for Act One, a very powerful curtain.

Almost all of the "Matinee Theater" plays are presented live. This posed somewhat of a problem in respect to the transformation scenes. If the play were on film, Jekyll and Hyde could readily be played by the same character. Here, Jekyll and Hyde are played by two different actors. This is acceptable because Hyde in physical appearance is completely different from Jekyll. Note how the transformation sequence is accomplished by the use of a duplicate set in this first act curtain scene, where Utterson has come to the doctor's laboratory looking for Edward Hyde.

DISSOLVE TO . . . . LABORATORY
(SOUND: DOOR OPENED SLOWLY.)
(LIGHT STRIKES CHEMICAL APPARATUS.)
(UTTERSON MOVES IN, TURNS UP LAMP AND LOOKS AROUND HIM.)
UTTERSON: Mr. Hyde — Are you here, sir? (CROSSES TO CORNER) Mr. Hyde.
(HE TURNS AS:)
(SOUND: DOOR IS SLAMMED — FAR BACK — FOOTSTEPS HURRY IN.)
(HENRY ENTERS, MOVES TO A SHELF IN CABINET, FILLS HIS VIAL FROM A GREAT DARK BOTTLE AND CROSSES TO DESK, HOLDING HAND TO HIS THROAT.)
UTTERSON (FRIGHTENED): Henry!
HENRY (WHIRLS): What are you doing here?
UTTERSON: Are you in pain? What's wrong with you?
HENRY: Get out! Get out of here! (AT HIS GESTURE, VIAL FALLS
    FROM HIS HAND BEYOND DESK) No — (HE BOWS HEAD TO
    DESK AND HIS HANDS WRITHE OUT TO ITS EDGE) No —
UTTERSON: Is it something you need?
(CUT TO: FLOOR BELOW — DUPLICATE — DESK AND ANOTHER
    VIAL, SMASHED, LIQUID SPILLED.)
UTTERSON: I'll get it for you. (ENTERS TO KNEEL) Is there more?
    This is gone. Can I get you more? Tell me where — (HE
    LOOKS OVER DESK AND HIS EYES GROW WIDE) Henry.
    What's happening to you?
(MUSIC: STRONG.)
(PULL BACK TO INCLUDE GNARLED HANDS GRASPING THE DESK
    EDGE AND THEN MR. HYDE, LIFTING HIS HEAD.)
UTTERSON (IN HORROR): Henry — !
                    DISSOLVE TO . . . . COMMERCIAL

The device of a double for Polly is utilized where Polly is to make the horrendous discovery that Jekyll and Hyde are one. Henry Jekyll and she have been discussing the imprisonment of an old man for the murder of Utterson. Polly believes the old man is not the criminal.

HENRY: You were ready to have them pick up Hyde for the way he looks. This other man has been identified.

POLLY: It frightens me, somehow. Someone else, on so little evidence, he'll die.

HENRY (TIGHTER CLOSE-UP, CUTTING OUT POLLY): And then it will be over. Finally. For good.

(HE CROSSES TO ANOTHER COUCH, WHERE DOUBLE FOR POLLY SITS, BACK TO CAMERA, ONLY HER HAIR AND SHOULDERS SEEN.)

HENRY (FACING HER, AND CAMERA): I don't want us to wait through the ugliness of a trial and hanging. They've found the killer. You'll marry me now, if you love me. You'll leave with me now and help me forget this thing. Do you love me?

(DOUBLE FOR POLLY HESITATES, THEN LIFTS HER ARMS TO EMBRACE HIM AND DRAW HIS FACE TO HER OWN.)

(CUT TO: TIGHT CLOSE-UP — POLLY)

(ON ORIGINAL COUCH, HYDE IN HER ARMS NOW, HIS BACK TO CAMERA.)

POLLY: You know the answer. I will help you. We'll travel to the sunlight and water, if that's what you want. We'll marry whenever you say. (DRAWING BACK TO KISS HIM) Our lives can begin now — together.

(HER JAW FALLS. EYES WIDEN. PARALYZED, SHE RECOILS.)

(MUSIC: STRONG)

(HYDE TURNS INTO CAMERA, LIFTING HANDS TO HIS FACE. HE REACHES OUT TO POLLY, WHO BACKS AWAY.)

(HE RUNS FROM ROOM.)

(CAMERA MOVES IN TO POLLY, WHO STAYS FROZEN FOR A MOMENT, THEN GIVES IN TO THE SCREAM SHE'S BEEN HOLDING.)

DISSOLVE TO . . . . COMMERCIAL

We have a powerful crisis to end Act Two, a sequence, by the way, which is not present in the original story since, as we stated, the love motif is not part of Stevenson's tale. Act Three is also largely the invention of the adaptor. In the original story, Dr. Jekyll realizes that he must take the restorative potion more often now to transform himself from Hyde, his evil self, to Jekyll. A dreadful situation has arisen since the doctor finds himself turning into Hyde now without any use of the evil-inducing potion. Hyde is being hunted by the police for the murder of Carew. The doctor locks himself in his laboratory and communicates with his butler, Poole, only by messages. Most of these messages are requests for a certain chemical which is now unavailable. When Poole and Utterson break open the laboratory door, on the assumption that Dr. Jekyll has been murdered, they discover instead the dead body of Mr. Hyde, who has committed suicide. A letter left by Henry Jekyll explains the mystery and reveals the tragic details.

The adaptation has Polly and the butler, Poole, hunting for Edward Hyde who has fled the Jekyll residence. Polly knows she is actually hunting for Dr. Jekyll. She finds Hyde at the waterfront and faces him bravely even as he attempts to strangle her. She tells him that she has full faith that love can conquer evil. She is willing to die for that faith. As she makes this statement, Hyde is transformed into Jekyll. At the close of the play, Henry Jekyll gives himself up to the police.

Adaptor Robert Esson has also introduced a new concept to the "Strange Case of Dr. Jekyll and Mr. Hyde": that of love conquering evil. The original story was a study in schizophrenia, Stevenson advancing the theory that man is two selves: good and evil, and that once evil is given a foothold, it will destroy the good in us.

The revelations in the Stevenson story are handled in a passive manner, that is, by the device of Jekyll and Lanyon leaving letters explaining the transformations. In the TV play, the revelations come about actively with both Utterson and Polly actually witnessing the changes, and Jekyll explaining the metamorphosis directly to Utterson.

The task of the adaptor, then, is not a simple one. True, he has a basic story, an imaginative theme to begin with. But more often than not, he has to call upon his own inventiveness, to a great degree, as Robert Esson did. He has to be able to make important decisions as to what to keep and what to eliminate. And as a craftsman, he has to be able to tailor his work to meet the requirements of a very exacting taskmaster: the television drama.

The series plays

17

Slowly at first and then very rapidly, television enticed into its own more lucrative airwaves most of the successful radio presentations. These included the Series Plays: Situation Comedies, Mysteries, Westerns, Science Fiction, Adventure, and so on. Some of the stalwarts of radio became mainstays of the new medium. But television soon bred its own creations, a multitude of them. Many of them stayed but a season. Some of them appeared destined to run unto eternity.

Undoubtedly the series programs are highly popular, yet so fickle is the taste and the loyalty of the viewer that if we were to mention a dozen or so series plays on this page, it is altogether possible that half of them might not be on the air by the time this book reaches the reader.

Nevertheless, for the writer, the series play offers a highly lucrative field. Sometimes no more than one or two writers may be assigned to a weekly series and for at least thirty-nine weeks during the year, these writers may be assured of an excellent income, especially if the series is as successful and long running as "I Love Lucy." Some writers develop a TV series of their own and sell it as a package so that they actually become entrepreneurs and derive an additional profit from their share in the program.

Almost all series plays are filmed and by far the majority of them are Hollywood productions. These film series may be fairly economical or very expensive. Costume dramas shot on location with large casts require vast budgets. On the other hand, family situation comedies may use the same sets continually and confine most of their shooting to interiors. Filming the plays also permits setting up a backlog which would take care of any unforeseen emergency such as the illness of the star.

Rather than spend much time on generalities regarding the series plays, we will explore several specific types with script illustrations. We believe, in that way, we will be able to give you a better insight into this phase of television writing. Permit us, however, to offer one sweeping generality: the series plays revolve about the same character or characters who appear in each episode, and the success of a series depends on the degree of acceptability of the character or characters by the home audience.

One more point: there are some programs on the air which may appear to be of the series type but are more properly classed as anthologies. The two Ziv produced programs "West Point" and "Annapolis," for example, use the same historic locale every week but each story presents different characters.

The anthologies generally employ many different writers or buy scripts on the free lance market whereas the series plays usually have the same writer or a small stable of writers preparing scripts. However, the anthologies and the series do have one element in common: both present a different and complete play each week.

THE SITUATION COMEDY

Situation comedies were highly successful on radio and are equally so on television. There are many readily apparent reasons for their success. Situation comedies, when well written, are highly entertaining, wholesome and relaxing, and often mirror some of the common problems or obvious absurdities of our daily living.

Most of the top rated situation comedies tend to be of the "family" type: "Father Knows Best," "I Love Lucy," "Ozzie and Harriet," "Life of Riley," "Mama." There are others written around a central character such as "Private Secretary," "December Bride,"

"Our Miss Brooks." A minority fall into the miscellaneous category: "It's a Great Life," "The Brothers." From the long-run aspect, the family series appears to have the edge.

There are variations of appeal within the same category. "I Love Lucy" engenders hilarity, has no compunctions about employing slapstick and its emphasis is on farce rather than comedy. Lucille Ball is a delightful comedienne and Desi Arnaz an excellent foil. Their antics have amused countless millions for many years. The farcical approach necessitates fast pacing and anyone who has viewed an "I Love Lucy" program must be aware of the constant rapidity of movement, the flow of gags and puns and the vaudeville type of situation. There is no attempt at any verisimilitude. The humor is broad and guaranteed for merriment.

Any potential situation comedy writer must be conscious of facing a constant challenge to turn out a mirth-provoking play week after week. The ability to do this will insure a steady and rather lucrative future for the writer. It is a most difficult task, as witness the many situation comedies which rise and shine for a brief span only to find their ratings suddenly fallen to low estate and their sponsors grown apathetic.

Although "I Love Lucy" and "Father Knows Best" are both situation comedies using the family as a nucleus, their approach differs considerably. "Father Knows Best" relies on familiar situations, family problems recognizable to the majority of viewers. It is comedy and not farce and there is a good deal of verisimilitude. The family is typical: Jim Anderson, an insurance broker, played by Robert Young, his wife, Margaret, played by Jane Wyatt, and their three children, Betty and Bud, who are teenagers and Kathy, who's a bit younger. The Andersons would find their counterpart in almost any fair-sized city.

"Father Knows Best" — a typical episode

"Spaghetti for Margaret," written by Roswell Rogers, is a typical episode in the life of the Andersons. It opens breezily, good-humoredly and sets up a seemingly unimportant incident which eventually proves the key to the resolution of the play.

"SPAGHETTI FOR MARGARET"

FADE IN:

INT. KITCHEN — DAY

CLOSE SHOT MARGARET (PATIO DOOR IN BG)

SHE HAS ON RUBBER GLOVES AND IS CLEANING THE STOVE, AS THE PATIO DOOR FLIES OPEN, AND BUD BARGES IN, CAUSING MARGARET TO CRINGE IN FEAR OF HER LIFE. HE IS WAVING A SMALL CARD.

BUD: Hey, mom! Guess what, mom! You — *you are a winner!* An E-flat, gold-plated, souped-up winner!

MARGARET: I am? Winner of what?

BUD: Winner of what, she says. Mom, don't you remember the chance I sold you for a buck? You know, when we were raising money for the Hi-Y, and the merchants put up prizes and all that?

MARGARET: Oh, yes . . . that.

BUD: Yes, that. And today we had the drawing, and you — oh little gray haired mother of mine — you are a big, fat winner!

MARGARET: You mean I actually won that television set?

BUD: Oh no, that was *first* prize.

MARGARET: Oh. Well what was the second prize?

BUD: Second prize was a hickory-smoked, sugar-baked Virginia ham!

MARGARET: Oh, really?!

BUD: But you didn't win that either. You got the thirteenth prize.

MARGARET: Thirteenth?

BUD: And here's the little beauty right here. (SHOWS HER THE CARD) A spaghetti feed for one at Lazarro's Pizza House. Pretty cool, huh?

MARGARET (TAKING CARD): Downright freezing.

BUD: And look — not just once can you go there, but *every week!* See — *fifty-two free feeds!* How about that? I guess you're just lucky, huh, mom?

MARGARET: I guess so.

BUD (LEAVING): I'm gonna call dad. Tell him your good news.

MARGARET: Oh no, don't bother your father at work.

BUD (HALTING): Listen, he'll be *glad* to be bothered with news like this. Think how comforting it'll be to know that even if he goes broke, his little wife can eat free spaghetti for the next fifty-two weeks!

BUD EXITS. MARGARET LOOKS AT THE CARD, SHAKES HER HEAD IN AMAZEMENT. SHE FOLDS IT AND TOSSES IT IN THE WASTEBASKET UNDER THE SINK.

The scene shifts to the office of Jim Anderson who is seen handing an insurance loan application and some money to an elderly man, carrying an old frayed briefcase. This is Harper Eames, who used to be Jim's teacher in grammar school but is now evidently destitute. Mr. Eames has illusions of being a famous author and dreams that some day a great banquet will be held in his honor. When Eames leaves, Jim tears up the loan application and we discover that this bit of kindly deception has been going on for some time. This exposition comes to us from Miss Thomas, Jim's secretary.

MISS THOMAS: I know it's none of my business, Mister Anderson, but how much longer are you going to go on financing that old — What I don't understand is how he has enough nerve to keep coming in here, pretending to borrow money on an insurance policy that lapsed at least sixteen years ago.

JIM (TAKES DESK PEN): Oh, don't be so hard on old Harper Eames. He's not a bad sort. He never could bring himself to walk in here and say, "Look, I'm broke and hungry; I need some money." But this way — well, it keeps his dignity intact. In his mind, it keeps him honest.

MISS THOMAS (SNORTS): Honest!

JIM: He doesn't do any harm with his illusions. If he didn't keep on thinking his book — which he's been writing for thirty years — would be published, and that some day the town would honor him with a banquet, — what would he have? (TRIES TO SIGN LETTER, BUT PEN WON'T WORK) Oh, this thing! Always out of ink. (PUTS IT ASIDE, REACHES IN POCKET FOR FOUNTAIN PEN, BUT NOT THERE) Now what did I do with that pen?

MISS THOMAS: Probably Mister Eames stole it.

JIM (FEELING AROUND ON DESK): Oh no, he'd never do a — (SUDDENLY REMEMBERS) By George, he did borrow it . . .

HE LOOKS ON FLOOR WHERE EAMES WAS SITTING, THEN UP AT

Miss Thomas, who has an i-told-you-so look on her
face.
Jim: But he didn't steal it!
She stares at him a moment, then heads for the door.
Miss Thomas: I'll get some ink for your desk pen . . . which you'll
have to use until your fountain pen turns up . . . *at some pawn
shop.*
She exits. Jim sits there, staring off thoughtfully, as
we:

Fade out.

First Commercial

The discovery of the missing pen is a minor crisis and brings
down the curtain for the first commercial. "Father Knows Best," as
we can see, opens with a dramatic sequence rather than a commercial. This is calculated to capture immediate audience attention.

Scene Three finds us back in the Anderson home and we discover another part of the plot taking shape. At first, like the prize-
winning ticket, it appears to have no direct bearing on the basic
plot. Kathy, the youngest of the Andersons, comes home from
school in a fret. She had been unaware of a rip in the back of her
dress and when she stepped to the blackboard, the class laughed at
her. Her discomfiture wasn't alleviated by the fact that on her way
back to her seat, she tripped and fell sprawling to the floor. She
believes herself now the laughing stock of the school and she wants
to do something heroic to save her face.

Kathy: Oh, I wish I could do something to show 'em! I wish I
could swim nine miles out in the ocean and save five people
from drowning and get my name in all the newspapers!
Betty: What good would that do?
Kathy: That'd show 'em! Make 'em sorry they ever laughed at
me. I wish there was a parade and the mayor'd ask me to lead
it on a white horse, and all those little smart alecs would be
lined up watchin' me ride by. And I'd throw 'em some cheap
candy.

Later, Kathy goes to answer the doorbell. It is Harper Eames
coming to the Andersons to return the pen he had inadvertently taken
with him. Jim Anderson is on the phone at the moment and Kathy
talks to Eames who tells her he is a famous author, a good friend

of her daddy's. What's more, he continues, a big banquet is going to be thrown in his honor and he will invite Kathy as his personal guest. This sequence has two pronounced effects. The return of the pen vindicates Jim's faith in old Eames and the invitation to Kathy from a "famous" author now gives her a place in the sun. Without further ado, Kathy runs out to tell her friends the wonderful news. Then, still agog, she returns home to regale her parents, as Jim is showing the pen triumphantly to Margaret.

MARGARET (SURPRISED): Eames? Here? What's the matter, didn't he get enough from you at the office today?
JIM, SMILING CONFIDENTLY, SHOWS HER THE PEN.
JIM: I know very few people who would take the trouble to walk clear across town just to return a little pen. Very few.
MARGARET IS LOOKING AT THE PEN, A LITTLE TAKEN ABACK, AS THE DOOR BANGS OPEN AND KATHY BARGES IN, EXCITED.
KATHY: Boy, you shoulda seen Patty when I told her. Her old eyes bugged out! At first she wouldn't believe I was going to this banquet!
MARGARET: Banquet? What banquet?
KATHY: The banquet they're giving for the famous author — daddy's friend. He invited *me* to be *his guest!*
MARGARET: Oh, no!
KATHY: Boy, this is the greatest thing that ever happened to me! And just when I needed it too! (HEADS TOWARD KITCHEN) Hey, Betty! Betty! Guess what!
MARGARET TURNS TOWARD JIM, LOOKS AT HIM ACCUSINGLY. HE HAS NO ANSWER FOR HER.

FADE OUT.
MIDDLE COMMERCIAL

And so the first act ends with a big crisis. Certainly, not an earth shaking crisis. There never is one in a situation comedy. But it is a crisis all the same and it keeps us tuned in to discover the outcome.

The second act opens with Kathy relaying the news about the banquet to more and more of her friends. Naturally enough, Jim and Margaret are now worried about the snowballing situation. Bud enters while his father and mother are debating the situation and this leads to an important facet of the plot.

During Margaret's speech, Bud drifts into the scene.

Bud: What about Kathy? What's she been goofin' up now?

Margaret: Oh — nothing. Why don't you go burn the trash. You've been neglecting that lately.

Bud: Okay, but what's Kathy —

Margaret: Go burn the trash!

Camera pans Bud to the sink where he takes the waste-basket from under it.

Bud: Okay, okay, okay. If I wasn't so loveable, witty and popular, I'd think you were trying to get rid of me.

He heads toward the patio door, but then stops as he sees something in the wastebasket. he reacts, then takes the crumpled spaghetti feed ticket out of the basket and turns back toward the others. camera pans him back.

Bud (continuing): Hey! Look, mom! Your free spaghetti ticket got thrown in the wastebasket! It's all bent up! How do you suppose that happened?

He hands it to Margaret.

Margaret: Oh — uh — must have been an accident.

Bud: Lucky thing I happened to see it, eh, mom?

Margaret: Very lucky.

Bud: If I hadn't seen it, it woulda got burned up, and then you wouldn't have gotten to go to Lazarro's Pizza House every week for —

Margaret: Bud, go burn the trash!

Bud: Okay, I'm going, I'm going.

He exits.

The winning ticket is brought into focus again but we are still not aware of its implications. Even if we do begin to surmise, we are confronted now by Kathy's plight. A couple of her friends have thrown cold water on her banquet dreams by doubting that Eames is a famous author. Margaret is also upset and is angered at Eames for having lied to her daughter. But Jim explains to his wife what Eames' teaching meant to him.

Margaret: All right — there's no banquet — so now let's talk sense. How can we tell her the truth without hurting her any more than she already has been . . .

Jim (thoughtfully as he sits down): I wonder what a banquet would cost —?

MARGARET: Oh, now, Jim! Let's don't be ridiculous. Think of all the money that old Harper has already cost you. In fact, *that's* what's caused this whole thing.

JIM: Huh?

MARGARET: If you hadn't kept him going all these years, he would have gotten a decent job and stepped out of his world of illusion.

JIM: Yes, I guess so . . . But — that would have been no life for him. Besides, I couldn't let him down.

MARGARET: Exactly what do you mean — let him down? This I've often wondered about.

JIM: Well — I don't know — when I was a kid in his class, he tried to make me understand what the true values of life were. I still remember the last couple of lines of a little poem he taught me — "Of all best things upon earth, I hold that a faithful friend is the best."

BETTY (WRYLY): That's a far cry from "Eames, Eames, full of beans . . . "

MARGARET: And I think it's been a fairly one-sided friendship, too.

JIM: No, it hasn't. I remember days in college when I didn't think I was going to make it. You know what kept me going? It was things old Harper had taught me. (PAUSE) And when I opened the insurance office, and there were some pretty black days, it was thoughts Harper had given me that helped me keep on struggling.

It is then that Margaret, who has been nervously twisting the winning spaghetti ticket in her hands, has an inspiration. But she refuses to tell Jim what she has in mind. The next scene finds her at Lazarro's Pizza House. In a very humorous sequence, Margaret arranges for a remarkable banquet.

MARGARET: Now tell me, Mister Lazarro, how many people can you serve here? At one time, I mean.

LAZARRO: Oh — forty-five — fifty if we squeeze a little.

MARGARET: That's fine. Now here's what I would like: I would like all my fifty-two free dinners this Friday night.

LAZARRO: All right, fine, we'll — (BIG TAKE) What??? What you say??? All fifty-two — in one night?

MARGARET: That's right. It's to be a sort of a banquet.

LAZARRO (JUMPING UP, STABBED TO THE SOUL): No, no, no, you got the wrong idea! *One* a *week!* That's it. One a week!
MARGARET: The ticket doesn't say that. Read it. It just says "fifty-two free spaghetti feeds."
LAZARRO TRIES TO FOCUS HIS EYES ON THE TICKET IN HIS HAND, AND WHAT HE READS IS PRETTY PAINFUL TO HIM.
LAZARRO: Well, this — this — anybody knows this means one a week. Not all in one — What are you trying to do? Bankrupt me? Why don't you like me?
MARGARET: I like you fine. Now, I wonder if you could put several tables together — (INDICATES) say, right over there —
LAZARRO SLUMPS DOWN IN HIS CHAIR, DEFEATED.
LAZARRO: Signora, I don't think you're gonna like it here. My spaghetti is — just —
HE SHRUGS, GESTURES TO INDICATE HIS SPAGHETTI IS NOT SO HOT.
LAZARRO (CONTINUING): It's miserable.
MARGARET: It'll be fine. And don't look so glum. You may be playing host to some very important people.
LAZARRO: Important people. That makes going broke better?
MARGARET (RISES, SMILING): You won't. Besides, you'll get some publicity out of this you couldn't buy for *two hundred* plates of spaghetti. Thank you, Mister Lazarro. You've been very sweet.

When Margaret tells Jim what she has done about arranging for an unexpected banquet, he is joyfully amazed. Hurriedly, invitations are extended but there remains one significant problem: the guest of honor cannot be found! When Bud suggests that his father look up Mr. Eames in the phone book, Jim replies:

JIM (LAUGHS): Phone book? The phone company never heard of Harper Eames, famous author. He lives around in little rooms, moving every time the rent is due. Let's see — Where would I find him — ?
THE SCENE DISSOLVES TO THE EXTERIOR OF LAZARRO'S PIZZA HOUSE.
EXT. SIDEWALK IN FRONT OF LAZARRO'S PIZZA HOUSE — DAY

CLOSE SHOT SIGN IN WINDOW
THIS IS A BLEAK, BRICK FRONT WITH AN ANCIENT SIGN DECLAR-

ING THIS TO BE LAZARRO'S PIZZA HOUSE ABOVE A WOODEN
DOOR WITH HEAVY IRON FITTINGS. BENEATH THE ONE
WINDOW IS A NARROW WINDOW BOX WITH A FEW WEARY
PLANTS IN IT. CAMERA HOLDS ON CRUDELY HAND-PRINTED
SIGN IN WINDOW:

> WANTED
> EXTRA WAITER
> EXTRA DISHWASHER
> FRIDAY NIGHT ONLY

CAMERA PULLS BACK TO INCLUDE AN OLD MAN LOOKING AT THE
SIGN. AS HE TURNS SLIGHTLY WE SEE THAT IT IS HARPER
EAMES. HE THINKS A MOMENT, TAKES OUT COIN PURSE,
CHECKS IT; IT'S EMPTY. HE PUTS IT BACK IN HIS POCKET,
STEPS TO THE DOOR AND GOES INSIDE THE RESTAURANT.

So in a poignant, visual sequence, Harper Eames applies for
the job of dishwasher and the threads of the plot are being tied
together. In the next scene, which takes place at the Anderson home,
we have a foreshadowing of the resolution.

JIM: Oh, and here's something else. Dan Thaw said he was familiar
with Harper's so-called book, and though it rambles around it
has a few good thoughts. So he's talked his newspaper into
running a little box in the paper every night under the heading
"Harper Eames says." He'll even get paid for it.

Actually, this statement of Jim Anderson's reveals that Harper
Eames will have a bright, though modest, future. It answers the
question of what is going to happen to Eames once the banquet is
over. This will satisfy the demands of the audience which is very
sympathetic to the old man. However, if it had been placed after
the banquet scene, it would definitely have been anticlimactic, as
you will see.

The final scene takes place at Lazarro's Pizza House.

The guests arrive at the restaurant but the author still cannot
be found. The dinner is held up, with Mr. Lazarro becoming more
wrathful by the minute. The play is now approaching its climax.
Suddenly, when the kitchen door opens, Jim spies old Eames. He
corners Lazarro and insists that Eames be fired. An explanation will
be forthcoming, Jim promises. The restaurant owner, already driven

to desperation, complies. Jim then meets Eames, as, saddened and bewildered, he leaves the restaurant, and the old man is brought back in triumph.

MEDIUM CLOSE SHOT   MARGARET   BETTY   BUD AND KATHY
THEY ARE SEATED AT THE SPEAKER'S TABLE, WITH TWO EMPTY
  CHAIRS BESIDE THEM. A WAITER IS SERVING THE ANTI-
  PASTO. KATHY LOOKS RADIANT AND EXCITED. THE OTHERS
  LOOK APPREHENSIVE. UNDER ALL THIS WE HEAR THE
  BUZZ OF CONVERSATION AND DISHES.
BETTY (WHISPERS TO MARGARET): What did father mean —
He's *almost* here.
MARGARET: I don't know. I just don't know.
SUDDENLY KATHY'S EYES LIGHT UP AS SHE SEES SOMETHING O.S.
KATHY: There he is! There he is!
SHE STANDS UP. ALL LOOK IN THAT DIRECTION. KATHY STARTS
  APPLAUDING.
MEDIUM CLOSE SHOT   MISTER EAMES AND JIM
MISTER EAMES, CARRYING HIS HAT, AND JIM, CARRYING THE
  BRIEFCASE, WALK FORWARD PAST ONE OR TWO OF THE
  TABLES, AND PAST THE ASTOUNDED LAZARRO, CAMERA
  PULLING BACK. GRADUALLY THE OTHERS JOIN IN THE
  APPLAUSE, WHICH MOUNTS IN VOLUME. MUSIC SNEAKS IN
  AND BUILDS TO A HELL OF A CLIMAX, AS THE CAMERA
  PLAYS ON THE FACE OF MISTER EAMES, WHO REFLECTS
  ALL THE WONDERFUL REALIZATION OF A HOPED FOR BUT
  UNATTAINABLE MOMENT, THE SUBLIME CULMINATION OF
  A LIFE-LONG DREAM.
                                          FADE OUT.

After every episode of "Father Knows Best," we are left with a heart-warming feeling. We have smiled a good deal and sometimes we have laughed outright. At the very least, we spend a pleasant evening with the Andersons and many times a rewarding one. The stories are always within the realm of probability and the protagonists are people we can recognize and understand. Most important, they are people who win our sympathy.

THE CRIME DRAMA

We are using the term "crime" in an all-inclusive sense to cover the multitude of sins, at least those permitted on the TV screen.

From time immemorial, stories of mystery and crime have held a strange fascination for man beginning with the most celebrated crime of all: the slaying of Abel by Cain. Crime abounds in the plays of Shakespeare: the murder of the king by Macbeth; the children cruelly smothered in "Richard the Third"; Othello strangling Desdemona.

Up until the middle of the nineteenth century, the emphasis in literature dealing with crime was on the crime itself and seldom introduced the element of detection. However, history's earliest detective was probably Daniel the Prophet who proved to an idol-worshipping king that his pagan god did not actually consume the quantity of food offerings set before him. By strewing ashes in the temple, Daniel was able to detect the footprints of the priests and their families who came in the dead of night via an underground passage to eat the food.

But the detective in crime fiction, as we know him today, was the conception of Edgar Allan Poe, whose Dupin proved the prototype of many a latter-day sleuth. The growth of the detective story rather parallels the establishment of detective bureaus in the organization of our police departments: Scotland Yard in England, the Sûreté in France, our own FBI, and, of course, the many efficient state and city detective bureaus.

Today, crime stories form an overwhelming body of our literature. Detective fiction readers are a true cross section of our population, from ditch diggers to presidents. For some readers, it is the highest form of relaxation; others find mental stimulation in trying to discover the culprit before the detective protagonist does.

It is no surprise then, that a great many of our television plays fall into the category of crime dramas. Some of them are of the anthology type, such as "Alfred Hitchcock Presents." Many of the half-hour or hour dramatic anthologies present plays that deal with crime. The hour plays, particularly, strive for full-blown characterizations which are the exception rather than the rule in the crime series.

Broadly speaking, we may classify the television crime series in three categories:

1. Private Detective;
2. Police Files;
3. Amateur Sleuth.

The first type features the familiar "private eye": "Richard Diamond," "Boston Blackie," "Martin Kane," "The Fat Man," etc. These detectives are offspring of the master "private eye," Sherlock Holmes. We cannot say how proud the old master is of his TV progeny. The fact is, Holmes and his omnipresent Watson have both invaded television, finding it a lucrative field for the retelling of their suspenseful tales. However, the modern "private eye," assuredly, is made of much sterner stuff, physically, than Holmes. Sherlock often found himself in tight spots, but could he have withstood the constant beatings of the modern private detective! In each episode, the "private eye" is invariably slugged by some blunt instrument; but he bounces back the next week, hale and hearty, completely indestructible.

Another very popular form of crime dramas are those whose stories are culled from police files. They are sometimes referred to as crime documentaries since they are based on actual cases. The most successful of this type is "Dragnet" which obtained its material from the police files of Los Angeles. "The Lineup" uses case histories from San Francisco police files. The high ratings of these programs have led to a host of imitators: "Highway Patrol," "State Trooper," etc.

"Dragnet" and its ilk probably can trace their origin to the classic writer of crime stories, Wilkie Collins. For it is related of Collins that once walking in Paris he came upon some worn records of French criminal cases in an old book shop. In them, he confessed, he found some of his best plots. Crime writers have been searching court records ever since.

Although there are not many amateur sleuths ferreting out criminals on the airwaves, this type of series must be considered in a special category. Probably the most popular of the amateur sleuths was "The Thin Man," so ably played in films by William Powell. On television we have had the "Mr. and Mrs. North" series. Both "The Thin Man" and "Mr. and Mrs. North," you will note, present a husband and wife as the protagonists. Mr. North is in the publishing business, but to all intents and purposes most of his time and Mrs. North's is spent in tracking down crimes that baffle a presumably efficient police force. To the amateur sleuth, detecting is a hobby, but one to which he is devoted and one which he enjoys hugely, especially since his livelihood doesn't depend on it. Usually, in the amateur sleuth series, therefore, a good deal of humor is present.

Plot formula

We advise the writer who is interested in the possibilities of crime dramas to read *The Mystery Writer's Handbook,* edited by Herbert Brean. Although there is only one chapter devoted to the broadcast medium, and that to radio, the comments, observations, admissions and helpful hints by established mystery writers are of great value to the neophyte. It should not be difficult for you to translate the essays into terms of television. Watching current video crime dramas is essential in order to discover not only what is being produced but the formulas that are being used in each instance.

The murder mystery, for example, generally has the corpus delicti found at the first act curtain. There is no rule in the book, however, which states that the victim may not be discovered as the curtain rises. This does have shock value. However, discovering the body at the end of the first act provides a cliffhanger for the commercial. There are then two avenues of approach for detection: (1) the audience knows who the killer is and is engrossed in watching the police untangle the evidence; (2) the audience doesn't know who the killer is and enjoys a vicarious experience in tracking down the clues with the detective.

Characterization

The average video crime drama is light on characterization and heavy on plot. In some of the series, after many episodes, we begin to get an inkling of the protagonist's character as we do in "Dragnet." Sgt. Joe Friday eventually begins to emerge as a person. In so many of the crime series, the protagonists are symbols rather than people.

What part does romance play in the crime series? Very little in the series based on police files. The detectives are too busy chasing criminals to find time for romance in the space of the average half-hour script. If any boy-girl angle is brought into the script, more often than not it takes the form of the man driven to crime in order to provide luxuries for the woman with whom he is infatuated. There is a hint of the romantic angle that sometimes appears in a "Dragnet" script, such as this sequence:

FRANK: You seen Ann lately?

JOE: Ann?

FRANK: The girl you used to go with. Ann Baker. You remember her, don't you?

JOE: Oh, sure.

FRANK: You two still dating?

JOE: I guess so.

FRANK: You haven't had any dates lately, have you?

JOE: We've been busy. You know that.

FRANK: Yeah. When *was* the last time, Joe?

JOE: The last time what?

FRANK: That you took her out?

JOE: I don't remember exactly.

FRANK: Approximately . . .

JOE: What difference does it make?

FRANK: Just kinda curious. That's all.

JOE: Oh, it wasn't so long ago. Around the holidays.

FRANK: What holidays?

JOE: Christmas . . . around in there.

FRANK: This is April, Joe.

JOE: I know it's April.

FRANK: Christmas is in December.

JOE: I'll keep that in mind.

THERE IS A PAUSE WHILE JOE REALIZES THAT IT HAS BEEN SOME MONTHS SINCE HE LAST CALLED ANN.

JOE (CONTINUING): Now that you mention it. . . .

FRANK: Yeah?

JOE: You and Fay doing anything Saturday?

FRANK: No, I don't think so. Why?

JOE: Maybe we can have dinner. The four of us.

FRANK: The four of us?

JOE (WITH GREAT PATIENCE): You and Fay; Ann and me. That makes four, doesn't it?

FRANK (SHAKES HIS HEAD): That makes five.

JOE: What are you talking about, Frank?

FRANK: You'd want to include her husband, wouldn't you?

JOE: Husband?

FRANK: She got married today, Joe.

JOE: Ann?

FRANK (NODS): It's in the paper.

JOE: Oh.

FRANK: I told you, Joe, but you wouldn't listen. You gotta follow through with a girl like that.

Generally, the romantic interest is more prevalent in the private detective and the amateur sleuth series. It is not unusual for the "private eye" to be called into a case that involves a beautiful blond with whom he, in turn, becomes involved. He always manages to extricate himself before the romance becomes too serious so that he may become involved in another tangle the following episode. Or he may have a secretary who is both romantic interest and detective assistant.

However, even when romance is injected into any of the crime series, it always plays a minor role. At times, the romantic interest serves to add additional suspense to the crime drama by using the ancient device of having the girl captured by the criminals and held as hostage.

"Dragnet"

Practically from its inception on the television airwaves, the popularity of "Dragnet" was phenomenal and brought fame and fortune to its producer-star, Jack Webb. For purposes of study, we are including several excerpts from a typical "Dragnet" script, "The Big Genius." This drama opens in standard fashion with Sgt. Joe Friday at police headquarters. Joe is the narrator setting the scene. You will note all through that the drama is underplayed. Joe Friday has a job. It happens to be that of a police sergeant dealing with criminals or suspected criminals. No need for histrionics. This is the story and this is how it happened. It's all told laconically. Short, pithy sentences. Technically, there is much use of the camera closeup. This is the beginning of the basic plot.

JOE (INTO PHONE): Juvenile, Friday . . . Yes, ma'am . . . Uh-huh . . . I see . . . Well, do you know the boy? . . . Uh-huh . . . Would you give me your address please? (REACHES FOR PENCIL AND PAD; MAKES NOTES) I've got it . . . What? . . . Yes, ma'am, we would . . . Will you be home? . . . All right, thank you very much.

JOE HANGS UP THE PHONE, TEARS PAPER FROM PAD AND TURNS TO FRANK.

JOE (TO FRANK): Lady up in the Hollywood Hills. She says some youngster's been stealing groceries out of her garage.

Sgt. Friday and Officer Smith drive out to a hillside address on Edgewood Drive, two miles north of Hollywood Boulevard, where Mrs. Ann Rillston lives. Mrs. Ann Rillston tells the police officers about a youngster stealing food cans out of her garage. She shouted at him and he dropped a bag he was carrying. She accompanies the policemen to the garage.

INT. GARAGE — DAY

As JOE, FRANK AND ANN ENTER. AT THE BACK OF THE GARAGE ARE A COUPLE OF SHELVES WHICH HOLD JARS AND CANNED GOODS. ALONG ONE WALL ARE A FEW TOOLS AND A STOOL. ON THE STOOL IS A PAPER BAG.

JOE: Just what was it he dropped, Mrs. Rillston?

ANN: That bag there. (INDICATES BAG ON STOOL)

JOE WALKS OVER TO THE STOOL AND OPENS THE PAPER BAG. HE TAKES OUT A COUPLE OF CANS OF FOOD, THEN FOUR OR FIVE HEAVY TEXT BOOKS.

INSERT — BOOKS

THEY BEAR SUCH TITLES AS: "THEORETICAL PHYSICS" . . . "PRINCIPLES OF DYNAMICS" . . . "FRONTIERS OF MOLECULAR STRUCTURE."

INT. GARAGE — DAY

JOE READS THE TITLES, FROWNS, THEN HANDS A COUPLE OF THE BOOKS TO FRANK WHO IS EQUALLY PUZZLED.

ANN (CONTINUING): Must be something he's studying. I couldn't make head nor tail of them myself.

JOE: Yes, ma'am.

JOE OPENS A COUPLE OF THE BOOKS TO CHECK THEIR OWNERSHIP.

FRANK: His name in any of them?

JOE (SHAKES HIS HEAD): Hollywood Library.

JOE TURNS TO MRS. RILLSTON.

JOE (CONTINUING): Could you tell us what he looks like, Mrs. Rillston?

ANN: Yes, I guess so. First off, I'd say he looks like books.

JOE: How's that?

ANN: You know, the studying type.

JOE: Oh.

ANN: Sorta thin and pinched.

JOE: I see.

The police are baffled by the type of books. Ann tells them that the boy headed up towards the hill but that he couldn't possibly live there because the street ends a hundred yards up. Sgt. Friday and Officer Smith exchange significant glances and decide to explore the woods.

EXT. CANYON — DAY — (SILENT)

UNIT 1K80 COMES TO THE END OF THE CANYON ROAD. THERE ARE NO HOUSES IN THE IMMEDIATE AREA. A FEW YARDS UP THE SIDE OF THE NEARBY HILL IS A SMALL OPENING.

JOE'S VOICE: Frank and I left Mrs. Rillston and we drove up to the end of Edgewood Drive.

FRANK AND JOE GET OUT OF THE CAR AND LOOK AROUND. JOE SPOTS THE NEARBY CAVE ENTRANCE AND POINTS TO IT.

JOE'S VOICE (CONTINUING): About two hundred yards east of the road, we spotted what appeared to be the opening to a natural cave.

JOE AND FRANK START TOWARD THE CAVE, AS WE:

DISSOLVE TO:

INT. CAVE — DAY

JOE AND FRANK CRAWL INTO THE CAVE. IT IS A SMALL, SHALLOW OPENING ABOUT FIVE BY EIGHT. IN ONE CORNER IS A SLEEPING BAG AND SIX OR EIGHT CANS OF FOOD. ALONG

THE OPPOSITE WALL IS A STACK OF SOME FORTY TEXT BOOKS AND A PILE OF LOOSE-LEAF NOTEBOOKS.

JOE'S VOICE (CONTINUING): The boy we were looking for was not there but there was plenty of evidence that this was where he had been living.

JOE POINTS TO THE SLEEPING BAG AND CANNED GOODS. THEN HE AND FRANK START TO EXAMINE THE NOTEBOOKS AND TEXTS.

JOE'S VOICE (CONTINUING): We found six notebooks filled with hand-written mathematical equations and some forty texts on advanced physics and higher mathematics.

FRANK: Sure believes in making use of the public library.

JOE (AS HE EXAMINES A VOLUME): They aren't all library books.

FRANK: What've you got, Joe?

JOE (EXAMINING ANOTHER BOOK): A couple with book-plates.

FRANK: Oh?

JOE: Owner's name is in 'em.

JOE PASSES A BOOK TO FRANK. HE LOOKS AT IT.

INSERT — OPEN BOOK

WE SEE THE BOOK-PLATE: "EX LIBRIS KARL WINDERMAN."

The discovery of the books leads Sgt. Friday to check the public library and also the phone book for Winderman's address.

INT. JUVENILE SQUADROOM — DAY — 12:06 P.M.

CLOSE SHOT OF OPEN TELEPHONE BOOK. WE SEE FRANK'S FINGER ENTER THE SHOT, MOVE DOWN A COLUMN OF NAMES AND STOP. CAMERA PULLS BACK AS FRANK DIALS A NUMBER. WE SEE JOE GOING THROUGH ANOTHER TELE-PHONE DIRECTORY.

JOE'S VOICE (CONTINUING): We checked city phone directories for the name Karl Winderman. 12:06 P.M. we reached him at his office at Bradfield University.

FRANK (INTO PHONE): Yes, sir . . . I see . . . Uh-huh . . . That's up to you, sir . . . Anytime you say . . . Yes, sir. That'd be fine . . . Thank you very much. (HANGS UP PHONE; TURNS TO JOE) Head of the Physics Department. They're his books all right.

JOE: He know anything that might help us?

FRANK (NODS): He knows the boy.

FADE OUT:

(Allow extra footage for music)
(Commercial insert)

This is a good curtain scene because by now our curiosity is greatly aroused. What does Professor Winderman know about this boy who lives in a cave? The Professor is head of the Physics Department at Bradfield University. He explains that he loaned the books to the boy, Peter Siler. Peter, the Professor states, is a brilliant student. From his appearance, probably poor. The Professor does not know very much about the boy's antecedents. Peter said he was 18, but the Professor suspects he's only 16. The police try to get some more details from the Professor.

FRANK: Is there anything else you can tell us about him, Dr. Winderman?

KARL: Well, I would say he is an unhappy boy.

JOE: What do you mean?

KARL: Lonely . . . aloof. It must be very difficult for him . . . other people. Children his age, he would be unable to talk to them. They would have nothing in common. Even adults. . . .

JOE: I see.

KARL: A brilliant mind does not necessarily make for a well-adjusted person. Especially in one so young.

JOE: Uh-huh. (JOE AND FRANK RISE) Well, thank you very much, Doctor Winderman. (TAKES OUT A CARD; HANDS IT TO KARL) If you hear from him again, would you get in touch with us.

KARL (HE RISES, TAKING THE CARD FROM JOE): Yes, of course. If there is anything I can do for Peter . . .

JOE: That's very kind of you.

KARL: Is he . . . is he in some kind of trouble?

JOE: We don't know yet, sir.

KARL: I did not mean to pry. Forgive me.

JOE: The fact is he's been borrowing some books that don't belong to him.

KARL: Books?

JOE: Yes, sir. From libraries around town.

KARL: To want to read, to want to learn, is that such a serious crime? It does not seem like one to me.

JOE: Sure.

KARL: And is that all he has done?

JOE: He's taken some other things, too. Food, canned goods.

KARL (SUDDENLY GETTING AN IDEA): Of course, I should have known. When he was here I should have known.

JOE: Beg pardon?

KARL (REMINISCENTLY): It has been so long since I have seen one . . .

JOE: What's that, sir?

KARL: A boy who is hungry.

JOE REACTS SYMPATHETICALLY.

Sgt. Friday and Officer Smith return to the juvenile squadroom. A call comes in of a patrol car picking up a youngster hanging around a grocery store. The youngster answers Peter Siler's description. However, when Peter is brought in, he gives a fictitious name and volunteers no information. Sgt. Friday explains to the boy that they're trying to help him.

JOE (CONTINUING): You're in trouble, Pete. We want to help you if we can. That's just as much our job as picking you up. Maybe you had a reason for what you did. Maybe we'd be on your side if we knew what it was. But we can't get on your side unless you cooperate.

PETER LOOKS AT JOE, ALMOST WEAKENS, THEN CHANGES HIS MIND.

PETER: I don't know what you're talking about.

JOE: Okay, you won't tell us, we'll tell you. You didn't come to Los Angeles today. You've been here for a couple of weeks. You've been living in a cave up in the Hollywood Hills.

PETER: Yeah?

JOE: And this grocery store tonight isn't the first time you've gotten out of line.

FRANK: Why'd you take all those books, son?

PETER: What books?

JOE: Well, it just shows you how much these college professors really know.

PETER: Huh?

JOE: Take Doctor Winderman. Says you're a smart kid, got a good head on your shoulders. He's a pretty poor judge of brains, isn't he?

PETER: Lot you know about it.

JOE: Yeah?

PETER: Doctor Winderman's so far ahead of you guys that . . .
HE BREAKS OFF, REALIZING HE'S ADMITTED KNOWING WINDER-
    MAN.

Now that Peter realizes he is caught, he gives his true background to the police. His parents are dead. He had lived for a while
with his sister but when she married, her husband threw the boy
out. Peter says he always wanted to go to college and study.

JOE: Why'd you take all those books?
PETER: I wanted to study 'em. I was gonna return 'em when I was
    through. I couldn't get a library card . . . not without a real
    address.
JOE: What about the canned goods you've been stealing?
PETER: It wasn't much . . . just enough to eat.
JOE: Uh-huh.
PETER: What's gonna happen to me now?
JOE: That's not up to us.
PETER: Oh.
JOE: What d'you think ought to happen?
PETER: I dunno. I don't see where I did anything so wrong.
JOE: You stole books, you stole food. You caused us a lot of trouble.
PETER: Yeah.
JOE (PICKS UP THE PUZZLE): You're the whiz at math.
PETER: Huh?
JOE: You add it up.
HE TOSSES THE PUZZLE ON THE TABLE. CAMERA MOVES INTO
    A BIG CLOSE SHOT OF PUZZLE, AS WE:
FADE OUT:
(ALLOW EXTRA FOOTAGE FOR MUSIC)

The closing scene is standard technique on "Dragnet": the
resolution.

FADE IN:
(ALLOW EXTRA FOOTAGE FOR MUSIC)
TITLE CARD

> THE STORY YOU HAVE
> SEEN IS TRUE. THE NAMES
> WERE CHANGED TO PROTECT
> THE INNOCENT.

DISSOLVE TO:

TITLE

GIBNEY: On April 16th, a Hearing was held in Juvenile Court, the State of California, in and for the County of Los Angeles. In a moment, the results of that Hearing.

FADE OUT:

(COMMERCIAL INSERT)

FADE IN:

TITLE — OVER CLOSEUP — PETER ELLIS SILER

GIBNEY: The subject was made a ward of the Juvenile Court and was placed in a Home for Boys. Through the efforts of Dr. Karl Winderman, he was permitted to enroll in Bradfield University as a special student in the fields of physics and higher mathematics.

DISSOLVE TO:

TITLE CARD — OVER CLOSEUP — PETER ELLIS SILER

    PETER ELLIS SILER —

    Now attending Bradfield University.

FADE OUT.

ADVENTURE

           The Adventure series may be divided into two categories: Contemporary and Costume. The contemporary dramas include series such as "Waterfront," "Crunch and Des," "Jungle Jim," "Dangerous Assignment," "Soldiers of Fortune." Recently, the costume series have become the vogue. These are adventure tales based on historic events, historic legend, or purely fiction. They include such series as "Adventures of Robin Hood," "The Buccaneers," "The 77th Bengal Lancers," "Sir Lancelot," "The Count of Monte Cristo." Television programming rotates in imitative cycles similar to that of the motion pictures. Therefore, if one costume series receives a good rating, a dozen others are rushed into production.

    All the costume adventure series and most of the contemporary variety are characterized by a great deal of physical action. The hero is constantly beset by danger, often seriously wounded, and just as often held captive by the enemy, whether that enemy be a political figure plotting for power or bloodthirsty natives on the warpath. In a series such as "The 77th Bengal Lancers" there is generally a battle scene. In the "Adventures of Robin Hood" one of the men of Sherwood Forest, or Robin himself, is always being rescued from the clutches of the Sheriff of Nottingham or some other evil lord. In the first we witness a hail of flying bullets; in the second, flying arrows.

Romance plays a greater role in the adventure series than in the crime series. Either the hero himself is involved in a romantic escapade or he assists in the culmination of a romantic subplot involving other characters in the episode.

The adventure series, as you can see, are all highly formularized.

WESTERNS

Westerns have always been popular with both the small-fry and their parents. Long before the days of television, the now older generation idolized those stalwart heroes of the western films: Tom Mix, Hoot Gibson, William S. Hart, William Farnum. Today's younger generation has its Roy Rogers, Gene Autry, its tales of Wyatt Earp, Annie Oakley, Wild Bill Hickok, and that long time, perennial favorite, The Lone Ranger.

What accounts for the popularity of the western? There are many factors. Primarily, the western provides an action story which is pure entertainment. It affords a vicarious outlet for the bounding energies of the very young. And if we may be permitted some mind-searching, it goes even deeper than that. The child has great need of someone to love, someone to look up to, someone whose strength will give him security and protection. The western hero becomes a symbol, a father image. Witness the sudden and sweeping popularity of Davy Crockett. Youngsters spoke of him affectionately, worshipfully. In their games, they emulated the exploits of the hero of the Alamo.

Just as the normal child has faith that his father can do no wrong, so his western hero is a symbol of the "good man." And so for the general run of westerns, we find that there is no attempt at character delineation, rather there is stylization. The hero is always good, the villain always bad. True, the hero may suffer setbacks from the villain, and he usually does, but always, the young viewer knows, the hero will emerge triumphant and the "bad man" will be punished. So, despite the constant gunplay, and the number of corpses that may litter the plains, these westerns are actually moralistic in tone: the triumph of good over evil.

The chase

An essential ingredient of almost every western is the chase. The hero pursuing the villain, the posse hot on the trail of outlaws, the bandits capturing the stagecoach — these are sequences which engender a high pitch of excitement and suspense. The writer of the average western plans for at least one killing and one lengthy chase in every episode of the series.

The "Adult Western"

Lately, we have witnessed a new phase of the western. It has been prefixed by the term "adult." The intention clearly is to garner an even wider audience than the run-of-the-mill western, to draw the more adult viewer to whom the average video western has little or no appeal.

Basically, the "adult" western has the same elements as any western. The setting is the same. The horse is the prime method of transportation. There is the inevitable gunplay. Good triumphs over evil. But there are some major differences. Where the average western substitutes action for characterization, the "adult" western attempts to give its main characters substance and depth. Dialogue, in the average western, is at a minimum as if it were trying to prove the maxim that actions speak louder than words. There is a good deal more dialogue in the "adult" western which assists in character delineation and in more acceptable motivation. The chase in the "adult" western is not an essential ingredient. But all westerns, "adult" or not, are action dramas, the difference being that this type of western is not averse to the introduction of mental action.

"Gunsmoke"

The CBS series, "Gunsmoke," was the forerunner of the "adult" westerns. It began as a radio series and later expanded into a video counterpart. Its listeners and viewers are many and loyal and they have helped keep the "Gunsmoke" series running successfully for several years.

A complete "Gunsmoke" script is included in the chapter on Radio Drama. Any potential writer of "adult" westerns will do well to study it.

The daily serial

18

Lest the young college intellectual turn up his nose at the daily serial, we should observe that some of our highly applauded literary lights cut their writing teeth on the "soap opera."

The producers of the daily serial believe that they are giving the public, at least a very large segment of it, what it wants. The long life of the average "soap opera" proves their point. "The Guiding Light," for example, has been broadcast continuously for more than twenty years. It has recently made the transition from radio to television. The thought of plotting a five-day-a-week program for twenty years should give any writer pause.

But "The Guiding Light" is not alone in this marathon. Your radio log, at least at this writing, still lists such ancient favorites as: "Backstage Wife," "Helen Trent," "Our Gal Sunday," "Nora Drake," "Ma Perkins," "Road of Life," "Right to Happiness," "2nd Mrs. Burton." These programs may seem comparatively new to today's college student, who may be startled to learn that they were already much in vogue when mother was a girl.

The drawing power of the daily serial is not to be underestimated. Its listeners and viewers take their "soap opera" seriously. The characters are meaningful to them. They neither analyze nor criticize. They accept. They will discuss the current situation of their favorite serial as if they were speaking of their next door neighbors. They have been loyal listeners for two decades. They may remain loyal viewers for another two decades.

The potential serial writer must be aware of the type of audience this genre of programs attracts. He cannot come to it with tongue in cheek. He must accept the fact that he is not writing literature. It is essentially a hack job, with some rare exceptions, but as we have often reiterated, whatever job the writer has undertaken, he should perform to the best of his ability.

CHARACTERIZATION

Since the daily serial audience is composed mostly of women, the main character of these dramas is almost always a woman. Even a serial such as "Young Dr. Malone" places heavy emphasis on the women in the doctor's life.

The lead characters are either simple, familiar types whose home environment parallels that of the average housewife, or women who live in a world of glamor far removed from the daily routine of housekeeping chores. "Ma Perkins" is typical of the first; "Backstage Wife," of the second. No matter their environment, all characters have one element in common: trouble . . . lots of it!

There is no place in the daily serial for profundity. Characterization is oftentimes one-dimensional: the villain is thoroughly bad, the heroine a paragon of self-sacrifice. Both Horatio Alger and Burt Standish would have made their fortune as writers of daily serials.

Because of the long, involved plots and the many characters who weave in and out of the story, it is advisable for the writer to prepare a sort of family tree. At the very least, this family tree will help him to maintain the various relationships in his own mind. He can also make notes, more or less detailed, regarding the background and the outstanding characteristics, or more probably characteristic, of the participants. Whatever the limits of character delineation may be, it will be most helpful to the writer to maintain an actual brief biography, not merely mental notes, of the major characters. Possibly, he may endow them with a single quality: grasping, generous, dominating, indulgent, and so on.

PLOT STRUCTURE

Unlike the one-time half-hour or hour dramas which avoid subplots, the daily serial not only welcomes, but requires them. The "soap opera" bathes in conflict and sub-conflict. The rating of a daily serial is often in direct proportion to the difficulties which beset its heroine.

The plot, however, must be doled out. There are two very good reasons for this. First, there is the practical consideration of listening or viewing time. A great many women, although loyal to the program, cannot watch or listen every day at the same time. Possibly, they may miss one or two episodes during the week. Obviously, if a major plot action were to take place within one or even two episodes, the housewife, returning to the serial after having missed an installment, would be at a loss. If she is unable to follow the story line, she will lose interest. The writer, therefore, has to be ingenious enough to keep a single episode interesting but not vital to the overall plot structure. Within the course of a week, one tiny facet of the current plot is unfolded.

The second reason for this doling out process is that the daily serial is intended for long-run consumption. Remember that some serials are about to celebrate their silver anniversaries! If the writer did not stretch his plot, he would soon run dry. This may not be as forbidding as it sounds. There are writers who have been turning out "soaps" for ten and twenty years.

This author recalls a series on which he collaborated and which had begun as an experiment on a local station. The writing of the first few episodes was very broad and the episodes themselves were loaded with plot. Since the series was sustaining and had no time guarantee, there appeared to be no necessity for stretching the plot. Truth to tell, it was much easier writing it that way. However, when the series was bought by a network, the problem arose of how long we could keep going. Plot conservation was the answer. As a result, after twenty-six weeks on the network, only three of the original episodes were consumed!

There are many other factors the daily serial writer must bear in mind. Interest must be continually aroused so that the viewer or listener will be anxious to follow each episode. This necessitates a small crisis each day. In addition, since the serial runs from

Monday through Friday, there is a weekend hiatus. Friday is therefore the day of the big crisis sufficient to hold the audience over the two-day lapse. This big crisis has become known in broadcast parlance as the "cliffhanger," a term drawn from the serials of the silent movie days whose heroines such as Pearl White or Ruth Roland were often left dangling from a precipice until the following week's episode.

Since a plot, no matter how complicated it may be, must eventually reach a climax, it is incumbent upon the writer to start formulating a secondary plot while he is working on the first or, better still, have the plots outlined for months in advance. The secondary plot may appear as a subplot and then as the first plot reaches its climax, the subplot becomes the major plot with transitional ease.

The story-line is best carried forward in chronological sequence and it is wisest to avoid flashbacks entirely. The coincidental action device is preferable, that is, switching from one scene to another which is taking place simultaneously. Thought sequences may be employed but they should be the character's thoughts about the current situation so that even this device has the effect of moving the story along. For production economies and ease in following the story, the number of characters in each episode should be kept to a minimum, no more than six or seven generally, oftentimes less, depending on whether it is a quarter-hour or half-hour serial.

The daily serial is almost always contemporary although there have been one or two exceptions in the past. The plot therefore can take advantage of current trends. With so much being written today on psychiatry and the prevalence of mental disease, you will find psychiatrists playing major roles in the radio serial "Nora Drake" and in the television serial "As the World Turns."

Plotting is not always the province of the writer. The serials produced by the Hummerts were plotted by Frank and Anne Hummert. The writers of these serials were merely dialoguers. They would come in for their regular briefing on the story line and then go home to their typewriters to hack out the appropriate dialogue. Some writers began by writing their own serials, then became so successful that they now hire other writers to assist them.

LOCALE

The setting of the daily serial is usually in a typical small town where everybody knows everybody else or the very big urban centers like New York or Chicago where anything can happen.

The radio serial writer has no physical problem in regard to sets. Yet it is not advisable for him to have very many scenes. Too many scenes would invite choppiness. This is also true of the quarter-hour and the half-hour television serials, although the added factor of cost is apparent on television where physical sets are necessary.

Unfortunately, minimum sets and doled-out plot have a tendency to create static scenes. Many of the quarter-hour TV serials are in reality transplanted radio programs with the emphasis on the dialogue and not on the visual. This may be intentional since it is thus possible for the housewife to turn her attention from the screen and still follow the story via the audio. As a matter of fact, the script for "The Guiding Light" is still written in radio format as the following excerpt illustrates:

BILL: Thursday is Thanksgiving, yes.
BERT: We're all going over to Meta's.
BILL: That's the general idea. So?
BERT: Nothing.
BILL: Nothing?
BERT: Nothing, that's right.
SOUND: TELEPHONE
BERT: I'll get it.
BILL EDGES OVER TO THE PICTURES OF THE HOUSE AS BERT
   GOES TO THE PHONE. SHE TAKES A LOOK AT HIM, HE LOOKS
   AT HER, SHE SMILES, AND HE PUTS THE PICTURES DOWN.
BERT: Hello?
KATHY: (IN A PHONE BOOTH) Bert?
BERT: Kathy! How are you, honey?
KATHY: Oh, I — I'm all right.
BERT: Bill just talked with Meta.
KATHY: Oh?
BERT: She was worried about Papa Bauer. She was alone and — he

was going to go home around eight, but Bill talked him into a chess game, and you know Papa Bauer and chess?

KATHY: Yes. Yes I do.

BERT: Dan get away?

KATHY: Yes he did. Bert? I — I know it isn't — well it's a little late —

BERT: What do you mean late? Bill and I are just starting one of our long evening arguments. I guess I haven't talked to you too much about wanting a new home? (AND SHE LOOKS OVER AT BILL)

KATHY: We haven't talked too much since I got back, have we, Bert?

BERT: Well, I know you've been busy and all. Bill saw Dick today.

When "The Guiding Light" was making the transition from radio to television, the same scripts were actually used on both media, with expository dialogue added to the radio scripts to take care of any of the purely visual scenes.

DIALOGUE

Generally speaking, the dialogue in the daily serial will follow the precepts outlined in the previous section on dialogue in the broadcast drama. However, there are certain differences. Because of the necessity for plot conservation, the dialogue is not taut. It has a slower pace and more deliberation than the anthology drama. There is a great deal of repetition in order to maintain the story line in the minds of the viewers or listeners. This necessity for repetition presents a problem to the writer who must endeavor to keep the conversation going without making it sound like padding.

LEAD-INS AND LEAD-OUTS

From its inception, the radio serial has employed the recapitulation device known as the lead-in at the opening of each program. The "recap" serves a double purpose: the listener, who may have missed an episode, is thus kept abreast of events and the regular listener's memory is refreshed. It is at best, a top-heavy device, but admittedly has its practical purpose. In addition to the "recap," there is usually ample reference within the framework of the dialogue to preceding events.

The closing of each episode or lead-out usually brings in the announcer with that omnipresent, foreboding query: "What's going to happen now?" and an exhortation to the audience to be sure to tune in tomorrow.

It is interesting to note that on television the daily serials generally omit the opening recapitulation and the announcer's closing comments. Many use the device of opening cold with a brief sequence before the first full commercial. The half-hour series, "The Edge of Night," employs a teaser scene at the close of each episode, a brief and highly dramatic sequence from the next day's episode.

"THE EDGE OF NIGHT"

In April of 1956, two new daily serials made their debut on the television networks: "As the World Turns" and "The Edge of Night." The first, starring Ruth Warrick, is very much in the familiar style, tempo and plot structure of its radio predecessors. "The Edge of Night" however, with its protagonist police Lieutenant Mike Karr, is a combination of "soap opera" and crime drama. Both these serials are half-hour in length, a departure from the usual quarter-hour format.

From a study of current daily serials it will be apparent that "The Edge of Night" is faster in pacing, carries more suspense and makes better use of visuals. It is, admittedly, a far cry from any literary writing, nor will the viewer be troubled by any provocative ideas or treated to any deathless dialogue. But these programs must be taken for what they are and studied accordingly.

Here is an episode from "The Edge of Night," Script #180, telecast on a Friday, and reprinted by courtesy of Procter and Gamble.

Scene 1
(The hallway at the bottom of the stairs. Pan the
   scene to show Sgt. Vincent and Helen, with coat
   over her shoulders, sitting on the stairs, watching

WHITE AND ROSE, CHATTING ALONG, CIGARETTES, ETC.
ALERT ENOUGH, BUT THERE IS NO REASON TO BE CON-
CERNED. THEN COME IN ON WHITE AND ROSE TO A CLOSE
TWO-SHOT. HER HEAD DOWN BESIDE HIS. THE POSITION IS
AMOROUS RATHER THAN OMINOUS.)

WHITE: I got in this jam because I love you, Rose . . . If you love
me, you'll help me out of it . . .

ROSE: I — I don't want to know anything about slugging and
shooting —

WHITE: You don't need to know . . ! Those cops think I'm paralyzed
. . . Okay, I was . . . But — now I'm all right . . . I got my legs
back . . . The cops don't know that . . . Maybe you didn't cross
me — but if you let me down now, so they can lock me up —
I'm dead . . . I mean it, baby . . . I'd go nuts . . . I'd try to blast
my way out. . . . I'd wind up on a slab . . . This way — I got
a chance . . .

ROSE: What do you want me to do . . . ?

WHITE: Get that woman cop down the hall somewheres . . . Slug
her . . . Get her gun . . . Gimmie it . . . I stick up that other
cop and get the key to the cuffs . . . We walk out'a here free
like birds . . .

ROSE: I — I've never slugged anybody in my life . . .

WHITE: Goin' chicken on me . . . ?

ROSE: Listen, Larry . . . There's a better way . . . Okay — so they
got you . . . Robbery . . . Maybe you'll get a couple of years —
even five . . . I'll wait for you . . . When you come out —

WHITE: How many times I got to tell you . . . ? Stir would drive
me nuts . . . If I go in — I'll never come out . . . and if I *got*
to go — I'll take that Karr guy with me . . . Him, I got to
kill . . !

ROSE: Stop talking about killing like it was nothing . . . Lt. Karr
says you shot that grocer . . . *You* say you didn't . . . If you keep
on talking about killing like that, I'll begin to believe maybe
you did . . !

WHITE (CONCILIATORY): Baby, listen . . I *didn't* shoot that guy . . .
Now, all I want is to get away . . . Do you want me to —

ROSE: All I want is what's best for us . . . You *and* me . . .

WHITE: That's what you gotta decide . . . Help me — or kill me
. . . (ROSE IS TORN. SHE IS FRANTIC. SHE LOVES THE GUY.
BUT SHE HAS DOUBTS AND FEARS. SHE LOOKS TOWARD

Vincent and Helen . . . she looks down at Larry White. she starts to turn away — as though to leave, but she comes back. . . . puts her face down into Larry's neck)

Rose (whispering): I'll do anything you want me to do. . . .

First commercial

Scene 2A
(The hallway at the bottom of the stairs, continuing scene 1)

Rose: I love you . . . You're no good . . . But I love you . . .

White: Like I told you . . . Slug the dame . . . All right . . . Get her gun . . . Let me have it . . . I'll take it from there . . .

Rose: Larry — no shooting . . .

White: When a guy's got a gun he don't have to shoot, baby . . . Her gun and the key to these cuffs from the cop — and we're outa here like a breeze . . .

Rose: How can I — er — slug her . . . . ?

White: Get sick . . . You're ready to collapse on account of I'm paralyzed . . . You love me . . . Faint . . . Dames can always faint and who knows it better than another dame . . . ? Get me . . .

Split to —

Scene 2B
(Front hallway outside Rose's dressing room — in the telephone area. Mike is at the phone. he dials . . . and waits)

Split to —

Scene 2C

(Come in on the telephone at Mattie's home.)
Sound: the telephone.
(Sara picks it up quickly)
Intercut
Sara: Hello . . . hello —
Mike: Sara . . . It's me . . .
Sara: Oh, Mike — Mike, . . . are you — all right . . . ?
Mike: I couldn't be allrighter, darling . . .

SARA: Did you — I mean — have you — er — is he —

MIKE: Where do you want to go on your honeymoon . . . ?

SARA: Mike — you got him . . !

MIKE: Yes, darling . . . Yes . . . He's wearing a beautiful pair of steel bracelets . . . It's all over — except for a few details, this way and that . . .

SARA: Oh, I'm so glad . . . I've been so miserable and afraid for the last four hours . . .

MIKE: Don't. . . . It'll take a little while to go through the formalities and so I may not get to see you tonight —

SARA: Can't you stop by so that I can be sure you're — all in one piece . . . ?

MIKE: It's late . . . I don't want to keep you up . . . It's way after midnight . . .

SARA: After a night like this, do you think I could sleep until you've kissed me goodnight . . . ?

MIKE: That does it . . ! I'll be there even if it's at sunrise. . . .

SARA: Was there any — trouble . . . ?

MIKE: No — just routine . . . He came, we tapped him — he gave up . . . We'll take him in — and tomorrow morning I'll put in for extended leave and next week — right after the wedding, we'll start off for — Where *do* you want to go for a honeymoon . . . ?

SARA: I don't care . . . . as long as we both go there . . .

MIKE: I wouldn't go on my honeymoon with anyone else . . . (THEY LAUGH)

SARA: If you did, I'd scratch her eyes out . . . (CHARLIE COMES TO MIKE. MIKE TURNS, SEES HIM)

MIKE: Wait a minute, Sara . . . (TO CHARLIE) Want me, Charlie . . . ?

CHARLIE: I didn't know you were talking to Sara . . . Duncan wants to see you . . .

MIKE: Duncan . . . . ? What for . . . ?

CHARLIE: He wants to sing . . . He's so scared he's got palsy . . . He won't talk to anybody but you, and he wants to tell all he knows before we book him . . . I think you ought to let him, Mike . . .

MIKE: Yes . . . the d. a. might find him useful . . .

CHARLIE: Have you told Sara the news . . . ?

MIKE: Yes.

CHARLIE: Happy, I bet — huh . . . ?

MIKE (IN THE PHONE): Sara — Charlie wants to know if you're happy . . .

SARA: I'm up in the clouds, darling — floating on air. . . .

MIKE (TO CHARLIE): She said yes . . . (IN THE PHONE) I've got to go now, Sara . . I'll call you back so you'll know when to expect me . . .

SARA: Don't be long . . .

(MIKE HANGS UP. MIKE AND CHARLIE START AWAY.)

CHARLIE (AS THEY GO): I still say it was a dirty low-down thing to do, not letting *me* have that guy . . .

MIKE: Now, Sergeant . . . That's no way to talk to your superior . . .

THEY EXIT

SPLIT TO —

SCENE 2D

(THE HALLWAY AT THE FOOT OF THE STAIRS, CONTINUING)

[NOTE — ALTHOUGH VINCENT AND HELEN HAVE BEEN PLACED ON THE STAIRS, THEY WOULD NOT HAVE BEEN STATIC. THERE WOULD BE MOVEMENT, CIGARETTES, ETC. WE WOULD SEE OCCASIONAL SHOTS OF THEM, OBVIOUSLY WATCHING WHITE'S EVERY MOVE. THEY WALK ABOUT, TOO, ALWAYS IN SIGHT, AND EVEN COME TO WHITE AND STAND FOR A BEAT OR TWO, INTERRUPTING THE DIALOG. ANY SUCH INTERRUPTIONS WOULD BE COVERED BY KISSING. VINCENT AND/OR HELEN WOULD RESPECT SUCH INTIMACY BY MOVING AWAY.]

(COME IN ON A CLOSE SHOT OF WHITE AND ROSE)

WHITE: We ain't got much time, baby — once the ambulance gets here, the jig's up — so start acting . . .

ROSE: No shooting, Larry — remember — no shooting.

WHITE: Get on with it!

(ROSE SITS UP, APPEARS TO TRY TO GET UP, BUT SHE WEAVES UNSTEADILY. SHE HOLDS HER HEAD, AND STAGGERS TO HER FEET, ONLY TO SAG DOWN AGAIN)

WHITE (LOUDLY): Rose — what's the matter, baby . . . ? Rose . . !

(HELEN AND VINCENT ARE QUICKLY ALERT. THEY HURRY TO ROSE.)

VINCENT: What's wrong, here . . !

WHITE: Look at her . . !

HELEN: What's the matter, Rose . . . ?

(HELEN SUPPORTS ROSE, HELPING HER TO HER FEET)

ROSE: I — I thought I was going to — to faint, I guess.

WHITE: Do somethin' for her . . !

VINCENT: The doctor ought to be here any minute. . . .

WHITE: That don't do her no good now . . .

(HELEN IS NO FOOL. SHE STUDIES ROSE CLOSELY. IS SHE
   REALLY SICK? THE STRAIN OF IT ALL, TEARS, ETC. WOULD
   GIVE ROSE THE APPEARANCE OF HER FAINTING SPELL
   BEING GENUINE, AND HELEN DECIDES IT IS)

VINCENT (TO HELEN): Take her into her dressing-room, Helen . . .

ROSE (QUICKLY): No — no, I won't leave Larry . . . I want to
   be here when the doctor comes — I won't leave him . . .
   (ROSE'S NEAR HYSTERIA IS ALMOST REAL)

HELEN (TAKES HER COAT AND THROWS IT AROUND ROSE'S
   SHOULDERS): All right, all right, Rose . . . Come over and sit
   down on the stairs — it's cooler there . . . (HELEN STARTS
   TO LEAD ROSE TO THE STAIRS. THIS IS NOT ACCORDING TO
   PLAN. WHITE SCOWLS)

ROSE: No — no, I got to keep moving . . . I want to walk . . . I'll
   be all right in a few minutes . . . Sitting down is — no good . . .

HELEN: All right . . . Up and down the hall a few times . . . How's
   that . . . ?

ROSE: Could I have some fresh air . . . ? Could I go up to the
   roof . . . ? It's just nerves, that's all . . .

HELEN: You've had a rough night . . .

ROSE: You can say that again . . . (SHE STARTS TO CLIMB A STEP
   OR TWO, AND STAGGERS. HAND TO HEAD DIZZILY)

WHITE: Do somethin' for her . . .

VINCENT: She'll be all right . . . The doctor can give her something . . .

ROSE: I've got to keep moving . . . I'm that way when I get like this
   . . . I'm highstrung — fresh air's the best thing for me . . . Let's
   go to the roof . . .

HELEN: All right . . . Let's try the stairs again . . . (SHE SUPPORTS
   ROSE) Think you can make it now . . . ?

ROSE: Yes . . . Thanks for — for helping me . . . (ROSE CLIMBS
   THE STAIRS SLOWLY WITH HELEN'S HELP. VINCENT AND
   WHITE WATCH THEM WALK UP. WHITE'S FACE WOULD
   BE INTERESTING TO SEE AS HE REALIZES THAT HIS PLAN

IS WORKING . . . SO FAR, AT LEAST. WE SHOULD SEE THE
TWO GIRLS GOING OUT OF SIGHT.)
WHITE (SMILES — TO VINCENT): Let me have another butt . . .
(AS VINCENT OBLIGES, WE FADE.)
SECOND COMMERCIAL

SCENE 3A

(THE CORRIDOR NEAR THE ROOF. ROSE AND HELEN COME OUT
OF EXIT DOOR AND WALK TOWARD THE ROOF, BUT STOP AT
THE DOOR WHICH ENDS THE CORRIDOR. [MARK THE DOOR:
"PROPS — KEEP OUT"] THEY WALK SLOWLY. ROSE STOPS
A TIME OR TWO TO EMPHASIZE HER WEAK HELPLESSNESS.
HAVING STOPPED BEFORE, HELEN IS NOT SUSPICIOUS WHEN
ROSE STOPS AGAIN — AND RIGHT AT THE PROP-ROOM DOOR.
ROSE SUPPORTS HERSELF BY HOLDING ONTO THE KNOB OF
THE DOOR. ROSE'S FACE IS STRAINED, ALERT, AND CALCU-
LATING AS SHE PLANS WHAT SHE WILL DO. SHE TURNS THE
KNOB AND THE DOOR SWINGS OPEN. SHE LOOKS BEHIND
THEM TO BE CERTAIN THEY ARE ALONE, THEN SHE TURNS
AS THOUGH TO GO BACK. THIS THROWS HELEN OFF. . . .)
HELEN: This is not the door to the roof . . . It's that way . . . (SHE
POINTS)
ROSE (CASUALLY): I didn't mean to open the door . . . That's the
prop-room . . . I better close it . . . (AND SHE WAVERS)
HELEN: I'll do it . . . (SHE TURNS TO REACH IN FOR THE DOOR
KNOB. HER BACK IS TO ROSE. A QUICK LOOK UP AND DOWN
THE HALL, AND THEN ROSE PUSHES HELEN'S BACK WITH
BOTH HANDS. . . . PUSHES HARD ENOUGH FOR HELEN TO
FALL FORWARD INTO THE PROP ROOM. HELEN'S COAT
FALLS FROM ROSE'S SHOULDERS TO THE FLOOR. ROSE
STEPS QUICKLY INSIDE AND CLOSES THE DOOR. HOLD ON
THE CLOSED DOOR AND ON THE COAT LYING CRUMPLED JUST
OUTSIDE IT.)
[NOTE: THE COAT LYING THERE PERMITS OUR VIEWERS TO WON-
DER IF SOMEONE WILL SEE THE COAT THERE.]
(THEN THE DOOR OPENS SLOWLY — VERY SLOWLY. WHO WILL
COME OUT? ROSE APPEARS, DISHEVELED AND PANTING.
SHE HAS HELEN'S GUN IN HER HAND. SHE LOOKS BACK.
APPARENTLY HELEN HAS GONE BYE-BYE. SHE WONDERS

WHERE TO HIDE THE GUN. SHE SEES THE COAT. THANK
GOD FOR THE COAT. SHE HURRIEDLY THROWS IT OVER HER
SHOULDERS AS BEFORE, DRAWS IT AROUND HER AND AS SHE
WALKS BACK TOWARD THE STAIRS WE KNOW THAT THE GUN
IS IN HER POSSESSION. SHE DISAPPEARS IN THE STAIR-
WELL.)

SCENE 3B

(HALLWAY AND STAIRS IN BACK OF ROSE'S DRESSING ROOM.
WHITE ON THE FLOOR, VINCENT LEANING OVER WHITE
GIVING A ROUTINE CHECK-UP TO HIS CONDITION AND AD-
JUSTING HIS "PILLOW." ROSE (WHO HAS WALKED STAIRS
TO 6TH FLOOR) APPEARS AT THE STAIRS. VINCENT'S BACK
IS TURNED TO HER. LARRY WHITE SEES HER, AND WE
WATCH HIS EYES GLEAM AS HE NOTICES THAT ROSE IS
ALONE. SHE GIVES HIM AN OKAY SIGN AND POINTS TO HER
HIDDEN HAND. THIS COULD HAPPEN DURING FOLLOWING
DIALOGUE.)
VINCENT (PAYING PARTICULAR ATTENTION TO WHITE'S LEGS):
  Feel any better?
WHITE: No . . .
VINCENT: Well, the ambulance will be here any minute . . . Hurt
  at all . . . ?
WHITE: No . . . Numb . . . No feelin' down there . . . When's that
  doc goin' to get here . . . A guy could pass out waitin' . . !
VINCENT: Any minute, I just said . . . (ROSE DESCENDS STAIRS.
  VINCENT TURNS AND SEES HER. NOTHING SEEMS AMISS)
  Feel better, now . . . ?
ROSE: Yeah . . . Lots better . . .
VINCENT: That's good . . . (THEN HE NOTICES THAT HELEN
  ISN'T WITH ROSE. HE IS NOT ALARMED. EVEN CASUAL)
  Where's Sgt. Kilbourn . . . ?
ROSE: She's coming . . .
(VINCENT WOULD INSTINCTIVELY TURN TO FACE IN THE DIREC-
TION IN WHICH HELEN WOULD APPEAR. THIS TURNS HIS
BACK TO WHITE AND TO ROSE WHO HAS STEPPED CLOSER
TO WHITE. SHE HOLDS OUT HER HAND. WHITE TAKES IT
AND PULLS HIMSELF QUICKLY TO HIS FEET, GRABS THE GUN
AS QUICKLY AS HE CAN, BEING HANDCUFFED, AND HE STANDS

AT THE READY, WAITING FOR VINCENT TO TURN. HE HASN'T
LONG TO "WAIT" BECAUSE VINCENT HAD TURNED AWAY
ONLY FOR A FEW SECONDS. AS HE TURNS BACK, HE FACES
LARRY WHITE — AND THE GUN. HIS JAW FALLS, EYES POP.
HE STARTS TO REACH FOR HIS GUN.)

WHITE: Don't do it, cop . . . ! Reach up high . . . ! (VINCENT
STOPS. HANDS UP. WHITE IS A KILLER. THERE'S NO POINT
IN COMMITTING SUICIDE.)

VINCENT: Where — where's Sgt. Kilbourn . . . ?

WHITE: Yeah — where is she, Rose . . . ?

ROSE: In the prop-room . . .

VINCENT: What did you do to her . . . ?

ROSE: She's all right . . . She's not hurt — much . . .

WHITE: Get his gun, Rose — from behind — and *you* (TO VIN-
CENT) Don't you even breathe while she does it . . . (ROSE
OPENS VINCENT'S COAT, AND HOLSTER IS VISIBLE. SHE
TAKES THE GUN FROM IT.) Put it in my coat pocket, Rose
. . . (TO VINCENT) Now the key to these things . . . Which
pocket you got it in . . .

VINCENT: You can't get away with this, White . . . You ought to
know that . . .

WHITE: The key . . .

VINCENT: No . . .

WHITE: Then this is *it,* Sgt. . . . and it'll be a pleasure . . . I only
wish it was Karr . . . (WHITE'S GRIMNESS AND VINCENT'S
EXPRESSION INDICATE THAT WHITE IS GOING TO PULL THE
TRIGGER. BUT ROSE STILL DOESN'T WANT ANY SHOOTING
AND SHE GOES TO WHITE IMPULSIVELY.)

ROSE: Larry — no . . . No, Larry!

WHITE (BRUSHING HER ASIDE): Don't you get between us — (TO
VINCENT) And *you* don't you *move* . . . (THE SPLIT-SECOND
INTERVAL GIVES VINCENT THE IMPULSE TO GO FOR WHITE.
HAND STARTING FOR WHITE'S COAT POCKET, BUT WHITE
IS ON THE BALL.)

ROSE: No shooting, Larry — you promised . . . You promised . . !

VINCENT: You'd better take her advice, White . . . You can't get
away with it . . . Our men are all around the place. . . .

ROSE (TO PACIFY WHITE WHO GETS OBVIOUS PLEASURE OUT OF
THE SITUATION): I'll get the key from him, Larry . . . I'll find
it and you can get those things off and like you said — we can
get away . . .

WHITE: Shut up . . . (VICIOUS SNEER) Ready, Sgt. . . . ? Ready to go . . . ?

ROSE (HORRIFIED): Larry — you *want* to kill him . . !

WHITE: Like I said — it'll be a pleasure . . .

VINCENT: Suppose I give you the key . . . ?

ROSE (TO VINCENT): Will you . . . ?

WHITE (SNEER): Oh — you want to make a deal . . . ?

VINCENT: Let's talk about it . . .

WHITE: There's no time to talk . . .

ROSE: Listen to what he wants to say . . (SHE MAKES AN IMPULSIVE MOVE TOWARD HIM AGAIN. SHE COULD, OF COURSE, THROW WHITE ENOUGH OFF-BALANCE OR EVEN STEP BETWEEN THE MEN TO GIVE VINCENT A CHANCE TO FIGHT BACK. WHITE KNOWS THIS AND SO AS ROSE APPEARS TO INTERFERE, HE SHOULDERS HER AWAY ROUGHLY. THEN HE STEPS BACK ENOUGH SO THAT HE HAS HER COVERED, TOO)

WHITE: Stay away from me, Rose . . . Try that again and you'll get *yours*, too . . . !

VINCENT: I think he means it, Miss LaTour . . .

ROSE (UNDERSTATED SHOCK — TONELESS): Larry — what they said about you was right . . . You — *are* a killer . . . You *want* to kill . . !

VINCENT: But you want even more to have your chance to escape, don't you . . . ?

WHITE: Got something in mind, Sgt. . . . .

VINCENT: Suppose I give you the key. . . .

ROSE: Oh, do that . . . please — do that and then he won't shoot —

VINCENT: It would save you the trouble of searching for it . . .

WHITE: Yeah . . . Then give it to me . . (EYEING WHITE NARROWLY, VINCENT SLOWLY BRINGS HIS HANDS DOWN. WHITE DOESN'T LIKE THAT.) Oh, no — no, you don't . . . ! You don't catch me with a trick like that . . . Keep your hands up . . . Which pocket is it in . . . ?

VINCENT: What do I do — tell you and then get knocked off . . ?

ROSE: Promise him, Larry . . . Promise him you won't shoot . . !

[NOTE: — VINCENT IS NOT CRAVEN, NOR IS HE GOING TO MAKE A DEAL WITH WHITE THAT WOULD TURN HIM LOOSE AND PERHAPS MEAN THE DEATH OF ONE OR MORE OF HIS MEN. ON THE OTHER HAND, HE DOESN'T WANT TO DIE. HIS ONLY STRATEGY IS TO PLAY FOR TIME. THIS SHOULD BE CLEAR TO THE VIEWERS.]

WHITE (WITH A LEER): Sure — I'll promise . . . Which pocket . . . ?

VINCENT: I don't believe your promises are worth very much . . .

WHITE: Quit stalling . . ! There's no time to waste . . .

ROSE: I'll find it, Larry . . . I'll find the key . . . If I do — will you go — run away if you can — and not kill anybody . . .

WHITE: Go ahead . . . Hurry up . . . I got to get these things offa me . . . (ROSE SEARCHES VINCENT'S POCKETS — FROM BEHIND SO LARRY CAN COVER HIM — ALWAYS KEEPING A CLEAR SHOT AND STAYING FAR ENOUGH AWAY SO THAT VINCENT COULD NOT REACH HIM READILY. CLOSE SHOTS OF ALL COULD BE EFFECTIVE HERE. IN A PREVIOUS SCRIPT, VINCENT PUT WHITE'S GUN IN HIS POCKET. ROSE FINDS IT IN VINCENT'S COAT POCKET. SHE HOLDS IT UP.)

WHITE: So that's why you wanted to get your hand in your pocket . . ! (TO ROSE) Give it to me . . . (HE TAKES IT, LOOKS AT IT.) My gun . . . (ROSE SEARCHES AND FINDS THE KEY.)

ROSE: Is this it . . . ?

WHITE: Try it . . . (HE HOLDS OUT HIS HANDS, OF COURSE, KEEPING THE GUN POINTED AT VINCENT. ROSE — STILL CAREFUL NOT TO COME CLOSE TO LARRY — AND KEEPING TO ONE SIDE, FUMBLES WITH THE CUFFS AND THE KEY. HER HANDS TREMBLE. A CU OF THE WRISTS, GUN AND HER HANDS. IT IS THE KEY. THE CUFFS COME APART. WHITE IS FREE. HE PUSHES ROSE AWAY FROM HIM.)

WHITE (ELATED): Now . . . . now, Sgt. Got any more deals you want to make . . . ?

VINCENT: Any offers . . . ?

WHITE: No . . . Said your prayers yet . . . ?

(HE TENSES AND THE KILL IS IMMINENT)

VINCENT: Had you thought of this, White? The sound of a shot will be heard all over the building . . . Thirty seconds after the shot my men will be here . . . How far away can you get in thirty seconds . . . ?

WHITE (A BEAT): That's the first thing you've said that makes sense . . . (HE TOSSES THE HANDCUFFS TO ROSE) (TO VINCENT) Get over to the rail . . . Go on . . . Hurry up . . . (VINCENT OBEYS. ROSE STANDS UNCERTAINLY)

WHITE: Put one cuff on his wrist and clamp it shut. . . . (SHE DOES) Now, the other cuff on the rail. . . . (SHE

DOES) Give me the key . . . (SHE HANDS IT TO HIM. HE PUTS IT IN HIS POCKET. HE PLACES THE GUN IN HIS SHOULDER HOLSTER OR POCKET. [HE HAS THREE OF THEM NOW] HE GOES TO VINCENT, REMOVES WALLET, PAPERS, BADGE, ETC. FROM HIS POCKET.)

WHITE: Money, papers, badge — all very useful . . . (HE STARTS AWAY, THEN WITH A GESTURE TOWARD HIS GUN) I oughta let you have it . . (HE DOESN'T DRAW) I'm always goin' to be sorry I didn't . . . (HE STARTS AWAY AGAIN) Come on, Rose . . .

ROSE: No . . .

WHITE: I said come on. . . . We only got seconds —

ROSE: I said, no. . . .

WHITE: You'd better, baby . . ! Get goin' . . . .

ROSE: Get away if you think you can . . . but not with me . . . It's like I see you for the first time . . . How could I have been such a blind fool . . ! You're a killer, Larry — a dirty, no good killer —

THIRD COMMERCIAL

SCENE 4A

(HALLWAY AT THE FOOT OF THE STAIRS, CONTINUING.)

WHITE: You heard me, Rose . . . Put the coat on —

ROSE: I'm not going with you, Larry . . . You're a killer, a dirty killer who shoots for the fun of hearing the gun go off — and who likes to see people die . . . As far as I'm concerned you're dead . . . I thought I loved you, but now — well, go ahead — try to get away and if you do, just keep going . . . I never want to see you again . . .

WHITE: I need you, Rose . . .

ROSE: Beat it . . .

WHITE: I need you to go in front of me — so that if any cop tries to stop me, he's got to plug you first . . .

ROSE: No, thank you . . ! (HE TAKES HER ARM AS THOUGH TO FORCE HER) Take your hands off me . . . All that talk about how much you love me was nothing but lies . . . You've been using me for a good thing —

WHITE: Get goin' —

ROSE (STRUGGLING TO FREE HERSELF): No — you're not going

to use me to hide behind — you're a coward, and gun-crazy, that's what you are —

WHITE: I ain't got time to argue —

ROSE: — gun-crazy, and I hope they get you . . . I hope they get you good —

WHITE: Okay, baby — you asked for it . . ! (HE SOCKS HER. WE DON'T WANT TO SEE THE ACTUAL BLOW. THEN CUT TO A REACTION SHOT OF VINCENT, THEN BACK TO LARRY LOOK-ING DOWN. HE SEES THAT SHE IS OUT OF COMMISSION, AND AS HE TAKES A LOOK AT VINCENT, HE DRAWS HIS GUN AS THOUGH TO LET HIM HAVE IT AFTER ALL, THEN HE TURNS AND HURRIES DOWN THE HALL OPPOSITE THE STAIRS, OUT OF SIGHT)

SPLIT TO —

SCENE 4B

(THE FRONT HALLWAY AREA OUTSIDE ROSE'S DRESSING ROOM. MIKE AND CHARLIE ENTER THE FRAME, AND MIKE DROPS A COIN AND DIALS)

MIKE: Dismiss the detail, Charlie . . . All men back to their stations . . . And see what happened to that ambulance . . !

CHARLIE: Okay . . . I'll do the mop-up, Mike . . . Why don't you go and tell Sara goodnight . . . ?

MIKE: I will as soon as the ambulance gets here . . . I want to know how badly hurt White is . . .

CHARLIE: The doc ought to be here by now . . .

MIKE: Any minute . . .

CHARLIE: Yeah . . . (CHARLIE EXITS THE FRAME)

SPLIT TO —

SCENE 4C

(VARIED SHOTS OF WHITE ON HIS WAY TO ESCAPE ALONG LIGHT BOARD — NEXT TO FREIGHT ELEVATOR, CUT BACK TO MIKE DIALING, BACK TO WHITE GOING TOWARD MIKE'S AREA. HE IS VERY CAUTIOUS, HAVING HIS GUN READY FOR USE. HE STILL IS IN UNIFORM, OF COURSE. WE CUT IN SEVERAL OF THESE SHOTS DURING MIKE'S TELEPHONE CONVERSATION TO SHOW WHITE'S PROGRESS AND FEEDING

SCENE 4D

(HALLWAY AREA. MIKE, AT THE TELEPHONE.)
MIKE: Sara . . . ?
SARA: Yes, Mike . . ! Is everything all right . . . ?
MIKE: All clear, darling . . .
SPLIT TO —

SCENE 4E

(MATTIE'S TELEPHONE. A CLOSE SHOT OF SARA)
INTERCUT
SARA: Oh, I'm so glad . . . Grace and I have been telling each other
how wonderful it is, ever since you called before . . .
MIKE: Is Grace still there . . . ?
SARA: Yes, she was trying on her dress for the wedding — and then
she stayed on when I found out what you were doing . . . Is
Charlie all right . . . ?
MIKE: Yes . . . I'll be leaving in a few minutes . . . (WE ARE WITH
MIKE NOW . . . AND BEYOND HIM, AS HE TALKS, WE SEE
WHITE IN UNIFORM, PASS BY MIKE'S BACK AND EXIT STUDIO
DOOR, NEAR PAY PHONE) (WHITE TO USE STAIRS TO 6TH
FLOOR) I'm only waiting for the ambulance . . .
SARA: Ambulance . . ! Who's hurt, Mike . . . ?
MIKE: White fell down the stairs . . . Hurt his back . . . I want to
know what the doc says, then I'll stop by your house on the
way home and tell you goodnight —
SARA: I'll wait and if it takes all night . . . I'll have a pot of coffee
ready — and a cake mother baked . . .
MIKE: That sounds great . . . By the way, have you made up your
mind where we are going on our honeymoon . . . ?
SARA: We'll talk about it when you get here . . .
MIKE: Boy, am I glad this is over . . . Imagine, in one week, Mr.
and Mrs. Mike Karr will be setting sail for a distant isle in
the South Sea . . .
SARA (LAUGHS): You sound like a travelogue — but it sounds
wonderful . . .
MIKE: You bet it does . . . Tomorrow morning, you and I have a

date at the Acme Travel Agency . . . (USE AS MUCH OF THE ABOVE AS IS NEEDED TO GET WHITE TO BANNISTER AT 6TH FLOOR, OUTSIDE CONTROL ROOM, AND ESTABLISH HIM EXITING FROM DOOR, AND STEPPING OUT.)

WHITE (INTERRUPTS BY CALLING): Excuse me, Lieutenant, but it's urgent . . .

MIKE: Hold it a second, darling . . . (HE STEPS AWAY FROM PHONE WHICH HE LEAVES DANGLING TO SEE WHO CALLED HIM. HE SEES A UNIFORMED MAN UPSTAIRS, AND CALLS:) What is it, off — (HE RECOGNIZES WHITE, REACHES FOR HIS GUN, BUT IT'S TOO LATE.)

WHITE: Don't say I didn't warn you, Karr . . . (WHITE SHOOTS) (MIKE CRUMPLES, BUT EVEN AS HE FALLS, HE AIMS UP AND FIRES. WHITE RUNS OUT OF SIGHT INTO THE DOOR, APPARENTLY UNHURT. MIKE LIES STILL ON THE FLOOR NEAR THE PHONE. THE PHONE DANGLES FROM THE CORD.)

(CUT TO SARA AT THE PHONE)

SARA: Mike — are you there . . . ? (ALARMED) Mike — answer me . . . What happened . . . ? Hello, hello — Mike. . . .

(CUT TO THE HALLWAY. HOLD ON MIKE LYING STILL AS DEATH. THE PHONE DANGLES)

SARA (IN RASPING FILTER AS WE WOULD HEAR IT INDISTINCTLY, AWAY FROM THE PHONE): Mike — Mike — answer me . . . Are you there — what happened . . . Oh, dear God — MIKE . . ! !

FADE

FOURTH COMMERCIAL

TEASER SCENE ("NEXT MONDAY")

ROSE'S DRESSING ROOM. ROSE LIES ON COUCH, HIDING HER FACE, SOBBING UNCONTROLLED. CHARLIE STANDS OVER HER — HARD, STONE-FACED.

ROSE (BETWEEN SOBS): I'm sorry — I'm sorry — I didn't believe he would — I'm sorry —

CHARLIE: Too late for that, Miss LaTour . . . get up, and stop the hysterics . . . where's your boyfriend . . .

ROSE: I don't know — I swear . . .

CHARLIE: You'd better remember . . . Because you're in real trouble now, Rose . . . You saw him lying out there — and you know

who gave the gun to *White* . . . ? (SHARP AND COLD) *You*
did . . !

ROSE (CALMER NOW): Is he — is Lt. Karr — dead . . . ?
DISSOLVE TO CLOSING BILLBOARD FILM.

SCRIPT ANALYSIS

You will note that
"The Edge of Night" avoids cumbersome lead-ins. The scene picks
up immediately from the previous episode. Actually, the first scene
is in the nature of a teaser building up suspense to hold the audience
through the first commercial.

In the dialogue between Rose and Larry White, we have some
examples of exposition which tell us why Larry is being held prisoner.
Rose says: ". . . so they got you . . . Robbery. . . ." and a moment
later, "Lt. Karr says you shot that grocer." This is a reiteration of the
plot line so that even if we had missed a few previous episodes we
would be aware of the reasons for Larry's predicament.

We have mentioned that the daily serials avoid flashbacks but
do utilize simultaneous time sequences. Scenes 2B and 2C are illustrative of this technique.

One of the main story lines is played up in Scene 2C: the
romance between Mike and Sara. (The love affair of Rose and Larry
is a secondary or subplot.) The use of the telephone sequence serves
to keep the main characters in the framework of the episode. Although Mike and Sara's conversation may appear innocuous, it will
be seen that their joy about their forthcoming wedding makes the
curtain scene disaster more highly emotional.

As we follow the progress of this episode, we find that the
writer has a quadruple challenge. There are four commercials and
at each curtain, a minor crisis is introduced. At the second curtain,
for example, we are waiting to see what will happen between Rose
and Helen.

Scene 3A is extremely visual. We make a point of this because
the current crop of daily serials on television are actually more audio
than video. In utilizing the visual as it does, "The Edge of Night"
proves itself a television vehicle rather than a transplanted radio
program.

All through the episode we are made aware of Larry White's hatred for Lt. Mike Karr. In the very first scene, Larry says: "I'll take that Karr guy with me . . . Him, I got to kill . . . !" And again in Scene 3B when Larry is holding the gun on Sgt. Vincent, he mutters: "Then this is *it*, Sgt. . . . and it'll be a pleasure . . . I only wish it was Karr. . . ." All this, of course, is a buildup for White's eventual meeting with the Lieutenant.

The close of Scene 3B brings us to another crisis. The criminal, Larry White, has obtained his freedom through a ruse and through playing on Rose's love for him. But now Rose sees him for what he is; "You're a killer, Larry — a dirty, no good killer — " Curtain. Third commercial.

Scene 4B is another simultaneous time sequence and in Scene 4C we find extensive use of the visual, aptly indicated by the writer as "Feeding the viewer's anticipation of the inevitable meeting between Mike and Larry White."

Scene 4D is actually a repetition of Scene 2C: the eagerly awaited honeymoon. Obviously, this will play upon the sentimentality of the viewer, and you can see now how it heightens the tragic shooting of Mike Karr. Remember that this is a Friday script and so we have a big crisis: Is Mike dead? This will certainly hold the viewer's interest over the weekend hiatus. To additionally maintain suspense, "The Edge of Night" employs a Teaser Scene after each episode. Observe how the Teaser Scene punctuates the previous curtain scene.

For a daily serial, "The Edge of Night" has a rather surprising amount of action. Suppose we review the action highlights: (a) Larry White induces Rose to aid his escape; (b) Rose simulates a fainting spell, deceives Policewoman Helen Kilbourn and then pushes Helen into the prop room and takes the gun from her; (c) Rose gets the gun to Larry who forces Sgt. Vincent to relinquish the key to the handcuffs; (d) After handcuffing Sgt. Vincent, Larry goes on a prowl for Lt. Mike Karr; (e) Larry finds Mike and shoots him.

There are about four sets utilized in this episode with some fragments of sets such as those necessitated by the "Varied shots of White at doors and hallways." Since one sequence of the plot may last for a couple of weeks or more, the same sets, naturally, are used over and over. This has its value economically in relation to production costs and additionally in giving the actors familiarity with the setting.

THE WRITER'S STAKE

For the writer, the daily serial is an all-consuming task: five scripts a week, month in, month out, year in, year out. Although it is true that because of lead-ins and lead-outs, commercials, special offers, etc., the quarter-hour script may not consume more than eleven minutes of playing time, still the fact remains that this is a daily task. The half-hour television serial which does not utilize a lead-in but does make use of a teaser, such as "The Edge of Night," approximates twenty-three minutes of playing time.

The serial writer also has a measure of security. Because of the necessity of writing for the same characters and following a pre-set plot line, it is to the advantage of the producer to keep the same writer as long as the writer is able and willing to turn out the scripts. This means a steady income and, generally, a very liveable one for the writer.

If you are worried about cracking under the strain, there is the evidence of some daily serial writers who have earned their bread and butter, and caviar, too, for more than a decade, dramatizing the trials and tribulations of noble women enduring the follies of erring spouses. There are others who have dropped quickly by the wayside, the strain of keeping their characters in continual difficulties proving too much for them!

We do not know whether the daily serials will invade the television airwaves in as much abundance as they did radio. In radio's heyday, there were some two dozen odd serials broadcast every weekday. At this writing, there are about ten on television. The chances are there will be more by the time you read this book. Although there are a good many daily serials still being broadcast on radio today, their audience hold has slipped considerably which is attested to by the fact that many of them are only partially sponsored.

If you have an idea for a daily serial, generally, it would be necessary for you to prepare at least three scripts: the first and second episodes and a future episode, possibly number twelve or thirteen. You would also have to submit a complete synopsis of your first major story and include a subplot or two. Many daily serials are home-grown products of networks or advertising agencies. It is possible, however, that an independent producer might be interested in a serial which he in turn could sell to a sponsor through the latter's advertising agency. It would most certainly be advisable for the writer to contact producers to ascertain whether there is any interest before sitting down to formulate a plot and write any episodes for a daily serial.

The radio drama

19

Granted that the bulk of broadcast drama is being written for television, there are still quite a number of plays regularly scheduled on radio. To mention a few, CBS has its Columbia Workshop with its experimental dramas, its adult western, "Gunsmoke," and its daily quota of serials; NBC has been presenting "Five Star Matinee," half-hour adaptations of popular magazine stories; ABC and MBS both have their quota of across-the-board mystery and crime dramas, with Mutual still presenting such long-run series as "Counterspy" and "Treasury Agent." CBS does especially well in the latter field with "Suspense," "FBI," and "Yours Truly Johnny Dollar," among others. This means that there are still a good many writers tilling the radio fields and producing a fairly substantial crop.

On the local level, some radio stations are continuing to present dramatic programs. However, the drama has never been a strong point of the smaller stations. A 250-watter in a small town rarely has available any professional actors, and a dramatic series would normally be too expensive for local sponsorship. Some of the larger independents or network affiliates in the great urban centers do have the facilities and a few of them still present original dramas, notably, WMCA in New York and its "New World A'Comin'" series. Many college and university groups produce effective dramas either over the campus radio station or the nearby local outlet. The productions of the University of North Carolina were recently given network time by NBC. Station WTIC, 50,000-watter in Hartford, Connecticut, has been presenting a series called "Experimental Radio Theater" in cooperation with local little theater groups.

Naturally, the big money is in television. The radio play today has to be produced at a minimum budget with a minimum cast. The hour radio dramas with their star-studded casts are now a matter of history. All the mystery dramas, and they form the bulk of radio dramatic fare, are taped after minimum rehearsal time. The music, in most instances, is taken from recorded selections. These crime dramas have very rigid formulas and are mostly written on assignment. However, John Roeburt, in his contribution to the *Mystery Writer's Handbook,* has a word of hopeful and helpful advice to the radio writer with a penchant for "whodunits." "The writer-producer and the writer-producer-director," states Mr. Roeburt, "are a developing phenomenon in radio mystery. . . . He [the writer] can become his own packager; he can offer himself and his own book character for station programming at a flat price."

The concentration of existing radio drama is on the shorter form: the quarter hour and the half hour, the latter very frequently shortened to twenty-five minutes to permit the station an additional five-minute newscast. Since the quarter-hour programs are almost all daily serials, a subject which we have previously considered, our emphasis in this chapter will be on the half-hour drama.

THE TOOLS

The basic elements discussed in the chapters on the television drama apply equally to the radio drama. However, since radio lacks the all important advantage of the visual, the writer must use his three tools, *dialogue, sound, music,* with consummate skill. His pictures are verbal; his images conjured out of sound and music. Not only does the radio writer have the same problems of exposition as the television writer, but he must also describe his settings verbally. Where a character in a television play moves easily and quietly across a room to a desk to write a check or to a bookcase to choose a volume, the same action in a radio drama must be explained to the listener verbally and with sound. Yet the radio dramatist should not be obvious. His necessary explanations of time and place and action should appear to spring naturally from the dialogue. This is the ideal since it accomplishes the task of exposition while it moves the play. The writer may employ a narrator and tell his story in the first person. Or he may simply utilize the announcer to describe changes of scene and passage of time. This latter device is the most ineffective and the announcer is, in reality, a crutch.

DIALOGUE

Suppose we see how dialogue is used to describe three essential elements to the listener: Place, Time and Action.

Place

Here is a scene from one of the most popular "Family Theater" dramas, which has been broadcast for many years over the Mutual Network. It is a half-hour drama, "God and a Red Scooter," presented during the Christmas season.

MUSIC: OUT

ED (LATE TWENTIES): From this hill, you get a pretty good idea how it looks, Jeanie.

JEAN (TWENTY): The vines are beautiful, Ed. Nice dark green.

ED: Here, let me hold Eddie for ya.

JEAN: Be careful of his back, Ed. He's so wiggly.

ED: I got 'im.

JEAN: Is that our land all the way to the road?

ED: Straight clean to Route 99. That's twenty-six acres of good grapewood, Jeanie. Don't it make you feel kinda glad just to look at it?

JEAN (SMILING PROUDLY): Uh-huh. It almost makes you want to laugh and . . . and cry, Ed. Standin' here like this and lookin' down on our own land. . . . (HAPPY BREATH) It's nice to own something.

ED: Yeah. Cost me plenty of jack, too. But it's worth it.

JEAN: When'll the grapes be growin', Ed?

ED: Oh, three years. It takes at least three years.

JEAN: Seems so long to wait. I mean . . . you'd think they'd just pop out.

ED: Not grapes, Jeanie. You gotta build up grapes. You gotta work a vineyard. Then after three years . . . you know what it's gonna be like down there?

JEAN: What?

ED: They're gonna be out there on the wire trellises . . . those grapes. They're gonna be hangin' thick and heavy near the redwood stakes. And when the harvest comes, we're gonna be packin' . . . well . . . over two hundred tons of the best Red Emperors in California.

JEAN (BREATHING HAPPILY): . . . it's almost like a miracle, Ed.

ED: Yah.

JEAN: Eddie'll be three years old when we start pickin' our grapes.

From this brief scene, we learn many things. We know our locale is California and specifically, a vineyard. We know, also, that Ed and Jean are a young married couple with a newborn baby. This knowledge has come to us through natural dialogue. We feel that this is the way Ed and Jean would speak, that they are reacting naturally to the scene before them.

Time

Dialogue may be employed for several different phases of time exposition: (a) to convey the current time of an action; (b) to convey the passage of time; (c) to convey the time of a period drama. We will illustrate each one of these phases by examples from broadcast radio dramas.

(a) In the dramatization of "The Case of the Wondering Wife," from the Mutual Network's "Treasury Agent" series, a plane develops engine trouble and has to make a forced landing in the water. A Coast Guard cutter is on its way for rescue operations.

(MUSIC: UP AND HOLD UNDER)

SOUND: (SHIP'S ENGINE)

LT: Bridge! Bridge! Get this! One pip on the radarscope — been stationary for some time. That must be that plane! Change course to twenty-eight, quarter speed, and stand by for rescue operations!

SOUND: (ENGINES UP INTO)

(MUSIC: UP AND HOLD UNDER)

SOUND: (INTO WIND)

GIRL (STEWARDESS) (OFF) (UP): Everybody — please listen! A

Coast Guard cutter has come! They'll begin taking passengers off as soon as it's *daylight.* It'll be only a little while now! Then we'll be taken into Baltimore!

The stewardess in reassuring the passengers also conveys the current time of action to the listening audience.

(b) In this scene from "Together We Live" (WMCA), the survivors of a wrecked plane are taking turns to keep a fire going. One of the men, Crofton, awakens to relieve the man on watch, Hendesh.

CROFTON: I'll take over now, Hendesh.
HENDESH: Ah, you have come to relieve me, Crofton. Good. I could hardly keep my eyes open. Has it been only two hours?
CROFTON: Yeah. Just a couple of hours.
HENDESH: I guess it's because I'm so tired . . . it seemed so long . . .
CROFTON: Better get some sleep . . .

(c) A great many radio dramas employ the narrative technique and this use of a narrator provides an effective and straightforward means of setting time or place, as illustrated in this excerpt from "The Legend of the Great Hope" broadcast over WMCA, New York:

(MUSIC: UP AND OUT)
JOSHUA: It was in the year 1721 that the good ship "Great Hope" spread her huge sails and set forth to the New World. There were a hundred men and women aboard her, leaving England for new life and new freedom. There were some fleeing persecution; there were adventurers; there were myself and my daughter, Rebecca.

As this historic fantasy continues, the "Great Hope" is blown far off its course by a hurricane, and finally founders on the African coast. The survivors are made slaves and their many attempts to escape are frustrated. Dr. Joshua Maccabee, the narrator of the drama, again conveys the time period within the framework of the story.

(MUSIC: UP AND UNDER)
JOSHUA: But it was long before such opportunity did come. The Captain, who had managed to keep some sort of calendar told us one day that we were entering the year, 1722. There was no celebration in our hearts. A year had gone and yet we were no more than slaves. And the pall of hopelessness shrouded our prison.

Action

For dialogue descriptive of action, we have another scene from "The Case of the Wondering Wife." George and Lola, both smugglers, are on a flight from Lisbon to New York.

GIRL: Would you like some chewing gum? The flight's getting a little rough.

LOLA: No, thanks, Stewardess.

GIRL (GO OFF): You're welcome.

GEORGE: On a boat down there on the water, at least we'd be among five hundred other people. But here — well. If

(OFF: ENGINES MISS)

GEORGE: — we ever got off this plane in New York and out to Kansas City safely, it'll be dumb luck. Hey, something's wrong!

LOLA: What?

GEORGE: The engines! Listen to 'em! They're conking out!

LOLA: You're hearing things, George.

GEORGE: Like blazes I am! And it's pitch dark! There's a storm! What chance'll we have down there?

GIRL (OFF) (UP): Please, everybody! Put on your safety belts. One at each seat!

CAST: (SCARED AD LIBS)

(ENGINES OUT)

GIRL (OFF) (UP): We've got engine trouble! The pilot's going to set the ship down on the water!

CAST: (AD LIBS)

SOUND

In the early days of radio, almost every sound effect was performed manually. The sound effects man rivalled Rube Goldberg in inventiveness. He had to be prepared for effects ranging from a dam bursting to footsteps crunching on snow. Today the sound effects man still has much of his ingenious equipment but complete sound effects libraries are now available on discs. This is especially helpful to local groups who wish to present a series of radio plays and who might find themselves unable to reproduce, realistically, sounds such as thunder, jungle noises, artillery fire, and the like.

It is difficult to conceive of a radio play without sound effects. For that matter, the theater, the motion picture and television make frequent use of them. The radio writer, however, has to place more reliance on sound effects than does the writer for any other medium. The motion picture, for example, will show you the actual train running along the rails; even the "live" TV program may have a film insert. But the radio broadcast must depict the train by sound: the chugging of the wheels, the clickety-clack across the rails, the whistle. The wonder is, that given the proper sound, the audience will see the train in its mind's eye almost as vividly as if it were visually depicted.

But there is one pitfall the radio writer must avoid. If he is a beginner, he is apt to indicate the sound desired without any bolstering by the dialogue. Now there are many sound effects that can stand alone. The audience will have little difficulty recognizing a thunderclap, or a train leaving the station, or a dog barking. But there are many sounds that are not so readily identifiable, and so they must be defined by the dialogue.

In one radio play, a sound called for was the rattle of gourds. Without some exposition by the dialogue, most of the audience would have been left wondering what the sound was supposed to indicate. The scene was handled as follows:

SOUND: RATTLE OF GOURDS

JOSHUA: Two of the tribe's medicine men, or so they called them, were shaking weird gourds and muttering incantations. Surely, I thought, their grotesquely painted faces were enough to frighten the devil out of one were he actually possessed of the demon.

This is a situation the radio writer will have to decide for himself. Let him stop a moment and consider. Would he recognize the sound immediately upon hearing it? If not, or if he is not sure, he had better err on the side of exposition and see to it that his dialogue carries an explanation of the sound.

The sound effect, like music, can be employed as a bridge between scenes, and also, like music, it can be used for time transitions. For example:

SOUND: AUTOMOBILE STARTING THEN MOTOR RUNNING SMOOTHLY UP FOR A FEW SECONDS AND THEN FADING OUT IN THE DISTANCE. FADE IN MOTOR FROM THE DISTANCE AND BRING UP

FOR A FEW SECONDS THEN CAR COMES TO A STOP WITH SCREECH-
ING OF BRAKES.

Sound, used as in the foregoing, will give an excellent illusion
of time passage; a mind's-eye picture of an automobile travelling
down the highway and then coming to a sudden stop.

To heighten any illusion the writer wishes to achieve, he will
find it most effective to mix both sound and music. If his story
deals with the supernatural, he can call for weird, eerie music above
which is heard the creaking of a door. The sound effect then combines with the music for the creation of atmosphere.

SOUND: UP WITH RAIN . . . HOLD BEHIND MUSIC
MUSIC: SWEEP UP WITH DELUGE . . . FADE OUT FAST
SOUND: HOLD WELL UP BEHIND WITH RAIN AND WIND

MUSIC

Music, broadly
speaking, has two main functions: transitions and mood. Although
it is possible to make up a list of a dozen different functions of music,
an analysis would demonstrate that they are really subdivisions of the
aforementioned two categories.

Television people often refer to radio as being "blind," but it is
only the blindness of the man who closes his eyes and lets his dreams
play upon the stage of his imagination. With dialogue, music and
sound, the radio writer fashions settings, breathes life into characters,
inspires empathy.

Transitions

One advantage
radio drama may be said to have over television is that it may employ a vastly greater number of scenes. Each new set for the television drama means an added expense. But the radio drama may
travel the world on bridges of music.

Fortunately for the writer, the radio audience has been accustomed to accept a few bars of music as a magic carpet. Let us suppose
Agent X has discovered a nest of intrigue in an Istanbul Hotel. He

calls his headquarters in London. "I'll be there in the morning," he says, trying to keep his voice calm. The music sweeps up and out and, presto, he is in London. The audience is right there with him for the blessing of imagination is a wonderful gift which we all possess in greater or lesser measure.

Now Agent X is in London via the *space transition*. He is in a conference with his superiors. At the end of the conference he is asked to wait for further orders. The music sweeps in again and out, to effect the passage of several hours. This is the *time transition*.

The radio writer should observe the same caution when using music as with sound. Since he does not have any visual aids, he must rely entirely on the aural. This necessitates a bolstering of the music and sound by the dialogue. A music bridge, per se, can imply a passage of time. It cannot, by itself, convey the amount of time. Is it minutes, hours, days, weeks, months? Therefore the dialogue must work in conjunction with the music. Specifically, let us examine the situation regarding Agent X. We stated that the music sweeps in and out to effect the passage of several hours. It would be necessary then for the writer to indicate the time verbally and yet within dialogue that sounds conversationally natural.

MUSIC: FOR TIME PASSAGE . . . UP AND OUT
COLONEL (TO AGENT X): Sorry to have kept you waiting, but you know how these conferences are . . . take hours.

The music then has served its purpose as a time transition and it has been bolstered by the dialogue which, in essence, informs the audience that several hours have passed.

In the matter of music cues, the neophyte rightly poses the question of how far must he go in describing the type of music desired. There is no question but that it is helpful for the writer to have some musical knowledge. But he need not be a musician nor be able to tell a B flat from a C sharp. He should be able to identify, however, the type of music he desires: tense, foreboding, sentimental, agitated. A one-word description may serve the purpose or he may be somewhat more detailed:

MUSIC: . . . IT IS LYRIC . . . A LOVER'S MOOD. . . .

These brief descriptions will be sufficient for the music director to prepare the proper cues. If the writer desires to indicate a time transition he may simply state:

The music director will score the appropriate passage. If you are preparing a radio script for local presentation and will have to rely on a record library, you will find that a large percentage of stations subscribe to music libraries. And as part of such libraries, there is available a transcription of music cues which are adaptable for most purposes.

Mood

You write a comedy and you want to create an atmosphere of gaiety. You write a mystery and you want to build up suspense. You write a tale of romantic love and you want to endow it with a feeling of rapture. For each of these goals, music is an invaluable aid to the radio writer.

The listening audience is put in a mood for a mystery play by the very opening bars of music which are sinister in tone. For the comedy, the music is light and sparkling. For the romance, the music is sentimental.

Within the script itself, there will evidently be many changes of mood. You end Scene One with the young man professing his love for the girl. You call for music to portray the happiness of two young people. In a following sequence a conflict arises . . . the course of true love, of course, does not run smoothly . . . and so at the end of this scene, you would indicate music that is agitated in spirit.

If you use the device of a narrator to relate portions of the story, you will want, most always, to have music under the narrator's monologue. You will find that it not only makes for easier listening but helps immeasurably to set the mood. In the following passage, the Narrator is also the lead of the story.

MUSIC: MOOD . . . IT IS SOFT AND GENTLE . . . IT PORTRAYS THE
    QUIET OF A PRIVATE HOSPITAL ROOM . . . IT STAYS UNDER THE
    NARRATOR FOR A FEW SECONDS THEN FADES OUT

DAN: I looked around at the white walls of the hospital room.
(NARR) I breathed in the clean, deodorant smell. It was just after dinner and there was a beautiful quiet and peace in the room. I was pretty comfortable now and I began to wonder how the others were coming along. I wondered especially about Joan, who was all of seven. I kept thinking of her lying there in the snow, her leg broken, the astonished pain on her child's face. I kept thinking

about what had happened on the mountainside . . . how much it was going to affect my life. And as I stared at the white walls, they seemed to part suddenly like the curtains on a stage . . . I was back at the National Airport and the sound of (START FADE) revving motors filled the air . . .

SOUND: AIRPLANE MOTORS UP STRONG THEN BG

"GUNSMOKE"

The student will find it profitable to study the following episode from the very popular radio series, "Gunsmoke," written by John Meston and presented over CBS Radio. This episode, "Sins of the Fathers," * is a complete drama and beneath its mantle of "adult western," it carries a message against prejudice.

SOUND: HORSE FADES ON TO FULL MIKE . . . ON CUE: RECORDED SHOT

MUSIC: HOLD UNDER . . . TRACK 1

WALSH: GUNSMOKE . . . brought to you by L & M Filters. This is it! L & M is best — stands out from all the rest!

MUSIC: FIGURE AND UNDER . . . TRACK 2

WALSH: Around Dodge City and in the territory on West — there's just one way to handle the killers and the spoilers — and that's with a U.S. Marshal and the smell of — GUNSMOKE!

MUSIC: THEME HITS: FULL BROAD SWEEP AND UNDER . . . TRACK 3

WALSH: GUNSMOKE, starring William Conrad. The transcribed story of the violence that moved West with young America — and the story of a man who moved with it.

MUSIC: OUT

MATT: I'm that man . . . Matt Dillon . . . United States Marshal . . . the first man they look for and the last they want to meet. It's a chancey job — and it makes a man watchful . . . and a little lonely.

MUSIC: MAIN TITLE . . . TRACK 4

MATT: (FADES ON) Morning, Doc. Chester.

DOC: Hello, Matt.

* © Copyright by Columbia Broadcasting System, Inc. 1956.

CHESTER: I've been waiting for you, Mr. Dillon.

MATT: Something wrong?

CHESTER: It's Mr. Dobie . . . he's at the desk in the hotel there, sir. And he's real upset about something. He wants to see you.

MATT: All right. Wait here . . . I'll be right out.

CHESTER: Yes sir.

SOUND: MATT CROSSES TO DOOR . . . OPENS . . . ENTERS . . . CLOSE DOOR

DOBIE: (OFF) Marshal Dillon. I've sure been wanting to see you.

SOUND: MATT CROSSES TO DESK

MATT: What's the trouble, Mr. Dobie? You got a riot in here?

DOBIE: There'll be a riot if you don't get them people out of here, Marshal.

MATT: What people?

DOBIE: The Daggitts . . . that's who.

MATT: Who're the Daggitts?

DOBIE: Big Dan Daggitt, he calls himself. And he is big, too, Marshal.

MATT: I never heard of Big Dan Daggitt.

CHESTER: Me, neither.

DOBIE: He's only been in Dodge since yesterday. He's one of them mountain men from on West. He's a hunter or something — one of them real hairy fellas. Shouldn't be allowed around other white men.

MATT: Why not? What's he doing?

DOBIE: He's setting in my hotel. I let him in before he told me.

MATT: Before he told you what?

DOBIE: It's better you see for yourself, Marshal. Their room's right down the corridor there.

MATT: Well . . . okay, Dobie, let's go.

MUSIC: BRIDGE

SOUND: DOBIE FROM BEHIND DESK — THEN FS ALONG CORRIDOR UNDER:

DOBIE: It's true, ain't it, Marshal, I don't have to let nobody stay in my hotel I don't want . . . ?

MATT: I guess so. If you've got a good reason.

DOBIE: I got plenty of reason. Three men have moved out already.

MATT: Sounds to me like he must have a box of rattlesnakes with him.

DOBIE: It's worse'n that. This is his room here.

SOUND: FS STOP

MATT: Isn't this a double room?

DOBIE: He needs it.

SOUND: KNOCK ON DOOR . . . REPEAT

DOBIE: He needs the whole doggone prairie. And that's where he's going. Now you tell him, Marshal.

SOUND: DOOR OPENS

DAN: Hello.

DOBIE: I got the U.S. Marshal with me this time, Daggitt.

DAN: Oh.

MATT: I'm Marshal Dillon, Daggitt. Dobie wanted me to come over here and meet you.

DAN: Come on in.

SOUND: FS ENTER . . . CLOSE DOOR

MATT: Well, you were right about his being big, Dobie.

DAN: A man can't help being big.

MATT: No offense.

DAN: That's okay. But they's been times I wished I was smaller. Not that I can't move as fast as any man. I'm easier to see . . . that's the only bad part.

MATT: Tell me, Daggitt . . . what's the trouble between you and Dobie?

DAN: It ain't my trouble, Marshal.

MATT: All right, Dobie, I guess you'd better explain — there's nothing wrong here I can see.

DOBIE: It ain't him — it's his wife.

MATT: What —

DAN: He don't like my wife cause she's a Indian, Marshal.

DOBIE: That's a lie. What do I care if she's an Indian?

MATT: I don't understand.

DOBIE: Where is she, Daggitt?

DAN: In the other room.

DOBIE: Well, bring her in here.

DAN: Dobie, you know what I could do to you with the fingers of this one hand . . . just the fingers.

DOBIE: Don't forget I got the Marshal with me.

DAN: I'll use the other hand on him, he starts ordering me around, too.

MATT: Now wait a minute — this kind of talk isn't doing any good.

DAN: You're probably pretty good with that gun, Marshal — but

I've killed mountain lion with this knife. I ain't afraid of nothing alive and not many ghosts.

DOBIE: "Ghosts" — what a savage.

MATT: That's enough, Dobie. I didn't come here for a fight, Daggitt — I came to see what all this trouble's about. And if it has something to do with your wife, tell me —

DAN: It has to do with Dobie — not my wife.

DOBIE: That's a lie.

ROSE: (OFF) Dan. . . .

DOBIE: There she is — look, Marshal. . . .

ROSE: (FADES ON) If it's me they're talking about, Dan, why didn't you call me?

DAN: It's nothing to do with you. They was trying to order me around — at least he was — Dobie there.

DOBIE: I only told you to get her in here, so's the Marshal could see her.

DAN: Well, now he's seen her. What's all the fuss about?

DOBIE: You're playing dumb, ain't you, Daggitt?

MATT: Wait a minute — I don't think he is. Will you answer a question, Daggitt?

DAN: Not from him.

MATT: From me. Where'd you and Mrs. Daggitt meet?

DAN: Near Denver.

MATT: Near Denver?

DAN: I'm a mountain man, Marshal. I never been on the prairie before.

MATT: But what were you doing near Denver, Mrs. Daggitt?

ROSE: I was sent there four years ago to get an education. My father was a chief, Marshal.

DOBIE: A chief! What chief?

ROSE: His name was Yellow Horse.

DOBIE: That's worse! That's the worst yet!

DAN: I don't understand either of you men. What're you talking about?

MATT: Yellow Horse was a Kiowa, Daggitt. And anyway, from her dress, Dobie could tell Mrs. Daggitt was a Kiowa.

DAN: She's gotta come from some tribe, don't she?

MATT: Two years ago, the Kiowas killed some eighteen settlers on raids through the country near here. Yellow Horse led them. Until he was killed.

DAN: (TO HER) You never told me that. Is it true.

ROSE: I only heard my father was dead. They told me nothing else.

DAN: Well, what difference it make? You wasn't on them raids.

MATT: The feeling's still high against Kiowas around here, Daggitt. But you're right — she had nothing to do with them.

DOBIE: A Kiowa's a Kiowa. We won't stand for them in Dodge.

MATT: Don't be a fool, Dobie. How can you blame her for what somebody else did?

DOBIE: I blame that whole tribe — and especially her father. And I won't stand for her being here. She's probably as murdering as he was.

SOUND: DAN MAKES MOVE . . . MATT STEPS BETWEEN THEM.

MATT: Hold it, Daggitt. I'd like to apologize to Mrs. Daggitt for bothering her.

DOBIE: "Apologize!"

MATT: Let's get out of here, Dobie . . . now.

DOBIE: No. You come here to throw them out, and you're going to do it.

MATT: Dobie — I guess I'm a little like Dan Daggitt — I don't take orders very well either.

DOBIE: (BEAT) All right, Marshal. If the law won't help me . . .

MATT: The law won't help you. And don't you try anything else. Now come on . . . we're getting out of here.

MUSIC: FIRST ACT CURTAIN

CHESTER: Mr. Dillon. . . .

MATT: What, Chester?

CHESTER: Would you mind stopping in to Mr. Jonas' store here? It won't take but a minute or two.

MATT: You going to spend your betting money on clothes again, Chester?

CHESTER: Oh no sir. I mean . . . aw, Mr. Dillon, I need a little string tie . . . for Sunday kinda. They don't cost more'n a quarter.

MATT: In that case, I'll go with you.

SOUND: FS TO DOOR . . . OPEN . . . BELL . . . CLOSE

CHESTER: Why, there's Miss Kitty. (UP) Hi, Miss Kitty.

KITTY: (OFF) Hello, Chester.

CHESTER: The ties are hanging back over there, Mr. Dillon. (FADES) I won't be long . . .

SOUND: MATT WALKS OVER TO KITTY

MATT: You're as bad as Chester, Kitty — always buying clothes.

KITTY: As Chester!? Matt, if Chester's always buying clothes, how come ever since I've known him, he's worn that same pair of striped pants.

MATT: Well, he's careful with them. He never gets them torn, I guess.

KITTY: He'd have to go to bed if he ever did.

MATT: Where's Mr. Jonas?

KITTY: Out back. He's showing Dan Daggitt and his wife something.

MATT: Are they here?

KITTY: Sure. He introduced me to them. Big Dan Daggitt — like you said last night, Matt, he earned the name. He's a buffalo, that man.

MATT: Yeah . . . he is.

KITTY: His wife's name is Rose. He said you couldn't pronounce it in Indian, so he made it English. She's a beautiful little thing.

MATT: She's prettier than most women around here.

KITTY: Thanks.

MATT: Now, Kitty.

KITTY: No . . you're right — she really is. I guess Dan Daggitt can't be all brute or a girl like that would never have married him.

MATT: It's too bad Dobie over at the Dodge House can't see it your way, Kitty.

KITTY: Dobie's just not thinking very straight.

SOUND: DOOR OPENS OFF . . . BELL . . . CLOSE . . . FS ENTER

RODIN: (OFF) Where's Jonas?

MATT: (UP) He's out back, Rodin.

RODIN: Oh, hello, Marshal. I didn't recognize you. Ah, here he comes . . .

SOUND: RODIN WALKS ACROSS TO JONAS ET AL

CAST: FADE ON JONAS SAYING 'YOU LIKE IT, ROSE?' ROSE: 'IT'S FINE, MR. JONAS' . . . STUFF LIKE THAT

KITTY: Who's that, Matt?

MATT: His name's Rodin. He works over at one of the stables.

KITTY: Oh . . . that explains why he's too poor ever to come into the Long Branch.

RODIN: (AT COUNTER, MAYBE FIFTEEN FEET FROM OTHERS) (UP) Jonas . . . . hey, Jonas . . .

JONAS: (UP) I'll be right with you, Rodin.

RODIN: I'm in a hurry.

JONAS: Won't be a minute.

RODIN: Well, I ain't waiting while you sell beads to her. Say — wait a minute — What's she doing in here anyway?

MATT: Stay here, Kitty.

SOUND: MATT WALKS SLOWLY CLOSER AND STOPS AS:

JONAS: She's got as much right to be here as you have, Rodin.

RODIN: A Kiowa woman . . ! ? You gone crazy . . .

JONAS: No.

RODIN: Then throw her out of here. Or I will.

DAN: (COMES CLOSER TO RODIN) (GENTLY THROUGHOUT) The woman's my wife, mister.

RODIN: Your wife. . . . ! *Your* wife. . . . ?

DAN: You'll have to throw me out, too.

RODIN: Now look here . . . I . . . I didn't mean nothing.

DAN: If you don't mean nothing, don't talk.

RODIN: Sure . . . sure . . . what do I care? It's your business. I don't care.

DAN: Even if you do care, you shouldn't say nothing about it out loud.

RODIN: I ain't saying nothing. I gotta go now . . . (FADES) I gotta go.

SOUND: HE WALKS TO DOOR . . . EXITS UNDER:

DAN: Hello, Marshal. I didn't know you was here.

MATT: You handled that pretty well, Daggitt.

DAN: I can't fight every man in the world.

MATT: No you can't.

DAN: And I don't aim to . . . long as they don't push me too far.

MATT: Dobie leaving you alone?

DAN: Oh, he's doing a lot of talking around — trying to stir up trouble. But before it comes, we'll probably be gone — back to Colorado. The mountains.

MATT: Oh. . . .

DAN: Marshal, you come see us sometime the next day or so. Rose'd kinda like that.

MATT: It'd be a pleasure, Daggitt.

MUSIC: BRIDGE

CHESTER: Where's Doc this morning, Mr. Dillon? I been up to his office twice and he ain't there.

MATT: He was called out to the Duke place last night.

CHESTER: Somebody sick?

MATT: Doc doesn't get many social calls, Chester.

CHESTER: Well, I was calling on him socially.

MATT: He'll appreciate that. But I think I'll go up to the Dodge House and make a call on Jim Dobie.

CHESTER: More trouble, Mr. Dillon?

MATT: There will be if somebody doesn't stop him. I heard more about how he's been talking to everybody who'll listen to him about Rose Daggitt being Yellow Horse's daughter, and how they oughta run her out of town.

CHESTER: It's like he's looking for help, ain't it?

MATT: Yeah.

CHESTER: He oughta know better than that, a man like Dobie.

MATT: That's what I'm going to try to explain to him, Chester.

SOUND: DOOR OPENS . . . FS ENTER

CHESTER: Why, it's Dan Daggitt.

DAN: (FADES ON) It's me, Chester.

MATT: Hello, Daggitt.

DAN: Marshal, I'm kinda worried.

MATT: What's the matter?

DAN: It's Rose. I can't find her nowhere.

MATT: You can't find her . . . ?

DAN: Well, I ain't seen her since about four o'clock this morning. I feel like a fool coming here and telling you that . . .

MATT: Daggitt, I don't think you would come here if you weren't real worried.

DAN: Maybe you and Chester'll help me look for her. I been everywhere . . .

MATT: Of course we'll help you. Where'd you see her last?

DAN: It ain't like Rose to go off like that. Especially here, with all the talk people are making. She wouldn't do that. I'm getting worried, Marshal.

MATT: Where'd you see her last?

DAN: In our room. I'll tell you — I woke up real early and I couldn't get back to sleep. So I got dressed and went out on the street and walked around. I didn't want to bother her. I wasn't gone more'n an hour, Marshal. I shouldn't never of left her.

MATT: Did you ask them at the hotel? Did anybody see her leave?

DAN: There wasn't nobody at the hotel. Not when I went out and not when I came back. So nobody coulda seen her.

CHESTER: Well, where would she of gone that hour of the morning?

DAN: She wouldn't've gone nowhere, Chester. Not Rose. That's what I can't understand.

MATT: (GETS UP) Well, let's start looking for her.

SOUND: THEIR FS TO DOOR . . . OPEN . . . FS ONTO BOARDWALK

DAN: I sure do thank you, Marshal. And you, too, Chester.

CHESTER: We'll find her. Don't worry. Hey, that's Doc's buggy coming there.

MATT: Yeah.

CHESTER: Look — he's got somebody with him.

SOUND: HORSE AND BUGGY FADE ON

DAN: That's Rose. That's Rose in that buggy.

SOUND: BUGGY PULLS UP . . . THEY RUN OUT

DAN: Rose . . . Rose, what're you doing there?

ROSE: (IN BUGGY) Hello, Dan.

DAN: Well, get down. Here . . . I'll take you.

SOUND: HE LIFTS HER DOWN

ROSE: You'll have to carry me, Dan.

DAN: Where you been? What happened to your feet?

DOC: (IN BUGGY) Chester —

CHESTER: What, Doc?

DOC: Do me a favor take this buggy, will you?

CHESTER: Sure I will, Doc. (MOVES)

DOC: And you, Daggitt — take Rose into the Marshal's office. She shouldn't be on the street out here.

DAN: We'll go.

SOUND: HE WALKS OFF . . . DOC'S FS FADE ON

DOC: (FADES ON) She told me about her husband, Matt, but she didn't tell me he was that big. Come on, let's follow them.

SOUND: THEY WALK TO OFFICE, UNDER:

MATT: What's Rose doing with you, Doc?

DOC: I found her out on the prairie — about ten miles East of here.

MATT: What was she doing out there?

DOC: I'll let her tell you that.

SOUND: THEY ENTER OFFICE . . . CROSS TO DAGGITTS

DAN: (FADES ON) You sit right there, Rose.

ROSE: (SITS) I'm all right, Dan. Doc — this is my husband, Dan.

DOC: I kinda gathered that, Rose. Glad to know you, Dan.

DAN: Good thing you come along, Doc.

DOC: You feel up to telling the whole story, Rose? I expect the Marshal here'll be interested too.

ROSE: All right.

DOC: And then I want you to come up to my office with me.

ROSE: Sure, Doc.

MATT: Has she been hurt?

DOC: Go ahead, Rose — tell them . . .

ROSE: Well, early this morning I woke up when somebody tied a bandana over my face — of course, I knew it wasn't Dan . . .

DAN: I never shoulda left you alone —

ROSE: That's foolish talk, Dan. It wasn't your fault.

DOC: Go on, Rose. . . .

ROSE: Well, it was two men. They never said a word the whole time. They never talked once. But they had a big sack of some kind and they put me in that and carried me out the back way. And then they tied me onto a horse and led it away out into the prairie.

DOC: Why didn't you yell or something, Rose?

ROSE: Oh, I fought, but they were a lot stronger.

DOC: But why didn't you yell?

MATT: Indian women don't yell, Doc. Go on, Rose.

ROSE: So they finally stopped and took me off the horse and untied me. And then they took my shoes away and rode off. I finally got the blindfold off, and I walked and walked — till I saw Doc's buggy coming. I couldn't have walked much farther.

DAN: Rose . . . Rose . . .

MATT: Wait a minute, Dan. Rose, you never saw those men . . . and you never heard their voices . . . ?

ROSE: No. But I heard them walk. Everybody has a different walk.

MATT: Did you recognize either of them from hearing their walks?

ROSE: No. It wasn't Dobie, or that man in the store.

DAN: We'll find them, Rose. We'll sit on the street and listen till we find them. And when we do I'll cut them — I'll cut them awful before I kill them.

MATT: No, Daggitt. You let Rose find them, if she can — and then I'll take them.

DAN: They're mine, Marshal. They're just as much mine as Rose is mine. I wouldn't let nobody else in the world touch them but me.

MATT: It'll be murder.

DAN: Is that what you call it? Rose, Doc wants you in his office, you go along now. And then we'll start listening — it's as good a way to hunt as any.

MUSIC: SECOND ACT CURTAIN

MATT: For the next few days the Daggitts took up their post on the boardwalk halfway down Front Street. Rose'd sit there for hours, her head down, her eyes half-closed, listening to the footsteps of hundreds of men as they passed. And Big Dan Daggitt would stand at her side, his bowie knife in his belt, waiting with animal patience for a sign from his wife. But it didn't come, and I began to hope that for his sake the kidnappers had left the country, and nothing would happen . . . And then, the morning of the third day, Chester and I were loafing around on the porch of the General Store . . .

CHESTER: Where's the Daggitts this morning, Mr. Dillon? They ain't over there where they usually are.

MATT: I guess they haven't started yet, Chester.

CHESTER: Every man in Dodge must've walked past there by now.

MATT: All but two, maybe.

DOBIE: (FADES ON) Morning, Marshal . . . Chester.

CHESTER: Hello, Mr. Dobie.

MATT: Dobie.

DOBIE: I'm looking for the Daggitts, Marshal. You seen them?

MATT: No, I haven't Dobie, but Dan Daggitt isn't taking things as easy as he was. If I were you, I'd stop looking right now.

DOBIE: Doc told me what happened, Marshal.

MATT: Doc did?

DOBIE: He knew nobody else would. So he took it on himself.

MATT: What for?

DOBIE: For my own good — the way he put it.

MATT: Well . . . did it do you any good, Dobie?

DOBIE: It made me mad, Marshal. Mad at myself, mostly. I've been a fool.

CHESTER: Mr. Dillon — there's Rose now. In the street there. She's got a shotgun. What's she doing?

MATT: It looks like she's following those two men.

CHESTER: She sure is. She's stopped them. She's got them turned around . . . why, she's gonna shoot them . . .

MATT: Come on . . .

SOUND: THEY WALK INTO STREET

CHESTER: She's sure got the drop on them. They ain't making a move.

MAN: (FADES ON) How do you know it was us? And what if it was? Now you put that gun down . . . or we'll do it again . . .

MATT: (UP) Don't shoot, Rose. I'll take them.

SOUND: TWO SHOTGUN BLASTS . . . TWO MEN FALL . . . MATT WALKS UP TO ROSE

MATT: Give me that shotgun, Rose.

ROSE: (HANDS IT OVER) It's empty, Marshal.

MATT: Why'd you do it? I'd have arrested them.

ROSE: Dan would've found a way to kill them, even if you had.

CHESTER: (OFF) They're dead, Mr. Dillon — both of them.

MATT: Who are they, Chester?

CHESTER: Never saw them before in my life. Couple of strangers, I guess.

DAN: (RUNS UP) Rose . . . Rose, was that them? (ON) Why didn't you tell me? What'd you run away for? Why'd you kill them?

ROSE: That's them, Dan.

DAN: How'd you know? Where'd you spot them?

ROSE: They walked past our table, while we were eating breakfast.

DAN: You said you was going up to our room.

ROSE: I did go. Long enough to get the shotgun.

DAN: Why didn't you tell me? Why'd *you* have to kill them?

ROSE: I couldn't see you hang for what happened to me, Dan.

DAN: I'd gladly hung for it. Anything's better'n your going to jail.

ROSE: I won't mind, Dan.

DAN: It'll kill you. I won't let it happen . . . it ain't right. Don't you try to take her, Marshal . . . don't you try.

MATT: I know how you feel, Daggitt, but I've got to arrest her.

DAN: You gonna put her in jail?

MATT: Not if you promise you'll stay in Dodge. Rose has got to stand trial.

DAN: What'll they do to her?

MATT: There's no judge in Kansas who'd convict a woman who did what Rose did.

DOBIE: (FADES ON) Marshal Dillon . . .

MATT: What, Dobie?

DOBIE: I gotta say something, Marshal.

MATT: All right.

DOBIE: Them two men she killed. I just looked at them, and I don't know who they are . . . but I've seen them.

MATT: So . . .

DOBIE: I seen them the other day when I was talking the way I was. They heard me . . . they was listening.

MATT: Go ahead . . .

DOBIE: I had to tell you that. I don't feel very proud.

MATT: You're the one that oughta go to jail, Dobie.

DOBIE: That's what I'm trying to tell you, Marshal. It's mostly my fault — what happened to her, and this killing, and all. . . .

MATT: Well, you've learned something now, anyway.

DOBIE: But there's nothing I can do about it. It's too late, I feel like hiding.

ROSE: Mr. Dobie . . .

DOBIE: Yes . . . ma'am. . . .

ROSE: Would you walk back to the hotel with me and my husband?

DOBIE: Would I . . . Thank you . . . I'd be proud to —

MUSIC: CURTAIN

The religious drama

20

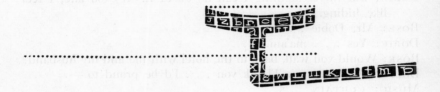

There are today numerous religious programs on radio and television. Many of them consist of a very simple format: liturgical music and a sermon. These types of programs are generally "remotes," that is, they are broadcast directly from the point of origin, in this instance, the church or synagogue. But the networks themselves, and many local stations, in cooperation with religious groups, present programs of a more ambitious nature, namely, the religious drama. You may be familiar with "Lamp Unto My Feet," "Frontiers of Faith," "The Catholic Hour," "The Greatest Story Ever Told," and "Family Theater."

At first glance, it may appear that the religious drama is a highly specialized field for the writer. Actually, although the religious drama presents a moral issue, it must meet the requisites of any effective dramatic presentation. Therefore, the writer, whether he be a churchman or a layman, must first have a knowledge of dramatic principles and be cognizant of radio and television techniques.

The audience in the church is a captive audience. It has come voluntarily to take part in the services, to listen to the sermon. It will stay in its pews throughout the service. But the home audience is not homogeneous. Some may be shut-ins, in which case religious programs constitute their church-going. But the majority will stay tuned in for only as long as the program interests them. The religious drama then must be on a par with other adult drama. It must be able to catch and hold interest and its message should be an integral part of the drama.

Sig Mickelson, Vice President in Charge of News and Public Affairs for CBS, made some pertinent observations about the religious drama in an address before the National Conference of Radio, Television, Film, Commission of the Methodist Church.

> . . . too often, in the case of drama, the message does not lend itself to dramatic treatment, and we end up with a dramatization of some minor problem in every-day life, and the religious message is dragged in by the hair, articulated out of context, or by some stereotype, so that not only is the drama vitiated, but the message itself is made meaningless. This is a common failing of many "religious dramas." And I have a feeling that it is because we have no basic understanding of — or at least no common agreement on — what constitutes religious drama.
>
> Drama can have a message, and a theme, drama can have a religious message, and a religious theme. But these must be inherent in the basic situation and in the believable actions of believable people. Neither message nor theme can be dealt with in pedantic fashion as from a pulpit.

Many religious organizations, cooperating in the presentation of network programs, have recognized these principles as stated by Mr. Mickelson. They have contracted with professional writers for their series of religious dramas. "The Eternal Light," produced for many years over NBC radio and now also seen on NBC television, is an outstanding example. Morton Wishengrad, one of our most sensitive radio and video playwrights, has written many successful dramas for "The Eternal Light." A representative collection of his scripts is available in book form and is noted in our bibliography. "Eternal Light" scripts for study may also be obtained by writing to the Jewish Theological Seminary of America, 3080 Broadway, New York 27, New York.

There are, of course, practical considerations, which must be taken into account in writing the religious drama for network television. Since these programs are sustaining, costs must be kept down to a minimum. This means few sets, two or three, probably, and small casts. The religious drama on radio has no problems of sets but here, too, casts are comparatively small.

We have chosen for study three network-produced religious dramas, one video and two radio scripts. All three vary in theme and will give you an idea of the wide scope of material which offers possibilities for religious dramas. The Bible, of course, is an endless source of material for dramatization and this has been done, most successfully, by the radio series, "The Greatest Story Ever Told." But many current religious dramas use contemporary themes as will be illustrated by the following scripts.

"LAMP UNTO MY FEET"

The CBS television series, "Lamp Unto My Feet," produced by Pamela Ilott, has won deserved critical acclaim. "The Back of His Head," by Steven Gethers, is a typical script from this series. It is a quarter-hour script, and in keeping with the requirements of the sustaining religious drama, it has a small cast of six, including an off-screen narrator. There are only three sets, all interiors. The play opens in the living room of the Parker home.

FADE IN ON:
(A WELL FURNISHED LIVING ROOM OF AN AFFLUENT LOOKING HOME. A BOY OF ABOUT TWELVE IS IN AN EASY CHAIR READING A BOOK ON SCIENCE. OFF TO ONE CORNER IS HIS FATHER. WE SEE ONLY THE BACK OF HIS HEAD SINCE HE NEVER TURNS OUR WAY TO ANSWER A QUESTION. HE IS BUSILY ENGAGED IN FILLING OUT TAX FORMS AND BUSINESS PAPERS. OUR NARRATOR'S VOICE COMES OVER THE SCENE.)

NARRATOR: This is a story of a family . . . and the tale is based on an old joke which I am sure you've heard many times. (PAUSE) The boy in the corner is Warren Parker . . . twelve years old. He is reading a book about science. Across the room is his father, Richard Parker. We see only the back of his head because this is how Warren sees him most of the time. Richard is busy. You know how it is . . . close to tax time . . . getting his business affairs in order. . . . You know how it is. (PAUSE) The joke? It goes something like this. . . .

WARREN: Dad? (NO ANSWER) Dad!
RICHARD: Mmmmm?
WARREN: What causes the moon to stay in the sky? How come it
  doesn't come crashing down to earth? What holds it up?
RICHARD (MUMBLING): I dunno. (PAUSE)
WARREN: And the sun. It says here that it's a big ball of fire. How
  come it doesn't burn up everything around it?
RICHARD (MUMBLING): I dunno.
WARREN: Where did the salt in the ocean come from?
RICHARD (IRRITATED): I dunno. (PAUSE)
WARREN: Dad?
RICHARD: Mmmm?
WARREN: You don't mind my asking you these questions, do you?
RICHARD: Of course not. How else will you learn? (THE NARRA-
  TOR COMES IN AS WE GO TO A CU OF THE BACK OF
  RICHARD'S NECK. HE IS STILL WORKING FURIOUSLY OVER
  HIS PAPERS.)
NARRATOR: An old joke . . . I warned you about it . . . except Mr.
  Parker doesn't know that the joke will be on him . . . five years
  later.

The next scene takes place five years later. Mr. Parker, as
usual, is buried in work at his desk. His son, Warren, is seventeen
now. Mrs. Parker is worried about Warren. Whenever she speaks
to him, he answers only in monosyllables. The effect of his father's
influence is apparent to Mrs. Parker, but Mr. Parker is unaware of
his own dereliction. In vain, Mrs. Parker warns her husband that
he is spending too much time at his desk and too little with his family.
His answer is that he has to stick to his desk in order to earn a living
for his family. He assures her there is no cause for anxiety about
Warren. Their son will be an honor student at State University,
Mr. Parker predicts, but his wife urges him to speak to the boy.

MILDRED: Talk to the boy, Richard.
RICHARD: Talk to him? What about?
MILDRED: Anything. Just talk to him. . . . Ask him about his plans
  . . . his . . . anything.
RICHARD: All right. (PAUSE) Will you sharpen these pencils, dear?
(SHE SIGHS AND TAKES THEM FROM HIM)
MILDRED: Fifty years from now Warren's son will ask him what he

remembers best about his father and he'll say, "The back of his head."

(BUT HE'S ALREADY AT WORK AND WE DOLLY IN FOR A CU OF . . . THE BACK OF HIS HEAD.)

DISSOLVE TO:

(INTERIOR OF A HIGH SCHOOL PRINCIPAL'S OFFICE. HE IS LOOK-ING OVER A STUDENT'S RECORD A BIT UNEASILY. HE FROWNS AS THERE IS A KNOCK ON THE DOOR.)

PORTER: Come in. (WARREN ENTERS) Hello, Warren. Sit down, son. (WARREN SITS WITHOUT A WORD. PORTER LOOKS AT HIM) Well . . . how are you getting along?

WARREN: Fine, sir.

PORTER: How are your folks? I haven't seen them in quite awhile.

WARREN: Fine, sir. (PORTER PAUSES FOR A MOMENT)

PORTER: Warren . . . what's happened to you this past semester?

WARREN: Mmmm?

PORTER: It seems inconceivable to me that a boy who was on the honor roll . . . the top of his class . . . should suddenly fall twenty points below his usual standards. Surely the work hasn't been *that* difficult. (PAUSE) Has it?

WARREN: No sir.

PORTER: You were such an . . . outgoing young man, Warren. Your instructors tell me that you're no longer . . . (HE FUM-BLES FOR THE RIGHT WORD) Er . . . curious.

WARREN: Mmmmm??

PORTER: No longer curious. You used to ask questions. Now you sit there rather listlessly.

WARREN: I'm passing.

PORTER: Is that all you want to do . . . pass?

We have seen now in this transition from the Parker home to the high school principal's office, the development of the theme: the influence of home environment on the growth of children. Warren's appetite for learning has been dulled by lack of intelligent feeding at home. Mr. Porter, the principal, decides to discover the reason for Warren's apathy and the sudden dip in his grades. He, therefore, visits the Parkers, and has a frank talk with them. Mr. Parker cannot understand his son's attitude and is shocked when the principal suggests that Warren see a psychiatrist.

PORTER: I'd like to have him talk to our school psychiatrist.

RICHARD: Psychiatrist? Are you serious? The boy's a normal, healthy . . .

PORTER: Disturbed young man. (PAUSE) Something's wrong, Richard. I don't know if it's with him or Mildred or . . . you. But something's wrong. And if you're not careful it can develop into something quite serious.

RICHARD: I don't understand, Phil. The boy's got everything. He's never felt any financial insecurity. I do quite well . . . always have. He's got friends . . . clothes . . . everything a kid could ask for. (PAUSE) A psychiatrist . . .

PORTER: Why does that frighten you?

RICHARD: I don't know. It just does.

PORTER: Well . . . think about it. If you want him to make State . . . think about it.

(HE RISES AND EXITS. MILDRED SEES HIM TO THE DOOR AND RETURNS. SHE STANDS LOOKING AT HIM FOR QUITE A WHILE.)

RICHARD: What . . . what do you think, Mildred?

MILDRED: I think he should, Richard. (PAUSE) I think he should talk to that psychiatrist.

RICHARD: Why?

MILDRED: Because . . . he won't talk to you.

It is his wife's blunt response which finally makes Mr. Parker realize that he must have a heart to heart talk with his son. He goes up to his son's bedroom, and knocks at the door.

WARREN (os): Come.

(RICHARD ENTERS, AS HE OPENS THE DOOR WE CUT TO THE FIRST SIGHT OF WARREN. HE IS AT HIS DESK WORKING OVER HIS HOMEWORK. HE DOESN'T MOVE AS ALL WE SEE OF HIM IS THE BACK OF HIS HEAD.)

RICHARD: Hello, Warren.

WARREN: Hello. (RICHARD CLOSES THE DOOR.)

RICHARD: May I sit down?

WARREN: Sure. (HE STILL DOESN'T TURN.)

RICHARD: Warren . . . (NO RESPONSE) Warren!

WARREN: Mmmmmmm?

The device here is obvious but it makes the point. We know that oftentimes the best method of teaching is by example. And

Warren is demonstrating to his father very specifically what is wrong. Mr. Parker finally becomes annoyed at speaking to the back of his son's head and asks the boy to turn around. Warren does. His father demands to know why his grades have dropped and warns that he will not be admitted to the highly rated State University. Mr. Parker is shocked to learn that his son doesn't want to go to State. Warren explains why.

WARREN: If I go out of town I'll live in a dormitory . . . a fraternity . . . somewhere . . . where after the day is over . . . they'll talk to me. (PAUSE) My average didn't drop in school. I dropped it . . . on purpose . . . because I don't want to be admitted to State University. (LONG PAUSE)

RICHARD: I . . . I've tried to give you everything, Warren.

WARREN: Yes, sir. But it always wound up like this. All I ever got from you was . . . *this*. . . .

(HE TURNS AWAY IN HIS CHAIR AND FACES HIS DESK. WE CUT TO A CU OF THE BACK OF HIS HEAD AND STAY ON IT FOR AWHILE. SLOWLY RICHARD RISES AND EXITS.)

Understanding has finally come to Richard Parker, and the play is resolved as he makes a somewhat shamefaced admission to his wife.

(WE FOLLOW HIM DOWN THE STEPS INTO THE LIVING ROOM. HE WALKS TO HIS DESK WHERE MILDRED IS STANDING. HE CAN'T LOOK AT HER.)

MILDRED: What did he say?

(RICHARD TAKES THE KEY AND LOCKS UP HIS DESK TIGHTLY.)

RICHARD: I'm the one, Mildred. I'm the one who should see the psychiatrist. There's nothing wrong with the boy. He's doing the right thing. (PAUSE) How else will he learn?

MILDRED: What?

(WE PULL BACK AS HE EMBRACES HER.)

NARRATOR (VOICE OVER): How else will he learn? . . . An old joke . . . the story of a family . . . and how a desk became a lethal weapon in the hands of an educated man. . . .

GO TO BLACK

"Family Theater" has been presented over the Mutual Network for many years. Hundreds of stars of stage, screen and radio have given unselfishly of their time and talent to appear on this weekly, half hour radio series, produced by Frs. Patrick Peyton and Philip A. Higgins. One of the finest plays of this series is Timothy Mulvey's "God and a Red Scooter."

MUSIC: THEME

ANNCR: Family Theater presents Mitzi Gaynor and Lyle Bettger.

MUSIC: THEME

ANNCR: From Hollywood, the Mutual Network, in cooperation with Family Theater, presents "GOD AND A RED SCOOTER" starring Lyle Bettger. And now, here is your Hostess — Mitzi Gaynor.

MUSIC: THEME

HOSTESS: Thank you, Tony La Frano —
Family Theater's only purpose is to bring to everyone's attention a practice that must become an important part of our lives if we are to win peace for ourselves, peace for our families, and peace for the world. Family Theater urges you to pray — pray together as a family.

MUSIC: THEME

ANNCR: And now to our transcribed drama, "GOD AND A RED SCOOTER" starring Lyle Bettger as "ED."

MUSIC: SOMETHING WITH MOONLIGHT AND VINEYARDS AND FAR HILLS . . . DOWN BEHIND

NARR (SLOWLY): Sleep is beautiful. . . . Sleep is a soft hand smoothing the frowns and frets on the tired faces of men. Sleep is a mother hand, rocking the cradle of the world . . . rocking it softly . . . rocking men and women and all the little children to sweet silence and peace. That's what sleep is. And do you want to know something? (PAUSE) *I pity the man who does not know how to sleep.*

MUSIC: SOFT PUNCTUATION . . . DOWN BEHIND

NARR: Consider little Eddie. I love children like Eddie. Eddie knows how to sleep. Before he went to bed tonight, he was having a talk, all by himself, down there in the garden. This is the way he spoke this afternoon as he sat dropping pebbles into a milk bottle.

MUSIC: OUT

EDDIE (FIVE YEARS OLD): And ya know what I said, God? Know what I said to Daddy? (PEBBLE PLINK) I said . . . "God *did* hear me!" That's what I said. (PEBBLE PLINK) And God, 'member when I said . . . "Please give me a red scooter like Stevie and Tony's got." (PEBBLE PLINK) 'Member when I said that? About the scooter. Didn't ya hear me, God? Huh? Didn't ya? (BEAT) Look, God . . . I got lotsa pebbles . . . a whole million. (PEBBLES PLINKING)

MUSIC: IN BEHIND

NARR: See what I mean? See why I love little children like Eddie? He wanted a red scooter . . . He went to sleep dreaming of a red scooter. And did he get the scooter? (LAUGHING SOFTLY) Well . . . I shall have to tell you the whole story. In a manner of speaking, the story begins with grapes.

MUSIC: OUT

ED (LATE TWENTIES): From this hill, you get a pretty good idea how it looks, Jeanie.

JEAN (TWENTY): The vines are beautiful, Ed. Nice dark-green.

ED: Here, let me hold Eddie for ya.

JEAN: Be careful of his back, Ed. He's so wiggly.

ED: I got 'im.

JEAN: Is that our land all the way to the road?

ED: Straight clean to Route 99. That's twenty-six acres of good grape-wood, Jeanie. Don't it make you feel kinda glad just to look at it?

JEAN (SMILING PROUDLY): Uh-huh. It almost makes you want to laugh and . . . and cry, Ed. Standin' here like this and lookin' down on our own land. . . . (HAPPY BREATH) It's nice to own something.

ED: Yeah. Cost me plenty of jack, too. But it's worth it.

JEAN: When'll the grapes be growin', Ed?

ED: Oh, three years. It takes at least three years.

JEAN: Seems so long to wait. I mean . . . you'd think they'd just pop out.

ED: Not grapes, Jeanie. You gotta build up grapes. You gotta work a vineyard. Then after three years . . . you know what it's gonna be like down there?

JEAN: What?

ED: They're gonna be out there on the wire trellises . . . those grapes. They're gonna be hangin' thick and heavy near the redwood stakes. And when the harvest comes, we're gonna be packin' in . . . well . . . over two hundred tons of the best Red Emperors in California.

JEAN (BREATHING HAPPILY): . . . it's almost like a miracle, Ed. . . .

ED: Yah.

JEAN: Eddie'll be three years old when we start pickin' our grapes.

ED: Yeah.

JEAN: He'll be walkin'.

ED: Yep. It takes time for kids and grapes to grow.

MUSIC: IN AND DOWN BEHIND

NARR: These plans . . . these husband wife plans, spoken in sunny places, are delightful. Invariably, delightful. But I must repeat. . . . I pity the man who does not know how to sleep.

MUSIC: OUT

NARR (OVER THE SHOULDER . . . EASILY): Just listen to him.

ED (WORRIED . . . THINKING): Maybe I made a mistake . . . it's a risky business . . . it's a gamble puttin' all your money into grapes.

NARR: The man is worrying, mind you, at one o'clock in the morning.

ED: Could be a shrinkage . . . could be a bad market, and then . . . well, I just can't afford to bump a tough market.

NARR: Look at him fidgeting with pencils and papers and doubts.

ED: Emperors should sell. Munson said Emperors was a good grape. But I don't know . . . maybe I should've stacked up with Muscats, or Rebiers. Norton did all right last year with Rebiers.

NARR: All this at *one* o'clock in the morning, when he should be asleep with his wife and babies.

MUSIC: UP AND DOWN BEHIND

NARR: You'd think the gentleman might allow himself the gentle privilege of getting tired. At least by *one* o'clock in the morning, you'd think he might yawn and go to bed. Why doesn't he stop fretting? Why doesn't he relax? Poor fellow. I pity the man who does not know how to sleep.

MUSIC: OUT

JEAN: You're not getting enough rest, Ed.

ED (TOUCHY): Now don't start fussin' again, Jean.

JEAN: You know what the Doctor said. All this worryin' will only make you. . . .

ED: Worryin' happens to be a part of a grape deal. Besides, a fella's got a right to get excited over his first harvest. We're pickin' in three weeks.

JEAN: But you're losin' weight. And, Eddie, grapes aren't everything. Not if you're gonna keep losin' your health and everything.

ED: That's what's worryin' ya?

JEAN: Yes.

ED (THE EXPLAINER): Look, Jeanie. I'm tryin' to figure this out. Maybe fifteen, twenty years from now we'll want to take it easy. We'll want a better house than this. And the kids . . . well, they got to get an education. College! Every kid we have goes to college. And then maybe — someday — you and me, we'll take a trip, Jeanie. All the way to Holland maybe. You always said you'd like to see kids in wooden shoes.

JEAN: It's so nice to hear you talk like that, Ed.

ED: All right. That's the picture. Now, do you know what's paintin' that picture?

JEAN: What?

ED: Grapes. . . . See those grapes out there tonight? I put four years into them. Every cent we own is in those grapes, and right now, this minute, I figure we got over two hundred and thirty tons on those vines. They're ready for the lug boxes in three weeks. Now, if anything goes wrong with those grapes, Jeanie . . . well . . . it's gonna put an awful big dent in things.

JEAN: Nothing's gonna be wrong with the grapes, Ed.

ED: A lot of things can go wrong with 'em.

JEAN: The trouble with you, Ed, is that you haven't got enough faith in God.

ED: Now, don't go into *that* again.

JEAN: Maybe if you got down on your knees once in awhile . . . instead of . . .

ED (VEXED): Listen, Jeanie, will you do the prayin' and let *me* look after the grapes. Will ya?

MUSIC: UP AND DOWN BEHIND

NARR: Well, that's the way it is with some people. Their heads are forever spinning plans and projects. You'd think Edward might

have a little more confidence in me. You'd think he'd stop
worrying for the space of a quiet sleep . . . and let me look
after the grapes. For I *do* have a way with grapes . . . with
vines and branches. . . . Understand me! I'm not against plans
and projects. I find no fault with the sweat on a man's brow
. . . for labor is a magnificent and courageous thing. I'm talking, rather, about something that is more courageous than
labor. I'm talking about relaxation. About confidence. About
trust and faith in *me*. I like the man who sleeps. I love the
man who relaxes, and who, like a child, rests easily in the arms
of my Providence. Not so with Edward. Edward is too full
of plans. As if the plans of men . . . were *merely* the plans of
men. . . . Listen to him!

Music: OUT

ED (BELLIGERENT): Sure I'm ready to start, Campbell. My grapes
can't wait. Where are those pickers ya promised me?

CAMP (BURLY GENT): We're comin' up the valley fast as can, Ed.
Don't blow your top, man.

ED: You got enough pickers for me?

CAMP: All you need. Only give me time.

ED: How soon do you figure to make it?

CAMP: We'll be cuttin' your vines by the seventeenth. I'll guarantee that.

ED: Okay. Only make it fast.

CAMP: Fast as I can.

Music: UP AND DOWN

NARR: Now . . . I like vineyards . . . vineyards and the fruit of the
vine . . . thick clustered grapes, all bursting black and purple
in the harvest time. . . . These are among some of the lovelier
aspects of my creation. I bear no grudges against vineyards . . .
having regard for the littlest grape. But once in a while . . . by
design . . . clouds will gather for reasons sufficient to the
ultimate purpose of things.

Music: THUNDER DRUM . . . ONE BOOM . . . FEATHER IN WITH
GATHERING STORM BEHIND

NARR: I gather a breeze at Burbank . . . and scoop a cool breath off
the High Sierras. Northeasterly, my gales go playing with
canyon dust and the sea sands at San Diego. And quite suddenly . . . quite perceptibly, there is mist in the midlands, and
in the valley of San Gabriel, and out around the mountains,

and down from the mountains . . . down around the flatlands of San Fernando. Nor is it any surprise that there is mist also in the eyes of a woman in Fresno.

MUSIC: OUT

JEAN (ANXIOUS): It won't rain, Ed. Don't keep staring like that out the window.

ED (HE'S BEEN HIT . . . TENSE): You heard what it said on the radio.

JEAN: But that's just mist, Ed. You know how it is with mists. They come and go. It'll be dry tomorrow. The grapes'll be dry, wait and see.

ED: Listen!

SOUND: MIX RAIN AND WIND . . . BUILD BEHIND

JEAN: It's only a little flurry of rain, Ed.

ED: Listen.

JEAN (BEGINNING TO BREAK): God won't spoil everything by letting it rain now, Ed. I know He won't. (CRYING IN) Oh, God, don't let it rain.

SOUND: UP WITH RAIN . . . HOLD BEHIND MUSIC

MUSIC: SWEEP UP WITH DELUGE . . . FADE OUT FAST

SOUND: HOLD WELL UP BEHIND WITH RAIN AND WIND

ED (COLD AND BITTER): Yeah. . . . God won't let it rain!

JEAN: Oh, Eddie . . . don't let it hurt you.

ED: Three days . . . three days to harvest. . . . And look at it tonight. (LAUGHING BITTERLY) You work for years . . . prune . . . cultivate. You put every red cent ya own into grapes and whatta ya get? Washout! A man ain't supposed to cry. (BREAKING SLIGHTLY) Yeah. A man ain't supposed to cry.

MUSIC: IN SOFTLY . . . SAD BEHIND

NARR: Believe me, I hold no grudges against vineyards. I like vineyards. But more than all the vineyards in the world, I like man. I love man. I know man well . . . yet never do I cease to wonder at him. He is capable of so much . . . of kindness, of charity, and of sacrifice . . . and yet, so often, he is incapable of hope. All things you can ask of him at times — save this — a little faith . . . a little confidence. It was so with you, Edward. . . . It was so with you those nights.

MUSIC: OUT

EDDIE: But Tony and Steve's got scooters, Mom.

JEAN: Yes, I know, Eddie. But you don't want a scooter.

EDDIE: I want a red one.

JEAN: Maybe on your next birthday you'll get one.

EDDIE (LIP TREMBLING): But Tony and Stevie's got scooters, and. . . .

JEAN: Now, no baby stuff. You're a big man now. You just pray to God and next year he'll send you a scooter.

EDDIE (A QUICKIE): God send me a scooter tomorrow like Stevie's got. A red one. I don't want to wait till next year, God. Hurry up and send me a scooter. (BACK TO NORMAL) Did He hear me, Mom?

SOUND: OPEN DOOR OFF

JEAN: Hello, Ed.

EDDIE: Daddy, did God hear me?

ED (OFF): What're you talkin' about, Eddie?

SOUND: DOOR CLOSES

EDDIE: I ast God to send me a scooter. Did He hear me on account of it's my birthday tomorrow?

ED (WEARY . . . COLD . . . FADE IN): I wouldn't know, Eddie. I wouldn't know too much about *that.*

EDDIE: It's a red one.

JEAN: Tired, Ed?

EDDIE (FADING): Maybe God left it in the yard already.

ED (QUIET GROUCH): Have ya been givin' him ideas about birthday presents?

JEAN: He's been askin' for that scooter for over a year, Ed. You know that.

ED: Well, tell him to stop askin'.

JEAN (PAUSE) (QUIET): Ed, you've . . . you've changed so much lately.

ED: Sure. I know enough now not to go around askin' God for scooters. Maybe I should ask Him for a rebate on twenty-six acres of slip-skins.

JEAN (UNEASY): Oh . . . er . . . supper's ready.

ED: I saw Campbell today. We're ready to pick in a week. (SOUR) My *second* harvest.

JEAN: It'll be a good one, Ed.

ED: Maybe. But I'm not countin' grapes 'till I get 'em offa the vine. I'm only bankin' on Red Emperors, Jeanie . . . not red scooters.

MUSIC: BRIDGE

CAMP: What're you so jittery about, Ed. Heck, man, you're gonna do all right. You gotta nice crop out there.

ED: I had a nice crop, last year, too, Campbell.

CAMP: Forget last year. From the looks of them vines, Ed, I'm guaranteein' you'll be cuttin' three hundred lugs a day.

ED: Okay. Be seein' you tomorrow, Campbell.

CAMP: Right. And . . . Ed.

ED: Yeah?

CAMP (CONFIDENTIAL): This is between you and me, but have you been noticin' your wife lately?

ED: Jeanie?

CAMP: Yeah. That kid looks plenty tired out. She's worryin' about a lotta things.

ED (LAUGHING IT OFF EASILY): Nothin' wrong with Jeanie. You know how women are, Campbell. But she'll straighten out.

CAMP: I dunno, Ed. But if I was you, I'd . . .

ED: Listen, Campbell. I understand Jeanie. All I need is one good harvest, and then . . . maybe, we'll do a little celebratin'. That'll fix her up.

CAMP: Yeah. . . . I suppose. . . . Well . . . here's to a good harvest.

MUSIC: UP . . . CROSS FADE OUT BEHIND

SOUND: THUMPING OF FULL GRAPE BOXES BEING LOADED ON TRUCK BEHIND

ED (EXULTANT OVERLORD): Looka those grapes pilin' up, Campbell! Those are big lugs!

CAMP: Swell crop!

ED (VERY SLOW FADE): I'm goin' back home and pick up Jeanie and the kids. Gonna set them up there on that hill and let 'em look at a real harvest. That's worth lookin' at . . . ain't it Campbell?

MUSIC: BRIDGE

SOUND: OPEN DOOR QUICKLY . . . CLOSE DOOR . . . WALK RAPIDLY THRU ROOMS OF HOUSE

ED (CALLING HAPPILY): Jeanie! Oh, Jeanie. . . . Got a surprise for you and the kids. . . . (TO HIMSELF) Mmmmm . . . wonder if she's lyin' down again?

SOUND: STEPS TO STOP . . . OPEN BEDROOM DOOR

ED (SHORT LAUGH): Knew I'd find you in here, lazy bones. Jeanie, I wanta take you and . . . (STOP SUDDENLY) . . . What's the matter, Jeanie?

JEAN (SORT OF WEARY): Tired, Ed.

ED (SLIGHT WORRY): You don't look good. You don't look good at all. Maybe I better get Doc Hanley for ya.

JEAN: Wait a minute, Ed. (PAUSE) It's funny. (PAUSE) Somehow I've always had a feelin' I'd be lyin' here like this . . . talkin' here like this . . . tellin' you sooner or later that. . . .

ED: Whatta ya talkin' about?

JEAN (MATTER OF FACT): Ed, I'll be leavin' you for awhile.

ED: Now look here. You're just run down. Doc Hanley'll fix you up in a jiffy.

JEAN: Come here, Ed. (PAUSE) Sit on the bed. (PAUSE) Now look at me. (LAUGHING VERY SOFTLY) Do I look scared?

ED: No. You don't look scared but you look. . . .

JEAN: All right. Now, listen to me. The sheets are in the closet downstairs. And the kids' laundry . . . you'd better send it out every week. . . . Mrs. Abel. . . .

ED (HE IS GETTING SCARED): Whatta ya talkin' about, Jeanie?

JEAN (SLIGHT PAIN): Ed, maybe you better start prayin' for me. . . . (BREAKING EASILY) Don't leave me alone, Eddie. Don't ever leave me alone. Just keep prayin' for me . . . and . . . (TRYING TO GET BACK TO A SMILE) and maybe we'll still take that trip someday you and me, Ed . . . we'll go first class, huh . . . all the way to Holland to see the tulips and the kids with the wooden shoes.

MUSIC: IN SOFTLY. . . . BUILD . . . OUT . . .

ED: What about it, Doc?

DOC (OLD): Far as I know . . . and remember . . . I'm only *one* doctor . . . there's nothing much that can be done for Jeanie, Ed.

ED (GRIM): All right. I'll get her . . . I'll get the best specialists in this country if I have to.

DOC: Go right ahead. By the way, you can go in and see her now. She's conscious again.

SOUND: OPEN DOOR . . . FOOTSTEPS SLOW . . . STOP . . .

ED (SOFT): Hello, Jeanie, kid.

JEAN: Hello, Ed. . . .

ED (LYING): You're lookin' pretty good, Jeanie. Your face is . . . you're still beautiful, honey.

JEAN: How're the kids?

THE RELIGIOUS DRAMA   **385**

ED: Good. Listen, Jeanie. . . . I was just talkin' to Doc Hanley and. . . .

JEAN (UTTERLY WEARY): I know, Ed. It's all right.

ED: I'm goin' to get you the best specialists in the country.

JEAN: Ed. . . .

ED: Yeah?

JEAN: I asked you to do something for me once. Remember?

ED (IRONICALLY RESIGNED): Okay, Jeanie. You asked me to pray. Look. I'll get down on my knees right now. Do you really want me to start prayin'?

JEAN: Not that way, Ed.

ED: All right. Now, look. If I have to kidnap a half dozen of the best doctors, I'll do it. You're gonna get better, Jeanie. Hear me, Honey? You're gonna get better. You'll be outta here before you know it.

MUSIC: BRIDGE

SOUND: OPEN DOOR

ED: Excuse me for bargin' in like this, Doc. What did you find?

DOC: They're doing everything possible, Eddie. You'll have to be patient.

ED (SLIGHTLY BEATEN HERE): Yeah. That's what everybody says. Be patient.

DOC: Why don't you go home and rest? Get a little sleep?

ED: Sleep? Not now. . . . I can't sleep now.

MUSIC: IN SOFTLY . . . DEEP . . . ANGUISH . . . BEHIND. . . .

ED (LONG PAUSE): Are ya listenin' God. . . . I don't know the words you're supposed to use . . . but . . . but it's from the bottom of my heart. . . . I'm prayin' for Jeanie, my wife. I . . . I can't lose her, God. Not now. . . . We got kids, God . . . three kids . . . and we're tryin' to make a go of it with grapes. You gotta hear me, God. You gotta make Jeanie well. . . . Please, God . . . I'm askin' ya from the bottom of my heart.

MUSIC: BRIDGE . . . COMING UP . . . HOLD. . . . OUT. . . .

ED: What's her chances now?

DOC (PAUSE): Sorry. I think you'd better be prepared for the worst.

ED: You mean there's no chance.

DOC: She's getting weaker. I'm sorry. . . .

ED (WASHED OUT): I see. I understand. Okay, Doctor.

MUSIC: BRIDGE

BOARD: DEAD AIR . . . THREE SECONDS

EDDIE: What's the matter, Daddy?

ED: Nothin'.

EDDIE: Mom's sick, huh?

ED: Yes.

EDDIE: Whyn't ya ask God to send Mom home, huh? Want *me* to ask God for ya, Daddy?

ED: Maybe God's got cotton in His ears, Eddie.

EDDIE: Cotton?

ED: Yeah. You can't hear so good with cotton in your ears.

EDDIE: He can hear *me*.

ED: That so?

EDDIE: Yep.

ED: Once He *didn't* hear you, Eddie.

EDDIE: When?

ED: Remember when you asked him for that scooter?

EDDIE: Yeah. A *red* scooter.

ED: Well, God didn't hear your prayers then, Eddie.

EDDIE: Yes, he did. God *did* hear my prayers.

ED: Come over here . . . up on my knee . . . now what did you say?

EDDIE: I said God *did* hear my prayers.

ED: That so? What did He say to you?

EDDIE: God said. . . . He said, "No." Sometimes God says no, huh, Daddy. (PAUSE) What's matter, Daddy? What's matter, huh?

SOUND: PHONE. . . . LIFT RECEIVER . . .

ED: Hello.

DOC (FILTER): Is this the residence of. . . .

ED (EXCITED): Yes, yes, Doctor. What's the news?

DOC: Well, we wanted to let you know that. . . . (CUT)

SOUND: CLICKING RECEIVER

ED: Doctor . . . Doctor . . . operator . . . I've been cut off. . . . Operator . . . get me Mercy Hospital . . . (STOP) The line's dead!

SOUND: FOOTSTEPS QUICKLY ACROSS FLOOR

ED: Stay in the garden with the kids, Ed. I got to go to Mom.

MUSIC: PUNCTUATION CUT

SOUND: FADE IN AUTOMOBILE RUNNING HIGH SPEED . . . HOLD BEHIND

JEAN (FILTER): I asked you to do something for me once. Remember?

ED (BITING LIP): God Almighty . . . I dunno . . . I dunno how to pray to ya. I tried, Jean . . . so help me I tried. (SEEING IT) Ya can't die, Jeanie. Not alone . . . not up there in that room . . . alone. Ya can't die on me, Jeanie.

EDDIE (FILTER): Sometimes, God says no, huh, Daddy?

ED (HE'S STARTING TO BEND): All right. All right, God. Ya got me where you want me. Listen to me. Please, you gotta listen now. Sure, I wanted Jeanie. When ya love somebody, ya don't want to see them die. Ya want to have them. . . . God . . . ya want to have them close enough to put your arms around. Okay . . . maybe I did want her. . . . Maybe I *did* want ya to say yes . . . just like I wanted ya to say yes to that first harvest.

EDDIE (FILTER): Sometimes, God says no, huh, Daddy?

ED: All right. Sometimes ya say no, too. If . . . if that's the way it's gonna be . . . well . . . all right. You're the boss. . . . I'm admittin' it. You're the boss. . . . Only listen to me now. I don't want Jeanie to die all alone . . . without me. Hear me, God? (BREAKING) I can take it. I can take anything . . . (CHILD NOW) only don't let it be all alone for Jeanie. I'm askin' ya, God. Honest to God, I'm askin' ya. . . .

MUSIC: SNEAK IN ON TAIL END OF ABOVE SPEECH . . . WASH CAR . . . UP OUT

SOUND: OPEN DOOR QUICKLY . . . QUICK FOOTSTEPS . . . SLOW DOWN . . . STOP

ED (BREATHING IN UNBELIEF): Jeanie!

JEAN (SUNSHINE ON THE PILLOW): Hello, Eddie.

ED: What . . . ! You're not . . . !

JEAN: What's the trouble, Ed?

ED (SMILING THRU TEARS): You're smilin' at me, Jeanie! You're lookin' at me . . . talkin' to me.

JEAN (LAUGHING WEAKLY): I'm really feeling much better today. Come and put your arms around me . . . and stop lookin' like a baby.

ED (IN HER ARMS): Maybe . . . maybe God is sayin' yes, Jeanie. Maybe he's sayin' yes!

MUSIC: GOD'S QUIET MUSIC OVER A TIRED WORLD . . . SOFTLY BEHIND

NARR (LAUGHING VERY SOFTLY): The night tonight is beautiful over California.

For the first time in a long time, a tired man sleeps.

Resting at last in the Shadow of My hand, he sleeps.
I might have said "No." I have said "No."
To some of My loveliest children, My best beloved.
But know this always, Edward.
There are times when My refusals are necessary.
To a plan you cannot understand.
The little Eddie, being Wiser in his innocence,
seems to understand.
That storm upon your vineyard,
that storm that drew your curse,
was blessing to a thousand other Edwards,
in pasture lands parched by the drought
six hundred miles to the North.
So tragedy, the tragedy of today, is but the pruning
and the preparation
of a lovelier tomorrow.
Yes, there are times I have said "No"
as many fathers have said no to their dearest,
their best beloved children. But tonight,
tonight, Edward, I have said "Yes."

MUSIC: SOFT PUNCTUATION . . . THEN DOWN BEHIND

NARR: O night . . . rest lightly on the tired eyes of the man. . . .
And concerning Eddie . . . five years old. . . . (Listen to him
mixing his prayers tonight)

EDDIE (SLEEPING ON MIKE): Our Father who are in heaven . . .
the Lord's with thee . . . and blessed is the fruit . . . and . . .
and give us this day our daily bread . . . and ever . . . and ever.
Amen. . . . And send me a scooter like Stevie's got. (YAWN)

NARR: I tell you. . . .
I have seen all the beauties of My creation. . . .
but there is nothing so beautiful. . . .
as the small face of a child . . . the small lips of a
child
fumbling with prayer . . . getting it mixed up . . . getting
it tangled,
and sweetly muddled with sleep.
Listen to him. . . .

EDDIE: A red scooter, huh, God?

NARR: And all the while, the soft fingers of sleep are smoothing
his eyelids . . . closing them easily. . . .

EDDIE: A red . . . (YAWN . . . VERY SLEEPILY NOW) . . . red scooter, huh, God?

MUSIC: OUT

NARR (QUIETLY ON MIKE): All right, Eddie. It'll be a *red* scooter. I have willed it, Eddie. A red scooter. Now sleep, Eddie . . . Sleep.

MUSIC: TO RESOLUTION

HOSTESS: This is Mitzi Gaynor again — In everyone's life there is an interesting story. A story that tells not only what has happened to us but a story of our doubts, hopes, and desires — our personal life story. And in each one's life there is a reaching out, a seeking for happiness. All of us long for the joy that comes from friendship and kindness and love. We all seek for peace and understanding. Would it not indeed be a better and more wonderful world if in every family there could be found true love and understanding and joy. There are many influences that in one way or another can turn or shape our way of life, but the most important influence in our life is love of God. It is the basis of our love of neighbor, the inspiration for our tolerance, for our faith in our fellowmen. It gives us the sublime power to rise above petty difficulties and differences. It brings to our homes and children a true appreciation of the purpose and meaning of life. And the simple expression of our Love of God, through family prayer brings the most wonderful blessings on our homes, because the family that prays together, stays together.

ECHO: MORE THINGS ARE WROUGHT BY PRAYER THAN THIS WORLD DREAMS OF

ANNCR: From Hollywood, Family Theater has brought you transcribed, "GOD AND A RED SCOOTER" starring Lyle Bettger; Mitzi Gaynor was your Hostess. Others in our cast were: Lawrence Dobkin, Alice Backes, Richard Beals, Bill Forrester and Bill Lally. The script was written for Family Theater by Timothy Mulvey and directed by John T. Kelley, with music composed and conducted by Harry Zimmerman.

This series of Family Theater broadcasts is made possible by the thousands of you who feel the need for this type of program, by the Mutual Network, which has responded to this need, and by the hundreds of stars of stage, screen and radio who give so unselfishly of their time and talent to appear on our Family Theater stage — to them and to you, our humble thanks.

This is Tony La Frano expressing the wish of Family Theater that the blessing of God may be upon you and your home and inviting you to join us next week when Family Theater will present:

Join us, won't you.

MUSIC: THEME

ANNCR: Family Theater is broadcast throughout the world and originates in the Hollywood studios of the world's largest network — THIS IS MUTUAL — THE RADIO NETWORK FOR ALL AMERICA.

Analysis

"God and a Red Scooter" is a believable story about believable people. Ed, his wife, Jeanie, and his boy, Eddie, are warm, sympathetic people. Ed is beset by problems we can understand. He has the strength and the shortcomings of any father. And, as any good father, he wants to provide the very best for his family. . . .

"... we'll want a better house than this. . . . Every kid we have goes to college. And then maybe — someday . . . you and me, we'll take a trip, Jeanie. All the way to Holland maybe."

But there are conflicts, with the elements: the first harvest wiped out by rain. And a subtler conflict, between Ed and his wife. Jean wants her husband to have more faith, to believe in prayer, but he is scornful of prayer and the ruination of the first harvest makes him bitter. Ed finds that a successful harvest is not an end in itself. And, finally, the seriousness of his wife's illness and the danger of losing her makes him turn to a Higher Power and raise his voice in prayer.

The poignancy and the power of this play lie in Eddie, the child, and the symbolism of the Red Scooter. For Eddie believes in prayer and with the intuitive wisdom of a child, he knows that sometimes God says "no." Here then note the moral teaching: we cannot doubt the efficaciousness of prayer, but we must understand that the way of the Lord is often inscrutable.

The device of the Narrator is used skillfully and the narration is written with a great deal of sensitivity.

"PILGRIMAGE: AMONG OUR OWN!"

The ABC radio network schedules a quarter hour series of transcribed religious dramas called "Pilgrimage: Among Our Own!". Typical of this series is "Skypilot of the Lumberjacks," written by Vera Eikel. This script utilizes, to good advantage, the dramatic devices for capturing and holding interest. The program opens "cold" with an effective "teaser."

FERRELL (VIGOROUS MAN IN HIS SIXTIES AND EX-PRIZEFIGHTER WHO CAN TALK UP TO THE TOUGHEST CUSTOMER): They told me I was a fool with a fool's faith. Maybe I was, but I stuck by it and even got some pretty tough lumberjacks to believe in these words — "Come unto me, all ye that are weary and heavy laden, and I will give you rest."
MUSIC: THEME UP AND UNDER:

This "cold" opening is followed by the program theme music and the standard announcer's introduction. The drama employs the device of telling the story in both first and third person, in other words, the protagonist of the play, Dick Ferrell, is also the narrator.

HIGGINS (OLD MAN, EDUCATED AND WITH AUTHORITY): Go into the lumber camps, where there are no preachers and no churches, and do what you can to spread the Gospel and *help* the men.
MUSIC: OUT
FERRELL: That's what I heard when I was a young feller — before I came out here to the Northwest. But that isn't the beginning of my story. I was born in "bloody" Hardin County back in Illinois — a coal mining place so tough that men fought with everything from fists and pistols to coal scuttles and spittoons. Sometimes they fought to kill. Before I was ten, I was working for my father. He was a blacksmith. I left school after the eighth grade and went to work in the mines. Nights I spent in saloons and pool halls boxing with the boys. It was all in fun until I knocked out our local champion. After that I made

fighting my business. People said I was headed for the welter-weight championship. All I know is that I won my fights, made a lot of money — and went broke! Trouble was — I spent lots moren'n I made — until I owed everybody I knew.

The use of the narrative device, in the above sequence, is a simple and effective method of exposition. We learn immediately who Dick Ferrell is, where he came from and we can visualize the physical strength of the fighter. This is essential for our understanding and acceptance of Ferrell's ability to handle the assignments he is given.

Also, by means of the same narrative device, we discover how Ferrell came to join the church.

FERRELL: One cold, sleety Sunday in Chicago, I was broke and mighty tired — something deep inside me was tired — and I happened to wander into a church to sit and rest — and think. I hadn't come to listen, but a man by the name of Stone — John Stone — was preaching. He had been a big football star. But nobody could sit in church and not listen to John Stone. He made you feel that every word he said he said straight at you! (SOLEMNLY) He cut me to pieces! — he never let up — just kept throwing jabs and hooks at me the whole time. After he got through talking, I went up to him —

MUSIC: OUT

FERRELL (YOUNGER SOUNDING NOW IF POSSIBLE): You don't know me, Dr. Stone — name's Dick Ferrell. I'm a prize-fighter — or I was until this morning.

STONE (BRISK — YOUNGISH): Glad to meet you, Mr. Ferrell —

We have here a typical transition from first to third person, from narrator to character.

The drama moves on. Dick Ferrell tells us how he was sent to the Moody Bible Institute for three years and then tackled a skid row mission. Soon, he was called in for his most important assignment. John Stone brings a mission official, Frank Higgins, to meet Ferrell.

HIGGINS: Ferrell, I'm looking for a tough man to go into the logging camps. John's told me about you.

STONE: What I said, Dick, was that you were an ex-mule-shoer and pug, you like the open-air life and — you've got a horror of growing fat and becoming a bishop!

HIGGINS: It's only fair to tell you — every man I've sent out into the woods has come back a-running. Will you take the job?

FERRELL: Suppose John and I do a little praying over this before I give you an answer, Mr. Higgins.

In this brief scene, we see foreshadowed the impending conflict: Ferrell against the tough loggers. This is an assignment no missionary has been able to accomplish successfully. You will note also that as the play moves along to critical action, the moral atmosphere is maintained. Ferrell states that he wants to do a little praying before he gives his answer.

Ferrell, of course, does go to the lumber camp and finds that the Boss wants men, not preachers. The missionary proves he's a workman by taking on the blacksmith's job. And when Ferrell preaches his first sermon, he speaks to the men in a language they can understand.

FERRELL (SOME PROJECTION AS HE PREACHES): After those fellers — those gamblers and saloonkeepers — cleaned out this young boy, what'd they do? (OMINOUSLY) I'll tell you what they did. They told him to go lie down in the sty with the rest of the hogs and eat husks! . . . (WARM) But there's a happy ending to that story! The Prodigal Son went home to his old Pappy, and straightened out. And he was a good, steady, sober feller after that. But let me warn you! — (LOWERS VOICE WITH FOREBODING) so long as the hog's still in a man he'll go to the swill! . . . Let us pray. . . .

MUSIC: TAG AND OUT

Since Ferrell could work as well as they could and talk to them in their own language, the lumbermen came to trust him and came to him with their troubles. The missionary listened and advised them. Sometimes, he had to use his fists to help them.

FERRELL (AS NARRATOR): One way I tried to help the boys was to look after 'em when they came to town on the spring drive down the river, their pockets full of money. Every gin mill tried to get 'em drunk and then roll 'em of their poke. When whiskey wouldn't do it, the barkeep would slip 'em a mickey to knock 'em out. . . . Sometimes I had to back up the Lord's work with my fists —

MUSIC: OLD TIME PIANOLA IN AND HOLD IN BG

FERRELL: Barkeeps didn't like for me to be pokin' my nose in their places, but that didn't stop me. Larsen was one of my boys, so I went looking for 'im —

MUSIC: UP A LITTLE ON PIANOLA

FERRELL: You got Larsen in here?

BARKEEP (TOUGH): Keep away from that door! This is a saloon! — not church! No preacher's goin' into my back room!

FERRELL (EVENLY BUT NOT GIVING AN INCH): Larsen's in there . . . He wants me to get his poke for him.

BARKEEP: Keep outa there, or I'll crack your skull wide open with this bung starter!

FERRELL: I'm goin' in —

SOUND: HEAVY CRASH OF BUNG STARTER THROWN AGAINST WALL: COUPLE OF SHARP FIST CRACKS AND GROAN: HEAVY FALL OF BODY

Ferrell retrieved Larsen's pay and then saw to it that the money was sent to Larsen's wife. Still there were many lumberjacks who were not ready to accept the preacher. But Ferrell went about his daily tasks, helping anyone who needed his help and holding prayer meetings. There was one old timer, dying of cancer. Ferrell came to see him daily, despite the old man's unfriendliness.

OLD TIMER (GRUFF AND UNFRIENDLY): I never paid any attention to you in camp. Why do you bother with me?

FERRELL: Because it's my business.

OLD TIMER (SCORNING): Business?

FERRELL: The biggest business in the world. The Company I work for will never fail, and it pays the biggest dividends. So I can afford to come to see you.

OLD TIMER (TRYING TO LAUGH OFF THE TEARS THAT HAVE COME TO HIS EYES): Sounds — sounds like one of them big blast-powder outfits that I don't know much about . . . still — (TIMIDLY) I'd like to go to work for that Company, if the Big Push will still have me.

FERRELL: He'll have you.

OLD TIMER: How do you go about joining that kind of outfit?

FERRELL: You start with a prayer.

OLD TIMER: Never said one in my life — don't know how to begin.

FERRELL: I'll begin and you finish. (PRAYING) Dear Lord, this feller was a good man in every camp he ever worked — he just never worked in yours before. It's not too late now, and I promise you he'll drive himself as hard as any jack, or logger, or push in your crew. Take him on now . . . and thank you, Lord. . . .

OLD TIMER (SWALLOWING): It's like the Pilot here says — I never asked for anything from any man or from you . . . but I do now. I know I'm on my last log jam. I'd like to work for an outfit like yours . . . and when the time comes and I get to the Big Camp up yonder — I promise you . . . I'll cut all the timber you need. . . .

FERRELL: Amen.

MUSIC: UP ON TAG AND OUT

Dick Ferrell is a Paul Bunyanesque character, and like the legendary figure, the missionary helped his people and fought for them. He undertook a mission that required the utmost of courage and faith. This sort of theme lends itself to compelling dramatization.

Local productions

Many church groups present religious dramas locally. These are generally works of love with the writer, director and cast all contributing their services. These local religious dramas are usually presented on occasion rather than as a weekly series, such as the network programs we have previously discussed.

If you are a beginning writer with a desire to write video dramas, you might do well to associate yourself with an active church group in your community. When you can write a religious drama which predicates without preachment, you will have advanced yourself considerably as a creative writer. You will find *Religious Radio* by Parker, Inman, Snyder and *The Television-Radio Audience and Religion,* by Parker, Barry, Smythe, of considerable value to you.

Special types

PART

4

The documentary

The documentary might well be called the public conscience of the broadcasting industry. It has sometimes approximated editorializing. Within its scope, causes have been fought, problems analyzed, issues dramatically portrayed. Whatever its approach, its technique, the documentary deals entirely with facts. Pare Lorentz defined the documentary as the "dramatic presentation of factual material."

Generally speaking, we may classify documentaries into three categories:

1. Action;
2. Information;
3. Dramatization.

You will find some overlapping in these categories. In any creative field, rules are flexible rather than rigid, but this simplified breakdown will be helpful for purposes of study.

The *Action* documentary portrays a problem of the contemporary scene and shows what you the audience can do about it. It may be a study of how one community solved its teacher shortage problem with a pointed reference that your community can do the same. It may be a documentary on traffic accidents with an admonition to drive safely and a lesson on how to avoid fatalities. Or it may be a depiction of a hurricane ravaged area with an appeal for Red Cross funds. The Action documentary, then, not only has something to say to you but has something for you to do.

The *Information* documentary is a study in exposition, a delver into background. "Victory at Sea," produced by the National Broadcasting Company in cooperation with the Navy, used actual World War Two footage to show the role of the Navy in the war. In similar vein, but broader in scope, was CBS's "Air Power." The "Johns Hopkins Review," produced by Lynn Poole on the former Dumont Television Network, was an explanation to laymen of scientific principles. The primary purpose of such documentary programs is to inform and often by informing, to inspire.

The *Dramatized* documentary may be either informative or it may inspire a call to action. But where the foregoing types deal with actualities, recording or filming actual events, and utilizing the actual people who took part in these events, the dramatized documentary recreates a situation *based* on actuality. The Armstrong Theater which recently changed its programming from dramas to documentaries veers generally towards the dramatized type. Some of you may recall the story of the New England town faced by the loss of its main industry and a probable depression and the battle of one man to transfuse new business into the town's economic veins. This was the basis for a dramatized documentary in which actors were used to portray the townspeople and, except for a few permissible liberties, events were depicted as they occurred. To add a further note of authenticity, the actual hero of the story was presented at the conclusion of the program to both verify the events of the story and to deliver a brief message of hope to any community faced by a similar problem.

One of the finest of dramatic documentaries was the series on the Constitution of the United States, presented on "Omnibus." The unique CBS series, "You Are There," utilizes a documentary presentation of historic events.

The documentary may include every form of broadcast writing: dramatic, interview, talk, announcement, narration, etc. The documentary writer should therefore have a knowledge of all these forms. He may be called upon, within the same documentary program, to recreate a scene as drama, to prepare pertinent questions for an interview, to write narration for silent film sequences. If the documentary is one that requires an appeal for funds, he may be asked to write the announcement, unless it is specifically furnished by the agency. Even then he may be asked to rewrite or edit the announcement. There is one chore that will not be his: if the program is sponsored, he will not be asked to write the commercials!

LIVE AND FILM

Actually, the amount of writing the television documentary writer is assigned will depend on the live and film aspects of the program. Where there is a good deal of sound on film, for example, scenes where many people voice their opinion or there are several interviews, the task becomes one for the film editor rather than the writer. However, documentaries based on historic episodes, such as a depiction of events leading to the rise of communism, fascism, or Nazism, will depend largely on silent film culled from archives or the film libraries of the military services. These films will require written narrative.

There is one rule the documentary writer will be wise to observe: wherever possible, let the picture tell the story. We cannot blame the writer for feeling that his words are all-important but prejudiced as we may be in favor of writers, the fact remains that one picture can equal a thousand words or at least a hundred. Scenes of a flood devastated area speak eloquently by themselves. In such scenes, background music can replace narration.

NARRATIVE TECHNIQUE

Narration is required where the scenes are unfamiliar and must be explained to the viewer.

In this scene from a "See It Now" documentary on the new Navy, there are shots of the aircraft carrier Forrestal.

EDWARD R. MURROW

This is the aircraft carrier Forrestal, named in honor of America's first Secretary of Defense. Length, a fifth of a mile — sixty thousand tons or twice the weight of the old Lex — the Fighting Lady of World War Two — five times the length of Old Ironsides.

Breadth at main deck, one hundred and twenty-nine feet. Angled deck gives it the equivalent of two runways. Height from keel to mast top equals that of a twenty-five story building. Number of crew, thirty-five hundred. Speed — anything more than thirty knots classified. Completely air conditioned.

Its hangar deck resembles the assembly line at Willow Run. Has storage and complete maintenance facilities for the F3H jet fighter and the A3D jet bomber and the new F8U Crusader.

The size of this steel cavern so dwarfs the planes that it's easy to forget that these jet bombers weigh sixty thousand pounds or half the weight of a B29. Four elevators shuttle the planes up to the flight deck in a matter of seconds.

You can readily see that the information narrated by Mr. Murrow would not be made apparent by film alone. Therefore the narration has added to the film.

RESEARCH

Research is the essential ingredient of all documentaries. Without adequate research, the documentary will lack body and integrity. The amount of research will vary according to the scope of the subject and the size of the budget.

Research may be divided broadly into two classifications: live and library.

Live research

By our definition, live research consists in actually filming or recording of events, as they occur, or of people who are or have been involved in those events. Let us say you are assigned to write a documentary on prison conditions. Live research would then include personal visits to a prison or prisons and filming or recording scenes on the spot. This might also include an interview with the prison warden.

Perhaps one of the most outstanding examples of live research was the work done for one of the "March of Medicine" documentaries, "Monganga." Lou Hazam, the writer, spent many weeks in South Africa engaged in on the scene research and filming actual instances of medical progress in that far off land. The complete story of the filming of "Monganga" and portions of the script will be found later on in this chapter.

Library research

The term "library" is here used in its widest sense to include film libraries, tape libraries, as well as collections of books. The military departments, for example, have extensive libraries of films of World War I, World War II, and the Korean conflict. For the presentation of documentaries concerning those wars, the writer would have to spend hours viewing films and choosing appropriate scenes. Series, such as "Air Power," "Victory at Sea," "The Big Picture," made extensive use of the film footage available through the Army, Navy and Air Force.

A series such as "You Are There," which recreates historic events, requires the writer to delve into history books, manuscripts, and any other memorabilia of the period.

THEME

A documentary, like a play, must first and foremost have a theme, but unlike a play, it must have definite informational value. The drama's primary function is to entertain; the documentary's, to inform.

The choice of theme is all important. Are you planning a series of action documentaries on current problems? Then you must have an awareness of the issues which are troubling the nation.

Are you planning a series of informational documentaries on a subject such as modern medicine? Then you will need to know the newest findings of medical research.

It is wisest, if at all possible, to confine the theme of your documentary to one phase of your subject. Thus, an informational documentary on medicine will prove more enlightening if it treats of only one ailment, such as cataracts, and explores the work being done to effect cures. Covering too many subjects within the scope of a single documentary will spread your material thin and may often result in confusion rather than enlightenment.

In choosing a theme, the question must inevitably arise: how controversial can your subject matter be? How stringent are the taboos? The answer lies both in the Television Code and the temper of the times. Many of the "See It Now" programs deal with controversial issues and have received excellent response. A topic, such as the treatment of venereal disease, might ordinarily fall into the range of taboos. But a series on this subject was successfully produced for radio broadcast by Erik Barnouw. "Among Ourselves" was a CBS Documentary Unit production on race and minority relations. Under the able direction of Robert Saudek, later the guiding genius of "Omnibus," ABC presented a suspenseful documentary treatment of the Federal security program.

In tackling a controversial subject, it is essential that both sides of the issue be detailed, otherwise the network or station may find that individuals or groups opposing the documentary's viewpoint will seek equal time.

THE MAKING OF "MONGANGA"

On the night of November 27, 1956, an announcer for the National Broadcasting Company TV network spoke these words into the microphone: "Smith, Kline & French Laboratories presents a world première — the first coast to coast medical program ever produced in RCA's compatible color." And so a documentary which had been months in the making and which had been filmed entirely in the Belgian Congo reached fruition with this first American showing to millions of people. The response was magnificent; the critical reviews, laudatory. The writer-producer, Lou Hazam, one of the most perceptive writers in the documentary field, took a long deep breath and relaxed for the first time in many months.

"Monganga" is the story of an American medical missionary in Africa. And the story behind this story reveals so dramatically the unusual trials, the amazing experiences and the heart-warming rewards of a documentary writer that we believe it will be of especial interest and value to every potential writer of documentaries.

Lou Hazam had already written several outstanding documentaries under the general title of the "March of Medicine." These were sponsored jointly by the Smith, Kline & French Laboratories and the American Medical Association. The object of these documentaries, presented some four or five times during the year, is to show both the progress of medical research and the dedication of medical men. Certainly, you could find no more dedicated man than a medical missionary in the wilds of Africa. Once the decision had been made to do the story, the question immediately arose: which medical missionary do you choose?

That choice had to be guided by the following requirements:

The medical missionary must be representative of all men of his calling. He must have a warm personality and a sincere dedication. (The camera is all revealing.) He must be a lone missionary, not a member of a group. He must have a strong story, both in regard to his person and his activity. It was also important that the surroundings in which he worked have "camera interest," that is, the terrain, preferably, should be varied, not flat and monotonous. The people he ministered to should be colorful. And in addition some means of quick transportation was essential for film shipment. The African heat could prove detrimental to the film.

A very large order, indeed. But after many talks with practically every missionary society in the United States, Hazam and Bill Eiman, TV coordinator for SKF, finally came upon their man: Dr. John Ross. Who is Dr. Ross? Let writer Hazam tell you as he did so well in this passage from the script of "Monganga."

         1st Narrator:
And now,
Perhaps you'd like to know
Our doctor's name.
He says it's unimportant
And he would rather remain
                nameless —
It's his *work* that counts. . . .
And that is *one good measure*
Of this man.
But his name is Ross . . .
            Dr. John Ross,

And he has been in the Congo
For six years . . .
Six years
With only one furlough home.

(Music: americana theme, in
and under)

Behind John Ross
Lies Kansas, where he was born,
One of four children.
Then California,
Which he calls home —
Where his father sold insurance
And he went to Fresno High
                    School.
Life was not easy . . .
A hundred odd jobs,
Necessary to provide bread and
                    butter,
Stand between him then,
And where he now stands —
Factory worker, grocery clerk,
                    milkman.
Then his love of God and his
                    fellow man
Sent him to working his way
                    through college
To prepare for the ministry.
Years of preaching
In country churches . . .
The staggering loss
Of his first four children to
                    illness —
Two within ten days.
Then, concerned with how others
                    in the world
Must be faring
With no medical care at all,
On to medical school at the ripe
                    age of 36,
Ignoring all who said
"You're too old."
Overcoming this age handicap
                    there,

CU AS HE TURNS OFF RADIO,
WALKS OUT OF PICTURE.
FULL SHOT AS HE WALKS
INTO LIVING ROOM WHERE
SON IS PLAYING ON FLOOR,
AND SQUATS DOWN TO PET AND
PLAY WITH DOG . . . RISES AND
WALKS OUT . . .

CUT TO MS DR. WORKING
AT HIS DESK, WHICH IS PILED
HIGH WITH PAPERS. HE
FINISHES A LETTER, SEALS
IT, PUTS OUT THE DESK
LIGHT AND WALKS OFF . . .

And later also —
When it interfered with his
                        desire
For foreign mission service —
He finally came to the Belgian
                        Congo
In 1950 —
Assigned to the
Disciples of Christ Mission at
                    Lotumbe . . .
Lotumbe,   CUT TO WS OF DOCTOR AT
Which for ten long years   WATER PUMP ON PORCH, LIGHT
Had been without a doctor.   HANGING DOWN ABOVE AS HE
This is the man   PUMPS. HE STOPS, PICKS UP
Who pauses to take his lamp,   LIGHT AND EXITS . . .
                        now,
For one last-minute check
Before bedtime . . .
Monganga John Ross
Whose life-purpose is crystal
                    clear —

Hazam found, as many documentary writers will find, that in many instances the script has to wait until the film is shot. You may have a general idea or a very specific idea of what you'd like to get into your documentary, but when you are dealing with a vast unknown like a mission in deepest Africa, you have to depend on time and circumstance. Time is precious and circumstance, you hope, will be propitious.

One primary decision was the choice of a Belgian camera crew which, obviously, would have easier access to the Belgian Congo. Officialdom was rather touchy about who it admitted to the territory. Both Hazam and Eiman, in addition to their passports, had to provide a written statement from their home county authorities to the effect that they had no police record!

Wisely considering the sponsor's budget, orders went out that the camera crew join them a week after their arrival at their destination. Hazam would need the time to orient himself to his surroundings and map out the shots. And Eiman would need to work out the logistics of shipping film, etc. Only the director, André Cauvin — who had previously filmed the Belgian King's tour of the Belgian lands in Africa — accompanied them. They had gone by air as far as the little town of Coquilhatville. From there it was necessary to hire a truck which after an eight hour drive took them to a river point. Then it was a long boat ride, 110 miles, to Dr. Ross's mission. The river was the only road.

Hazam's first step, on arrival, was to check the physical surroundings for background shooting. Then he sat down with Dr. Ross and discussed in detail the doctor's daily routine. His next step was to accompany the doctor on his rounds. He made notes on what would prove interesting to the camera. An operation? Yes. The leprosarium? Undoubtedly. "Monganga" was to be an hour show. It would need a story line, a beginning, a middle and an end. Also, it had to be borne in mind, this documentary was to be filmed in color.

The best way to do the story, Hazam decided, was to follow a number of patients through their treatment at the hospital. But the camera crew could not stay on for months. It was essential therefore to find out what tropical disease responded most quickly to treatment. Dr. Ross said that yaws would respond to penicillin in a week and a half. Very well then, one sequence could deal with the treatment of yaws.

But the basic story was life itself, the beginning of life: birth. In the mission clearing, surrounded by ancient jungle, inhabited by primitive people, Dr. Ross had established a modern pre-natal and post-natal clinic. The clinic sessions were perfect pictorially. They were the inspiration, too, for a story line: a native woman, about to give birth, attending a pre-natal clinic; the birth itself; the healthy mother and child at a post-natal clinic. Hazam's schedule called for four weeks in the Belgian Congo. Little enough time. He asked Dr. Ross whether any births were imminent. Dr. Ross said he knew of two cases; one of them was probably due in two weeks, the other he could not pinpoint the date exactly. This was not calculated to make Hazam's task any easier. Then the long arm of coincidence . . . the fiction writer's delight . . . but fortunately for Hazam, actuality and not a device . . . brought a young married woman, her husband, her mother and her brother to the mission. She was a totally unexpected patient and she was due to give birth in a very few days. What is more, she lived up to her billing as "leading lady" for she was one of the prettiest of the natives.

By the end of the first week, Hazam had begun to work out his story line, and over the weekend he had turned out eighteen pages of script. This was as far as he could go script-wise. Once the camera crew arrived, the script would be written on a sort of film as you go basis. In many instances, events determined the changes in the script. When it rained, there was no shooting. And yet even that day had its compensations, for Hazam, standing in the shelter of the mission eaves, saw a procession of children following a native pastor down the jungle road and singing what was evidently a hymn. They were on their way to a baptism. It was a colorful, inspiring ceremony and when the sun shone again, Hazam asked the pastor to recreate the ceremony. The pastor and the children complied happily.

The visit to the leprosarium was most rewarding both from the camera and the medical angles. Pictorially, there was a wealth of material and the many cases in different stages demonstrated vividly the progress Dr. Ross was making. Striking evidence of the former lack of medical attention was shown in shots of some of the older natives who were, unfortunately, in very advanced stages of the disease.

Hazam was anxious to include some sequences of the work Dr. Ross was doing in even more remote areas of the jungle, particularly with the pygmy and the semi-pygmy tribes. He also wanted to include, if at all possible, a scene of a funeral procession. The latter, Dr. Ross informed him, was difficult. A funeral in the Congo area was the occasion of a seemingly unending wild wailing on the part of the mourners. This went on for two or three days. The natives, Dr. Ross explained, believed that an impassioned show of remorse would keep the spirit of the dead one from haunting the village. If a death occurred, perhaps it could be filmed; if not, well, this was hardly the sort of incident that could be staged.

Planning was concentrated now on a trip to the semi-pygmy village. This required some rather diplomatic arrangements. Hazam discovered that the natives had their own type of bureaucracy. There was a major chief of the tribes who had to be contacted and convinced first. The major chief then conferred with the lesser chiefs. A favorable decision was arrived at when the chiefs were convinced that the cameras were not dangerous instruments. They were also given a fifty pound bag of salt, a luxury to the natives.

When Lou Hazam, Eiman, Dr. Ross and the Belgian camera crew arrived at the pygmy village after some ten hours travelling, they found to their horror that the village was deserted except for the local chief and one or two natives. The chief nonchalantly informed the doctor that he would get in touch with his tribe which he proceeded to do via the native drum telegraph. The message came back that the tribesmen would return to their village in an hour and a half. This was cutting it very fine since there were only four hours of daylight left. Hazam told the camera crew to get their equipment in readiness and then they would just have to stand around and wait. But the cameras had hardly been set up when the sound of wailing was heard coming from the nearby jungle. Dr. Ross, Hazam and the local chief went into the jungle to search for the source and found a funeral procession, complete with all the trappings. Again, the long arm of coincidence. The local chief was pressed into service to try to get the procession to come through the village past the cameras. At first the chief frowned on the suggestion. If the procession did come through the village, it would mean that the ghost of the departed would haunt the village. That was why such processions avoided any habitations. It took a good deal of persuasion to change the chief's mind. He finally acceded on the basis that this was a very special occasion. And this was how the funeral procession became part of the documentary, "Monganga."

Soon after the procession was on its way, the pygmy tribesmen came flocking into the village and the cameramen were ready to go again. Hazam wanted a scene of the entire tribe welcoming the doctor on his regular visit. The welcome ritual was a ceremonial dance which Dr. Ross had described. There was only one problem. All the women of the tribe were naked from the waist up. The network censors would probably have a word for it: delete. Hazam explained the delicate situation to Dr. Ross. When word got to the native women, they stared at Hazam with a mixture of disbelief and disgust. He wished he could tell them that it was none of his doing, just the sensitivities of his own civilization. Obviously, since there was no Macy's handy, the women couldn't put in an immediate order for a couple of hundred Mother Hubbards. But their native ingenuity came to the fore. They dashed into the jungle and reappeared shortly, their "offending" bosoms covered by huge banana leaves. The cameramen were ready to grind away when suddenly the men of the tribe scurried into the jungle. In a few minutes they also returned, banana leaves turned into garlands around their heads, vines trailing from their waists. Evidently, they believed what the producer wanted was a little more festooning!

Every week, as film was shot, Bill Eiman carried it down river via Dr. Ross's speedboat for transshipment to London. Hazam had no way of knowing how the shots were turning out. He had to pray that the cameras were doing their job and that no harm would come to the films en route. During his month in the Belgian Congo, he received only one report. It came one morning via the radio station in Coquilhatville, a message immediately following the morning news roundup. It was addressed to the camera crew informing them that the first shipment of film had arrived safely and in good order. As a safety precaution, Hazam filmed several extra sequences. Budget-wise, there was a limit to how much footage could be taken.

All the film editing was done in London and it was there that Hazam completed the entire script except the portions for John Gunther, who was to be the guest narrator. The filming of "Monganga" is a saga in itself. The completed production cost in the neighborhood of a quarter of a million dollars. "Monganga" is a classic of its kind. It has since been given a repeat showing on the NBC network and there will probably be many more. It is television at its finest.

And now let us turn to the script itself, of which we have chosen several representative scenes.

"MONGANGA"

Here is the opening scene of "Monganga." The narration is written with poetic simplicity. It sets a mood of sympathy and understanding. The scene takes us immediately into the locale of the documentary.

> FULL SHOT OF PIROGUE ON
> RIVER; TWO MEN, ONE AT
> EACH END, STAND PADDLING
> . . . A PREGNANT WOMAN AND
> HER OLD MOTHER ARE SEATED
> IN THE CENTER OF THE
> PIROGUE . . . WE HEAR THE
> PADDLES IN THE WATER. . . .
> (10")

1ST NARRATOR:
Her name is Bolafa Malia.
She is an Nkundu,
And she is big with child
And now her husband,
Who gave 100 iron bracelets
                    for her
And a bolt of cloth and a
                    goat . . .
And her brother
Take her —
And her old mother to care for
                    her —
To the white missionary doctor
                    on the river . . .
To the —
"Monganga."

CUT TO CU OF PREGNANT
WOMAN . . .

CUT TO MS OF HUSBAND AT
PROW . . .

CUT TO WS OF BROTHER AT
STERN . . . FOLLOWED BY CU
OF BOLAFA MALIA AND
MOTHER . . .

The commentator on the program is John Gunther, a very wise choice, since his *Inside Africa* was a very widely read volume. He appears immediately after the first scene and gives us some interesting and informative background about "the great dark continent."

GUNTHER:
How do you do. I'm John Gunther.
I'm here to introduce a special
program that has been almost six
months in the making.
Behind me is the enormous shape
of Africa — the great dark continent which is the background for
our story — a continent where I've
recently travelled almost 40,000
miles.
Africa, packed with mystery, majesty and the great unknown among
continents is so vast that you can
lose the United States in it four
times over. (TURNS TO FACE MAP,
THEN BACK TO CAMERA AGAIN)
Yet many of us — even today —

UP ON JOHN GUNTHER
MCU STANDING BEFORE CUT
OUT MAP OF AFRICA.

HE CROSSES IN FRONT OF MAP
AND WALKS AS CAMERA DOL-
LIES BACK FOR MLS.

CROSSES TO DESK DECORATED

know as little about it as did the
geographers in Jonathan Swift's
time . . . who —

"In Afric maps,
With savage pictures filled
their gaps. . . ."

Well, we plan to fill a gap *not* with
"savage pictures," but with the inspiring, challenging report of the
work of an American medical missionary.

We Americans have every reason
to be proud of our doctors here at
home. Often we owe them our
health, happiness — sometimes
even life itself. But when they
choose to carry the practice of their
wonderful art — and science — to
undeveloped people in remote parts
of the earth, they become more
than doctors. They become unoffi-
cial American educators and am-
bassadors to whom our debt is even
greater.

I have met these dedicated men
inside Latin America . . . inside
Asia. But nowhere have I been
more impressed with the quality of
their devoted work than *inside
Africa.*

Fittingly, our story was filmed in
the Belgian Congo (INDICATES),
lying astride the equator like a
mighty giant — the same land we
first came to hear about in the days
of another medical missionary, the
celebrated Dr. Livingstone.

And now, we begin our story — in
the hot moist sky over Leopoldville. . . .

WITH AFRICAN CARVINGS AND
SITS ON EDGE.

PICKS UP MASK
(CU MASK IN GUNTHER'S HAND)

CUT TO MS OF GUNTHER ON
DESK

GUNTHER RISES, CROSSES TO
MAP

CAMERA DOLLIES IN PAST
GUNTHER AS HE INDICATES
THE CONGO . . .

CAMERA CONTINUES PAST
GUNTHER TO LEOPOLDVILLE.
DISSOLVE THROUGH TO AFRICA
FILM.

There are shots of Leopoldville, its apartments, industries, hospitals with descriptive narration. And then we are taken to Lotumbe,

the tiny village where the medical missionary lives and works. We see some patients on their way to the doctor. The doctor's young son, Ernest, greets them.

NATIVE SPOKESMAN:
(NATIVE TONGUE)
Good morning. Where do we find the doctor?
ERNEST:
(NATIVE TONGUE)
You go to the clinic. It is that way. (POINTS)
NATIVE SPOKESMAN:
Thank you.

CAMERA FOLLOWS NATIVES AS THEY MOVE AWAY IN THE DIRECTION ERNEST POINTS. CUT TO MS OF ERNEST AS HE LEAVES HURRIEDLY BY A DIFFERENT WAY.

(MUSIC IN AND UNDER — ESTAB-LISHING IDENTIFYING THEME FOR EACH PATIENT)
1ST NARRATOR:
When a doctor,
In the spirit of
Him who cured the sick and the
    lame and the blind,
Sets down his lamp in a dark
        forest,
Its glow can be seen for miles
        around.

FADE OUT.

FADE IN: LONG SHOT OF LEPER WALKING ALONG RIVER BANK . . . TURNING AND CLIMBING UP TOWARD CAMERA, SCRAM-BLING UP BANK, CU OF FEET. . . .

The patients come without pause: a mother with her boy who is suffering from yaws, a crippled native carried by two of his cousins, the woman about to give birth. They are all given living space in the compound. Now we are taken to the doctor's office as he is ready to see his first patient.

2ND NARRATOR:
You remember this little child . . .
He came with his family
Through miles of swamp
To reach the Monganga. . . .
(SOF DOCTOR AND CHILD IN NA-

CUT TO LS, INTERIOR OF DOC-TOR'S OFFICE AS HE CALLS OUT FOR 1ST PATIENT. ENTER YAWS BOY . . . . WS AS DOCTOR GREETS AND EXAMINES. DOCTOR

TIVE TONGUE AS DOCTOR EXAM-
INES AND PRESCRIBES: THEN
DOWN FOR:)

2ND NARRATOR:
The doctor's diagnosis is prompt,
He prescribes penicillin,
Sends the child to the infirmary,
And turns to the next case. . . .

(SOF NATIVE TONGUE AS DOCTOR
DISMISSES BOY, CHECKS RECORD
AND CALLS NEXT PATIENT.)

2ND NARRATOR:
This is our friend
Who arrived by the river bank.
(SOF UP, DOCTOR AND PATIENT
IN NATIVE TONGUE, THEN DOWN
FOR:)
The doctor now informs him
That he has leprosy — Hanson's
disease —
And directs that he go to the
mission leprosarium
For treatment
Three miles away. . . .
Sometimes,
When it is necessary for the
patient
To undergo extensive treatment,
His relatives —
Like this group of fishing folk
From far up river —
Build for themselves nearby
The kind of habitat they are
used to,
And do their waiting
As they carry on
The kind of life they know
best. . . .

PRESCRIBES, HANDS CHILD SLIP
FOR MEDICATION AND PATIENT
LEAVES. LS, DOCTOR MARKS
RECORD AND TURNS PAPERS
OVER TO NSAKA, HIS ASS'T.
RETURNS TO DESK, PICKS UP
NEW RECORD

DOCTOR CALLS NEXT PATIENT.
ENTER LEPER. DOCTOR GREETS
AND EXAMINES HIM . . . DIS-
CUSSES PROBLEM WITH PA-
TIENT AND SENDS HIM TO
LEPROSARIUM. PATIENT EXITS
AS DOCTOR RETURNS TO
DESK. . . .

CUT TO VARIED SHOTS OF
FISHING FAMILY ON RIVER
BANK NEAR VILLAGE. . . .
WS AS CAMERA FOLLOWS
NATIVE DELIVERING CATCH
TO WIFE.
. . . CU OF FISH AS IT IS
PLACED IN PAN . . .

We follow the doctor in his daily rounds: the pre-natal clinic, the children's ward. We see the man afflicted by elephantiasis, the skin of his leg as tough as an elephant's. We see the woman wasting away from the dread African sleeping sickness. And then in a scene that is purely visual we observe the doctor demonstrating the use of crutches to the crippled patient.

(SOF, DOCTOR IN BRIEF CONVER-
SATION WITH PATIENT)
    DOCTOR:
    (CONTINUING UNDER FILM)
Ah, Nsaka, my head nurse and good right arm, has brought me the crutches I ordered for the crippled man. I told this man there was nothing I could do for his deformity, but I *could* help him to walk erect like a man. Did he want to? He said "yes," so I had Nsaka dig up some crutches for me. (PAUSE) See for yourself what happens. . . ."
(SOF NATIVE TONGUE UP FILL)

CUT TO EXTERIOR VIEW FROM INSIDE HUT, SHOWING NSAKA STANDING OUTSIDE THE HUT WITH A PAIR OF CRUTCHES WAITING FOR DOCTOR TO COME OUT.

DOCTOR EMERGES AND GREETS NSAKA, TAKING THE CRUTCHES FROM HIM.

THE CAMERA FOLLOWS THEM AS TOGETHER THEY PASS OUT OF SCENE.

CUT TO NEW EXTERIOR WHERE WE SEE THE CRIPPLED MAN SEATED ON DIRT BANK IN FRONT OF LAB. PORCH. DR. AND NSAKA ENTER. THEY EX-CHANGE GREETINGS, THE DR. APPARENTLY ASKING TO SEE THE CRIPPLE MOVE. THE PATIENT DEMONSTRATES HOW HE GETS ALONG WITH THE HELP OF A STICK.

THE DR. SPEAKS TO HIM, SHAKING HIS HEAD AS IF TO SAY HE WILL NOT NEED TO WALK THAT WAY ANY MORE. EXPLAINS THAT HE HAS BROUGHT HIM CRUTCHES THAT WILL ENABLE HIM TO WALK ERECT LIKE A MAN.

THE DR. THEN DEMONSTRATES THE CRUTCHES FOR THE PATIENT. CLOSE SHOT OF THIS AND CU OF PATIENT'S REACTION. WIDE SHOT, NOW, SHOWS THE DR., WITH NSAKA'S HELP, LIFT THE PATIENT AS THEY PLACE A CRUTCH UNDER EACH ARM.

MS OF PATIENT ON CRUTCHES, STILL SUPPORTED BY DOCTOR AND NSAKA . . .

(MUSIC, MODIFIED CRIPPLE THEME, IN AND UNDER.)

WIDE SHOT AS DOCTOR AND NSAKA STEP AWAY, LEAVING THE PATIENT TOTTERING UNCERTAINLY ON HIS CRUTCHES . . . FULL SHOT OF PATIENT AS HE TAKES HIS FIRST STEP AWKWARDLY AND FALLS, LAUGHING GOOD NATUREDLY. WIDE SHOT AS DOCTOR HELPS HIM INTO SITTING POSITION AGAIN AND HANDS HIM THE CRUTCHES, EXPLAINING ENCOURAGINGLY THAT IT IS JUST A MATTER OF TIME AND PRACTICE BEFORE HE WILL BE USING THEM WELL. MS OF DOCTOR GIVING A FEW LAST INSTRUCTIONS, AS HE LEAVES WITH NSAKA, WAVING GOODBYE TO THE CRIPPLE. AFTER THEY'VE GONE, CRIPPLE LIFTS HIMSELF UPON THE CRUTCHES TO TRY AGAIN. . . .

But the medical missionary has a rival, an ancient rival, in whom many of the natives still have faith, the witch doctor.

(SOF OF WITCH DOCTOR UP FOR 7″, THEN DOWN UNDER:)

CUT TO WS WITCH DOCTOR, FRAMED BY A GNARLED TREE STUMP, TREATING A NATIVE WOMAN WHO LIES SPRAWLED

AGAINST THE STUMP. SPOTTED
WITH PAINT, HE RATTLES BONES
TOGETHER, INVOKING THE
SPIRITS WITH INCREASING
FERVOR AS HE RUBS HER
BODY WITH LEAVES AND
HERBS. HOLD. . . .

1ST NARRATOR:
(OVER SOUND)
Always,
Deep in the dark recesses of
              the forest,
There are those who would
              ward off illness
Another way . . .
For a fee
Vastly higher than that assessed
          by the medical doctors,
They claim to intercede with
              the spirits
Who strike and cripple, swell
              and torture
The human body,
Often delaying real help.
              (15″)
(SOF OF WITCH DOCTOR UP FOR
ABOUT 10″)

2ND NARRATOR: (32″)
Hastening to repair the damage
          caused by such delay,
Are hands
Whose color alone
Speak volumes
For the increasing medical
          teamwork in Africa
              (10″)

CUT TO CU, FOLLOWED BY MS,
OF THE HANDS OF DR. ROSS
AND HIS NATIVE ASSISTANT AS
THEY SCRUB, PRELIMINARY TO
SURGERY
              (05″)
CUT TO WS, DOCTOR AND STAFF
IN OPERATING ROOM, GATH-
ERED ABOUT THE PATIENT,
HEAD BOWED IN PRAYER. . . .
(PRAYER BEGINS AT 04″ IN,
CONTINUES FOR 13″)

Always
Surgery is preceded
With a prayer. . . . (04″)

(SOF UP, AS DOCTOR LEADS STAFF
IN PRAYER IN NATIVE TONGUE)
              (13″)

DR. ROSS:
"The tumor which we have today is a fibroma.

(39")

DR. ROSS:
"It is quite large as you may see, as I press it back and forth like this. You will note the markings on the skin. This is quite common in this area."

WS AROUND TABLE AS DOCTOR EXAMINES THE ABDOMINAL GROWTH BY OUTLINING IT WITH HIS HANDS. . . .

There are actual shots of an operation to remove a tumor. The doctor invites the natives to watch the operation from the outside of the operating room. This is to dispel their fear of surgery. As the operation progresses, the doctor explains the details of the surgery. The operation is a success. The tumor, fortunately, is not cancerous.

Now we are about midway in our story. We return to John Gunther who, this time, describes native life in the Belgian Congo.

GUNTHER:
Dr. John Ross fights disease in the Congo. This is his great personal contribution toward preserving the health of more than 12 million people.
Who are these people? How do they live?
Well, to begin with, we must remember that Africans are divided into amazing and fantastic numbers of different tribes. They speak more than 700 different languages, and often have cultures completely different — even from their next-door neighbors. Dr. Ross's patients are known as the Nkundus. . . .
(GUNTHER CONTINUES, UNDER FILM, NARRATING "NATIVE LIFE AND ASSISTANT")

UP ON GUNTHER STANDING BEFORE AFRICA MAP.

DISSOLVE TO NATIVE LIFE SEQUENCE.

We learn that manioc, a tuberous root plant, bananas, palm nuts and fish form the staple diet of the natives. Protein is scarce and malnutrition is prevalent.

Gunther also explains the type of schooling available to the natives with particular emphasis on the background of Nsaka, the medical missionary's male nurse, who has learned a great deal about medicine from careful observation of the doctor. The commentary is tied in, of course, with appropriate footage.

Now we meet Dr. Ross again, this time at the leprosarium.

DOCTOR:

We have about 150 patients in our leprosarium. These patients are being isolated until the disease is stabilized. Then they will return to their homes to live normal lives, and to follow regular treatment in our dispensaries.

ESTABLISHING SHOTS I.E., LS STREET SHOWING FLAGS BEING RAISED . . . PEOPLE PASSING CAMERA AS THEY GO ABOUT THEIR BUSINESS. . . .

Now let me tell you something about leprosy. In the first place, it is not as infectious a disease as tuberculosis.

CUT BACK TO DOCTOR, MS.

The picture in recent years has been made very hopeful by the introduction of sulfone drugs. But still, it is one of the most prevalent diseases that we have in this part of Africa . . . affecting perhaps 5% of the people.

CUT TO CU OF DOCTOR

(AS HE WALKS)

Don't be surprised at the presence of the children. Leprosy is no respecter of age. We have cases here from six to eight years on up. We have about 27 in our leprosarium, many who have been with us for some time. We have built a school building in order to take care of their educational needs. This is Mbula Joseph who is our teacher and also has leprosy.

CUT OF WIDE SHOT OF CHILDREN SEATED ON GROUND. DOCTOR STEPS INTO PICTURE. MBULA JOSEPH SHORTLY JOINS HIM.

Now let me show you a few of the various types of leprosy we have in our leprosarium.

DOCTOR WALKS OUT OF SCENE. MBULA JOSEPH ORDERS CHILDREN TO RISE AND ACCOMPANIES THEM AS THEY LEAVE. . . .

Dr. Ross describes the different types of leprosy as the camera follows him on his visit to the patients. We leave the leprosarium on a note of hope.

DOCTOR:

The *vast majority* of people who are here, once their cases are arrested, will return to their villages . . . healthier and happier.

CUT BACK TO DOCTOR IN ORIGINAL SETTING, THE DISPENSARY, PATIENTS COMPLETED, SEATED AT EDGE OF TABLE . . .
PUTS ON CAP . . .

(MUSIC OUT)

2ND NARRATOR:

And so,
With the inevitable washing of
                          hands
That precedes his departure —
A never-omitted ritual for all
            who visit here —
The doctor
Returns to the problems he left
                          behind,
Shouting the familiar native
                          parting —
"You stay well!"

CUT TO WS BOKA SETTING DOWN A PAN OF WATER AND SOAP. DOCTOR STEPS INTO SCENE AND WASHES HANDS.

CUT TO WIDE SHOT OF DOCTOR ON HIS BICYCLE AND WAVING GOODBYE TO STAFF AND OTHERS GATHERED TO SEE HIM OFF

DOCTOR: (CALLING OUT)
Locikala-o!

For the next sequence, writer Lou Hazam brings us a study in contrasts: birth and death.

PART 7 — DELIVERY SEQUENCE

LS . . . THEN MS AND CUS OF LONG SINGLE-FILE FUNERAL PROCESSION, CARRYING COFFIN. ESTABLISH FOR ABOUT 10″ BEFORE NARRATION AND CONTINUE OVER NARRATION. . . .

1ST NARRATOR:

Death —
Indifferent to the color of man —
Visits the people of the forest
As it visits *all* folk . . .

Oft' giving rise
To such a funeral procession as
this . . .
Returning the body of its victim —
A woman —
To her native village,
Amid the din of drums
And the sound of their
bereavement. . . .

CUT OR DISSOLVE TO WS
DELIVERY ROOM IN HOSPITAL,
WOMAN ON TABLE DOCTOR
DELIVERING CHILD. . . .

But here, too,
As everywhere in the world,
Death must meet its inevitable
challenger —
Birth . . .

CUT TO NEWBORN CHILD BEING
LIFTED, WRAPPED AND PLACED
ON MOTHER'S ABDOMEN. . . .

2ND NARRATOR:
This is Bolafa Malia,
Whose baby has come at last
Into the world of Lotumbe . . .
Come to be born
Where all the science of
modern medicine
Can be brought to bear
To assure his safe arrival . . .
As his *grandmother* looks on.
Quickly the doctor
Pursues his post-natal activities,
Seeing to the hundred-and-one
things
That must be done —
All brought to a fitting climax
When he carries the baby in
his arms
To the mother herself.
(SOF, DOCTOR AND MOTHER UP)

CUT TO MOTHER ON OPERATING
TABLE . . . THEN TO CU OF BABY
IN COT AS DOCTOR CLEARS NOSE
AND MOUTH PASSAGES . . . (12")

CUT TO CU GRANDMOTHER
LOOKING ON . . . (02")
CUT TO BABY IN COT AS
DOCTOR TIES NAVEL . . . CU OF
MOTHER . . . BABY IN COT BEING
WRAPPED . . . CU ASS'T NURSE
WATCHING . . . THEN CUT TO
DOCTOR SHOWING BABY TO
MOTHER . . . (19")

SOF OF DOCTOR AND MOTHER
& CU MOTHER   (09")

2ND NARRATOR:
And again the doctor honors
An old custom at Lotumbe.

CUT TO CU OF GRANDMOTHER,
THEN TO WS OF DR. ROSS

He presents the infant child
Before the grandmother,
Announcing —
With the joyful word "Aobika,"
"She lives . . . the mother lives!"
(SOF FOLLOWS WITH DOCTOR AND
GRANDMOTHER RE "AOBIKA.")

AND GRANDMOTHER AS HE
SHOWS HER THE BABY. . . .
(14″)

At the conclusion of this scene, we return again to John Gunther. Now we are told about the many activities undertaken by Dr. Ross which are far removed from the purely medical: showing the natives how to make bricks, doing his own carpentry work, repairing his outboard motor. And on Sunday, Dr. John Ross, accordionist, is the "organist" of the church.

The 1st Narrator picks up the story with a lead-in to the baby clinic presided over by Mrs. Ross. Then we are off on a trip to a remote tribe of semi-pygmies, who are also the doctor's patients.

2ND NARRATOR:
A small clearing
That is the home
Of a tribe of semi-pygmies
Known as the Batswas.
(NATIVE MUSIC SNEAK UNDER)
The news of the Monganga's
                            arrival
Has preceded him.
There is the usual greeting
From the Chief . . .
And then he pauses
To listen to the Batswas
Sing his welcome. . . .

CUT TO DR. AND NURSE
ENTERING BATSWA VILLAGE,
DUCKING UNDER FRAMEWORK
OF NATIVE HUT. . . . (14″)
CUT TO NATIVES DANCING AND
SINGING IN THE BG AS CHIEF
COMES FORWARD TO SHAKE
DOCTOR'S HAND TO WATCH
DANCING (18″) CUT TO
VARIED SHOTS OF SINGING
AND DANCING . . . (57″)

(MUSIC, WILD TRACK, UP . . .
HOLD THEN DOWN)
Having saluted the greeting,
The doctor moves on
To the purpose of his visit.
With microscope set up,
To examine blood smears.
He starts on the long line of

CUT TO DOCTOR, NURSE, AND
CHIEF PASSING ON TO HUT IN
BACKGROUND. CUT TO HUT
WITH TABLE SET UP WITH
MICROSCOPE . . . DR. AND NURSE
BEHIND TABLE . . . PATIENT'S

patients who deem
A consultation with a doctor
A rare event indeed,
And can count the time-between
In years. . . .
As Dr. Ross describes the
                    Batswas. . . .

AWAITING EXAMINATION TWO
LONG LINES TO ONE SIDE . . .
PATIENTS MOVE IN FOR
EXAMINATION, ONE AFTER THE
OTHER, AS THE DOCTOR
MOTIONS FOR THEM TO COME
FORWARD

DR. ROSS: (WILD SOUND)
"These people are generally the
most primitive people we have, living in the most primitive condition.
While they are more prolific than
the more advanced peoples, they
also are more subject to the inroads
of malaria . . . pneumonia . . . and
other diseases. We find more yaws
in this group than we commonly
do, but on the other hand, less
venereal disease."

This is one man's contribution to his fellow men. This is modern medicine come to heal the ills of an ancient people, far removed
from the centers of civilization. In the same poetic vein with which
Hazam opened this documentary, "Monganga," he writes the moving
conclusion.

CLOSING SEQUENCE

(MUSIC: COMPOUND MEETING IN
. . . HOLD UNTIL ESTABLISHED,
THEN DOWN FOR NARRATION)

DISSOLVE TO CROWD AND
STAFF GATHERED AROUND
PASTOR IN COMPOUND SINGING

1ST NARRATOR:
Thus do we return,
As each succeeding day
                    inevitably returns —
To *another* dawn
At Lotumbe's mission compound.
Many of the faces have changed,
For those with old aches are
                              gone,
And others with new pain are
New come.

But some faces you remember . . .
Those we have followed here.
The little boy
Who came covered with yaws
Festering his sad face. . . .
Bolafa Malia,
Who came to have her baby,
And who — only yesterday —
May have borne her child in
                                    the jungle
Surrounded by all the fetishes
                            of ignorance,
Our crippled man
Whose twisted legs
Could not hold him. . . .
They await now
Only the benediction. . . .

    PASTOR:
(GIVES BENEDICTION)
(MUSIC SWELLS OUT OF BENE-
DICTION AND UNDER)

    1ST NARRATOR:
And so has come
Their time to go. . . .
The woman with her newborn . . .
Turning her steps
Toward the Momboyo. . . .
The cured boy
With his mother . . .
Toward the swamp
That leads to home. . . .
And our friend
Down the path to the forest,
Reflecting — as he walks
                            unaided —
The words of the Greatest
                            Healer . . .
"Arise, And go thy way". . . .
All well,
By the skill of the American
                            Monganga. . . .
    (PAUSE)
And by the grace of God.

CUT TO YAWS BOY WITH
MOTHER, STANDING

CUT TO BOLAFA MALIA
AND FAMILY SEATED, SINGING

CUT TO CRIPPLED MAN SEATED
SINGING

CUT TO PASTOR IN CENTER
WHO RAISES HIS HAND AND
GIVES THE BENEDICTION. . . .

CUT TO LONG SHOT OF CROWD
BREAKING UP. . . .
CUT TO:
BOLAFA MALIA AND FAMILY
LEAVING CROWD AT BREAK-UP.
CUT TO YAWS CHILD AND
MOTHER DEPARTING FOR HOME

CUT TO CRIPPLED MAN
WALKING ERECT ON HIS
CRUTCHES ALONG PATH . . .
HIS BACK TO CAMERA. . . .

CUT TO BOLAFA MALIA AND
FAMILY IN PIROGUE, AS IT
IS PADDLED AWAY FROM
CAMERA UPON THE BOSOM OF
THE MOMBOYO. . . .

(THE QUIET SOUND OF THE PAD-
DLES IN THE WATER)

THE BOAT ON THE RIVER
GROWING SMALLER AND SMALLER
AS TITLES AND CREDITS
ARE SUPERIMPOSED. . . .

(MUSIC RISING TO WARM CON-
CLUSION AND AMERICANA THEME
UNDER TITLES.)

ON THE LOCAL LEVEL

When we consider
the time, the effort, the personnel and the vast sums of money required
to produce an effective TV network documentary, it may seem to
be an impossible project for a local station. Actually, this is not the
case. Several local stations have produced both one-shot and series
documentaries with minimum personnel, equipment and cost. What
they have possessed is imagination, courage and an issue.

For a definitive picture of how a local station can produce a successful documentary and the role the writer plays, let us study a
specific example.

The nation's capital is a beautiful city. Tourists from vast
metropolitan centers like New York or Chicago, are undoubtedly impressed by the cleanliness of Washington, by its tree lined streets and
avenues, by its monuments and public buildings. Yet Washington,
unfortunately, has its share of ugliness, its slums, which it is slowly
eradicating, and a river, which should be a ribbon of beauty but instead is a conveyor of filth.

Here then is an issue: pollution.

The station that took up the cudgels in the fight against pollution was WRC-TV, the NBC outlet in Washington. It instituted a
series of half-hour documentaries called, ironically enough, "Our
Beautiful Potomac," for which it received the highly prized Sylvania
award.

Now, pollution is not a pretty subject. It would be difficult
enough to handle on radio but for a television documentary, the question naturally arises: how far can you go visually? The Potomac River
is polluted because of the amount of sewage which flows into it.
Would it be too shocking, or in bad taste to show films of sewage

flowing into the river? The WRC-TV staff decided there was no middle ground here. If you were going to tackle this problem, you had to show how serious it was. If people were shocked then maybe they would be aroused enough to do something about the situation. That was the avowed purpose of this documentary series. It was, in every sense, an action documentary.

WRC-TV organized a documentary unit consisting of a producer, writer, film editor and director, all of whom participated equally in decisions. As far as the writer was concerned, he did more than prepare the script. He took part in the planning of shots, in the editing of the script and in the production of the program. In other words, this was a closely knit group which made up in extra activity what it lacked in number of personnel.

Because of the particular problems it faced, the WRC-TV documentary unit decided it would have to do without a shooting script. Camera work was dependent on the flow of sewers, the tide, the wind, and the light. In striving for naturalism, for example, to catch people fishing in the polluted waters without giving the effect of posing, the cameraman had to be quick on the shutter. Once a picture was set up, the participants were usually self-conscious and posed. It was decided therefore to shoot first and obtain releases later. Written releases are essential from individuals who have been photographed, otherwise the station may be liable on grounds of invasion of privacy.

Many of the shots taken were stark and of definite shock value: a pan shot from the Lincoln Memorial to a sewer outfall; a fisherman hauling a catch out of a fly-covered river area; a couple of youngsters wading and splashing water oblivious to the warning sign: "No Wading — Polluted."

Many of these shots were taken "wild," that is, without specific relation to script but with the probability of use. Film limitations required that the copy be adapted to the available film. A rough edit of the film was prepared from which the writer turned out a first draft. This served to show up the story line deficiencies due in the main to the original film edit. Revisions were therefore in order until script and film told a coherent, powerful story.

All through the script the general rule was followed to let the pictures tell the story whenever possible. When script was utilized for obvious scenes, it was written to offer additional information to the viewer. For instance, a sequence showing men fishing in the Potomac, would require no identifying script to the effect that:

"These men are fishing." But the script did explain that the fish the men were catching were carp and catfish, the scavengers.

Music played an important part in the documentary. The producer's rule of thumb was "To allow the music to come up full when the picture was powerful and to supplement relatively weak pictures with narration." The music consisted of recorded selections taken from the station's library of recordings. Mostly, these selections were from the lesser known classical works. Familiar music as background has a tendency to be distracting.

As we have stated previously, the essential ingredient of any successful documentary is thorough research. The documentary unit at WRC-TV had to be sure of its facts. In some instances, it was treading on political toes and it therefore had to be certain that every statement the writer used in the script was accurate.

This series on "Our Beautiful Potomac" did not confine itself to shots of the river and narration. Interviews were recorded with city officials. The local citizenry was invited to air its opinions and suggestions. Since the Potomac River also borders the neighboring communities of Arlington County in Virginia and Montgomery County in Maryland, officials from those suburban areas were asked to appear on the program to tell the public what plans, if any, they had to clear the pollution. The producer-narrator of the program series, Stuart Finley, did not pull any punches during the interviews.

Two questions must inevitably arise: one, how costly was this program series to WRC-TV? The answer is that the cost was extremely nominal. Since this was a constructive public service series, many agencies assisted the station. The United States Public Health Service, the Potomac River Commission and the local Health Department supplied the unit with film, additional cameramen, visual aids and plenty of advice.

What results did the documentaries achieve? First of all, the newspapers took up the lead of WRC-TV. There were columns of copy following each telecast. Broadcast interviews were quoted. Editorials were written. The public conscience was awakened with pressure being placed on the proper officials to literally clean up the situation. Progress was definitely being made.

The United States Public Health Service thought so highly of the series that it, in turn, has produced an overall documentary film utilizing the salient features of the original series. This film has been processed for showing throughout the country. It will be helpful to other cities which are faced with an identical pollution problem.

Here now are excerpts from one of the scripts of the prize-winning documentary series, "Our Beautiful Potomac," co-authored by John Dewitt and Stuart Finley.

VIDEO	AUDIO
	(MUSIC)
CLOSE-UP OF AN OAR BEING ROWED THROUGH SEWAGE FLOATING ON SURFACE OF A STREAM.	God decreed that Pharaoh must let his people go. He commanded Moses and Aaron to pollute the river Nile . . . and make it abominable. Moses and Aaron did as God commanded. The Bible records: "And the fish that was in the river died. And the river stank. And the Egyptians could not drink of the water of the river." God could think of no greater punishment to inflict upon the people of Egypt. Today, Americans inflict this punishment upon themselves. (MUSIC)
(DISSOLVE) CAPITOL BUILDING WHITE HOUSE	Washington, D.C., our Nation's Capitol. Home of the President of the United States and nearly two million other Americans.
POTOMAC RIVER (SUPER TITLES)	And this is the beautiful Potomac River. (MUSIC)
PAN FROM LOVELY SHOT OF JEFFERSON MEMORIAL TO WATER OF TIDAL BASIN COVERED WITH SEWAGE AND DEBRIS.	Washington's historic shrines form a panorama of beauty — with a background of filth. Human thoughtlessness has converted the Potomac River into one of the ten dirtiest rivers in all America.
PAN FROM AN AIRPLANE COMING IN AT NATIONAL AIRPORT TO SEWAGE IN WATER NEARBY.	Thousands of visitors arrive at Washington's National Airport every day. The river looks lovely (PAUSE) until they get a closer look. This is human sewage, dumped raw into the beautiful Potomac.
CU — BUBBLES COMING UP.	Gas bubbles up to the surface, polluting the air as well as the water. (MUSIC)

PAN FROM FISH-ERMAN CASTING TO SEWAGE AND DEBRIS IN WATER.	The people who live here have to relax some-where. And what's more fun than fishing in the river. But the Potomac is a quagmire . . . a dump-ing place for junk and filth. (MUSIC)
SEVERAL FISHER-MEN FISHING OVER SEWER OUTFALL.	Incredible! These fishermen are huddled over a flowing sewer . . . because this is where the fish bite best. Carp . . . catfish . . . muck-dwellers . . . scavengers. Easy to catch . . . but not very appe-tizing.
FISH IN BOX COV-ERED WITH FLIES.	These fish weren't caught for sport. They're for supper tonight.

This was the opening sequence. The documentary continued with additional scenes: a couple swimming in the polluted river, a group holding a picnic on the river bank. Then followed taped com-ments by some of the local residents.

MONTAGE OF BEAUTIFUL MONU-MENTS OF WASH-INGTON USUALLY SHOWING THEIR PROXIMITY TO THE WATER. (NO FILTH SHOWN HERE.)	"I've owned two cabin cruisers located here on the river in the past. I've had discussions with my wife on the subject and she won't let me take the children out on the Potomac River." (MUSIC) "The fish were dying. There were 500 or so fish floating by dead because there was no oxygen in the river." (MUSIC)

There were other equally indignant comments. The script then explained some of the background of the problem including matched film and narration describing the existing facilities of the District of Columbia.

PUMPING STATION EXTERIOR	Here is Washington's big pumping station where billions of gallons of wastes converge from all over the city and are funneled down to the treat-ment plant. Just to keep the stuff moving takes huge facilities and engineering skill. It costs big money, too.
EMPTY BAR SCREENS	In dry weather, everything works just fine. These bar screens remove rags, sticks, and other junk that might clog the pumps and the liquid is pushed along.

FULL BAR SCREENS	But when it rains, there's trouble. Pumps overload, bar screens clog, and everything is shunted out to the river instead of being sent down to Washington's treatment plant.
OUTFALL BLUE PLAINS TREATMENT PLANT SIGN	
WIDE SHOT OF PLANT SETTLING TANKS & CU	Actually, it is only HALF a plant. This is what they call "primary treatment." These big settling tanks permit the heavy stuff to settle out and the light material to be skimmed off. Here the treatment ends. A "complete" disposal plant would include "secondary" treatment too. Additional processes can remove as much as 95% of the pollution load before returning the liquid to circulation. But with primary treatment like this, only about a third of the harmful effects is removed.

An explanation of treatment continued, this time describing the facilities of the neighboring communities. Then the script delved into the causes of the pollution and the all-important question: what can be done about it?

SEWAGE SHOTS	There are two schools of thought about cleaning up the Potomac. One group would like to remove the lumps. They talk in terms of "permissible loading" . . . in other words: "how much sewage can the river carry away without it showing?"
BEAUTIFUL SCENE	Other people think the river should be really clean . . . in the interest of health and recreation. Earnest men are working to clean it up. The water pollution control agencies and the health departments of the surrounding States and cities are trying valiantly to do their share. There is an Interstate Potomac River Commission to help in overall planning.
GREAT FALLS PAN	When you view a majestic-looking river from a distance . . . it actually looks clean enough. It's easy to disregard water pollution. This is what makes it so difficult. The citizens themselves most often don't comprehend.

The script moved on to a specific example of action. It showed

how the city of Alexandria, Virginia, with its own Potomac waterfront, remedied its situation.

CONSTRUCTION SCENES . . . SEVERAL SCENES . . . EARLY CONSTRUCTION	Gradually, as the citizens read the editorials in the newspaper . . . watched television . . . and, most important, visited their own waterfront . . . they began to wake up. This was an emergency. Something had to be done. And they did it. They created an Alexandria Sanitation Authority and floated a bond issue to pay for a big new sewage treatment plant. Once they'd made up their minds, the work went quickly. (MUSIC)
AERIAL SHOT OF PLANT	And now it's in operation.
SETTLING TANKS FILTERING TANKS SHOT TOWARD MEMORIAL	Today, the sewage from 85,000 people goes to the treatment plant . . . instead of to the river. (MUSIC)
HOOFF'S RUN OUTFALL FLOWING	And look at the difference. Sewage used to pour out here . . .
HOOFF'S RUN DRY PENDLETON OUTFALL FLOWING	And it doesn't any more. It used to emerge here.
PENDLETON MANHOLES	Now, it flows through interceptor sewers under these manholes.

The program concluded with a statement by an official of the United States Public Health Service to the effect that the polluted Potomac was not an isolated instance, that other large cities faced similar problems and that there were adequate solutions: bond issues to pay for treatment plants and assistance to small communities by means of the Federal Water Pollution Control Act.

IN THE PUBLIC INTEREST

A local station can serve both the community and itself by the presentation of a forceful documentary, or a series of documentaries, on an issue of vital concern to the community. This type of programming, more than any other, makes a radio or television station an integral part of the area it serves and is substantial proof that the station is operating in the public interest.

Generally, documentaries on the local level, as on the network level, are staff-conceived. Nevertheless, students of radio and television writing may find it to their interest to explore the possibility of preparing a documentary radio or television script for the local station. A study would have to be made of any problems affecting the local area and then an outline formulated for presentation purposes.

The writer will have to bear in mind the probability that the local documentary will be presented on a sustaining basis and therefore costs must be kept to a minimum. As in the case of "Our Beautiful Potomac," enlisting the aid of local or Federal agencies should prove helpful.

Radio documentaries can be presented at a bare minimum of cost by any station that has a portable tape recorder. One of this author's students produced a series of weekly documentaries sponsored by a cooperative organization. It was an informational series explaining the different types of cooperatives, how they were formed and how they operated. Some of the documentaries were historical in nature, delving into the origin of cooperatives and their growth in various lands. The producer was a young lady with drive and imagination. She was given an inelastically thin budget and a minute expense account for travel. She was allotted an adequate tape recorder. The productions were entirely her own. She wrote and narrated the script, arranged interviews and pickups of pertinent events. It was not an easy assignment but it was always an interesting one. She discovered that this business of broadcasting is often nerve-wracking but seldom dull.

Television presents greater problems to the local documentary producer or writer and the interest of the station in putting on a series will vary in proportion to its area coverage and financial standing. Technically, a television documentary can rarely be a one-man or one-woman production. A capable cameraman is a necessity. But the writer can also be the producer, and narration and interviews can be handled by one of the station's staff announcers.

THE RADIO DOCUMENTARY

The radio documentary has a notable history. It reached its zenith during 1947 and 1948 with the CBS Documentary Unit leading the way. Such productions as "The Eagle's Brood," a probe of juvenile delinquency, "The Sunny Side of the Atom," a study of the peaceful uses of atomic energy, "Among Ourselves," an inquiry into race relations, attracted nation-wide attention and critical acclaim. Of comparable stature was the NBC series, "Living." This was radio for adults. All networks contributed their share of outstanding provocative documentaries.

The Fund for Adult Education sponsored a series of dynamic documentaries under the title of "The People Act." This recorded series showed what communities could do to remedy local problems through united action whether it was routing racketeers in Gary, Indiana, or fighting for good schools in Arlington, Virginia. "The People Act" radio programs are now on deposit with the Educational Television and Radio Center and are available for distribution to all educational stations.

Whether the radio documentary will ever again have such a resurgence is problematic because we must admit that the visual advantage of television makes it a far superior medium for the documentary. Obviously, if you were to produce a documentary on the ravages of floods, one film sequence of a stricken community will have vastly greater impact than any number of words, no matter how dramatically written.

Essentially, the observations we have made concerning the writing of the television documentary apply equally to the radio documentary with one important exception: in television, a film segment may make a dramatic point without the use of any narration or dialogue; in radio, words must paint the picture. Both media can, and do, use sound and music to good effect.

The radio documentary is alive and kicking today and although not as widespread or as vocal as its predecessors of a decade ago, it still has an important job to do. Witness the award-winning series, "Disaster," presented by the American Broadcasting Company radio network in cooperation with the Red Cross. This series of dramatic documentaries is written by one of the network's top writers, Ira Marion. We have selected portions from one of the programs in the series: "The Tampico Hurricanes." This is the opening sequence utilizing a narrator:

NARR: They are born at the eastern edge of the Caribbean, these whirling winds. They are disciples of the ancient god Hurakan, he of the thunder and lightning.

    (ONE CRACK OF LIGHTNING AND THUNDER)

    (CUE) They travel out of the southeast, spinning north and west. The young men in the aircraft find them, flying the Gull Tracks out of Bermuda, flying the search patterns out of Miami, and Key West.

    (RADIO BUG SNEAKS IN UNDER)

They report what they find, out there over blue water, those young men. The air is busy, whining and crackling with their reports.

    (RADIO BUG SEGUES TO TELETYPE)

Their terse, concise, cogent words are translated at the Miami Office of the United States Weather Bureau, and speed northward on the chattering teletypes, to reach the big room in Washington — twenty-four hundred M Street in Washington — where the maps are made, and, in their own turn, transmitted, by the code numbers on the teletype,

    (TELETYPE SEGUES TO FACSIMILE WHINE)

on the facsimile transmitters, to all the receiving stations on the continent. The forecasters observe the maps, send out their "advisories" . . .

    (SOUND OUT)

VOICE: (FILTER) United States Weather Bureau advisory . . . Hurricane Alice is building up east of the Lesser Antilles. Winds approximately 80 miles per hour. Course, uncertain at this time.

(MUSIC: HEAVY CHORD AND RESUME WIND THEME UNDER)

NARR: Hurricane Alice — or Bertha — or Carol — or Diane — or Edna. No matter the name, save for the first letter, which tells us, each time, how many have gone before. Just — watch the winds from the aircraft; chart the course of the whirlwind; transmit the advisories; send out the warnings. No stopping this power. No halting the whirlwind. Northward and westward they track, over the sea, curving landward.

(MUSIC: SPINS TO HUGE CACOPHONOUS CHORD. CUTS OUT SHARPLY)

    (TELEGRAPH KEY)

VOICE: (FILTER) Mexican Red Cross, Mexico City, Mexico . . . O T 1306. Amcross receiving reports major disaster caused by floods Tampico area and energetic relief action your society and Mexican Government. Red Cross chapters and community leaders in Texas and elsewhere this country inquiring if they can help. Amcross

prepared assist with relief supplies and would be pleased to send
Carlos Patterne who worked closely with Mexican Red Cross and
Governor Teran in Nuevo Laredo floods last year. Please advise if
Amcross can help with relief supplies and services of Patterne. . . .
Amcross.

NARR: (SOFTLY) "Amcross." American National Red Cross. You!
(MUSIC: SHARP, BRIEF CHORD. OUT)

The scenes immediately following describe the assistance forthcoming from the Red Cross, particularly the dispatch of two experienced Red Cross workers, Carlos Patterne and Harris Austin. In
narrative fashion, Austin tells of the establishment of an airlift.

AUSTIN: I departed from Fort Sill, Oklahoma, at noon, September 28,
1955, arriving at Harlingen Air Force Base, Texas, on the afternoon of September 29. I found that plans were under way to establish an airlift. Ten thousand pounds each of rice, beans and flour
were to be lifted directly to Tampico by elements of the 14th Air
Force. A carload of cheese, butter, oil and powdered milk was en
route. On Saturday, October 1, 1955, I boarded the second plane
loaded with cheese and went with it to Tampico.

(MUSIC: RESOLVE PROGRESSION OF CHORDS. SEGUE TO MEXICAN
THEME, AND GO BEHIND)

The aid to the stricken Mexicans has now been given the title
of "Operation Brotherhood." Brief, cogent scenes describe the
assistance rendered by all branches of the Armed Forces. Then we
pick up a bit of local color which adds contrast to the grim situation.

(MUSIC: A MEXICAN MARCH IN BRASS AND WOODWINDS. FADE TO
BG BUT HOLD UNDER)
(CROWD BG WITH SOME LAUGHTER)

AUSTIN: What's this, Carlos?
PATTERNE: The "paseo," Cy.
AUSTIN: (SMILE) Educate me, Carlos.
PATTERNE: This is — Sunday. Always, on Sunday the girls — you see
them — in their best clothes, si? — they walk around the square.
The young men walk in the other direction, and say romantic words
to their sweethearts. A — si — tradition.
AUSTIN: (GENTLY) Even with the water coming down from the moun-
tains.
PATTERNE: (QUIETLY) The water is not here yet. It is not necessary
to disturb the people. Not yet.
(SMALL BURST OF LAUGHTER, OFF)

(MUSIC: SURGE BRIEFLY AND BACK)

NARR: (QUIETLY) Twenty-four hours later, there was no electricity in Tampico, and the water supply was cut off.

There are scenes of heroic Mexicans, such as the Reverend Andres Perez, working unceasingly to help the stricken people. A tense moment follows as the mobs are angered at the sight of soldiers with rifles when the hungry people are crying for bread. The situation suddenly changes when an American duck arrives on the scene.

VOICES: (CONFUSED) What is this? . . . Americanos? . . . With telephones on their backs? . . . Strange men . . . Norte Americano soldiers. . . . Telephones . . . *No rifles!* . . . Telephones!

AUSTIN: (OFF. FADING IN. MAKING A SPEECH) Ladies and gentlemen . . . please . . . Amigos . . . I will explain . . .

WOMAN 1: (CAN BE HEARD IN BG, THROUGHOUT, TRANSLATING HIS WORDS ROUGHLY INTO SPANISH.)

AUSTIN: This is . . . a duck. It is a truck which goes on water as well as on land! The American Red Cross . . . you see . . . here, on my shoulder . . . the sign . . . The American Red Cross . . . we have brought this duck and many like it . . . with the young men to drive them. They will bring food into the city. In a short time now . . . there will be places all over the city where you will receive hot food. At the street corners, our friends of the U.S. Army will give you water that is safe to drink. All will be well! Please let us through, so we can begin work. Let us through. (ASIDE) Sergeant. Sound your horn. Move forward slowly.

SERGEANT: (GRIN) Yes SIR!

(HORN, INSISTENTLY. DUCK CREEPS FORWARD)

MAN 2: (OFF. SHOUTING) Let them through! Let them through.

WOMAN 1: (OFF. SHOUTING) These are good men. Let them through. There is food on the duck!

VOICES: (ON AND FADING) The duck . . . A duck! . . . A strange duck! (LAUGHTER STARTS IN THE CROWD) Good men! . . . With telephones . . . And food . . . ! Water . . . !

(HEAVY APPLAUSE FADES IN. THE DUCK'S HORN. IT PICKS UP SPEED.)

And there is a touching tribute by a Mexican waiter in Tampico.

NARR: And there was the waiter in the hotel, who served the American Red Cross personnel in Tampico. One day, toward the end of their stay, at lunch time . . .

(SMALL RESTAURANT BG)

WAITER: With your permission, señors, I wish to make a brief speech.
PATTERNE: But of course, señor.
WAITER: (PAUSE. CLEARS THROAT. WITH GREAT FLOURISH, TO THE ROOM) Señoras, señors. Permit me to say . . . I have been a waiter for forty years. All my life, I have served the dinners. Here, in this hotel, have come the turistas . . . of many nations. Very many are not with the courtesy of Mexicans. Many are inconsiderate, ill-bred. When the Norte Americanos came to Tampico in this bad time, I expect they will be the same. I must now . . . apologize. The distinguished members of the United States Army and the American Red Cross, whom it has been my honor to serve, are muy simpático. Sí, muy simpático. They are modest, hard-working men who demand nothing. Nothing. The great generosity of the people of North America who have sent these gentlemen to us in our time of trouble, will never be forgotten. (FADING) They have shared the suffering and made it easy. They are . . . God Bless. . . .

The documentary ends with a scene at the Tampico airport as the natives shout their thanks to their benefactors.

NARR: No wonder then . . . six thousand people jamming the airport, to make their farewells, as the band played "La Golondrina" . . . the song of parting . . . as hands were clasped, and the last "abrazo" was given. No wonder then . . . that YOU may feel that you were there, indeed . . . that you had been there when you were needed most . . . that true friends had been made in your name. No wonder then, that all Harris Austin could say, as the airplane lifted from the runway, was . . .
AUSTIN: (ECHO. DEEPLY MOVED) Well . . . Operation Brotherhood now is history!
(MUSIC: SWELLS TO CURTAIN)

Children's programs

22

If there is any one issue which is bound to arouse controversy, it is the effect of television programs on children. There is wide disagreement on whether television viewing is detrimental or beneficial to the child. Educators, social workers, parents, child psychologists, all have varying opinions. The only safe view, it appears to us, is to admit that television has its faults and its benefits. If this sounds like fence-straddling, the reader is referred to the many articles written on television and the child. He will find therein all shades of opinions. However, there is common agreement on one point: television does influence the child.

In the previously quoted article from *U.S. News and World Report*, there is a section on "TV and the Child." "Most studies of TV habits," the article states, "agree that the average youngster spends from 20 to 30 hours a week in front of a television set while he is between 7 and 13 years of age." That is about as much time as the average child spends in school in full time sessions. Little wonder why parents and educators are disturbed about the magnetism of the home screen.

If we were to attempt any sort of tabulation of effects, we might discover the following:

Detriments: Less active play;
Less reading;

439

                    Less creative work;
                    Less group activity;
                    More emotional disturbance.
Benefits: More knowledge of the world geographically;
                    Understanding of various peoples and their cultures;
                    Favorable attitudes toward others;
                    Increased vocabulary;
                    Learning games and skills;
                    Mental stimulation.

Any one of these categories is arguable — "Less reading," for instance. Nancy Larrick, Education Director for Random House Children's Books, reported in a newspaper article that television has actually produced an upsurge in children's reading. She pointed out that when Walt Disney presented his Davy Crockett series on "Disneyland," "libraries and bookshops were swept bare and publishers fell over themselves reprinting their old titles about Davy Crockett or bringing out new ones." Even the weather reports have been influential in fostering reading. They have boosted to the best seller lists books for children and teen-agers such as "Everybody's Weather," "Hurricanes and Twisters," "Everyday Weather and How It Works," etc. Miss Larrick's article concluded, "Once a child's curiosity has been aroused by television, he finds it very satisfying to turn to a book which can say so much more."

The fact is that children do a tremendous amount of viewing and since they are especially impressionable, children's programs are extremely important.

We have been using the term "children's programs." It would be more accurate to state, "programs children watch." Broadly, there are programs which appeal both to the adult and the child and there are programs specifically geared to children. Of the first category, "Disneyland" is an outstanding example. In the latter category, there is a breakdown according to age group: programs for pre-school age children, elementary school children and teen-agers. These include such programs as "Ding Dong School," "Mr. Wizard," "Captain Kangaroo," "Mickey Mouse Club," and "Zoo Parade," all of which provide a wealth of information for children and which have been highly commended. Many of these programs are of an extemporaneous nature and are not scripted. But the school age child also watches crime dramas, situation comedies, western movies, and many dramas their parents watch depending on how late the children are permitted to stay up.

CONTROVERSIAL CRIME PROGRAMS

Much of the controversy about children's programs centers around the crime programs. Every crime program is expected to follow the precepts of the Television Code: crime does not pay; the forces of good always triumph over the machinations of evil; the law is upheld.

No one disputes the fact that programs like "Dragnet" and "The Lineup" portray the excellent work of our police departments in preventing and ferreting out crime. But the argument against many crime programs is that they are much too detailed concerning methods of committing a crime and often motivate emulation on the part of juvenile viewers and listeners. Indeed, the inventiveness of the crime writer is startlingly fertile.

There have been instances, recorded in the newspapers, where some juvenile miscreants have admitted they were influenced by a television program. However, some psychologists support the theory that crime programs, if at all injurious, affect only those youngsters who are maladjusted, either mentally or socially. Poor home environment, lack of recreational activities, inadequate schooling, lack of religious influence, may be some of the causes that lead to juvenile delinquency. Slum areas are prone to breed crime. But juvenile delinquents come also from homes which are economically stable. The chances are, however, that those homes are socially unstable. A youngster with the proper home environment, with the love of his parents, with sufficient recreational outlets will seldom resort to crime. Viewing crime programs will have little effect on him, except as a form of entertainment, and, as these child psychologists have held, as a vicarious outlet.

Other authorities, such as psychiatrist Isadore Ziferstein, writing in the Journal of the Association for Education by Radio-Television (AERT), believe that the great number of crime programs on the airwaves is detrimental to children. "This large and overwhelming dosage of violence," states Dr. Ziferstein, "rather than produce a release of emotions, results in an increase of tension and anxiety. This is most obvious in five and six year olds and in children who are already moderately disturbed, taking the form of fears, nightmares, disturbed sleep, and appetite disturbances. In children who are borderline psychopaths, these programs may precipitate them over the border into overt delinquent behavior. In the large majority of older children who are relatively healthy the effects are not obvious or immediate. They are subtle and long range."

As in every life activity, there is a danger in excess. That, it seems to us, is the crux of the problem as it concerns television viewing by children. Many parents have acquired a tendency to utilize the television set as a new-fangled baby-sitter. Not enough effort is made to guide the child along the route of more active endeavors, to have more planned family activities, to get the child to read more. It is much the easiest way out to get little Willie off a harassed mother's hands by having him park for hours in front of the TV screen.

But lest the impression be gained that the onus is entirely on the parents — heaven knows how many sins of omission and commission have been fastened on parents — the writer must come in for his share of criticism. Ideally, the writer might use as a guide this question: is this the sort of program I'd want my child to watch? Too often a compromise is made between conscience and pocketbook. The writer may know what he wants to write but more often he is forced to write what the producer, agency or network believes will attract and hold an audience. Blood and thunder is an old reliable. Count the corpses in a week's video and radio dramas. Enough to keep the nation's morgues bulging!

The program producers insist they are giving the public what it wants, whether that public is adult or juvenile. As long as a program retains a high rating, it will remain on the air. But the public, except in a few instances, is evidently unaware of its power. A wholesome family-appeal program such as "Father Knows Best" was threatened with cancellation but the combined protests of viewers and TV columnists kept it on the airwaves. Very well then, it is true that the public may get what it wants. The writer, if he has not been reduced to the status of out-and-out hack, will welcome the opportunity to write finer, more creative programs, but he must have the support of the audience.

It is doubtful whether the crime writer is afflicted with a guilt complex and spends weekly sessions on the psychoanalyst's couch. He knows that the crime story has long been accepted as a part of our literature, ever since Edgar Allan Poe brought a new type of writing to the American scene. He knows, too, that many of the mystery and suspense programs he writes are mild and innocuous compared to many of the so-called fairy stories that almost every child reads or has read to him. No continuity acceptance department would permit such scenes of sadism and brutality on any crime program that appear in many of Grimm's Fairy Tales.

Let us examine two famous classics, "Cinderella" and "Hansel and Gretel." This is how "Cinderella" concludes:

"As the bridal party was going to the church, the elder [sister] was on the right side, the younger on the left, and the doves picked out one of the eyes of each of them. Afterwards when they were coming out of the church, the elder was on the left, the younger on the right, and the doves picked out the other eye of each of them. And so for their wickedness and falseness they were punished with blindness for the rest of their days."

That is a scene which the television version of "Cinderella" never included!

And from "Hansel and Gretel":

"Although the old woman appeared to be so friendly, she was really a wicked old witch who was on the watch for children, and she had built the bread house on purpose to lure them to her. Whenever she could get a child in her clutches she cooked it and ate it, and considered it a grand feast."

Later on in the story:

"She [the witch] hobbled up and stuck her head in the oven. But Gretel gave her a push which sent the witch right in, and then she banged the door and bolted it.

" 'Oh! Oh!' the witch began to howl horribly. But Gretel ran away and left the wicked witch to perish miserably."

Is it conceivable that any television script writer could insert a scene in his script of an old woman being pushed into an oven and have it presented on the air? Definitely not.

The point is that wise parents will certainly not bring up their children on a steady diet of fairy stories. Nor should they permit their children to watch a steady stream of crime stories. As there is a great variety of books, so there is a great variety of television programs, some of which may help to inform and enlighten the growing youngster.

FACTORS FOR MAINTAINING INTEREST

The most popular children's programs on television generally include three basic elements:

1. A strong story;
2. Constant action;
3. Personal identification.

These elements characterize such programs as "Lassie," "My Friend Flicka," "Rin Tin-Tin," "Fury," and "Circus Boy." All of these programs are strong on plot, move forward swiftly from crisis to crisis, and one of the main characters is a youngster with whom the child viewer may identify himself. Note also that in four of the children's programs we have mentioned, the title character is an animal. Children love pets and often have strong attachments to a dog, or if they are in rural areas, to both a horse and a dog.

Children are normally hero worshippers. They look upon their parents as towers of strength. You have often heard a child remark: "My Pop can do anything!" That hero worship is carried, empathically, to his television viewing. The child in the story has a father, a guardian, a friend who performs heroically and who always wins out in the end.

Morally, children's programs always demonstrate the triumph of good over evil. The child at home, in school and in church has been taught this precept. He expects it and he must never be disappointed. With his very vivid imagination, he becomes part of the play he is watching. It is a living thing to him. And is not the art of playwriting the ability to create an atmosphere of verisimilitude?

THE IDEAL

Surely, the ideal children's program would be one that combines sufficient action to hold the child's attention and sufficient information to stimulate him for the good. Disney's remarkable films of the animal, the insect and the flower world are as close to the ideal as we can get. They are so far above the general run of television film fare that they must be considered in a class by themselves. Their appeal is universal.

"MICKEY MOUSE CLUB"

When Walt Disney was asked to produce a television series specifically for children, the result was the "Mickey Mouse Club," presented daily on the ABC network. The nation's radio and television critics voted it the best children's program for 1956. It is a happy admixture of songs, dances, games and educational films. The Disney organization has been kind enough to grant us permission for the reproduction of one of their typical shooting scripts. It is called "Fun with Music" and presents "Basketballet," a clever and frolicking juxtaposition of basketball and ballet dancing. In the "Eileen" sequence that follows "Basketballet," note how the children are introduced to classical music. The children viewing the program will react sympathetically to the applause of the basketball players and the ballet dancers at the conclusion of Eileen's playing.

(*The format of this script is also typical of video film scripts and should serve as a guide to the writer. Note the numbering of shots, single spacing, and use of lower case for stage directions.*)

MICKEY MOUSE CLUB TV SHOW
FUN WITH MUSIC — Prod. 8206-083
"BASKETBALLET & EILEEN SHOW"
Larry Orenstein/Sid Miller/
Tom Mahoney —

PART I
   FADE IN:
  1. INT. — ONE END STYLIZED GYM — MED. SHOT — FIVE GIRLS
     (DOREEN, DARLENE, SHARON, MARGENE, CHERYL)

There is a suggestion of high large grilled windows in the bg. Basket and board hang from what appears to be an overhanging balcony. Area in front of basket is taped to resemble basketball court. The five girls in ballet costumes are practicing a ballet step, as EILEEN accompanies them on the old beat up upright piano, which is off to one side. MUSIC: A FEW BARS of the waltz, "High

School Romance." The phrase comes to a conclusion, and the girls hold a pose with their arms extended.

Suddenly a basketball is bounced into the outstretched hands of the lead girl (Doreen). Immediately o.s. VOICES of boys in high excitement, AD LIBBING: "Okay, Bobby," "Come on Lonnie, let's go," "Come on guys, let's get a little pep into it," etc.

MUSIC SEGUES immediately into high school rouser type song. BOBBY, LONNIE, LARRY, J.J., DENNIS, come running out onto the court from the direction presumably of the locker room, bouncing basketballs, jumping, etc. CUBBY is with them as mascot.

BOBBY

(*stopping boys'
activity*)

Hold it fellows —

(*takes ball from
Doreen, passes it.
— To girls*)

What are you doing here?
We're scheduled to practice
today!

DOREEN

What are *you* doing here?
We're scheduled to *rehearse*
today!

BOBBY

But — we've got a game Friday!

DOREEN

We've got a show Friday!

Cubby leaves group and goes over to piano with Eileen. The basketball players are on one side, ballet dancers on the other.
MUSIC: BELL TONE. The two groups sing "THE PROBLEM."

2. BASKETBALL PLAYERS & BALLET DANCERS

BOYS
WE GOTTA PRACTICE SHOTS!

GIRLS
WE GOTTA LEARN GAVOTTES!

BOYS
(to girls)
WE'VE GOT A GAME IN A COUPLE O' DAYS!

GIRLS
(to boys)
WE'VE GOTTA PRACTICE TOUR JETÉS!

4 bar fill, during which two groups walk away FROM CAMERA.
They stop, boys huddle, girls lean over trying to overhear.

BOYS
(to each other)
WE CAN'T PRACTICE FOR ANY GAMES,
TRIPPING OVER THE DANCING DAMES!

(to girls)
WE'RE ASKIN' YOU POLITELY,
WON'T YOU KINDLY GO?

Both groups are back up front, they stop.

GIRLS
WE WON'T LEAVE AND RIGHTLY,
WE MUST REHEARSE OUR SHOW!

They turn backs to each other.

ALL
IT'S A

BOYS
PROBLEM!

GIRLS
PROBLEM!

BOYS
PROBLEM!

GIRLS
PROBLEM!

BOYS
PROBLEM!

GIRLS
PROBLEM!

BOYS
PROBLEM!

GIRLS
PROBLEM!

ALL
(to audience)
WE'RE ASKIN' EVERY BOY AND EVERY MISS!

BOYS
PROBLEM!

GIRLS
PROBLEM!

BOYS
PROBLEM!

GIRLS
PROBLEM!

BOYS
PROBLEM!

GIRLS
PROBLEM!

BOYS
PROBLEM!

GIRLS
PROBLEM!

ALL
(to audience)
'D'JEVER SEE A PROBLEM TOUGH AS THIS?

Boys and girls face each other and sing Fugue simultaneously:

GIRLS	BOYS
(practicing steps)	(each going behind girl)
WE — MUST —	WE REFUSE TO GIVE AN OUNCE —
TRY — OUR —	WE GOTTA HAVE SOME ROOM TO
	BOUNCE —
GRANDE — JETÉS	WE — ARE — RIGHT, RIGHT, RIGHT!
WE — MUST —	WE GOT A BIG GAME COMIN' UP —
PRACTICE — OUR —	WE GOTTA WIN THE LOVIN' CUP —
PLIÉS!	WE MUST — FIGHT, FIGHT, FIGHT!

4 BAR fill.

BOYS
WE GOTTA HAVE THE GYM!

GIRLS
(*pose*)
WE GOTTA STRETCH OUR LIMB!

BOYS
WE GOTTA STAY AND PRACTICE DRIBBLING!

GIRLS
PLEASE GO 'WAY AND STOP YOUR QUIBBLING!

4 BAR fill.

3. BOYS
in huddle.

BOYS
(*to each other*)
WE CAN'T PLAY WITH THE GIRLS ON THE COURT!

CUT TO:

4. GIRLS
in huddle.

GIRLS
(*to each other*)
WE CAN'T DANCE WHILE THE BOYS CAVORT!

CUT TO:

5. BOYS

BOYS
(*to girls*)
GIRLS, WE'VE MADE OUR MIND UP,
WE'RE HERE AND GONNA STAY!

CUT TO:

6. GIRLS

GIRLS
(*to boys*)
FINE, AND HERE'S THE WIND UP:
WATCH US DO BALLET!

7. MED. SHOT — BOYS AND GIRLS

ALL
IT'S A —

BOYS
PROBLEM!

GIRLS
PROBLEM!

BOYS
PROBLEM!

GIRLS
PROBLEM!

BOYS
PROBLEM!

GIRLS
PROBLEM!

BOYS
PROBLEM!

GIRLS
PROBLEM!

ALL
WE'RE ASKIN' EVERY BOY AND EVERY MISS —

BOYS
PROBLEM!

GIRLS
PROBLEM!

BOYS
PROBLEM!

GIRLS
PROBLEM!

BOYS
PROBLEM!

GIRLS
PROBLEM!

BOYS
PROBLEM!

GIRLS
PROBLEM!

ALL
'D'JEVER SEE A PROBLEM TOUGH AS THIS?

Boys and girls sing Fugue simultaneously as before:

GIRLS	BOYS
WE — MUST —	WE REFUSE TO GIVE AN OUNCE —
TRY — OUR —	WE GOTTA HAVE SOME ROOM TO BOUNCE
GRANDE — JETÉS	WE — ARE — RIGHT, RIGHT, RIGHT!
WE — MUST —	WE GOT A BIG GAME COMIN' UP —

PRACTICE — OUR —   WE GOTTA WIN THE LOVIN' CUP!
PLIÉS!   WE — MUST — FIGHT, FIGHT, FIGHT!

MUSIC into INTRO of "THE PROBLEM."

8. MED. SHOT — BASKETBALLET

As it progresses, it becomes a mixup in which the boys and girls
simultaneously try to dance and play basketball in the same area.
It builds to a mixup finish, with the boys doing ballet, and the
girls playing basketball, triumphantly.

FADE OUT:

COMMERCIAL

PART II
    FADE IN:
9. INT. GYM (AS BEFORE) — MED. SHOT — PLAYERS AND DANCERS

MUSIC of the Basketball Ballet has just come to a conclusion. There
is excitement and AD LIB VOICES: "Gee that was great!", "See you at
the game Friday," "See you at the show," etc. . . . As they exit,
CAMERA PUSHES IN to MED. SHOT of Eileen and Cubby. Eileen is
still sitting on the piano bench. Cubby is leaning against the piano.
As the excited VOICES DIE AWAY O.S., Eileen looks up, sees Cubby.

EILEEN
Aren't you going to be in
the game Friday?

CUBBY
Naw . . . I'm just a substitute.
Are you going to be in the show
Friday?

EILEEN
I — I don't think so.

CUBBY
But you play piano real
good!

EILEEN
Thanks — but the kids like
jazz, and — I only play
the classics.

CUBBY
Oh. — Say, why don't you
learn to play jazz? I'm

a drummer, and we could
play together!

               EILEEN
              (*brightening*)
Could we? That's a wonderful
idea, Cubby!

           VOICE (O.S.)
Come on, Cubby!

              CUBBY
          (*to* O.S. *player*)
Okay — okay! — See you
later, Eileen.
           (*he leaves*)

               EILEEN
          (*watching him go*)
S'long, Cubby.

She quickly turns around at the piano and plays a few bars of what
she intends to be a great boogie woogie. Somehow the left hand
doesn't care what the right hand is doing.

It doesn't sound right to her. She stops playing. Still thinking of
Cubby, she realizes that he'll have to like her as she is. She starts
playing her favorite classical selection, "FOR ELISE" by Beethoven.

As she becomes lost in the mood of the piece, CAMERA PUSHES IN
to her hands.

                 MATCH DISSOLVE TO:

10. CLOSE SHOT — EILEEN'S HANDS

playing continuation of "For Elise." CAMERA PULLS BACK revealing
Eileen in a formal, playing a concert grand piano. The set is still
the Gym, but now the lighting reveals it to be a very enchanting
place. CAMERA PUSHES IN TO CLOSE SHOT of Eileen's hands for
final notes of concert. O.S. APPLAUSE and CHEERS are heard as we

                 MATCH DISSOLVE TO:

11. CLOSE SHOT — EILEEN'S HANDS

on keyboard of beat up upright piano. LIGHTING, etc. is the same
as in the opening Gym SHOT. APPLAUSE and CHEERS continue, as we

                     CUT TO:

who have been listening o.s. They press in to congratulate Eileen. CAMERA PUSHES IN to THREE SHOT as the kids AD LIB their excited reactions to her playing.

> DOREEN
> Eileen, we want you on the
> show, Friday!

Cubby comes over and gives Eileen the "okay" sign, and shakes her hand in congratulations.

> GIRL
> And please play that same
> number! You're great!

> BOBBY
> And Cubby — in the game
> this Friday, you start at
> center!

Eileen gives Cubby the "okay" sign and shakes hands with him, as the kids react with unbounded enthusiasm. CAMERA PUSHES IN to TIGHT TWO SHOT of Eileen's and Cubby's beaming faces, and Cubby does a double take. AND FAINTS.

> FADE OUT.

The educational
program

23

The drama of television does not lie entirely in the play. There is an extensive new field opening and its possibilities are indeed limitless. We have accepted television as an unparalleled medium of entertainment and of information. It is now also becoming an instrument of education.

When, in 1952, the Federal Communications Commission reserved a part of the broadcasting spectrum for educational television stations, the door was opened for pioneering, for experimentation, and for a new fulfillment. Now we know this may sound overly optimistic. But as the October 1956 report of the Joint Council on Educational Television (JCET) observes: "While the full utilization of reserved television channels by no means has as yet been realized, what has already happened represents one of the greatest achievements in the history of American education."

There have been 258 channels reserved for educational use, largely in Ultra-High Frequency (UHF) channels. As of this writing, twenty-three educational television stations are now on the air and eight stations under construction. This is a promising figure when we consider the high cost of constructing television transmitters and studios and the expense of the equipment. The problem of financing these stations is a formidable one since by regulation they must be operated on a non-profit basis. But the JCET reports that during the past four years, educational stations have received more than $40,000,000 from both public and private interests. In addition, more than thirty states have appointed commissions to report on the use of educational channels.

EDUCATION ON TELEVISION

Why special educational television stations? There are, of course, programs which we may classify as educational on the networks.

"Omnibus" produces many excellent cultural features. The documentary series on the Federal Constitution with the vibrant commentary of Joseph Welch, the dramatic events in the life of Abraham Lincoln, the brilliant discourses by Leonard Bernstein on the nature of jazz, the classics and musical comedy — all this is television of a very high order. On a comparable scale was "The Search," produced by CBS, a 26-week series dealing with vital research projects in progress at the country's leading universities. And NBC's "Wide, Wide World," as its title implies, is literally broadening our horizons.

Many stations have Educational Directors. There are also instances of college professors scheduled on commercial stations for courses of instruction, an outstanding example of which is "Shakespeare on TV," a course of televised lectures by Dr. Frank C. Baxter, Professor of English at the University of Southern California. These programs were begun on Station KNXT in Los Angeles and received such wide acclaim that they were carried by the CBS network. As a result, Dr. Baxter has been called upon for other educational efforts, notably, as narrator for the Bell Telephone Company's enlightening documentary, "Our Mr. Sun."

The recent report, prepared by a staff member of the U.S. Office of Education and published by NARTB, shows the extent to which commercial stations are cooperating with local educators. Some 531 programs were presented during the 1956 school year in 144 cities over 198 local TV stations.

We can only hope that with the educational level of the country steadily rising, the audience for educational programs will increase.

Nevertheless, commercial stations depending on advertising revenue for their existence must, perforce, present programs which have a large mass appeal. These programs must be scheduled at an optimum time which means that non-revenue programs are scheduled, generally, at non-saleable times or when the least audience is available. There is little point in presenting an adult education program at eight o'clock Sunday morning. Also, full commercial schedules prevent stations from devoting any substantial amount of time to truly educational programs. Therefore, in order to present any kind of concrete and continuous programming, it is imperative that special channels be made available to educational television.

Today, educational television stations are providing a wide variety of programs: adult education series, college courses for credit, children's programs, cultural improvement programs designed to stimulate the reading of good books and to enhance public interest in museums, art galleries, parks and gardens, good music, fine drama and similar subjects.

Unlike the commercial networks, which are highly competitive, and whose program ideas are labeled top secret while in the conceptual stage, the educational stations are anxious to help each other and to exchange ideas and programs. Through the facilities of the Educational Television and Radio Center in Ann Arbor, Michigan, programs developed by educational stations are made available for national distribution. Recently, the Ford Foundation gave the Center a grant of $6,000,000 to expand its program service. At this writing, the Center has developed or acquired more than one hundred series totaling more than 1200 television programs. And so, instead of exclusivity, there is wholehearted cooperation.

A most exemplary decision was revealed by NBC at its thirtieth anniversary celebration in Florida. The network stated it was going to produce a special series of programs for educational TV stations, to encompass the fields of mathematics, music, government, literature, world geography and economics.

The first of these educational programs was on the subject of American literature, and featured Walter D. Edmonds' novel, *Drums Along the Mohawk*. Mr. Edmonds read a selection from his book and several scenes were acted out by a stellar cast, including Julie Harris, James Daly and Ed Begley. The lecturer on this initial program was Dr. Albert B. Van Nostrand, Associate Professor of English at Brown University. This NBC series, produced in cooperation with the Educational TV and Radio Center, is fed live to the educational network daily at 6:30 to 7:00 P.M. It is presented in 13-week segments and is an invaluable contribution to educational television.

The writer should find educational television a true challenge. He will have to combine the intellectuality of scholarship with the showmanship of entertainment. It is not by any means a simple task but it is always a stimulating one. In helping to create programs, he may be working more with ideas than scripts, for he is apt to find himself a combined writer-producer-director. Many of his programs will be aimed at a very specific audience to meet the needs of particular age groups. Assuredly, he will discover that there is room for experimentation, much of which will depend on his own ingenuity in overcoming the obstacles of budgetary limitations.

What we have been discussing briefly, thus far, in relation to programming may be termed education *on* television. Now, suppose we examine education *by* television, or television as a teaching tool. Here, too, the writer plays his part.

EDUCATION BY TELEVISION

There has been so much said and written about the shortage of teachers that by now any thinking person must be aware that we are faced with an overwhelming problem. Skyrocketing school enrollment is intensifying the shortage and unless there is a concerted recruiting campaign, we are going to find ourselves either limiting education or increasing our already overcrowded classrooms. Colleges may feel justified in raising their requirements to limit enrollments but it is manifestly unfair to deny educational facilities to those who desire it. The point has been raised that not everybody needs a college education anyway. But this may result in a denial of opportunity. Business has steadily raised its employment requirements so that over the years a high school education is practically mandatory and many firms today require their employees to have college degrees. The standards are bound to rise.

In any event, elementary education is compulsory and it is in the elementary schools that the teacher shortage is most acute. It is our not very original opinion that bringing teachers' salaries up to the level of bricklayers and truck drivers would do much to alleviate the situation. However, since this entails higher taxes . . . unless some bright young economist has meantime discovered an alternative method . . . the question of teacher pay will always involve a long drawn-out battle between the salary liberals and the salary conservatives.

The question arises now: can television help this situation? Can teaching be done effectively by television? And what specifically is the writer's role?

The fact is that teaching by television is being done successfully in many cities. A great deal of experimentation is also taking place over closed-circuit such as the Hagerstown, Maryland, project, where the entire county school system participated. Alexander J. Stoddard recently completed a report entitled, "Schools for Tomorrow — an Educational Blueprint." This study of television's effect on the classroom was sponsored by the Fund for the Advancement of Education. Mr. Stoddard predicted that closed-circuit television would be the best solution for teacher shortages and skyrocketing enrollments. He envisioned classrooms of 150 to 300 pupils taught by specialists. Not all subjects could be taught in this manner but physical education, art, music, modern languages and many phases of other subjects, he believes, are readily adaptable to TV instruction. However, television must be regarded as a tool to assist the teachers, not supplant them. To learn how this teaching tool does function, let us study, in brief, how one community operates.

CHANNEL NINE — ST. LOUIS

For several years now, the city of St. Louis has been taking giant strides in its development of education by television. It has tackled some difficult problems and proved that television can be a highly effective teaching tool. It has proved also that teaching by television does not mean simply placing a camera before a teacher. Many teachers, who are more than adequate in the classroom, are completely ineffective before the camera. The point is, that as in any other phase of television, educational programs require special planning and skilled personnel.

The School Programs Department of KETC, Channel Nine, St. Louis, is under the direction of Clair R. Tettemer. His staff consists of nine people including two writer-producers, two production assistants, an elementary program consultant and a spelling teacher, all on a full-time basis. Seven other teachers participate, on a part-time basis. Studies are made continually to determine in what areas television can do the best job and is most needed.

A specific instance is the state requirement that the Missouri Constitution and the Federal Constitution be taught in the eighth and ninth grades. There were comparatively few problems relating to the teaching of the Federal Constitution. A multitude of textbooks thoroughly cover all its aspects. However, the study of the Missouri Constitution did present problems. First of all, the State Constitution is itself a complex instrument. Secondly, of the two paper-bound textbooks on the subject, one was already out of print. As a result, teachers found the Missouri Constitution a most difficult subject for the classroom.

The School Programs staff met with several teachers to discuss ways and means of visualizing the difficult concepts of the State Constitution. Finally, these concepts were refined to twelve. The writer-producers, who were educationally oriented, then set about to develop visual methods. Many teachers were auditioned until one was found with sufficient talent to handle the program on the air. This teacher, working closely with the production staff, prepared a basic outline of the subject matter. This, in actuality, was his script: a detailed outline. Instructing monologues were also outlined. The television teacher was an instructor who had taught the subject, who had considerable audio-visual background, and the talent to explain abstract ideas in concrete form.

The Missouri Constitution series is presented as a seven-week series of fourteen programs. Two different lessons are telecast each week and study guides are issued as an adjunct to the television programs. In the Foreword of the Study Guide, there is a cogent explanation of the relation of the television program to the classroom:

"The television program is not intended to be an end in itself, nor may it be the most important element in the total learning process that occurs in the classroom. Pre-program and post-program activities will add much to the effectiveness of the broadcasts. However, what is done and how much is done must be left to the discretion of the individual teacher."

The Missouri Constitution is only one of many programs produced by KETC. These programs include "The Science Shelf," and "The Storyteller," both of them making excellent use of a visual medium that has unlimited potentialities in the teaching field.

"THE ART CART"

Educational television programs for children appear to be especially successful and this is very heartening. "The Children's Corner," produced by WQED, Pittsburgh's Educational Television Station, met with such an enthusiastic response that it was selected for nationwide viewing by the National Broadcasting Company. In Houston, Texas, a series called "The Art Cart" has recently been awarded the Ohio State Institute's first award for children's programs (out-of-school viewing).

"The Art Cart" is an outstanding example of cooperation between a school system and a commercial television station. The programs are presented each Saturday morning by the Department of Audio-Visual Education and the Department of Art Education of the Houston Public Schools over the facilities of KPRC-TV. It is described as an "out-of-school television experience for boys and girls in the upper elementary grades." Response to this program series has shown, however, that it has a very wide appeal ranging from kindergarten to junior high. It also serves to assist teachers and parents in furthering the child's interest in art both at school and at home. Guides, which include brief outlines of the programs, and many reference aids have been made available to parents and teachers.

The television teacher for "The Art Cart" is Mrs. Audrey Wrye who appears on every program, but the children are chosen from different classes which gives every school a chance to participate. The typical "working script" reproduced below will give you an idea of how these programs are handled. But first, a few observations before we get to the script.

The questions, answers and comments as they appear in the script are really a draft. However, they serve an important function. They give the program a beginning, a middle and an end. The television teacher and her performers know where they are going, and what they are going to do. There are adequate rehearsals but there is no memorizing of script. You will note, as you read the script, that there are blank spaces after certain questions which indicate ad lib answers by the children. Mrs. Dorothy Sinclair, Supervisor of Radio and Television for the Houston Independent School District, explains the program procedure as follows: "We rehearse until we have an idea of where the program should be at every point but we ask the children not to memorize any portion of the proceedings, and to keep their responses natural. Each day, we try to ask questions that are worded differently but have the same essential meaning. It is a technique which we have found to be quite effective, sometimes surprising, but always fun for the participants and the viewers."

Astronomical costs of television programming to the contrary, Mrs. Sinclair further notes that the entire outlay for supplies and materials for a year's series was $200!

OPEN WITH FILM CLIP 35 SEC SOF
CUT TO ART CART WITH OPEN LID ON WHICH IS SIGN: "FROM TOES TO TIPS" WITH MRS. LAURA LEE'S FIFTH GRADE PUPILS FROM POE SCHOOL

0:15 ANNCR. OVER MUSIC ON FILM

ANNCR: Yes, here comes The Art Cart — filled with all sorts of materials that you will need to create pictures and objects that are fun to make and give you a chance to exercise your imagination. Today the program is called, "From Toes to Tips" and it's time to see what Mrs. Wrye has in The Art Cart for us. . . .

OPEN ON TOES OF TWO DANCERS IN THE SET PAN UP TO DANCERS AS THEY BEGIN TO DANCE
OVERALL OF DANCERS. . . . TIME WRYE AND PAINTERS WILL BE AT TABLE WATCHING DANCERS
CU OF #5
CU OF #3
DANCERS WILL JOIN THE SET AND STAND BEHIND THE PAINTERS AND WRYE

MUSIC IN STUDIO
WRYE: How does it make you feel?

BETSY: It makes me want to move.
STEVE: I feel good inside.

WRYE: How do you suppose the

CU OF #4 STANDING

CU OF #5 STANDING
OVERALL OF GROUP

CU OF #1 STANDING

OVERALL OF GROUP

CU OF #2 STANDING

OVERALL OF GROUP

CU OF #3 STANDING
OVERALL OF GROUP

CU OF #5 STANDING

MUSIC UP — DANCE OF THE
CLOWNS 1 MINUTE. SOUND IN
STUDIO

dancers feel besides tired? Maybe
we had better ask them.

DONNA: I feel like I'm in a fairy
land.

SUE: I just feel whirly.

WRYE: What kind of dancing
were you doing?

SHERRY: It is really interpretive
dancing.

WRYE: What do you mean by interpretive dancing?

SHERRY:

SUE: We have studied ballet a
little and. . . .

WRYE: Could anybody do this
kind of dancing?

SHERRY:

WRYE: How do you know what to
do to the music?

STARR: If the music sounds like
twirls, you twirl. . . .

SUE: We don't lead the music, the
music leads us.

WRYE: Have you ever seen a famous ballet?

DONNA:

MIKE:

WRYE: Interpreting music with
dancing sounds very exciting. If I
play another record do you think
that you would do the same thing
that you did to the Nutcracker
Suite?

SUE: We don't lead the music, the
music leads us so I don't imagine
we would.

WRYE: Let's try it. Did you feel
the rhythm of the music, and did
you make your feet move to the
rhythm? Is there any other way to

CU OF #1 SITTING

CU OF #5 SITTING

CU OF #2 SITTING

OVERALL OF GROUP

CU OF #1 SITTING
CU OF #4 STANDING

OVERALL OF GROUP

CU OF #5 SITTING
OVERALL OF GROUP

interpret music other than dancing to it?

VALERIE: That's where we come in. You can get the same feeling on paper.

WRYE: How can you do this, Valerie?

VALERIE: By painting to it.

WRYE: How did you combine music, dancing and painting at school?

BETSY:

WRYE: How do you know what to put down on your paper?

WAYNE: You really have to stop, look and listen, then you are ready to paint.

WRYE: If you are going to paint ballet, what does every picture need to have in it?

STEVE: People.

WRYE: In drawing ballet figures, what part of the figure gives you the most trouble?

MICKEY: The legs. . . .

WRYE: Any other trouble?

VALERIE: The feet.

DONNA: Toes are important, but only one of us dances on her toes, because to do that you must have on special shoes. The rest of us just dance on the balls of our feet.

WRYE: Whether you are on your toes or the balls of your feet though, your legs still look long and your feet are pointed.

SUE: Anybody can dance like we dance.

WRYE: Does anything else about this figure give you trouble?

BETSY: The arms. . . .

WRYE: Does this picture need anything else?

STEVE: Ballet is full of movement

so your picture should look like this movement.

VALERIE: Your picture should fit the space of the paper.

WRYE STRAIGHT TO CAMERA

Let's play all of the Nutcracker Suite now, and let our dancers dance, and our painters paint. You do what you feel like doing at home, will you? If you feel like moving with the music dance with us, but if you want to try your hand at painting ballet figures, get your water colors, tempera paints, crayons, or chalk, and watch our figures. Get plenty of this motion in your pictures, will you?

PLAY FIRST HALF OF THE NUTCRACKER SUITE WITH ALTERNATE SHOTS OF THE DANCERS AND CU'S OF THE PICTURES BEING PAINTED

CHILDREN WILL DANCE AND PAINT FOR ONE SIDE OF THE RECORD.

MUSIC IN STUDIO

AUDIO IN STUDIO AS RECORD IS BEING CHANGED.

WRYE: Steve, what kind of ballet picture is this?

2-SHOT OF WRYE AND STEVE WHILE RECORD IS BEING TURNED OVER
CU OF STEVE'S PICTURE
RESUME MUSIC IN STUDIO AND ALTERNATE DANCERS AND PAINTERS

STEVE:
WRYE: Let's finish our pictures. I believe our dancers have had a chance to catch their breath.

MUSIC WILL RESUME AND CHILDREN WILL COMPLETE THEIR PICTURES.

DANCERS WILL JOIN WRYE AT SMALL EASEL ADJOINING BOOKCASE TO DISCUSS BOOKS

WRYE: While the pictures are being finished we'll sit over here with the ballet dancers. Some of these steps you were doing looked like real ballet steps. Have there been any books written that we could read to help explain different positions for your feet?

CU OF BOOK HELD BY STARR

STARR: I found this book named "A Dance for Susie." . . .

OVERALL OF GROUP

WRYE: Ballerinas live such an ex-

CU OF BOOK

CU OF BOOKLET HELD BY SUE

CU OF BOOK HELD BY SHERRY

CU OF BOOK

OVERALL OF GROUP

CU OF SHERRY

CU OF DEGAS PRINT ON
SMALL EASEL. THE CHILDREN
DISCUSS IT

WRYE AND CHILDREN WILL

citing life, have you ever read anything about their experiences?

STARR: The name of this book is
"Prima Ballerina" and . . .

WRYE: Who was Prima Ballerina
for the Ballet Russe?

SUE: _____ was ill, and so _____
took her part in the ballet, and the
most beautiful thing about the ballet was when the lights. . . .

WRYE: I wish that we could have
all seen the ballet but at least you
gave us a sample of it. Do you
know any books giving stories
about ballet?

SHERRY: This book "Tales from
Ballet" gives the stories for many
of the most famous ballets.

WRYE: Sherry, what is this book?
Look at these beautiful pictures.

SHERRY: This book is "The Little
Ballet Dancer," and it's the story
about a little girl who lives in
France and wants to be a ballet
dancer.

WRYE: These pictures remind me
of a famous French painter who
painted ballet dancers. His name
was Degas. Do any of you know
anything about him?

SHERRY: He was born in Paris
and. . . .

WRYE: Degas was famous for his
pastel ballet dancers and I have a
print of the Ballerinas over on the
bulletin board. Where do you think
they are?

SHERRY: It looks as if they are
back stage.

WRYE: What makes you think
that?

DONNA: See the curtains and the
stage manager?

WRYE: Two of the girls who were

JOIN PAINTERS ON FLOOR IN
FRONT OF LARGE EASEL TO
EVALUATE PAINTING

painting your pictures while you
were dancing were using colored
chalk. Do you suppose we have
several budding Degas over here?
Let's look at the finished pictures,
should we?

WRYE AND CHILDREN WILL SIT
IN FRONT OF THE EASEL AND
EVALUATE THE FINISHED
PICTURES
WRYE STRAIGHT TO CAMERA

WRYE: I hope that if you painted
at home with us today, you will
take your pictures to school so we
can show them on The Art Cart
next Saturday. Last Saturday we
worked with clay and some boys
and girls from Pugh School dug
clay out of the yard like we suggested.

CU OF ARTICLES IN BOOKCASE
AS WRYE DISCUSSES

WRYE WILL WALK TO THE BOOKCASE WHERE ARTICLES SENT IN
WILL BE SHOWN AND TALKED ABOUT.

SLIDE: "SELF-ADDRESSED
ENVELOPE"
SLIDE: "1300 CAPITOL"
WRYE STRAIGHT TO CAMERA

WRYE: Have you sent for your
booklet yet? . . . .
The name of our program next
Saturday is "The Egg and Eye."
We are going to use our eyes to
discover how to decorate Easter
Eggs. See you next Saturday at
11:00.

SLIDE #1: "PRESENTED AS A
PUBLIC SERVICE BY KPRC-TV"
SLIDE #2: "WITH THE AUDIO-
VISUAL AND ARTS DEPTS. OF
HOUSTON SCHOOLS"
SLIDE #3: "ON TODAY'S
SHOW. . . ."
SLIDE #4: "PRODUCTION
SUPERVISED BY
MRS. DOROTHY SINCLAIR"
MUSIC UP AND OUT TO CLOSE

THE WRITER AND THE TEACHER

In many of our large cities, educational television stations are filling a need both in and out of school. Their programs may never reach the astronomical ratings of a variety show on commercial TV, but their audience is growing, which is proof positive that at least some segment of our population not only likes to be entertained but also likes to learn.

The writer should not overlook the educational television field. He will not get rich, but not all profits are counted in gold. He will help others to gain knowledge and by doing so he will gain more knowledge himself. He will have the satisfaction of knowing that unlike the gag-line programs laughed at today and forgotten tomorrow, the programs he works on will have staying power. He can have the hope, too, that as the intelligence level of the nation keeps rising, the demand will increase for more meaningful programming.

Parenthetically, we may observe that the maturity of teaching by television will develop a special breed of instructors. They may be found within the current teaching ranks, as some are now. Others will undoubtedly have to be recruited. They will have to have camera presence and an ability to hold attention. These specialized and talented instructors may even bring a certain glamor to the teaching profession and inspire other talented men and women to join their ranks. They will have to possess the wit, the discernment, the knowledge of the medium of a Frank C. Baxter. Perhaps you have been fortunate enough to obtain a copy of the Outline Guides for "Shakespeare on TV." If not, we should like to quote a paragraph or two from Professor Baxter's Foreword:

These telecasts will not be "academic," in the malign sense of the word. Very little will be said about dates, Shakespeare's sources, textual criticism, and the thousand and one problems that are the valid concern of the research scholar. Shakespeare has had many bad friends: pedantic critics, parsers, and elocutionists; people who regard him as a mine to be worked for quotations ("To thine own self be true"!); producers who have overproduced and overdressed his plays into circus spectacles; and people who, like the "Bardolators" of the late eighteenth century, see Shakespeare as a superman without flaw. The star system in the theater has cut and slashed the texts to heighten one man's part ("My kingdom for a horse"!) at the expense of the play the author intended. There are people who believe that Shakespeare was somebody else; two other fellows, or Francis Bacon, or the Earl of Oxford, or Marlowe, or thirty Rosicrucians — and discern puzzles where no puzzles exist. There are hot-eyed patrons of Shakespeare who see him as a writer of political and religious allegory; there are those who read into his writing more than the author ever intended; there are those who see him as a prophet of Sigmund Freud.

Let us forget all of these noisy people, and read these plays as vital and fresh literary adventures. The lecturer intends to read a great deal with you. Have your book with you during the telecast, whether you are with us in the studio classroom or sitting comfortably at home, for it is much more profitable to follow the text as you listen. Your lecturer hopes that these telecasts will be a pleasant and exciting experience. If it is not, he extends his condolences and apologies. But it will not be Shakespeare's fault.

EDUCATIONAL RADIO

It is natural that the emphasis today is on television. But radio has played and is still playing an important part in education. The introduction of FM bands somewhat parallels the utilization of Ultra-High frequency TV channels. FM gave educators a second chance in radio. In the early days of radio, many AM frequencies were allotted for educational use but only a few stations actually made full use of them. This meant that the AM frequencies were turned over to commercial outlets. It was not a very auspicious beginning for educational radio. But with the advent of FM and its vastly greater spectrum than AM, new channels could be reserved for educational stations. The prospects began to look bright. Predictions were made that eventually FM would supplant AM radio almost entirely. This prediction might well have come true were it not for the sudden mushrooming of television. Hardly had the American public become aware of the rising star of FM, when it was abruptly eclipsed by a star of even greater magnitude, TV.

Nevertheless, as we have pointed out, radio still commands a very large audience and educational radio is today performing valiant service. FM is particularly useful in broadcasts to school audiences, since it eliminates the electrical disturbances that interfere with AM broadcasting, and schedules may be maintained despite what would otherwise be atmospheric disturbances.

Since our particular interest is that of the writer, we will explore briefly the writer's role in educational radio. Many educational radio stations present special news programs which make current events come alive. Script writers prepare these programs to meet the needs of various school levels: elementary, junior high, secondary and college. Several stations present dramatizations of selected children's stories. As an aid to vocational guidance, script writers have prepared a series of interviews with men and women engaged in many types of occupations.

FM educational radio also functions as a direct teaching tool just as does teaching by television. Obviously, television has a distinct advantage over radio as a teaching device because of its ability to use all types of visual aids. But current events programs, talks, interviews, musical programs can be presented with great effectiveness in teaching by radio.

The Educational Television and Radio Center has set aside funds for the "stimulation and development of educational radio programs of national significance." In line with this aim, the Center has made grants available to educational organizations for the production of programs to be distributed nationally, thus acting as a spur to the creative talents of writers and producers in the educational field.

The National Association of Educational Broadcasters, which was organized several years ago for the mutual assistance of educational radio broadcasters, makes possible an exchange of the finest programs of each member station through a tape network.

There is, as you can see, a good deal of activity in the educational radio field, too, and if radio does lack the power of the visual, it can count on the impetus of imagination.

Writing the government program

24

One autumn, recently, a group of foreign journalists, free-lance writers and radio and television broadcasters were being escorted through the unending corridors of the Pentagon. They had come to the United States, by invitation, to study our methods of mass communication. This was one phase of their tour: government operations.

In the studio at the Pentagon they were given a briefing on how the military services produce their own programs. Most of the visitors were from countries where the broadcast media were government-owned, and there was one aspect of the briefing that puzzled them greatly: the means by which a United States government agency obtained time on the air for a series of programs. They could not understand that it was necessary for the agency to prepare a complete representative program, and have it auditioned by a network which would then make a decision as to whether or not it wanted to schedule the program. They wondered why the government agency could not simply call any network and arbitrarily command a time period.

It was explained to them that under our system of free enterprise, broadcasting is private industry, and as such, its own master. True, they were told, there is a degree of government regulation of the broadcasting industry by the Federal Communications Commission. This was made necessary by the technical limitations of frequencies and the fact that unless there were some equitable method of allocating those frequencies, the end result would be confusion.

However, the point of the above story is that government-produced programs must meet broadcast standards whether on a network or local level. In other words, they must be professional. The listener or the viewer is not prone to make any allowances. If the program fails to hold his interest, a flick of the wrist will turn the dial.

Government broadcasts fall into three broad categories:

1. Programs written and produced by the agency for United States consumption: the Public Information Program.

2. Programs written and produced by the agency for overseas consumption: the Overseas Information Program.

3. Programs written and produced by the Armed Forces at their world-wide bases: the Troop Information Program.

PERSONNEL

Radio and television writers are hired by the government through its regular civil service procedures. An Information Specialist Register was set up about 1940 for the employment of writers who had experience in one of the mass communication fields. There was an optional classification for radio which at present also includes television. The work description is outlined briefly as follows:

(Announcement No. 27. Issued: October 25, 1955. No closing date.)

"Information Specialists in the fields of radio and television plan, develop and prepare materials and conduct the necessary liaison with radio and/or television officials to arrange for dissemination of information by radio or television. In some cases they present and/or direct programs or supervise this work."

The Grades to be applied for (according to Announcement

No. 27) range from $5,440 to $11,610 a year (Grades GS–9 to GS–15). From five to six years' experience in radio or television are required. For television, however, experience in radio, visual or motion picture work may be cited. Of special interest to the student is the fact that a college degree with a major in communications may be substituted for three years of experience. A Master's degree in the same field will earn another year's experience. For a government career, therefore, your college degree is invaluable.

Note that professional experience is required for every one of the Information Specialist ratings. As a professed radio or television writer, you will be asked to submit scripts that have been broadcast. Once you have obtained a position, you may find, depending on the size of the Information Division of the Agency, that your duties are not confined to writing. In the smaller agencies you may be writer, producer, public relations advisor, and liaison official with the networks and local stations.

If your position is at the seat of government, Washington, you may find that because your activities are nation-wide, you may be doing a good deal of travelling which you should find an interesting and broadening experience. In a small sense, you are also a part of history for the information you send out, in its proper sphere, should be of vital concern to the public.

Perhaps this is as good a place as any to take up the question that you may be asking yourself. Why a government career in radio or television? Are not the opportunities and the emoluments infinitely greater in private industry? Assuredly, they are. In the matter of earning power, the government salary is limited. But in many instances, government writers' salaries are above those paid to staff writers at the larger independent stations and compare favorably with network staff salaries.

Remember, we are comparing *staff* salaries. Contract writers for the networks are paid a great deal more, depending to a large extent on the reputation of the writer. But the neophyte with his illusions of grandeur does not consider the staff writer nor the contract writer as his goal. He sets his sights on the Chayefskys, the Roses, the Serlings, the Gore Vidals, the top-notch free-lance writers whose earnings run into the six-figure category, and whose television scripts find a golden vein in other media: the movies and the theater. We would be the last to destroy the illusion. Ambition has sometimes been looked upon as more vice than virtue. But a writer should have ambition and there is nothing wrong whatever in the desire to make money, lots of it.

Still, the top of the ladder is a narrow place and there is not room for many. Without the rungs there would be no ladder and if the writer will consider that every rung is essential he may find one that will bring him an inner satisfaction, even if it is not the very top. On one of those rungs stands the government writer.

INFORMATION GOALS

When the Department of Agriculture was established in 1862, it was authorized by the Congress "to acquire and diffuse, among the people of the United States, information on subjects connected with agriculture in the most general and comprehensive sense of that word." The United States Office of Education, in 1867, was given the duty to disseminate "such information respecting the organization and management of schools and school systems and methods of teaching as shall aid the people of the United States in the establishment and maintenance of efficient school systems and otherwise promote the cause of education throughout the country."

These are true information goals. They are not propaganda or publicity in the press-agentry sense. You may be aware of the criticism that has been leveled, from time to time, at government information programs. It is neither the intent, nor does it come within the scope of this book, to enter into such controversy. Suffice it to say that much of the controversy centers around the definition of information and propaganda and this was explored rather thoroughly by the House Propaganda and Publicity Subcommittee in 1947. The Subcommittee stated that it was not "unlawful or improper for officials or employees of the federal government to express opinions or to impart factual information, if distinguished from propaganda."

Information, the Subcommittee defined as "The act or process of communicating knowledge; to enlighten"; whereas propaganda is "A plan for the propagation of a doctrine or a system of principles."

The question has also arisen as to whether government information divisions encroach on the commercial communications media and usurp some of their functions. The answer to this question is that the government information divisions exist to serve the established communications media: the press, radio and television, magazines, books. They operate as adjuncts to these media and in the case of radio and television, in which we are primarily interested, they produce their own programs in those areas which, for various reasons, the broadcasters are unable to cover fully.

There are also specialized internal areas, such as the programs produced for troop consumption and broadcast over the facilities of the Armed Forces Radio and Television Service. And, of course, there is the vast program structure of the Voice of America.

THE WARTIME PROGRAM

Although we are confining our observations on government broadcasting to the current peacetime scene, uneasy as it may be, we believe some mention should be made of the government's role in wartime as it concerns the writing and producing of radio and television programs.

Obviously, a tremendous expansion occurs in the government structure during wartime and this includes the information divisions of all agencies. There is also a great deal of difference in the personnel picture. Many of the outstanding broadcast writers are drawn into the armed forces. The majority of them perform some battle function as they did in World War II but a substantial number were requested, at least on a temporary assignment, to write and produce government programs. Many writers were assigned, as civilians, to the Office of War Information (OWI), Office of Defense Mobilization, the American Red Cross, and other agencies.

These programs played their part in helping to apprise the American public of the actual progress of the fighting through such vehicles as "The Army Hour" and "The Navy Hour." Government programs were also written and produced to maintain the morale of the American people and to obtain their fullest cooperation in donating to blood banks, in buying bonds, in saving fats, in becoming air raid wardens, in cultivating "victory gardens" and a host of other activities calculated to assist the war effort. These multitudinous campaigns were channeled through the Office of War Information. To reach the American public with the greatest impact, the four radio networks cooperated with the government in presenting a thirteen-week series under the title "This is War!" These programs, which were in format dramatic documentaries, were carried simultaneously by all the networks and reached an estimated twenty million listeners each week. They were produced by H. L. McClinton and directed by Norman Corwin, who also wrote six of the programs. The others were written by such gifted writers as Stephen Vincent Benet, Maxwell Anderson, Philip Wylie, George Faulkner, Ranald MacDougall, William N. Robson and John Driscoll. Some of our finest acting talent, in and out of uniform, helped make "This is War!" a memorable series: Paul Muni, Robert Montgomery, James Stewart, Frederic March, Raymond Massey, to name just a few. The programs were designed "to express the attitudes and aims of the government, to present and elucidate national policies to the country, and at the same time to arouse and unify the people emotionally."

There is also in wartime the need for strict censorship. Government writers were and still are subjected to security clearances, the type of clearance depending on the sensitivity of the job. All scripts were primarily reviewed by the agency's own review board, as in the War Department, and final clearances were obtained through the Office of Censorship. This was an attempt to obviate any possibility of a writer consciously or inadvertently including material in his script which would be of value to the enemy. Often the writer may have felt he was plagued and circumscribed by censorship and that deletions were picayune and needless. But he soon learned that an alert enemy could make much of what on the surface appeared to be harmless bits and pieces. However, and this is true of the government writer in peacetime or wartime, no matter what restrictions may be placed on the content of his script there are no restrictions on the quality of his writing.

By Armistice Day (now Veterans Day) 1945, most of the purely war programs left the air. There was a resurgence, however, with the outbreak of the Korean conflict. Although this was not a full-scale conflict such as World War II, many broadcasters who had retained their reserve commissions were called back to duty with the military forces. The Information Divisions of many agencies, which had been cut severely immediately after World War II, began to expand. Among other programs, the Defense Department produced two radio series, "Time for Defense," presented over the American Broadcasting Company network; "The Armed Forces Review," broadcast over the Mutual network; and a television series "Pentagon: Washington," over the Dumont network.

You may note that during World War II the only broadcast medium utilized was radio. Television had begun experimental broadcasts prior to that war, but the conflagration that swept the world halted temporarily any commercial ventures. During the period between World War II and Korea, many television stations rushed into operation and network competition began in earnest. Thus, for the first time in a war period, the United States government began utilizing the television medium. Its efforts in that direction, let us admit, were not as successful or rewarding as in radio for two reasons: lack of personnel and lack of funds.

Perhaps it may seem strange to the reader to speak of the lack of funds in respect, particularly, to the astronomical budget of the Defense Department. Nevertheless, the fact is that funds for informational activities are one of the smallest items in the governmental budget. The entire yearly allotment for public information activities of the Defense Department (Army, Navy, Air Force) is one hundredth of one per cent of the total defense budget.

Radio programs are produced at infinitely less cost than comparable television programs which explains why a small staff of professional writers and producers can prepare a satisfactory series of government documentary radio programs at a minimum cost. The budget for a series of comparable television programs is almost a thousand per cent higher.

There is an additional asset which accrues to the government program in wartime: the availability, at no cost, of leading stars of stage, screen, radio and television. These stars are constantly requested to give their services for all manner of causes during wartime or peacetime and they offer their time and their talent without stint.

Generally, because of the innumerable requests the stars receive for public appearances, they have found it wise and equitable to channel these requests through the Hollywood Coordinating Committee. This avoids burdening a few stars with impossible requests and saves embarrassment for the star and disappointment for the requesting organization.

Most veterans of World War II remember with some warmth the one radio program, produced by the War Department, which featured each week the greatest gathering of entertainers ever to appear on a radio series. It was called "Command Performance" and, as its title implied, it was a performance requested by servicemen and women. They were asked to send in their requests for any performer or any selection and these requests ran the entire gamut from having screen star Carole Landis sigh, to hearing Leopold Stokowski conduct the Philadelphia Symphony. The recording sessions were held before a "live" audience, consisting mostly of service personnel. All the entertainment unions contributed freely of their services. There was one stipulation: "Command Performance" was to be broadcast only to our troops overseas.

One of the most unusual and hilarious of the "Command Performance" series was a takeoff on the widely syndicated Dick Tracy comic strip. Its casting was fabulous: Bing Crosby as Dick Tracy; Bob Hope as Flattop; Frank Sinatra as Shakey; Dinah Shore as Tess Trueheart; Jimmy Durante as The Mole; Frank Morgan as Vitamin Flintheart; Judy Garland as Little Snowflake; Jerry Colonna as the Chief of Police; Cass Daley as Gravel Gertie; the Andrews Sisters as the Summer Sisters; and Harry Von Zell as Old Judge Hooper. Top ranking screen writers and radio writers contributed the scripts for the "Command Performance" programs.

THE WARTIME AUDIENCE

Obviously, government-produced programs during wartime command a much greater audience than they reach in peacetime. The public is anxious about the war front, about sons, husbands, and sweethearts in battle. Even the daily newscasts are not enough to satisfy their anxiety. And so they tuned in a full hour program such as "The Army Hour," which brought them a great deal more detail than a quarter-hour newscast could and on which most of the participants were service personnel at the battlefront or in training.

The appearance of stars of the entertainment world on government programs, with their tremendous "marquee" value, naturally attract a large audience. On its second anniversary program, during the Korean conflict, "Time for Defense" presented three guest stars: Ray Milland, Sid Caesar and Eddie Fisher, whose combined talents must have increased the listening audience a hundredfold.

A vigorous democracy demands that the public be fully informed of its government's activities. There are, of course, some phases of government activity, military and diplomatic, which require absolute secrecy: a new type of bomb, a radically designed jet, a hazardous diplomatic mission are examples. Agencies such as the Atomic Energy Commission, the Defense Department, the State Department, and naturally, the Central Intelligence Agency, maintain rigid security regulations. But a democracy such as ours, based on freedom of the press and freedom of inquiry, insists that the people know all the facts of government life short of those details which might palpably endanger the security of the nation. Granted that there are many differences of opinion as to where the security line should be drawn — and the arguments pro and con are endless — the commercial writer, if he differs with the agency's concept, may take his grievance to the White House or to the Congress.

On the other hand, how free is the government writer? Is he hidebound by security and policy regulations? Naturally, as a trusted employee of the government, he is expected to abide by his agency's regulations and certainly not to impart any classified information. But there is a great deal of to-do about government "red tape" and "channeling." The inference, as it concerns the government writer, is that he is enmeshed in getting clearances and having his script pass through so many hands that it becomes a most frustrating and unrewarding task. Presumably, the commercial writer is comparatively unfettered. But is he? His choice of material is limited by radio and television taboos. The government writer is necessarily confined to the activities of his particular agency. But the writer of commercial television drama, for example, finds it not unusual to have his script mauled by editors, deletions insisted upon by the sponsor's representative, changes made by the director, until at times the play that appears on the screen is far different from the original manuscript. There have been some angry letters by video dramatists to the columns of *Variety* or the New York *Times* attesting to the foregoing.

And what of the government writer's — shall we say allegiance — to his agency? Remember that the government writer is not a creator of fiction, although there are many times when that label has been hurled at him! He deals with facts, with informational and educational material. He takes what is known in public relations parlance as the positive approach. He is duty bound to avoid controversy, although this is not always possible. He is neither a tool of press-agentry nor has he been hired to ferret out the shortcomings of his agency and make those shortcomings public. The journalist or the Congressional Committee will take care of that soon enough. But he has often been criticized for presenting the positive activities of his agency, as if he were some miscreant. Would a newspaper run an editorial each week informing its readers that they were subscribing to a poorly managed, ineffectively edited paper? Would a network produce a series on its airwaves devoted to castigating the program policy of that network? Assuredly, if a newspaper reporter or a network writer disagrees with the policy of his organization, he will look for another job. The government writer must be equally honest with himself. If he is not in agreement with the policies of his agency, or feels that it is not being run to the best interest of the public, then it is more prudent for him to find a niche in another agency or return to the commercial field.

On the other hand, the government writer must not be swayed by every carping criticism of his agency. Much of the criticism may be purely political. Much of it may be justifiable. But he should understand that any large organization, no matter how efficient it appears to be, has its failings. There are very few, if any, total villains or spotless paragons of virtue. He must weigh the good against the bad and make a decision with which he can live.

TYPES OF PROGRAMS

Government radio and television programs embrace all types: documentary, interview, talk, musical, even the drama. But whereas the primary purpose of commercial programs is entertainment, the government program's raison d'être is information. This does not prevent the government program from utilizing entertainment features in order to attract an audience. There are also some government programs which may be considered pure entertainment, such as broadcasts of concerts by the official military bands. Ever since 1854, when the Marine Band began to give open air concerts at the Capitol and the White House, such concerts have become an accepted tradition in the United States.

Actually, the existence of these military bands provides a unique asset for the Defense Department in preparing radio or television programs. No other government agency has such a large body of professional musicians at its disposal. Most permanent military posts have military bands which can be effectively utilized in the presentation of local or regional programs. Many of these bands have choruses and vocalists to lend variety to musical presentations. This is a great asset to the writer, who is often writer-producer, in planning an effective broadcast series.

TALENT IN UNIFORM

Many military installations are able to put to good advantage the youthful talent that comes to it from broadcasting stations or from universities and colleges which offer courses in radio and television. This presents an interesting possibility to college students facing military service. Writers for the university radio or television outlet may find continuing opportunities for their creative talents in the public information office of a military installation.

It goes without saying that the young serviceman's primary duty is to become an efficient soldier, sailor, airman or marine. Certainly, his basic training is concentrated entirely on learning the elements of modern warfare. His mission is to learn how to defend his country, should the need arise. But the armed forces are vast in size and scope and they cover almost every conceivable type of activity, from buying food to flying jets. Public information is one of its many missions. But the personnel allotted to public information duties is a tiny fraction of the military force and cannot possibly begin to include every young man or woman with broadcasting experience. The writer who cannot obtain a public information berth while in uniform should certainly not act frustrated. If he is truly a writer, then every experience he undergoes, pleasant or unpleasant, is grist for his mill. He will find that the more varied his experience, the more he has to draw upon for his creative output.

THE RECRUITING PROGRAM

The majority of the military programs are devoted to recruitment, and almost all of the recruiting programs are musical in format. On the local level, they may be simply a series of quarter-hour recordings interspersed with a couple of recruiting announcements. On the regional level, the programs may at times be more ambitious, such as a documentary series on the opportunities available in the Women's Army Corps. Network programs have been produced using a vocalist backed by one of the official bands or a dance unit from the band, such as the "Eddie Fisher Sings" series, produced when that young singing star was serving his stint in the Army. This latter program series illustrates another aspect of talent available to the armed services, courtesy of the draft or enlistment.

The writer for government-produced recruiting programs finds himself handling mainly two types of copy: spot announcements and musical continuity.

In respect to musical continuity, the principles expressed in Chapter 11 apply equally to government programs. However, the approach to recruiting announcements, although they have some elements in common with commercial, and the general run of "public interest" announcements, must be unique. Recruiting announcements are selling careers, not products. Each military service also has its own particular assets and liabilities. The copywriter should be furnished with adequate research in order to combat negative reactions.

Today, careers in the service are open to women as well as men. It must be remembered, however, that all women who join the service do so on a voluntary basis, that is, they enlist. Therefore, the writer's approach to campaigns for recruitment of servicewomen must vary somewhat from that of recruitment of men. We must consider, also, that some segments of the population are still opposed to women serving in the armed forces. During the Korean conflict, an Advisory Committee on Women in the Service was formed by the then Assistant Secretary of Defense, Anna M. Rosenberg. The dynamic drive of Mrs. Rosenberg and the presence on the Committee of the distinguished actress, Helen Hayes, gave impetus to the creation of several radio and television scripts on the role of women in the service. This author had the good fortune to write and produce programs in which both these remarkable women participated. One of the more successful programs was a radio documentary entitled "A Letter to Joan," originally broadcast over the Mutual network and then, due to innumerable requests, made available via transcriptions to every radio station in the United States.

THE ARMED FORCES RADIO AND TELEVISION SERVICE

Wherever American servicemen and women are stationed overseas, radio goes with them. Currently, Armed Forces television stations are beginning to make their appearance even in remote outposts. Broadcasting to the troops overseas via their own radio stations began about January, 1943, when low-powered transmitters were made available in some quantity. In this way, the network programs, so familiar to the fighting men when they were back home, reached them on the continent of Europe and on the islands of the Pacific. The morale value of these programs was incalculable.

The broadcasting industry cooperated wholeheartedly then, as it still does today, in making all its radio programs available, sans commercials. It is evident that a Marine sweating it out on Guadalcanal would hardly have appreciated an exhortation to stop at the neighborhood grocery for a carton of coke! However, there appears to be a modicum of truth to the claim that many of the troops would have preferred the programs intact with commercials. Certainly, the programs would sound more like home. Nevertheless, the practice of deleting commercials from radio programs for overseas rebroadcast still continues today. It is interesting to note that television programs, on the contrary, are shipped overseas with commercials intact. The practical reason is that it entails too much expense to attempt to delete commercials from television kinescopes.

We must assume that as long as the world continues in a "cold war" status, the size of our military forces will remain comparatively large. Our troops will be stationed in many corners of the world, either on occupation duty, or, for defensive purposes, at many strategic outposts. Since broadcasting has proved itself an unparalleled morale factor in bringing entertainment and information to service personnel, it is safe to predict that radio and television stations will always be available to our overseas contingents. As of this writing, there are some 140 Armed Forces radio facilities in existence. A precise figure for television stations cannot be given since many are still either in the planning or construction stage.

Many of these overseas stations are individual broadcasters such as the radio station at Asmara, Eritrea. Others form part of various networks, such as the American Forces Network in Europe (AFN), the Far East Network (FEN), the American Forces Korea Network (AFKN), and the Caribbean Forces Network (CFN). Although the bulk of the schedule of these stations is devoted to rebroadcast of programs from the United States, there is a good deal of original, local programming. Both the network in Europe, with its headquarters in Frankfurt, and the Far East Network, with its headquarters in Tokyo, have civilian writers on their staffs. These writers are hired through the civil service and are under the jurisdiction of the Troop Information Divisions of the various military services. Military personnel at these stations are classified as broadcast specialists, and may be writers, producers or announcers.

The programs produced locally vary from on-the-scene pickups of maneuvers to full-scale historical dramatizations. A Signal Corps anniversary may provide the inspiration for a half-hour drama which portrays the development of communications in the Army. Or a dramatized documentary will deal with the "Code of Conduct." The American Forces Network in Europe produced several weekly series of radio dramas and documentaries, among which were "Command Theater," "Assignment in Europe" and "You in Europe."

Many of the "Command Theater" productions were based on Troop Information Pamphlets, such as the one entitled "Defense Against Enemy Propaganda." An excerpt from the "Command Theater" production is given below.

SOUND: BATTLE NOISES. UP AND FADE UNDER
NARRATOR: The sounds of the battlefield are not pleasant sounds . . .
SOUND: BATTLE NOISES UP AND FADE UNDER
NARR: The sounds of the battlefield are loud . . . and menacing . . .
SOUND: WHISTLE AND BOOM OF DROPPED BOMB
NARR: . . . and insistent . . .
SOUND: MACHINE GUN
NARR: . . . and *deadly*. . . .

SOUND: DEAD SILENCE. LONG PAUSE.

NARR: Have you ever heard the sounds of the *other* battlefield? Not so loud, perhaps . . . nor so menacing . . . nor so insistent . . . but, yes . . . just as deadly! More than one war has been won . . . or lost . . . on this . . . the *other* battlefield!

MUSIC: THEME

ANNCR: Command Theater!

MUSIC: THEME

ANNCR: Welcome to Command Theater . . . a weekly radio theater of drama and high adventure, reflecting the events, both past and present, which make up the exciting history of our times. Listen now to "The *Other* Battlefield," tonight's presentation on Command Theater.

MUSIC: OMINOUS-TYPE CURTAIN

NARR: The *other* battlefield. It's quiet on the *other* battlefield. The bomber and the bazooka . . . the machine gun and the mortar . . . their harsh voices are not to be heard here. Occasionally, one hears the restless chatter of the typewriter, or the ubiquitous voice of the radio . . . but even these are not necessary. Wars have been won and lost on this battlefield with little more than a whisper . . . (FADE)

SPY #1: (WHISPERING) Your Majesty, it is a sight one's eyes can scarce believe . . . they are more like monsters than men . . . (FADE)

NARR: More than seven hundred years ago, one of the greatest conquerors the world has ever set loose his Mongol forces against Europe and the Near East. This Asiatic invasion sent a shudder of fear throughout the Western World. Temujin . . . or Ghengis Khan, as we know him . . . was reputed to have at his command limitless hordes of wild Tartar Horsemen, ready to flood the world in a tidal wave of fierce attacks.

MUSIC: VERY SHORT BRIDGE

NARR: *Now,* we know that Ghengis Khan did not have such a huge army at his disposal. But he knew how to fight his war on the *other* battlefield. And, so . . . when the worried rulers of the West sent spies into the camp of Temujin, the whispering began. And when the agents returned to give their reports, the whispering continued . . .

SPY #1: (WHISPERING) . . . And they look like wrestlers, sire . . . they breathe nothing but war and blood, and show so great an impatience to fight, that the Generals can scarce moderate it . . .

SPY #2: (INTERRUPTING, ALSO IN A WHISPER) . . . And yet, sire, though they appear thus fiery, they keep themselves within the bounds of a strict obedience to command, and are entirely devoted to their prince . . .

SPY #1: (AS ABOVE) . . . And they are contented with any sort of food . . . they are not particular in the beasts they eat, like the Mohammedans. They eat not only swine's flesh, your Majesty, but feed upon wolves, bears, and dogs, when they have not other meat . . .

SPY #2: (AS ABOVE) . . . And as to their number, sire, Ghengis Khan's troops seemed like the grasshoppers, impossible to be numbered!

MUSIC: BRIDGE AND MOOD. HOLD UNDER

NARR: Ghengis Khan's troops frequently were numerically inferior to those of their opponents. They often had poorer equipment. Yet, they overran nearly all of Europe. For they faced a frightened enemy. Ghengis Khan had already won the war . . . on the *other* battlefield!

Although overseas productions permit of a wide latitude so that the writer may, for example, dramatize the short stories of Edgar Allan Poe, the productions are generally concerned with military activities. Dramatizing information pamphlets, such as the example quoted above, offers a challenge to the writer to present a militarily important message in an interesting and palatable form.

He must try to present a point of view without preachment. He is precisely in the same position as any stateside writer in creating a vehicle that will attract and hold attention. The serviceman may have only one kilocycle or channel to tune in, but there is nothing to prevent him from tuning out. Therefore, the overseas writer, although he may be somewhat limited in subject matter, must be fully cognizant of all the basic principles that make for good radio or television programming.

"The Army Hour"

In September, 1953, "The Army Hour" radio series was revived in a somewhat different format from that of its predecessor. There were more entertainment features on this new edition than its World War II counterpart. It was now a production of the Troop Information Division broadcast on all Armed Forces stations overseas. Soon after its inception, a request was made by the Mutual Broadcasting System for rebroadcast of "The Army Hour" stateside. This was rather a reversal of the usual situation but it meant that the program was now truly being broadcast world-wide.

The format of "The Army Hour" generally includes two recorded "documents," culled from the many tapes which come from far-flung Army installations to the Troop Information headquarters at the Pentagon. These "documents," which may vary from interviews with Hungarian refugees at Camp Kilmer to a reporter's eyewitness account of the firing of a guided missile, form the body of the program. The entertainment frame includes selections by the official military bands and choruses and a weekly feature, called "Guest House," on which appear outstanding entertainers currently in the Army.

Since the tape recorded "documents" are generally extemporaneous, the usual continuity for the program consists of introductions to the musical selections, and background material concerning the time, place and significance of the "documents." However, on many occasions special programs are written such as those in observance of the Army's anniversary. Since large dramatic casts are not available, the script format is that of a dramatic narrative with appropriate musical background. One of the recent Army anniversary programs, written by "Army Hour" scripter David B. Eskind, and narrated by screen, stage and TV star Dane Clark, was awarded the Freedoms Foundation Honor Medal as "an outstanding achievement in helping to bring about a better understanding of the American way of life." Although restricted to the use of one voice for the half-hour program, the broadcast had a powerful impact thanks to the combination of a sensitively written script and the perceptive delivery of the narrator.

The script tells the story of the soldier from the days of Valley Forge to the present. This is the opening:

MUSIC: TYMPANY ROLL. SUSTAIN UNDER
NARR: I am the men born of freedom and bred in liberty. . . .
I am the men of a hundred million names who marched to war and came home again. . . .
I am the lost and nameless men who fell somewhere along the way. . . .
I am the American soldier!
MUSIC: BIG STING. THEN, THE REVOLUTIONARY WAR THEME. ESTABLISH AND UNDER
NARR: Today, April 19, 1775 — the long tension is ready to break. The word has come: the British are marching on

Lexington. My choice is clear; I would make no other,
for —
>My forefathers came to this country
>To establish a land for the free.
>So my heart knows only one thing to do.
>If an honorable man I would be,
>Is to walk this land with head held high
>For the blood that runs in me.

At Lexington we say farewell to some of our slain
Minutemen, but at Concord the enemy leaves 200 dead
on the field of battle.

MUSIC: UP BRIEFLY AND UNDER

NARR: It is June — I am at Bunker Hill.
Twice they storm us; twice we exact a fearful price.
Again they come — and now, out of powder, we are beaten
back. And so, the long road of fight-and-retreat begins.
At Quebec — disaster. At Long Island — defeat.
Northward now — under General Washington's command:
Harlem Heights . . . White Plains . . . Fort Washington —
humiliating delaying actions all.
Christmas of '76 — the tide turns. With Washington we
cross the ice-ridden Delaware and take Trenton.
The New Year begins well: on January 3, Trenton is ours.

The story continues in this narrative vein: the War of 1812,
the Mexican War, the Civil War, the Spanish American War, World
War I and II and then Korea.

MUSIC: KOREAN WAR THEME, THEN UNDER

NARR: July 1, 1950 — Korea.
I am the American Soldier — the Regular, the recalled veteran,
the draftee,
Fighting again — against the Communists in North Korea.

MUSIC: UP VERY BRIEFLY, THEN UNDER

NARR: July 4th — we meet the enemy for the first time at Osan . . .
Then land unopposed at Pohang. . . .
Two days later we withdraw from Taejon.
And General Dean is listed as missing in action.
Hemmed in at Taegu. We are reinforced at the last desperate
moment; with a major landing at Inchon, we begin a
steady pushing back of the invaders:
We retake Seoul . . . cross the 38th parallel,
And capture Pyongyang, the capital of North Korea.

Now in November, we meet a strong counter-offensive
As the Chinese Communists, with 24 divisions enter the conflict.
Thru December we steadily fall back under increasing pressure . . .
Pyongyang is abandoned . . . and we fight out of a trap at Changjin Reservoir. . . .
Against terrific odds, in bitter cold, we march and fight 60 miles along a narrow, dangerously steep road. . . .
At Hungnam a hundred thousand soldiers, and as many civilians, are evacuated by sea. . . .
New Year's Eve, the Communists launch a general offensive,
And, badly outnumbered, we give up the capital city of Seoul.

MUSIC: UP BRIEFLY AND UNDER

NARR: The Communists continue to advance — south, west, and thru the center.
But in "Operation Killer" we gradually roll them back, retake Seoul on March 14.
And cross the parallel north of Chunchon in force.
Then as they unleash their spring offensive on a hundred-mile front,
Hwachon falls . . . then Nunsan — the enemy is 7 miles from Seoul.
But in June we turn loose our own offensive.
Exacting a ghastly toll of a 100,000 casualties, and 12,000 prisoners.
There is talk now of peace negotiations, but also reports of large Communist reinforcements,
So we continue the attack around Kumson. . . .
Fierce fighting for Little Gibraltar and The Punchbowl. . . .
And when we take "Heartbreak Ridge," we say it is aptly named . . . for the many lives it cost.
December now — mostly company-size actions,
But we patrol continuously —
While we wait and hope . . . for peace.
Finally, the official word has come:
Yesterday — Sunday, July 26 — the Armistice was signed,
And now, in just a few more seconds, at ten hundred hours, Tokyo Time —
Fighting will cease. . . .
It is almost here: ten . . . nine . . . seven . . . four . . . three . . . two . . . one —
The fighting in Korea is over!

MUSIC: UP TO CLOSE, SEGUE TO FINAL THEME, HOLD UNDER

NARR: From Lexington and Concord to Panmunjom . . .
        I have served my country in the cause of freedom,
        And, to have and to hold, now and forever —
            I serve her still,
            For — I am The American Soldier!
MUSIC: UP TO CLOSE

THE MILITARY AUDIENCE

It may appear at
first glance that the overseas military audience is a unique body.
Actually, it is not. It is composed of Americans of varying ages:
youngsters, fresh out of high school, or with only a smattering of
education, career non-coms with their families, lieutenants on their
first tour overseas, officers with ten to thirty years' service bringing
their families with them. They enjoy "Gunsmoke" in Heidelberg or
Sendai just as much as they did in Milwaukee or Brooklyn.

The hillbilly fans are as populous, percentage-wise, on Okinawa
as they are in the United States. The tours overseas have brought
many new experiences to the serviceman but his program tastes have
remained unchanged. And of one thing the writer may be certain:
if the program is dull, the American serviceman will simply flick the
switch. He is no slave to any ideology. He will listen to his radio or
watch his TV set because he wants to and not because he is forced to.

THE VOICE OF AMERICA

Less than three
months after the infamous attack at Pearl Harbor, the Voice of
America began its historic short-wave broadcasts from one tiny studio.
The date was February 24, 1942, and that first broadcast was directed to the German people.

Today, the Voice of America (VOA) is the radio arm of the
United States Information Agency (USIA). It has more than a
dozen specially designed studios in Washington. It broadcasts
"around the clock and around the globe" in forty-three languages.
It produces some forty program hours of direct short-wave broad-

casts each day beamed to penetrate the Iron and the Bamboo Curtains. By presidential directive, its mission is to inform all peoples throughout the world of the policies and objectives of the United States government and to counter the distortions of hostile propaganda.

The USIA uses every communication medium to bring the truth about America to other nations. However, except in rare instances, the only way to reach the countries behind the curtains is by radio. That explains why 75 per cent of the Voice's direct, short-wave broadcasts are beamed to Communist-controlled countries. Most of these broadcasts are factual news reports. Naturally, since these newscasts must be voiced in the language of the country to which they are directed, a large part of the Voice's staff is composed of linguists.

However, there are seven English broadcasts daily prepared by writer-producers or writer-announcers. Most of the newscasts for the foreign language programs are originally written in English and then translated. Major wire services are available to the VOA, including a direct line to the United Nations. In addition, the Voice has its own reporters and commentators to supplement the services of the Press Associations.

Television

In 1954, the USIA began its television activities in earnest. Before that time, most of the broadcast activities were devoted to radio which still carries the lion's share of programming. However, with the tremendous upsurge of TV in this country and the growth of television stations in overseas areas, the USIA could now turn its attention to the utilization of this new and powerful medium of communication. Experienced television personnel were available in this country, and transmitters and receivers were appearing with some rapidity overseas.

The first phase of USIA television programming consisted of weekly newsreels and a number of commercial and public interest programs, such as "Industry on Parade," "World Through Stamps," "The Firestone Hour," etc., which could be adapted, readily, for overseas presentation. All commercials were eliminated so that the "Firestone Hour," for example, became "Concert of the Air."

1955 was the transition year for USIA. Its television activities expanded greatly. Many original productions were planned and presented. One of the most successful, thus far, is a monthly series called "Report from America" and produced under contract with the National Broadcasting Company. It is a people's-eye-view of life in the United States, the everyday problems of everyday people; their jobs, their common interests, the highways they motor on, the traffic jams they gripe about, the smog in Pittsburgh and what's being done about it. "Report from America," first presented as a regular series on the BBC, elicited so many favorable comments that the programs may be expanded to reach additional audiences via French, Italian, Spanish and Portuguese productions.

A "Latin-American Round Table" which, as its name implies, is a discussion program, has been filmed for distribution to our southern neighbors. Nationals of the various Latin-American countries participate in discussions of subjects of mutual interest.

Other types of programs include a series in which a foreign commentator reports back to his native country his observations of the American scene. This may take the form of a documentary on elementary education with the reporter actually visiting American schools and talking with teachers, pupils and parents.

The potential of TV in presenting the story of America is so vast and exciting that it is impossible to predict at this early stage how tremendous its influence will be. The USIA's Sixth Review of Operations for 1956 observed that "To reach a television audience estimated at 40 million persons, USIA supplied more than 460 TV programs for telecast by 150 stations in the free world. The programs included news and special events, adaptations of domestic shows and 34 original productions."

News

The VOA newsroom is organized in the same manner as any network operation. Although, as we have stated, the VOA does make use of the major wire services, it has its own house wire service with its own editors, rewrite men, and reporters. These reporters cover the White House, and also the news conferences of any Executive Agency which may furnish items of international import. VOA reporters are stationed at the "Hill" to cover the Congressional sessions, and they are also present at the all important Summit meetings.

Staff functions vary in importance and in pay much as they

would in private industry. There are writers whose job it is to cull the daily newspapers and summarize editorial opinion. There are cub reporters who begin with the more routine assignments. Top reporters cover important "beats" such as the White House. Rewrite men and editors polish the copy for the VOA's house wire service.

The VOA newsroom is a busy place where activity never ceases. Three shifts keep the newsroom humming twenty-four hours a day, seven days a week.

Talks and features

In this branch, writers supply basic commentaries and features to each language service which, in turn, selects those most suitable for its area. These commentaries and features explain the official policies and objectives of the government and implement the basic themes of the USIA such as "Peaceful Use of the Atom," "People's Capitalism," and "The President's Aerial Inspection Plan." The following commentary, "Power for Peace," is typical.

"Power for Peace"

ANNCR: And now, here is _____ with a comment on the news:

COMM: The closing of the Suez Canal has resulted in an oil shortage in Western Europe — a matter of grave concern not only for the people of Europe, but also for Americans. If Western European economy were to suffer deep damage as a result of this shortage, the economy of the whole free world would suffer. Therefore, it is of primary importance that an unimpeded supply of fuel be available to Western Europe, whose industry plays such an important part in the economic health of many nations, both East and West.

It is hoped that the oil supply will soon return to normal, and that the nations of the Middle East — by increasing their defensive strength — will be able to fully protect the source of that supply from possible Communist encroachment. Nevertheless, the fuel shortage problem is one with long-range implications. The fact of the matter is that conventional sources of fuel, no matter how fully developed or exploited, will — in the near future — be insufficient to fill the needs of Western Europe. A recent study by the European Organization for Economic Cooperation — the EOEC — points out that by 1975 the situation could become critical.

The Suez crisis, then, merely serves to dramatize a problem which Western Europe — and, eventually, the whole world — must face: the problem of finding new sources of energy. And, long before the Suez crisis, many nations had underway programs for the development of power from nuclear reactors. An indication of the progress of such a program here in the United States may be seen in tomorrow's (February 9) opening of the first experimental nuclear power plant, at Argonne National Laboratory, in the midwestern state of Illinois. This is the first reactor built in this country solely for the experimental generation of electric power. It is part of a broad program of power for peace, which calls for the construction — under auspices of the Atomic Energy Commission — of five different types of reactors between 1954 and 1959.

In the United States, nuclear power has not yet reached what economists would call the "competitive" stage — that is, it is not yet an economically feasible or economically necessary alternative to coal, oil or even water power. In Europe, nuclear power is "competitive." It is approaching the point where it will be both necessary and scientifically and economically feasible. But at the same time, it is evident that the cost of developing an atomic energy industry is beyond the means of the countries concerned if they act individually. What is needed, it is believed, is a regional mechanism which will provide Western Europe with an atomic industry and the opportunity to build an atomic foundation for the whole economy.

Americans have watched, with the keenest interest, the development of the proposed organization known as Euratom — by which six Western European countries would combine to form an atomic co-operative. The Foreign Minister of Belgium is now in Washington, discussing the possibility of United States co-operation in the program. Earlier this week, he conferred with President Eisenhower, and reviewed the main lines of the proposals.

Such proposals, for the regional application of nuclear power toward industrial uses, would seem to reflect the spirit of Mr. Eisenhower's Atoms-For-Peace program. In his State of the Union message, last month, he declared that the United States welcomes European co-operative efforts in the field of atomic energy. For there can be little doubt that Mr. Eisenhower — like many other statesmen — sees, in European integration, at many levels, one of the best assurances of world peace and free world security.

Special events

The USIA maintains a Central Service which arranges for all coverage of special events which have international significance: a presidential election, a trade fair, an art exchange program. The event may be of special interest to an individual country. For example, if a German movie star were to appear in a Broadway production, arrangements could be made by the Central Service for a German language specialist to conduct an interview with the star.

Package programs

In some instances, the USIA will contract with a writer to prepare an entire series on a particular subject, let us say, the peaceful use of the atom. Or perhaps the package may be a series of dramatic programs. These programs generally are of greater length than those used on the regular language service. They are packaged for placement in a specific country, or countries, where the Agency's overseas officer may be able to obtain more air time over the native station.

Special services

For some time now, the VOA has been broadcasting a music series under the simple but expressive title of "Music — USA." This is a two-hour program of "pop" and jazz, the VOA's only regular music program. In order to avoid possible distortions by short-wave atmospheric conditions, tapes of "Music — USA" are sent to relay bases within easy reach of the foreign countries. Evidently, there are "pop" fans and "bop" fans everywhere, including the iron curtain countries, for "Music — USA" averages a thousand letters a month!

Religious programs are broadcast in each language on Sundays and on denominational holidays.

Language services

Each language service is a small radio station in itself. It does its own programming and has a designated number of hours assigned to it each week. Its major source of programming comes from the News Branch and the Talks and Features Branch so that the primary job of the foreign language writers is that of selection, adaptation and translation. These writers may have to make major changes in the copy provided them in order to meet the requirements of the specific area. They may take the basic idea and write completely new copy or prepare scripts of their own.

As you can understand, the foreign language writers are highly specialized. They must be well versed in the language of the country to which the broadcasts are beamed. Many of these writers are foreign born or first generation Americans.

The writer

There are many interesting and challenging career opportunities for the writer both with the USIA in the United States and overseas where the Agency is known as the United States Information Service (USIS). For job requirements, the reader is referred to the International Information Specialist Examination, issued by the United States Civil Service Commission. On assignment to the USIA, the writer faces no problem of having something to say. Every line he writes is a message in itself. He is a warrior whose greatest weapon is the truth. He will find that his factual newscasts are termed "distortions" by the Communist-controlled radio and his on-the-scene documentaries labeled "vile propaganda." But these verbal castigations are high praise to the writer for he knows he has hit home.

His scripts also face a technical obstacle known as "jamming," a method by which a Communist radio station transmits on the same frequency in order to make the broadcast unintelligible. But the VOA has its own devices to overcome "jamming" and the proof of their success lies in the many thousands of letters and word-of-mouth underground that bear ample testimony to the program's penetration.

The USIS radio or television officer may find himself stationed in any of a hundred different countries. His job overseas calls for both knowledge and diplomacy. He will work closely with the native broadcasters in placing the specially packaged radio and television programs and in assisting the station staff with any of its production or writing problems. He will also write and produce programs of his own for local consumption: perhaps a newscast of particular interest to that area or he may prepare a series of interviews with officials of his own embassy and with the native population. For a writer, this opportunity to get to know a foreign country and its people intimately is an invaluable experience.

INFORMING THE FARMER

The farmers, indispensable to the nation's welfare, have their special problems, their specific requirements. And ever since its establishment in 1862, one of the prime missions of the Department of Agriculture has been to keep the nation's farmers informed of any new developments that will make their task of tilling the soil less burdensome and more productive.

As radio transmitter towers sprang skyward in state after state, in urban and rural communities, the Department of Agriculture took advantage of this new medium to reach every farmer no matter how remote his situation. In 1928, the National Broadcasting Company, in cooperation with the Department, produced the "Farm and Home Hour" and for three decades now, Agriculture's Office of Information has been supplying the program with live and taped features and news items of special interest to farmers and homemakers. For many years, the program has also been sponsored. A companion radio series, "The American Farmer," has been scheduled weekly by the American Broadcasting Company.

Each week an "RFD Letter" is sent to hundreds of radio farm directors, bringing them news which is not readily available to them from other sources.

With the advent of television, the Department's Radio and Television Service expanded its activities. Here was a natural medium for teaching, for demonstrations, for reaching farmers with most effectiveness. Yet the Department is aware that, although its primary service is to farmers, a good deal of the viewing audience is urban. This is true because most television stations are located in urban centers. Whenever possible, therefore, scripts are tailored to include items of interest to all segments of the population. This is not too difficult since food is of common interest. With urban areas mushrooming into suburbia and extending even unto exurbia, there is a pronounced trend to more private dwellings with gardens of various sorts and sizes. To these home dwellers, programs on how to grow better vegetables and how to get rid of those pesty, parasitic insects, should be welcome, certainly not on a scale of interest to match the farmer, but welcome, nonetheless.

For concentrated local coverage, the Department of Agriculture furnishes information to County Agents stationed throughout the country. They cooperate with the local radio and television stations much in the same manner as do the military services Public Information Officers. For these County Extension Agents, the television service has prepared a succinct and very informative handbook, called "Television for You," which is a guide for the presentation of effective video programs.

In Washington, the Department of Agriculture's Television Service prepares a package series of programs for use by any individual who is producing a farm television program or series. These programs generally run anywhere from five to eight minutes in length to be used as part of the station's farm program. Topics range from a photo report on foreign trade fairs to improved methods of processing milk. This is a weekly service which includes scripts plus visuals. The visuals may be narrated film or, as many of them are, still photos and cartoons.

The portion of a typical film script, reproduced below, will give the reader a precise picture of this service.

VIDEO	AUDIO
TITLES U.S. DEPARTMENT OF AGRICULTURE FADE OUT	The United States Department of Agriculture presents . . .
FADE IN BELTSVILLE NEWSREEL FADE OUT	Beltsville Newsreel!
FADE IN PAN SHOTS OF GREENHOUSES	A report to the nation from the Agricultural Research Center near Beltsville, Maryland. From the fields, the laboratories, and the greenhouses of the Research Center come improvements for

the American farmer and gardener. Here . . . near Washington, D.C. . . . scientists in every phase of agriculture develop new and better ways to produce the food and fiber needed by a growing nation. Fifteen thousand people visited the Research Center last year.

One out of every eight came from a foreign country. And here comes another group by bus. They are bankers and soil conservation district supervisors from Louisiana. Every year these bankers and farmers go on tour together to learn more about farming. This summer they came to Beltsville. Let's join them. (NO AUDIO)

CUT TO 46 SECS.
BUS TOUR ARRIVING
MS-SAME

CUT TO
CU OF ATOMIC
ENERGY SIGN
CUT TO
1:10 SECS.
ISOTOPE
STORAGE AREA

Yes, their first stop is to study atomic energy as a research tool. Dr. Maurice Fried shows how radioactive isotopes are used as tracer bullets to learn more about the use of fertilizer by crops. Scientists fully understand the *unseen* danger of the radioactive materials they use to help build a better agriculture.

CUT TO
CU OF DANGER
SIGN
CUT TO
LS IN GREENHOUSE
CUT TO
1:53 SECS.

Here in the greenhouse, the tagged atoms are put to work. Dr. J. C. Brown is trying to learn why some crops can take iron from the soil . . . and why others can't. Radioactive iron is added to the soil in these buckets.

CU EXAMINATION
OF SOYBEANS

Two different varieties of soybeans are growing in the *same* soil. One fails to get iron from the soil. It's a light yellow . . . and stunted, but another variety is green because it gets enough iron. Dr. Brown wants to know why.

CUT TO

EXT CU
GRAFTED
SOYBEANS

Is there some weakness in the root which keeps one soybean from getting iron? Or is the problem in the top growth? These grafts may answer those and other questions. Dr. Brown believes the answer will help farmers solve some fertilizer problems . . . and also help plant breeders develop better soybean varieties.

CUT TO
2:30 SECS.
CU OF MOUNTED
PLANTS

Research men can determine *how* the plant used radioactive iron . . . through the use of X-ray film. A radioactive plant will take its own X-ray picture.

TILT DOWN TO X-RAY PIX CUT TO TITLE — KEEPING PLANTS AWAKE CUT TO 2:51 SECS. TOUR GROUP	The yellow soybean on the *left* contained no radioactive iron. So the X-ray negative on the *left* is blank. But the radioactive soybean on the *right* made a clear picture. (NO AUDIO)

Our visitors stop for the latest news on research with light and plants. These two plants are the same age. But one is short . . . and is full of flower buds. The other is tall . . . yet shows no sign of blooming. Research proved that you can force plants into flower out-of-season by shortening their daylight hours.

CUT TO

PLANTS INSIDE GREENHOUSE

In the greenhouse, we get the details. The short plants receive only eight hours of light. That forces them into early maturity. This research gives us chrysanthemums . . . the year around. The tall plants are kept awake sixteen hours. . . . They continue to grow. The two pine trees are the same age, too . . . but doubling the hours of light more than doubled the height.

CUT TO
3:30 SECS.
PLANTS BEING PLACED IN LIGHT ROOM

Dr. R. J. Downs believes that pine seedlings may be grown faster . . . by placing lights over *outdoor* seedbeds. But more research is needed.

It's time to put the short plants to bed . . . while the tall plants are kept growing under ordinary light bulbs for eight more hours behind the black curtain.

BLACK CURTAIN IS LOWERED

LIGHTS OFF

The short plants will sleep . . . for sixteen hours, thus they are fooled into believing that the long nights of winter are near.

As Dr. Downs switches off the light, some plants get ready to flower . . . others slow down their growth . . . prepare to become dormant for winter. Quiet, please. Research plants asleep!

DOOR CLOSED
CUT TO

The radio-television activities of the Red Cross fit into the scope of this chapter because the Red Cross is a quasi-governmental agency. Its Board Chairman is appointed by the President of the United States and its functions are both national and international in scope. There are hundreds of chapters throughout the country aiding the distressed in local areas and coordinating through the national headquarters in the event of any regional or national disaster. Most of us are prone to think of the Red Cross in terms of great national emergencies and we may not be aware of the many day-to-day activities of the agency that add to our health, welfare and security. These activities may vary from teaching youngsters how to swim, to helping a soldier get home to a seriously ill parent.

Ninety-eight per cent of the Red Cross workers are volunteers who give of their time and their talent without stint. But there are paid staff workers at the national headquarters and at the larger local offices.

The work of the Audio-Visual Division (Radio-TV and Motion Pictures) has three main purposes: (1) year-round interpretation of Red Cross services at national and local levels; (2) recruitment of volunteers; (3) enlisting public support during campaigns.

The radio-television branch has for many years scripted a quarter-hour dramatic series depicting the various ways in which the Red Cross services affect the life and well being of the public. The scripts were written in Washington and produced in Hollywood, and the transcriptions were then made available to stations throughout the nation. The quarter-hour scripts have since been converted to a five-minute dramatic series, in keeping with the current trend of radio programming, that is, a preference for flexibility in scheduling rather than rigid time slots.

A monthly television kit is provided for individual chapters for local placement. These kits include film spots running twenty seconds and one minute, plus a slide to be used with live announcements.

Although in some cities the Red Cross has joined the United Givers Fund, the bulk of its contributions are still received from an individual campaign traditionally run during the month of March.

This campaign is generally kicked off with an all-network television and radio program on which the President of the United States and many guest stars of the entertainment world appear.

These are the planned activities of the American National Red Cross radio-television branch. But since disaster often strikes without warning in many parts of the world and in our own nation, the Red Cross finds itself called into overnight action to help alleviate a stricken area. It may be a flood in the midwest, an earthquake in Greece or a campaign to assist Hungarian refugees. In these instances, the Red Cross radio and television writers supply spot announcements, films, and complete scripts to networks and individual stations for the duration of the emergency.

THE GOVERNMENT CONTRACT WRITER

In some instances, a government agency becomes a sponsor with an advertising agency serving its needs, much as any commercial industry. This is particularly true in the recruiting drives. The military services, including the National Guard, all have advertising agencies handling the bulk of their recruiting promotion. These agencies bid for the military accounts by making client presentations before military boards.

Spot announcements, scripts for musical programs such as the National Guard's "Let's go to Town" series, are either written by the advertising agency or by a production agency with which the advertising agency has a sub-contract. The Treasury Department contracts with agencies for the production of programs, such as "Treasury Star Parade," on behalf of the sale of United States Savings Bonds.

The Voice of America often contracts for scripts, both radio and television. These may be dramatizations, documentaries or interviews.

Free-lance writers are also hired directly by the government for special programs. The military recruiting services, on occasion, contract for free-lance scripts. The Army's television series, "The Big Picture," utilizes contract writers for its documentaries. The pattern of "The Big Picture" scripts is generally informational or dramatic narrative. Both historic film clips and contemporary on-the-scene shots are included. Most of the programs deal with a single subject: "Exercise Arctic Night," describing paratroop training in icy Greenland; "The Guns are Silent," the story of soldiers on patrol duty in the Demilitarized Zone of Korea; "Operation Friendly Hand," the reactions of a young German girl invited to live with an American soldier's family for a month.

SUMMARY

We hope this chapter has given you a fairly coherent picture of the information activities of your federal government in relation to the broadcast media. As we stated, towards the beginning of this chapter, we chose only a few representative agencies, those with the most active information programs. To include each federal department would require a volume in itself. Practically every government agency has an information staff which may vary from one to a hundred. In the smaller agencies, a single information officer may have to handle all media.

In most of the federal departments, the information specialist's primary job is to answer queries or channel the queries to the proper source. Only in the larger departments is there much opportunity for creative programming. However, even though you may not be called upon for creative programming, there may be many opportunities for contacts with network officials which may prove invaluable to you. If your agency should happen to be in the news because of a current situation in regard to housing, civil aeronautics, atomic energy, etc., the chances are that network news departments, or program producers, will request the head of the agency to appear on one of their programs. The request may come from "Meet the Press," "American Forum of the Air," "Capitol Cloakroom," "Face the Nation," "Reporter's Roundup," or "Press Conference." As the information officer or radio-TV officer for your agency, you will be called on to coordinate all details relative to the appearance of your chief.

There is a common impression that the bulk of federal workers are stationed in the District of Columbia. Actually, there are about a quarter of a million federal workers in Washington, who comprise approximately 10 per cent of the total federal employment. The concentration of top officials is at the nation's capital. However, many federal departments have information officers in their field branches in various of the nation's cities.

Many state and city governments also employ information personnel whose tasks may vary from publicizing the state's or city's tourist attractions to coordinating information regarding local civil defense activities.

If you have received a civil service appointment, you have proved that you possess the qualifications to be an information specialist. If you take your duties lightly, you may turn into a drone seeking only a modicum of security. We say a modicum because budgets are dependent on the will of Congress and a job is only secure as long as there is an appropriation for it. It is true that the civil service employee has many protective rights, but he can lose his job because of unsatisfactory work.

In most instances, the job will be what you make it. You may find yourself limited in actual programming but not in ideas. Your government information job may be a continual challenge to your ingenuity and ability. It is never a sinecure. It can be a stimulating career.

Copyright and marketing information

PART

5

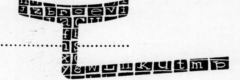

Copyrights and releases

25

There is a perennial question students in writing classes, and presumably all budding writers, ask. How can I protect my masterpiece?

The simplest and most inexpensive method is to seal a copy of your manuscript in an envelope, addressed to yourself, and take it to the registered mail window of the nearest post office. The date stamped across the flap of the envelope by the registry clerk is the birth certificate of your brainchild. It is wise to write the title of your script or idea across the back of the envelope so that in future months, or perhaps years, you will know what the envelope contains. To serve any protective purpose, the envelope, of course, must remain sealed.

The Writers Guilds offer a registry service to their members for a small fee.

THE COPYRIGHT OFFICE

The legal way to register your manuscript is to submit it to the Copyright Office in

Washington. However, there are many misconceptions as to what can and cannot be copyrighted. For example, you can copyright the manuscript of a play before it is produced, but a book, such as a novel, biography, history, and the like, has to be published before it can be copyrighted. A minister may copyright a sermon; an artist, a painting; a photographer, a still. Maps, models or designs for works of art, commercial prints and labels may be registered for protection. Titles, by themselves, cannot be copyrighted. But, of course, the Copyright Office wants a title submitted with each work. It makes it easier to index the millions of registrations. And titles, naturally, are of great importance to the author or composer since a catchy title can definitely increase sales. However, your title may have protection because you have a right to plead unfair competition if someone tries to duplicate your title or use one so similar to it that the value of your work might be affected. Recently, the columnists who wrote the vast selling "Confidential" series threatened to sue a new television program which was going to use the word "confidential" in its title in a manner similar to the columnists' books. As a result of the threatened suit, the TV series eliminated "Confidential" from its title.

Many embryo radio and TV writers have written to the Copyright Office asking whether their precious manuscripts may be registered. Actually, there is nothing in the copyright law which mentions radio or television. But fortunately, the present Register of Copyrights, and his predecessors, have not been burdened by narrow concepts. Plays are plays, they ruled, whether written for the so-called legitimate stage, for radio or for television, and the same regulations are applied to each medium.

PROTECTION OF IDEAS

But the advent of broadcasting brought an avalanche of inquiries: "I've got an idea for a new children's series" . . . "I am planning a TV series that will outrate 'Dragnet' " . . . "I've just worked up something really new in quiz programs." The queries come from people in all walks of life; from professional writers and amateurs, from housewives, doctors, mechanics. They all end with the same refrain. "Can I copyright the idea?" The answer is, no. You can't copyright ideas. Neither can you copyright a synopsis. If, for instance, you have an outline for a wonderful movie, you'll have to submit a reasonably complete scenario in order to have it copyrighted.

How then are you going to safeguard that idea? It's not too difficult. Write a one-act play or a radio or TV drama in which you incorporate your idea. Then submit the play for registration. In this case, the play's not the thing. It's the gimmick in it that counts.

COPYRIGHT FILES

This is probably as good a place as any to clear up the common misconception that the Copyright Office keeps in its own files all the works sent to it for registration. It is true that a complete copy of each unpublished work and two complete copies of each published work must be deposited with the Copyright Office for proper registration. But all periodicals, published maps and music, and most of the books, pamphlets and prints are transferred to the Library of Congress. Selected motion pictures also go into the Library's collections. Although the Copyright Office is somewhat autonomous, it does come under the jurisdiction of the Librarian of Congress. In 1870, the business of copyrighting was all centralized in the Library of Congress, but when the volume of copyrights requested grew by leaps and bounds, a separate Office was established in 1897. It is located today in the modern Annex Building of the Library of Congress where it takes up most of the first floor and has a staff of some 240.

SLOGANS

Slogan devisers are continually searching for that elusive catch phrase and naturally want to protect their ingenuity. However, slogans, like titles, are not copyrightable, but amateur sloganeers persist in sending their inventions to the Copyright Office. It is curious how many slogans received by the Copyright Office from different parts of the country are alike in thought and phrasing and how often they resemble or are exact duplicates of slogans used by major manufacturers years ago.

The oddest slogan came from the Planning Commission of a New England state. The Commission claimed its state's lovely scenery was being used in Chamber of Commerce ads for Middle Atlantic and Western states. It wanted to know whether it could copyright the legend: "Most Stolen State in the 48."

COST OF COPYRIGHT

Inflation has affected the Copyright Office just as it has any other phase of our national life, though perhaps not as strongly. The first article copyrighted in this country was the Philadelphia Spelling Book in 1790 and the fee was then fifty cents. Today, the registration fee is $4.00, but if you take into account the number of years the copyright may be held, the fee is minute: about fourteen cents a year. In the United States, a copyright is valid for 28 years and may be renewed for another 28 years. That makes a total of 56 years before the work enters the public domain. That renewal is important and must be received by the Copyright Office within the 28th year. If it isn't, the copyright will lapse and the work become public domain in its 29th year. There are hundreds of works on record whose authors have unwittingly permitted their copyright to lapse. It may be that many authors are unaware that the renewal of a copyright is not automatic. It must be applied for just as the original copyright was and it must be in the name of the person entitled to claim the renewal.

FOREIGN RIGHTS

A good deal of confusion also exists in the minds of many authors regarding copyrights in foreign countries. On December 6, 1954, the United States ratified the Universal Copyright Convention with an effective date of September 16, 1955. One of the most important principles set forth by the Convention is that authors of any country adhering to

_____

_____

_____

_____

_____

_____

_____

_____

(If space is insufficient, please complete summary on reverse side)

Received in accordance with
the foregoing,

By _____

Release forms from the networks and advertising agencies vary considerably. Some producers of comedy programs, who claim to be in the market for new writers, have their own variation of the release. In one or two cases, these releases practically placed the writer in the situation of forfeiting his script. Nevertheless, if you do wish to submit your script and you feel the release is too binding you may request that a paragraph or paragraphs be changed or deleted. An individual producer may comply. Networks and advertising agencies generally will not.

Perhaps the release form can best be summed up as a necessary evil. However, it should not be a deterrent to your submission of scripts.

Markers

26

When we speak of markets, we mean the free-lance field, and, primarily, the television drama, for in the video drama lies the greatest opportunity for the free-lance writer. Several thousand scripts are presented each year. This includes the half-hour, hour, and ninety-minute anthologies, the series plays and the daily serials. You have probably read time and again in the radio and television column of your hometown newspaper or in the trade publications that television has an insatiable appetite, that it consumes scripts and writers with such rapidity that it must be fed constantly and urgently. This is true enough, yet the beginning writer must not be deceived into thinking that there is such a dearth of scripts that almost anything he writes, as long at it looks like a television play, will be accepted. This is definitely not the case.

Yes, the producers are always looking for new talent but it must give promise of being better than the professionals with whom they are now working. This may seem to place an unfair burden on the beginner but it is a fact of creative life which he must face. Therefore, the neophyte must curb his impatience to sell, and his desire to turn out a large quantity of scripts. He must concentrate on quality. He must not be misled by the multitude of mediocre scripts he has seen on his television screen. They only prove the point that producers can get all the mediocrity they want. They don't have to look to new writers for that!

Another element the writer should bear in mind when submitting scripts is that "professional look." At first thought, the neat appearance of a script may seem of very minor importance. After all, the story's the thing. But remember, you are competing against professionals who, generally, have their scripts typed by expert typists. A slipshod looking script or one that has too many erasures may very well denote the amateur. No matter how objective an editor may be, a badly typed, sloppy looking script will evoke an unfavorable psychological reaction. Be sure your script is adequately bound. When you type your script, leave enough margin to allow for binding. In other words, make your script as easily readable as you can. And if your script is doing the rounds, be sure it looks fresh every time you send it out. Most editors handle manuscripts carefully and they have no objection to reading scripts which have been to another source, but, again, a dog-eared, worn looking manuscript tells an editor all too plainly: seen but not wanted. Creating the illusion of a primary submission may not win you an acceptance, but it will help.

TELEVISION DRAMA MARKETS

We are going to speak of these markets in general terms. With programs changing from season to season, it is difficult to make a satisfactory listing except in periodicals which carry market data. The various writers' magazines, such as "The Writer's Digest," "The Writer," and "Author and Journalist," have sections devoted to television and radio which list current programs, and addresses for submissions, along with script requirements. A very handy guide is issued each year by Albert R. Perkins of New York University. It is called "The Freelance Writers' List of Television Script Markets" and copies may be obtained by writing directly to Mr. Perkins at P.O. Box 371, Grand Central Annex, New York, New York. Single copies are $2.50 but there are discounts available for classroom use.

The Writers Guild of America (East and West) provides current market information to its members and you will undoubtedly want to join the Guild when you become a selling writer. A writer is eligible for the Guild if he has had material produced in radio, television or motion pictures during the past two years, or if he presently has a contract for employment in one of these three media. The Guild has a registration bureau for the protection of non-copyrightable material, group hospitalization plans and business counsel on professional craft matters. Its New York office is at 22 West 48th Street; its Hollywood office at 8782 Sunset Boulevard.

You may also garner a great deal of information on market trends by reading the trade publications: *Variety, Billboard, Radio and Television Daily, Broadcasting, Sponsor,* and others. A subscription to *Variety,* "The Bible of Showbusiness," will be particularly helpful. But if you can't afford a subscription at the moment, make a weekly trip to your public library.

Most important of all, keep a watchful eye on your television screen. If you have an idea for a half-hour drama, observe some of the current half-hour anthologies to see what types of plays are being used. If you're planning an hour drama, watch the hour programs. On occasion, some writers have remarked that this is not always a helpful routine since you may submit a play too close in subject matter to the ones you have been viewing and the editor will want something new. In the main, however, you will be advised by editors to "watch our productions and you'll see what we want."

THE RADIO DRAMA MARKET

Since TV now presents the bulk of the drama on the air, the market for radio dramas is rather limited for the free-lance writer. Most of the radio dramatic series are written on assignment, which means the market is one for professionals rather than the beginner. However, a program such as the "CBS Radio Workshop" has been receptive to scripts and ideas. The "Workshop" has the advantage of permitting the writer full imaginative sway. Many of the programs are "offbeat," that is, they present stories with unusual themes, or treat a familiar theme in an unusual approach. Again, if you wish to write for the "Workshop," it is advisable to listen to some of its programs. Then write for a release form to "CBS Radio Workshop," 485 Madison Avenue, New

York 22, New York. The "Workshop" is successor to the famed "Columbia Workshop" which brought to the fore some of the finest writers in radio.

THE LOCAL MARKET

The writer may have an opportunity to begin his career at home. If he lives in a fairly large city which has its full complement of network affiliates plus a couple of independent stations, he may find an occasional market. Sometimes a local organization will "sponsor" a series of radio plays. We have placed the word "sponsor" in quotations because more often than not there are no fees involved for the writer. He may be asked to dramatize a cause, a charity campaign. It is good experience for the writer and it does get his name known in the local area.

The more ambitious local outlet may present a series of documentaries for which it may employ a free-lance writer or, on occasion, it may produce an historical drama related to the region. A special event, a centennial celebration, or the birthday of a local hero may also inspire a local production. Here, the idea may come from the writer and he can approach the local radio or television station with a program suggestion.

AGENTS

With rare exceptions, the professional writer is represented by an agent. Although there have been some discussions regarding the advisability of having an agent, the pros generally outweigh the cons. A good agent is a decided asset to the writer. As a matter of fact, many of the top TV programs, such as "Kraft Theatre," will not accept scripts unless they come from an accredited agent. Therefore when you are ready to market, your first step, after your script is completed, is to shop around for an agent. How do you shop around?

You may start by going to your public library and asking for the latest edition of the "Literary Marketplace." There you will find a section listing some of the more active literary agents. Usually, there is a notation as to whether these agents handle dramatic scripts for the theater and for television. Write to two or three of them, giving some of your background and stating that you have a script you want to market. Is the agency interested in seeing your script for possible handling? You may receive an answer from one, from all three or from none. The best procedure is to send the script to the first agent who responds. Don't be too impatient, however, if the response seems long in coming. Good agents are busy agents and it may be some time before you receive an answer. It may come within a week. It may be a month or more.

You should also bear in mind that, with few exceptions, the very top agents are not interested in newcomers unless they are introduced by one of their selling writers. If you have a friend who is selling and has an agent, ask him for an introduction to his agent. Your friend will want to, or should, read your script before he contacts his agent. If he doesn't think much of your script, don't blame him if he gently tries to dissuade you from submitting it. Nevertheless, you must be the final judge of your work. If you believe it is good, then go ahead and submit it on your own.

Albert Perkins' Freelance Writers' List has a section devoted to agents who will accept newcomers. You will note that some of these agents charge fees, which brings that question to the fore. If you pick up any writer's magazine, you will see advertisements by dozens of literary agents located in all parts of the country. These agents, with a possible exception or two, all charge reading and criticism fees. Many of them state that after they have sold a designated number of your scripts, you will then be handled on a professional basis. The professional basis means that the agent receives 10 per cent of all income resulting from his sale of your scripts. Sometimes, the commission may be 15 per cent for foreign sales. The 10 per cent is standard among agents and is fair enough, considering that the agent receives no income unless he is able to sell your script.

Now, what about fees? Those agents who charge reading and criticism fees evidently feel they are justified. It takes time to read a script and most agents will receive thousands of scripts during a year, many of which are patently unsaleable. If the criticism these agents offer is of value, it is therefore worth some tangible return. Most agents are people of integrity. We may, however, offer one note of caution. If you find your script is being returned many times for suggested changes with a fee being charged for each suggested change, you may be throwing money down the drain. Don't let your over-anxiety to be a selling writer destroy your sense of practicality.

The competent agent knows the market picture and is aware of current requirements. Producers and editors welcome scripts from recognized agents, many of whom are members of the Society of Authors Representatives. A script from an agent means that some one with knowledge of program requirements has read the script and believes it has possibilities. An agent also helps ease the shock of rejections, because he is the one who receives the rejected script and sends it out again. This is also a burden of expense borne by the agent.

Once an agent has accepted your work for sale, you may naturally feel very exhilarated. But having an agent is not an end-all or be-all for the writer. There will be weeks and months of waiting. The agent cannot afford the time and the expense of writing to an author every time a script is returned and sent out. The best antidote for the waiting period is to begin work immediately on another script. An agent's judgment is not infallible. If it were so, all literary agents would be riding around in Cadillacs and living in Park Avenue penthouses. However, your highly competent agent will not market a script which he does not believe is saleable. He will return it to the writer. Other agents are not so critical and if the work has any merit at all, they will market it on the assumption that you can never tell about an editor. If some months pass by without a word from your agent, it will do no harm to drop him a line and inquire about the current status of your script. Bear in mind that producers and editors may take from two to six weeks before making a decision about a script. Also, if you have any marketing suggestions of your own, don't hesitate to mention them to your agent. They may prove helpful. Agents, as we have said, are not infallible, neither are they omniscient.

Script fees

There is only one definite statement we can make about script fees: they vary! This is an area where a good agent really earns his money, for he will nego-tiate for the best possible price. However, we will mention some figures which will at least give an indication of fees paid. It must be borne in mind that fees for sustaining programs are much lower than those paid for commercial programs.

A half-hour sponsored video drama may run from $500 to $1,000.

An hour sponsored video drama may run from $1,100 to $3,000.

The 90-minute video dramas pay considerably higher, and rates are negotiable.

Sustaining video dramas may receive $300 to $500 for quarter-hour and half-hour scripts.

Half-hour radio dramas may be paid for at a scale ranging from $350 to $500.

These are fees for network or syndicated programs. Local fees, naturally, are not at all comparable. Some local stations have paid from $75 to $100 for half-hour dramas or documentaries.

Remember, these are general figures. Almost all script fees are negotiable, the rate paid varying in proportion to the writer's reputation, or his agent's bargaining power.

SCRIPT CONTESTS

Unfortunately, script contests are few and far between. Contests are of especial value to the beginning writer because he knows that at least his script will be read, and judged for the script's content, not the writer's reputation. Most script contests, besides the desirable financial reward, also offer production of the winning script or scripts which gives the writer a chance to be seen and heard. The writers' magazines carry details of any such contests.

For college and university students taking radio and television courses, there is the annual Victor Frenkl TV Script Award conducted by the University of Maryland. The prize for the winning script is $500. Students may receive details by writing to: George F. Batka, Director, Radio-Television Division, Department of Speech, University of Maryland, College Park, Maryland.

Appendixes

PART

6

Assignments

CHAPTER 7

1. As a TV commercial copywriter, you are assigned the task of preparing a one-minute commercial utilizing two characters. Write it.
2. Write an Institutional type of radio commercial for a major industrial corporation. The subject of the commercial should be the high morale of its employees. Time: One minute.
3. Create a slogan for an imaginary or actual product, in ten words or less.
4. Describe six types of TV commercial announcements. Which of these do you believe is most effective? Give your reasons.
5. As a staff writer for a local TV station, you are called on to write a commercial announcement for a bank. You are asked to meet two essential requirements in the one-minute announcement: (a) appeal for new depositors; (b) keep the writing on a level with the dignity of an old established banking institution.
6. Prepare two ten-second station break radio announcements for a local soft drink bottling concern.
7. Write a one-minute multi-voiced radio commercial for a soap product.
8. Write a one-minute TV commercial for a local retail sponsor, bearing in mind that the sponsor's budget is low in relation to the high cost of TV commercials. Plan your visual material accordingly.
9. Prepare a one-minute radio commercial for a cigarette manufacturer, then write a one-minute TV commercial based on the same selling copy.
10. Your advertising agency has given you the assignment of writing an integrated commercial for a situation comedy which one of its clients is sponsoring. Write the commercial and also include the lead-in and lead-out lines from the situation comedy preceding and following the commercial.

CHAPTER 8

1. The following are four types of public service announcements: Informational, inspirational, recruiting, warning. Write a one-minute radio announcement for each category.

2. Prepare a one-minute TV announcement for the Heart Fund including an appeal for donations.

3. Your local civic association is having its annual outing. Write a 30-second radio announcement calling attention to the fact that the public is invited.

4. Your church or school is sponsoring a book fair. Write a 20-second radio announcement about the fair.

5. A disaster has occurred in your area. Write a one-minute announcement asking for volunteers.

6. Prepare a one-minute TV announcement for either the Crusade for Freedom or Care utilizing imaginative visual material.

CHAPTER 9

1. You are a public relations assistant to a business executive who has been asked to deliver a brief statement, one to one and a half minutes in length, over the local radio station in behalf of a charitable cause. You are asked to write the talk for him which is to include an appeal for funds.

2. You are conducting a five-minute series of book reviews. Write a review of a current best seller, fiction or non-fiction.

3. Prepare a quarter hour TV talk on a scientific subject. Incorporate appropriate visual material.

4. Imagine yourself campaigning for a seat in the House of Representatives. Write a quarter hour campaign speech for TV.

5. Imagine yourself campaigning for Mayor or Councilman. Write a quarter hour campaign speech for radio.

CHAPTER 10

1. You are called upon to write a daily series of five-minute interviews. Describe the pitfalls you must avoid and explain some of the elements that are essential to maintain interest.

2.   Write a 3-minute interview with a celebrity in each of the following fields: (a) Sports; (b) Screen; (c) Fiction Writing.

3.   Prepare a five-minute interview with a presumably well known TV writer in which he or she gives some pointers on how to write a saleable TV dramatic script.

4.   Write a brief interview with a leading "pop" singer in which you integrate one or two of the singer's hit recordings.

5.   Your state's Civil Defense Authority asks you to prepare a quarter-hour interview on Civil Defense activities for distribution to all stations in the state. This interview is to be between a local civic official and the station announcer.

CHAPTER 11

1.   You are assigned to write the continuity for a quarter-hour program of American music to include the following: a spiritual, a Stephen Foster melody, a patriotic song, a folk song.

2.   With the Yuletide season approaching, you are called upon to write the continuity for a half-hour radio Christmas program. Since you are aware that the airwaves will be filled with similar programs, you will attempt to write continuity that avoids the usual clichés. Note: Plan to have six musical selections appropriate to the season.

3.   Write the continuity for a half-hour popular musical program consisting of the top hits of the week.

4.   As part of your tryout for a staff position at a radio station, you are asked to write an introduction to an operatic aria; an introduction to a semi-classical number; an introduction, in disc jockey style, to a popular hit. The introductions should run from 20 to 30 seconds in length.

5.   The TV network has just sold a half-hour weekly musical series to a steamship line which specializes in Latin American and South American cruises. The program is to be in the nature of a musical travelogue. Prepare the continuity for the opening program, making full use of visuals, such as film clips.

6.   Your radio station is presenting a weekly hour series devoted to the music of American composers. Prepare the continuity for a program featuring one of the following composers: George Gershwin, Jerome Kern, Richard Rodgers, Cole Porter.

7.   You are announcing and writing the copy for a late evening program of mood music. Prepare continuity in keeping with the mood.

8.   Your good music station is presenting a series of complete symphonies played by the world's leading orchestras. Choose a symphony and write a two-minute introduction.

CHAPTER 12

1.   Write a two-minute news item for radio, reporting on the results of either presidential or congressional elections. Use fictitious or actual quotations of public and/or party officials. Pay particular attention to the identification of officials, the use of quotes and of figures.

2.   Describe the basic similarities and differences in preparing news copy for the press, radio and TV.

3.   Write a one-minute radio news item based on any current headline. Explain what visuals could be used to adapt this item to TV.

4.   Prepare a five-minute newscast for radio and for TV utilizing the same news items. This is to be a daily sponsored newscast so allow for commercials.

5.   Prepare a quarter-hour TV newscast which employs three reporters, one each for the international scene, the national scene and local happenings.

6.   Choose at least six items from a daily newspaper and rewrite them: (a) for a radio newscast; (b) for a TV newscast.

7.   You are employed as a radio network news analyst and have a daily five-minute spot following a ten-minute summary of the news. Choose a topic of current international or national interest and write a five-minute analysis.

8.   You are a reporter for a weekly newspaper and as an additional assignment, you are to present a weekly series of newscasts over a local radio station. Write a five-minute newscast confining yourself to community news.

9.   One of your assignments for the college or university radio station is a weekly roundup of news of particular interest to the students. Write this as a quarter-hour program.

10.   There has been a good deal of discussion on how to present a TV newscast most effectively. Many stations just have an announcer reading the news with a minimum of visuals. Outline a series incorporating your ideas on how to utilize television most effectively for the presentation of news.

CHAPTER 13

1. Discuss a one-hour television play which you have seen, commenting on the following elements: (a) plot structure; (b) characterization; (c) motivation; (d) resolution.

2. Write approximately thirty lines of dialogue which will establish for television viewers, the following situation: An airplane has crashed in the Rocky Mountain area. There are only three survivors: a young man, the airline hostess, and a child of about ten who is badly hurt.

3. In any discussion of television drama, the phrase "slice of life" technique often arises. Explain its meaning and give your views of this technique.

4. You are assigned to write a half-hour TV drama utilizing four characters: an old man, his grandson, a widow, a young girl. Write a brief biography of each character.

5. Define a "cover" scene. Write a brief sequence for a TV drama utilizing a "cover" scene.

6. Prepare a synopsis for a half-hour TV drama whose action takes place in 24 hours.

7. For a TV drama, write a sequence which is to be played entirely in pantomime.

8. Write the opening scene for a TV drama in which you demonstrate how exposition is carried out through natural dialogue.

9. You are working on a TV drama in which the heroine is having a difficult time deciding between two suitors. In one scene, she is alone in her room, thinking about one of the suitors. Write a flashback sequence in which she recalls the time he proposed.

10. Outline a plot for each of the three basic conflicts as discussed in this chapter.

CHAPTER 14

1. Prepare a scene-by-scene outline of a half-hour filmed drama using a maximum of six characters and four sets.

2. Write an original half-hour drama of the contemporary scene: comedy or serious.

3. Write a half-hour video drama set in one of the following periods: (a) England during the Victorian era; (b) United States during the Civil War; (c) California during the gold rush.

4. Write a half-hour dramatic fantasy.
5. Write a half-hour drama which has a social theme.

CHAPTER 15

1. Write an original hour drama to meet "Matinee Theater" requirements. Your play should be divided into three acts plus an opening "teaser." Keep your characters to a maximum of eight.
2. Study several current hour dramatic programs such as "Kraft Theatre" or "Studio One." Write an hour original for one of these programs.
3. Prepare a scene-by-scene outline for a 90-minute drama.
4. Prepare a scene-by-scene outline for a filmed hour drama with a western locale.
5. Develop an outline and then write an hour drama, for live presentation, based on an experience in your own life.

CHAPTER 16

1. Choose a short story from any current magazine. Adapt it for a half-hour live TV program.
2. The stories of Edgar Allan Poe and Guy de Maupassant are in the public domain. Choose one of your favorites and adapt it for a filmed half-hour TV program.
3. Adapt a Somerset Maugham novel for an hour filmed TV program.
4. Adapt a John Galsworthy play for an hour live TV program.
5. Adapt Nathaniel Hawthorne's "Dr. Heidegger's Experiment" for a half-hour filmed program.

CHAPTER 17

1. Prepare a synopsis of a situation comedy series including descriptions of your main characters and outlines of two episodes.
2. Write one of the above episodes.
3. Prepare an outline of a crime drama series based on detective

bureau files and write an episode of the series. This may be a fictional or factual series.

4. Try inventing a character such as "Perry Mason," "The Fat Man," "The Saint," etc. Write an episode of a mystery drama featuring your protagonist.

5. Create a character in the tradition of the westerns. The character may be fictional or based on an actual western hero. Write a synopsis of an episode for your projected series.

6. Prepare an outline for an historical adventure series which does not duplicate any such series currently on television.

CHAPTER 18

1. Prepare a synopsis for a quarter-hour daily serial, of your own invention, for radio. Include your major plot and a subplot.

2. Write the opening episode for a half-hour daily TV serial. Use a "teaser" scene at the close of the episode.

3. Plan a quarter-hour daily TV serial utilizing any set of the following basic characters: (a) a husband and wife who both have careers; (b) a widow and her teen-age daughter living in a small town; (c) a housewife whose husband is having difficulties making ends meet.

4. Write an episode for one of the above serials.

5. Make a study of the daily serials now on radio and TV. List the main characters of each serial. Prepare a synopsis which will utilize characters and plot differing in many respects from the current offerings.

CHAPTER 19

1. Choose a short story from a current magazine and adapt it for a half-hour radio drama.

2. Write an original half-hour radio drama with an unusual theme, suitable for the CBS Radio Workshop type of program.

3. Write an episode of a quarter-hour dramatic series of a public service nature based on one of the following: (a) Red Cross achievements; (b) Civil Defense activities; (c) Ground Observer Corps; (d) A Veterans' organization or Fraternal Order's contribution to the community.

4. Write a half-hour radio mystery drama.
5. Write a 25-minute radio romantic drama.
6. Adapt a Bret Harte or Jack London short story for a half-hour radio dramatic program.

CHAPTER 20

1. Write a quarter-hour radio drama based on a problem of ethics.
2. Prepare a half-hour TV dramatization of a biblical episode.
3. Write a quarter-hour TV drama whose protagonist is a missionary. This may be fictional or based on fact.
4. Outline a half-hour original radio drama whose theme is faith.
5. Write an historical half-hour radio drama based on the life of a religious leader.

CHAPTER 21

1. Outline the scenes for an hour TV informational documentary on a medical or scientific subject.
2. Write a half-hour documentary for radio in which you describe a local civic problem and present a possible solution.
3. Write a dramatized half-hour TV documentary in the manner of "You Are There," based on an event in American history.
4. Prepare a half-hour TV documentary using narrator and film in the manner of "See It Now." Write the continuity for the narrator and indicate the film to be used. Choose a topic of national or international significance.
5. Prepare an hour TV documentary on one of the following subjects: (a) Slum Clearance; (b) Juvenile Delinquency; (c) Statehood for Alaska and Hawaii; (d) The Teacher Shortage.

CHAPTER 22

1. Prepare a presentation for your idea of a successful children's program.
2. Prepare a synopsis for a children's program which will deal with current events.

3. Write a half-hour drama for radio or TV which you feel would appeal to children from ages 7 to 10.
4. Adapt an episode from "Little Women" or "Black Beauty" for a half-hour children's TV program.
5. Prepare a synopsis of a series of stories, of your own choosing, for a children's TV program. Use the device of a narrator as a storyteller.

CHAPTER 23

1. Discuss several college level subjects which you believe suitable for educational TV programming. Choose one of the subjects and prepare an outline for a half-hour presentation of the subject.
2. Write a half-hour children's program based on folklore of the United States. This may be a dramatic series for TV or radio.
3. Choose an elementary school subject and prepare an outline for TV presentation of that subject.
4. Prepare the same type of outline for a high school subject.
5. Prepare a synopsis for a quarter-hour weekly radio series based on the history of your town or city.
6. Plan a weekly half-hour TV series that deals with civic affairs.
7. Prepare an outline for a documentary series based on the operations of your state government.

APPENDIX 2

Glossary

AD-LIB: From the Latin *ad libitum* meaning "at pleasure," or "without restriction." In broadcast parlance, speaking without script, extemporizing.

ANIMATION: The process by which an illusion is created of moving figures in a cartoon or other visual device. This is accomplished by filming drawings one frame at a time to produce the illusion of continuous movement.

ATMOSPHERE: Radio: Background sounds which aid in giving the illusion of an event, such as crowd noise and cheering at a football game, boxing match, etc. TV: Atmosphere shots are comparable to the foregoing with the addition of camera views.

AUDIMETER: An electronic rating research device.

AUDIO: The sound portion of a TV program.

BACKGROUND: (BG) In TV, the framework at the back of the set which may be a drape, a backdrop, etc. In radio, the sound behind the primary scene, e.g., a background of voices at the site of an accident. Music played under a scene, for radio or TV, may be referred to as background music.

BALOP: Abbreviation of Balopticon, a projector for stills.

BLACK: Going to Black or Fade to Black figuratively means ringing down the curtain for a scene or an act. Literally, the screen is dark for an instant.

BOOM: A metal arm used for suspending a microphone in mid-air so that it can readily be moved from one part of the studio to another.

BRIDGE: Radio: a transition from one scene to another usually by means of music.

BUSINESS: Incidental stage action, such as smoking a cigarette, picking up a book, etc.

CAMERA ANGLE: Placement of the camera for a particular shot.

CLOSED CIRCUIT: A channel for television or radio transmission within a special area, not for public reception, e.g., a telecast confined to in-school receiving.

CLOSE-UP: (CU) A shot of an individual with the camera moved in close so that only the head and shoulders fill the screen. A Big Close-Up (B.CU.) may include only the head or perhaps just the eyes. A Close-Up shot may also be taken of an object, such as a revolver or a knife.

COLD: Without introduction, e.g., beginning a program with a statement taken out of the context of the script, then followed by the standard opening credits.

COMPATIBILITY: Refers to reception of color transmissions on black and white receivers and vice versa.

CONTINUITY: The written portion of a program, generally used when referring to non-dramatic scripts.

CREDITS: The names of the writer, director, producer, cast, etc., given at the opening and close of a program.

CROSS-FADE: TV: The fading-out of one picture and the simultaneous fading-in of another. Radio: The fading-out of dialogue, sound or music, while fading-in other dialogue, sound, or music, simultaneously.

CUE: A line of dialogue, a measure of music or a sound effect which alerts response.

CUT: (a) To switch instantaneously from one camera to another; (b) to stop action; (c) to delete a portion of a script.

DIALOGUE: In drama, the conversation between characters.

DIORAMA: A miniature scene, used to create the illusion of a large set.

DISSOLVE: To fade from one picture to another by the use of two cameras. Both pictures are on screen momentarily.

DOLLY: A trolley on which a camera is set permitting it to be moved at will around the studio. Hence, to Dolly In or Dolly Out means to move the camera forward or back.

DRY RUN: A rehearsal of action and dialogue without the use of the camera, or in radio, a pre-recording rehearsal.

ESTABLISHING SHOT: Generally used at the opening of a program; a long shot to orient the viewer to the locale of a drama.

EXPOSITION: Explanation of details essential to the progression of a program, usually accomplished through dialogue or narration.

EXTERIOR: An outdoor set.

EXTRA: A player who appears in a program but has no lines, except for mob scenes, etc., where many voices in unison may be called for.

FADE: TV: A gradual decreasing or increasing of the intensity of the picture; Fade In, to increase; Fade Out, to decrease. Radio: The gradual increase or decrease in volume of sound, voice or music.

FILTER: A screen of glass or gelatin used to control the intensity of light and the balance of color.

FILTER MIKE: A type of microphone for controlling sound waves to achieve special effects, e.g., speaking over a telephone.

FLASHBACK: A device for recreating a scene from the past.

FLUFF: An error.

FRAME: A single rectangle of film.

GAIN: The increase in power of a signal by means of an amplifier.

GOBO: A non-transparent black screen.

HITCH-HIKE: A brief commercial advertising another product of the same sponsor in addition to the main product advertised on the program.

IN THE CLEAR: Without background accompaniment, such as narration without underscoring music or sound.

INGENUE: A young girl lead in a drama or musical.

INTERCUT: To cut from one camera to another.

JUVENILE: A youthful role.

KILL: To eliminate, as a bit of action or dialogue, or to do without some lighting or staging previously utilized.

KINESCOPE: A process of filming a television program directly from the tube, usually for repeat performances.

LAP DISSOLVE: A slow dissolve.

LEAD: The protagonist of a play.

LIP SYNC: Abbreviated form of "lip synchronization"; recording of actors' dialogue at the same time that the program is being filmed.

LIVE: A program actually presented at the time it is seen, as differentiated from a film presentation.

LOCATION: An exterior scene for filming action remote from the studio.

LONG SHOT: (L.S.) A full shot of the scene so that we may obtain a complete view of the background as well as the foreground.

MC: Abbreviation for "Master of Ceremonies."

MEDIUM CLOSE-UP: (M.CU.) A shot in between the close-up and the long shot.

MINIATURE: A small model used to give the illusion of a full set.

MONITOR: A TV receiver in the control room on which the program of the telecast can be seen; to monitor means to check a TV or radio program for quality.

MONTAGE: A rapid succession of voices relating to a connected idea; in TV, a series of brief scenes in quick succession.

NEMO: A remote pickup.

OFF: TV: Off stage or off screen (o.s.). Radio: Away from the microphone, to give the impression of distance.

ON THE NOSE: On time.

OPTIONAL CUT: A scene, or lines of dialogue, which the writer has indicated may be deleted for time.

OVER FRAME: A voice heard off screen.

PACKAGE: A complete program usually prepared by an independent producer for possible sponsorship.

PAN: Abbreviation of panorama. Movement of the camera, horizontally, across a scene from left to right or right to left.

PANTOMIME: An expression of meaning by visual action.

PLATTER: A transcription or recording.

PROPS: Abbreviation of properties. Refers to all objects on a TV set: furniture, telephone, books, etc.

RATING: A method of radio and TV audience measurement.

REAR PROJECTION: A special effect device which consists of projecting a still picture or a film clip onto a semi-transparent screen placed behind a set. This effect is then photographed and when used on a TV program, the viewer is given the impression that the set is placed within the projected area; e.g., a train stalled by an avalanche.

REMOTE: A program or portion of a program broadcast away from the studio.

RESOLUTION: The final unraveling of the plot. The denouement.

SEGUE: To follow immediately, as one musical selection following another without interruption.

SET: The physical surroundings of a scene.

SLIDE: A picture or title on a single frame of film, which is projected into the camera.

SNEAK: To bring in softly, almost imperceptibly, as music sneaking in under narration.

SOAP OPERA: A daytime serial.

SPECIAL EFFECT: Any device to create illusions.

SPLIT SCREEN: A special effect utilizing two or more cameras so that two or more scenes are visible simultaneously on each part of the screen; e.g., two people holding a telephone conversation.

STET: To let stand; a notation to retain a previously deleted line or passage in a script.

STING: A brief musical chord, generally used to punctuate an important line of dialogue or a powerful visual action.

STOCK SHOT: A film clip readily available from a film library.

STRETCH: To lengthen a program which is running short.

SUPERIMPOSITION: Overlapping of the image of one camera by the image of another camera.

SUSTAINING: Unsponsored.

SYNCHRONIZATION: Picture and sound going on together.

TAG LINE: The final speech of a program.

TAKE: An acceptable or completed shot.

TELEPROMPTER: The trade name of a mechanical prompting device used on TV.

TELOP: A projector for opaque slides.

TILT: The up and down movement of a camera.

TRANSITION: Passage from one scene to another.

TRUCKING: The camera moving beside a character or object which is in motion.

TWO SHOT: A shot of two people.

UNDER: A direction, usually referring to music or sound, meaning to bring the volume down and keep behind dialogue.

UP: A direction to raise the volume.

VIDEO: The visual portion of a television program. Often used now as a synonym for television.

VIDEO TAPE: A new form of magnetic tape for recording pictures and sound which can then be played back immediately, without processing.

WILD TRACK: To record sound or music separately for possible later use in a program.

ZOOM: The change in focal length of a special lens (Zoomar Lens) which gives the effect of moving right up to an object, such as a baseball in flight.

Bibliography

American Research Bureau, *A New Look at the Television Viewer Diary.* Washington, D.C., 1956.

Baker, George Pierce, *Dramatic Technique.* Boston: Houghton Mifflin Company, 1919.

Barnouw, Erik, *Handbook of Radio Writing.* Boston: Little, Brown & Co., 1939.

Battison, John H., *Movies for TV.* New York: Macmillan Company, 1950.

Brean, Herbert, *The Mystery Writer's Handbook.* New York: Harper & Brothers, 1956.

Bretz, Rudy, and Edward Stasheff, *Television Scripts.* New York: A. A. Wyn, 1953.

Butcher, S. H., *Aristotle's Theory of Poetry and Fine Art.* London: Macmillan & Co., Ltd., 1911.

Callahan, Jennie Waugh, *Television in School, College and Community.* New York: McGraw-Hill Book Company, Inc., 1957.

Chayefsky, Paddy, *Television Plays.* New York: Simon and Schuster, 1955.

Crews, Albert, *Professional Radio Writing.* Boston: Houghton Mifflin Company, 1946.

Egri, Lajos, *Art of Dramatic Writing.* New York: Simon and Schuster, 1946.

Ewbank, Henry L., and Sherman P. Lawton, *Broadcasting: Radio and Television.* New York: Harper & Brothers, 1952.

Greene, Robert S., *Television Writing* (Revised Edition). New York: Harper & Brothers, 1956.

Head, Sydney W., *Broadcasting in America.* Boston: Houghton Mifflin Company, 1956.

Heath, Eric, *Writing for Television* (Third Edition). Englewood Cliffs, N.J.: Prentice-Hall, Inc., 1953.

Highet, Gilbert, *People, Places and Books.* New York: Oxford University Press, 1953.

Highet, Gilbert, *A Clerk at Oxenford.* New York: Oxford University Press, 1954.

Hodapp, William, *The Television Manual.* New York: Farrar, Straus & Young, 1953.

Hubbell, Richard, *Television Programming and Production* (Third Edition). New York: Rinehart & Co., 1956.

Kirby, Edward M., and Jack W. Harris, *Star-Spangled Radio*. Chicago: Ziff-Davis Publishing Company, 1948.

McMahan, Harry Wayne, *The Television Commercial*. New York: Hastings House, 1956.

Mickelson, Sig, Vice President Columbia Broadcasting System, "Television and the Church," an address. October 9, 1956.

National Association of Radio and Television Broadcasters, *Is Your Hat In the Ring?* Washington, D.C., 1956.

Nielsen, Arthur C., *Television Audience Research*. Chicago: A. C. Nielsen Company, 1955.

Parker, Everett C., Elinor Inman, and Ross Snyder, *Religious Radio*. New York: Harper & Brothers, 1948.

Parker, Everett C., David W. Barry, and Dallas W. Smythe, *The Television-Radio Audience and Religion*. New York: Harper & Brothers, 1955.

Pimlott, J. A. R., *Public Relations and American Democracy*. New Jersey: Princeton University Press, 1951.

Poole, Lynn, *Science via Television*. Baltimore: Johns Hopkins Press, 1950.

Roberts, Edward Barry, *Television Writing and Selling*. Boston: The Writer, Inc., 1954.

Rose, Reginald, *Six Television Plays*. New York: Simon and Schuster, 1956.

Roslow, Sydney, *Pulse Pluses in Radio/TV*. New York: The Pulse, Inc.

Seldes, Gilbert, *Writing for Television*. Garden City, New York: Doubleday & Company, Inc., 1953.

Sheen, Fulton J., *Life Is Worth Living*. New York: McGraw-Hill Book Company, Inc., 1953.

Spring, Samuel, *Risks and Rights in Publishing, Television, Radio, Motion Pictures, Advertising and the Theater*. New York: W. W. Norton, 1952.

Stasheff, Edward, and Rudy Bretz, *The Television Program*. New York: A. A. Wyn, 1951.

Trendex Audience Measurement Services. New York: Trendex, Inc.

U.S. News and World Report, *What TV Is Doing To America*. September 2, 1955. Washington, D.C.

Vidal, Gore, Editor, *Best Television Plays*. New York: Ballantine Books, 1956.

White, Paul W., *News on the Air*. New York: Harcourt, Brace & Co., 1947.

Wylie, Max, *Radio and Television Writing*. New York: Rinehart & Co., 1952.

Index

the moment they dig into the broadcast fields, he will find the odds are very much against him. If Dr. Gallup were to take a nation-wide poll, it is fairly probable he would discover that 90 per cent of the literate population either has written a television or radio script or made a mental note to write one. And, of course, one that would be far superior to the current crop!

Editors, despite the constant cry of a dearth of scripts, are literally bombarded with scripts and if they become weary and jaded and reach rather hurriedly for a rejection slip, who is to blame them? The dearth actually is not of scripts but of good scripts.

On the other hand, there is the instance of the young man who took a year's course in writing for television and at the end of that time not only sold two hour dramas to the networks but had one of them purchased by a major Hollywood film producer. This is a heartening experience and one which, undoubtedly, will have every aspiring TV playwright saying to himself: "Perhaps this can happen to me."

Perhaps it can, but the writer should realize that the above instance is the very rare exception. He may have to write a dozen scripts before one is accepted. And here let us offer a word of caution: do not in a fit of temperament destroy anything you have written. If you get beyond the golden door, you will find that you will need all your ideas. As long as you have faith in your script, hold on to it; a bit of skillful rewriting may turn the previously rejected manuscript into an eminently saleable one. Story editors come and go. The "climate" of the times may change and you may find that the script that came back is suddenly welcomed with open check book.

Your faith in your work, however, must be tempered by an ability for self-criticism. This faculty for judging your own script is difficult. If you have just taken a page of dialogue hot from your typewriter, your mood is one of elation and every word may seem to have the sound of genius. Put it aside till the next day, at least. Return to it cold and if then the feeling of elation still persists, maybe you've got something.

The writer is a creature of compulsion. He may write every day. Sometimes, he may not write for weeks or months but event-ually he will find himself compelled to put words on paper. The degree of persistence is in direct ratio to the degree of compulsion. It spells the difference between the dilettante and doer.

Audience
and measurement

2

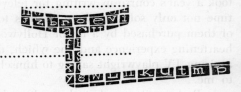

If you were to ask the broadcast writer what audience he is writing for, his answer might well be "everybody." With the vast number of television and radio stations blanketing the country, any program at any given time has some audience. The Annual Report of the Federal Communications Commission (FCC) for the fiscal year of 1956 tells us that there are approximately 500 commercial television stations, more than 20 educational TV stations, some 2900 Amplitude Modulation (AM), 530 Frequency Modulation (FM) and 160 educational FM radio stations on the air. The FCC estimates that ". . . over 90 per cent of the nation's population is now within range of two or more stations and that nearly 39 million TV sets are now in use."

This chapter will deal with the composition of that audience and describe how its viewing and listening habits are measured.

THE TELEVISION AUDIENCE

In September 1955, U.S. News and World Report published a comprehensive

Executed on behalf of _____

as duly authorized agent. (Insert owner's name)

Name of agency _____

By _____
        (Name of Agency Representative)

Address _____

City _____

Telephone No.: _____

Please indicate form of material submitted:

Outline ☐   Transcription ☐

Script ☐   Film ☐

Brochure ☐   Other _____

_____

SUMMARY OF MATERIAL SUBMITTED:

_____

_____

_____

_____

_____

_____

_____

1. I represent that the features which I have specifically described on page two hereof are original with me and that no persons other than those whose names appear below have collaborated with me in creating this material. I limit my claim of rights to such features and acknowledge that I do not, and will not, claim any rights whatsoever in any other elements of the program material which are not so described, unless such material embodies concrete literary expression in which case I claim rights in the manner of such expression. I claim exclusive rights in the title only as regards its use in connection with the elements of the program material submitted hereunder.

2. You will not use the material submitted by me hereunder unless (i) you shall first negotiate with me compensation for such use, or (ii) unless you shall determine that you have an independent legal right to use such material which is not derived from me, either because the material submitted hereunder is not new or novel, or was not originated by me, or has not been reduced to concrete form, or because other persons including your employees have submitted, or may hereafter submit, similar or identical suggestions, features and material which you have the right to use.

3. In the event that, pursuant to paragraph 2 above, you determine that you have the legal right to use any of the material submitted by me hereunder without the payment of compensation to me and proceed to use the same, and if I disagree with your determination, I agree that, if you so elect, the dispute between us shall be submitted to arbitration, the arbitrator to be a person experienced in the radio or television fields, and mutually selected by you and me, or, if we cannot agree, then to be selected as provided by the rules of the American Arbitration Association. The Arbitration shall be controlled by the terms hereof, and any award favorable to me shall be limited to the fixing of a royalty which shall not exceed royalties normally paid for a comparable program suggestion in the regular course of business.

Very truly yours,

(a) Name _____   (b) Name _____

Address _____   Address _____

City _____   City _____

Telephone No.: _____   Telephone No.: _____

Note: Sole owner should complete section (a). In a case of collaboration, one owner should complete section (a) and the other owner should complete section (b).

the Convention are to enjoy the same protection granted by each member country to its own citizens. This marks the first time the United States has been a party to a copyright convention outside the Western Hemisphere. The Congress did ratify a Pan-American copyright agreement at Buenos Aires, Argentina, in 1910, which is still in effect. Since the Buenos Aires Copyright Convention is open to adherence only by Western Hemisphere republics, the nations of the Eastern Hemisphere are excluded. Canada is also excluded from this particular Convention.

There are a great many countries, predominantly European, which are members of the International Union for the Protection of Literary and Artistic Works, more informally known as the Berne Union. The United States is not a member of the Berne Union. However, United States authors may obtain copyright protection in countries adhering to the Berne Union by having their works published simultaneously in one of those countries. For example, Canada is a member of the Berne Union.

In addition, the United States has bilateral copyright relations with a number of foreign countries which may not be parties either to the Universal Copyright Convention or the Buenos Aires Convention. If the writer is interested he may obtain lists of the countries with which the United States has agreements from the Copyright Office, the Library of Congress, Washington, D.C. In the event that the television or radio playwright has a book of his plays published, these copyright matters are generally thoroughly attended to by the publisher.

The Copyright Office is now receiving about a quarter of a million applications for registration each year. From the turn of the century, it has recorded more than eight million creative efforts of the average and not so average American. One conclusion is therefore evident: no one can accuse this nation of a lack of creative endeavor.

RELEASES

The copyright protects your work. But now, let's look at this matter of protection from the viewpoint of the buying agency: the network, the package producer, the advertising agency. Suppose you were to submit a script, have it rejected and then some time later hear or see a radio or teleplay very similar to yours broadcast over a network. Your natural reaction would be one of indignation. You would be certain your script was stolen and you would be inclined to call a lawyer and begin a suit. In this hectic, highly competitive field of entertainment where ideas pay off in handsome fortunes, there are instances, shall we say, of slight irregularities. But the search for new talent is constant — although the struggling writer may often believe it's a myth. Nevertheless, if your script is good and meets the approbation of the story editor, the chances are it will be bought at current rates. However, it may be that a script written on the same theme as yours — and that does happen — is already in the play file. That may account for the rejection of your script no matter how well written. If the agency were not protected by your signed release, it might be vulnerable for a suit. Plagiarism is hard to prove but it has had its day in court. A jury recently awarded a writer more for his script than the fee he would have been paid under current commercial rates.

Any network, advertising agency of any size, or package producer will require a signed release before reading an unsolicited idea or script. Years ago, many agencies issued release forms of such complexity that it required an astute legal mind to unravel the technicalities. The gist of the release was that you, the writer, were offering a manuscript which the agency, with great magnanimity, deigned to look at. The complete decision of acceptability and amount of payment was left up to the agency and according to some of the release forms, your script could be used for practically no payment and you, also magnanimously, were supposed never to bring suit under any circumstances.

The Radio Writers Guild, now absorbed by the Writers Guild of America (East and West), fought, with some notable success, to modify the release form.

Here is a typical release form:

Date: _____

Title of material

submitted: _____

_____

Gentlemen:

I am today submitting to you program material upon the following express understanding and conditions: